HMH SOCIAL STUDIES

WORLD HISTORY

Teacher's Guide

HISTORY.

Educational Advisory Panel

The following educators provided ongoing review during the development of prototypes and key elements of this program.

Jose Colon
Berkeley High School
Berkeley, California

Bethany Copeland
Peach County High School
Fort Valley, Georgia

Darrel Dexter
Egyptian Community Unit School
Tamms, Illinois

Charles Dietz
Burnett Middle School
San Jose, California

John Hogan
Brevard High School
Brevard, North Carolina

Jeffrey Kaufman
Aspirations Diploma Plus High School
Brooklyn, New York

Beth E. Kuhlman
Queens Metropolitan High School
Forest Hills, New York

Beatrice Nudelman
Aptakisic Junior High School
Buffalo Grove, Illinois

Kyle Race
Greene High School
Greene, New York

Gretchen Ritter Varela
Northville High School
Northville, Michigan

Sharon Shirley
Branford High School
Branford, Connecticut

Yvette Snopkowski
Davis Junior High School
Sterling Heights, Michigan

La-Shanda West
Cutler Bay Senior High School
Cutler Bay, Florida

ISBN 978-0-544-91588-6

5 6 7 8 9 10   0607   25 24 23 22 21 20 19

4500767168   C D E F G

Table of Contents

Table of Contents

Table of Contents

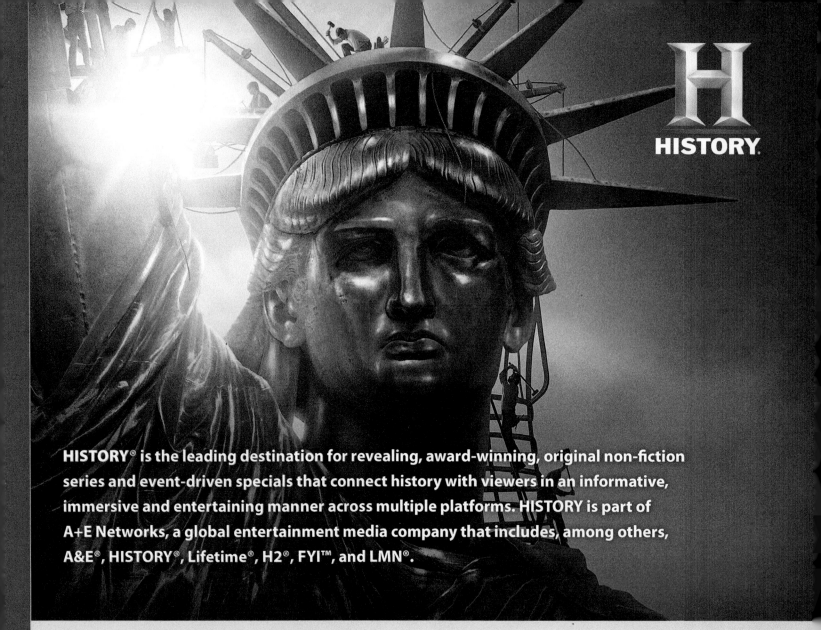

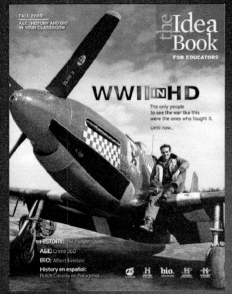

The Idea Book for Educators

Classroom resources that bring the past to life

Live webcasts

HISTORY Take a Veteran to School Day

In addition to premium video-based resources, **HISTORY** has extensive offerings for teachers, parents, and students to use in the classroom and in their in-home educational activities, including:

- *The Idea Book for Educators* is a biannual teacher's magazine, featuring guides and info on the latest happenings in history education to help keep teachers on the cutting edge.

- **HISTORY Classroom (www.history.com/classroom)** is an interactive website that serves as a portal for history educators nationwide. Streaming videos on topics ranging from the Roman aqueducts to the civil rights movement connect with classroom curricula.

- **HISTORY email newsletters** feature updates and supplements to our award-winning programming relevant to the classroom with links to teaching guides and video clips on a variety of topics, special offers, and more.

- **Live webcasts** are featured each year as schools tune in via streaming video.

- **HISTORY Take a Veteran to School Day** connects veterans with young people in our schools and communities nationwide.

In addition to **Houghton Mifflin Harcourt**, our partners include the *Library of Congress*, the *Smithsonian Institution*, *National History Day*, *The Gilder Lehrman Institute of American History*, the Organization of American Historians, and many more. HISTORY video is also featured in museums throughout America and in over 70 other historic sites worldwide.

Keeping the **Story** in History

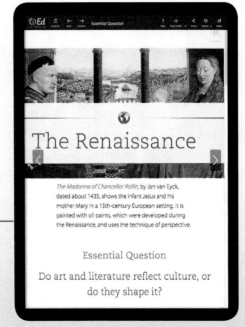

Houghton Mifflin Harcourt delivers a powerful and personal narrative to captivate students' curiosity and help them connect their learning to their lives and interests.

Essential Questions begin every Module in *HMH Social Studies World History* to help spark students' curiosity about the content.

HISTORY® Videos, introduced in Module openers, embedded within the narrative, and highlighted in Multimedia Connections, bring the content to life through primary source footage, dramatic storytelling, and expert testimonials.

Setting the Stage
Lesson introductions place lesson content in a broader historical context.

Interactive Features, Maps, and Games, at point of instruction in the Online Student Edition, provide quick entertaining activities and assessments that present important content in a fun way.

HMH Current Events gives students regularly updated articles organized by disciplinary themes on today's news and offers access to safe, trustworthy news sources for further exploration and research. The HMH Current Events site offers unparalleled access to the latest world developments tailored for students, helping them to connect what they learn in history class to the world around them.

Supporting Inquiry and Active Learning

HMH Social Studies offers the tools and support necessary to challenge students to approach history through active inquiry.

Online Student Edition

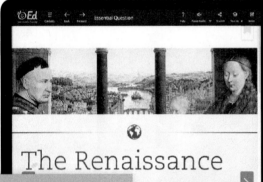

Essential Question Preview

Do art and literature reflect culture, or do they shape it?

Have students consider the Essential Question and capture their initial responses.

Teacher's Guide

Essential Questions open every Module in *HMH Social Studies World History* to help students kick off the inquiry process by modeling the development of key questions. The **Teacher's Guide** provides support to help students create and answer supporting questions to driving their understanding of the Big Idea and Why it Matters Now for every Lesson.

Essential Question Preview

Do art and literature reflect culture, or do they shape it?
Have students consider the Essential Question and capture their initial responses.

Explore the Essential Question

- Explore with students the difference between art and literature reflecting culture versus shaping it.
- Describe to students ways that art and literature reflect culture, using current examples of both to begin a discussion. For example, display images of street art and ask students how it reflects or shapes culture.

Help students plan inquiries and develop their own supporting questions such as

What new ideas and values led to the Renaissance?

How did humanism play a key role in the artistic achievements of the Renaissance?

You may want to assign students to write a short essay in response to the Essential Question when they complete the module. Encourage students to use their notes and responses to inform their essays.

▶ Explore the Online Video

ANALYZE VIDEOS

Da Vinci's World
Invite students to watch the video to learn about the transformation of the world in which Leonardo da Vinci lived: Florence, Italy.

History What is the name of the family that restored Florence? *the Medici family*

PLAY VIDEO 2:18
▶ Da Vinci's World

536   Module 14

Module 14

The Renaissance

Essential Question
Do art and literature reflect culture, or do they shape it?

About the Painting: *The Madonna of Chancellor Rollin*, painted by Jan van Eyck in about 1435, shows the infant Jesus and his mother Mary in a 15th-century European setting. It is painted with oil paints, which were developed during the Renaissance, and uses the technique of perspective.

In this module you will learn how European society was revitalized as classical art and ideas were embraced and improved upon.

Explore ONLINE!
VIDEOS, including...
• Da Vinci's World
• Da Vinci and the Code He Lived By

HISTORY.
☑ Document Based Investigations
☑ Graphic Organizers
☑ Interactive Games
☑ Image Compare: Perspective
☑ Image with Hotspots: Printing Press

What You Will Learn ...
Lesson 1: Birth of the Renaissance 538
The Big Idea The Renaissance was a rebirth of learning and art.
Lesson 2: The Italian Renaissance 546
The Big Idea The Italian Renaissance was a rediscovery of learning that produced many great works of art and literature.
Lesson 3: The Northern Renaissance 554
The Big Idea In the 1400s, the ideas of the Italian Renaissance began to spread to northern Europe.
Lesson 4: Renaissance Achievements 562
The Big Idea The Renaissance was a period of striking achievements in many areas.

536   Module 14

Lesson 1 Big Idea
The Renaissance was a rebirth of learning and art.
Why It Matters Now
Renaissance art and ideas still influence thought today.

Lesson 2 Big Idea
The Italian Renaissance was a rediscovery of learning that produced many great works of art and literature.
Why It Matters Now
Renaissance art and literature still influence modern thought and modern art.

Lesson 3 Big Idea
In the 1400s, the ideas of the Italian Renaissance began to spread to northern Europe.
Why It Matters Now
Renaissance ideas such as the importance of the individual are an important part of modern thought.

Lesson 4 Big Idea
The Renaissance was a period of striking achievements in many areas.
Why It Matters Now
The achieve...
writers, scie...
affect peop...

536   Module 14

Lesson 2 Big Idea
The Italian Renaissance was a rediscovery of learning that produced many great works of art and literature.

Why It Matters Now
Renaissance art and literature still influence modern thought and modern art.

Program Highlights

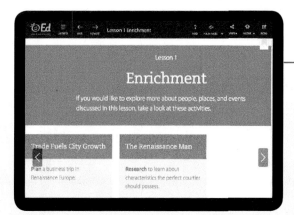

Enrichment Activities close every Lesson giving students an opportunity to explore additional topics in depth to deepen their understanding of the content studied and apply it actively in their community.

Document-Based Investigations build throughout every Module featuring documents in each Lesson with practice and short answers. In the Module Review, a unified Document-Based Investigation asks students to re-examine the featured documents and to draw upon the entire set of documents to demonstrate their understanding of the Module's main concepts through a presentation or essay.

Lesson DBI   **Module Review DBI**

Skills Support links analyzing visuals, sources, writing, and other tasks accompany activities at point of use to help students tackle these challenging and critical social studies skills.

Providing **Choice** and Supporting **Learning Needs**

HMH Social Studies World History *presents material and activities in a variety of ways to allow students and teachers to choose the path that works best for them. Differentiated instruction and assessments with built-in feedback provide support for all students.*

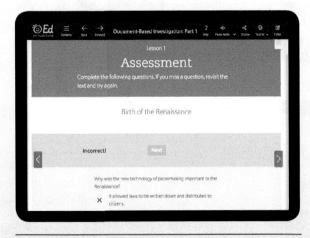

Differentiated Instruction Activities in the Teacher's Guide offer further options for varying lessons to meet the needs of every student.

Lesson-Level Assessments serve to inform instruction rather than simply assign grades to students. If a student misses a question, the system gives the student the option to pause, review instructional material, and then go back to the assessment. Teachers can further guide this process through reports on their students' performance, tied to standards and curriculum, to provide personalized intervention.

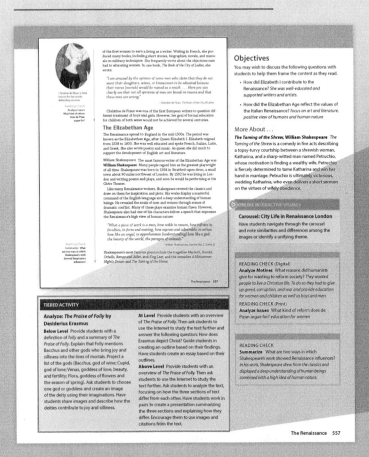

Enrichment Activities at the end of every lesson provide avenues for students to stretch their curiosity and explore select topics in greater depth than called for by the standards.

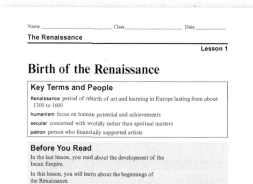

Name _____ Class_____ Date_____

The Renaissance

Lesson 1

Birth of the Renaissance

Key Terms and People

Renaissance period of rebirth of art and learning in Europe lasting from about 1300 to 1600

humanism focus on human potential and achievements

secular concerned with worldly rather than spiritual matters

patron person who financially supported artists

Before You Read

In the last lesson, you read about the development of the Incan Empire.

In this lesson, you will learn about the beginnings of the Renaissance.

As You Read

Use a chart to describe the cause-and-effect relationships that led to the birth of the Renaissance.

A TIME OF CHANGE
What factors led to the birth of the Renaissance?

The years 1300 to 1600 saw a rebirth of learning and culture in Europe called the **Renaissance**. This rebirth involved an explosion of creativity in art, architecture, and writing. The Renaissance had its roots in an effort to bring back the culture of classical Greece and Rome. However, new ideas and values also developed and gained influence.

The Renaissance grew out of important changes in society, economics, learning, and politics. First, famine and disease caused Europe's population to become much smaller. With fewer people to feed, the general standard of living was higher. People were also becoming better educated. Second, an increase of trade led to the growth of a middle class made up of merchants, bankers, and tradespeople. People in the middle class had extra money to spend on luxuries. Third, Europeans also regained access to learning from classical times. Greek texts, which had been preserved by Byzantine and Islamic scholars, became more available. This spread of classical knowledge was helped along by the introduction of new technologies. Papermaking, for example, helped make possible the development of printing. The ability to create and store books led to the growth of libraries and the spread of knowledge. Finally, a long period of almost constant warfare was brought to a close. Peace returned to much of the continent

© Houghton Mifflin Harcourt Publishing Company

109

Guided Reading Workbook

**Guided Reading Workbook
Lesson Summary**

Note-Taking Support exists throughout the program:

- Within the **Modular Online Edition,** students can complete and save a graphic organizer for every Lesson.

- In print, the **Guided Reading Workbook** provides lesson summaries and note-taking templates that serve as scaffolds for learning.

- The **Spanish/English Guided Reading Workbook** supports students who are more proficient in Spanish with lesson summaries and note-taking templates in side-by-side Spanish and English language versions.

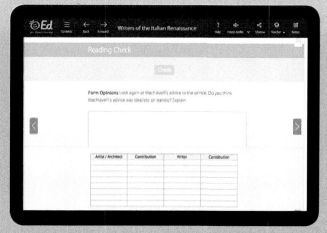

Online Student Edition: Graphic Organizer

Giving the **Freedom** **To Teach** Your Way

Designed for flexibility, HMH Social Studies World History provides resources in a variety of formats to allow you to easily address content in the manner that best fits students' needs and your instructional style.

The **Teacher's Guide** serves as the starting point for teachers to blend their instruction how they see fit, with as much print and digital as they choose, and tying all of the program's pieces, such as the printed Student Edition and fully digital Modular Online Edition, together.

Lesson 1 Planner

Birth of the Renaissance

- Islamic Cultural Influences in Spain

Visuals

Video

LESSON 1

Big Idea
The Renaissance was a rebirth of learning and art.

Maps, Graphs, and Charts

- Map: Europe, 1500

- **Biography:** Lorenzo de Medici
- Trade Fuels City Growth
- The Renaissance Man

Extend and Enrich

Historical Sources

- **Document-Based Investigation:** Patrons of the Arts
- Renaissance Man

Assessment

- Key Terms Review
- Reading Check
- Graphic Organizer Activity
- Lesson Assessment

537a   Module 14, Lesson 1

Built for maximum compatibility, *HMH Social Studies World History* provides digital resources with options to support various levels of connectivity and devices. The Modular Online Edition resides on a responsive platform enabling it to function across operating systems and devices. *HMH Social Studies World History* allows students and teacher to download material, work offline, and re-sync with the system upon reconnecting.

image credit: *computer monitor* ©Yahia Loukkal/Fotolia

Program Highlights

Flexible Assessment options appear at the Lesson, Module, and Benchmark levels. *HMH Social Studies World History* includes a robust writing strand to allow students to demonstrate their learning through a variety of essay types, such as informative and argumentative. Online assessments offer quizzes and tests that are scored automatically.

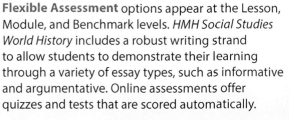

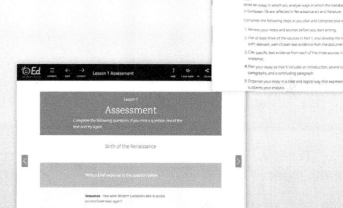

Flexible Arrangement with *HMH Social Studies World History's* modular format allows schools to purchase exactly the content that they want. While the material can always be bought with its full, pre-set table of contents, customers now also have the option to order individual Modules to build and sequence a program that follows their exact curriculum.

image credit: *computer monitor* ©Yahia Loukkal/Fotolia

Content Structure

In HMH Social Studies World History, the structure of content is shared in digital and print. This enables seamless navigation and content synchronization whether digital, print, or both are used.

Modules are the broadest content category and cover historical eras, seminal events, and/or essential social studies concepts and themes. Each Module opens with an Essential Question to spark student interest and provide connections between content and context. Rich imagery, HISTORY© videos, and timelines are also used to engage students. These elements are reinforced in the Module Review through essays and activities and are followed by Module Assessments that gauge understanding.

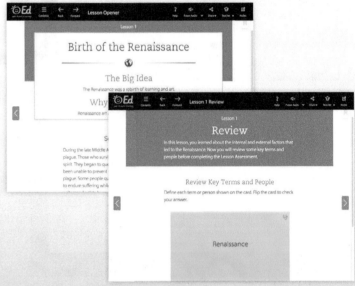

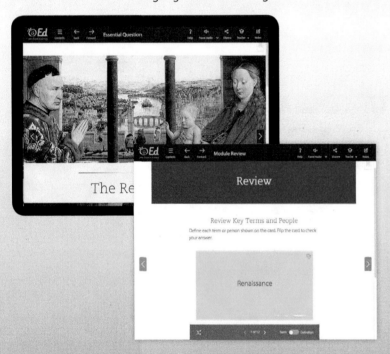

Lessons present Module content in focused, manageable divisions based on subtopics and/or contributing events. Each Lesson opens with a Big Idea, encapsulating the primary point of the Lesson. *Setting the Stage* places lesson content in a broader historical context. Key Terms and People are presented throughout Lessons, and graphic organizers and flip cards in Lesson Reviews prepare students for Lesson Assessments.

Segments organize Lesson content into discrete sections and are the smallest content category. Each segment ends with a Reading Check question to check comprehension.

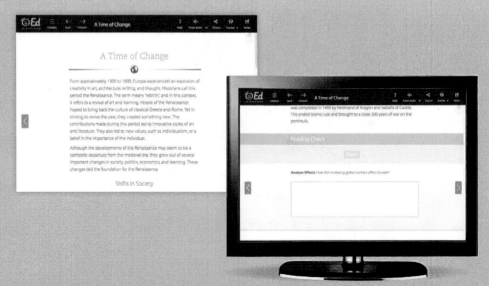

image credit: *computer monitor* ©Yahia Loukkal/Fotolia

Teacher's Guide

Content alignment allows instructors to use the print Teacher's Guide to steer instruction whether students are using digital, print, or both.

Module Planner

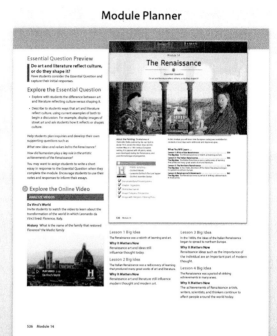

Lesson Planner

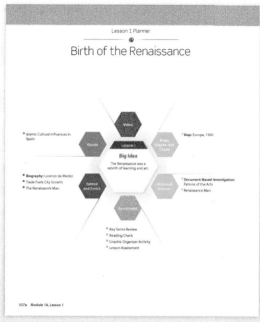

Planning is simplified through clean, at-a-glance planners detailing elements of Modules and Lessons. Color-coding visually identifies print-only components and organizes Module, Lesson, and Segment content.

Module Highlights

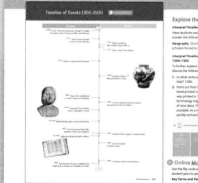

Lesson Highlights

Module and Lesson Highlights provide overviews of integral Module and Lesson elements. Features detailing overarching Module themes, skills instruction, whole class collaborative activities, and review tools including flip cards, graphic organizers, sequencing activities, and more are included.

How to Use This Program

Instruction is presented at point of use for ease of navigation and discovery. Content extension, differentiated activities, instructor scaffolding, questions, answers, suggestions on engaging students, help with program features and more are all presented in sequence with student materials. The Teacher's Guide bridges student digital and print editions, providing seamless instruction for both environments.

Teacher's Guide: Core Instruction

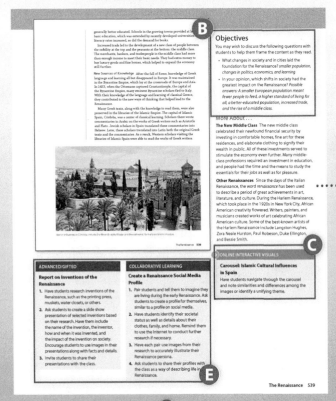

Online Student Edition

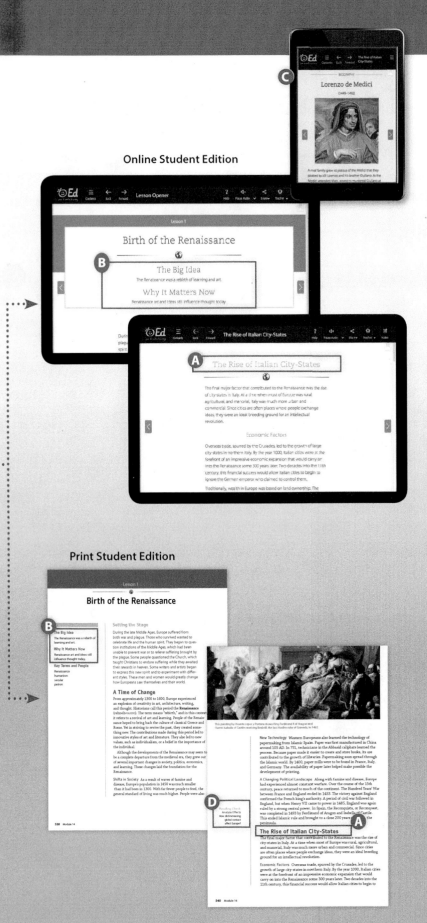

Module, Lesson, and Segments Ⓐ *are synchronized in the digital and print student editions, so core instruction unpacking Big Ideas* Ⓑ *serves both environments. Instruction for elements including visuals, maps, graphs, and Document-Based Investigations* Ⓒ *is provided in the Teacher's Guide, and all elements are identified as digital, print, or shared. Assessment items and answers* Ⓓ *are presented at point of use, and differentiated individual and whole-class activities* Ⓔ *are provided throughout.*

Teacher eBook and Resources

HMH Social Studies World History instruction can also be accessed in a digital-only environment. Additional resources provide even more options and tools for instructors.

Teacher eBook

Student eBook

The Teacher eBook presents the same instructional content as the print Teacher's Guide, but is focused solely on digital content. In addition to core instruction provided in the print Teacher's Guide, links to completed graphic organizers, rubrics, and other resources are provided in the Teacher eBook overlay.

Presentations

Resources beyond the Teacher's Guide and Teacher eBook include presentations, skills instruction, online assessments, rubrics, activities, and more. These resources supplement instruction, provide additional channels for differentiation, and aid in planning and delivery.

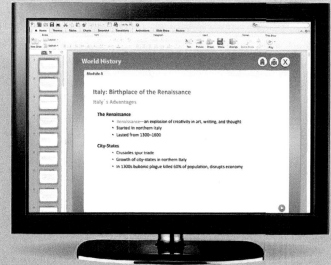

HMH Social Studies World History
Dashboard

Designed for today's digital natives, **HMH Social Studies** offers you and your students a robust, intuitive online experience.

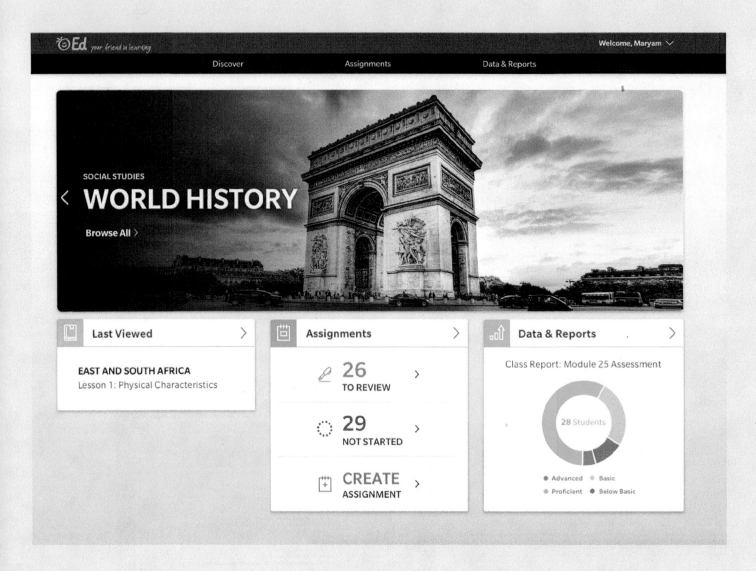

Your personalized Teacher Dashboard is organized into three main sections:

1. **Discover**—Quickly access content and search program resources
2. **Assignments**—Create assignments and track progress of assignments
3. **Data & Reports**—Monitor students' daily progress

Explore Online ⊳
to **Experience** the **Power** of
World History

Houghton Mifflin Harcourt® is **changing**
the way students **experience** social studies.

By delivering an immersive experience through compelling narratives
enriched with media, we're connecting students to history through experiences
that are energizing, inspiring, and memorable activities. The following pages
highlight some digital tools and instructional support that will help students
approach history through active inquiry so they can connect to the past while
becoming active and informed citizens for the future.

The Student eBook is the primary learning portal.

More than just the digital version of a textbook, the
Student eBook serves as the primary learning portal
for students. The narrative is supported by a wealth of
multimedia and learning resources to bring history to life
and give your students the tools they need to succeed.

Bringing Content to Life

HISTORY® videos and Multimedia Connections bring
content to life through primary source footage, dramatic
storytelling, and expert testimonials.

In-Depth Understanding

Close Read Screencasts model an analytical conversation about primary sources.

Content in a Fun Way

Interactive Features, **Maps**, and **Games** provide quick, entertaining activities and assessments that present important content in a fun way.

Investigate Like a Historian

Document-Based Investigations in every lesson build to end-of-module DBI performance tasks so students can examine and assess primary sources as historians do.

Full-Text Audio Support

Students can listen while they read.

Skills Support

Point-of-use support is just a click away, providing instruction on critical reading and social studies skills.

Personalized Annotations

Notes encourages students to take notes while they read and allows them to customize their notes to their preferences. Students can easily access their notes to review later as they prepare for exams.

Interactive Lesson Graphic Organizers

Graphic organizers help students process, summarize, and keep track of their learning for end-of-module performance tasks.

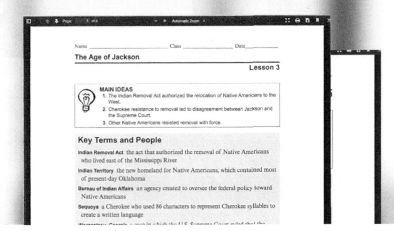

The **Guided Reading Workbook** and **Spanish/English Guided Reading Workbook**
offer students lesson summaries with vocabulary, reading, and note-taking support.

Current Events features trustworthy articles
from today's news that connect what students
learn in class to the world around them.

No Wi-Fi®? No problem!

HMH Social Studies World History allows you to connect to
content and resources by downloading them when online
and accessing them when offline.

Essential Question Preview

How did interactions with other cultures shape African societies?

Have students consider the Essential Question and capture their initial responses.

Explore the Essential Question

- Point out that major migrations helped spread African culture.

- Point out the central role that Islam played in the development of societies in North Africa.

Help students plan inquiries and develop their own supporting questions such as:

How did the movement of Bantu-speakers affect African lands and peoples?

What were causes and effects of the spread of Islam in Africa?

You may want to assign students to write a short essay in response to the Essential Question when they complete the module. Encourage students to use their notes and responses to inform their essays.

Explore the Online Video

ANALYZE VIDEOS

The Sahara

Invite students to watch the video to learn why Africans migrated out of the Sahara.

Geography Where did the people who lived on the North African savanna go as the Sahara developed? *They moved south to Central African grasslands or north to the Mediterranean Sea.*

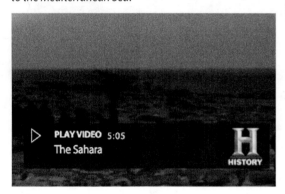

▶ **PLAY VIDEO** 5:05
The Sahara

HISTORY

Module 12

Societies and Empires of Africa

Essential Question
How did interactions with other cultures shape African societies?

About the Photo: This rock painting in northwestern Africa shows a line of calves tied to a rope in a pastoralist camp.

In this module you will learn how African civilizations adapted to various environments and developed complex civilizations and trading networks.

▶ *Explore ONLINE!*

HISTORY.
VIDEOS, including...
- The Sahara
- Masai People of Africa
- Trans-Saharan Trade
- Timbuktu: Thriving Songhai Empire Metropolis

☑ Document-Based Investigations
☑ Graphic Organizers
☑ Interactive Games
☑ Image with Hotspots: African Ironworking
☑ Carousel: The Ruins of Great Zimbabwe

What You Will Learn ...

Lesson 1 Big Idea

African peoples developed diverse societies as they adapted to varied environments.

Why It Matters Now

Differences among modern societies are also based on people's interactions with their environments.

Lesson 2 Big Idea

Relocation of large numbers of Bantu-speaking people brings cultural diffusion and change to southern Africa.

Why It Matters Now

Migration continues to shape the modern world.

Lesson 3 Big Idea

The kingdom of Aksum became an international trading power and adopted Christianity

Why It Matters Now

Ancient Aksum, which is in modern-day Ethiopia, is still a center of the Ethiopian Orthodox Christian Church

Lesson 4 Big Idea

North and West Africa contained several rich and powerful states, including Muslim states in the north and Ghana, Mali, and Songhai in the west.

Why It Matters Now

These civilizations demonstrate the richness of African culture before European colonization.

Timeline of Events 1500 BC–1500

▶ *Explore ONLINE!*

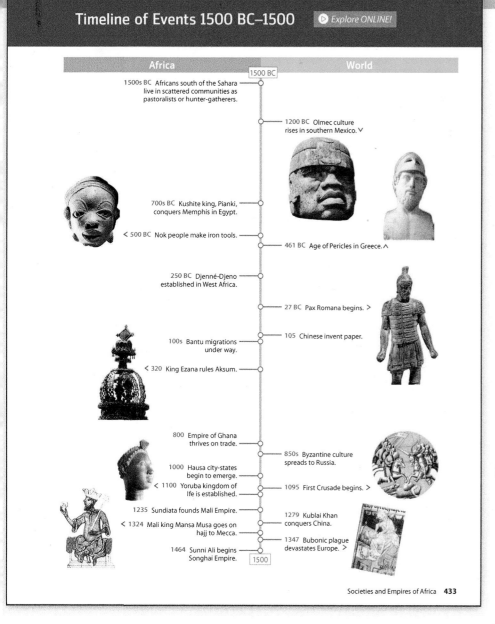

Africa

1500s BC	Africans south of the Sahara live in scattered communities as pastoralists or hunter-gatherers.
700s BC	Kushite king, Pianki, conquers Memphis in Egypt.
< 500 BC	Nok people make iron tools.
250 BC	Djenné-Djeno established in West Africa.
100s	Bantu migrations under way.
< 320	King Ezana rules Aksum.
800	Empire of Ghana thrives on trade.
1000	Hausa city-states begin to emerge.
< 1100	Yoruba kingdom of Ife is established.
1235	Sundiata founds Mali Empire.
< 1324	Mali king Mansa Musa goes on hajj to Mecca.
1464	Sunni Ali begins Songhai Empire.

World

1200 BC	Olmec culture rises in southern Mexico. ∨
461 BC	Age of Pericles in Greece. ∧
27 BC	Pax Romana begins. >
105	Chinese invent paper.
850s	Byzantine culture spreads to Russia.
1095	First Crusade begins. >
1279	Kublai Khan conquers China.
1347	Bubonic plague devastates Europe. >

Societies and Empires of Africa **433**

Lesson 5 Big Idea

African city-states and empires gained wealth through developing and trading resources.

Why It Matters Now

The country of Zimbabwe and cities such as Mogadishu and Mombasa have their roots in this time period.

Explore the Timeline

Interpret Timelines: African Societies and Empires, 1500 BC–1500

Have students examine the timeline and then answer the following question:

History About how long after the Empire of Ghana emerged did Sundiata conquer it? *about 435 years*

Interpret Timeline of Events: Timeline of Events 1500 BC–1500

To further explore the timeline, have students discuss the following questions:

1. What was happening elsewhere in the world during the Bantu migrations? *Chinese invent paper.*
2. How many years passed between the beginning of Sundiata's reign and Mansa Musa's hajj to Mecca? *89*

▶ ## Online Module Flip Cards

Use the flip cards as a whole-class activity or in student pairs to preview the module's Key Terms and People. Students can guess the meaning of each word, then review its definition, or do the reverse, using the flip card's toggle button to switch from Term to Definition mode. Students can also use the flip cards at the end of the module as a review tool before taking the Module Assessment.

▶ ## Online Sequencing Activity

Students can use this sequencing activity to review the chronology of events in the Societies and Empires of Africa module. To complete, have students drag each event to the correct year on the timeline

Year	Event
500 BC	*Nok people make iron tools.*
100s	*Bantu migrations under way.*
320	*King Ezana rules Aksum.*
800	*Empire of Ghana thrives on trade.*
1100	*Yoruba kingdom of Ife established*
1324	*Mali king Mansa Musa goes on hajj to Mecca.*

Diverse Societies in Africa

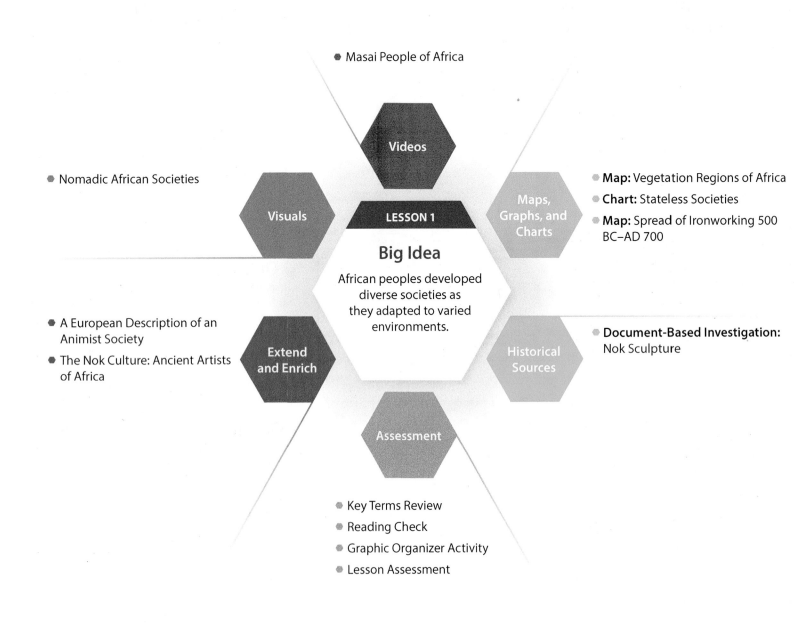

- Masai People of Africa

Videos

LESSON 1

Maps, Graphs, and Charts

- **Map:** Vegetation Regions of Africa
- **Chart:** Stateless Societies
- **Map:** Spread of Ironworking 500 BC–AD 700

- Nomadic African Societies

Visuals

Big Idea

African peoples developed diverse societies as they adapted to varied environments.

Historical Sources

- **Document-Based Investigation:** Nok Sculpture

- A European Description of an Animist Society
- The Nok Culture: Ancient Artists of Africa

Extend and Enrich

Assessment

- Key Terms Review
- Reading Check
- Graphic Organizer Activity
- Lesson Assessment

Online Lesson 1 Enrichment Activities

A European Description of an Animist Society

Account Students read and analyze an early English account of southern African animist beliefs from the 1874 book *Africa: Geographical Exploration and Christian Enterprise* by A. Gruar Forbes.

The Nok Culture: Ancient Artists of Africa

Article Students read about how and what archaeologists have learned about the Nok peoples of West Africa. Then they contrast the Nok method of sculpting and the lost wax process used by Benin sculptors.

Teach the Big Idea

1. **Whole Class Open/Introduction** Explain that the ancient peoples of Africa adapted creatively to their environment. Ask students how people today adapt to their environment. *Possible answers: air conditioning, central heating, specialized clothing*

2. **Direct Teach** Read students the Big Idea: *African peoples developed diverse societies as they adapted to varied environments.* Review the following lesson objectives with students to aid in their understanding of the Big Idea.

   - Identify the different geographic regions of Africa.

   - Explain how early Africans adapted to their environments.

   - Describe how a stateless society is run.

   - Trace the growth of African ironworking.

3. **Whole Group Close/Reflect** Review with students the features of a graphic novel. Ask students to imagine that they are writing and illustrating a graphic novel about Africa. Have them create several panels that show the transition from African hunting-gathering societies to settled lifestyles.

▷ ONLINE DOCUMENT-BASED INVESTIGATION

Societies and Empires of Africa

Nok Sculpture is the first of five historical sources that students will analyze in the Societies and Empires of Africa module. A Nok sculpture in the classical elongated style shows that the Nok had skilled artisans who created sophisticated artifacts. Have students study the image to observe characteristics of Nok sculpture.

▷ ONLINE GRAPHIC ORGANIZER

Diverse Societies in Africa

As students read the lesson, have them use the graphic organizer to take notes. Students can review their graphic organizer notes at the end of the lesson to answer the following question.

Draw Conclusions How did the geography of Africa affect the development of early African societies? *The geographic regions that had more natural resources, like the savanna, could support larger communities. Because the geography and climate were hospitable, agriculture could flourish there. People who lived in areas with fewer resources, such as the Sahel, continued to be nomadic, moving around to find what they needed to live.*

Diverse Societies in Africa

The Big Idea
African peoples developed diverse societies as they adapted to varied environments.

Why It Matters Now
Differences among modern societies are also based on people's interactions with their environments.

Key Terms and People
Sahara
Sahel
savanna
lineage
stateless society
patrilineal
matrilineal
animism
griot
desertification
Nok
Djenné-Djeno

Setting the Stage

Africa spreads across the equator. It includes a broad range of Earth's environments—from steamy coastal plains to snow-capped mountain peaks. Some parts of Africa suffer from constant drought, while others receive over 200 inches of rain a year. Vegetation varies from sand dunes and rocky wastes to dense green rain forests. Interaction with the African environment has created unique cultures and societies. Each group found ways to adapt to the land and the resources it offers.

A Land of Geographic Contrasts

Africa is the second largest continent in the world. It stretches 4,600 miles from east to west and 5,000 miles from north to south. With a total of 11.7 million square miles, it occupies about one-fifth of Earth's land surface. Narrow coastlines (50 to 100 miles) lie on either side of a central plateau. Waterfalls and rapids often form as rivers drop down to the coast from the plateau, making navigation impossible to or from the coast. Africa's coastline has few harbors, ports, or inlets. Because of this, the coastline is actually shorter than that of Europe, which is one-third Africa's size.

Challenging Environments Each African environment offers its own challenges. The deserts are largely unsuitable for human life and also hamper people's movement to more welcoming climates. The largest deserts are the **Sahara** in the north and the Kalahari (kahl•uh•HAHR•ee) in the south.

Stretching from the Atlantic Ocean to the Red Sea, the Sahara covers an area roughly the size of the United States. Only a small part of the Sahara consists of sand dunes. The rest is mostly a flat, gray wasteland of scattered rocks and gravel. Each year the desert takes over more and more of the semiarid region at the southern edge of the Sahara Desert, the **Sahel** (suh•HAYL).

COLLABORATIVE LEARNING

Public Service Announcement

1. Review with students information related to water in Africa. Point out that drought has been an ongoing problem that has made finding clean water increasingly difficult.

2. Organize the class into small groups. Ask each group to conduct Internet research about the problems associated with obtaining clean water. Have groups begin a two-column chart that lists the problems on one side. After they have completed their research about problems related to water, tell them to discuss possible solutions and add them to the second column of their chart.

3. Have each group prepare a 30-second public service announcement video on the importance of dealing with Africa's water problems. Tell groups to identify a hook to begin their announcement. Then they should focus on two or three important points they want to make. Remind them to present accurate information.

4. Have each group play their announcement for the class. Invite peers to provide feedback.

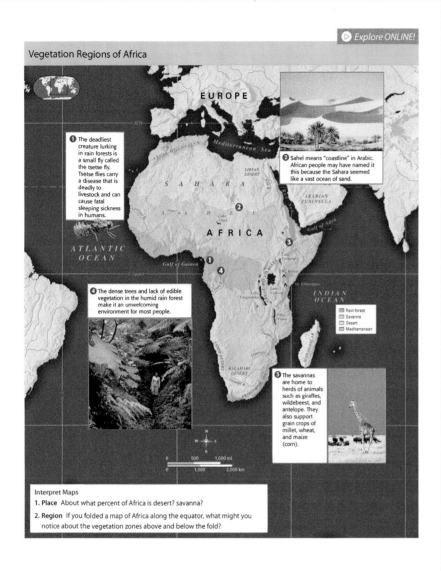

Vegetation Regions of Africa

Explore ONLINE!

1 The deadliest creature lurking in rain forests is a small fly called the tsetse fly. Tsetse flies carry a disease that is deadly to livestock and can cause fatal sleeping sickness in humans.

2 Sahel means "coastline" in Arabic. African people may have named it this because the Sahara seemed like a vast ocean of sand.

4 The dense trees and lack of edible vegetation in the humid rain forest make it an unwelcoming environment for most people.

3 The savannas are home to herds of animals such as giraffes, wildebeest, and antelope. They also support grain crops of millet, wheat, and maize (corn).

EUROPE

Mediterranean Sea

SAHARA

LIBYAN DESERT

ARABIAN PENINSULA

AFRICA

ATLANTIC OCEAN

Gulf of Guinea

INDIAN OCEAN

KALAHARI DESERT

- Rain forest
- Savanna
- Desert
- Mediterranean

0   500   1,000 mi
0   1,000   2,000 km

Interpret Maps

1. **Place** About what percent of Africa is desert? savanna?

2. **Region** If you folded a map of Africa along the equator, what might you notice about the vegetation zones above and below the fold?

Objectives

You may wish to discuss the following questions with students to help them frame the content as they read.

- What problems might the expansion of the Sahara cause? *Possible answer: push people off the land, crowd people into smaller livable areas, limit food production*

- Why might the rain forest be called "nature's greenhouse"? *The dense tree cover creates a sheltered area underneath where many plants can grow, much like a greenhouse.*

More About . . .

Life in Mali The nation of Mali includes part of the inhospitable Sahara and a swath of the dry Sahel. The remainder of the country follows the course of the Niger River and its tributaries. In the Sahel, people live far apart so their animals can take advantage of the sparse vegetation. Farther south, there is more water but infertile soil. Subsistence farmers manage to grow just enough millet, sorghum, corn, rice, cassava, and yams to feed themselves, with a little more to trade. Some are able to grow a few cash crops such as cotton, rice, peanuts, tobacco, and kola nuts. Though trade was lively in early Africa, today most people in Mali are subsistence farmers.

▶ ONLINE INTERACTIVE MAPS

Vegetation Regions of Africa

Have students explore the map using the interactive features and answer the associated questions.

Region About what percent of Africa is desert, and what percent is savanna? *about 30 percent desert and 50 percent savanna*

In print edition, see map of same title.

1. **Place** About what percent of Africa is desert? savanna? *about 30 percent desert; about 50 percent savanna*

2. **Region** If you folded a map of Africa along the equator, what might you notice about the vegetation zones above and below the fold? *The zones more or less match up: rain forest with rain forest, savanna with savanna, desert with desert, and Mediterranean with Mediterranean.*

▶ ONLINE LESSON FLIP CARDS

Review Key Terms and People

Students can use the flip cards in the Lesson Review at any time to review the lesson's key terms and people: *Sahara, Sahel, savanna, lineage, stateless societies, patrilineal, matrilineal, animism, griot, desertification, Nok,* and *Djenné-Djeno.*

STRUGGLING READERS

Map Game

1. Have students refer to a political map of Africa and the map Vegetation Regions of Africa. Students should use the lesson map to identify the desert, Mediterranean, rain forest, and savanna regions on the political map.

2. Organize the class into teams. Tell them they will play a game that requires them to compare the two maps.

3. Explain that the first team to supply the name of a present-day African country that is partly or completely within the vegetation you call out will get a point. Then start the game by beginning to call out vegetation regions.

COMPARE AND CONTRAST

Africa's Environment Poster

1. Ask groups of students to research either the savanna, Sahel, Sahara, or rain forest to find out about its location, climate, vegetation, and wildlife.

2. Have each group create a poster or multimedia presentation to display their information. Then have groups share their information with the class.

3. Guide students in a discussion of the similarities and differences of each region.

Objectives

You may wish to discuss the following questions with students to help them frame the content as they read.

- To what might the Efe attribute their long success as a hunting-gathering society? *a highly organized social system, defined roles within the group, a designated leader, plenty of resources in the forest*

- Why would complex settlements require more government than smaller communities? *Possible answer: to organize who would do which tasks*

- What happened to pastoralists of the Sahara 8,000 years ago? Why did this happen? *Many migrated east into the Nile Valley and south into West Africa because the Sahara became drier.*

More About . . .

African Music Early Africans developed varied and rich cultural traditions. Traditional African music was performed with a variety of instruments, including stringed and wind instruments as well as drums. The Efe, in particular, are known for making animal sounds, chanting, playing the *likembi* (an instrument with a wooden board with metal tines played by plucking the tines with thumbs) and singing songs that tell of their love for the Ituri Forest. Their music involves complex rhythms and harmony and is tied to religious expression.

Political Conflict Affecting the Efe For more than 40 years, the Democratic Republic of Congo (DRC) has been plagued by civil war. During the 1980s, government forces and rebels clashed over differences in economic opportunities and basic freedoms. Finally, the dictator Mobutu Sese Seko was ousted in 1997. While the Efe have stayed out of these political conflicts, the Ituri Forest has seen an influx of immigrants from both the DRC and Rwanda. This has caused issues for the Efe, who have no legal claim to the Ituri Forest and surrounding areas.

READING CHECK
Find Main Ideas Why do most people in Africa live on the savannas? *The savannas are suitable for agriculture, but the deserts and rain forests are not.*

Another very different—but also partly uninhabitable—African environment is the rain forest. Sometimes called "nature's greenhouse," it produces mahogany and teak trees up to 150 feet tall. Their leaves and branches form a dense canopy that keeps sunlight from reaching the forest floor. The tsetse (TSET•see) fly is found in the rain forest. Its presence prevented Africans from using cattle, donkeys, and horses to farm near the rain forests. This deadly insect also prevented invaders—especially Europeans—from colonizing fly-infested territories.

Welcoming Lands The northern coast and the southern tip of Africa have welcoming Mediterranean-type climates and fertile soil. Because these coastal areas are so fertile, they are densely populated with farmers and herders.

Most people in Africa live on the **savannas**, or grassy plains. Africa's savannas are not just endless plains. They include mountainous highlands and swampy tropical stretches. Covered with tall grasses and dotted with trees, the savannas cover over 40 percent of the continent. Dry seasons alternate with rainy seasons—often, two of each a year. Unfortunately, the topsoil throughout Africa is thin, and heavy rains strip away minerals. In most years, however, the savannas support abundant agricultural production.

Early Humans Adapt to Their Environments

The first humans appeared in the Great Rift Valley, a deep gash in Earth's crust that runs through the floor of the Red Sea and across eastern Africa. People moved outward from this area in the world's first migration. They developed technologies and social systems that helped them survive in—and then alter—their surroundings.

Hunting-Gathering Societies Nomadic hunting-gathering societies—the oldest form of social organization in the world—began in Africa. In Africa today, hunting-gathering societies form an extremely small percentage of the population. Scattered throughout the continent, these groups speak their own languages and often use their own hunting techniques. By studying these groups, scholars learn clues about how hunter-gatherers may have lived in the past.

The Efe (AY•fay) are one of several hunting-gathering societies in Africa. They live in the Ituri Forest in the Democratic Republic of Congo (formerly Zaire). Like their ancestors, the modern-day Efe live in small groups of between 10 and 100 members, all of whom are related. Each family occupies its own grass-and-brush shelter within a camp, but their homes are rarely permanent. Their search for food causes them to be somewhat nomadic. As a result, the Efe collect few possessions and move to new camps as they use up the resources in the surrounding area.

In the Efe society, women are the gatherers. They search the forest for roots, yams, mushrooms, and wild seeds. Efe men and older boys do all the hunting. Sometimes they gather in groups to hunt small antelope called duikers. At other times, hunters go solo and use poison-tipped arrows to

Reading Check
Find Main Ideas
Why do most people in Africa live on the savannas?

An Efe camp

ENGLISH LANGUAGE LEARNERS

Main Idea and Supporting Details Chart

1. Have students partner-read the text under the headings "Pastoral Societies" and "Transition to a Settled Lifestyle."

2. Have partners make a T-chart, labeling the two columns "Main Idea" and "Supporting Details."

3. Have partners reread the text under "Pastoral Societies" and identify the main idea. They should write it in the left column. Then have them identify details that support their main idea and write it in the right column. Repeat for "Transition to a Settled Lifestyle."

LINK TO MATH

African Societies Bar Graph

1. Have students work in pairs to find recent population figures for the following societies in Africa: Efe, Aka, Twa, Masai, Turkana, and Afar. Tell students that Efe, Aka, and Twa societies are nomadic hunting-gathering societies and the others are pastoralists. Have partners make a bar graph showing each population.

2. Then have partners draw two conclusions about the information on the bar graph and write four questions relating to the bar graph that others can answer.

kill mammals such as monkeys. The Efe also trade honey, wild game, and other forest products for crops grown by farmers in nearby villages.

A respected older male, such as a father, uncle, or father-in-law, typically serves as group leader. Although members of the group listen to and value this man's opinion, he does not give orders or act as chief. Each family within the band makes its own decisions and is free to come and go. Group members settle arguments through long discussions. If conflicts cannot be settled by talking, a group member may decide to move to a different hunting band. Daily life for the Efe is not governed by formal written laws.

In most African pastoral societies, young boys were responsible for watching over the herds.

Pastoral Societies Other early Africans eventually learned to domesticate and raise a variety of animals for food. Called herders, or pastoralists, these people kept cattle, goats, or sheep. They were nomads who drove their animals to find water and good pastures for grazing during the dry season. Millions of modern Africans are pastoral herders as well. The Masai (mah•SEYE) of Tanzania and southern Kenya, for example, still measure their wealth by the size of their herds. The Masai diet consists mostly of meat, blood, and milk. The Masai live in small bands that traditionally included up to 12 households, although bands are smaller today. As among the Efe, each Masai family within a band makes its own decisions and is free to come and go. Multiple bands work together to oversee use of grazing and watering facilities.

Transition to a Settled Lifestyle Experts believe that agriculture in Africa probably began by 6000 BC. Between 8000 and 6000 BC, the Sahara received increased rainfall and turned into a savanna. But about 6000 BC, the Sahara began to dry up again. To survive, many early farmers moved east into the Nile Valley and south into West Africa. Some settled on the savannas, which had the best agricultural land. Grain grew well in the savannas. In addition to growing grain, Africans began to raise cattle. In areas where the tsetse fly was found, it was not possible to keep cattle. However, south and east of the rain forests, cattle raising became an important part of agricultural life. Other Africans learned to farm in the rain forest, where they planted root crops that needed little sun.

Agriculture drastically changed the way Africans lived. Growing their own food enabled them to build permanent shelters in one location. Settlements expanded because reliable food supplies led to longer, healthier lives and an increased birthrate. The increased food supply also freed some members of the community to practice activities such as working metal, making pottery, and crafting jewelry.

These increasingly complex settlements of people required more organization than smaller communities. Various types of governing bodies developed to fill this need. Some governments consisted of a village chief and a council of the leaders of individual family groups. As strong groups moved to extend their land and conquered weaker settlements, they centralized their power and their governments. Some of these societies eventually developed into great kingdoms.

Reading Check
Make Inferences
Why might some Africans continue living a nomadic lifestyle?

▷ **ONLINE INTERACTIVE VISUAL**

Carousel: Nomadic African Societies

Have students navigate through the carousel and note similarities and differences among the images or identify a unifying theme.

▷ **ONLINE ANALYZE VIDEOS**

Masai People of Africa

Have students watch the video individually or as a class. You may wish to use the associated question as a discussion prompt.

Analyze Videos What do Masai males do when they become *morrans,* or warriors? *They travel for seven years, learning to be an adult, live off the land, and hunt buffalo.*

▷ PLAY VIDEO 4:13
Masai People of Africa

READING CHECK

Make Inferences Why might some Africans continue living a nomadic lifestyle? *They have no reasons to change a lifestyle that has suited their culture for thousands of years.*

Objectives

You may wish to discuss the following questions with students to help them frame the content as they read.

- How is lineage important to stateless societies? *determines inheritance and property distribution; elders of lineages govern the community*

- What were some religious beliefs of many early Africans? *Many believed in a supreme god and several secondary gods; they believed that spirits play an important role in regulating daily life; they honored the spirits of their ancestors.*

- Why were oral traditions important in early Africa? *Many societies did not develop systems of writing, so oral traditions kept history alive.*

More About . . .

Animism In ancient Buganda, in what is now south-central Uganda, each village recognized the existence of many local spirits. Beliefs stated that these spirits could do harm if displeased, so people left offerings of food or observed taboos such as bans against interacting with sacred places and objects. Stream spirits were thought to bathe at certain times, so people avoided the village well at those times. Similarly, wood gatherers avoided areas where wood spirits were thought to dwell. Tales of the terrible consequences of violating such taboos are told to this day.

▷ ONLINE INTERACTIVE CHARTS

Stateless Societies

Have students explore the graph and answer the associated question.

Interpret Charts If *h* is in conflict with *2*, who will meet to negotiate? *A and B*

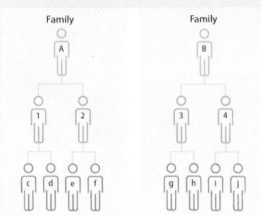

Stateless Societies

The societies south of the Sahara—like all human cultures—shared common elements. One of these elements was the importance of the basic social unit, the family. In many African societies, families are organized in groups called lineages. The members of a **lineage** (LIHN•ee•ihj) believe they are descendants of a common ancestor. Besides its living members, a lineage includes past generations (spirits of ancestors) and future generations (those not yet born). Lineage members are very loyal to one another.

South of the Sahara, many African groups developed systems of governing based on lineages. In some societies, lineage groups took the place of rulers. These societies, known as stateless societies, did not have a centralized system of power. Instead, authority in a **stateless society** was balanced among lineages of equal power so that no one family had too much control. The Igbo (IHG•boh) people—also called Ibo—of southern Nigeria lived in a stateless society as early as the ninth century. (Although the Igbo lived in West Africa, their political structure was similar to stateless societies found in central Africa.) If a dispute arose in an Igbo village, elders from different lineages settled the problem.

Tracing Family Descent In African societies, the way a society traces lineage determines how possessions and property are passed on and what groups individuals belong to. Members of a **patrilineal** society trace their ancestors through their fathers. Inheritance passes from father to son. When a son marries, he, his wife, and their children remain part of his father's extended family.

In a **matrilineal** society, children trace their ancestors through their mothers. Young men from a matrilineal culture inherit land and wealth from their mother's family. However, even in a matrilineal society, men usually hold the positions of authority.

Age-Set System In many African societies, young people form close ties to individuals outside their lineage through the age-set system. An age set consists of young people within a region who are born during a certain time period. Each age set passes together through defined life stages, such as warrior or elder. Ceremonies mark the passage to each new stage.

Social History

Negotiating Conflict in Stateless Societies

In a stateless society, the power to negotiate conflicts shifts from generation to generation as circumstances demand.

Look at the diagram of two lineages. If **d** is in conflict with **f**, then **c** will side with his brother **d**, and **e** will side with his brother **f**. Therefore, the parents—**1** and **2**—will meet to negotiate.

If **f** is in conflict with **g**, both entire lineages will take sides in the dispute. Therefore, the members of the oldest surviving generation—**A** and **B**—must meet to negotiate.

ENGLISH LANGUAGE LEARNERS

Focus on Vocabulary: Understand Word Origins

1. State that *patrilineal* comes from the prefix *patri-* meaning "father" or "paternal." The root word *lineal* means "in the direct line of descent from an ancestor."

2. Ask student pairs to break down the word *matrilineal* in the same way you have just modeled.

3. Next, request that students find other words in the dictionary with the two prefixes and write the words and their definitions in a chart.

Men and women have different life stages, and each stage has its own duties and importance. Societies like the Igbo use the age-set system to teach young people discipline, community service, and leadership skills.

Local Religions African peoples organized themselves into family groups. They also developed belief systems that helped them understand and organize information about their world. Many of these local religions were polytheistic, involving belief in one divine creator or supreme god in addition to several secondary gods or semi-divine spirits. African religions generally also included elements of **animism**, a belief system in which spirits play an important role in regulating daily life. Animists believe that spirits are present in animals, plants, and other natural forces. In addition to nature spirits, Africans honored the spirits of their ancestors.

In most African religions, the supreme god was not involved in humans' lives. Instead, nature spirits and spirits of ancestors were responsible for many of life's events, such as a plentiful harvest or an illness. This belief led Africans to develop many religious practices and ceremonies to ask the spirits for health, fertility, and wealth. Other rituals were to protect people from bad spirits. Africans did not separate religion from other areas of life. Instead, spiritual beliefs and practices were integral to all of life.

Keeping a History Few African societies had written languages. Instead, storytellers shared orally the history and literature of a culture. In West Africa, for example, these storytellers, or **griots** (gree·ohz), kept this history alive, passing it from parent to child:

> *"I am a griot . . . master in the art of eloquence. Since time immemorial the Kouyatés have been in the service of the Keita princes of Mali; we are vessels of speech, we are the repositories [storehouses] which harbor secrets many centuries old. . . . Without us the names of kings would vanish into oblivion, we are the memory of mankind; by the spoken word we bring to life the deeds . . . of kings for younger generations. . . . For the world is old, but the future springs from the past."*

—Djeli Mamoudou Kouyaté, from *Sundiata, an Epic of Old Mali*

Collecting Water

Finding and collecting water has traditionally been the job of women, whether they have a settled lifestyle or a nomadic one. Each day they must find clean water for their families, but drought in Africa has increased the difficulty of this task. In the past, it was estimated that women spent an average of nine minutes a day collecting water, but that time has increased in recent years. In some places, women have to walk as far as 6 miles (about 10 kilometers) to find water. Obtaining clean water will continue to be a difficult task, even for those who have made the transition to a settled lifestyle on small plots of land.

Societies and Empires of Africa **439**

ADVANCED/GIFTED

Explore Oral Traditions by Telling a Story

1. Have students reread Djeli Mamadou Kouyate's quotation about the importance of the spoken word and the role of the griot. Ask students to brainstorm possible topics for griots' tales: *real and legendary leaders, beginning of culture, creation of world*

2. Ask students to research some stories from an African oral tradition.

3. Invite students to select a story to retell in a dramatic presentation and plan their presentations.

4. Ask students to make their presentations to the class, using gestures and movements for emphasis.

Objectives

You may wish to discuss the following questions with students to help them frame the content as they read.

- How do artifacts provide a picture of daily life? *Possible answer: Tools reveal how people worked and help identify their daily tasks.*

- What major changes affected societies during Africa's Iron Age? *The spread of iron technology changed farming and hunting practices. Society changed as a result.*

- What are some possible reasons that Djenné-Djeno was abandoned? *Possible answer: Drought caused famine, war.*

More About . . .

Ironworking Some peoples in the Middle East had begun to smelt iron and make tools by about 3500 BC. They even decorated some of the tools. The oldest iron tools in existence are Egyptian sickle blades and a crosscut saw. By 1500 to 1000 BC, ironworking had spread over much of Asia, Africa, and Europe. The Greek poet Homer speaks of iron as something precious, like gold. The people of Scandinavia, however, knew very little about iron before the time of Julius Caesar.

Nok Sculpture More than 150 Nok figurines have been excavated. Many are stylized heads such as the one shown in the lesson. Others show elephants, which played a role in the people's daily lives. From the detailed study of these terra cotta figures, scholars suggest that some figures represent rulers, priests, or other members of an upper class. The figures may also have been memorials to ancestors.

▷ ONLINE DOCUMENT-BASED INVESTIGATION

Nok Sculpture

Nok artifacts show evidence of a sophisticated culture. Their sculptures are made of terra cotta and include animals as well as people. Have students study the image and answer the associated question.

Analyze Sources What questions would you ask if you could speak with the creator of this sculpture? *Does the sculpture represent a real person? Why and how was it made?*

READING CHECK
Analyze Sources Why were griots important to West African societies? *They provided the links between the past and the present in societies that did not have written histories.*

Recent discoveries in West Africa have proved how old and extensive the history of this part of Africa is. Archaeologists believe that early peoples from the north moved into West Africa as **desertification**, or drying of the soil, forced them south to find better farmland. Discoveries in the areas of present-day Mali and Nigeria reveal that West Africans developed advanced societies and cities long before outsiders came to the continent.

West African Iron Age

Archaeologists' main source of information about early West African cultures has been from artifacts such as pottery, charcoal, and slag—a waste product of iron smelting. By dating these artifacts, scientists can piece together a picture of life in West Africa as early as 500 BC.

Unlike cultures to the north, the peoples of sub-Saharan Africa seem to have skipped the Copper and Bronze Ages and moved directly into the Iron Age. Evidence of iron production dating to around 500 BC has been found just north of the Niger and Benue rivers. The ability to smelt iron was a major technological achievement of the ancient Nok of that region.

The Nok Culture West Africa's earliest known culture was that of the **Nok** (nahk) people. They lived in what is now Nigeria between 500 BC and AD 200. Their name came from the village where the first artifacts from their culture were discovered. Nok artifacts have been found in an area stretching for 300 miles between the Niger and Benue rivers. They were the first West African people known to smelt iron. The iron was fashioned into tools for farming and weapons for hunting. Some of the tools and weapons made their way into overland trade routes.

DOCUMENT-BASED INVESTIGATION   Historical Source

Nok Sculpture

Nok artifacts show evidence of a sophisticated culture. Their sculptures are made of terra cotta, a reddish-brown baked clay. Sculptures include animals as well as people. This Nok figure features a classical look called "elongated" style.

Most Nok figurines have these characteristics:

- distinctive features such as bulging eyes, flaring nostrils, and protruding lips
- an elongated style, especially used for the head
- the hand or chin on the knee in some figures
- hairstyle still common in Nigeria

Analyze Historical Sources
What questions would you ask if you could speak with the creator of this sculpture?

ENGLISH LANGUAGE LEARNERS

Understand Artifacts

1. Explain to students that the Copper, Bronze, and Iron Ages do not represent exact periods of time. Each is defined by the materials—copper, bronze, iron —with which tools were made. The phases lasted different lengths of time for different cultures. Some early African cultures appear to have skipped from stone tools directly to iron tools.

2. To help students apply this background to the discussion of early African culture, review the words and phrases shown here. List each term or phrase in the left column of a horizontal chart. Then invite students to share a suggested definition.

Word	Definition
artifacts	*things made by people*
fashioned	*shaped*
refining metal	*making metal pure*
dating artifacts	*figuring out when artifacts were made*
smelting iron	*using a furnace to separate iron from unwanted materials*
oasis	*fertile area where water is located in a desert*
make their mark on history	*influence people who come after them in time*
techniques	*ways of doing something*

3. Ask students to each choose one word or phrase and make an illustrated vocabulary card, showing the word or phrase, the definition, and a picture that helps them understand the meaning.

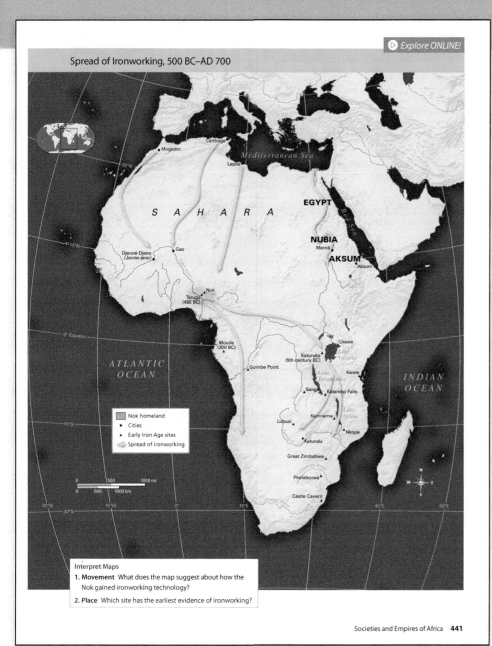

Spread of Ironworking, 500 BC–AD 700

▶ Explore ONLINE!

Interpret Maps

1. **Movement** What does the map suggest about how the Nok gained ironworking technology?

2. **Place** Which site has the earliest evidence of ironworking?

Spread of Ironworking, 500 BC–AD 700

Have students explore the map and answer the associated questions.

Movement What does the map suggest about how the Nok gained ironworking technology? *Ironworking spread from North Africa to West Africa.*

In print edition, see map of same title.

Movement What does the map suggest about how the Nok gained ironworking technology? *Ironworking spread from North Africa to West Africa.*

Place Which site has the earliest evidence of ironworking? *Katuruka*

ARCHAEOLOGIST RECORDS

Below Level Have students paraphrase information from the text to record findings made by archaeologists about early West African cultures. Students should include details about how the archaeologists gained their information and what they learned.

At Level Have students examine the text to write a summary of what archaeologists discovered about early West African cultures and Djenné-Djeno. Students should draw conclusions about the use of technology and its effect on these early cultures.

Above Level Have student synthesize information in the text to write an analysis about the West African Iron Age and its effect on Africa. Students should include information about archaeological findings, the implications of these findings, and the impact the West African Iron Age had on civilizations at the time.

African Ironworking

Discuss the process of ironworking with students to help them understand its value and importance to early African societies. Ironworking represented a significant technological advance, which enabled these cultures to make more durable and thus more useful tools.

Connect to Today

1. **Hypothesize** What advantages would iron tools give a civilization? *Possible answer: Stronger tools that last longer and do heavier work means that workers don't have to produce as many tools, saving time and resources. Also, the iron tools and technology are valuable and might bring a civilization income through trade.*

2. **Compare and Contrast** Use the Internet to research the history of modern ironworking techniques. What improvements have been made, and how do they benefit our life today? *Possible answer: Encourage students to look at the progression of technology in ironworking, noting, for example, the difference between iron and steel. Benefits to daily life might include more resilient buildings and better and stronger tools/products.*

African Ironworking

Refining metal was an important technological advance in every civilization. Africa was no exception. Iron tools were stronger than copper or bronze tools, so iron tools and the technology to produce them were very valuable.

Producing iron began by mining the iron ore. The iron itself was bound up with other minerals in rocks. The trick was separating the iron from the unwanted minerals. That was the function of the furnace shown below. This process is known as smelting.

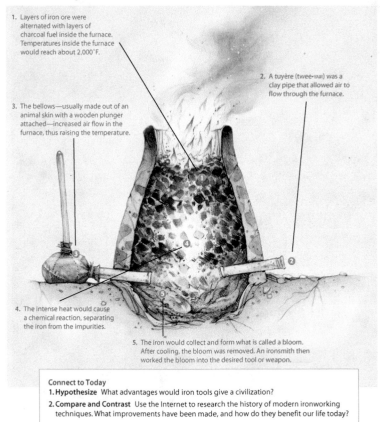

1. Layers of iron ore were alternated with layers of charcoal fuel inside the furnace. Temperatures inside the furnace would reach about 2,000°F.

2. A tuyère (twee-YAIR) was a clay pipe that allowed air to flow through the furnace.

3. The bellows—usually made out of an animal skin with a wooden plunger attached—increased air flow in the furnace, thus raising the temperature.

4. The intense heat would cause a chemical reaction, separating the iron from the impurities.

5. The iron would collect and form what is called a bloom. After cooling, the bloom was removed. An ironsmith then worked the bloom into the desired tool or weapon.

Connect to Today
1. **Hypothesize** What advantages would iron tools give a civilization?
2. **Compare and Contrast** Use the Internet to research the history of modern ironworking techniques. What improvements have been made, and how do they benefit our life today?

Djenné-Djeno In the region south of the Sahel, most Africans lived in small villages. However, cities began to develop sometime between 600 BC and 200 BC. Usually they were in areas along rivers or at an oasis. One of these cities was Djenné-Djeno.

Djenné-Djeno (jeh·NAY-jeh·NOH), or ancient Djenné, was uncovered by archaeologists in 1977. Djenné-Djeno is located on a tributary of the Niger River in West Africa. There, scientists discovered hundreds of thousands of artifacts. These objects included pottery, copper hair ornaments, clay toys, glass beads, stone bracelets, and iron knives.

A modern artist, Charles Santore, has pictured life in Djenné-Djeno around 1000.

The oldest objects found there dated from 250 BC, making Djenné-Djeno the oldest known city in Africa south of the Sahara. The city was abandoned sometime after AD 1400.

At its height, Djenné-Djeno had some 50,000 residents. They lived in round reed huts plastered with mud. Later, they built houses made of mud bricks. They fished in the Niger River, herded cattle, and raised rice on the river's fertile floodplains. By the third century BC, they smelted iron. They exchanged their rice, fish, and pottery for copper, gold, and salt from other peoples who lived along the river. Djenné-Djeno became a bustling trade center linked to other towns by the Niger and by overland camel routes.

The early inhabitants of West Africa were developing cities, cultures, and technologies that would make their mark on history. Meanwhile, other groups in West Africa were beginning to make an historic move out of West Africa. The Bantu-speaking people would take their culture and ironworking techniques with them to parts of eastern and southern Africa.

Reading Check
Compare
In what ways were the cultures of Djenné-Djeno and the Nok alike?

Lesson 1 Assessment

1. **Organize Information** Use an outline like the one below to organize your notes about early African societies.

```
Africa
    I. A Land of Geographic
       Contrasts
        A.
        B.
    II. Early Humans Adapt to
        Their Environments
```

Write a paragraph explaining how hunting-gathering societies are different from pastoral societies.

2. **Key Terms and People** For each key term or person in the lesson, write a sentence explaining its significance.
3. **Analyze Causes** Why did diverse cultures develop in Africa?
4. **Recognize Effects** How did agriculture change the way Africans lived?
5. **Hypothesize** Why were elders from each lineage responsible for solving disputes amongst lineages of stateless societies?
6. **Summarize** Why did African societies develop age-set systems?
7. **Draw Conclusions** What evidence shows that Djenné-Djeno was a major trading city in West Africa?

Compare In what ways were the cultures of Djenné-Djeno and the Nok alike? *Both peoples were farmers and iron-makers, and they created similar artifacts.*

Print Assessment

1. **Organize Information** Use an outline to organize your notes about early African societies. Write a paragraph explaining how hunting-gathering societies are different from pastoral societies. *Students' answers will vary, but students should mention that hunting-gathering societies live by gathering the plants and hunting the animals in their environment, and pastoral societies live by raising livestock.*

2. **Key Terms and People** For each key term or person in the lesson, write a sentence explaining its significance. *Explanations of the lesson's key terms can be found on the following pages: Sahara, p. 434; Sahel, p. 434; savanna, p. 436; lineage, p. 438; stateless societies, p. 438; patrilineal, p. 438; matrilineal, p. 438; animism, p. 439; griot, p. 439; desertification, p. 440; Nok, p. 440; Djenné-Djeno, p. 443.*

3. **Analyze Causes** Why did diverse cultures develop in Africa? *They developed because of diverse climates and natural resources; groups adapted to suit resources and climates; migration introduced different adaptation techniques.*

4. **Recognize Effects** How did agriculture change the way Africans lived? *settled in one location, reliable food supplies, longer and healthier lives, increased birthrate, increased social and political organization required*

5. **Hypothesize** Why were elders from each lineage responsible for solving disputes amongst lineages of stateless societies? *Possible answer: The people of each lineage would automatically side with their own lineages in any dispute; elders had advanced through the life stages; they were considered wise because of their experience; they were closer to the ancestors.*

6. **Summarize** Why did African societies develop age-set systems? *to educate people, to encourage bonding in the community, and to award status*

7. **Draw Conclusions** What evidence shows that Djenné-Djeno was a major trading city in West Africa? *artifacts, e.g., pottery, copper, gold, iron; evidence of overland camel trade*

▷ Online Assessment

1. What are **two** reasons that the northern coast and the southern tip of Africa are densely populated?
   - ○ fertile soil
   - ○ grassy plains
   - ○ natural resources
   - ◉ welcoming climate
   - ○ tropical rain forests
   - ○ swampy landscape

   Alternate Question *Select the answer choice from the drop-down list to complete the sentence correctly.* Certain areas of Africa have uninhabitable environments. However, the [northern coast and southern tip of the continent ⬍] have a welcoming Mediterranean-type climate and fertile soil.

2. What is the primary difference between the Efe and Masai people?
   - ◉ how they get their food
   - ○ the types of homes they live in
   - ○ how they record their histories
   - ○ the way they travel from place to place

   Alternate Question *Select the answer choice from the drop-down list to complete the sentence correctly.* The Efe people and Masai people are similar and different in certain ways. One of the primary differences is that the Masai people [raise animals ⬍] for food while the Efe people hunt for their food.

3. What led early Africans to develop many religions, practices, rituals, and ceremonies?
   - ○ a belief in having a matrilineal society
   - ○ a belief in a supreme god that controlled nature spirits
   - ○ a belief that there was a main god and manyminor gods
   - ◉ a belief that spirits were responsible for many of life's events

   Alternate Question *Select the answer choice from the drop-down list to complete the sentence correctly.* Africans believed that [spirits ⬍] were responsible for many of life's events. This belief led the Africans to develop many religious practices, rituals, and ceremonies focused on health, fertility, and wealth.

4. What did the Nok, Djenné-Djeno, and Bantu-speaking people have in common with one another?
   - ◉ They all worked with iron.
   - ○ They all lived along major rivers.
   - ○ They all were hunters and gatherers.
   - ○ They all frequently invaded their neighbors.

   Alternate Question *Select the answer choice from the drop-down list to complete the sentence correctly.* The Nok, Djenné-Djeno, and Bantu-speaking people were all known for their [ironworks ⬍].

5. **Compare and Contrast** How are the desert and the rain forest similar to and different from each other?

   Possible answer: The desert and the rain forest are similar because they are both partly uninhabitable. The desert is uninhabitable because of no rain and a lack of vegetation, and the rain forest is uninhabitable because of the opposite reasons—too much rain and too much vegetation. The two are different because of the varied vegetation and rainfall totals. Also, the desert doesn't have the tsetse fly and the rain forest does.

6. **Cause and Effect** How did agriculture change the way early Africans lived?

   Possible answer: Agriculture drastically changed how Africans lived. They were able to grow their own food instead of hunting and gathering for it. This allowed them to stay in one place and build permanent shelters. Settlements grew from small villages to larger cities because reliable food sources were now available. Africans lived longer lives and had increased birthrate. The increased food supply allowed people to do other things rather than just search for food— pottery makers, metalworkers, and jewelry artisans became part of the culture.

7. **Compare and Contrast** What is the difference between patrilineal and matrilineal societies?

   Possible answer: Patrilineal societies trace lineage through the fathers. Possessions and property are passed from father to son. People in patrilineal societies also trace their lineage through their father's line. When a son marries, he and his family (wife and children) become part of the father's household. Matrilineal societies, on the other hand, trace their ancestors through the mother's side of the family. A son receives land and possessions from his mother's family.

8. **Elaborate** Who were the Djenné-Djeno people, and how was their civilization discovered?

   Possible answer: Djenné-Djeno was a civilization of 50,000 people south of the Sahel. This civilization was located on a tributary of the Niger River in West Africa. The people first lived in round reed huts plastered with mud and then built enclosed houses made of mud bricks. The civilization was discovered in 1977 by archaeologists who found artifacts including toys, hair ornaments, pottery, and glass beads.

Migration: Case Study: Bantu-Speaking Peoples

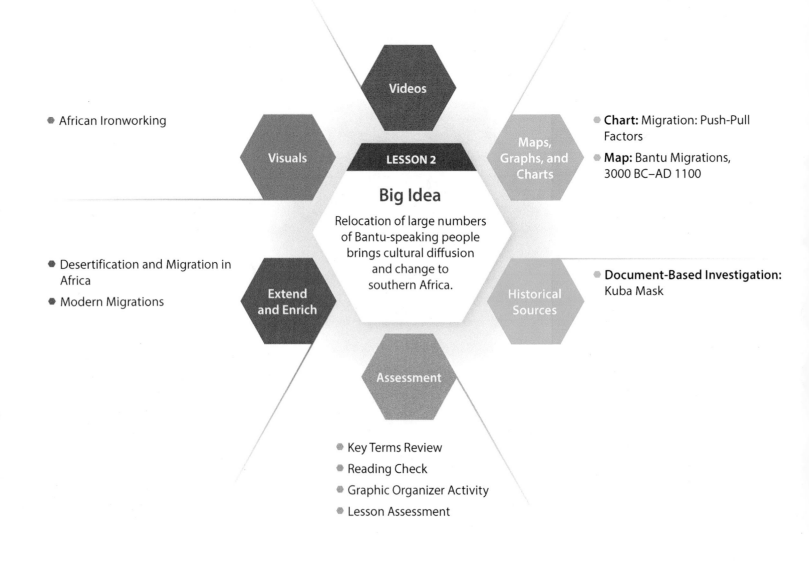

Videos

● African Ironworking

Visuals

LESSON 2

Maps, Graphs, and Charts

● **Chart:** Migration: Push-Pull Factors
● **Map:** Bantu Migrations, 3000 BC–AD 1100

Big Idea

Relocation of large numbers of Bantu-speaking people brings cultural diffusion and change to southern Africa.

● Desertification and Migration in Africa
● Modern Migrations

Extend and Enrich

Historical Sources

● **Document-Based Investigation:** Kuba Mask

Assessment

● Key Terms Review
● Reading Check
● Graphic Organizer Activity
● Lesson Assessment

▶ Online Lesson 2 Enrichment Activities

Desertification and Migration in Africa

Article Students first study how the desertification of North Africa causes movement of populations in Africa. Then they draw a thematic map of North Africa before 10,000 BC, showing climate, vegetation, and animal life.

Modern Migrations

Presentation Activity Students research a recent or current migration involving push-pull factors. Then they create an informative presentation to tell about it.

Teach the Big Idea

1. **Whole Class Open/Introduction** Tell students that Bantu-speaking peoples migrated over huge distances, bringing their culture to new groups. Ask students how movements of people into the United States have changed their culture and community. *Possible answer: increased variety in foods, businesses, languages, customs, and religions*

2. **Direct Teach** Read students the Big Idea: *Relocation of large numbers of Bantu-speaking people brings cultural diffusion and change to southern Africa.* Review the following lesson objectives with students to aid in their understanding of the Big Idea.

   • Summarize the causes and effects of human migration.

   • Describe the Bantu migrations into the southern half of Africa.

3. **Whole Group Close/Reflect** Have each student write a two-paragraph cause-and-effect explanation of the Bantu migrations.

▷ ONLINE DOCUMENT-BASED INVESTIGATION

Societies and Empires of Africa

Kuba Mask is the second of five historical sources that students will analyze in the Societies and Empires of Africa module. Like most sub-Saharan African cultures, the people of the Kuba kingdom traditionally used masks for rituals and ceremonies. Have students study the image.

▷ ONLINE GRAPHIC ORGANIZER

Migration

As students read the lesson, have them use the graphic organizer to take notes. Students can review their graphic organizer notes at the end of the lesson to answer the following question.

Draw Conclusions What are the push-pull factors encountered by Bantu-speaking peoples that historians believe motivated them to continue moving east and south through Africa? *Push factors were depleted soil from their farming techniques and population too large. Pull factors were resources such as good soil, water, and trees.*

▷ ONLINE LESSON FLIP CARDS

Review Key Terms and People

Students can use the flip cards in the Lesson Review at any time to review the lesson's key terms and people: *migration, push-pull factors, Bantu-speaking peoples.*

Case Study
Bantu-Speaking
Peoples

Migration

The Big Idea
Relocation of large numbers of Bantu-speaking people brought cultural diffusion and change to southern Africa.

Why It Matters Now
Migration continues to shape the modern world.

Key Terms and People
migration
push-pull factors
Bantu-speaking peoples

Setting the Stage

Human history is a constantly recurring set of movement, collision, settlement, and more movement. Throughout history, people have chosen to uproot themselves and move to explore their world. Sometimes they migrate in search of new opportunities. Other times, migration is a desperate attempt to find a place to survive or to live in peace.

People on the Move

As an important pattern in human culture, migrations have influenced world history from its outset. **Migration** is a permanent or semipermanent move from one country or region to another.

Causes of Migration Aside from the general human desire for change, the causes of migrations fall into three categories: environmental, economic, and political. In the early history of human life, environmental factors were most likely the strongest. Later, economic and political causes played a greater role. For example, in the 15th century, the Ottomans' drive for power pushed them to move all over the ancient world to create a massive empire. As the world became more industrialized, more people moved to cities where work in factories was available. Elsewhere, religious or ethnic persecution supported by governments often drove groups of people to flee in order to survive. Seventeenth-century European settlers were pulled to America by the hope of religious tolerance, land for farming, or better economic conditions.

When looking at migration, historians and geographers speak of **push-pull factors**. These factors can either push people out of an area or pull them into an area. An example of an environmental pull factor might be abundant land that attracts people. On the other hand, the depletion of natural resources forces people away from a location—a push factor. Employment or the lack of it is an economic push or pull

---

COLLABORATIVE LEARNING

Create a Bantu-Language Use List and Map

1. Review with students that Swahili is a Bantu language spoken by about 50 million people in Central and East Africa. Point out that in addition to Swahili, there are other Bantu languages.

2. Have students work in groups. Explain that they are to use online or library resources to find information on the most widely-spoken Bantu languages and the African countries in which they are spoken.

3. After they have gathered their information, they should create a database of the information. Explain to students that their database can be a listing of the information in easy-to-use form.

4. Suggest that groups divide the tasks by assigning students the roles of researcher, recorder, anddatabase organizer.

5. After groups have created their database, have them use it to identify on a map of Africa where eachlanguage is spoken.

Migration: Push-Pull Factors

Push Examples	Migration Factors	Pull Examples
Climate changes, exhausted resources, earthquakes, volcanoes, drought/famine	Environmental	Abundant land, new resources, good climate
Unemployment, slavery	Economic	Employment opportunities
Religious, ethnic, or political persecution, war	Political	Political and/or religious freedom

Interpret Charts
1. **Develop Historical Perspective** Are environmental factors still a cause of migration in the modern world? Explain.
2. **Analyze Causes** Which cause do you think is most important in modern migrations? Why?

factor. Political conditions such as freedom or persecution can encourage people to move or to stay where they are. Urbanization also causes migration because job opportunities and other benefits attract people. The chart shows how causes of migration are related to push-pull factors.

Effects of Migration Life in a newly populated area changes because of the influx of new people. The results of migration may be positive or negative.
- Redistribution of the population may change population density.
- Cultural blending of languages or ways of life may occur.
- Ideas and technologies may be shared.
- People's quality of life may be improved as a result of moving.
- Clashes between groups may create unrest, persecution, or even war.
- Environmental conditions may change, causing famine or depleted natural resources.
- Employment opportunities may dry up, creating unemployment and poverty.

Migration changes the lives of those who migrate and also of the people in communities where they settle. Both groups may need to make adjustments in the way they live. Some adjustments may be relatively easy to make. For example, more advanced technology may improve living conditions. Other adjustments may be more difficult and may occur over a longer period of time. One of these adjustments may include language.

Tracing Migration Through Language One way experts can trace the patterns of movement of people over time is by studying the spread of languages. People bring their languages with them when they move to new places. And languages, like the people who speak them, are living things

Objectives

You may wish to discuss the following questions with students to help them frame the content as they read.

- Why would environmental migration factors be most important to early peoples? *Possible answer: great dependence on nature for survival*

- What does the spread of Bantu languages suggest about Bantu migrations? *They were quite widespread.*

More About . . .

African Migration Today Push and Pull factors affect present-day migration in Africa. For example, lack of educational opportunities, jobs, and basic freedoms push many people out of Zimbabwe. People from Somalia, Ethiopia, and Eritrea are pushed from their homelands for such reasons as conflict, mistreatment, and poverty. In contrast, many people are pulled to South Africa because of its strong economy and its job market.

Anthropologist Root and Suffix The word *anthropologist* combines the root *anthropo* with the suffixes *-ology* and *-ist. Anthropo*, from the Greek *anthropos*, means "human being." The suffix *-ology* means "branch of learning," while *-ist* means "one who specializes in an area." Together, these word parts create a word that means "one who specializes in the study of human beings."

▷ **ONLINE INTERACTIVE CHARTS**

Migration: Push-Pull Factors
Have students explore the chart and answer the associated questions.

Interpret Charts Which cause do you think is most important in modern migrations? Why? *Since fewer people raise their own food, finding employment is a powerful force in modern migrations.*

In print edition, see chart of same title.

1. **Develop Historical Perspective** Are environmental factors still a cause of migration in the modern world? Explain. *Yes, floods, famine, earthquakes, and volcanic eruptions still force people to leave a region.*

2. **Analyze Causes** Which cause do you think is most important in modern migrations? Why? *Since fewer people raise their own food, finding employment is a powerful force in modern migrations.*

ENGLISH LANGUAGE LEARNERS

Evaluate Migration Factors

1. Ask students to brainstorm positive and negative migration factors and list these on the board. For each factor listed, help students identify why that factor is either positive or negative.

2. Discuss with students whether any factor could change categories, from negative to positive or vice versa. For example, clashes between groups might lead to people overcoming their preconceptions and developing greater tolerance.

STRUGGLING READERS

Identify Cause and Effect

1. Have students create a cause-and-effect chart. Also, create one on the board to serve as a model.

2. As students begin to read the lesson, pause and ask them to identify a cause of migration and an effect. Write the first cause and effect in the chart as an example.

3. Have students continue reading the lesson to complete their cause-and-effect chart. After students complete their cause-and-effect chart, have them quiz each other by asking questions about causes and effects of migration.

Bantu Migrations, 3000 BC–AD 1100

Have students explore the map using the interactive features and answer the associated questions.

Human-Environment Interaction What geographic features did the Bantu speakers encounter in the course of their migrations? Choose the most complete answer. *lakes, rivers, rain forest, and deserts*

In print edition, see map of same title.

1. **Human-Environment Interaction** What geographic features did the Bantu speakers encounter in the course of their migrations? *lakes, rivers, rain forest, and deserts*

2. **Movement** Why didn't the Bantu speakers migrate northward? *They were blocked by the Sahara.*

READING CHECK

Form Opinions Which of the effects of migration do you think are most negative? Explain. *clashes between groups because people may be injured or killed; environmental degradation, which hurts all people living in an area; unemployment, which causes hardships in families*

---

that evolve and change in predictable ways. If two languages have similar words for a particular object or idea, for example, it is likely that the people who spoke those languages probably had close contact at one time.

Experts have studied languages in Africa. One group of African languages, the Niger-Congo, includes over 900 individual languages. A family of languages in this group developed from a single parent tongue, Proto-Bantu. Many anthropologists believe that the language spread across Africa as a result of migration. Today in Africa, Bantu speakers live in a region from Cameroon east to Kenya and south to the southern tip of Africa. A Bantu language is the first language of nearly one-third of all Africans.

Reading Check
Form Opinions
Which of the effects of migration do you think are most negative? Explain.

A mask of the Kuba, a Bantu-speaking people, from Congo and Zaire

▷ *Explore ONLINE!*

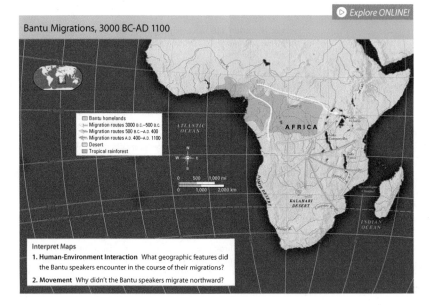

Bantu Migrations, 3000 BC-AD 1100

Bantu homelands
Migration routes 3000 B.C.–500 B.C.
Migration routes 500 B.C.–A.D. 400
Migration routes A.D. 400–A.D. 1100
Desert
Tropical rainforest

ATLANTIC OCEAN
AFRICA
NAMIB DESERT
KALAHARI DESERT
INDIAN OCEAN

0   500   1,000 mi
0   1,000   2,000 km

Interpret Maps
1. **Human-Environment Interaction** What geographic features did the Bantu speakers encounter in the course of their migrations?
2. **Movement** Why didn't the Bantu speakers migrate northward?

Massive Migrations

Early Africans made some of the greatest migrations in history. When the migrations were over they or their descendants populated the southern third of the continent. Starting in the first few centuries AD and continuing over 1,500 years, small groups moved southward throughout Africa, spreading their language and culture. Historians refer to these people as the **Bantu-speaking peoples**. (The word *Bantu* itself means "the people.") The Bantu-speaking peoples originally lived in the savanna south of the Sahara, in the area that is now southeastern Nigeria.

Migration Begins Bantu speakers were not one people, but rather a group of peoples who shared certain cultural characteristics. They were farmers and nomadic herders who developed and passed along the skill of iron-working. Many experts believe they were related to the Nok peoples.

Beginning at least 2,000 years ago or earlier, small groups of Bantu speakers began moving to the south and east. The farming technique used by these people forced them to move every few years. The technique is called slash and burn. A patch of the forest is cut down and burned. Then the ashes are mixed into the soil, creating a fertile garden area. However, the land loses its fertility quickly and is abandoned for another plot in a new location.

When they moved, the Bantu speakers shared their skills with the people they met, adapted their methods to suit each new environment, and learned new customs. They followed the Congo River through the rain forests. In the rain forests, they farmed the riverbanks—the only place that received enough sunlight to support agriculture.

As they moved eastward into the savannas, they adapted their techniques for herding goats and sheep to raising cattle. Passing through the area that is now Kenya and Tanzania, they learned to cultivate new crops. One such crop was the banana, which came from Southeast Asia via Indonesian travelers.

Causes of Migration Although it is impossible to know exactly what caused the Bantu-speaking peoples to migrate, anthropologists have proposed a logical explanation. These experts suggest that once these peoples developed agriculture, they were able to produce more food than they could obtain by hunting and gathering. As a result, the population of West Africa increased. Because this enlarged population required more food, the earliest Bantu speakers planted more land. Soon there wasn't enough land to go around. They couldn't go north in search of land because that area was densely populated. The areas that once had been savanna were becoming more desertlike. The Sahara was slowly advancing toward them. So the people moved southward.

The Bantu people probably brought with them the technology of iron smelting. As they moved southward, they were searching for locations with

Objectives

You may wish to discuss the following questions with students to help them frame the content as they read.

- Why do you think the Bantu migrations split into eastern and southern streams? *to avoid the tropical rain forest; because their land had been depleted*

- How might the Bantu migrations have been different if the people had not had iron weapons? *Possible answer: Bantu would have been less dominant, would have assimilated more with existing cultures.*

More About . . .

The Mbuti The Mbuti people of the Ituri Forest in what is now the Democratic Republic of the Congo are nomadic hunter-gatherers. Much of their diet consists of roots, nuts, fruits, and fungi they gather in the forest. Snails, termites, fish, and snakes provide nutritious animal protein. Honey is also an important part of the diet because it is considered a delicacy. Although adept at hunting forest animals, such as wild pigs, antelope, and monkeys, the Mbuti smoke most of the meat and trade it to farming villages at the forest fringes for yams, corn, peanuts, and beans.

Slash-and-Burn Agriculture Slash-and-burn agriculture causes many problems, including deforestation, loss of habitat and species, an increase in air pollution, and an increase in accidental fires. However, it has been practiced throughout the world for centuries. It is estimated that approximately 300 million farmers practice this type of agriculture today.

ADVANCED/GIFTED

Effects of Bantu Migration

1. Have students review the effects of Bantu migration.

2. Tell each student to choose three effects that he or she thinks were the most significant.

3. Students should then write a justification for each choice, providing details that support their position.

4. Ask volunteers to share their effects and justifications. Then poll the class to determine the top three effects chosen by most members of the class. Initiate a class discussion on the merits of their choices.

Kuba Mask

Like most sub-Saharan African cultures, the people of the Kuba kingdom traditionally used masks for rituals and ceremonies. Have students study the image and answer the associated question.

Analyze Sources Why might cowrie shells and beads have been an indication of elite status among the Kuba? *They were imported, so only people with enough wealth to trade for luxuries would have been able to get them.*

DOCUMENT-BASED INVESTIGATION HISTORICAL SOURCE

Kuba Mask

Most sub-Saharan African cultures used masks for rituals and ceremonies, such as funerals or initiations. Masks may represent a variety of entities, including spirits and ancestors. Both those who create the mask and those who wear the masks in ceremonies enjoyed special status in their communities.

Image with Hotspots: African Ironworking

Have students explore the image using the interactive hotspots. You may wish to use the associated question as a discussion prompt.

Analyze Visuals What advantages would iron tools give a civilization? *Stronger tools will last longer and do heavier work so workers don't have to produce as many tools. That saves time and resources. Also, the iron tools and technology are very valuable and might bring a civilization wealth through trade.*

READING CHECK

Analyze Effects How did the Bantu migrations change the history of Africa? *They brought new techniques for agriculture, ironworking, language, and other ideas to the southern half of Africa.*

---

iron ore resources and hardwood forests. They needed the hardwood to make charcoal to fuel the smelting furnaces.

As you can see from the map, the migrations split into eastern and western streams. Eventually, the Bantu speakers worked their way around the geographical barriers of the Kalahari and Namib deserts. Within 1,500 years or so—a short time in the span of history—they reached the southern tip of Africa. Bantu speakers now populated much of the southern half of Africa.

Effects of the Migration When the Bantu speakers settled into an area, changes occurred. The lands they occupied were not always unpopulated. Some areas into which the Bantu moved were sparsely populated by peoples such as the Mbuti and the San. These groups were not Bantu speakers. They were not engaged in agriculture but were instead hunter-gatherers. They had to find ways to get along with the Bantu, get out of their way, or defend their lands and way of life.

As the Bantu speakers spread south into hunter-gatherers' lands, territorial wars often broke out. Fighting with iron-tipped spears, the newcomers easily drove off the Mbuti and the San, who were armed only with stone weapons. Today, the Mbuti are confined to a corner of the Congo Basin. The San live only around the Kalahari Desert in northwestern South Africa, Namibia, and Botswana. Both groups live a very simple life. They do not speak a Bantu language, and their culture does not reflect the influence of the Bantu-speaking peoples.

The Bantu speakers exchanged ideas and intermarried with the people they joined. This intermingling created new cultures with unique customs and traditions. The Bantu speakers brought new techniques of agriculture to the lands they occupied. They passed on the technology of ironworking to forge tools and weapons from copper, bronze, and iron. They also shared ideas about social and political organization. Some of these ideas still influence the political scene in eastern and southern Africa. Although the Bantu migrations produced a great diversity of cultures, language had a unifying influence on the continent.

In the next lesson, you will see how cultures on the east coast of Africa experienced growth and change. These changes came about as a result of human migrations from Arabia and cultural interaction with traders from North Africa and the Indian Ocean trade routes.

Reading Check
Analyze Effects
How did the Bantu migrations change the history of Africa?

This Kuba mask represents the sister of the founding ancestor of the Kuba culture group, a Bantu-speaking people.

LINK TO ART

Design a Mask

Materials: images of Kuba masks, art paper, pencils, markers, blank outline of a face

1. Ask students what they noticed about the images of the Kuba masks. Guide them to recognize that when Kuba artists created masks, they did not leave any empty spaces between the forehead, cheeks, chin, eyes, nose, and mouth as is the case with their own face.

2. Have each student decide what ritual or ceremony their mask will be for and whether it will represent an entity such as a spirit or an ancestral hero.

3. Have students use a blank outline of a face to design their Kuba mask. Suggest they divide the face into sections and then fill in each area with some kind of repetitive pattern. Remind them to fill in all the spaces.

4. Have students write a description of their mask that includes what it shows and how and when it is to be used.

5. After students have completed their designs, have small groups share their mask designs and descriptions. Have students identify any common characteristics found in the masks, such as patterns, eyes, lines, and so on.

Now and Then

Bantu Languages: Swahili

An estimated 240 million people in Africa speak one of the Bantu languages as their first language. Of that number, about 50 million people in central and east Africa speak Swahili (also known as Kiswahili). The word *swahili* means "the coast." Swahili is widely used on the east coast of Africa but is found elsewhere, too. It is the official language of Kenya and Tanzania.

In fact, after Arabic, Swahili is the most commonly spoken language in Africa. Swahili uses Bantu basics along with Arabic and Persian words. It probably developed as people of East Africa interacted with Arabic traders and with traders from the Indian Ocean trade networks.

Lesson 2 Assessment

1. **Organize Information** Complete a graphic organizer like the one below by adding the effects of the Bantu-speaking migrations.

Bantu Migrations

Effect · Effect · Effect

Which effects of the Bantu-speaking migrations do you think had the most long-term impact? Explain.

2. **Key Terms and People** For each key term or person in the lesson, write a sentence explaining its significance.
3. **Synthesize** How did the Bantu deal with the problems they encountered in their migrations?
4. **Make Inferences** How can the effects of one migration become a cause of another migration?
5. **Recognize Effects** How does migration shape the modern world?
6. **Hypothesize** How might the population of Africa be different today if the Bantu-speaking migrations had not taken place?

NOW & THEN

Bantu Languages: Swahili

Africa's languages fall into three main groups. Swahili and all the Bantu languages are in the Black African language group. Arabic falls into the Afro-Asian group, as does Berber, spoken by about 20 million Africans. Finally, more than 4 million Africans speak Indo-European languages such as English and Afrikaans (related to Dutch).

Print Assessment

1. **Organize Information** Complete a graphic organizer by adding the effects of the Bantu-speaking migrations. Which effects of the Bantu-speaking migrations do you think had the most long-term impact? Explain. *Possible answer: Bantu languages are still spoken by millions of people in central and southern Africa.*

2. **Key Terms and People** For each key term or person in the lesson, write a sentence explaining its significance. *Explanations of the lesson's key terms can be found on the following pages: migration, p. 444; push-pull factors, p. 444; Bantu-speaking peoples, p. 447.*

3. **Synthesize** How did the Bantu deal with the problems they encountered in their migrations? *They adapted their old ways to new environments and learned new ways from the people they encountered.*

4. **Make Inferences** How can the effects of one migration become a cause of another migration? *Possible answer: Increased population causes unemployment and resource shortages, thus migration.*

5. **Recognize Effects** How does migration shape the modern world? *Possible answer: Movements change both the areas people join and those they leave.*

6. **Hypothesize** How might the population of Africa be different today if the Bantu-speaking migrations had not taken place? *Possible answer: Bantu languages might be more localized. Ironworking might have been delayed.*

▷ Online **Assessment**

1. In the early history of human life, what was the strongest factor affecting migration?
   - ○ political
   - ○ religious
   - ○ economic
   - ◉ environmental

   Alternate Question *Select the answer choice from the drop-down list to complete the sentence correctly.* Early humans first began to migrate from place to place mainly for [*environmental* ⬍] reasons.

2. Why did early Bantu-speaking peoples of Africa use the slash-and-burn method of farming in the forests?
   - ○ to open up land for industry
   - ◉ to increase fertility in the soil
   - ○ to obtain rare natural resources
   - ○ to provide more land for grazing

   Alternate Question *Select the answer choice from the drop-down list to complete the sentence correctly.* The Bantu-speaking peoples of Africa used the slash and burn method of farming [*in the forests* ⬍] as a way to increase fertility in the soil.

3. **Compare and Contrast** What is the difference between push factors and pull factors?

   Possible answer: In migration, a push factor is something that drives settlers away from a place. A pull factor, on the other hand, is something that draws people toward a location. Push factors are generally negative things—such as political unrest, religious persecution, and famine. Pull factors are generally positive things— such as new job opportunities, promises of land, and religious freedom.

4. **Cause and Effect** What do experts believe caused the Bantu-speaking people to migrate?

   Possible answer: Once agriculture was developed, the Bantu-speaking people were able to produce more food than they could obtain by hunting and gathering. As a result, the population of West Africa increased, creating a need for more food and more land to grow the food. Soon, there wasn't enough land to go around. The people couldn't go north because that area was already densely populated, so they migrated southward.

The Kingdom of Aksum

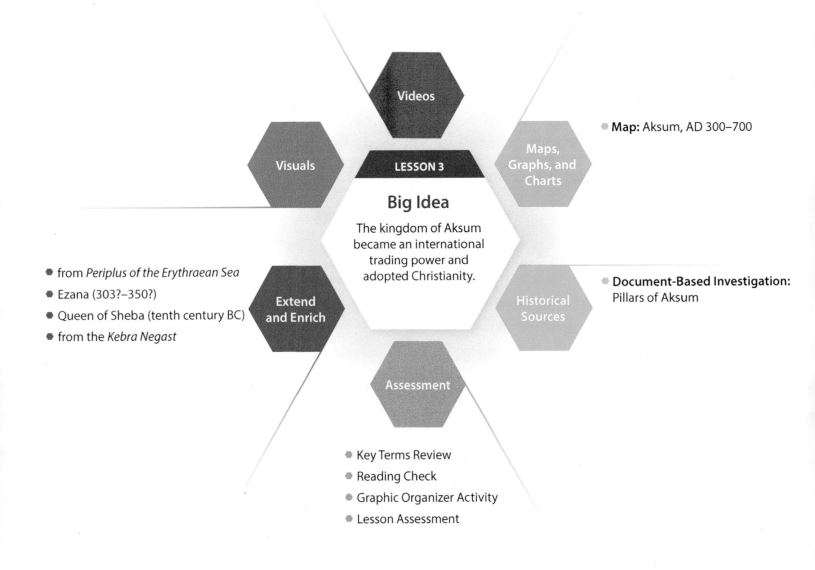

Videos

Visuals

LESSON 3

Maps, Graphs, and Charts

● **Map:** Aksum, AD 300–700

Big Idea

The kingdom of Aksum became an international trading power and adopted Christianity.

- from *Periplus of the Erythraean Sea*
- Ezana (303?–350?)
- Queen of Sheba (tenth century BC)
- from the *Kebra Negast*

Extend and Enrich

Historical Sources

● **Document-Based Investigation:** Pillars of Aksum

Assessment

- Key Terms Review
- Reading Check
- Graphic Organizer Activity
- Lesson Assessment

Online Lesson 3 Enrichment Activities

from *Periplus of the Erythraean Sea*

Excerpt Students read what an ancient Greek writer had to say about the East African coast on the Red Sea and the Aksumite port, Adulis. They then imagine they are merchants planning a trading trip to Adulis. Next, they write two paragraphs to explain what they will offer to the people of Adulis, what they hope to acquire from them, and any additional information that they may need before traveling.

Ezana (303?–350?)

Biography Students read about the king whose conversion led to the Christianization of ancient Aksum and analyze sources that provide information about the king's campaign.

Queen of Sheba (tenth century BC)

Biography Students read about the famed queen, whom legends say ruled an Arabian kingdom but whom scholars believe ruled an area in modern-day Ethiopia. Then they explain the traditions or beliefs expressed in the story about the queen, as revealed in several sources.

from the *Kebra Negast*

Excerpt Students read about King Menelik I's return to Aksum to be king. Then they find out more about legends and write a summary of one of their choice.

Teach the Big Idea

1. **Whole Class Open/Introduction** Explain that the kingdom of Aksum built its influence on trading power. Ask students to think about trade in the world today. How are we affected by our global economy? *Goods come from around the world, jobs depend on trade, U.S. power comes from the economy.*

2. **Direct Teach** Read students the Big Idea: *The kingdom of Aksum became an international trading power and adopted Christianity.* Review the following lesson objectives with students to aid in their understanding of the Big Idea.

   • Explain how maritime trade led to Aksum's growth.

   • Give examples of Aksum's achievements.

   • Explain the effects of the Muslim invasion of Aksum.

3. **Whole Group Close/Reflect** Have students use their own words to write a summary of the rise and fall of the Kingdom of Aksum.

▷ ONLINE DOCUMENT-BASED INVESTIGATION

Societies and Empire of Africa

Pillars of Aksum is the third of five historical sources that students will analyze in the module. Aksumites developed a unique architecture that included stone pillars as tall as 100 feet. Have students study the image.

DOCUMENT-BASED INVESTIGATION   HISTORICAL SOURCE

Pillars of Aksum

Aksumites developed a unique architecture. They carved stones that fit together without mortar to construct palaces and public buildings. Stone pillars as tall as 100 feet were erected as monuments or tomb markers. The carvings on the pillars are representations of the architecture of the time.

▷ ONLINE GRAPHIC ORGANIZER

The Kingdom of Aksum

As students read the lesson, have them use the graphic organizer to take notes. Students can review their graphic organizer notes at the end of the lesson to answer the following question:

Hypothesize How might Aksum's history have been different if its leaders had not moved their capital after the arrival of Muslims? *The city might have been occupied by Muslims, and Ethiopia would not have remained a Christian nation.*

The Kingdom of Aksum

The Big Idea
The kingdom of Aksum became an international trading power and adopted Christianity.

Why It Matters Now
Ancient Aksum, which is in modern-day Ethiopia, is still a center of the Ethiopian Orthodox Christian Church.

Key Terms and People
Aksum
Adulis
Ezana
terraces

Setting the Stage

While migrations were taking place in the southern half of Africa, they were also taking place along the east coast. Arab peoples crossed the Red Sea into Africa perhaps as early as 1000 BC. There they intermarried with Kushite herders and farmers and passed along their written language, Ge'ez (GEE•ehz). The Arabs also shared their skills of working stone and building dams and aqueducts. This blended group of Africans and Arabs would form the basis of a new and powerful trading kingdom.

The Rise of the Kingdom of Aksum

By 715 BC, the East African kingdom of Kush had become powerful enough to push north and conquer Egypt. During the next century, fierce Assyrians swept into Egypt and drove the Kushite pharaohs south. However, Kush remained a powerful kingdom for over 1,000 years. Finally, a more powerful kingdom arose and conquered Kush. That kingdom was **Aksum** (AHK•soom). It was located south of Kush on a rugged plateau on the Red Sea, in what are now the countries of Eritrea and Ethiopia.

In this area of Africa, sometimes called the Horn of Africa, Arab traders from across the Red Sea established trading settlements. These traders were seeking ivory to trade in Persia and farther east on the Indian Ocean. They brought silks, textiles, and spices from eastern trade routes. Eventually, the trading settlements became colonies of farmers and traders. Trade with Mediterranean countries also flowed into seaports located here.

The Origins of Aksum A legend traces the founding of the kingdom of Aksum and the Ethiopian royal dynasty to the son of King Solomon (of ancient Israel) and of the Queen of Sheba (a country in southern Arabia). That dynasty lasted into the 20th century when the last ruler, Haile Selassie, died in 1975.

COLLABORATIVE LEARNING

Economic Partnership Presentations

1. Remind students that Aksum was a Christian kingdom that traded peacefully with its Muslim neighbors. Tell students that they will research other instances of diverse groups coexisting peacefully as economic partners.

2. Each group should choose an example of partnership from the past or present that illustrates two diverse political or religious groups practicing tolerance and cooperating economically. Groups should gather data including the length of the partnership, brief descriptions of the groups involved, geographic locations, and economic value of the partnership.

3. Have students create multimedia presentations about their partnership and deliver to the class.

The first mention of Aksum was in a Greek guidebook written around AD 100, *Periplus of the Erythraean Sea*. It describes Zoskales (ZAHS•kuh•leez), thought to be the first king of Aksum. He was "a stickler about his possessions and always [greedy] for getting more, but in other respects a fine person and well versed in reading and writing Greek." Under Zoskales and other rulers, Aksum seized areas along the Red Sea and the Blue Nile in Africa. The rulers also crossed the Red Sea and took control of lands on the southwestern Arabian Peninsula.

Aksum Controls International Trade Aksum's location and expansion made it a hub for caravan routes to Egypt and Meroë. Access to sea trade on the Mediterranean Sea and the Indian Ocean helped Aksum become an international trading power. Traders from Egypt, Arabia, Persia, India, and the Roman Empire crowded Aksum's chief seaport, **Adulis** (AHD•uh•luhs), near present-day Massawa.

Aksumite merchants traded necessities such as salt and luxuries such as rhinoceros horns, tortoise shells, ivory, emeralds, and gold. In return, they chose from items such as cloth, glass, olive oil, wine, brass, iron, and

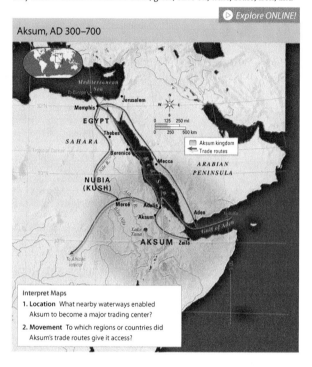

▶ *Explore ONLINE!*

Aksum, AD 300–700

Interpret Maps

1. **Location** What nearby waterways enabled Aksum to become a major trading center?

2. **Movement** To which regions or countries did Aksum's trade routes give it access?

Societies and Empires of Africa **451**

STRUGGLING READERS

Understand Primary Sources

1. Organize students in groups of two or three to analyze the primary source text from Cosmas.

2. Have students take turns reading aloud a sentence and deciding its meaning. Instruct students to record the meaning in their own words. Invite a volunteer to read aloud his or her paraphrase.

3. Ask students to respond to the description of the trading. What do they think makes successful trading relationships? *If both sides agree on the value of the items being traded, the relationship will be a success.*

LINK TO GEOGRAPHY

Explore Aksum's Trading Empire

1. Have students name the exports and imports of Aksum.

2. Pair students and assign one product to each pair. Have students find where their product was probably produced and the routes such products traveled. Then have students show these locations on a large map.

3. Have students list and explain what they learned about Aksum's trade and trading partners.

Objectives

You may wish to discuss the following questions with students to help them frame the content as they read.

- How did Aksum rise to power? *developed as a wealthy trading kingdom along the Red Sea; conquered the Kushites; had a strong leader*

- Aksumite merchants traded necessities and luxuries. What does this suggest about the Aksumite economy? *It was thriving if people could trade away necessities.*

More About . . .

Caravans Remind students that caravans were made up of groups of men, who were merchants, and camels carrying trade goods. Camels were used because they could go without water for several days. They could also hold large loads, with half being placed on each side of the camel's back. Some camels carried passengers who were in baskets, called panniers, that were found on each side of the camel.

Ezana Ezana had his exploits recorded on stone victory thrones placed throughout his kingdom. Many were written in several languages including Ge'ez—an old Ethiopian language—and Greek. The stone messages reported on events of the times. However, they were probably slanted to reflect favorably on the kingdom.

▶ **ONLINE INTERACTIVE MAPS**

Aksum, AD 300–700

Have students explore the map and answer the associated question.

Location Which nearby body of water gave Aksum access to the Arabian Peninsula and to Egypt? *the Red Sea*

In print edition, see map of same title.

1. **Location** What nearby waterways enabled Aksum to become a major trading center? *Red Sea, Gulf of Aden, Blue Nile, White Nile*

2. **Movement** To which regions or countries did Aksum's trade routes give it access? *African interior, Egypt, Mediterranean countries, countries along the Indian Ocean*

▶ **ONLINE LESSON FLIP CARDS**

Review Key Terms and People

Students can use the flip cards in the Lesson Review at any time to review the lesson's key terms and people: *Aksum, Adulis, Ezana,* and *terraces.*

Objectives

You may wish to discuss the following questions with students to help them frame the content as they read.

- Why might an international language be necessary for trading? Why is it English today? *so traders can communicate; Because of the economic and cultural strength and influence of the United States and the United Kingdom, English today is the international language of business, many people around the world speak it as a first or second language.*

- How did Ezana's promise to rule justly and righteously fit with his actions toward Kush? How might he have justified these actions? *Perhaps his promise was only to his own people. He saw Kush as the enemy.*

- How did trade and religion influence the development of Aksum and Ethiopia? *Aksum's location was ideal for trade, which brought it wealth and cultural influences, such as Christianity and Islam, from Greece, India, and Persia.*

More About . . .

Aksum's Relationship with Empires of the Time Aksum's close economic and religious ties to the Roman and Byzantine Empires meant it was often asked by the empires to help curb the growth of their rival, Sassanid Persia. But Aksum mostly kept out of this power game, perhaps because the Persian army was near and Aksum's allies were far away.

Aksumite Coins The first Aksumite coins bear an image of the king along with the pagan symbols of a disc and a crescent. An inscription attests to the king's divine descent from Mahrem. Beginning with Ezana, the disc and crescent are replaced with a cross, and inscriptions such as "By this cross [the king] will conquer" appear. At first, inscriptions were in Greek, the language of the eastern Mediterranean. While Greek continued to be used on coins for world trade, Ge'ez came to be used for local trade.

READING CHECK

Analyze Effects How did Aksum's location and interactions with other regions affect its development? *Its location on water and land trade routes gave it access to new ideas and products, markets for its own products, and the means of expanding its kingdom.*

---

copper. Around AD 550, an Egyptian merchant named Cosmas described how Aksumite agents bargained for gold from the people in southern Ethiopia:

> *"They take along with them to the mining district oxen, lumps of salt, and iron, and when they reach its neighborhood they . . . halt . . . and form an encampment, which they fence round with a great hedge of thorns. Within this they live, and having slaughtered the oxen, cut them in pieces and lay the pieces on top of the thorns along with the lumps of salt and the iron. Then come the natives bringing gold in nuggets like peas . . . and lay one or two or more of these upon what pleases them. . . . Then the owner of the meat approaches, and if he is satisfied he takes the gold away, and upon seeing this its owner comes and takes the flesh or the salt or the iron."*
>
> —Cosmas, quoted in *Travellers in Ethiopia*

A Strong Ruler Expands the Kingdom The kingdom of Aksum reached its height between AD 325 and 360, when an exceptionally strong ruler, **Ezana** (AY·zah·nah), occupied the throne. Determined to establish and expand his authority, Ezana first conquered the part of the Arabian peninsula that is now Yemen. Then, in 330, Ezana turned his attention to Kush, which had already begun to decline. In 350, he conquered the Kushites and burned Meroë to the ground.

An International Culture Develops

From the beginning, Aksumites had a diverse cultural heritage. This blend included traditions of the Arab peoples who crossed the Red Sea into Africa and those of the Kushite peoples they settled among. As the kingdom expanded and became a powerful trading center, it attracted people from all over the ancient world.

The port city of Adulis was particularly cosmopolitan. It included people from Aksum's widespread trading partners such as Egypt, Arabia, Greece, Rome, Persia, India, and even Byzantium. In the babble of tongues heard in Aksum, Greek stood out as the international language of the time, much as English does in the world today.

Reading Check
Analyze Effects How did Aksum's location and interactions with other regions affect its development?

Global Patterns

A Road Paved with Gold: Aksum to Rome

The kingdom of Aksum had a tremendous impact on the ancient Mediterranean world. It particularly influenced one of the most important powers of the time, the Roman Empire. Roman ships came to Adulis weekly to trade with the Aksumites. Many Roman merchants lived in Adulis and in the capital city, Aksum.

One of the chief commodities that linked the two powers was gold. The Aksumites had access to it from inland gold mines, and the Romans needed it to support the monetary system of their growing empire. Rome and Aksum were linked not only by gold, however. They also shared a spiritual link in Christianity.

LINK TO ART

Create a Stele

Materials: cardstock strips, scissors, tape

1. Have students read the Pillars of Aksum text. Then ask students to identify a word in the source that is another word for *pillar*. Write *stele* on the board along with its plural *stelae*. Explain that Ezana and others created stelae as a permanent record of history. Encourage students to locate images of stelae on the Internet.

2. Distribute cardstock strips, and have students create their own three-dimensional stelae. Students should inscribe their stelae with a fact about Aksum or Ezana.

Aksumite Religion Early Aksumite religion probably resembled the polytheistic religion practiced in southern Arabia at the time. Aksumite gods included Astar, Mahrem, Beher, and Medr. Aksumites were also animists, however, and worshiped the spirits of nature and honored their dead ancestors. They offered sacrifices—often as many as a dozen oxen at a time—to those spirits, to Mahrem, and often to the Greek god of war, Ares.

Merchants exchanged more than raw materials and finished goods in Aksum. They shared ideas as well. One of these ideas was a new religion, Christianity. Based on the teachings of Jesus and a belief in one God—monotheism—Christianity began in Judea about AD 30. It spread throughout the Roman Empire and then to Africa, and eventually to Aksum.

Aksum Becomes Christian Ezana succeeded to the throne as an infant after the death of his father. While his mother ruled the kingdom, a young Christian man from Syria who had been captured and taken into the court educated him. When Ezana finally became ruler of Aksum, he converted to Christianity and established it as the kingdom's official religion. He vowed, "I will rule the people with righteousness and justice and will not oppress them, and may they preserve this Throne which I have set up for the Lord of Heaven." King Ezana's conversion led to the conversion of the royal court, but for many years people outside of the court continued to practice indigenous religions. As Christianity spread amongst the Aksumite people, they blended the new beliefs and practices with traditional religious practices, such as dancing ceremonies and use of the sistrum during worship, to form a unique expression of Christianity. The establishment of Christianity was the longest-lasting achievement of the Aksumites. Today, the land of Ethiopia, where Aksum was located, is home to millions of Christians.

Vocabulary
sistrum a handheld percussion instrument that includes a frame with rods or loops attached to it and is shaken to make sound

This mural depicting Bible stories is located on the wall of one of the oldest Christian churches in Aksum.

Investigate Ethiopian Art

1. Have students comment on the mural depicting Bible stories. Ask: How can the figures be described? *Possible answers: They have simple outlines, limited shading, and bland expressions.*

2. Organize students into small groups. Each student will gather information on an aspect of Aksumite art and draw conclusions about how the art reflects Ethiopian traditions and ideas.

3. Have each group summarize its findings in a report accompanied by representative images.

Pillars of Aksum

Aksumites developed a unique architecture that included stone pillars as tall as 100 feet. Have students study the image and answer the associated question:

Analyze Sources How would constructing these pillars be similar to constructing the pyramids in Egypt? *Both would require government planning and funding to pay hundreds of workers; stone was quarried off site and moved to the site.*

DOCUMENT-BASED INVESTIGATION   HISTORICAL SOURCE

Pillars of Aksum

Aksumites developed a unique architecture. They carved stones that fit together without mortar to construct palaces and public buildings. Stone pillars as tall as 100 feet were erected as monuments or tomb markers. The carvings on the pillars are representations of the architecture of the time.

READING CHECK
Analyze Causes What conditions led to Aksum's becoming Christian? *status as a trade center where ideas were exchanged and Ezana's conversion to Christianity*

Aksumite Innovations The inscription on Ezana's stele is written in Ge'ez, the language brought to Aksum by its early Arab inhabitants. Aside from Egypt and Meroë, Aksum was the only ancient African kingdom known to have developed a written language. It was also the first state south of the Sahara to mint its own coins. Made of bronze, silver, and gold, these coins were imprinted with the saying, "May the country be satisfied." Ezana apparently hoped that this inscription would make him popular with the people. Every time they used a coin, it would remind them that he had their interests at heart.

In addition to these cultural achievements, the Aksumites adapted creatively to their rugged, hilly environment. They created a new method of agriculture, terrace farming. This enabled them to greatly increase the productivity of their land. **Terraces**, or steplike ridges constructed on mountain slopes, helped the soil retain water and prevented it from being washed downhill in heavy rains. The Aksumites dug canals to channel water from mountain streams into the fields. They also built dams and cisterns, or holding tanks, to store water.

Reading Check
Analyze Causes
What conditions led to Aksum's becoming Christian?

DOCUMENT-BASED INVESTIGATION   Historical Source

Pillars of Aksum

Aksumites developed a unique architecture. They put no mortar on the stones used to construct vast royal palaces and public buildings. Instead, they carved stones to fit together tightly. Huge stone pillars were erected as monuments or tomb markers. The carvings on the pillars are representations of the architecture of the time.

This towering stone pillar, or stele, was built to celebrate Aksum's achievements. Still standing today, its size and elaborate inscriptions make it an achievement in its own right. The pillars have many unique features:

- False doors, windows, and timber beams are carved into the stone.
- Typically, the top of the pillar is a rounded peak.
- The tallest stele was about 100 feet high. Of those steles left standing, one is 75 feet tall and is among the largest structures in the ancient world.
- The stone for the pillar was quarried and carved two to three miles away and then brought to the site.
- Ezana dedicated one soaring stone pillar to the Christian God, "the Lord of heaven, who in heaven and upon earth is mightier than everything that exists."

Analyze Historical Sources
How would constructing these pillars be similar to constructing the pyramids in Egypt?

454 Module 12

The Fall of Aksum

Aksum's cultural and technological achievements enabled it to last for 800 years. The kingdom finally declined, however, under invaders who practiced the religion called Islam (ihs•LAHM). Its founder was Muhammad; by his death in 632, his followers had conquered all of Arabia. This territory included Aksum's lands on the Arabian coast of the Red Sea.

Islamic Invaders Between 632 and 750 Islamic invaders conquered vast territories in the Mediterranean world, spreading their religion as they went. Aksum protected Muhammad's family and followers during their rise to power. As a result, initially the invaders did not seize Aksum's territories on the African coast of the Red Sea. Retaining control of that coastline enabled Aksum to remain a trading power.

Before long, though, the invaders seized footholds on the African coast as well. In 710 they destroyed Adulis. This conquest cut Aksum off from the major ports along both the Red Sea and the Mediterranean. As a result, the kingdom declined as an international trading power. But it was not only Aksum's political power that weakened. Its spiritual identity and environment were also endangered.

Aksum Isolated As the invaders spread Islam to the lands they conquered, Aksum became isolated from other Christian settlements. To escape the advancing wave of Islam, Aksum's rulers moved their capital over the mountains into what is now northern Ethiopia. Aksum's new geographic isolation—along with depletion of the forests and soil erosion—led to its decline as a world power.

Although the kingdom of Aksum reached tremendous heights and left a lasting legacy in its religion, architecture, and agriculture, it never expanded outside a fairly small area. This is a pattern found in other cultures, both in Africa and around the world.

Reading Check
Analyze Effects
How did the Muslim conquest of Africa affect the kingdom of Aksum?

Lesson 3 Assessment

1. **Organize Information** Use a web like the one below to record the significant achievements of Aksum.

Aksum's Achievements

In your opinion, which of Aksum's achievements was most impressive? Why?

2. **Key Terms and People** For each key term or person in the lesson, write a sentence explaining its significance.

3. **Draw Conclusions** How did Aksum's location and interaction with other regions affect its development?
4. **Analyze Causes** Why did the kingdom of Aksum decline?
5. **Evaluate Decisions** What impact did Ezana's decision to become a Christian have on the kingdom of Aksum?
6. **Form Opinions** Write a two-paragraph opinion on the following statement: The kingdom of Aksum would have reached the same heights even if Ezana had not become king.

Objectives

You may wish to discuss the following questions with students to help them frame the content as they read.

- What can you conclude about the importance of Aksum's location to both its rise and its decline? *Possible answer: Its location on the Red Sea helped make Aksum an important trading center, but it also made it vulnerable to attack.*

- Why did Aksum not expand into a large area? How are the challenges to such an expansion different for today's nations? *Possible answer: geographic, communication, and transportation obstacles; fewer obstacles today*

More About . . .

The City of Adulis Adulis was destroyed in 710, but it was one of the first Aksumite sites to be excavated. Beginning during the 1860s and continuing into the early 1900s, excavations showed the importance and value of the site. Monumental buildings, coins, columns, figures on marble slabs, and other artifacts were uncovered. The fact that people who once lived in Adulis were in contact with foreigners who visited and traded in the city indicates its global significance. Today, much of Adulis remains buried.

READING CHECK
Analyze Effects How did the Muslim conquest of Africa affect the kingdom of Aksum? *The conquest cut Aksum off from trading ports, reducing its power. It forced Aksumite leaders to move the capital.*

Print Assessment

1. **Organize Information** Use a web to record the significant achievements of Aksum. In your opinion, which of Aksum's achievements was most impressive? Why? *Students' answers will vary. Some may say the conversion to Christianity because the religion is still important in Africa today. Others may say international trade because that achievement was so remarkable for the time. Still others may say terraces because it was a creative solution to a problem.*

2. **Key Terms & People** For each key term or person in the lesson, write a sentence explaining its significance. *Explanations of the lesson's key terms can be found on the following pages: Aksum, p. 450; Adulis, p. 451; Ezana, p. 452; terraces, p. 454.*

Categorize Proper Nouns

1. Review with students the difference between common and proper nouns to help students who may have difficulty identifying the proper nouns in the segment "The Fall of Aksum."

2. Have students work in mixed-ability pairs and take turns reading aloud the paragraphs from the segment. Instruct students to categorize each proper noun as a person, place, thing, or idea.

3. Then ask student pairs to select five proper nouns and write a sentence that describes each one.

Explore Aksum's Trading Empire

Below Level Have students make a list of the reasons for the decline of the Aksum kingdom.

At Level Have students write a paragraph that outlines the causes for the decline of the Aksum kingdom.locations on a large map.

Above Level Have student identify the causes for the decline of the Aksum kingdom, choose one cause, and then use the Internet or other reference materials to find more about it. Students should prepare an oral presentation about this cause and share it with the class.

(continued)

Print Assessment *(continued)*

3. **Draw Conclusions** How did Aksum's location and interaction with other regions affect its development? *Location on water and land trade routes offered Aksum access to new ideas and products, markets for its own products, and means of expanding its kingdom.*

4. **Analyze Causes** Why did the kingdom of Aksum decline? *spread of Islam; geographic and religious isolation; depletion of natural resources*

5. **Evaluate Decisions** What impact did Ezana's decision to become a Christian have on the kingdom of Aksum? *Possible answer: It created ties to other Christian nations, then led to isolation and decline.*

6. **Form Opinions** Write a two-paragraph opinion on the following statement: The kingdom of Aksum would have reached the same heights even if Ezana had not become king. *Paragraphs will vary but should provide evidence to support their hypothesis related to whether Aksum would have reached the same heights even if Ezana had not gained the throne.*

Online Assessment

1. According to legend, what is the connection between Israel's King Solomon and Arabia's Queen of Sheba?
   - ○ They are said to be the parents of Aksum's first king.
   - ○ They are believed to be responsible for Aksum's demise.
   - ○ They are said to be the owners of much of Aksum's land.
   - ○ They are believed to be responsible for Aksum's chief seaport.

   Alternate Question *Select the answer choice from the drop-down list to complete the sentence correctly.*
   King Solomon of Israel and Queen Sheba of Arabia are, according to legend, the [*parents* ⬍] of Aksum's first king.

2. Why did Christianity become the official religion of Aksum?
   - ○ King Ezana converted to the faith.
   - ○ Christianity began in Judea in AD 30.
   - ○ The early Aksumite religion honored ancestors.
   - ○ Animal sacrifices were performed by early Aksumites.

   Alternate Question *Select the answer choice from the drop-down list to complete the sentence correctly.*
   [*Christianity* ⬍] became the official religion of Aksum because the country's leader converted to the faith after learning the teachings from a Syrian man.

3. Which group conquered vast territories in the Mediterranean world between 632 and 750?
   - ○ Muslims
   - ○ Christians
   - ○ Buddhists
   - ○ Aksumites

   Alternate Question *Select the answer choice from the drop-down list to complete the sentence correctly.*
   The Mediterranean world was conquered by [*Islamic invaders* ⬍] between the years 632 and 750. Aksum, however, was spared from invasion at first because this country had protected family members of the religion's founder.

4. **Make Inferences** What can be determined about Aksum based on its trading patterns?

   Possible answer: It can be inferred that Aksum was rich in natural resources and things of the earth but lacking in humanmade products. This can be determined based on the types of things that Aksum exported, including salt, rhinoceros horns, tortoise shells, ivory, emeralds, and gold. All of these are natural resources or objects obtained from animals. In contrast, Aksum imported cloth, glass, olive oil, wine, brass, iron, and copper. Many of these are humanmade items.

5. **Elaborate** How did the Aksumites adapt to their geographical environment?

   Possible answer: The Aksumites adapted to their geographical environment by developing terrace farming. This helped them live in their rugged mountain environment by greatly increasing the productivity of the land that they lived on. On the mountain slopes, steplike ridges were constructed. This helped the soil retain water and prevented the soil from being washed down in heavy rains. The Aksumites also dug canals to channel water from the mountain streams into the fields. They built dams and cisterns to store water for later use.

6. **Draw Conclusions** What factors ultimately caused the fall of the Aksum kingdom?

   Possible answer: First, the Aksumites lost control over the Red Sea coastline. This cut them off from their major ports, which decreased their ability to easily trade. They wanted to stay more connected to other Christian nations, so they moved their capital to what is now northern Ethiopia. They no longer had access to forests as they did before, and they were now in a place with frequent soil erosion, so the industries they had always relied on were no longer available.

North and West African Civilizations

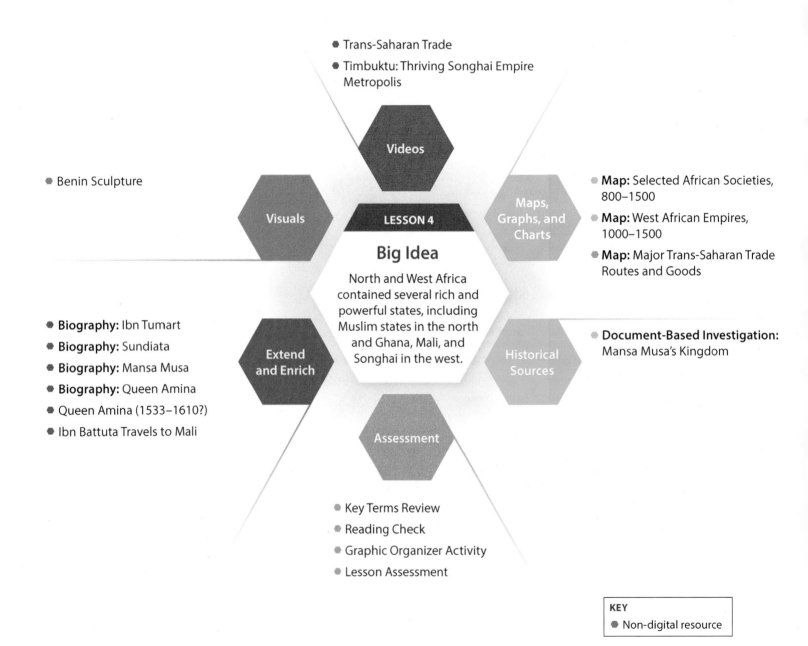

- Trans-Saharan Trade
- Timbuktu: Thriving Songhai Empire Metropolis

Videos

- Benin Sculpture

Visuals

LESSON 4

Maps, Graphs, and Charts

- **Map:** Selected African Societies, 800–1500
- **Map:** West African Empires, 1000–1500
- **Map:** Major Trans-Saharan Trade Routes and Goods

Big Idea

North and West Africa contained several rich and powerful states, including Muslim states in the north and Ghana, Mali, and Songhai in the west.

Historical Sources

- **Document-Based Investigation:** Mansa Musa's Kingdom

- **Biography:** Ibn Tumart
- **Biography:** Sundiata
- **Biography:** Mansa Musa
- **Biography:** Queen Amina
- Queen Amina (1533–1610?)
- Ibn Battuta Travels to Mali

Extend and Enrich

Assessment

- Key Terms Review
- Reading Check
- Graphic Organizer Activity
- Lesson Assessment

KEY
- Non-digital resource

▷ Online Lesson 4 Enrichment Activities

Queen Amina (1533–1610?)

Biography Students read about Queen Amina, who ruled the Hausa city-state of Zazzau in the late 1500s and expanded its territories to their largest extent ever. Then they design a military medal that pays tribute to Queen Amina and explain their design in writing.

Ibn Battuta Travels to Mali

Article Students study the travel routes of 14th-century traveler Ibn Battuta as he journeyed through West Africa during his 75,000-mile tour of the Muslim world. Then they explain why he took the route he traveled.

Teach the Big Idea

1. **Whole Class Open/Introduction** Ask students what they think living in a kingdom or empire would be like. *Possible answer: might need to obey the whims of a ruler, might be able to obtain goods from faraway lands*

2. **Direct Teach** Read students the Big Idea: *North and West Africa contained several rich and powerful states, including Muslim states in the north and Ghana, Mali, and Songhai in the west.* Review the following lesson objectives with students to aid in their understanding of the Big Idea.

   - Explain effects of Islam in North Africa.

   - Explain how the gold-salt trade led to the rise of Ghana.

   - Describe how Sundiata and Mansa Musa advanced Mali.

   - Describe the Songhai Empire.

   - Identify Benin and the Hausa and Yoruba city-states.

3. **Whole Group Close/Reflect** Have each student make a fact card with at least four bulleted points about one of the kingdoms or empires discussed in the lesson.

▷ ONLINE DOCUMENT-BASED INVESTIGATION

Societies and Empires of Africa

Mansa Musa's Kingdom is the fourth of five historical sources that students will analyze in the Societies and Empires of Africa module. At its height, the Empire of Mali was known throughout much of Africa, the Middle East, and Europe. Students can enlarge the map to see portions in greater detail.

▷ ONLINE GRAPHIC ORGANIZER

North and West African Civilizations

As students read the lesson, have them use the graphic organizer to take notes. Students can review their graphic organizer notes at the end of the lesson to answer the following question.

Compare and Contrast How was the growth of Islam in North Africa similar to and different from the growth of Islam in West Africa? *Islam spread in North Africa through military conquest; in West Africa it spread through trade. In both regions, Muslim rulers used religious scholars as government advisers.*

North and West African Civilizations

The Big Idea
North and West Africa contained several rich and powerful states, including Muslim states in the north and Ghana, Mali, and Songhai in the west.

Why It Matters Now
These civilizations demonstrate the richness of African culture before European colonization.

Key Terms and People
Maghrib
Almoravids
Almohads
Ghana
Mali
Sundiata
Mansa Musa
Ibn Battuta
Songhai
Hausa
Yoruba
Benin

Setting the Stage

In the seventh century, the new religion Islam appeared in Arabia and quickly spread through Egypt and into North Africa. Many African rulers converted and established strong states based on Islamic law. While these states developed in North Africa, three powerful empires flourished in West Africa. These ancient African empires arose in the Sahel, the savanna region just south of the Sahara. They grew strong by controlling trade. In this section you will learn about the Almoravid and Almohad empires of North Africa and the West African empires of Ghana, Mali, and Songhai.

Muslim States

While stateless societies developed south of the Sahara and the Christian state of Aksum developed in the Horn of Africa, Islam played a vital role in North Africa. After Muhammad's death in 632, Muslims swept across the northwest part of the continent. They converted many by the sword of conquest and others peacefully. By 670, Muslims ruled Egypt and had entered the **Maghrib**, the part of North Africa that is today the Mediterranean coast of Libya, Tunisia, Algeria, and Morocco.

As Islam spread, some African rulers converted to Islam. These African Muslim rulers then based their government upon Islamic law. Muslims believe that God's law is a higher authority than any human law. Therefore, Muslim rulers often relied on religious scholars as government advisers.

Islamic Law In Islam, following the law is a religious obligation. Muslims do not separate their personal life from their religious life, and Islamic law regulates almost all areas of human life. Islamic law helped to bring order to Muslim states.

However, various Muslim states had ethnic and cultural differences. Further, these states sometimes had differing

---

COLLABORATIVE LEARNING

Empires of Ghana, Mali, and Songhai Presentations

1. Divide the class into three groups, and assign each group one of these empires: Ghana, Mali, or Songhai.

2. Have groups use the Internet or other reference sources to gather information about their empire with regard to its influence, achievements, and lasting impact on future societies.

3. Have groups consider these questions to help them focus their research: What factors contributed to the growth of the kingdom? What factors led to the decline of the kingdom? What are the legacies of the kingdom?

4. Ask groups to design a computer slideshow or multimedia presentation that describes their empire. They should use images to illustrate their presentation as well.

5. Have groups present their slideshows or presentations to the class. Elicit feedback from other groups about the presentations.

interpretations, or schools, of Islamic law. Nonetheless, Islamic law has been such a significant force in history that some states, especially in North Africa, are still influenced by it today.

Among those who converted to Islam were the Berbers. Fiercely independent desert and mountain dwellers, the Berbers were the original inhabitants of North Africa. While they accepted Islam as their faith, many maintained their Berber identities and loyalties. Two Berber groups, the Almoravids and the Almohads, founded empires that united the Maghrib under Muslim rule.

Almoravid Reformers In the 11th century, Muslim reformers founded the Almoravid (al•muh•RAHV•uhd) Empire. Its members came from a Berber group living in the western Sahara in what is today Mauritania. The movement began after devout Berber Muslims made a hajj, or pilgrimage, to Mecca. On their journey home, they convinced a Muslim scholar from Morocco named Abd Allah Ibn Yasin to return with them to teach their people about Islam. Ibn Yasin's teachings soon attracted followers, and he founded a strict religious brotherhood, known as the **Almoravids**.

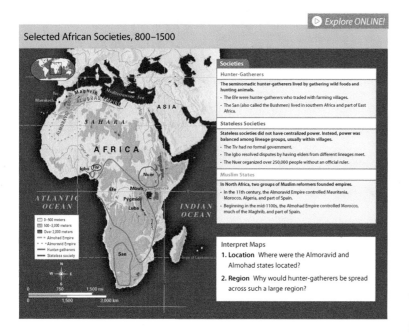

▶ Explore ONLINE!

Selected African Societies, 800–1500

Interpret Maps

1. **Location** Where were the Almoravid and Almohad states located?

2. **Region** Why would hunter-gatherers be spread across such a large region?

You may wish to discuss the following questions with students to help them frame the content as they read.

- How do states governed by Islamic law differ from the United States? *Under U.S. law, religion and government are separate.*

- How did the Almoravids and the Almohads differ? *interpreted Islamic beliefs differently*

More About . . .

Tip for Struggling Readers Remind students that Islam is a religion and a Muslim is a person who follows that religion. The word *Islam* is an Arabic word meaning "surrender" or "submission."

Impact of Muslim Conquest A major effect of the Almoravid and Almohad conquests was the spread of literacy to North and West Africa. Converts to Islam had to learn Arabic to read the Qur'an. Mosques became centers of learning. Trade and visits by Muslim scholars spread knowledge of Muslim intellectual achievements in mathematics, medicine, and astronomy to people in North and West Africa.

▶ **ONLINE INTERACTIVE MAPS**

Selected African Societies, 800–1500

Have students explore the map and answer the associated questions.

Location Where were the Muslim states located? *in North Africa*

In print edition, see map of same title.

1. **Location** Where were the Almoravid and Almohad states located? *north and northwest Africa*

2. **Region** Why would hunter-gatherers be spread across such a large region? *had to move constantly to look for food*

▶ **ONLINE LESSON FLIP CARDS**

Review Key Terms and People

Students can use the flip cards in the Lesson Review at any time to review the lesson's key terms and people: *Maghrib, Almoravids, Almohads, Ghana, Mali, Sundiata, Mansa Musa, Ibn Battuta, Songhai, Hausa, Yoruba,* and *Benin.*

Propose a System of Government

1. Have students form small groups and decide on the best system of government for a group the size of the class. Students should assume there is no pre-assigned leader, and the group must effectively address the challenges of daily life in the first century AD: solving conflict among members, organizing hunting and gathering expeditions, and distributing food. What would be the best way to go about these tasks? Would one leader who offers counsel, a small group of leaders who make the decisions for the group, or a democracy work best? Tell students not to designate themselves or any of their

classmates as leaders but rather to focus on a concept of leadership that would work for a group that size.

2. Ask students to create a poster or other graphic explaining their proposed system. Graphics should include the total number in the group, the number of leaders, how problems would be solved, and an overall explanation of their system.

3. Have groups present their ideas to the class.

Ibn Tumart

Have students read the biography of Ibn Tumart, a Muslim spiritual leader who declared himself a messiah and claimed that he would lead humankind back to righteousness.

Islamic Law

Maliki, the main school of religious law in North Africa, gained its name from its founder Malik ibn Anas. It spread from his homeland of Saudi Arabia. Sources of Maliki law include the Qur'an, shared ideas of Muslim scholars, and practices and customs of the early people of Medina.

READING CHECK

What was the main effect of Almohad rule on the Maghrib? *It unified the region through Islamic teaching.*

Carpets for sale in Marrakech, Morocco

According to one theory about the name's origin, the group lived in a *ribat*, or fortified monastery. They were therefore called the "people of the *ribat*," or *al-Murabitun*. This eventually became "Almoravid."

In the 1050s, Ibn Yasin led the Almoravids in an effort to spread Islam through conquest. After Ibn Yasin's death in 1059, the Almoravids went on to take Morocco and found Marrakech. It became their capital. They overran the West African empire of Ghana by 1076. The Almoravids also captured parts of southern Spain, where they were called Moors.

Almohads Take Over In the mid-1100s, the **Almohads** (AL·moh·HADZ), another group of Berber Muslim reformers, seized power from the Almoravids. The Almohads began as a religious movement in the Atlas Mountains of Morocco.

The Almohads followed the teachings of Ibn Tumart. After a pilgrimage to Mecca, Ibn Tumart criticized the later Almoravid rulers for moving away from the traditional practice of Islam. He urged his followers to strictly obey the teachings of the Qur'an and Islamic law. The Almohads, led by Abd al-Mumin, fought to overthrow the Almoravids and remain true to their view of traditional Islamic beliefs.

By 1148 the Almohads controlled most of Morocco and ended Almoravid rule. The new Muslim reformers kept Marrakech as their capital. By the end of the 12th century, they had conquered much of southern Spain. In Africa, their territory stretched from Marrakech to Tripoli and Tunis on the Mediterranean. The Almohad Empire broke up into individual Muslim dynasties. While the Almohad Empire lasted just over 100 years, it united the Maghrib under one rule for the first time.

Stronger empires were about to emerge. Societies in West Africa created empires that boasted economic and political power and strong links to trade routes.

Reading Check
Analyze Effects
What was the main effect of Almohad rule on the Maghrib?

Empire of Ghana

By AD 200, trade across the Sahara had existed for centuries. However, this trade remained infrequent and irregular because of the harsh desert conditions. Most pack animals—oxen, donkeys, and horses—could not travel very far in the hot, dry Sahara without rest or water. Then, in the third century AD, Berber nomads began using camels. The camel could plod steadily over much longer distances than other pack animals, covering as much as 60 miles in a day. In addition, it could travel more than ten days without water, twice as long as most pack animals. With the camel, nomads blazed new routes across the desert and trade increased.

Other technologies and developments also facilitated interregional trade between North and West Africa. The ironmaking technologies that had developed by 500 BC in West Africa enabled trade as people manufactured agricultural tools, weaponry, and other implements. The iron weapons helped West African empires keep order on the trade routes, providing safe passage to merchants. Iron tools also helped increase agricultural production, and agricultural surplus could be traded. Plentiful food also meant that more people could specialize in areas such as metalworking, trading, or administration. By the 11th century, Arabic writing became important for recording contracts, sharing information, and keeping other records. Pottery made locally could be used to store and transport goods, and canoes were used to carry materials and goods along the Niger (NY•juhr) River to trading towns.

The trans-Saharan trade routes crossed the savanna through the region farmed by the Soninke (soh•NIHN•keh) people. The Soninke people called their ruler *ghana*, or war chief. Muslim traders began to use the word to refer to the Soninke region. By the 700s, **Ghana** was a kingdom, and its rulers were growing rich by taxing the goods that traders carried through their territory.

Gold-Salt Trade The two most important trade items were gold and salt. Gold came from a forest region south of the savanna between the Niger and Senegal (SEHN•ih•GAWL) rivers. Miners dug gold from shafts as deep as 100 feet or sifted it from fast-moving streams. Some sources estimate that until about 1350, at least two-thirds of the world's supply of gold came from West Africa. Although rich in gold, West Africa's savanna and forests lacked salt, a material essential to human life. The Sahara contained deposits of salt. In fact, in the Saharan village of Taghaza, workers built their houses from salt blocks because it was the only material available.

Arab and Berber traders crossed the desert with camel caravans loaded down with salt. They also carried cloth, weapons, and manufactured goods from ports on the Mediterranean. After a long journey, they reached the market towns of the savanna. Meanwhile, African traders brought gold north from the forest regions. African traders also exported spices, kola nuts, shea butter, animal hides, leather goods, cloth (starting in the 11th century), and slaves.

Societies and Empires of Africa **459**

Objectives

You may wish to discuss the following questions with students to help them frame the content as they read.

- What discovery first allowed successful trade routes through the Sahara? *use of camels*

- How did limiting the supply of gold nuggets prevent their price from falling? *kept people from flooding the market by spending lots of gold at one time*

- How did temporary control by the Almoravids cause the decline of the kingdom of Ghana? *The gold-salt trade was disrupted, and this led Ghana to lose power.*

More About . . .

Land Disputes For thousands of years, North African Berbers repelled Roman, French, and Arab invaders, preserving their language, land, and culture. In 2000, a joint American-Moroccan company discovered oil fields in Morocco. Not all Berbers are nomadic, so many strongly objected to the arrival of oil workers, who were claiming land for their own use. Morocco's King Mohammed VI faces the difficult task of managing the new wealth, satisfying displaced people, and negotiating with neighboring Algeria, across whose border the field may extend. His actions so far have shown he is up to the many challenges. For example, he has worked to improve the life of poor Moroccans and has made the country more democratic.

Scarcity, Supply, and Demand Scarcity, the lack of a particular resource, exists because the world's resources are limited. The scarcity of resources affects everyone but not always in the same way. For example, scarcity benefits those who can supply a desired limited resource, if those who demand the resource can pay the price.

ENGLISH LANGUAGE LEARNERS

Understand a Quote

Materials: white paper, colored pencils or markers

1. Read aloud the quotation attributed to Al-Bakri describing the lavish lifestyle of Ghana's kings. Work with students to paraphrase it so they grasp its meaning.

2. Have students draw the scene described in the quotation. Review student drawings as a class. Ask them what the drawings suggest about who controlled the supply of gold in Ghana.

3. Guide students in a discussion of the importance of gold to Ghana and its kings. Remind students that Ghana was rich in gold but that only the king could own large pieces of it; the rest of the people could only own gold dust.

Trans-Saharan Trade

Have students watch the video individually or as a class. You may wish to use the associated question as a discussion prompt.

Analyze Videos What were the three items traded most across the Sahara? *gold, salt, and slaves*

▷ **PLAY VIDEO** 4:51
Trans-Saharan Trade

Slaves were a part of the trans-Saharan trade from the sixth century to the 19th century. Slaves taken from West Africa were sold in North Africa, Egypt, Arabia, what is now Iraq, and India, although most African slaves in Arabia, Iraq, and India came from east African societies and were traded along the Indian Ocean routes.

Merchants met in trading cities, where they exchanged goods under the watchful eye of the king's tax collector. In addition to taxing trade, royal officials made sure that all traders weighed goods fairly and did business according to the law. Royal guards also provided protection from bandits.

Land of Gold By the year 800, Ghana had become an empire. Because Ghana's king controlled trade and commanded a large army, he could demand taxes and gifts from the chiefs of surrounding lands. As long as the chiefs made their payments, the king left them in peace to rule their own people.

In his royal palace, the king stored gold nuggets and slabs of salt (collected as taxes). Only the king had the right to own gold nuggets, although gold dust freely circulated in the marketplace. By this means, the king limited the supply of gold and kept its price from falling. Ghana's African ruler acted as a religious leader, chief judge, and military commander. He headed a large bureaucracy and could call up a huge army. In 1067, a Muslim geographer and scholar named al-Bakri wrote a description of Ghana's royal court:

> "The king adorns himself . . . wearing necklaces and bracelets. . . . The court of appeal is held in a domed pavilion around which stand ten horses with gold embroidered trappings. Behind the king stand ten pages holding shields and swords decorated with gold, and on his right are the sons of the subordinate [lower] kings of his country, all wearing splendid garments and with their hair mixed with gold."
>
> —al-Bakri, quoted in *Africa in the Days of Exploration*

Social Organization At its height, the Empire of Ghana included many peoples, some of which had their own customs and language. However, as Ghana's rule strengthened and trade continued to connect peoples and communities, the empire's cities, at least, began to develop similarities. In all of Ghana, the king was considered the supreme ruler. An administrative class helped the king run the government. Other segments that emerged in Ghana's society included miners, agricultural laborers, metalworkers, and leather crafters. Skilled craftsmen such as blacksmiths and leather crafters enjoyed a privileged place in society. Some were supported by the king's court.

Ghana was a matrilineal society, meaning that ancestry was traced through the mother's lineage. Inheritances also passed through the mother's lineage. For example, the king's son was not the king's heir. The son of the king's sister was the heir.

460   Module 12

Chart Main Ideas

1. Review the concept of identifying main ideas with students.

2. Tell students that you would like them to make a Main Idea chart with the following column headings: Year, Kingdom/Ruler, Description. You may want to show them a sample chart without answers.

Year	Kingdom/Ruler	Description
700–800	Ghana, kingdom turned empire	Soninke people; taxed traders; king stored gold
1076	Muslim Almoravids	took over Ghana
1235	Mali, kingdom Sundiata, ruler of Mali	Mali's wealth came from gold; Sundiata became Mali emperor.
1312	Mansa Musa	ruled after Sundiata; made Timbuktu an important city

3. Explain that students will fill in the information about this segment on Ghana after they have read it. They will then follow the same process as they read the remaining segments.

Islamic Influences While Islam spread through North Africa by conquest, south of the Sahara, Islam spread through trade. Muslim merchants and teachers settled in the states south of the Sahara and introduced their faith there.

Eventually, Ghana's rulers converted to Islam. By the end of the 11th century, Muslim advisers were helping the king run his kingdom. While Ghana's African rulers accepted Islam, many people in the empire clung to their animistic beliefs and practices. Animism is the belief that spirits living in animals, plants, and natural forces play an important role in daily life. Much of the population never converted. Those who did kept many of their former beliefs, which they observed along with Islam. For example, people might celebrate both Islamic festivals and festivals of local African religions. Among the upper class, Islam's growth encouraged the spread of literacy. To study the Qur'an, converts to Islam had to learn Arabic.

In 1076 the Muslim Almoravids of North Africa completed their conquest of Ghana. Although the Almoravids eventually withdrew from Ghana, the war had badly disrupted the gold-salt trade. Ghana never regained its power, but it had helped Islam to gain a foothold in the region, and the West African–North African trade that Ghana developed would continue for centuries, although the trade routes would shift.

Reading Check
Analyze Causes Why would the disruption of trade destroy Ghana's power?

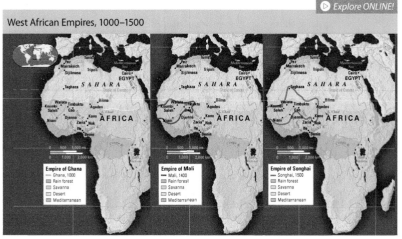

West African Empires, 1000–1500

▶ *Explore ONLINE!*

Empire of Ghana
— Ghana, 1000
☐ Rain forest
☐ Savanna
☐ Desert
☐ Mediterranean

Empire of Mali
— Mali, 1400
☐ Rain forest
☐ Savanna
☐ Desert
☐ Mediterranean

Empire of Songhai
— Songhai, 1500
☐ Rain forest
☐ Savanna
☐ Desert
☐ Mediterranean

Interpret Maps
1. **Region** Compare the regions occupied by the Ghana, Mali, and Songhai empires in terms of size and location.
2. **Human-Environment Interaction** How did the environment both contribute resources to and cause problems for traders?

Societies and Empires of Africa **461**

West African Empires, 1000–1500
Have students explore the map using the interactive features and answer the associated questions.

Movement Which settlement traded slaves and ivory south to Gao? *In Salah*

In print edition, see map of same title.

1. **Region** Compare the regions occupied by the Ghana, Mali, and Songhai Empires in terms of size and location. *Ghana was smallest and Songhai largest. Songhai encompassed most of Ghana and Mali and stretched farther east and north.*

2. **Human-Environment Interaction** How did the environment both contribute resources to and cause problems for traders? *The environment contributed salt but caused a problem because it lacked water.*

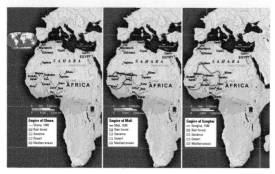

READING CHECK
Analyze Causes Why would the disruption of trade destroy Ghana's power? *because Ghana's power was based on wealth gained from controlling trade*

SUMMARIZE INFORMATION

Write a Summary of the Salt Trade

1. Remind students that the salt-for-gold trade created great wealth in West African kingdoms and that salt is still a valuable commodity to sub-Saharan peoples.

2. Organize students into small mixed-ability groups, or have them work individually. Have students conduct research about the significance of the salt trade to various African cultures. Suggest to students that they search with keywords such as *cultural survival* and *salt trade*. Have students create an annotated bibliography to accompany their research.

3. Have volunteers share their findings and their research techniques with the class. Have students take notes during the presentations.

4. Then ask students to write a brief summary of the continuing importance of salt to indigenous people.

Objectives

You may wish to discuss the following questions with students to help them frame the content as they read.

- What governing institution did Mansa Musa introduce to his empire? *divided it into provinces and appointed governors*

- Why are Ibn Battuta's travels worth noting? *Possible answer: He was a historian who had traveled widely throughout the Islamic world. His comparisons and critiques of different societies help us understand them.*

More About . . .

Building in Mali A poet and architect from Andalusia, Spain, named Abu-Ishaq Ibrahim-es-Saheli met Mansa Musa during the ruler's famous hajj. Es-Saheli was well versed in techniques of mud and burnt-brick construction. The king offered him payment to encourage him to travel to Mali to build a vast royal palace and a mosque. Es-Saheli agreed to come to complete Mansa Musa's building projects. He also constructed the great Djingareyber Mosque at Timbuktu, another one at Djenné, and a third in Gao. Es-Saheli is credited with the introduction of burnt bricks, flat roofs, and pyramid-shaped minarets to the area's architecture.

Priceless Manuscripts Between 200,000 and 300,000 ancient manuscripts dating back to the 13th century were once kept in the library of Mansa Musa at Timbuktu. These documents prove that Africa did not rely solely on oral tradition. The manuscripts, letters, and books cover topics from history to religion, philosophy, math, sciences, medicine, and justice. The valuable manuscripts have been spread among various libraries over the years. People around the world can read the priceless manuscripts thanks to the Tombouctou Manuscripts Project. As part of the project, many of the manuscripts have been digitized and are available online.

BIOGRAPHY

Sundiata

Have students read the biography of Sundiata, the founder and ruler of Mali, who organized an army and defeated the other kingdoms of West Africa.

BIOGRAPHY

Mansa Musa

Have students read the biography of Mansa Musa, the leader of Mali who held power from 1312 to 1332. He is remembered for expanding trade and supporting and promoting the arts.

Empire of Mali

By 1235 the kingdom of **Mali** had emerged. Its founders were Mande-speaking people who lived south of Ghana. Mali's wealth, like Ghana's, was built on gold. As Ghana remained weak, people who had been under its control began to act independently. In addition, miners found new gold deposits farther east. This caused the most important trade routes to shift eastward, which made a new group of people—the people of Mali—wealthy. With this wealth they acquired horses and crafted iron weapons and leather goods, all of which enabled them to seize power.

Sundiata Conquers an Empire Mali's first great leader, **Sundiata** (sun•JAHT•ah), came to power by crushing a cruel, unpopular leader. Then, in the words of a Mande oral tradition, "the world knew no other master but Sundiata." Sundiata became Mali's *mansa,* or emperor. Through a series of military victories, he took over the kingdom of Ghana and the trading cities of Koumbi Saleh and Walata. A period of peace and prosperity followed.

Sundiata proved to be as great a leader in peace as he had been in war. He put able administrators in charge of Mali's finances, defense, and foreign affairs. From his new capital at Niani, he promoted agriculture and reestablished the gold-salt trade. Niani became an important center of commerce and trade. People began to call Sundiata's empire Mali, meaning "where the king lives."

Mansa Musa Expands Mali Sundiata died in 1255. Some of Mali's next rulers became Muslims. These African Muslim rulers built mosques, attended public prayers, and supported the preaching of Muslim holy men. The most famous of them was **Mansa Musa** (MAHN•sah moo•SAH), who

--- BIOGRAPHY ---

Sundiata
(?–1255)

Sundiata came from the kingdom of Kangaba near the present-day Mali-Guinea border. According to tradition, he was one of 12 brothers who were heirs to the throne of Kangaba.

When Sumanguru, ruler of a neighboring state, overran Kangaba in the early 1200s, he wanted to eliminate rivals, so he murdered all of Sundiata's brothers. He spared Sundiata, who was sickly and seemed unlikely to survive.

However, as Sundiata grew up, he gained strength and became a popular leader of many warriors. In 1235, Sundiata's army defeated Sumanguru and his troops.

Mansa Musa
(?–1332?)

Mansa Musa, the strongest of Sundiata's successors, was a devout Muslim. On his hajj, Mansa Musa stopped in Cairo, Egypt. Five hundred slaves, each carrying a staff of gold, arrived first. They were followed by 80 camels, each carrying 300 pounds of gold dust. Hundreds of other camels brought supplies. Thousands of servants and officials completed the procession.

Mansa Musa gave away so much gold in Cairo that the value of this precious metal declined in Egypt for 12 years.

ENGLISH LANGUAGE LEARNERS

Use Context Clues and Word Parts to Unlock Meaning

1. Direct students' attention to the quotation by Ibn Battuta. Explain that when faced with an unfamiliar word, a skilled reader looks for context clues and tries to break unfamiliar words into parts.

2. Ask individual students to choose a challenging word in the quote and try to determine its meaning. Then have them check a dictionary to see if their determination is correct.

3. Have several students say their word and definition aloud. Then work together as a class to restate the primary source. *Possible answer: They are rarely unfair, and they hate unfairness more than anybody else. Their king punishes anyone who is unfair. Nobody gets robbed there. Travelers and those who live there are safe.*

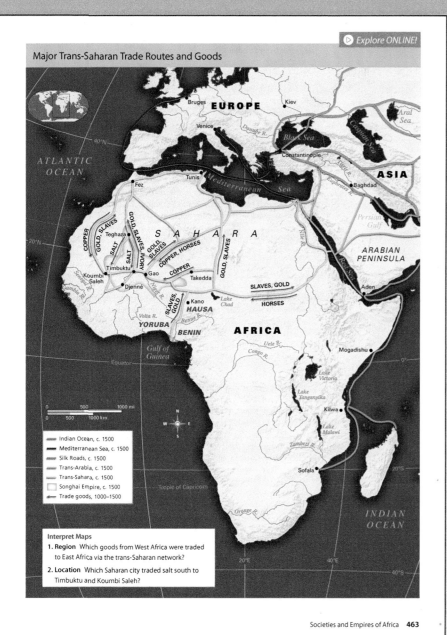

Major Trans-Saharan Trade Routes and Goods

Explore ONLINE!

Interpret Maps

1. **Region** Which goods from West Africa were traded to East Africa via the trans-Saharan network?

2. **Location** Which Saharan city traded salt south to Timbuktu and Koumbi Saleh?

MAPS

Major Trans-Saharan Trade Routes and Goods

Have students explore the map and answer the associated questions.

1. **Region** Which goods from West Africa were traded to East Africa via the trans-Saharan network? *slaves, gold*

2. **Location** Which Saharan city traded salt south to Timbuktu and Koumbi Saleh? *Teghaza*

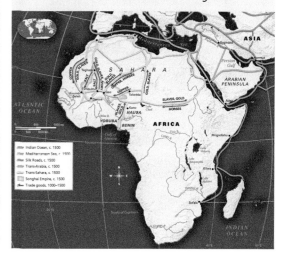

LINK TO MUSIC

Write a Song or Rap

1. Remind students that in West Africa, griots were a community's record keepers. Tell students that a griot would pass on historical knowledge by reciting long poems or stories about generations of ancestors.

2. Explain that an oral history often began with an elaborate introduction. A griot might have begun this way: "Listen to my word. I am going to tell you about . . ." Griots recited rhyming poems about warriors and kings. Some people believe that these poems were the conceptual ancestors of modern rap music.

3. Have small groups of students create a poem, song, or rap describing the achievements of Sundiata or Mansa Musa.

4. Ask groups to perform their oral histories. Encourage observers to provide feedback on the presentations.

Analyze Effects Why did Islam flourish in urban centers of West Africa? *Mansa Musa built mosques in cities; Muslim North African merchants settled in West African cities; Muslim scholars and traders came from other countries to Mali's cities; Africans had contact with many foreign Muslims in cities.*

▷ ONLINE DOCUMENT-BASED INVESTIGATION

Mansa Musa's Kingdom

In 1375, a Spanish mapmaker created a map showing Mansa Musa's kingdom, which includes an illustration of Mansa Musa holding a gold nugget. Students can enlarge the map to see portions in greater detail.

Analyze Sources How might Mali's (and Africa's) wealth have influenced interactions between Africans and Europeans? *Europeans might have wanted the wealth and tried to acquire the territory.*

In print edition, see map of same title.

1. **Determine Main Ideas** What was a major source of wealth for the Empire of Mali? *gold*
2. **Make Inferences** How might Mali's (and Africa's) wealth have influenced interactions between Africans and Europeans? *Europeans might have wanted the wealth and tried to acquire the territory.*

DOCUMENT-BASED INVESTIGATION   HISTORICAL SOURCE

Mansa Musa's Kingdom

In 1375, a Spanish mapmaker created a map showing Mansa Musa's kingdom. The map shows Mansa Musa holding a gold nugget. At the top of the map is Spain. Below Spain, the Mediterranean meets the Atlantic at the Strait of Gibraltar. Further south is Africa. Filling most of the map is North Africa.

---

may have been Sundiata's grandnephew. Mansa Musa ruled from about 1312 to 1332.

Between the reigns of Sundiata and Mansa Musa, Mali had experienced turmoil. There had been seven different rulers in approximately 50 years. Like Sundiata, Mansa Musa was a skilled military leader who exercised royal control over the gold-salt trade and put down every rebellion. His 100,000-man army kept order and protected Mali from attack. Under Mansa Musa, the empire expanded to roughly twice the size of the Empire of Ghana. To govern his far-reaching empire, Mansa Musa divided it into provinces and appointed governors, who ruled fairly and efficiently.

A devout Muslim, Mansa Musa went on a hajj to Mecca from 1324 to 1325. When he returned, he ordered the building of new mosques at the trading cities of Timbuktu (TIHM•buhk•TOO) and Gao. Timbuktu became one of the most important cities of the empire. It attracted Muslim judges, doctors, religious leaders, and scholars from far and wide. They attended Timbuktu's outstanding mosques and universities. These intellectual and religious centers helped to integrate Islam into the society of Mali, an effect of Mansa Musa's rule that would endure for centuries.

Although Mali's urban centers flourished under Mansa Musa, their residents represented a small minority of the empire's population. Most people were farmers. Many others were skilled craftspeople, such as carpenters and metalworkers, and still others were religious leaders. The governing class of Mali and the scholars of its intellectual centers were Muslim, but most people believed in and practiced traditional African religions, especially outside of the urban centers. While Mansa Musa supported Islamic studies and religious practices, he did not force the faith on his subjects.

Travels of Ibn Battuta In 1352, one of Mansa Musa's successors prepared to receive a traveler and historian named **Ibn Battuta** (IHB•uhn-ba•TOO•tah). A native of Tangier in North Africa, Ibn Battuta had traveled for 27 years, visiting most of the countries in the Islamic world.

After leaving the royal palace, Ibn Battuta visited Timbuktu and other cities in Mali. He found he could travel without fear of crime. As a devout Muslim, he praised the people for their study of the Qur'an. However, he also criticized them for not strictly practicing Islam's moral code. Even so, Mali's justice system greatly impressed him:

"One of the best things in these parts is, the regard they pay to justice; for, in this respect, the Sultan regards neither little nor much. The safety, too, is very great; so that a traveller may proceed alone among them, without the least fear of a thief or robber."
—Ibn Battuta, *The Travels of Ibn Batūta, 1829*

Ibn Battuta left Mali in 1353. Within 50 years, the powerful empire began to weaken. Most of Mansa Musa's successors lacked his ability to govern well. In addition, the gold trade that had been the basis of Mali's wealth shifted eastward as new goldfields were developed elsewhere.

Mansa Musa's Kingdom

In 1324, Mansa Musa left Mali for the hajj to Mecca. On the trip, he gave away enormous amounts of gold. Because of this, Europeans learned of Mali's wealth. In 1375, a Spanish mapmaker created an illustrated map showing Mansa Musa's kingdom in western Africa. Drawn on the map is Mansa Musa holding a gold nugget.

At the top of the map is Spain. At the bottom of Spain, the Mediterranean meets the Atlantic Ocean at the Strait of Gibraltar. South of Gibraltar is Africa. Filling most of the map is North Africa, with the Mediterranean extending east and the Atlantic west of Gibraltar.

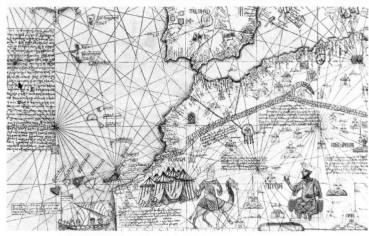

Analyze Historical Sources
1. What was a major source of wealth for the Empire of Mali?
2. How might Mali's (and Africa's) wealth have influenced interactions between Africans and Europeans?

Empire of Songhai

As Mali declined in the 1400s, people who had been under its control began to break away. Among them were the **Songhai** (SAWNG·HY) people to the east. They built up an army and extended their territory to the large bend in the Niger River near Gao. They gained control of the all-important trade routes. Gao was the capital of their empire.

Sunni Ali, a Conquering Hero The Songhai had two extraordinary rulers, both of whom were Muslims. One was Sunni Ali, who built a vast empire by military conquest. Sunni Ali's rule began in 1464 and lasted almost 30 years.

Societies and Empires of Africa   **465**

Objectives

You may wish to discuss the following questions with students to help them frame the content as they read.

- Based on what you have read, what can you conclude about Sunni Ali as a ruler? *He was fierce, persistent, and skilled.*

- What would motivate the Moroccans to overtake the Songhai? *to control trade routes across the Sahara*

More About . . .

Askia Muhammad Like Mansa Musa, Askia Muhammad made a pilgrimage to Mecca. On his return, he revived Timbuktu as a center of Muslim learning. A Moroccan traveler who used the name Leo Africanus provided a detailed description of Timbuktu. He told what the shops there sold, what the women typically wore, and how trade took place. He also noted that the king paid to support doctors, judges, and priests.

▶ **ONLINE ANALYZE VIDEOS**

Timbuktu: Thriving Songhai Empire Metropolis

Have students watch the video individually or as a class. You may wish to use the associated question as a discussion prompt.

Analyze Videos Why was Timbuktu's location ideal for trade? *It was situated at the point where the desert met the Niger River, and trade goods could be transferred from camels to canoes.*

LINK TO LANGUAGE ARTS

Write a History of the Songhai Empire

1. Have students review the information about Songhai rulers and Songhai decline.

2. Have each student write a brief history of the Songhai Empire in 300 words or fewer. Tell students to include both highlights of the kingdom's history and its problems.

3. Then have volunteers read their histories aloud. Have students compare and contrast the ideas.

ADVANCED/GIFTED

Compare Women's Roles in Different Societies

1. Request that students summarize the difference between the status of women in West Africa and in Muslim societies during the 15th century. Ask why students think these differences existed.

2. Tell students that differences exist today for Muslim women depending on where they live. Have student pairs research how Muslim women in a selected non-Muslim country practice their traditional customs and interact socially. Have pairs compare and contrast what they have learned about women's roles in different places.

READING CHECK
Make Inferences Why might the people who had been conquered by Mali want to break away? *because they resented being controlled by Mali; because they wanted to take over trade for themselves*

Sunni Ali built a professional army that had a riverboat fleet of war canoes and a mobile fighting force on horseback. He expanded Songhai into an empire through his skill as a military commander and his aggressive leadership. In 1468, Sunni Ali achieved his first major military triumph. He captured the city of Timbuktu, which had been an important part of Mali's empire.

Five years later, he took Djenné, also a trade city that had a university. To take Djenné, Sunni Ali surrounded the city with his army for seven years before it fell in 1473. Sunni Ali completed the takeover of Djenné by marrying its queen.

Askia Muhammad Governs Well After Sunni Ali's death in 1492, his son succeeded him as ruler. Almost at once, the son faced a major revolt by Muslims who were angry that he did not practice their religion faithfully. The leader of the revolt was a devout Muslim named Askia Muhammad. He drove Sunni Ali's son from power and replaced him.

Askia Muhammad conquered the Mossi people, whose territory bordered Songhai to the south. Then he turned west, to the Hausa kingdoms, and conquered them. He permitted the king of the Hausa city-state Kano to remain on his throne as a vassal. In some lands that he annexed, Askia established a Songhai colony to ensure efficient governance and collection of taxes and tribute. Annexing neighboring kingdoms increased the power and wealth of the Songhai Empire by expanding control of trade routes, increasing tax revenues, and increasing receipt of tribute.

During his 37-year rule, Askia Muhammad proved to be an excellent administrator. He set up an efficient tax system and chose able officials. Adding to the centralized government created by Sunni Ali, he appointed officials to serve as ministers of the treasury, army, navy, and agriculture. In addition to the king and the elites who worked in his government, Songhai society included a class of artisans such as metalworkers, farmers, and slaves. Under his rule, the well-governed empire thrived.

Despite its wealth and learning, the Songhai Empire lacked modern weapons. The Chinese had invented gunpowder in the ninth century. About 1304, Arabs developed the first gun, which shot arrows. In 1591, a

---

SOCIAL HISTORY

Islam in West Africa

South of the Sahara, many converts to Islam also kept their African beliefs. They found ways to include traditional rituals and customs in their new religion.

The status of women in West African societies demonstrates how local custom altered Muslim practice. In many 15th-century Muslim societies, women seldom left their homes. When they did, they veiled their faces. Muslim women in West Africa, however, did not wear veils. They mingled freely with men in public, which shocked visiting Muslim religious leaders.

Reading Check
Make Inferences
Why might the
people who had been
conquered by Mali
want to break away?

Moroccan fighting force of several thousand men equipped with gunpow-der and cannons crossed the Sahara and invaded Songhai. The Moroccan troops quickly defeated the Songhai warriors, who were armed only with swords and spears. The collapse of the Songhai Empire ended a 1,000-year period in which powerful kingdoms and empires ruled the central region of West Africa.

Other Peoples of West Africa

While empires rose and fell, city-states developed in other parts of West Africa. As in Ghana, Mali, and Songhai, Muslim traditions influenced some of these city-states. Other city-states held to their traditional African beliefs.

Hausa City-States Compete The **Hausa** (HOW•suh) were a group of people named after the language they spoke. The city-states of the Hausa people first emerged between the years 1000 and 1200 in the savanna area east of Mali and Songhai in what is today northern Nigeria. Songhai briefly ruled the Hausa city-states, but they soon regained their independence. In such city-states as Kano, Katsina, and Zazzau (later Zaria), local rulers built walled cities for their capitals. From their capitals, Hausa rulers governed the farming villages outside the city walls.

Each ruler depended on the crops of the farmers and on a thriving trade in salt, grain, and cotton cloth made by urban weavers. Because they were located on trade routes that linked other West African states with the Mediterranean, Kano and Katsina became major trading states. They profited greatly from supplying the needs of caravans. Kano was noted for its woven and dyed cloth and for its leather goods.

Zazzau, the southernmost state, conducted a vigorous trade in enslaved people. Zazzau's traders raided an area to take captives and then sold them to traders in other Hausa states. These traders sold the captives to other North or West African societies in exchange for horses, harnesses, and

History in Depth

Queen Amina's Reign

In the 1500s, the Hausa city-state of Zazzau (later called Zaria) was governed by Queen Amina. She was remembered as the "headdress among the turbans." Her rule was distinguished for its military conquests.

The *Kano Chronicle,* a history of the city-state of Kano, records:

> "At this time Zaria, under Queen Amina, conquered all the towns as far as Kawarajara and Nupe. Every town paid tribute to her. . . . Her conquests extended over 34 years."

Queen Amina's commitment to her Muslim faith also led her to encourage Muslim scholars, judges, and religious leaders from religious centers at Kano and Timbuktu to come to Zazzau.

Societies and Empires of Africa **467**

COLLABORATIVE LEARNING

Explore West African Art

1. Divide students into heterogeneous groups of three or four.

2. Have each group choose one piece of West African art from any of the cultures studied in this lesson. Students can use images included in this module, or they can use images from the Internet or library resources.

3. Instruct each group to research the artwork to find out the artist's method, materials, purpose, and what the work suggests about the society it came from.

4. Have groups take turns presenting their findings. Encourage the audience for each presentation to provide constructive feedback to the presenters.

Objectives

You may wish to discuss the following questions with students to help them frame the content as they read.

- Why were Yoruba kings considered divine? *descendants of first Ife ruler; believed to have been sent by the creator, according to legend*

- What evidence of the relationship between artists and rulers can be seen in Ife art? *favorable portrayal of rulers—positive relationship*

- Why do you think these African societies did not rival the power of the other kingdoms and empires in this segment? *Possible answer: They were not located where they could control or profit from the Saharan trade.*

More About . . .

Queen Amina's Reign Zaria prospered under Queen Amina. After her soldiers invaded Nupe in the south, Zaria's trade in slaves and kola nuts grew. The river that separated the Hausa kingdoms from Nupe became known as the "river of washing away poverty" because those who crossed it to trade grew rich. Today, girls' schools in northern Nigeria celebrate Amina Day. During the festival, students play sports and wear special clothes in Amina's honor.

Ife Artists Ife artists drew figures of humans to a specific proportion. The head was one-third to one-fourth the size of the body. Artists made the head larger because they believed it was the seat of the life force.

Europeans in West Africa The Portuguese established a chain of trade settlements on the "Gold Coast" of West Africa. The most important settlement was El Mina, where European ironware, cloth, food, and firearms were exchanged for African gold, ivory, and food beginning in the early 1400s.

BIOGRAPHY

Queen Amina

Have students read the biography of Queen Amina, who ruled over the Hausa city-state of Zazzau in the 1500s.

The Lost-Wax Process

Many of the Benin sculptures were made using the lost wax process.

Create Clay Core

The artist forms a core of clay that is roughly the shape of the planned sculpture.

guns. The Hausa kept some enslaved captives to build and repair city walls and grow food for the cities.

All the Hausa city-states had similar forms of government. Rulers held great power over their subjects, but ministers and other officials acted to check this power. For protection, each city-state raised an army of mounted horsemen. Although rulers often schemed and fought to gain control over their neighbors, none succeeded for long. The constant fighting among city-states prevented any one of them from building a Hausa empire.

This Yoruba crown made of glass beads and grass cloth stands about 20 inches high.

Yoruba Kings and Artists Like the Hausa, the **Yoruba** (YAWR•uh•buh) people all spoke a common language. Originally the Yoruba-speaking people belonged to a number of small city-states in the forests on the southern edge of the savanna in present-day Benin and southwestern Nigeria. In these communities most people farmed. Over time, some of these smaller communities joined together under strong leaders. This led to the formation of several Yoruba kingdoms.

Considered divine, Yoruba kings served as the most important religious and political leaders in their kingdoms. All Yoruba chiefs traced their descent from the first ruler of Ife (EE•fay). According to legend, the creator sent this first ruler down to earth at Ife, where he founded the first Yoruba state. His many sons became the heads of other Yoruba kingdoms. All Yoruba chiefs regarded the king of Ife as their highest spiritual authority. A secret society of religious and political leaders limited the king's rule by reviewing the decisions he made.

Ife and Oyo were the two largest Yoruba kingdoms. Ife, developed by 1100, was the most powerful Yoruba kingdom until the late 1600s, when Oyo became more prosperous. As large urban centers, both Ife and Oyo had high walls surrounding them. Most rural farms in the surrounding areas produced surplus food, which was sent to the cities. This enabled city dwellers to become both traders and craftspeople.

The Ife were gifted artists who carved in wood and ivory. They produced terra cotta sculptures and cast in metal. Some scholars believe that the rulers supported artists. Many clay and metal casts portray Ife rulers in an idealistic way.

Vocabulary
terra cotta a reddish-brown clay, hard ceramic

Kingdom of Benin To the south and west of Ife, near the delta of the Niger River, lay the kingdom of **Benin** (buh•NIHN). Like the Yoruba people of Ife and Oyo, the people of Benin made their homes in the forest. The first kings of Benin date from the 1200s. Like the Yoruba kings, the oba, or ruler, of Benin based his right to rule on claims of descent from the first king of Ife.

In the 1400s, an oba named Ewuare made Benin into a major West African state. He did so by building a powerful army. He used it to control an area that by 1500 stretched from the Niger River delta in the east to what is today Lagos, Nigeria. Ewuare also strengthened Benin City by building walls around it. Inside the city, broad streets were lined by neat rows of houses.

The huge palace contained many courtyards and works of art. Artists working for the oba created copper figurines and magnificent brass heads of the royal family. Brass plaques on the walls and columns of the royal palace of the oba showed legends, historical scenes, and the deeds of the oba and his nobles. According to tradition, Benin artists learned their craft from an Ife artist brought to Benin by the oba to teach them.

In the 1480s, Portuguese trading ships began to sail into Benin's port at Gwatto. The Portuguese traded with Benin merchants for pepper, leopard skins, ivory, and enslaved persons. This began several centuries of European interference in Africa, during which Europeans enslaved Africans and seized African territories for colonies. Meanwhile, East Africans prospered from trade and developed thriving cities and empires.

This ivory mask is one of four taken from the king of Benin in 1897. It was worn on the belt of a ceremonial costume.

Reading Check
Analyze Causes
What was the main reason that the Hausa did not develop an empire?

Lesson 4 Assessment

1. Organize Information Create a timeline like the one below to trace the growth and decline of the empires you read about in this lesson.

```
        event two    event four
  ──────○──────○──────○──────
    event one     event three
```

Write a paragraph describing how any two of these events are related.

2. Key Terms and People For each key term or person in the lesson, write a sentence explaining its significance.

3. Analyze Motives Why did Berber leaders want to make changes to their society?

4. Summarize How did the trans-Saharan trade practiced by Ghana, Mali, and Songhai work?

5. Compare What are some of the similarities between Sundiata and Mansa Musa?

6. Evaluate Impact How did the expansion of the Songhai Empire affect the people and the economy of West Africa?

7. Compare What are some of the similarities between the Hausa city-states and other city-states you have read about?

Print Assessment

1. **Organize Information** Create a timeline to trace the growth and decline of the empires you read about in this lesson. Write a paragraph describing how any two of these events are related. *Students' answers will vary, but students should describe text evidence of the relationship between the two events. Possible pairs of events might include Muhammad's death and Muslim rule in Egypt; Almoravid expansion and Almohad takeover; Berber use of camels and the development of ironmaking technologies; West African growth of trade and the creation of the empire of Ghana.*

2. **Key Terms and People** For each key term or person in the lesson, write a sentence explaining its significance. *Explanations of the lesson's key terms can be found on the following pages: Maghrib, p. 456; Almoravids, p. 457; Almohads, p. 458; Ghana, p. 459; Mali, p. 462, Sundiata, p. 462; Mansa Musa, p. 462; Ibn Battuta, p. 464; Songhai, p. 465; Hausa, p. 467; Yoruba, p. 468; Benin, p. 469.*

3. **Analyze Motives** Why did Berber leaders want to make changes to their society? *Possible answer: They had traveled to Mecca and saw that Islam was practiced differently in other places; they wanted a more devout society.*

4. **Summarize** How did the trans-Saharan trade practiced by Ghana, Mali, and Songhai work? *Possible answer: Traders took salt and other goods from Sahara, crossed the desert by camel, and traded for gold, slaves, and other goods in market towns of West Africa.*

5. **Compare** What are some of the similarities between Sundiata and Mansa Musa? *Possible answer: strong rulers, skilled military leaders and administrators*

6. **Evaluate Impact** How did the expansion of the Songhai Empire affect the people and the economy of West Africa? *Possible answer: Smaller kingdoms were conquered and had to pay tribute; more people had to pay taxes and follow the Songhai way of trading; new cities grew, power and wealth shifted from older cities to new ones.*

7. **Compare** What are some of the similarities between the Hausa city-states and other city-states you have read about? *Possible answer: Cities were walled; rulers governed farming villages; workers grew food for the city; city-states fought one another.*

▷ Online Assessment

1. Why did the Almohads fight to seize power from the Almoravids?
   ○ The Almohads desired to live in the fortified monastery.
   ○ The Almohads wanted to be more lenient on Islamic law.
   ○ The Almohads believed it was important to take pilgrimages to Mecca.
   ◉ The Almohads thought they were better observers of Islamic teachings.

   Alternate Question *Select the answer choice from the drop-down list to complete the sentence correctly.* The Almohads believed that the Almoravids weren't strong enough followers of [Islam ▾], so the Almohads wanted to seize control of the government.

2. What contribution did the Sahara provide in the trans-Saharan trade route?
   ◉ salt
   ○ gold
   ○ spices
   ○ leather

   Alternate Question *Select the answer choice from the drop-down list to complete the sentence correctly.* Each region in Africa provided different goods and resources for the trans-Saharan trade route. The southern regions provided gold, and the Sahara provided [salt ▾].

3. Where did most people in Mali practice Islam during the reign of Mansa Musa?
   ○ coastlines
   ○ rural areas
   ○ mountains
   ◉ urban centers

   Alternate Question *Select the answer choice from the drop-down list to complete the sentence correctly.* Most of the people in Mali's urban centers practiced [Islam ▾] during the reign of Mansa Musa.

4. What did the takeover of Djenné show about Sunni Ali?
   ○ He was greedy.
   ○ He was educated.
   ◉ He was persistent.
   ○ He was diplomatic.

   Alternate Question *Select the answer choice from the drop-down list to complete the sentence correctly.* The takeover of Djenné showed that Sunni Ali was persistent because he surrounded the city for [seven years ▾] before the city finally surrendered in 1473.

5. How were the people of Yoruba and the people of Benin similar to each other?
   ○ They both followed the Islamic faith.
   ○ They both spoke a common language.
   ◉ They both made their homes in the forest.
   ○ They both fought the Hausa Empire for land.

   Alternate Question *Select the answer choice from the drop-down list to complete the sentence correctly.* The people of Benin and the people of [Yoruba ▾] were similar because they both made their homes in the forest.

6. **Apply Concepts** What is the connection between the Islamic religion and Islamic law?

   Possible answer: The Islamic faith requires that its followers are strict observers of the law. Muslims do not separate their personal everyday life from their religious life—they are one and the same. Islamic law regulates almost all areas of human life.

7. **Elaborate** How did the king act in Ghana's royal court?

   Possible answer: In Ghana's royal court, the king controlled the trade and commanded a large army. He required the chiefs of surrounding lands to pay him a tribute if they wanted to live in peace. The king stored all of his gold and salt inside the palace. He wouldn't let anyone else in the kingdom own any gold. He was the military commander, chief judge, and religious leader.

8. **Make Inferences** Why did the people of Mali most likely revere Sundiata?

   Possible answer: Sundiata was as great a leader in peace as he was in war. He appointed administrators to be in charge of the country's finances, defense, and foreign wars. He encouraged advancements in agriculture. He reestablished the gold-salt trade. The new capital of Niani therefore became an important center of commerce and trade.

9. **Draw Conclusions** Why did other peoples find it easy to conquer the Songhai?

   Possible answer: The Songhai Empire lacked modern weapons, which were utilized by other peoples who fought them. The Songhai tried to battle the Moroccans with swords and spears, for example, while the Moroccans had gunpowder and cannons. The Songhai simply could not compete with that.

10. **Draw Conclusions** What was the importance of art in the kingdom of Benin?

    Possible answer: Art was of great importance in Benin. The people believed that artists learned their craft from an Ife artist who was brought to Benin by the oba to teach them. The king's palace contained many courtyards full of art. Artists worked directly for the oba and created brass heads of the royal family and copper figurines. Art was a way for the people to show their history. Brass plaques on the walls of the palace showed the legends, historical scenes, and deeds of the nobles and the oba.

History Through Art

Benin Bronzes

- Ask students why they think many societies make sculptures of rulers, leaders, and heroes. *Possible answer: to honor achievements, remember people after death, please rulers*

- Have students consider why historians put so much emphasis on the art created by early cultures of Benin. *Possible answer: few or no written records of the period, so have to rely on art to find out about culture*

Benin Bronzes

Benin is famous for its bronze and brass sculptures. Benin sculpture was made by guilds controlled by the king. One of the main functions of Benin art was to please the ruler by recording his history or by displaying his power. For instance, brass plaques commemorating the ruler's great achievements adorned the palace walls. Busts of the ruler and his family showed them as idealized figures.

▶ **QUEEN MOTHER**
Perhaps the most widely known type of Benin sculpture was the royal head, such as this one. In Benin, the Queen Mother held a lot of power. To symbolize that power, she wore a woven crown called a "chicken's beak."

◀ **PLAQUE**
Plaques such as this decorated the palace of the oba, or ruler, of Benin.

470   Module 12

▼ **LEOPARD**
Admired for its power, fierceness, and intelligence, the leopard was depicted on many royal objects. This snarling leopard is a symbol of the king's power. It is also a water vessel that was used on ceremonial occasions.

▲ **MUSICIAN**
This figure was probably made in the late 16th or early 17th century. It shows an attendant of the king blowing a horn or flute. This type of figure was often found on altars.

THE LOST-WAX PROCESS

Many of the Benin sculptures were made using the lost-wax process.

1. The artist forms a core of clay that is roughly the shape of the planned sculpture.

2. The artist applies a layer of wax over the core, then carves fine details into the surface of the wax.

3. A layer of fine clay is spread over the wax surface. This creates a smooth finish and captures the small details.

4. Several layers of coarse clay are applied to create the mold.

5. The entire object is fired in a kiln (oven). The clay hardens and the wax melts away, leaving a clay mold. (The melted wax is the origin of the name "lost-wax.")

6. Melted bronze is poured into the mold and left to harden.

7. The clay mold is broken off, revealing the finished bronze sculpture.

Now and Then

1. **Make Inferences** Why do you think the figure of a servant blowing a horn was found on an altar?
2. **Compare and Contrast** Use library resources or the Internet to identify a sculpture of a U.S. leader. What quality about that leader does the sculpture portray? How is it similar to or different from Benin's royal sculptures?

NOW & THEN

1. **Make Inferences** Why do you think the figure of a servant blowing a horn was found on an altar? *Horns and music may have been used in religious ceremonies. Also, horns may have been used to announce a ceremony or to signal the presence of the king at a ceremony.*

2. **Compare and Contrast** Use library resources or the Internet to identify a sculpture of a U.S. leader. What quality about that leader does the sculpture portray? How is it similar to or different from Benin's royal sculptures? *Possible answer: Some students might name the statue in the Lincoln Memorial and say that it portrays Lincoln's goodness or compassion. This is quite different from the Benin emphasis on showing power.*

Eastern City-States and Southern Empires

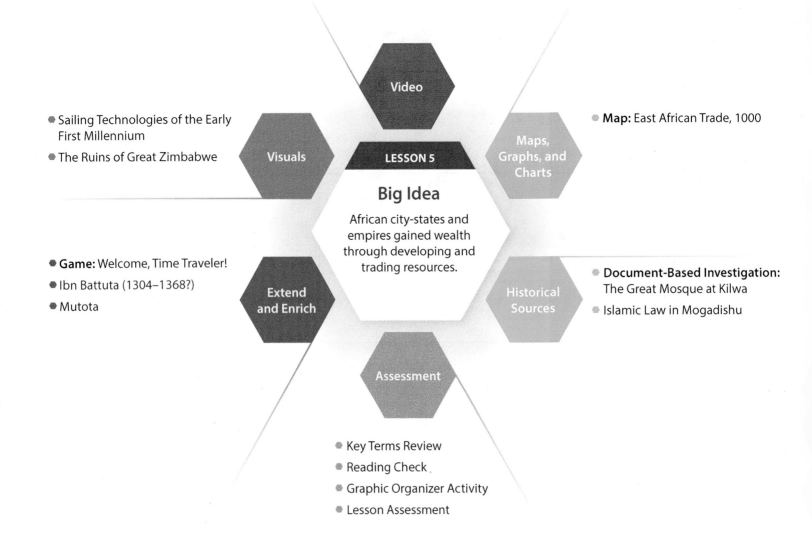

- Sailing Technologies of the Early First Millennium
- The Ruins of Great Zimbabwe

Visuals

Video

LESSON 5

Maps, Graphs, and Charts

- **Map:** East African Trade, 1000

Big Idea

African city-states and empires gained wealth through developing and trading resources.

- **Game:** Welcome, Time Traveler!
- Ibn Battuta (1304–1368?)
- Mutota

Extend and Enrich

Historical Sources

- **Document-Based Investigation:** The Great Mosque at Kilwa
- Islamic Law in Mogadishu

Assessment

- Key Terms Review
- Reading Check
- Graphic Organizer Activity
- Lesson Assessment

Online Lesson 5 Enrichment Activities

Ibn Battuta (1304–1368?)

Biography Students read about the voyager who traveled tens of thousands of miles around the world in the 14th century. Then they tell why his journeys were so important.

Mutota

Biography Students read about how the African leader established a powerful empire in southern Africa and write a scene for a movie about his life.

Teach the Big Idea

1. **Whole Class Open/Introduction** Ask students to share what they know about international trade today. *Possible answer: many everyday products imported*

2. **Direct Teach** Read students the Big Idea: *African city-states and empires gained wealth through developing and trading resources.* Review the following lesson objectives with students to aid in their understanding of the Big Idea.

   • Describe the role of east coast trade cities in the economy of East Africa.

   • Explain how Islam influenced East African peoples.

   • Identify Great Zimbabwe and explain its significance.

   • Describe how the Mutapa Empire was established.

3. **Whole Group Close/Reflect** Have each student write a summary of the development and growth of the Mutapa Empire.

▷ ONLINE DOCUMENT-BASED INVESTIGATION

Societies and Empire of Africa

The Great Mosque at Kilwa is the fifth of five historical sources that students will analyze in the Societies and Empires of Africa module. Built of stone and coral, the Great Mosque of Kilwa is a fine example of Kilwa architecture. Have students study the image.

▷ ONLINE GRAPHIC ORGANIZER

Eastern City-States and Southern Empires

As students read the lesson, have them use the graphic organizer to take notes. Students can review their graphic organizer notes at the end of the lesson to answer the following question:

Summarize Were Ibn Battuta's impressions of the coastal cities that he visited favorable? Use evidence from the text to support your answer. *Possible answer: Ibn Battuta "admired" the way the people of Kilwa lived in "fine houses of coral and stone." His excerpt about Mogadishu doesn't show if he favored their legal methods or not, but his writing makes their process seem well organized.*

Eastern City-States and Southern Empires

Ruins of the Great Mosque at Kilwa

Setting the Stage

By the third century AD, Aksum was part of an extensive trade network. From its Red Sea port, Aksum traded with Arabia, Persia, India, and Rome. In the 600s, Muslim forces gained control of Arabia, the Red Sea, and North Africa. They cut off the Aksumites from their port. The Aksumites moved their capital south from Aksum to Roha (later called Lalibela) before 1100. Meanwhile, other cities on the east coast were thriving because of Indian Ocean trade. In this lesson, you will learn about East African trade, Islamic influences in East Africa, and the peoples of southern Africa.

East Coast Trade Cities

Villages along the east coast began to develop into important trade cities. By 1100, waves of Bantu-speaking people had migrated across central Africa to the east coast. There they established farming and fishing villages. Slowly, the coastal villages grew into bustling seaports, built on trade between East African merchants and traders from Arabia, Persia, and India. As trade increased, many Muslim Arab and Persian traders settled in the port cities. Arabic blended with the Bantu language to create **Swahili** (swah•HEE•lee).

Persian traders moved south from the Horn of Africa, a triangular peninsula near Arabia. They brought Asian manufactured goods to Africa and African raw materials to Asia. In the coastal markets, Arab traders sold porcelain bowls from China and jewels and cotton cloth from India. They bought African ivory, gold, tortoiseshell, ambergris, leopard skins, and rhinoceros horns to carry to Arabia.

By 1300, more than 35 trading cities dotted the coast from Mogadishu in the north to Kilwa and Sofala in the south. These seaports grew wealthy by controlling trade. Some cities also manufactured trade goods for export. For example, weavers in Mogadishu and Sofala made cloth. Workers in Mombasa and Malindi made iron tools.

COLLABORATIVE LEARNING

Africa's Eastern City-States and Southern Empires Articles

1. Divide students into small groups. Tell students that you would like each group to plan and write a series of articles for a web page that describes one of Africa's eastern city-states or southern empires. Explain that the articles should highlight significant changes that have occurred over a number of centuries. Assign groups different city-states/empires.

2. Tell each group to divide roles among themselves. Allow time for students to brainstorm ideas before they begin their specialized tasks.

3. Have group members compile their articles and share them with other groups. Have groups discuss the similarities and differences among the city-states/empires.

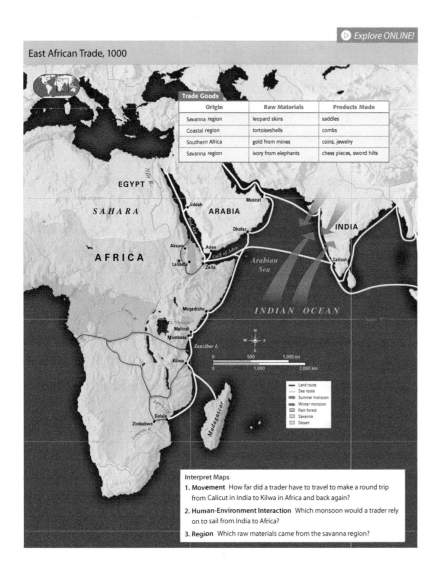

East African Trade, 1000

Trade Goods

Origin	Raw Materials	Products Made
Savanna region	leopard skins	saddles
Coastal region	tortoiseshells	combs
Southern Africa	gold from mines	coins, jewelry
Savanna region	ivory from elephants	chess pieces, sword hilts

Land route
Sea route
Summer monsoon
Winter monsoon
Rain forest
Savanna
Desert

Interpret Maps

1. **Movement** How far did a trader have to travel to make a round trip from Calicut in India to Kilwa in Africa and back again?

2. **Human-Environment Interaction** Which monsoon would a trader rely on to sail from India to Africa?

3. **Region** Which raw materials came from the savanna region?

Societies and Empires of Africa **473**

Objectives

You may wish to discuss the following questions with students to help them frame the content as they read.

- Why did Kilwa become the wealthiest and most powerful of East Africa's coastal city-states? *It was the southernmost city traders could reach in a single monsoon season.*

- Why would merchants from southern regions send their goods north to Kilwa? *so Asian merchants could buy them*

- What role did technology play in the conquests by the Portuguese? *Portuguese had shipboard cannon, East Africans did not.*

More About . . .

Fed by the Sultan When Ibn Battuta arrived in Mogadishu, he was sent food by the sultan. He was fed rice topped with ghee (clarified butter) and a sauce of meat, chicken, fish, and vegetables. Green bananas cooked in milk were served as well, along with sour milk with pickled lemon, pickled chilies with vinegar and salt, green ginger, and mangoes.

Ivory Trade Ivory trade was important to East Africa and other parts of Africa for centuries. Eventually, this trade greatly reduced the populations of elephants and rhinoceros in Africa. While ivory trading was outlawed in 1975, illegal trade of ivory continues to be a problem in Africa. The elephant population was estimated to be at about 1.3 million around 1979. By 2007, the estimate was from about 472,000 to 690,000. It is believed that more than 100,000 African elephants were poached from 2010 to 2012, with about 24,000 elephants being poached from East Africa.

⊳ **ONLINE INTERACTIVE MAPS**

East African Trade, 1000

Have students explore the map using the interactive features and answer the associated questions.

Human-Environment Interaction During which month might a ship captain choose to sail from Calicut to Africa in order to make the best use of the wind conditions? *January*

In print edition, see map of same title.

1. **Movement** How far did a trader have to travel to make a round trip from Calicut in India to Kilwa in Africa and back again? *about 6,000 miles*

2. **Human-Environment Interaction** Which monsoon would a trader rely on to sail from India to Africa? *the winter monsoon*

3. **Region** Which raw materials came from the savanna region? *leopard skins and ivory*

LINK TO ART

Chart Kilwa's Rise

1. Ask students to reread the paragraphs entitled "The City-State of Kilwa."

2. Tell students that you would like them to identify two sets of causes and effects in the reading.

3. Have students create a poster that creatively shows one cause-and-effect relationship on one side and the other cause-and-effect relationship on the other side.

4. Encourage students to pair up and compare and discuss their posters.

⊳ **ONLINE LESSON FLIP CARDS**

Review Key Terms and People

Students can use the flip cards in the Lesson Review at any time to review the lesson's key terms and people: *Swahili, Great Zimbabwe, and Mutapa.*

Carousel: Sailing Technologies of the Early First Millennium

Have students navigate through the carousel and note similarities and differences among the images or identify a unifying theme.

Islamic Law in Mogadishu

Have students read the excerpt and answer the associated question.

Analyze Sources What were the four types of people who decided legal matters, and what types of cases did each one judge? *Qadi, or judge—religious cases; wazirs, or government ministers, and amirs, or military commanders—nonreligious cases; Shaikh, or sultan—any case that was referred to him*

In print edition, see historical source of same title.

1. **Summarize** Who were the four types of people who decided legal matters? *Qadi—judges; Wazirs—government ministers; Chief amirs—military commanders; Shaikh—sultan*

2. **Synthesize** What types of cases did they judge? *Qadi—religious cases; Wazirs and amirs—nonreligious cases; the sultan (or Shaikh)—cases that were specially referred to him*

HISTORICAL SOURCE

Islamic Law in Mogadishu

In 1331, Ibn Battuta, traveling by caravan, visited the African city of Mogadishu. He described how Muslim officials decided legal

READING CHECK

Analyze Causes What were the two main reasons Kilwa became so wealthy? *Its favorable location caused trade to funnel into the city; it controlled Sofala and its gold trade.*

The City-State of Kilwa In 1331, Ibn Battuta visited Kilwa. He admired the way that its Muslim rulers and merchants lived. Rich families lived in fine houses of coral and stone. They slept in beds inlaid with ivory, and their meals were served on porcelain. Wealthy Muslim women wore silk robes and gold and silver bracelets.

Kilwa grew rich because it was as far south as a ship from India could sail in one monsoon season. Therefore, trade goods from southerly regions had to funnel into Kilwa, where Asian merchants could buy them.

In addition, in the late 1200s Kilwa had seized the port of Sofala, which was a trading center for gold mined inland. By controlling Sofala, Kilwa was able to control the overseas trade of gold from southern Africa. As a result, Kilwa became the wealthiest, most powerful coastal city-state.

Portuguese Conquest In 1488, the first Portuguese ships rounded the southern tip of Africa and sailed north, looking for a sea route to India.

Historical Source

Islamic Law in Mogadishu

In 1331, Ibn Battuta, traveling by caravan, visited the African city of Mogadishu. He described how Muslim officials decided legal matters.

Analyze Historical Sources
1. Who were the four types of people who decided legal matters?
2. What types of cases did they judge?

"The Shaikh [sultan] takes his place in his hall of audience and sends for the Qadi [judge]. He takes his place on the Shaikh's left and then the lawyers come in and the chief of them sit in front of the Shaikh. . . . Then food is brought and . . . those who are in the audience chamber eat in the presence of the Shaikh. . . . After this the Shaikh retires to his private apartments and the Qadi, the wazirs [government ministers] . . . and . . . chief amirs [military commanders] sit to hear causes and complaints. Questions of religious law are decided by the Qadi, other cases are judged by the . . . wazirs and amirs. If a case requires the views of the [Shaikh], it is put in writing for him. He sends back an immediate reply."

—Ibn Battuta, *Travels of Ibn Battuta*

STRUGGLING READERS

Map the Origins of Trade Goods

1. Distribute a blank outline map to students, or have them draw their own.

2. Ask students to label the cities along Africa's east coast. Then have them draw and label land and sea routes, using the East African Trade, 1000 map as a guide. Also have students use color to shade in the savanna region, Southern Africa, and the coastal region.

3. Next, have students use the digital map content or the Trade Goods chart to determine which cities may have sold which products.

4. Tell students to add the products sold in the appropriate places on their maps. *Possible answer: saddles—Askum, Lalibela, Zimbabwe; combs—Mogadishu, Mombasa, Kilwa, Zeila, Sofal; coins/jewelry—Zimbabwe, Sofala, Kilwa*

Reading Check

Analyze Causes
What were the two
main reasons Kilwa
became so wealthy?

They wanted to gain profits from the Asian trade in spices, perfumes, and silks. When the Portuguese saw the wealth of the East African city-states, they decided to conquer those cities and take over the trade themselves.

Using their shipboard cannon, the Portuguese took Sofala, Kilwa, and Mombasa. They burned parts of Kilwa and built forts on the sites of Kilwa and Mombasa. The Portuguese kept their ports and cities on the East African coast for the next two centuries.

Islamic Influences

Muslim traders introduced Islam to the East African coast, and commerce caused the religion to spread. Even the smallest towns had a mosque for the faithful. A Muslim sultan, or ruler, governed most cities. Most government officials and wealthy merchants were Muslims. However, the vast majority of people along the eastern coast held on to their traditional religious beliefs. This was also true of the people who lived in inland villages.

Enslavement of Africans Along with luxury goods, Arab Muslim traders exported enslaved persons from the East African coast. Traders sent Africans acquired through kidnapping to markets in Arabia, Persia, and

An Arab slave market in Yemen, 1237

Societies and Empires of Africa **475**

Objectives

You may wish to discuss the following questions with students to help them frame the content as they read.

- Why would the growth of commerce cause Islam to spread? *As wealthy merchants and rulers did business with traders, they shared their religion as well.*

- Why might the development of plantations affect the slave trade? *A plantation requires more laborers than a house or estate does.*

More About . . .

Enslaved Africans In the 1300s, some African slaves were shipped to Europe, where they replaced Russian slaves on Italian sugar plantations. In the 1400s, Portuguese sailors arrived on the coast of West Africa. Having started sugar plantations of their own on islands off the coast of West Africa, the Portuguese enslaved Africans and shipped them to the islands as laborers. However, a few enslaved Africans sent to Muslim societies were able to rise to political power through domestic or military service. In the 1490s, for instance, a man named Sidi Badr briefly seized the throne of Bengal.

The Great Mosque at Kilwa Today, the Great Mosque is located at the edge of modern Kilwa. It was built in the 11th and 12th centuries and made larger in the 14th century. In fact, up until the 16th century it was the largest mosque in sub-Saharan Africa.

▶ **ONLINE DOCUMENT-BASED INVESTIGATION**

The Great Mosque at Kilwa

The Great Mosque is built of stone and coral. Have students study the image.

Analyze Sources What resources would the leaders and residents of Kilwa have needed to build this mosque? *They needed stone, coral, porcelain for the décor, and skilled builders and carvers.*

DOCUMENT-BASED INVESTIGATION   HISTORICAL SOURCE

The Great Mosque at Kilwa

Many buildings in Kilwa were built of stone and coral. The Great Mosque is a fine example. Erected in the 11th century and expanded in the 14th, the mosque has many domes and vaulted ceilings. It was decorated with stone carvings, engraved coral plaster, and embedded porcelain from China.

Analyze Primary Sources

1. Organize students in groups of two or three to analyze the primary source text from Ibn Battuta.

2. Have students scan the source to identify words that are unfamiliar to them such as *Shaikh, Qadi, wazirs,* and *amirs.* Instruct them to find the meaning of each word within the source.

3. Have groups make a sequence chart and write each event that happens according to the source.

4. Ask students to pose questions within their group such as the following: What happens first? What happens after the food is eaten? What happens if the views of the Shaikh are needed?

Objectives

You may wish to discuss the following questions with students to help them frame the content as they read.

- What are some reasons the people of Great Zimbabwe may have abandoned the site? *The land may have become overgrazed by cattle; the soil may have lost its fertility; the people left to find new sources of salt and timber, which had been used up where they were.*

- What evidence is there to support the idea that Great Zimbabwe was an organized state? *The city was near important trade routes and eventually gained control of them. Its capital was thriving as shown by the fact that its leaders taxed traders and demanded payments from less powerful chiefs.*

More About . . .

Building Great Zimbabwe Large granite boulders originally covered the site of Great Zimbabwe. Workers incorporated some of the boulders into structures and cut others into smaller blocks. Workers split some boulders by heating them with fire, then quickly cooling them with water.

The Role of Intermediary Great Zimbabwe lay along a trade route linking Africa's interior gold mines to the city-states on the coast. In this location, Great Zimbabwe served as a intermediary between gold miners and ivory hunters in southern Africa and the traders on the coast. A intermediary is a person who buys something from one person and sells it to another, making a profit on the sale.

Archaeological discoveries support this role for Great Zimbabwe. For example, archaeologists have found glass beads from India and a coin minted in Kilwa at the site of Great Zimbabwe. The kingdom's rulers likely taxed the trade goods that passed through their territory.

READING CHECK

Summarize How extensive was the trade in enslaved persons from East Africa before 1700? *Although it was widespread geographically, the numbers were small compared to those after 1700.*

Iraq. Wealthy people in these countries often bought slaves to do domestic tasks. Muslim traders shipped enslaved Africans across the Indian Ocean to India, where Indian rulers employed them as soldiers. Enslaved Africans also worked on docks and ships at Muslim-controlled ports and as household servants in China.

Although Muslim traders had been enslaving East Africans and selling them overseas since about the ninth century, the numbers remained small—perhaps about 1,000 a year. The trade in slaves did not increase dramatically until the 1700s. At that time, Europeans started to buy captured Africans for their colonial plantations.

Southern Africa and Great Zimbabwe

The gold and ivory that helped the coastal city-states grow rich came from the interior of southern Africa. In southeastern Africa, the Shona people established a city called **Great Zimbabwe** (zihm·BAHB·way), which grew into an empire built on the gold trade.

Great Zimbabwe By 1000, the Shona people had settled the fertile, well-watered plateau between the Zambezi and Limpopo rivers in present-day Zimbabwe. The area was well suited to farming and cattle raising. The location also had other economic advantages. The city of Great Zimbabwe stood near an important trade route linking the goldfields with the coastal trading city of Sofala. Sometime after 1000, Great Zimbabwe gained control of these trade routes. From the 1200s through the 1400s, it became the capital of a thriving state. Its leaders taxed the traders who traveled these routes. They also demanded payments from less powerful chiefs. Because of this growing wealth, Great Zimbabwe became the economic, political, and religious center of an empire.

Almost everything that is known about Great Zimbabwe comes from its impressive ruins, which include a complex of walled enclosures on a large hill, another group of enclosures south of the hill, called the Great Enclosure, and more recent ruins in the valley between. In addition to the stone walls of the enclosures, there are ruins of many huts that were constructed of mud or stone, both within and without the walls of the enclosures. Most of the stone structures in Great Zimbabwe were probably built between 1250 and 1450.

Excavations of the ruins suggest that Great Zimbabwe's society included multiple social and economic classes. Huts outside of the city's enclosures were very close together, but inside the enclosures, they were not—showing that those living inside the enclosures enjoyed elite status. Some huts inside the hill enclosure seemed to be for special purposes, such as religious ceremonies. Additionally, most cattle bones on the site were found near the wall of the Great Enclosure, an indication that the elite of the

---

LINK TO LANGUAGE ARTS

Hypothesize about Great Zimbabwe

1. Organize students into small groups to discuss possible reasons for the rise and fall of Great Zimbabwe.

2. Have each student write a mystery story that offers a theory of how Great Zimbabwe came to an end. Students should include facts from the segment and information from the group's discussion. Encourage students to think creatively about the role of the story's characters and plot and how the mystery will be solved.

3. Invite volunteers to read their stories to the class.

Great Zimbabwe

Great Zimbabwe was an important city in southern Africa. The word *zimbabwe* comes from a Shona phrase meaning "stone houses." The ruins consist of two complexes of stone buildings that once housed the royal palace of Great Zimbabwe's rulers. There are great curving walls around the ruins. Because there was no way for soldiers to climb to the top of the walls, archaeologists theorize that they were not used primarily as defenses. The massive walls were probably built to impress visitors with the strength of Zimbabwe and its ruler.

Inside the walls stands a cone-shaped tower. Among the ruins were found tall figures of birds, carved from soapstone. Archaeologists believe the construction of Great Zimbabwe may have taken about 400 years.

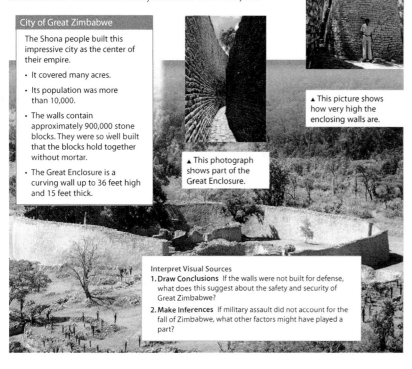

City of Great Zimbabwe

The Shona people built this impressive city as the center of their empire.

- It covered many acres.
- Its population was more than 10,000.
- The walls contain approximately 900,000 stone blocks. They were so well built that the blocks hold together without mortar.
- The Great Enclosure is a curving wall up to 36 feet high and 15 feet thick.

▲ This picture shows how very high the enclosing walls are.

▲ This photograph shows part of the Great Enclosure.

Interpret Visual Sources
1. **Draw Conclusions** If the walls were not built for defense, what does this suggest about the safety and security of Great Zimbabwe?
2. **Make Inferences** If military assault did not account for the fall of Zimbabwe, what other factors might have played a part?

▷ **ONLINE INTERACTIVE VISUALS**

Carousel: The Ruins of Great Zimbabwe

Today, Great Zimbabwe National Monument is a World Heritage site. This means that it is protected by law against destruction or theft of artifacts. For example, workers make sure that the site does not become overgrown by plant life. Also, they make sure that the building materials do not continue to decay and are preserved. Still modern visitors may explore the site.

In print edition, see Analyze Architecture: Great Zimbabwe.

1. **Draw Conclusions** If the walls were not built for defense, what does this suggest about the safety and security of Great Zimbabwe? *It suggests that Great Zimbabwe was relatively safe and secure from attack.*

2. **Make Inferences** If military assault did not account for the fall of Zimbabwe, what other factors might have played a part? overgrazing of grasslands, overfarming of soil, overuse of salt and timber

LINK TO ECONOMICS

Demonstrate Intermediary Role

1. Remind students that intermediaries acted as a go-between by purchasing goods from merchants in one place and selling the goods to merchants in another place far away.

2. Ask two students to serve as traders and one to serve as a intermediary. Provide fake currency and something to serve as the traded good. In private, tell the intermediary to charge the buyer more for the object than what he or she pays for it. Have Trader A sell the product to the intermediary. Then have the intermediary sell it to Trader B.

3. Ask the class to explain how the intermediary profited from the sale.

Objectives

You may wish to discuss the following questions with students to help them frame the content as they read.

- What enabled Mutota's takeover of the northern Shona people to remain successful? *Mutota forced them to give money to support his army.*

- Why did the Portuguese believe *mwenemutapa* was a title of respect? *They probably did not know the Shona language, but they could see the title was used to refer to the leader.*

More About . . .

Swahili Today, those in East Africa who speak Swahili as their only language are often referred to as Waswahili. This term denotes only their mother tongue and not ethnicity. Today, Swahili is spoken in Tanzania, Kenya, the Democratic Republic of the Congo, and Uganda, and there are as many as 15 main Swahili dialects.

READING CHECK
Analyze Events Why did the people of Great Zimbabwe settle on the plateau between the Limpopo and Zambezi Rivers? *It was fertile and had water; it was near trade routes.*

---

community were probably the only ones who ate beef; commoners may have eaten goat or mutton, if they ate meat at all.

The people of Great Zimbabwe probably practiced a traditional religion similar to the Shona religion of today. This religion's dominant feature is devotion to the spirits of ancestors, who the Shona believe protect and guide the community.

By 1450, Great Zimbabwe was abandoned. No one knows for sure why it happened. According to one theory, cattle grazing had worn out the grasslands. In addition, farming had worn out the soil, and people had used up the salt and timber. The area could no longer support a large population.

Portuguese explorers knew about the site in the 1500s. Karl Mauch, a German explorer, was one of the first Europeans to discover the remains of these stone dwellings in 1871.

Reading Check
Analyze Events
Why did the people of Great Zimbabwe settle on the plateau between the Limpopo and Zambezi rivers?

The Mutapa Empire

According to Shona oral tradition, a man named Mutota left Great Zimbabwe in about 1420 to find a new source of salt. Traveling north, he settled in a valley with fertile soil, good rainfall, and ample wood. There he founded a new state to replace Great Zimbabwe. As the state grew, its leader, Mutota, used his army to dominate the northern Shona people living in the area. He forced them to make payments to support him and his army.

Mutapa Rulers These conquered people called Mutota and his successors *mwene mutapa*, meaning "conqueror" or "master pillager." The Portuguese who arrived on the East African coast in the early 1500s believed *mwene mutapa*—or *monomotapa*, as they wrote it—to be a title of respect for the ruler. The term is also the origin of the name of the **Mutapa** Empire. By

Global Patterns

Swahili

Over the centuries, contacts between two peoples—Bantu speakers and Arabs—led to the creation of a new people and a new language. Many Arab traders married African women. People of mixed Arab and African ancestry came to be called Swahili. The word comes from an Arabic term meaning "people of the coast" and refers to the East African coast.

Although Swahili peoples do not share a single culture, they do speak a common language. Swahili is a Bantu language with many words borrowed from Arabic. Swahili cultures are also dominated by Bantu characteristics, although many Swahili peoples practice Islam.

The Swahili peoples traded the gold and ivory of Africa for goods from India and China. At least some Indian and Chinese goods made it back to the inland Africans who supplied the gold: archaeologists have discovered fragments of Chinese porcelain in sites related to Great Zimbabwe. During the 1500s and 1600s, the Portuguese looted Swahili cities and damaged Swahili trade as they sought to take control of Indian Ocean trade.

478 Module 12

ADVANCED/GIFTED

Interview Mutota

1. Group students into pairs, and tell them that they will imagine that Mutota is being interviewed by a journalist.

2. Ask pairs to review what they have read about Mutota in this lesson and conduct additional research on the leader.

3. Tell the partners to decide which role each will play—Mutota or a journalist interviewing him. The student posing as the journalist should prepare a list of interview questions based on information they have read. The student portraying Mutota should also review that information.

4. Then have the journalist read the questions to the student posing as Mutota or relay them in writing. The classroom Mutotas should then answer the questions orally or in writing.

Modern ships such as this are similar to those historically used in trading along the East African coast.

the time of Mutota's death, the Mutapa Empire had conquered all but the eastern portion of what is now Zimbabwe. By 1480 Mutota's son Matope claimed control of the area along the Zambezi River to the Indian Ocean coast. Matope established vassal states in the southern areas that he conquered.

The Mutapa Empire controlled most of the gold mines in this region of Africa and the trade routes to and from the coast. Its people were able to mine gold deposited in nearby rivers and streams. In addition, Mutapa rulers forced people in conquered areas to mine gold for them. The rulers sent gold to the coastal city-states in exchange for luxuries. Even before the death of Matope, the southern vassal states of his empire broke away. However, the Mutapa Dynasty remained in control of the smaller empire.

In the 1500s, the Portuguese tried to conquer the empire. When they failed to do so, they resorted to interfering in Mutapa politics. They helped to overthrow one ruler and replace him with one they could control. This signaled increasing European interference in Africa in centuries to come.

Reading Check
Make Inferences
Why do you think the Portuguese wanted to conquer the Mutapa Empire?

Lesson 5 Assessment

1. Organize Information Create a chart to list the effects of intercultural interactions between two groups of people discussed in this lesson.

cultural group	cultural group

resulting interaction

Write a paragraph analyzing the results of the cultural interaction. Were the effects mostly positive or mostly negative?

2. Key Terms and People For each key term or person in the lesson, write a sentence explaining its significance.
3. Compare Compare the Portuguese who arrived in East Africa with the rulers of the Mutapa Empire.
4. Synthesize What were some of the effects of East African trade on different cultural groups?
5. Draw Conclusions How is Swahili an example of cultural interaction?
6. Summarize Based on the archaeological evidence, what was the society of Great Zimbabwe like?

Print Assessment

1. **Organize Information** Create a chart to list the effects of intercultural interactions between two people groups discussed in this lesson. Write a paragraph analyzing the results of the cultural interaction. Were the effects mostly positive or mostly negative? *Students' answers will vary, but students might focus on any of the following: positive events: trade, new language of Swahili, improvements in lifestyle, increased wealth for some places; negative events: take over of trade by others such as the Portuguese, enslavement, taxation, conquest of some regions and peoples, countries interfering in the politics of other places.*

2. **Key Terms and People** For each key term or person in the lesson, write a sentence explaining its significance. *Explanations of the lesson's key terms can be found on the following pages: Swahili, p. 472; Great Zimbabwe, p. 476; Mutapa, p. 478.*

3. **Compare** Compare the Portuguese who arrived in East Africa with the rulers of the Mutapa Empire. *Possible answer: both conquerors; interested in dominating trade and acquiring wealth*

4. **Synthesize** What were some of the effects of East African trade on different cultural groups? *Possible answer: Swahili created; Islam introduced; Europeans involved in politics, trade, and conquest*

5. **Draw Conclusions** How is Swahili an example of cultural interaction? *Possible answer: interaction of Arabic speakers and Bantu speakers, Asia and Africa, traders and merchants with local villagers*

6. **Summarize** Based on the archaeological evidence, what was the society of Great Zimbabwe like? *Possible answer: There were several social classes. The elites lived in separate compounds and ate beef. The commoners raised cattle and farmed; they ate goat or sheep.*

▷ Online Assessment

1. Why did Portuguese sailors round the southern tip of Africa in 1488?
   ○ They wanted to find a sea route to India.
   ○ They wanted to trade with the people of Kilwa.
   ○ They wanted to control the trade in East Africa.
   ○ They wanted to introduce Christianity to the Africans.

   Alternate Question *Select the answer choice from the drop-down list to complete the sentence correctly.* The Portuguese's original purpose for [rounding the southern tip of Africa ⬍] in 1488 was to find a sea route to India. However, their plans changed once they saw the wealthy port cities. They decided instead to take over these cities and control the trade in this region.

2. Which of the following did the Arab Muslim traders on the East African coast do?
   ○ They imported gold from Arabia and Iraq.
   ○ They organized the city-states under one government.
   ◉ They exported enslaved persons to other Muslim nations.
   ○ They took control of Kilwa and built their own forts there for protection.

   Alternate Question *Select the answer choice from the drop-down list to complete the sentence correctly.* Arab Muslim traders in East Africa exported luxury items to other Muslim nations. In addition to these items, they also exported [enslaved Africans ⬍] to work in homes, on ships, and as soldiers.

3. What is one theory as to the abandonment of Great Zimbabwe?
   ○ A drought forced the people to relocate.
   ○ A famine caused a depletion of the city's population.
   ○ The Portuguese enslaved all of the people living there.
   ◉ The people depleted the natural resources and moved on.

   Alternate Question *Select the answer choice from the drop-down list to complete the sentence correctly.* One theory as to the disappearance of the people from [Great Zimbabwe ⬍] is that the people had used up all the natural resources in the area, so they moved on to find better opportunities elsewhere.

4. What strategy did the Portuguese use to gain control of the Mutapa Empire?
   ○ They took over the gold fields.
   ○ They barraged it with cannon fire.
   ○ They enslaved all of the residents.
   ◉ They interfered in Mutapa politics.

   Alternate Question *Select the answer choice from the drop-down list to complete the sentence correctly.* The Portuguese tried to take control of the Mutapa Empire by [conquering ⬍] it, but they were unsuccessful after several attempts. So, they opted to interfere with the empire's politics by helping to overthrow one ruler and replace him with one they could control.

5. **Draw Conclusions** Why was Kilwa the wealthiest and most powerful city-state?

   Possible answer: Kilwa was the most wealthy and powerful city-state for several reasons. For one, it was as far south on the coast as a ship from India could sail in one monsoon season. Therefore, trade goods from southerly regions had to funnel into Kilwa, where Asian merchants could buy them. This strategic location made Kilwa very important and very wealthy. Also, Kilwa had control of the port city of Sofala, a trading center for the gold that was mined inland. As a result, Kilwa was able to control the overseas trade of gold from southern Africa.

6. **Elaborate** What role did the Arab Muslim traders have in the slave trade in Africa?

   Possible answer: The Arab Muslim traders were exporting enslaved Africans to Arabia, Iraq, Persia, India, and China long before the Europeans arrived on the continent. These slaves were purchased by people who wanted domestic servants in their houses. They were bought by rulers in India who wanted to increase the size of their armies by adding enslaved soldiers. They were put to work on Muslim-controlled ports and as household servants in China.

7. **Analyze Information** Why was the location that the Shona people chose for their civilization an ideal one?

   Possible answer: The location chosen by the Shona people for their civilization was ideal because it was in an area between the Zambezi and Limpopo Rivers that had fertile soil and plenty of water. This allowed them to farm and raise cattle. This area was also close to an important trade route that linked the goldfields with the coastal city of Sofala. When Great Zimbabwe took control of these trade routes, its leaders taxed the traders who traveled the route and demanded payment from less powerful chiefs in the area. This made Great Zimbabwe an economic, political, and religious center of its empire.

8. **Draw Conclusions** Why were the rivers and streams in the Mutapa Empire of particular importance to the rulers? Include evidence from the text to support this conclusion.

   Possible answer: The rivers and streams were of particular importance to the Mutapan rulers because they contained gold. The rulers forced people in conquered areas to mine gold for them. They sent gold to the coastal city-states and traded it for luxury items.

Print Assessment

Key Terms and People

For each term or person below, write a sentence explaining its connection to Africa in the period from 1500 BC to AD 1500.

1. Sahara
2. animism
3. push-pull factors
4. Bantu-speaking peoples
5. Aksum
6. Ghana
7. Mali
8. Songhai
9. Swahili
10. Great Zimbabwe

Explanations of the lesson's key terms can be found on the following pages: Sahara, p. 434; animism, p. 439; push-pull factors, p. 444; Bantu-speaking peoples, p. 447; Aksum, p. 450; Ghana, p. 459; Mali, p. 462; Songhai, p. 465; Swahili, p. 472; Great Zimbabwe, p. 476.

Main Ideas

Use your notes and the information in the module to answer the following questions.

Diverse Societies in Africa

1. How did geographic features affect the settlement of Africa? *Areas with good soil and climate were populated more heavily than those with challenging conditions.*
2. What technology did the Nok introduce to West Africa? *ironworking*
3. What circumstances enabled Djenné-Djeno to become a bustling trade center? *The Niger River and overland camel routes linked Djenné-Djeno to other towns, providing easy trading access.*
4. How is a dispute settled in Efe society? *Older male serves as group leader, offering opinions; families make own decisions; members resolve argument through long discussions.*
5. What is an age-set system? *Society is organized into groups of people who are about the same age; they go through life stages and have clearly defined responsibilities for each stage.*

Case Study: Migration

6. What are three general causes of migration? *environmental causes, economic causes, political causes*
7. How are push-pull factors related to migration? *They create conditions that encourage movement.*
8. What caused the Bantu-speaking peoples to migrate? *increase in population, need for more land, and Sahel desertification*
9. Why were the migrations of Bantu speakers so extensive and successful? *Bantu speakers adapted to new environments, spread skills for agriculture and ironworking, and kept moving east and southward.*

Module 12 Assessment

Key Terms and People

For each term or person below, write a sentence explaining its connection to Africa in the period from 1500 BC to AD 1500.

1. Sahara
2. animism
3. push-pull factors
4. Bantu-speaking peoples
5. Aksum
6. Ghana
7. Mali
8. Songhai
9. Swahili
10. Great Zimbabwe

Main Ideas

Use your notes and the information in the module to answer the following questions.

Diverse Societies in Africa

1. How did geographic features affect the settlement of Africa?
2. What technology did the Nok introduce to West Africa?
3. What circumstances enabled Djenné-Djeno to become a bustling trade center?
4. How is a dispute settled in Efe society?
5. What is an age-set system?

Case Study: Migration

6. What are three general causes of migration?
7. How are push-pull factors related to migration?
8. What caused the Bantu-speaking peoples to migrate?
9. Why were the migrations of Bantu speakers so extensive and successful?

The Kingdom of Aksum

10. Why was Aksum able to control international trade?
11. In what ways did Ezana contribute to the rise of his kingdom?
12. Why did Aksum fall?

North and West African Civilizations

13. How were the beginnings of the Almovarid and Almohad empires similar?
14. What accounted for Ghana's financial success?
15. What were two ways that Islam spread through Africa?
16. How did Sunni Ali build an empire?
17. What was the economy of the Hausa city-states like?

Eastern City-States and Southern Empires

18. How did the Swahili language evolve?
19. Why was it important for Kilwa to control Sofala?
20. Who was most affected by the introduction of Islam to East Africa?
21. What was the relationship of Great Zimbabwe to the Mutapa Empire?

480 Module 12

▶ ONLINE DOCUMENT-BASED INVESTIGATION

Societies and Empires of Africa

Have students complete and review all the DBI activities in **Part 1**.

Use this Informative Essay Rubric to score students' work in **Part 2**.

RUBRIC Students' essays should

- focus on the topic and support it with explanations and facts
- present information logically, clearly, and accurately
- cite multiple sources of relevant, informative text evidence from Part 1 in support of their topic
- be organized into a distinct introduction, a main body consisting of several paragraphs, and a conclusion that sums up the main points

Write an Informative Essay

Across the African continent, art and architecture were integral to communal life. How did African art and architecture reflect the trade-related changes experienced by African societies? Write an Informative Essay exploring this question. Be sure to cite specific evidence from each of the three sources in your response.

Module 12 Assessment, continued

Critical Thinking

1. **Compare** Use a chart like the one below to describe and compare the social, economic, and political aspects of African societies you read about in this module.

Description of Society or Empire	How They're Alike

2. **Make Inferences** How are the spread of ironmaking technology to East and South Africa and the Bantu migrations related?
3. **Evaluate** What were some of Ezana's most crucial leadership decisions?
4. **Form Opinions** Do you think cultural characteristics or personal qualities determine how individuals act toward migrating people who settle among them? Explain.
5. **Compare and Contrast** What are some positive and negative effects of migration?
6. **Recognize Effects** In what way did Islam encourage the spread of literacy?
7. **Recognize Effects** How did people adapt to the harsh conditions of the Sahara? Discuss traders who crossed the Sahara and people who lived in the Saharan village of Teghaza.
8. **Summarize** How are group membership, inheritance rights, and positions of authority usually decided in a matrilineal society?
9. **Synthesize** Why was the location of Great Zimbabwe advantageous?
10. **Compare and Contrast** In what ways was Great Zimbabwe's growth similar to and different from that of Kilwa?

Engage with History

Consider what you learned in this module about trading states in both West and East Africa. How might trade benefit both sides? Now that you've read the module, reevaluate what makes trade beneficial. How did environmental conditions affect which items had value in Africa? Did government policies have any effect on value?

Focus on Writing

Review the causes for migration you learned about in this module. Think about which of the causes might affect you personally. Write a paragraph describing a cause that would force you to migrate to another part of the country or the world. Be sure to identify either the push or pull factor that might influence your decision. Consider the environmental conditions in the area in which you live and the economic or political factors that might have a direct effect on your life.

Multimedia Activity

Today, much of eastern Africa still relies heavily on trade. Work with a group to create an electronic presentation about trade in Africa. Have each member choose one East African country to research in terms of its trade and culture. Use this module and the Internet as resources for your research. Issues to investigate might include what goods present-day East African nations trade and who their trading partners are. Remember to confirm your information by checking multiple sources. Next, create an electronic presentation of information on exports and imports, quantities shipped, where the goods are going, and how they are being transported. How did this project contribute to your understanding of the interrelationship between prosperity and trade?

The Kingdom of Aksum

10. Why was Aksum able to control international trade? *It was located along key trade routes between Asia, Africa, and Europe.*
11. In what ways did Ezana contribute to the rise of his kingdom? *Ezana united his people under Christianity and expanded his kingdom through conquest and trade.*
12. Why did Aksum fall? *It was isolated religiously and geographically by Muslim invasion.*

North and West African Civilizations

13. How were the beginnings of the Almovarid and Almohad Empires similar? *Muslim reformers began both.*
14. What accounted for Ghana's financial success? *It regulated and taxed the gold-salt trade.*
15. What were two ways that Islam spread through Africa? *by conquest and trade*
16. How did Sunni Ali build an empire? *military conquest*
17. What was the economy of the Hausa city-states like? *based on both agriculture and trade; trade goods: salt, grain, cotton cloth, leather goods, enslaved persons, harnesses, guns*

Eastern City-States and Southern Empires

18. How did the Swahili language evolve? *mixing of Arabic-speaking and Bantu-speaking peoples*
19. Why was it important for Kilwa to control Sofala? *to control the gold trade*
20. Who was most affected by the introduction of Islam to East Africa? *rulers, government officials, wealthy merchants*
21. What was the relationship of Great Zimbabwe to the Mutapa Empire? *Great Zimbabwe came first. Mutota left the area, traveled north, and founded the Mutapa Empire, which eventually included most of Zimbabwe.*

Critical Thinking

1. **Compare** Use a chart like the one below to describe and compare the social, economic, and political aspects of African societies you read about in this module.

Description of Society or Empire	How They're Alike
Aksum: diverse heritage; Christian; written language; terrace farming; ruled by king; expanded kingdom; controlled trade; traded salt and gold	African kingdoms or empires; made up of diverse people; strong rulers; controlled trade; lost control over time
Ghana: controlled many peoples; matrilineal; early empire with king; controlled trade; taxed trade goods; traded gold for salt	
Mali: people practice various faiths; rulers became Muslim; Sundiata, Mansa Musa expanded empire; Muslim; profited from gold trade	
Songhai: controlled many peoples; Muslim; leaders built empire, expanded it, ruled wisely; controlled trade routes; collected taxes; did not have modern weapons	
Mutapa: controlled people in captured areas; leader Mutapa built empire; mined gold and traded it; taxed subjects; weakened by European influence	

Essential Question ESSAY

How did interactions with other cultures shape African societies?

RUBRIC Students' essays should

- respond to the Essential Question with a specific position
- illustrate valid reasoning supporting their position
- cite persuasive evidence supporting their position
- identify key people, events, and/or turning points that demonstrate understanding of the module content
- be organized into a distinct introduction, main body, and conclusion

Write an argument answering this question. Your essay should include key people, events, and turning points in the history of Africa. Be sure to cite evidence to support your position and organize your essay into an introduction, body, and conclusion.

Alternative Activity Instead of writing essays, address the Essential Question through activities such as holding debates, creating multimedia presentations, or writing journal entries.

(continued)

Print Assessment (continued)

2. **Make Inferences** How are the spread of ironmaking technology to East and South Africa and the Bantu migrations related? *The Bantu-speaking peoples carried this technology wherever they went and shared it with people in the lands they occupied.*

3. **Evaluate** What were some of Ezana's most crucial leadership decisions? *Conquering Kush led to expansion of his kingdom and his power. Embracing Christianity linked him to the Mediterranean cultures but eventually cut Aksum off from Muslim Africa.*

4. **Form Opinions** Do you think cultural characteristics or personal qualities determine how individuals act toward migrating people who settle among them? Explain. *Possible answer: Characteristics such as isolation, self-sufficiency, protectiveness, and openness to new ideas or people will influence the attitudes of individuals or societies in their responses to migrating people who settle in the area.*

5. **Compare and Contrast** What are some positive and negative effects of migration? *Possible answer: Positive—greater economic development, enhanced skills and technology, cultural blending. Negative—overuse of resources, crowding, prejudice and discrimination, possibly war*

6. **Recognize Effects** In what way did Islam encourage the spread of literacy? *Muslims needed to be able to read Arabic in order to study their sacred book, the Qur'an.*

7. **Recognize Effects** How did people adapt to the harsh conditions of the Sahara? Discuss traders who crossed the Sahara and people who lived in the Saharan village of Teghaza. *Traders learned to use the camel, which could travel long distances without water. Villages in Teghaza built their homes from the salt available there.*

8. **Summarize** How are group membership, inheritance rights, and positions of authority usually decided in a matrilineal society? *In a matrilineal society, membership and inheritance rights are based on descent from women, although men usually hold positions of authority.*

9. **Synthesize** Why was the location of Great Zimbabwe advantageous? *located in a fertile plateau between rivers that was well suited to farming and cattle raising; near an important trade route*

10. **Compare and Contrast** In what ways was Great Zimbabwe's growth similar to and different from that of Kilwa? *Similar—Both gained power by controlling trade routes in their regions, constructed large buildings, traded gold; Different— Leaders in coastal towns practiced Islam, while in Zimbabwe they practiced the Shona religion; Some coastal cities manufactured goods for export, while Zimbabwe traded natural resources and taxed those who traveled the trade routes of their territory; Merchants in Kilwa interacted with Asian merchants, those in Great Zimbabwe did not.*

Engage with History

Consider what you learned in this module about trading states in both West and East Africa. How might trade benefit both sides? Now that you've read the module, reevaluate what makes trade beneficial. How did environmental conditions affect which items had value in Africa? Did government policies have any effect on value? *Answers will vary, but students should show an understanding of why societies engage in trade and how African environments and African governments affected trade.*

Focus on Writing

Review the causes for migration you learned about in this module. Think about which of the causes might affect you personally. Write a paragraph describing a cause that would force you to migrate to another part of the country or the world. Be sure to identify either the push or pull factor that might influence your decision. Consider the environmental conditions in the area in which you live and the economic or political factors that might have a direct effect on your life.

> **RUBRIC** Paragraphs should
> - clearly describe the issue or cause that would result in the student's migration
> - include push and pull factors
> - describe environmental, political, and economic conditions in the student's homeland

Multimedia Activity

Today, much of eastern Africa still relies heavily on trade. Work with a group to create an electronic presentation about trade in Africa. Have each member choose one East African country to research in terms of its trade and culture. Use this module and the Internet as resources for your research. Issues to investigate might include what goods present-day East African nations trade and who their trading partners are. Remember to confirm your information by checking multiple sources. Next, create an electronic presentation of information on exports and imports, quantities shipped, where the goods are going, and how they are being transported. How did this project contribute to your understanding of the interrelationship between prosperity and trade?

> **RUBRIC** Presentations should
> - contain up-to-date information on present-day East African trade
> - present information in a clear, easy-to-read format
> - list the sources of information used in building the database

For help creating presentations, refer students to the Skillbuilder Handbook.

▷ Online Assessment

1. *Drag the name of each geographical region into the box next to the correct description.*

This area is characterized by grassy plains, mountainous highlands, and swampy tropical stretches.	savanna
This region has a semiarid climate and is located at the southern edge of a vast desert.	Sahel
Known as "nature's greenhouse," this region has a dense canopy that prevents light from reaching the forest floor and is also home to the dreaded tsetse fly.	rain forest
Stretching from the Atlantic Ocean to the Red Sea, this area is roughly the size of the United States.	Sahara

2. What is the role of women in the Efe society?
   - ○ They are hunters.
   - ○ They are farmers.
   - ○ They are herders.
   - ○ They are gatherers.

3. *Select the correct button in the table to show whether each statement about the age-set system used by the Igbo is true or false.*

	True	False
This system forbade special ceremonies.	○	○
This system was used to teach discipline.	○	○
This system discouraged community service.	○	○
This system taught that men and women have different life stages.	○	○

4. What is one way that experts study the patterns of human migration?
   - ○ by looking at religious rituals
   - ○ by carbon dating rocks in an area
   - ○ by studying the spread of languages
   - ○ by exploring agricultural advancements

5. Which natural resource was of particular interest to migrating Bantu-speaking people?
   - ○ iron ore
   - ○ volcanic rock
   - ○ elephant ivory
   - ○ rhinoceros horns

6. What advantage did the Bantu-speaking people have over the Mbuti and San?
   - ○ The Bantu-speaking people had a written language.
   - ○ The Bantu-speaking people were hunter-gatherers.
   - ○ The Bantu-speaking people lived in an unpopulated land.
   - ○ The Bantu-speaking people used iron-tipped spears as weapons.

7. How did King Ezana expand his authority when he first took the throne?
   - ○ He established a seaport at Adulis.
   - ○ He conquered part of the Arabian Peninsula.
   - ○ He set up a trade network with Arab merchants.
   - ○ He built caravan routes between Aksum and Egypt.

8. *Drag each description of a religion into the correct column in the table. Each description will be used only once.*

Early Aksumite Religion	Christianity
offered animal sacrifices	began in Judea was monotheistic
was polytheistic	spread throughout the Roman Empire and then to Africa
honored dead ancestors	claimed King Ezana as a convert
worshiped nature spirits	

9. *Select the correct button in the table to show whether each statement about Aksum is true or false.*

	True	False
Aksum was primarily a Muslim nation.	○	○
Aksum had protected Muhammad's family.	○	○
Aksum was cut off from its major ports by Muslim invaders.	○	○
Aksum moved its capital to what is now northern Zimbabwe.	○	○

10. How were Sundiata and Mansa Musa similar to each other?
    - ○ They were both animists.
    - ○ They both built elaborate mosques.
    - ○ They both ruled the Empire of Songhai.
    - ○ They were both skilled military leaders.

11. *Select the correct button in the table to show whether each statement about Askia Muhammad is true or false.*

	True	False
He developed the first gun.	○	○
He ruled Songhai for 37 years.	○	○
He overtaxed his people to pay for his elaborate lifestyle.	○	○
He appointed excellent administrators to run branches of the government.	○	○

12. *Select the correct button in the table to show whether each characteristic is associated with the civilization of Hausa, Yoruba, or Benin.*

	Hausa	Yoruba	Benin
located in the savanna	○	○	○
high walls surrounded the city	○	○	○
were gifted artists in wood and ivory	○	○	○
rulers depended on farmers' crops and the salt trade	○	○	○
located in the forests on the edge of the savanna	○	○	○
were known for their brass works	○	○	○
supplied the caravans on the trade routes	○	○	○
located near the Niger River delta	○	○	○
was ruled by an oba, or king	○	○	○

13. Why did Ibn Battuta feel admiration when he visited Kilwa?
    - ○ The buildings were built out of pure gold.
    - ○ The merchants had an organized market.
    - ○ The port was open to ships from East Asia.
    - ○ The Muslim residents had a wealthy lifestyle.

14. How did the slave trade change in Africa in the 1700s?
    - ○ It increased with European involvement.
    - ○ It included the enslavement of Arabic Muslims.
    - ○ It focused on domestic workers more than agricultural workers.
    - ○ It shifted from enslaving West Africans to enslaving East Africans.

15. *Select the correct button in the table to show whether each statement about Great Zimbabwe is true or false.*

	True	False
Great Zimbabwe was known for its stone buildings.	○	○
The ruins of Great Zimbabwe were discovered by the British in 1871.	○	○
Salt was an important commodity for the people of Great Zimbabwe.	○	○
There was just one social and economic class in Great Zimbabwe.	○	○

Essential Question Preview

> **How did early American civilizations influence future societies and cultures before the arrival of Europeans?**
> Have students consider the Essential Question and capture their initial responses.

Explore the Essential Question

How did early American civilizations influence future societies and cultures before the arrival of Europeans?

- Explain that the culture of early Mesoamerican civilizations influenced later cultures.

- Point out that complex societies existed across North America long ago.

Help students plan inquiries and develop their own supporting questions such as:

What influences of early North American cultures are seen in the United States today?

What influence did Incan government have on later governments?

You may want to assign students to write a short essay in response to the Essential Question when they complete the module. Encourage students to use their notes and responses to inform their essays.

▶ Explore the Online Video

ANALYZE VIDEOS

Secret Mounds of Pre-Historic America
Invite students to watch the video to learn about the Mound Builders.

Geography Why did early peoples use the earth to make the mounds? *It was a plentiful resource, and they probably did not have to travel far to find the resource.*

▶ **PLAY VIDEO** 8:51
Secret Mounds of Pre-Historic America
HISTORY

Module 13

People and Empires in the Americas

Essential Question
How did early American civilizations influence future societies and cultures before the arrival of Europeans?

About the Photograph: This photograph shows the ruins of Machu Picchu, an ancient Inca city high in the Andes Mountains. It was all but forgotten for hundreds of years before its rediscovery in 1911.

▶ *Explore ONLINE!*

HISTORY. VIDEOS, including...
• Secret Mounds of Pre-Historic America

✓ Document-Based Investigations
✓ Graphic Organizers
✓ Interactive Games
✓ Image Compare: Comparing Nazca Lines
✓ Carousel: Aztec Calendar

In this module you will learn about the first Americans and the complex cultures that arose in Mesoamerica, the Andes, and North America in the period before contact with Europeans.

What You Will Learn ...

482 Module 13

Lesson 1 Big Idea

The cultures of the first Americans, including social organization, developed in ways similar to other early cultures.

Why it Matters Now

The Americas' first inhabitants developed the basis for later American civilizations.

Lesson 2 Big Idea

The Olmec created the Americas' first civilization, which in turn influenced later civilizations.

Why it Matters Now

Later American civilizations relied on the technology and achievements of earlier cultures to make advances.

Lesson 3 Big Idea

In the Andes Mountains, various groups created flourishing civilizations.

Why it Matters Now

Like the early Andean civilizations, people today must adapt to their environment in order to survive.

Lesson 4 Big Idea

Complex North American societies were linked to each other through culture and economics.

Why it Matters Now

Traditions and ideas from these cultures became part of the cultures of North America.

Timeline of Events 30,000 BC–AD 1500 ▶ Explore ONLINE!

Americas	World

30,000 BC

17,000 BC Pre-Clovis blades used at Meadowcraft Rockshelter in what is today Pennsylvania.

10,000 BC Last Ice Age ends; land bridge to Asia disappears.

< 7000 BC Agriculture begins in central Mexico.

1200 BC Olmec Civilization emerges in southeast Mexico.

1200 BC Egyptian Empire begins to decline. ∧

900 BC Chavín culture arises in Peru.

500 BC Zapotec build Monte Albán.

< 200 BC Nazca civilization arises in southern Peru.

480 BC Golden Age of Greece begins.
202 BC Han Dynasty begins in China.

AD 120 Roman Empire reaches its height. >

< AD 500s. Teotihuacán reaches population peak in central Mexico.

618 Tang Dynasty begins 289-year rule in China.

800 Anasazi culture develops in the Southwest.

800 Charlemagne crowned Holy Roman Emperor by the pope. >

900 Classic period of Maya civilization ends.

1066 Normans invade England.

1100 Mississippian culture thrives at Cahokia.

1300 Renaissance begins in Italy. >
1324 Mansa Musa, king of Mali, goes on hajj to Mecca.

< 1325 Aztecs build Tenochtitlán.

1438 Pachacuti becomes Incan emperor.

1492 Columbus makes first voyage to the Americas.

1502 Montezuma II crowned Aztec emperor.

AD 1500

People and Empires in the Americas **483**

Explore the Timeline

Interpret Timelines: People and Empires in the Americas 30,000 BC–AD 1500

Have students examine the timeline and then answer the following question:

Geography In which hemispheres did early civilizations and empires rise? *all hemispheres: northern, southern, eastern, and western*

Interpret Timeline of Events: Timeline of Events 30,000 BC–AD 1500

To further explore the timeline, have students discuss the following questions:

1. Consider the span of time from the end of the Ice Age to the time agriculture began. What geographical changes may have taken place during those 3,000 years to create a hospitable environment? *As ice melted, more water in oceans created a life-sustaining ecosystem. Melting ice also left fertile, dry land where plants could grow.*

2. Compare the Aztec and Renaissance sculptures represented on the timeline. *The Aztec sculpture seems to portray a type rather than an individual, while the Renaissance sculpture seems more realistic. The Renaissance piece appears to be made out of marble, while the Aztec piece appears to be made out of clay.*

▶ Online Module Flip Cards

Use the flip cards as a whole class activity or in student pairs to preview the module's key terms and people. Students can guess the meaning of each word, then review its definition, or do the reverse, using the flip card's toggle button to switch from Term to Definition mode. Students can also use the flip cards at the end of the module as a review tool before taking the Module Assessment.

▶ Online Sequencing Activity

Students can use this sequencing activity to review the chronology of events in the People and Empires in the Americas Module. To complete, have students drag each event to the correct year on the timeline.

Year	Event
-30000	*People begin to migrate across the land bridge connecting Asia to the Americas.*
-7000	*Agriculture is first used in central Mexico.*
-200	*Nazca civilization arises in southern Peru.*
250	*The Classic Period of the Maya begins.*
900	*The Anasazi begin to build Pueblo Bonito; the Toltecs rise to power in central Mexico.*
1325	*The Aztecs found their capital city, Tenochtitlán.*

Lesson 5 Big Idea

The Maya developed a highly complex civilization based on city-states and elaborate religious practices.

Why it Matters Now

Descendants of the Maya still occupy the same territory.

Lesson 6 Big Idea

Through alliances and conquest, the Aztecs created a powerful empire in Mexico.

Why It Matters Now

This time period saw the origins of one of the 20th century's most populous cities, Mexico City.

Lesson 7 Big Idea

The Inca built a vast empire supported by taxes, governed by a bureaucracy, and linked by extensive road systems.

Why It Matters Now

The Incan system of government was similar to some socialist governments in the 20th century.

The Earliest Americans

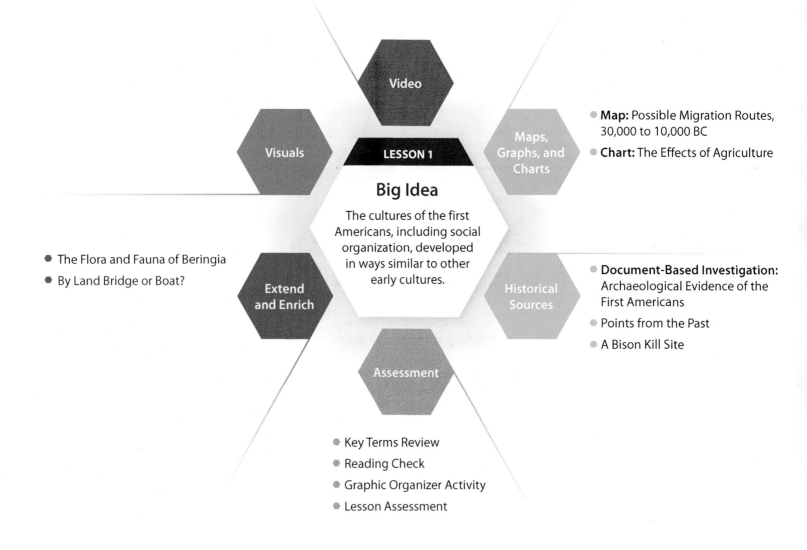

Video

Visuals

LESSON 1

Maps, Graphs, and Charts

- **Map:** Possible Migration Routes, 30,000 to 10,000 BC
- **Chart:** The Effects of Agriculture

Big Idea

The cultures of the first Americans, including social organization, developed in ways similar to other early cultures.

- The Flora and Fauna of Beringia
- By Land Bridge or Boat?

Extend and Enrich

Historical Sources

- **Document-Based Investigation:** Archaeological Evidence of the First Americans
- Points from the Past
- A Bison Kill Site

Assessment

- Key Terms Review
- Reading Check
- Graphic Organizer Activity
- Lesson Assessment

The Flora and Fauna of Beringia

Multimedia Presentation Students read about the flora and fauna of Beringia. They will use this information to create a multimedia presentation that includes graphics, images, and audio about the physical geography of Beringia and how the climate affected the environment.

By Land Bridge or Boat?

Article Students read an article about how the discovery of an early human changes theories about the land bridge connecting Asia and North America. They will use the events described in the article to create a timeline and sketch a map depicting how the discovery of Kennewick Man affected the land bridge theory.

Teach the Big Idea

1. **Whole Class Open/Introduction** Remind students that the continent's first inhabitants may have walked from Asia through harsh, icy conditions. What equipment and clothing do students think might be necessary for such a difficult journey today? *Possible answers: waterproof jackets, thermal underwear, hiking boots, sleeping bag, tents, a boat*

2. **Direct Teach** Read students the Big Idea: *The cultures of the first Americans, including social organization, developed in ways similar to other early cultures.* Review the following lesson objectives with students to aid in their understanding of the Big Idea.

   - Trace the route of the first inhabitants' migration to the Americas.

   - Describe how the earliest Americans lived as hunter-gatherers.

   - Explain the origins and impact of agriculture in the Americas.

3. **Whole Group Close/Reflect** Have students write a short essay comparing and contrasting the different theories on how the first Americans arrived on the continent. Invite students to share their work.

▷ ONLINE DOCUMENT-BASED INVESTIGATION

People and Empires in the Americas

Archaeological Evidence of the First Americans is the first of seven historical sources that students will analyze in People and Empires in the Americas module. Spearheads found by archaeologists have provided evidence for the tracking of early peoples in the Americas.

DOCUMENT-BASED INVESTIGATION HISTORICAL SOURCE

Archaeological Evidence of the First Americans

Spearheads found by archaeologists have provided evidence for the tracking of early peoples in the Americas.

▷ ONLINE LESSON FLIP CARDS

Review Key Terms and People

Students can use the flip cards in the Lesson Review at any time to review the lesson's key terms and people: *Beringia, Ice Age,* and *maize.*

The Earliest Americans

The Big Idea
The cultures of the first Americans, including social organization, developed in ways similar to other early cultures.

Why It Matters Now
The Americas' first inhabitants developed the basis for later American civilizations.

Key Terms and People
Beringia
Ice Age
maize

Setting the Stage

While civilizations were developing in Africa, Asia, and Europe, they were also emerging in the Americas. Human settlement in the Americas is relatively recent compared to that in other parts of the world. However, it followed a similar pattern. At first the ancient people of the Americas survived mainly by hunting. Over time, they developed farming methods that ensured a more reliable supply of food. This in turn led to the growth of the first civilizations in the Americas.

This illustration shows what some of the earliest people to migrate to the Americas may have looked like.

A Land Bridge

The American continents include North and South America. They are connected and span two hemispheres, from the frigid Arctic Circle in the north to the icy waters around Antarctica in the south. Although this land mass narrows greatly around modern-day Panama, it stretches unbroken for about 9,000 miles. This large and rugged land is isolated

---

COLLABORATIVE LEARNING

Early Settlements in America Presentation

1. Organize the class into three groups. Assign each group a site to research: Clovis, New Mexico; Monte Verde, Chile; and Tehuacan Valley, Mexico.

2. Have each group create an electronic slideshow presentation about the site that includes images of artifacts found there and explains the site's significance.

3. Have each group share their electronic slideshow presentation to the class. Tell them to be prepared to answer questions from the class.

4. Allow time for students to view the electronic slideshow presentations on their own.

from the rest of the world by vast oceans. Yet, thousands of years ago, the Americas were connected by a land bridge to Asia, called **Beringia**. Hardy Ice Age people migrated from Asia to the Americas over this land bridge. However, the Americas were not unoccupied. Recent evidence shows that people had arrived much earlier, possibly by boat.

Peopling the Americas The first Americans arrived sometime toward the end of the last **Ice Age**, which lasted from roughly 1.9 million years ago to about 10,000 BC. Huge sheets of moving ice, called glaciers, spread southward from the Arctic Circle. They covered large portions of North America. The buildup of glaciers locked up huge amounts of the earth's water. It lowered sea levels and created a land corridor between Asia and Alaska across what is now the Bering Strait.

Herds of wild animals from Siberia, including mammoths, migrated across the plains of the Beringia land bridge. Gradually, Siberian hunters followed these animals into North America. They most likely were unaware that they were entering a new continent. These migrants became the first Americans.

No one knows for sure when the first Americans arrived because there are no written records or other available sources to consult. Some scholars contend that the migration across the land bridge began as early as 30,000 BC. Others argue it occurred as late as 10,000 BC. For years, many researchers have regarded the discovery of spearheads dating back to 9500 BC near Clovis, New Mexico, to be the earliest evidence of humankind in the Americas.

Hunters killed mammoths and other large mammals using a spear-throwing device that gave them greater force and accuracy in hurling the spear from a distance.

Objectives

You may wish to discuss the following questions with students to help them frame the content as they read.

- What happened to the land corridor, Beringia? *became the Bering Strait when glaciers melted*

More About . . .

Monte Verde Archaeologists typically find only objects that don't decay easily, such as bones or stone tools, at ancient archaeological sites. At Monte Verde, however, organic materials—including mastodon meat—have been found preserved under a thick layer of peat.

▷ **ONLINE GRAPHIC ORGANIZER**

The Earliest Americans

As students read the lesson, have them use the graphic organizer to take notes. Students can review their graphic organizer notes at the end of the lesson to answer the following question:

Analyze Causes and Effects What were the causes and effects of the earliest Americans in the Americas? *The earliest Americans developed their cultures by using the resources in their environment to survive. As they developed, they influenced later cultures, which adopted aspects of their cultures.*

	Land Bridge	
Causes	→	Effects

	Hunters and Gatherers	
Causes	→	Effects

	Agriculture	
Causes	→	Effects

Migration Routes of the First Americans

1. Distribute copies of maps showing the Western Hemisphere and the Pacific Region.

2. Have students identify Asia, present-day Alaska, and former Beringia on the Pacific Region map. Students should draw in the land bridge.

3. Have students identify and label Clovis, New Mexico; Mexico City, Mexico; and Monte Verde, Chile, on the Western Hemisphere map.

4. Have students place the maps side by side with the Western Hemisphere map on the right. Then have them draw possible land and water routes from Asia to the locations they have identified on the map.

5. Have students create a label for each city, similar to the map in the text. Labels should cite information gathered from the text about each city, other than what is on the map. *Possible answers: Clovis—some experts think this site has the earliest evidence of people living in the Americas. Mexico City—Site of the oldest skull discovered in the Americas. Monte Verde—Researchers found pieces of animal skin, tools, a chunk of preserved meat, and the footprint of a child.*

Possible Migration Routes, 30,000–10,000 BC

Have students explore the map using the interactive features and answer the associated questions.

Location What two continents does the Beringia land bridge connect? *Asia and North America*

In print edition, see map of same title.

Location Which two continents does the Beringia land bridge connect? *Asia and North America*

Movement From where do scholars believe the first Americans came? How did they come? *Asia; either on foot over the Beringia land bridge*

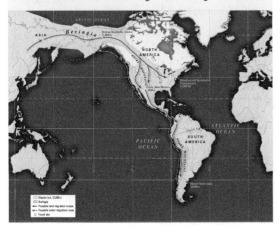

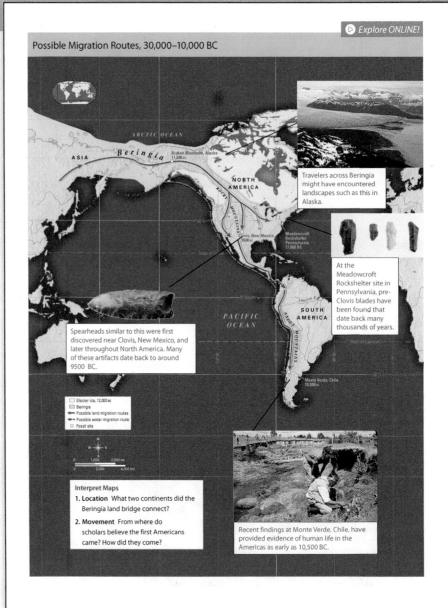

Explore ONLINE!

Possible Migration Routes, 30,000–10,000 BC

Travelers across Beringia might have encountered landscapes such as this in Alaska.

At the Meadowcroft Rockshelter site in Pennsylvania, pre-Clovis blades have been found that date back many thousands of years.

Spearheads similar to this were first discovered near Clovis, New Mexico, and later throughout North America. Many of these artifacts date back to around 9500 BC.

Glacier ice, 12,000 BC
Beringia
Possible land migration routes
Possible water migration route
Fossil site

Interpret Maps

1. **Location** What two continents did the Beringia land bridge connect?

2. **Movement** From where do scholars believe the first Americans came? How did they come?

Recent findings at Monte Verde, Chile, have provided evidence of human life in the Americas as early as 10,500 BC.

Many other pre-Clovis sites, from Texas to Brazil, reinforce what archaeologists learned at Monte Verde, Chile, near the southern tip of the Americas. Researchers there have found evidence of human life dating back to 10,500 BC. Underneath this site—a sandy bank near a creek—archaeologists discovered pieces of animal hide and various tools. They also found a preserved chunk of meat and a single child's footprint. The evidence at Monte Verde suggests that the first Americans arrived well before the Clovis era. To reach southern Chile at such an early date, some experts believe, humans would have had to cross the land bridge at least 20,000 years ago.

As more archaeological finds are examined, new theories emerge about the peopling of the Americas. Some scholars have proposed that people may have paddled from Asia to the Pacific Coast in small boats. A skull discovered near Mexico City has recently been dated to about 11,000 BC, making it the oldest skull ever found in the Americas. Some scientists studying the skull believe that it is related to the Ainu people of Japan and that these descendants of the Ainu reached the Americas by island-hopping on boats.

Reading Check
Analyze Issues
Why do scholars disagree about when the first Americans arrived?

Historical Source

A Bison Kill Site

The first hunters roaming North America hunted mammoths, deer, and bison. Researchers found the bones of bison at a kill site near Calgary, Alberta, in Canada. This kill site is believed to have been in use for more than 8,000 years.

Different layers of remains and artifacts have been found at the kill site, with different kinds of points—spears, arrows, knives, and so forth. The different styles of points can tell archaeologists about the age of a site and its various layers. Weapons and tools such as those shown here were used to kill and butcher animals for the hunters and their families to consume.

Analyze Historical Sources
What resources besides food might animals have provided to early hunters and their families?

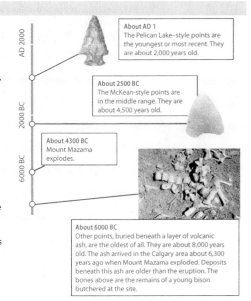

About AD 1
The Pelican Lake–style points are the youngest or most recent. They are about 2,000 years old.

About 2500 BC
The McKean-style points are in the middle range. They are about 4,500 years old.

About 4300 BC
Mount Mazama explodes.

About 6000 BC
Other points, buried beneath a layer of volcanic ash, are the oldest of all. They are about 8,000 years old. The ash arrived in the Calgary area about 6,300 years ago when Mount Mazama exploded. Deposits beneath this ash are older than the eruption. The bones above are the remains of a young bison butchered at the site.

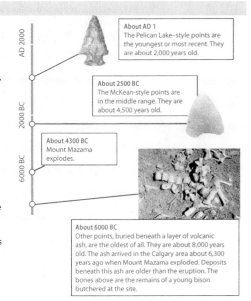 **ONLINE HISTORICAL SOURCES**

Points from the Past

Invite students to view the images and answer the associated question.

Make Inferences Based on these two points, what inference can you make about how points changed over time? *Technology improved and the points were shaped to be sharper in order to be more effective.*

In print edition, see historical source titled *A Bison Kill Site*.

Make Inferences What differences can you see between these two spear points? *Possible responses: The later point is leaf-shaped and less jagged than the early point. They are made from different types of stone.*

READING CHECK
Analyze Issues Why do scholars disagree about when the first Americans arrived? *They have made different discoveries and found evidence in different places in the Americas and have determined different dates based on these finds.*

Objectives

You may wish to discuss the following questions with students to help them frame the content as they read.

- How might the melting of the glaciers have affected early settlers? *Possible answer: Land could sustain more wild game and edible plant life, meaning there was more food available.*
- Compare the photographs of spearheads found near Clovis with the blades found in Pennsylvania. What might account for the difference between them? *Possible answer: Game may have varied among regions, requiring different-sized weapons; density of raw material may have determined size of objects; tools probably had different functions.*

More About . . .

Mammoths Mammoths are the ancestors of the modern elephant. The most recognized mammoth is the woolly mammoth, which first appeared in the Arctic region of Eurasia. These animals eventually crossed the Bering Strait to inhabit North America. These animals became extinct about 10,000 years ago. Mastodons were related to mammoths and were also hunted by early people. The most famous mastodon is known as the American mastodon. Remains have been found in present-day Ohio.

▷ ONLINE DOCUMENT-BASED INVESTIGATION

Archaeological Evidence of the First Americans

Spearheads have provided evidence for the tracking of early peoples in the Americas. Have students compare the images using the slider below the interactive images.

Analyze Sources How do you think these spearheads were made? *They probably used other stones or rocks to shape the spearheads.*

READING CHECK

Analyze Effects How did the earliest Americans adapt to the loss of large animals? *They hunted smaller prey, fished, and gathered edible plants.*

Hunters and Gatherers

Questions remain about how and when the first Americans arrived. What appears more certain—from the discovery of chiseled spearheads and charred bones at ancient sites—is that the earliest Americans lived as hunters. Perhaps their most challenging and rewarding prey was the mammoth. Weighing more than seven tons, this animal provided meat, hide, and bones for food, clothing, shelters, and tools.

Following the Game Eventually, large animals like the mammoth were overhunted and became extinct. Hunters soon turned to smaller prey, such as deer and rabbits, for their survival. They also fished and gathered edible plants and fruits. Because they were hunters, the earliest Americans found it necessary to move regularly in search of food. Whenever they did settle in one place for a short time, prehistoric Americans lived in caves or temporary shelters in the open air.

With the end of the Ice Age, around 12,000 to 10,000 years ago, came the end of land travel across Beringia. As the great glaciers melted, sea levels rose. The ancient land bridge disappeared under the Bering Strait. By this time, however, humans inhabited most regions of the Americas. Wherever they roamed, from the grassy plains of the modern-day United States to the steamy tropical forests of Central America, the first Americans adapted to the variety of environments they inhabited. In doing so, they carved out unique ways of life.

Reading Check
Analyze Effects
How did the earliest Americans adapt to the loss of large animals?

Agriculture Creates a New Way of Life

Gradually, the earliest Americans became more familiar with plant foods. They began to experiment with simple methods of farming. Their efforts at planting and harvesting led to agriculture. This dramatically changed their way of life.

The Development of Farming Around 7000 BC, a revolution quietly began in what is now central Mexico. There, people began to rely more on wild edible plants, raising some of them from seeds. By 5000 BC, many had begun to grow these preferred plants. They included squashes, gourds, beans, avocados, and chilies. By 3400 BC, these early farmers grew **maize**, or corn. Maize soon became the most important crop. This highly nourishing crop flourished in the tropical climate of Mexico. There, a family of three could raise enough corn in four months to feed themselves for a long time.

Gradually, people settled in permanent villages in the Tehuacan (tay•wuh•KAHN) Valley, south of present-day Mexico City. These people raised corn and other crops. The techniques of agriculture spread over North and South America. However, it is believed that people in some areas, such as Peru and eastern North America, may have discovered the secrets of cultivating local edible plants independently.

Over the next several centuries, farming methods became more advanced. In central Mexico native farmers created small islands in swamps and shallow lakes by stacking layers of vegetation, dirt, and mud.

Maize, or corn, was one of the most important crops in the Americas.

ADVANCED/GIFTED

Research Other Migration Theories

1. Have interested students research theories about the earliest migrations to the Americas, such as the Clovis theory, the sea-route theory, and the African-connection theory.

2. Have students find out how the discovery of archaeological sites that may predate Clovis, such as Monte Verde, Chile, and Pedra Furada, Brazil, support some of these theories. Students should report their findings orally, using maps or charts.

The Effects of Agriculture

Before Agriculture	After Agriculture
People hunted or gathered what they ate.	People enjoyed a more reliable and steady source of food.
Families continually moved in search of big game.	Families settled down and formed larger communities.
Groups remained small due to the scarcity of reliable sources of food.	Humans concentrated on new skills: arts and crafts, architecture, and social organization.
Humans devoted much of their time to obtaining food.	Complex societies eventually arose.

Interpret Charts
How might the establishment of agriculture have helped humans to develop new skills and interests?

They then planted crops on top of the island soil. The surrounding water provided irrigation. These floating gardens were very productive, yielding up to three harvests a year.

Farming Brings Great Change In the Americas, as in other regions of the world, agriculture brought great and lasting change to people's way of life. The cultivation of corn and other crops provided a more reliable and expanding food supply. This encouraged population growth and the establishment of large, settled communities. As the population grew, and as farming became more efficient and productive, more people turned their attention to nonagricultural pursuits. They developed specialized skills in arts and crafts, building trades, and other fields. Differences between social classes—between rich and poor, ruler and subject—began to emerge. With the development of agriculture, society became more complex. The stage was set for the rise of more advanced civilizations.

Reading Check
Make Inferences
Why might the development of agriculture be characterized as a turning point in human history?

Lesson 1 Assessment

1. Organize Information Complete the chart with the effects. Which effect do you think had the greatest impact on the Americas?

   [Beringia land bridge forms.] →

   [Experiments with farming begin.] →

2. Key Terms and People For each key term or person in the lesson, write a sentence explaining its significance.

3. Make Inferences What can you infer about the development of early farming?
4. Summarize How did human beings come to the Americas?
5. Analyze Effects What sorts of changes did farming bring?
6. Evaluate Why do you think early Americans, isolated from the rest of the world, developed in ways similar to other early humans?

Objectives

You may wish to discuss the following questions with students to help them frame the content as they read.

- What might have happened to people in this region had agriculture failed? *Possible answer: continued migration for food, few permanent communities, new skills may not have developed*
- How did geography and climate play a role in the success of these early communities? *warm climate ideal for crops; swamps and lakes made irrigation possible*

More About . . .

Early Farming Methods Early Mexican farmers learned to plant corn, beans, and squash in the same field. The climbing bean plants could support themselves on the cornstalks. The bean and squash plants also added nitrogen to the soil, keeping the land fertile. Ask interested students to investigate how many foods from the Americas, such as potatoes, squash, and corn, were added to the European diet.

▷ **ONLINE INTERACTIVE CHARTS**

The Effects of Agriculture

Have students explore the chart and answer the associated question.

Interpret Charts In what areas might the growth of agriculture have helped humans to develop new skills and interests? *All of the above (social organization, metalworking, art and crafts)*

In print edition, see chart of same title.

Interpret Charts How might the establishment of agriculture have helped humans to develop new skills and interests? *With a reliable food source, they no longer had to devote all their time and energy to obtaining food.*

READING CHECK
Make Inferences Why might the development of agriculture be characterized by some as a turning point in human history? *It led to a more reliable and increased food supply, population growth, settled communities, and the establishment of civilizations.*

ENGLISH LANGUAGE LEARNERS

Locate the Tropics

1. Ask students if they know what the term *tropical* means. *hot and humid*
2. Explain that *tropical* can also refer to a specific region.
3. Have students look at a physical map of the world. Ask them to find the equator at 0 degrees, the Tropic of Cancer at 23 degrees north of the equator, and the Tropic of Capricorn at 23 degrees south of the equator. Explain that the area between these lines of latitude is called *the tropics*.

4. Have students turn to a physical map of North America and locate Mexico City.
5. Ask students, Is Mexico City within the tropics? *yes* How do you know? *It is south of the Tropic of Cancer and north of the Tropic of Capricorn.* According to the text, what crops grew well in the tropical climate near Mexico City? *maize, squashes, gourds, beans, avocadoes, chilies*

Print Assessment

1. **Organize Information** Complete the chart with the effects. Which effect do you think had the greatest impact on the Americas? *Possible answer: Cause 1—Beringia land bridge forms. Effect 1—Siberian hunters enter North America; Cause 2—Experiments with farming begin, Effect 2—Crops provide reliable food supply. Most significant—Siberian hunters entering North America because it peopled the continent.*

2. **Key Terms and People** For each key term or person in the lesson, write a sentence explaining its significance. *Explanations of the lesson's key terms can be found on the following pages: Beringia, p. 485; Ice Age, p. 485; maize, p. 488*

3. **Make Inferences** What can you infer about the development of early farming? *Possible answer: It provided a reliable food supply, which meant communities could be settled, leading to population growth and the development of new occupations.*

4. **Summarize** How did human beings come to the Americas? *over the land bridge or by boat*

5. **Analyze Effects** What sort of changes did farming bring? *reliable food supply; population growth; settled communities; other occupations*

6. **Evaluate** Why do you think early Americans, isolated from the rest of the world, developed in ways similar to other early humans? *Possible answer: Early humans had to use what was readily available for survival, mainly plants and animals.*

Online Assessment

1. Which **two** pieces of evidence suggest that the first Americans arrived before the Clovis era?
   - ○ a child's footprint
   - ○ a chunk of preserved meat
   - ○ a paddle that originated in Asia
   - ○ a fossil of a wild animal from Siberia
   - ○ a land bridge across the Bering Strait
   - ○ a set of written records at Monte Verde, Chile

   Alternate Question *Select the answer choice from the drop-down list to complete the sentence correctly.*
   When archaeologists found a preserved chunk of meat and a child's single footprint in [Chile ◆], they concluded that humans would have needed to come across the land bridge much earlier than they had expected.

2. Why did prehistoric Americans begin to hunt deer and rabbits?
   - ○ Glacial ice melted.
   - ◉ Mammoths were overhunted.
   - ○ Tropical forests began growing.
   - ○ People inhabited most regions of the Americas.

   Alternate Question *Select the answer choice from the drop-down list to complete the sentence correctly.*
   At first, prehistoric Americans hunted large animals like the mammoth, but eventually these animals were [overhunted and became extinct ◆]. The hunters had to resort to smaller animals like deer and rabbit.

3. What was special about the farming methods developed in Mexico?
   - ○ They learned how to grow corn.
   - ◉ They grew crops on floating gardens.
   - ○ They set up preserves for wild animals.
   - ○ They used ocean water to water their crops.

   Alternate Question *Select the answer choice from the drop-down list to complete the sentence correctly.*
   In Mexico, the farmers used [floating gardens ◆] to grow their crops. The water surrounding these islands was used for irrigation.

4. **Draw Conclusions** What can be concluded about scholars' ideas of how the early Americans came to the continents? Use details from the text to support your conclusion.

   It can be concluded that historians do not have a solid idea of why the early Americans came here and how they arrived. There are many different theories (Bering Strait land bridge, paddling across the Pacific), but since there are no written records that the historians know about, there is no way to know these answers for sure.

5. **Make Inferences** What can be concluded about the homes of the prehistoric Americans? Use details from the text to support your answer.

   It can be concluded that the early Americans lived in homes that suited their environment. Some of the people lived in tropical forests, others lived in grasslands, and still others lived in cold northern climates. It also seems that they didn't live in permanent shelters since they were on the move to find food as hunters and gatherers.

6. **Cause and Effect** How did the development of agriculture impact the people living in the Americas?

   Because of the development of corn and other crops, people had a more reliable and expanding food supply. This encouraged population growth and made it possible for large civilizations, such as cities, to develop. Without everyone having to go out looking for their own food, more people were able to explore nonagricultural pursuits. They developed skills in the arts and crafts, building trades, and other fields. Social status began to develop with a ruling class and rich and poor.

Early Mesoamerican Civilizations

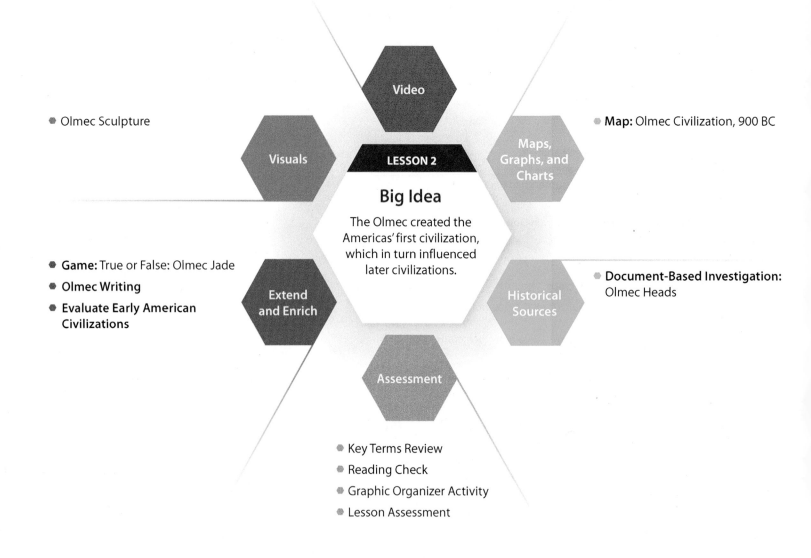

Video

● Olmec Sculpture

Visuals

Maps, Graphs, and Charts

● **Map:** Olmec Civilization, 900 BC

LESSON 2

Big Idea

The Olmec created the Americas' first civilization, which in turn influenced later civilizations.

● **Game:** True or False: Olmec Jade
● **Olmec Writing**
● **Evaluate Early American Civilizations**

Extend and Enrich

Historical Sources

● **Document-Based Investigation:** Olmec Heads

Assessment

● Key Terms Review
● Reading Check
● Graphic Organizer Activity
● Lesson Assessment

Olmec Writing

Article Students will read an article about the Olmec writing system. They will then create ten symbols that could have been part of Olmec writing and explain what they mean.

Evaluate Early American Civilizations

Writing Activity Students use multiple sources to gather and evaluate information about early American civilizations. The activity guides students as they evaluate civilizations, and as they write, review, and proofread their evaluations.

Teach the Big Idea

1. **Whole Class Open/Introduction** Remind students that many early civilizations had to adapt to environmental factors such as humid conditions and excessive rainfall. Ask students what environmental factors early settlers in their region may have had to adapt to. *Possible answer: dry climate, harsh winters, extreme heat.*

2. **Direct Teach** Read students the Big Idea: *The Olmec created the Americas' first civilization, which in turn influenced later civilizations.* Review the following lesson objectives with students to aid in their understanding of the Big Idea.

   • Describe the achievements of Olmec civilization.

   • Trace the rise and fall of the Zapotec.

   • Identify contributions to later Mesoamerican cultures.

3. **Whole Group Close/Reflect** Have students make a poster comparing the Olmec and Zapotec civilizations. Posters should include text and images, either hand-drawn or from the Internet. Invite students to share their work.

▷ ONLINE DOCUMENT-BASED INVESTIGATION

People and Empires in the Americas

Olmec Heads is the second of seven historical sources that students will analyze in People and Empires in the Americas module. Olmec stone heads may be portraits of Olmec leaders or of players in a sacred ball court. Students can use the interactivity to explore the image.

DOCUMENT-BASED INVESTIGATION   HISTORICAL SOURCE

Olmec Heads

Olmec heads such as this one may be portraits of Olmec leaders or of players in a sacred ball court.

▷ ONLINE GRAPHIC ORGANIZER

Early Mesoamerican Civilizations

As students read the lesson, have them use the graphic organizer to take notes. Students can review their graphic organizer notes at the end of the lesson to answer the following question:

Compare and Contrast How were the Olmec and Zapotec similar and different? *Both had pyramids, giant plazas, urban centers, and sculptures. They were different in that the Olmec had no form of writing or calendars, but the Zapotec had a system of writing as well as a calendar.*

Early Mesoamerican Civilizations

The Big Idea
The Olmec created the Americas' first civilization, which in turn influenced later civilizations.

Why It Matters Now
Later American civilizations relied on the technology and achievements of earlier cultures to make advances.

Key Terms and People
Mesoamerica
Olmec
Zapotec
Monte Albán

Setting the Stage

The story of developed civilizations in the Americas begins in a region called **Mesoamerica**. This area stretches south from central Mexico to northern Honduras. It was here, more than 3,000 years ago, that the first complex societies in the Americas arose.

The Olmec

Mesoamerica's first known civilization builders were a people known as the **Olmec**. They began carving out a society around 1200 BC in the jungles of southern Mexico. The Olmec influenced neighboring groups as well as the later civilizations of the region. They often are called Mesoamerica's "mother culture."

Many large carved heads such as this one have been found by archaeologists in two major Olmec centers along the Gulf Coast of southern Mexico.

COLLABORATIVE LEARNING

Ancient Civilizations Display

1. Organize the class into two groups. Assign each group a civilization: Olmec or Zapotec.

2. Have each group research and create a pictorial display, consisting of images and text explanations, about the written language, art, and architecture of each civilization. Students may either draw images or download them from online sources

3. Have each group present their display to the class.

4. Allow time for the class to compare the accomplishments of each civilization

The Rise of Olmec Civilization Around 1860, a worker clearing a field in the hot coastal plain of southeastern Mexico uncovered an extraordinary stone sculpture. It stood five feet tall and weighed an estimated eight tons. The sculpture was of an enormous head wearing a headpiece. (See History Through Art: Olmec Sculpture) The head was carved in a strikingly realistic style, with thick lips, a flat nose, and large oval eyes. Archaeologists had never seen anything like it in the Americas.

This head, along with others that were discovered later, was a remnant of the Olmec civilization. The Olmec emerged about 1200 BC and thrived from approximately 800 to 400 BC. They lived along the Gulf Coast of Mexico, in the modern-day Mexican states of Veracruz and Tabasco.

Gulf Coast Geography On the surface, the Gulf Coast seemed an unlikely site for a high culture to take root. The region was hot and humid and covered with swamps and jungle. In some places, giant trees formed a thick cover that prevented most sunlight from reaching the ground. Up to 100 inches of rain fell every year. The rainfall swelled rivers and caused severe flooding.

However, the region also had certain advantages. There were abundant deposits of salt and tar, as well as fine clay used in making pottery. There were also wood and rubber from the rain forest. The hills to the north provided hard stone from which the Olmec could make tools and monuments. The rivers that laced the region provided a means of transport. Most important, the flood plains of these rivers provided fertile land for farming.

The Olmec used their resources to build thriving communities. The oldest site, San Lorenzo, dates back to around 1150 BC. Here archaeologists uncovered important clues that offered a glimpse into the Olmec world.

The Olmec ball game was one of the first team sports in history.

Objectives

You may wish to discuss the following questions with students to help them frame the content as they read.

- Why might the Olmec have deemed natural elements, like the rain, and animals, like the jaguar, worthy of being worshipped as deities? *Possible answer: Weather and wildlife determined how successful crops and hunting would be and how secure life would be.*
- What might have initially prompted the Olmec to establish trade with groups in faraway regions? *Possible answer: certain natural resources or materials were available only in other areas.*

More About . . .

Olmec Sites The Olmec built their houses and temples out of wood and thatch, which decompose over time. For that reason, earthen mounds and stone monuments are mostly what remain of Olmec sites today, though experts can make out the outlines of temples and other buildingse.

▷ **ONLINE DOCUMENT-BASED INVESTIGATION**

Olmec Heads

Olmec stone heads may be portraits of Olmec leaders or of players in a sacred ball court. Have students study the image and then answer the question that follows.

Analyze Sources Why did the Olmec use heavy stones to create their sculptures? *They found the stones in their environment and found them to be durable.*

▷ **LESSON FLIP CARDS**

Review Key Terms and People

Students can use the flip cards in the Lesson Review at any time to review the lesson's key terms and people: *Mesoamerica, Olmec, Zapotec,* and *Monte Albán.*

Jaguar Artifacts of the Olmec

1. Ask students why they think the Olmec revered the jaguar. If students have difficulty answering, tell them that jaguars, which weigh up to 300 pounds and are up to nine feet long, are formidable predators.

2. Have students form small groups to study examples of Olmec art bearing the jaguar motif. Students can use the images in the text and library and Internet sources for research.

3. Have students design their own artifacts depicting jaguars. Artifacts can include drawings, sculptures, jewelry, or masks. Students should create labels for their artifacts, as if the object were on display at a museum.

Encourage students to think about what a museum-goer would want to know about the artifact, such as what it is made from and how it was created, what the artifact was used for, and how it is typical of Olmec culture.

Olmec Civilization, 900 BC

Have students explore the map using the interactive features and answer the associated questions.

Movement What two geographic features might the Olmec have found challenging in developing their trade routes? *rivers and mountains*

In print edition, see map of same title.

Movement Judging from the map, what was one way in which the Olmec spread their influence? *through the establishment of trade with other peoples of the region*

Movement What difficulties might the Olmec have encountered in developing their trade routes? *crossing rivers and climbing over mountainous terrain*

GAME

True or False: Olmec Jade

Have students play the game to test their knowledge of facts about the Olmec civilization.

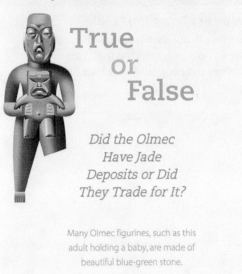

True
or
False

Did the Olmec Have Jade Deposits or Did They Trade for It?

Many Olmec figurines, such as this adult holding a baby, are made of beautiful blue-green stone.

Start

Olmec Society At San Lorenzo, archaeologists discovered earthen mounds, courtyards, and pyramids. Set among these earthworks were large stone monuments. They included columns, altars, and more colossal sculpted heads, which may have represented particular Olmec rulers. These giant monuments weigh as much as 44 tons. Some scholars think that Olmec workers may have moved these sculptures over land on rolling logs to the river banks. From there, they may have rafted the monuments along waterways to various sites.

To the east of San Lorenzo, another significant Olmec site, La Venta, rose around 900 BC. Here, researchers discovered a 100-foot-high mound

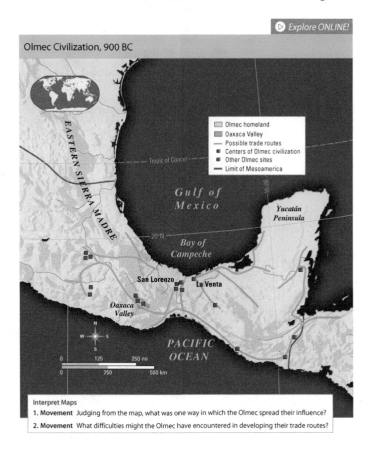

▶ Explore ONLINE!

Olmec Civilization, 900 BC

Interpret Maps

1. **Movement** Judging from the map, what was one way in which the Olmec spread their influence?

2. **Movement** What difficulties might the Olmec have encountered in developing their trade routes?

of earth and clay. This structure may have served as the tomb of a great Olmec ruler. Known as the Great Pyramid, the mound also may have been the center of the Olmec religion. Experts believe the Olmec prayed to a variety of nature gods.

Most of all, they probably worshiped the jaguar spirit. Numerous Olmec sculptures and carvings depict a half-human, half-jaguar creature. Some scholars believe that the jaguar represented a powerful rain god. Others contend that there were several jaguar gods, representing the earth, fertility, and maize.

Trade and Commerce Archaeologists once believed that sites such as La Venta were ceremonial centers where important rituals were performed but few people lived. In recent years, however, experts have begun to revise that view. The Olmec appear to have been a prosperous people who directed a large trading network throughout Mesoamerica. Olmec goods traveled as far as Mexico City to the north and Honduras to the south. In addition, raw materials—including iron ore and various stones—reached San Lorenzo from faraway regions. This trade network helped boost the Olmec economy and spread Olmec influence.

Decline of the Olmec For reasons that are not fully understood, Olmec civilization eventually collapsed. Scholars believe San Lorenzo was destroyed around 900 BC. La Venta may have fallen sometime around 400 BC. Some experts speculate that outside invaders caused the destruction. Others believe the Olmec may have destroyed their own monuments upon the death of their rulers.

Reading Check
Make Inferences
In what ways did the Olmecs' environment help in the creation of their civilization?

Zapotec Civilization Arises

By the time Olmec civilization had collapsed, another people—the **Zapotec**—were developing an advanced society to the southwest, in what is now the Mexican state of Oaxaca (wuh•HAH•kah). Though they showed traces of Olmec influence, the Zapotec built a unique civilization.

Peoples of the Oaxaca Valley Oaxaca is a rugged region of mountains and valleys in southern Mexico. In the center of the state, three valleys meet to form a large open area known as the Oaxaca Valley. This valley has fertile soil, a mild climate, and enough rainfall to support agriculture. As a result, various peoples have made the Oaxaca Valley their home, including the ancient Zapotec.

For centuries the Zapotec lived in scattered villages throughout the valley. By 1000 BC, however, one site—San José Mogote—was emerging as the main power in the region. At this site, the Zapotec constructed stone platforms. They also built temples and began work on monumental sculptures. By 500 BC they had developed early forms of writing and a calendar system.

Objectives

You may wish to discuss the following questions with students to help them frame the content as they read.

- Which features of the Zapotec urban center are similar to modern towns and cities? *central plaza or mall, places of worship, tall buildings*
- What is the main difference between modern buildings and those of the Zapotec? *Possible answer: Modern structures are built of steel, metal, or wood rather than simply stone.*

More About . . .

Monte Albán Monte Albán was later occupied by the Mixtec, another important culture of the Oaxaca region. Today, Monte Albán draws many visitors, who marvel at the size and magnificence of the ancient structures there.

READING CHECK

Make Inferences In what ways did the Olmecs' environment help in the creation of its civilization? *The region supplied abundant natural resources, and the surrounding floodplains provided fertile farmland*

Invite Tourists to Visit Monte Albán

1. Have students plan a travel brochure about Monte Albán.

2. Have students work in pairs to reread the text under "Zapotec Civilization Arises" and note facts and details to include in their brochures. Tell students to include:

   • Where is it located?

   • How old is it?

   • Why is it important?

3. Have students use their findings to make a brochure that will invite tourists to visit Monte Albán. Encourage them to use high-interest images, either hand-drawn or from the Internet. Students who need more help with the ideas and concepts in this section may complete the Guided Reading activity (also available in Spanish)

The Zapotec Flourish at Monte Albán Around 500 BC, Zapotec civilization took a major leap forward. High atop a mountain at the center of the Oaxaca Valley, the Zapotec built the first real urban center in the Americas, **Monte Albán**. This city, with its commanding view of the entire valley, grew and prospered over the next several centuries. By 200 BC, Monte Albán was home to around 15,000 people. The city eventually would reach a peak population of almost 25,000.

From AD 250 to AD 700, Monte Albán was truly impressive. At the heart of the city was a giant plaza paved with stones. Towering pyramids, temples, and palaces, all made out of stone, surrounded this plaza. There was even an observatory for observing the stars to establish a calendar. Nearby was a series of stone carvings of corpses. Their facial features show an Olmec influence.

Global Patterns

Pyramids

A number of ancient peoples used pyramids for temples, tombs, and observatories. The Egyptians built pyramids as tombs. Their pyramids had smooth sides and came to a point. In contrast, the pyramids built by the Zapotec at Monte Albán have stepped sides, with flat tops that served as platforms for temples.

LINK TO WORLD HISTORY

Research Pyramids

1. Display photographs of pyramids from the Egyptian, Mesopotamian, Nubian, Maya, and Chavín civilizations.

2. Organize the class into five groups and have each group research one of the pyramids. Students should find out the material used to build the pyramid, how the pyramid was made, and how the pyramid was used.

3. Have groups create a multimedia slide show to present their research to the class.

4. Once each group has shared their presentation, have them compare the materials and process used to build each pyramid. What is similar about each pyramid and what is different?

COLLABORATIVE LEARNING

Olmec and Zapotec Civilization Poster

1. Review with students the information in the text about the Olmec and Zapotec civilizations.

2. Organize the students into mixed-ability pairs and have each pair choose a civilization.

3. Have pairs plan and create a poster documenting their civilization. Posters should include images of cities and artifacts, and text explaining the images.

4. Display posters in a classroom exhibit. Have students compare the images on the posters and identify similarities and differences between the civilizations

For more than a thousand years the Zapotec controlled the Oaxaca Valley and the surrounding region. Sometime after AD 600, the Zapotec began to decline. Some scholars believe they may have suffered a loss of trade or other economic difficulties. As with the Olmec, the fall of Zapotec civilization remains a puzzle.

The Early Mesoamericans' Legacy

Although both the Zapotec and Olmec civilizations eventually collapsed, each culture influenced the Mesoamerican civilizations that followed.

The Olmec Leave Their Mark The Olmec contributed much to later Mesoamerican civilizations. They influenced the powerful Maya. Olmec art styles, especially the use of the jaguar motif, can be seen in the pottery and sculpture of later peoples in the region. In addition, future Mesoamerican societies copied the Olmec pattern of urban design.

The Olmec also left behind the notions of planned ceremonial centers, ritual ball games, and an elite ruling class. And while there is no clear evidence that the Olmec used a written language, their descendants or a related people carved out stone symbols that may have influenced later glyph writing.

Zapotec Contributions The Zapotec left behind their own legacy. It included a hieroglyphic writing system and a calendar system based on the movement of the sun. In addition, the Zapotec are noted as the Americas' first city builders. Monte Albán combined ceremonial grandeur with residential living space. This style influenced the development of future urban centers and became a hallmark of Mesoamerican civilizations.

As the Zapotec and Olmec flourished and then declined, civilizations were also taking shape in South America. Along the rough and mountainous terrain in what is now Peru, ancient peoples came together. There, they created more advanced and complex societies.

Lesson 2 Assessment

1. **Organize Information** Use a Venn diagram to record the characteristics that were similar and different among the Olmec and Zapotec. What was one of the most important characteristics that they shared?

Olmec   Zapotec

2. **Key Terms and People** For each key term or person in the lesson, write a sentence explaining its significance.
3. **Analyze Causes** Why did Olmec civilization collapse?
4. **Analyze Effects** What were some important Zapotec contributions to later cultures?
5. **Analyze Causes** What factors made the Oaxaca Valley a likely place for civilization to develop?
6. **Compare** What were some similarities between the Olmec and Zapotec cultures?

Objectives

You may wish to discuss the following questions with students to help them frame the content as they read.

- How was the structure of the Olmec social system similar to that of the Egyptian empire? *Both had an elite ruling class.*
- What did the Zapotec achieve in their urban center that would set a precedent for future urban development? *residential space in city center*

More About . . .

Hieroglyphic Language Hieroglyphics are pictures and symbols to represent objects or sounds. The word *hieroglyph* means "sacred carving" in Greek. While the Zapotec had a hieroglyphic writing system, hieroglyphic language is attributed primarily to ancient Egyptians, who called their writing system "gods' words."

Olmec Writing The discovery of an ancient stone tablet at an Olmec site in Veracruz, Mexico, dates the earliest writing in the Western Hemisphere to about 900 BC. Analysis of the stone slab, which was unearthed in 1999, has uncovered organized patterns of glyphs and symbols.

READING CHECK

Compare How does Monte Albán's population compare to the populations of today's major cities? *It was much smaller; many of today's large cities have several million residents*

READING CHECK

Summarize What do you consider to be the Olmecs' most important contributions to later cultures? *the Olmec's sculpture and planned ceremonial centers*

Print Assessment

1. **Organize Information** Use the Venn diagram to record the characteristics that were similar and different among the Olmec and Zapotec. What was the one of the most important characteristics that they shared? *Possible answer: Olmec—May have rafted monuments along waterways (unique), worshiped jaguar spirit, traded with faraway regions. Both—Built huge monuments, decline mysterious. Zapotec—Built urban center. Most important—huge monuments*

(continued)

⏵ ONLINE INTERACTIVE VISUALS

Carousel: Olmec Sculpture

Have students navigate through the carousel and note similarities and differences among the images or identify a unifying theme.

Analyze Visuals How are these images similar? *They are all made of some kind of stone and represent important aspects of Olmec culture.*

Print Assessment *(continued)*

2. **Key Terms and People** For each key term or person in the lesson, write a sentence explaining its significance. *Explanations of the lesson's key terms can be found on the following pages: Mesoamerica, Olmec, p. 490; Zapotec, p. 493; Monte Albán, p. 494*

3. **Analyze Causes** Why did the Olmec civilization collapse? *Possible answer: perhaps due to invaders*

4. **Analyze Effects** What were some important Zapotec contributions to later cultures? *hieroglyphic language, calendar system, great urban system*

5. **Analyze Causes** What factors made the Oaxaca Valley a likely place for civilization to develop? *fertile soil, mild climate, enough rainfall to support crops*

6. **Compare** What were similarities between the Aztec and Zapotec cultures? *pyramids, giant plazas, urban centers, sculptures*

Online Assessment

1. Why do scholars feel that Mexico's Gulf Coast was an unusual site for the establishment of a large civilization?
   - ○ The region had few navigable rivers to use as transport.
   - ○ The region was far away from necessary natural resources.
   - ○ The region had little freshwater available for the irrigation of crops.
   - ○ The region was hot and humid with dense tropical forests and swamps.

   Alternate Question *Select the answer choice from the drop-down list to complete the sentence correctly.*
   Mexico's Gulf Coast was hot and humid and covered with
   [dense tropical forests ⬍]. Even though the region seemed like an unlikely spot for development, the Olmec people still built large communities in this region.

2. What are three reasons that large civilizations developed in the Oaxaca Valley?
   - ○ fertile soil
   - ○ large rivers
   - ○ mild climate
   - ○ ocean harbors
   - ○ adequate rainfall
   - ○ abundant natural resources
   - ○ access to trade with other regions

   Alternate Question *Select the answer choice from the drop-down list to complete the sentence correctly.* The Oaxaca Valley was surrounded by mountains, yet it had fertile soil, a mild climate, and adequate rainfall to support agriculture. Thus, this area was suitable for
   [a home to various peoples ⬍]

3. What was significant about the Zapotec civilization in comparison with the Olmec civilization?
   - ○ The Zapotec civilization used jaguar motifs in its art.
   - ○ The Zapotec civilization played ritual ball games for sport.
   - ○ The Zapotec civilization had a hieroglyphic writing system.
   - ○ The Zapotec civilization built its cities on mountainous terrain.

   Alternate Question *Select the answer choice from the drop-down list to complete the sentence correctly.* The Zapotec civilization was different from the Olmec civilization in that the Zapotec had an
   [advanced hieroglyphic writing system ⬍].

4. **Elaborate** Why was the Gulf Coast of Mexico a suitable place for a large civilization to develop?

   The area had abundant natural resources such as tar, salt, fine clay for pottery, wood, rubber, and stone. The rivers in the region were used by the people for transportation and shipment. The flood plains near the rivers had very fertile soil, which was necessary for agriculture.

5. **Compare and Contrast** How were the Zapotec settlements at San José Mogote and Monte Albán similar to and different from each other?

   The San José Mogote and Monte Albán settlements were both established in the same area—the Oaxaca Valley. In both settlements, the peoples were advanced and established such things as calendar systems. They both worked with stone and built such structures as temples. San José Mogote was established about 500 years earlier than Monte Albán. Monte Albán was the first real urban center in the Americas.

6. **Elaborate** How did the Zapotec contribute to urban development in the Americas?

   They were considered the first city builders in the Americas. They combined ceremonial grandeur with residential living space. This style influenced the way other urban areas in Mesoamerican civilizations were later built.

History Through Art

Olmec Sculpture Explain that the Olmec stone heads may be sculptures of honored athletes. Ask students to think of modern athletes who have been honored in different forms of art or popular culture. *Possible answers: Michael Jordan—statue; Tony Hawk—video game, skateboards; Venus and Serena Williams—books, posters; Muhammad Ali—film*

1. **Hypothesize** The Olmec probably did not use the wheel. How do you think the Olmec transported the stone for the huge head sculptures? *Possible answers: building a road and then pushing or pulling the rocks over logs on the road; using rivers to transport rocks; roughly carving the rocks into a cylindrical shape at the quarry and then, using hundreds of people, rolling them along the road.*

2. **Compare and Contrast** Mount Rushmore in the United States also shows giant stone heads of leaders. Find out how it was made by using an encyclopedia or the Internet. What are similarities and differences between the way Mount Rushmore was made and the way the Olmec heads were made? *Possible answers: Both were carved from stone. Mount Rushmore was carved on a mountain; the stone for Olmec heads was transported. Mount Rushmore was created with 20th-century tools; Olmec stones were carved by hand with ancient tools.*

Olmec Sculpture

Around 1200 BC, the Olmec civilization appeared in southeastern Mexico. Over the next several hundred years, its culture spread into the Valley of Mexico and into parts of Central America. The Olmec are especially known for their huge sculptures of heads and their small, finely crafted stone carvings. Much of their art reflects a fascination with the jaguar.

OLMEC HEAD ▶
The Olmec Center at San Lorenzo, Honduras, contains several huge carved heads. Some of them are 9 feet high and weigh about 40 tons. The heads may be portraits of Olmec leaders or of players in a sacred ball game. The stone used for the sculptures came from a site more than 250 miles away. The Olmec transported this stone over mountain ranges, rivers, and swamps.

◀ JAGUAR FIGURE
The Olmec created many carvings of beings that were part human, part jaguar. Peter Furst, in "New Light on the Olmec" in *National Geographic*, explains why: "You can almost call the Olmec the people of the jaguar. In tropical America, jaguars were the shamans [medicine men] of the animal world, the alter ego [other identity] of the shaman." Olmec jaguar art greatly influenced later Mesoamerican cultures.

▲ OLMEC ALTAR
This Olmec altar has a carved figure at the base situated at the mouth of a cave. This figure's elaborate headdress shows that he is a ruler. The ruler holds a rope that winds around the base of the altar and binds a carved figure at the back. Scholars believe that the altar was used as a throne.

◄ JADE FIGURE
Many Olmec figurines are made of this beautiful blue-green stone, a fact that puzzled scientists for decades because they believed that no jade deposits existed in the Americas. However, in May 2002, a scientist discovered what he believes to be an ancient Olmec jade mine in Guatemala.

Critical Thinking

1. **Hypothesize** The Olmec probably did not use the wheel. How do you think the Olmec transported the stone for the huge head sculptures?

2. **Compare and Contrast** Mount Rushmore in the United States also shows giant stone heads of leaders. Find out how it was made by using an encyclopedia or the Internet. What are similarities and differences between the way Mount Rushmore was made and the way the Olmec heads were made?

Early Civilizations of the Andes

Video

Visuals

LESSON 3

Maps, Graphs, and Charts

- **Map:** Early Civilizations, 1200 BC–AD 700

Big Idea

In the Andes Mountains, various groups created flourishing civilizations.

- Uniting the Andes People
- Early Civilizations of Peru

Extend and Enrich

Historical Sources

- **Document-Based Investigation:** Comparing Nazca Lines

Assessment

- Key Terms Review
- Reading Check
- Graphic Organizer Activity
- Lesson Assessment

Researching the Moche

Article Students will read more about how some of the Moche were killed. They will then imagine that they are forensic anthropologists and develop hypotheses about why these killings happened. Students will give reasons that support their theories.

Early Civilizations of Peru

Multimedia Presentation Students will conduct research to learn more about the early Andean civilizations and use this research to create a multimedia presentation. The activity guides students through planning, creating, and reviewing their presentations.

Teach the Big Idea

1. **Whole Class Open/Introduction** Remind students that early Andean people traveled on foot in challenging geography in search of suitable places to settle. Ask students to list their criteria for an acceptable place to live. Then ask how their criteria might change if they had to search in an inhospitable environment for a place to live. *Possible answer: more concerned with survival, less concerned with the location's appearance or amenities*

2. **Direct Teach** Read students the Big Idea: *In the Andes Mountains, various groups created flourishing civilizations.* Review the following lesson objectives with students to aid in their understanding of the Big Idea.

   - Describe the first people of the Andes and the Chavín civilization.

   - Explain the rise of the Nazca and Moche societies.

3. **Whole Group Close/Reflect** Have students write a speech from the perspective of an archaeologist explaining the significance of one of the Andean civilizations. Invite students to share their work.

▷ **ONLINE DOCUMENT-BASED INVESTIGATION**

People and Empires in the Americas

Comparing Nazca Lines is the third of seven historical sources that students will analyze in People and Empires in the Americas module. The Nazca Lines are more than 1,000 drawings of animals, plants, humans, and geometric shapes etched on the plains of southeastern Peru. Most are so large that they can only be recognized from the air. Students can explore and compare the Nazca lines by using the interactive slider.

DOCUMENT-BASED INVESTIGATION HISTORICAL SOURCE

Comparing Nazca Lines

Etched on the plains of southeastern Peru are more than 1,000 drawings of animals, plants, humans, and geometric shapes. Most of them are so large that they can be recognized only from the air. Scientists believe that the Nazca people made the drawings between 200 B.C. and A.D. 600.

▷ **ONLINE LESSON FLIP CARDS**

Review Key Terms and People

Students can use the flip cards in the Lesson Review at any time to review the lesson's key terms and people: *Chavín, Nazca,* and *Moche.*

Early Civilizations of the Andes

The Big Idea
In the Andes Mountains, various groups created flourishing civilizations.

Why It Matters Now
Like the early Andean civilizations, people today must adapt to their environment in order to survive.

Key Terms and People
Chavín
Nazca
Moche

Setting the Stage

While civilizations were emerging in Mesoamerica, advanced societies were independently developing in South America. The early cultures of South America arose in a difficult environment, the rugged terrain of the Andes Mountains.

Societies Arise in the Andes

The Andes Mountains stretch about 4,500 miles down the western edge of South America, from Colombia in the north to Chile in the south. After the Himalayas in southern Asia, the Andes is the next highest mountain range in the world. The Andes has a number of peaks over 20,000 feet in elevation. South America's first civilizations emerged in the northern Andes region, in Peru.

Settlements on the Coastal Plain Peru was a harsh place to develop a civilization. The Andes are steep and rocky, with generally poor soil. Ice and snow cover the highest elevations year-round. Overland travel often is difficult. The climate is also severe: hot and dry during the day, and often freezing at night.

Between the mountains and the Pacific Ocean lies a narrow coastal plain. Most of this plain is harsh desert where rain seldom falls. In some places, however, rivers cross the desert on their path from the mountains to the sea. It was in these river valleys that the first settlements occurred.

COLLABORATIVE LEARNING

Museum Displays of Early Andean Civilizations

1. Organize the class into three groups. Assign each group a civilization: Chavín, Nazca, and Moche.

2. Have each group research the following questions:

   - What materials did the civilization use in art?

   - What motifs are common in the art of this civilization?

   - What types of crops did this civilization grow?

   - How did agriculture help this civilization?

3. Students will use their findings to create a museum display. Have them draw or download images from the Internet to support their research and write museum-style labels for each image.

4. Have each group present their displays to the class.

5. Assemble the finished displays in a classroom museum

Between 3600 and 2500 BC, people began to establish villages along the Pacific coast. These first inhabitants were hunter-gatherers who relied on seafood and small game for their survival. Around 3000 BC, these people began to farm. By 1800 BC, a number of thriving communities existed along the coast.

The Chavín Period The first influential civilization in South America arose not on the coast, however, but in the mountains. This culture, known as the **Chavín** (chah•VEEN), flourished from around 900 BC to 200 BC. Archaeologists named the culture after a major ruin, Chavín de Huántar, in the northern highlands of Peru. This site features pyramids, plazas, and massive earthen mounds.

Chavín culture spread quickly across much of northern and central Peru. Archaeologists have found no evidence of political or economic organization within the culture. Thus, they conclude that the Chavín were primarily a religious civilization. Nevertheless, the spread of Chavín art styles and religious images—as seen in stone carvings, pottery, and textiles—shows the powerful influence of this culture. Ancient Peruvians may have visited Chavín temples to pay their respects. They then carried ideas back to their communities. The Chavín are believed to have established certain patterns that helped unify Andean culture and lay the foundation for later civilizations in Peru. Thus, like the Olmec in Mesoamerica, the Chavín may have acted as a "mother culture" in South America.

Reading Check
Contrast
How did the environment of the Andes region differ from that of much of Mesoamerica?

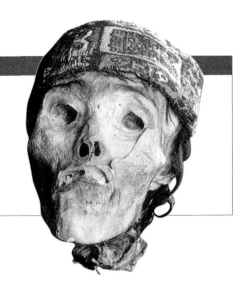

History in Depth

Headhunters

The striking images on their pottery indicate that the Nazca may have been headhunters. In numerous ceramic and textile designs, Nazca artisans depict the taking of human heads, probably from enemies in combat. Taking and displaying the head of an enemy was considered a way of increasing the strength and well-being of a community.

Early Cultures of South America

1. Have students work in mixed-ability pairs to set up a four-column, four-row chart to record information about the early cultures of South America: Chavín, Moche, and Nazca.

2. Have pairs complete their charts with information about the location of each civilization, how they adapted, and what they are well-known for.

3. Have volunteers share their charts with the class.)

Objectives

You may wish to discuss the following questions with students to help them frame the content as they read.

- Based on the first paragraph of "Settlements on the Coastal Plain," what can you predict about early societies in Peru? *Land would support few people; they would be isolated.*

- What similarities are there between pre-Chavín people and other early societies that you have studied? *settled in river valleys and along coast; hunter-gatherers became farmers.*

More About . . .

Chavín Gods The Chavín religion, like that of the Olmec, featured gods that were part human and part animal. An image called the Smiling God was found carved into a granite pillar at Chavín de Huântar. The figure has a human form but protruding fangs. For hair, it has several twisting snakes. This pillar is thought to have been key to Chavín religious life.

READING CHECK

Contrast How did the environment of the Andes region differ from that of much of Mesoamerica? *The Andes region was mostly dry, mountainous terrain with poor soil, while much of Mesoamerica was humid tropical forests with more fertile soil.*

▷ **ONLINE GRAPHIC ORGANIZER**

Early Civilizations of the Andes

As students read the lesson, have them use the graphic organizer to take notes. Students can review their graphic organizer notes at the end of the lesson to answer the following question.

Summarize What were the major achievements that early cultures shared along the Andes and northern Peru? *The Chavín created carvings, pottery, and textiles. The Nazca used irrigation and created textiles and pottery, and the Nazca lines. The Moche used irrigation and created jewelry and pottery. All excelled in ceramics and other crafts.*

	Chavín	Nazca	Moche
Location			
Time Span of Civilization			
Economic			
Cultural			

Comparing Nazca Lines

The Nazca Lines are more than1,000 drawings of animals, plants, humans, and geometric shapes etched on the plains of southeastern Peru. Most are so large that they can only be recognized from the air. Students can explore and compare the Nazca lines by using the interactive slider.

Analyze Sources What do the Nazca Lines reveal about the Nazca culture? *They were spiritual and relied on water for agriculture, which was challenging in a dry environment.*

In print edition, see History in Depth titled Nazca Lines.

Form and Support Opinions Do you think the purpose of the Nazca lines had something to do with water? Why or why not? *Yes—Dry region, so water was important. No—no one is certain of connection.*

Evaluate What might be the next step for researchers who wish to prove or disprove the aquifer theory? What are potential positive and negative consequences of such an action? *Drill to see if the lines really point to aquifers. Positive—Might discover water. Negative—Damage to the lines.*

DOCUMENT-BASED INVESTIGATION HISTORICAL SOURCE

Comparing Nazca Lines

Etched on the plains of southeastern Peru are more than 1,000 drawings of animals, plants, humans, and geometric shapes. Most of them are so large that they can be recognized only from the air. Scientists believe that the Nazca people made the drawings between 200 B.C. and A.D. 600.

History in Depth

Nazca Lines

Etched on the plains of southeastern Peru are more than 1,000 drawings of animals, plants, humans, and geometric shapes. Most of them are so large that they can be recognized only from the air. Scientists believe that the Nazca people made the drawings between 200 BC and AD 600. Since the lines were discovered in 1927, people have proposed many theories about their purpose, including the following:

- The Nazca people worshiped mountain or sky gods and created the drawings to please them.

- The lines indicated where surface water entered the plain and marked elevated land between ancient riverbeds.

- The lines are a huge map that marks the course of underground aquifers, or water sources. (This is the most recent theory.)

Size of the Nazca Lines

Many of the Nazca drawings are huge. Some of the wedges (below) are more than 2,500 feet long. The hummingbird (right) is 165 feet long. The Nazca people probably created small model drawings and used math to reproduce them at such a vast scale.

Durability of the Nazca Lines
This spider was created more than 1,000 years ago. It survived because the region has little erosion. The plains are one of the driest regions on earth with only 20 minutes of rain a year. Also, the ground is flat and stony, so wind rarely carries away the soil.

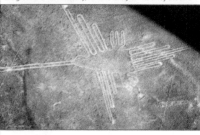

Nazca Water Cult
Some scholars think the lines were linked to a Nazca water cult, or religion. The straight lines may have led to ceremonial sites. The animals may have been symbols. For example, according to traditional beliefs, the hummingbird (above) represents the mountain gods. The mountains were a main source of water.

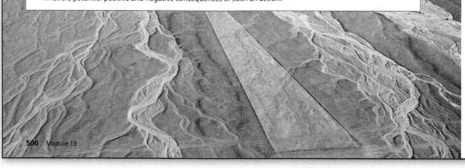

Interpret Visual Sources
1. **Form and Support Opinions** Do you think the purpose of the Nazca lines had something to do with water? Why or why not?
2. **Evaluate** What might be the next step for researchers who wish to prove or disprove the aquifer theory? What are potential positive and negative consequences of such an action?

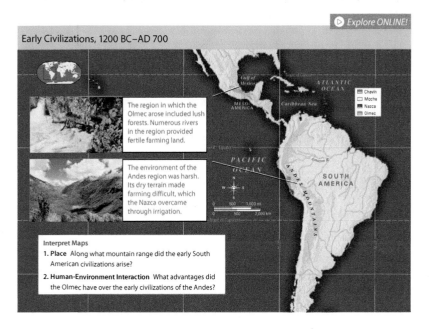

Early Civilizations, 1200 BC–AD 700

Explore ONLINE!

The region in which the Olmec arose included lush forests. Numerous rivers in the region provided fertile farming land.

The environment of the Andes region was harsh. Its dry terrain made farming difficult, which the Nazca overcame through irrigation.

Interpret Maps

1. **Place** Along what mountain range did the early South American civilizations arise?

2. **Human-Environment Interaction** What advantages did the Olmec have over the early civilizations of the Andes?

Other Andean Civilizations Flourish

Around the time Chavín culture declined, other civilizations were emerging in Peru. First the Nazca and then the Moche (MOH•chay) built societies that flourished in the Andes.

Nazca Achievements The **Nazca** culture flourished along the southern coast of Peru from around 200 BC to AD 600. This area is extremely dry. The Nazca developed extensive irrigation systems, including underground canals, that allowed them to farm the land. The Nazca are known for their beautiful textiles and pottery. Both feature images of animals and mythological beings. They are even more famous, however, for an extraordinary but puzzling set of creations known as the Nazca Lines.

Moche Culture Meanwhile, on the northern coast of Peru, another civilization was reaching great heights. This was the **Moche** culture, which lasted from about AD 100 to AD 700.

The Moche took advantage of the rivers that flowed from the Andes Mountains. They built impressive irrigation systems to water their wide range of crops, which included corn, beans, potatoes, squash, and peanuts. According to Peruvian archaeologist Walter Alva, the Moche enjoyed a variety of foods. These included both fish and game.

Objectives

You may wish to discuss the following questions with students to help them frame the content as they read.

- What does the art on Moche pottery reveal about their culture? *It was a complex culture that included doctors, musicians, and soldiers.*

- What can be inferred from the discovery of Nazca shrunken heads and the depiction of soldier on Moche pottery? *Both the Nazca and the Moche had enemies; some of their people were warriors.*

More About . . .

Moche Tombs In 1987, an elaborate tomb of a Moche ruler was discovered in Peru, which unearthed much valuable information about the Moche. Looters later raided the tomb, stealing or destroying priceless items. The FBI helped to recover one of the stolen artifacts.

Water Cults Explain that *cult* in this context means participants in a formal set of religious practices. Members of a "water cult" may have worshiped rain or bodies of water instead of animals or spirits.

▷ **ONLINE INTERACTIVE MAPS**

Early Civilizations, 1200 BC–AD 700

Have students explore the map and answer the associated questions.

Place Along what mountain range did the early South America civilizations arise? *Andes*

In print edition, see map of same title.

Place Along what mountain range did the early South America civilizations arise? *Andes*

Human-Environment Interaction What advantages did the Olmec have over the early civilizations of the Andes? *lush vegetation, fertile land*

Print Assessment

1. **Organize Information** Use the chart to show the achievements the early Mesoamerican cultures shared. Did they have any similar achievements?
Possible answer: Chavín —carvings, pottery, textiles; Nazca—textiles, pottery, Nazca Lines; Moche—jewelry, pottery. All excelled in ceramics and other crafts.

2. **Key Terms and People** For each key term or person in the lesson, write a sentence explaining its significance. *Explanations of the lesson's key terms can be found on the following pages: Chavín, p. 499; Nazca, Moche, p. 501.*

3. **Analyze** Why was Peru a difficult place for a civilization to develop? *rugged terrain, poor soil, travel difficult, harsh climate*

4. **Compare** How was the Chavín culture like the Olmec culture? *Both were "mother cultures.*

5. **Draw Conclusions** How did the Nazca and the Moche adapt to their environment in order to build flourishing societies? Give evidence. *They developed elaborate irrigation systems, allowing them to focus on cultural developments. Textiles, pottery, and jewelry from these civilizations still exist.*

Moche tombs uncovered in the recent past have revealed a civilization with enormous wealth. Archaeologists have found beautiful jewelry crafted from gold, silver, and semiprecious stones. The Moche were also brilliant ceramic artists. They created pottery that depicted scenes from everyday life. Moche pots show doctors healing patients, women weaving cloth, and musicians playing instruments. They also show fierce soldiers, armed with spears, leading enemy captives. Although the Moche never developed a written language, their pottery provides a wealth of detail about Moche life.

Nevertheless, many questions about the Moche remain. Experts still do not fully understand Moche religious beliefs. Nor do they know why the Moche fell. Like many early cultures of the Americas, the Moche remain something of a mystery awaiting further archaeological discoveries.

Unlike the lands you will read about in the next module—which were unified by the spread of Islam—the Americas would remain a patchwork of separate civilizations until the early 16th century. Around that time, the Europeans would begin to arrive and bring dramatic and lasting changes to the American continents.

Reading Check
Analyze Issues
How were archaeologists able to gain so much information about the Moche without the help of a written language?

Lesson 3 Assessment

1. Organize Information Use the chart to show the achievements that the early Mesoamerican cultures shared.

Chavín	Nazca	Moche

Did they have any similar achievements?

2. Key Terms and People For each key term or person in the lesson, write a sentence explaining its significance.

3. Analyze Why was Peru a difficult place for a civilization to develop?

4. Compare How was the Chavín culture like the Olmec culture?

5. Draw Conclusions How did the Nazca and the Moche adapt to their environment in order to build flourishing societies? Give evidence.

▷ Online Assessment

1. What was unusual about the Chavín culture that developed in the Andes between 900 BC and 200 BC?
   - ○ It was primarily a religious culture.
   - ○ It was a culture that left no written records.
   - ○ It was mainly an economic and political culture.
   - ○ It was a culture that prevented other cultures from developing.

   Alternate Question *Select the answer choice from the drop-down list to complete the sentence correctly.*
   The Chavín culture was unusual in comparison to other cultures in the Americas because it was a [*religious civilization* ⬍] rather than a culture that had an organized economic and political structure.

2. What has helped scholars learn more about Moche daily life?
   - ○ discovering their artisan jewelry
   - ○ finding their musical instruments
   - ○ translating their written language
   - ◉ studying the scenes on their pottery

   Alternate Question *Select the answer choice from the drop-down list to complete the sentence correctly.*
   Since the Moche people did not have a written language, scholars would have been unable to know about their culture if the Moche [*pottery* ⬍] hadn't been painted with detailed scenes of their everyday life.

3. **Elaborate** Why do scholars consider the Olmec and Chavín cultures to be "mother cultures"?

   Scholars consider the two cultures to be "mother cultures" because they both helped lay the foundation for later cultures. The Olmec helped lay the foundation for other Mesoamerican cultures that came after it, while the Chavín culture helped lay the foundation for later civilizations in Peru.

4. **Compare and Contrast** What significance did water play in both the Nazca and Moche cultures?

   In the Nazca culture, water was very important because it was so scarce. The southern coast of Peru where this civilization lived has a very dry climate. They developed extensive irrigation systems including underground canals that allowed them to farm the land. Water was also important to the Moche people. They took advantage of the rivers that flowed from the Andes Mountains and built impressive irrigation systems to water their wide range of crops. They also used the water to obtain food in other ways, specifically through fishing.

North American Societies

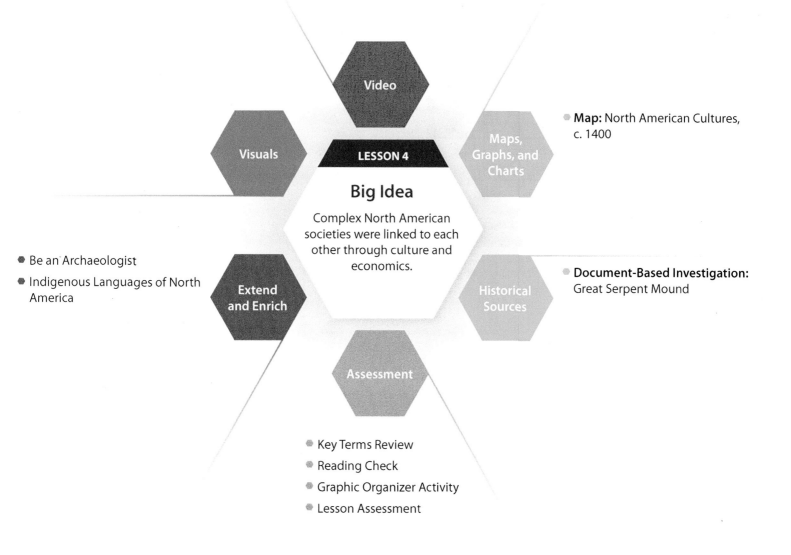

Video

Visuals

LESSON 4

Maps, Graphs, and Charts

● **Map:** North American Cultures, c. 1400

Big Idea

Complex North American societies were linked to each other through culture and economics.

● Be an Archaeologist
● Indigenous Languages of North America

Extend and Enrich

Historical Sources

● **Document-Based Investigation:** Great Serpent Mound

Assessment

● Key Terms Review
● Reading Check
● Graphic Organizer Activity
● Lesson Assessment

Be an Archaeologist

Writing Activity Students will imagine they are archaeologists who have uncovered a Hopewell artifact that is representative of a snake. They will write a report discussing what they observe and why a Hopewell might want to wear this piece of jewelry.

Indigenous Languages of North America

Multimedia Presentation Students will make a multimedia presentation highlighting the work of linguists or a Native American language that is spoken today. Guide students as they research their topic. Their presentations will include imagery, audio, and text.

North American Societies

The Big Idea

Complex North American societies were linked to each other through culture and economics.

Why It Matters Now

Traditions and ideas from these cultures became part of the cultures of North America.

Key Terms and People

potlatch
Anasazi
pueblo
Mississippian
Iroquois
totem

This headdress was used by the Kwakiutl in religious ceremonies. Carved of red cedar and painted, it shows a thunderbird, the highest of the spirits in the Kwakiutl religion. Like a huge eagle, the thunderbird flew high in the sky. When it was hungry, it swooped down to catch and eat killer whales.

Setting the Stage

Between 30,000 and 12,000 years ago, hunter-gatherers migrated across the Bering Strait land bridge from Asia and began to populate the Americas. Migrating southward, those first Americans reached the southern tip of South America by somewhere between 12,000 and 7000 BC. At the same time, they began to spread out east and west across North America. Over the centuries, the early North American peoples adapted to their environment, creating a very diverse set of cultures.

Complex Societies in the West

In some ways, the early North American cultures were less developed than those of South America and Mesoamerica. The North American groups created no great empires. They left few ruins as spectacular as those of ancient Mexico or Peru. Nevertheless, the first peoples of North America did create complex societies. These societies were able to conduct long-distance trade and construct magnificent buildings.

Cultures of Abundance The Pacific Northwest—from Oregon to Alaska—was rich in resources and supported a sizable population. To the Kwakiutl, Nootka, and Haida peoples, the most important resource was the sea. They hunted whales in canoes. Some canoes were large enough to carry at least 15 people. In addition to the many resources of the sea, the coastal forest provided plentiful food. In this abundant environment, the Northwest Coast tribes developed societies in which differences in wealth created social classes. Families displayed their rank and prosperity in an elaborate ceremony called the **potlatch** (PAHT•lach). In this ceremony, they gave food, drink, and gifts to the community.

Accomplished Builders The dry, desert lands of the Southwest were a much harsher environment than the temperate Pacific coastlands. However, as early as 1500 BC, the peoples of the Southwest were beginning to farm the land. Because of the climate, competition for farmland sometimes

Objectives

You may wish to discuss the following questions with students to help them frame the content as they read.

- Besides serving as a way to display social status, what other functions might have been served by the potlatch? *Possible answer: might have kept the poor from becoming too resentful of their lower status*

- Why would a people, such as the Anasazi, choose to live in the desert? *Possible answer: They had the skills to make the desert habitable, such as knowledge of irrigation.*

More About . . .

Connect to Geography Explain to students that a map of culture is just one way of showing what was happening in the Americas prior to the arrival of Europeans. Another map might show population density—which would indicate the greatest density along the Pacific Coast and in the farming areas of the Southwest and East.

Kivas Kivas were at the center of many clan and village activities and had both religious and political significance. Almost entirely underground, the circular kivas were entered by a ladder descending through the roof. Kiva walls were decorated with colorful murals that depicted sacred subjects or scenes of everyday life.

Teach the Big Idea

1. **Whole Class Open/Introduction** Ask students if they know of any U.S. place names based on Native American cultures. *Possible answers: Cheyenne, Delaware, Illinois, Lake Huron, Miami.*

2. **Direct Teach** Read students the Big Idea: *Complex North American societies were linked to each other through culture and economics.* Review the following lesson objectives with students to aid in their understanding of the Big Idea.

   - Describe various cultures of North America before Columbus.

   - Explain the unique traditions of Mound Builders and other woodland cultures.

   - Identify common features of Native American cultures.

3. **Whole Group Close/Reflect** Have students make a Venn diagram comparing and contrasting the culture of two Native American groups.

▷ **ONLINE DOCUMENT-BASED INVESTIGATION**

People and Empires in the Americas

Great Serpent Mound is the fourth of seven historical sources that students will analyze in the People and Empires in the Americas module. The Hopewell culture built the Great Serpent Mound in present-day Ohio for burials and other purposes. Students can use the interactive features to study the image of the Great Serpent Mound.

▷ **ONLINE GRAPHIC ORGANIZER**

North American Societies

As students read the lesson, have them use the graphic organizer to take notes. Students can review their graphic organizer notes at the end of the lesson to answer the following question.

Analyze Effects How did the environment affect the development of cultures on the Northwest Coast and of the Southwest? *The cultures on the Northwest Coast relied on the sea for the resources they needed, while the cultures of the Southwest used irrigation to grow crops because the environment was very dry.*

Review Key Terms and People

Students can use the flip cards in the Lesson Review at any time to review the lesson's key terms and people: *potlatch, Anasazi, pueblo, Mississippian, Iroquois,* and *totem.*

MAP

North American Culture Areas, c. 1400

Have students explore the map and answer the associated questions.

Region Which Native American culture groups had the largest number of tribes? *Great Plains, Northeast*

Human-Environment Interaction In which culture areas would movement of trade goods be made easier by river and lake connections? *Great Plains, Northeast*

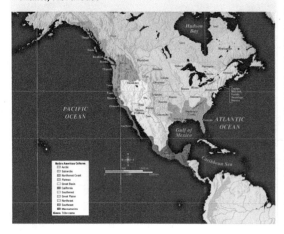

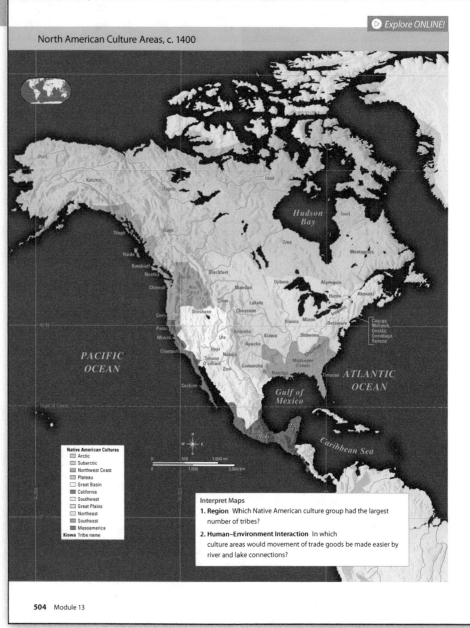

North American Culture Areas, c. 1400

Native American Cultures
- Arctic
- Subarctic
- Northwest Coast
- Plateau
- Great Basin
- California
- Southwest
- Great Plains
- Northeast
- Southeast
- Mesoamerica

Kiowa Tribe name

Interpret Maps

1. **Region** Which Native American culture group had the largest number of tribes?

2. **Human–Environment Interaction** In which culture areas would movement of trade goods be made easier by river and lake connections?

COLLABORATIVE LEARNING

Pueblos and Irrigation Systems

1. Review information about and show students images of Hohokam irrigation and Anasazi pueblos.

2. Organize students into pairs. Have each pair design a Hohokam irrigation system and an Anasazi pueblo. Have them sketch their designs and label each design feature with its name and purpose.

3. Have volunteers share their designs with the class.

ENGLISH LANGUAGE LEARNERS

North American Cultures and Peoples Flash Cards

1. Write the names of Native American cultures on the front of the cards. On the back of the card, write the phonetic spellings of the groups' names and the culture areas to which they belong.

2. Divide the class into two groups. Have one member from each team step forward and show them the first card. The student who raises his or her hand first gets to answer the question. If the student accurately pronounces the tribe's name and correctly identifies its culture area, his or her team is awarded one point.

3. If students answer the question incorrectly, allow the other team an opportunity to answer.

Cliff Palace, Mesa Verde, had 217 rooms and 23 kivas.

led to conflicts. Among the most successful of the early farmers in this area were the Hohokam (huh•HOH•kuhm) of central Arizona. They used irrigation to produce harvests of corn, beans, and squash. Their use of pottery rather than baskets, as well as certain religious rituals, showed contact with Mesoamerican peoples to the south.

A people to the north—the **Anasazi** (ah•nuh•SAH•zee)—also influenced the Hohokam. They lived in the Four Corners region, where the present-day states of Utah, Arizona, Colorado, and New Mexico meet. The Anasazi built impressive cliff dwellings, such as the ones at Mesa Verde, Colorado. These large houses were built on top of mesas—flat-topped hills—or in shallow caves in the sheer walls of deep canyons. By the AD 900s, the Anasazi were living in **pueblos** (PWEHB•lohs), villages of large, apartment-style compounds made of stone and adobe, or sun-baked clay.

The largest Anasazi pueblo, begun around AD 900, was Pueblo Bonito, a Spanish name meaning "beautiful village." Its construction required a high degree of social organization and inventiveness. The Anasazi relied on human labor to quarry sandstone from the canyon walls and move it to the site. Skilled builders then used a mudlike mortar to construct walls up to five stories high. Windows were small to keep out the burning sun. When completed, Pueblo Bonito probably housed about 1,000 people and contained more than 600 rooms. In addition, a number of underground or partly underground ceremonial chambers called kivas (KEE•vuhs) were used for a variety of religious practices.

Objectives

You may wish to discuss the following questions with students to help them frame the content as they read.

- Why might Cahokia's priest-rulers have been involved in the regulation of farming activity? *Possible answer: Individuals may have been made priests when they showed signs of being able to pinpoint the best time to plant or harvest.*

- Besides defense, what other benefits might the Iroquois have derived from joining together? *Possible answer: may have promoted trade among league members*

More About . . .

Cahokia In the early 1800s, in southern Illinois, a group of French monks founded a monastery near a 10-foot-high mound that covered about 15 acres. Later explorations would show that their settlement had been in the middle of one of the greatest pre-Columbian Native American cities. The large mound, eventually known as Monks Mound, was located inside a stockade that enclosed more than 100 acres of land.

Great Lakes Explain to students that the Great Lakes region refers to the area around the five large lakes in central North America: Superior, Michigan, Huron, Erie, and Ontario.

▷ ONLINE DOCUMENT-BASED INVESTIGATION

Great Serpent Mound

The Great Serpent Mound runs some 1,300 feet along its coils and is between 4 and 5 feet high. Have students study the image of the Great Serpent Mound and then answer the question that follows.

Analyze Sources What do mounds like this one reveal about mound-building cultures in the Americas? *They were spiritual and probably used them for religious ceremonies.*

READING CHECK

Hypothesize Why do you think no great empires developed in North America? *There were many different groups thavt developed in different regions of North America and used the available resources in their environment, which in some cases were limited so they had to trade with other groups to live.*

READING CHECK

Draw Conclusions Of what value would a political alliance be to an individual tribe? *It would provide protection from enemies.*

Reading Check
Hypothesize
Why do you think
no great empires
developed in North
America?

Many Anasazi pueblos were abandoned around 1200, possibly because of a prolonged drought. The descendants of the Anasazi, the pueblo peoples, continued many of their customs. Pueblo groups like the Hopi and Zuni used kivas for religious ceremonies. They also created beautiful pottery and woven blankets. They traded these, along with corn and other farm products, with plains Indians to the east, who supplied bison meat and hides. These nomadic plains tribes eventually became known by such names as the Comanche, Kiowa, and Apache.

Mound Builders and Other Woodland Cultures

Beyond the Great Plains, in the woodlands east of the Mississippi River, other ancient peoples—the Mound Builders—were creating their own unique traditions. Beginning around 700 BC, a culture known as the Adena began to build huge earthen mounds in which they buried their dead. Mounds that held the bodies of tribal leaders were often filled with gifts, such as finely crafted copper and stone objects.

Some 500 years later, the Hopewell culture also began building burial mounds. Their mounds were much larger and more plentiful than those of the Adena. Some of the Hopewell mounds may have been used for purposes other than burials. For example, the Great Serpent Mound, near Hillsboro, Ohio, may have played a part in Hopewell religious ceremonies.

The last Mound Builder culture, the **Mississippian**, lasted from around AD 800 until the arrival of Europeans in the 1500s. These people created thriving villages based on farming and trade. Between 1000 and 1200, perhaps as many as 30,000 people lived at Cahokia (kuh•HOH•kee•uh), the leading site of Mississippian culture. Cahokia was led by priest-rulers, who regulated farming activities. The heart of the community was a 100-foot-high, flat-topped earthen pyramid, which was crowned by a wooden temple.

These Mississippian lands were located in a crossroads region between east and west. They enjoyed easy transportation on the Mississippi and Ohio rivers. Items found in burial mounds show that the Mississippians had traded with peoples in the West and, possibly, Mesoamerica. Similar evidence shows that they also came into contact with peoples from the Northeast.

Eastern Woodland Tribes Build Alliances The eastern woodlands tribes developed a variety of cultures. These peoples often clashed with each other over land. In some areas, tribes formed political alliances to ensure protection of tribal lands. The best example of a political alliance was the **Iroquois** (IHR•uh•kwoy), a group of tribes speaking related languages living in the eastern Great Lakes region. In the late 1500s, five of these tribes in upper New York—the Mohawk, Oneida, Onondaga, Cayuga, and Seneca—formed the Iroquois League. According to legend, Chief Hiawatha helped to create this league. His goal was to promote joint defense and cooperation among the tribes.

Reading Check
Draw Conclusions
Of what value would a
political alliance be to
an individual tribe?

ADVANCED/GIFTED

The Iroquois and U.S. Constitutions

1. Have students research the history of the Iroquois and U.S. constitutions. Ask them to find and read the texts.

2. Have students prepare a presentation that contrasts the two constitutions. Presentations should describe the needs that gave rise to each constitution and the circumstances that allowed for their adoption, as well as similarities and differences in the documents.

3. Have students include the strengths and weaknesses of both constitutions in their presentations.

COLLABORATIVE LEARNING

Excavating a Hopewell Mound

1. Tell students that, in order to find artifacts, archaeologists must carefully sift through earth. Provide additional information about the process of excavation.

2. Organize the class into groups of three. Have groups use print and Internet sources to find out more about Hopewell mounds and archaeology.

3. Have students write a series of eight journal entries from the perspective of an archaeologist excavating a Hopewell mound in the Ohio River Valley. The journal entries should describe the process of excavation, the artifacts, and the clues those artifacts offer about the Hopewell civilization.

Great Serpent Mound runs some 1,300 feet along its coils and is between 4 and 5 feet high.

Cultural Connections

The Iroquois alliance was a notable example of a political link among early North American peoples. For the most part, however, the connections between native North Americans were economic and cultural. They traded, had similar religious beliefs, shared social patterns, and spread ideas.

Trading Networks Tie Tribes Together Trade was a major factor linking the peoples of North America. Along the Columbia River in Oregon, the Chinook people established a lively marketplace that brought together trade goods from all over the West. And the Mississippian trade network stretched from the Rocky Mountains to the Atlantic coast and from the Great Lakes to the Gulf of Mexico.

Religion Shapes Views of Life Another feature that linked early Americans was their religious beliefs. Nearly all native North Americans believed that the world around them was filled with nature spirits. Most Native Americans recognized a number of sacred spirits. Some groups held up one supreme being, or Great Spirit, above all others. North American peoples believed that the spirits gave them rituals and customs to guide them in their lives and to satisfy their basic needs. If people practiced these rituals, they would live in peace and harmony.

Native American religious beliefs also included great respect for the land as the source of life. Native Americans used the land but tried to alter it as little as possible. The land was sacred, not something that could be bought and sold. Later, when Europeans claimed land in North America, the issue of land ownership created conflict.

Shared Social Patterns The family was the basis for social organization for Native Americans. Generally, the family unit was the extended family, including parents, children, grandparents, and other close relatives. Some tribes further organized families into clans, or groups of families descended from a common ancestor. In some tribes, clan members lived together in large houses or groups of houses.

Objectives

You may wish to discuss the following questions with students to help them frame the content as they read.

- Why might different North American peoples have followed similar religious practices? *Possible answer: Traders carried beliefs from one region to another; beliefs were shaped by a similar way of life.*

- How might a totem help define group behavior and relationships? *Possible answer: Individuals may have been required to behave in specific ways in the presence of the totem. The totem may have been the focus of important rituals.*

More About . . .

Totem Poles Totem poles are carved and painted logs used as monuments by Northwestern tribes in the United States and Canada. Most totem poles were carved out of red cedar, which is readily available in the area. These carved logs showed a family's totem, which could be anything in nature, including an animal. Some totem poles are used as grave markers or tombstones. Others tell about a family's history. Totem poles were also a sign of a person's wealth and influence, since hiring an artist to carve a totem pole was expensive. The art of totem pole carving reached its height in the mid-1800s when chiefs had more money from trading fur with Europeans. European carving tools also made it easier to carve totems. The climate of the Northwest causes the red cedar to decay within 60 to 70 years, so most totem poles from that period no longer exist.

▷ **ONLINE INTERACTIVE MAP**

North America Culture Areas, c. 1400

Have students explore the map and answer the associated question.

Human-Environment Interaction In which culture areas would movement of trade goods be made easier by river and lake connections? *Great Plains, Southwest*

Cultural Connections Among Native Americans

1. Draw and display a concept map for students. Draw a large circle, with arrows pointing to three smaller circles. Draw two arrows and circles coming from each of the smaller circles. In the large circle at the top, write the phrase "Cultural Connections." In the three second-tier circles, write the following phrases: "Shared Social Patterns," "Trading Networks Tie Tribes Together," and "Religion Shapes Views of Life."

2. Have students review the text and fill in the empty circles with information from the text. Ask a volunteer to fill in information on the displayed concept map.

Make Inferences What artificial symbols are used by nations or organizations in a way similar to totems? *flags, mascots, religious signs*

Print Assessment

1. **Organize Information** Use the chart to compare the effect of the environment on the development of cultures of the Northwest coast and the Southwest. Write a paragraph to explain how the effects were different. *Possible answer: NW: near sea; SW: hot and dry; Both: high degree of social organization—NW people took advantage of nearby ocean resources; SW peoples adapted to dry conditions by irrigating.*

2. **Key Terms and People** For each key term or person in the lesson, write a sentence explaining its significance. *Explanations of the lesson's key terms can be found on the following pages: potlatch, p. 503; Anasazi, pueblo, p. 505; Mississippian, Iroquois, p. 506; totems, p. 508.*

3. **Summarize** For what purpose did the Mound Builder cultures use earthen mounds? *burying the dead; religious purposes*

4. **Analyze Causes** Why might location have been important to the power and wealth of the Mississippian culture? *The culture developed at the intersection of major trade routes.*

5. **Compare** In which ways did the peoples of North America share similar cultural patterns? *Most believed that their lives were guided by sacred spirits and that land was sacred and the source of all life. The family unit was central, and many tribes expressed tribal unity through totems.*

6. **Develop Historical Perspectives** Why did societies in North America interact with each other? *Possible answer: Interaction among societies provided security and exchange of goods.*

Global Patterns

Iroquois Women

Iroquois society was matrilineal. This means that all Iroquois traced their descent through their female ancestors. Clans of the mother controlled property, held ceremonies, and determined official titles.

The ability to grant titles to men was handed down from mother to daughter. The most important title given to men was that of "sachem," the peace, or civil, chief.

A council of sachems met once a year to decide on war and peace and other important matters. Since sachems could not go to war, they appointed warriors to lead a war party. Thus, in a way women had a say in warfare in the Iroquois tribes.

Common among Native American clans was the use of **totems** (TOH·tuhmz). The term refers to a natural object with which an individual, clan, or group identifies itself. The totem was used as a symbol of the unity of a group or clan. It also helped define certain behaviors and the social relationships of a group. The term comes from an Ojibwa word but refers to a cultural practice found throughout the Americas. For example, Northwestern peoples displayed totem symbols on masks, boats, and huge poles set in front of their houses. Others used totem symbols in rituals or dances associated with important group events such as marriages, the naming of children, or the planting or harvesting of crops.

There were hundreds of different patterns of Native American life in North America. Some societies were small and dealt with life in a limited region of the vast North American continent. Other groups were much larger and were linked by trade and culture to other groups in North America and Mesoamerica. Peoples in Mesoamerica and South America also lived in societies that varied from simple to complex. You will read about three of these cultures—the Maya, the Aztec, and the Inca—in the next three lessons. They would develop very sophisticated ways of life.

Reading Check
Make Inferences What artificial symbols are used by nations or organizations in a way similar to totems?

Lesson 4 Assessment

1. Organize Information Use the chart to compare the effect of the environment on the development of the cultures of the Northwest Coast and the Southwest.

Northwest Coast   Southwest

Write a paragraph to explain how the effects were different.

2. Key Terms and People For each key term or person in the lesson, write a sentence explaining its significance.

3. Summarize For what purpose did the Mound Builder cultures use earthen mounds?

4. Analyze Causes Why might location have been important to the power and wealth of the Mississippian culture?

5. Compare In what ways did the peoples of North America share similar cultural patterns?

6. Develop Historical Perspectives Why did societies in North America interact with each other?

508 Module 13

TOTEM POLES

Below Level Display images of totem poles and explain the significance of a totem, which could be anything in nature, including an animal. Have students design a totem pole for your school, using your school mascot.

At Level Explain that many images were carved on totem poles, including that of the clan's symbol totem. Totem poles could be used to show the history of a family or clan. Students can then design a totem pole for your school, choosing symbols that best represent your school's history.

Above Level Explain that totem poles were carved for various reasons. Have students research the different uses of totem poles and then design a totem pole for a landmark or an important historical figure in your state.

▷ Online Assessment

1. What evidence leads scholars to believe that the Hohokam had contact with the Mesoamerican peoples?
   - ○ The Hohokam lived in pueblos.
   - ○ The Hohokam used irrigation techniques.
   - ○ The Hohokam grew corn, beans, and squash.
   - ◉ The Hohokam used pottery rather than baskets.

   Alternate Question *Select the answer choice from the drop-down list to complete the sentence correctly.*
   The fact that the Hohokam [used pottery instead of baskets ⇕] showed that they had contact with the Mesoamerican people who lived to the south.

2. How do archaeologists know the extent of the Mississippian people's trade network?
   - ○ They interpreted cave drawings.
   - ○ They translated written records.
   - ◉ They found items in burial mounds.
   - ○ They studied the statues by the pyramids.

   Alternate Question *Select the answer choice from the drop-down list to complete the sentence correctly.*
   When archaeologists found items in the Mississippian people's burial mounds, they realized that the trade network of these people stretched throughout the present-day United States and even to [Mesoamerica ⇕].

3. What was one common characteristic of North American Native American religious beliefs?
   - ○ They all believed in a Great Spirit.
   - ○ They all believed in reincarnation.
   - ○ They all believed in ancestor worship.
   - ◉ They all believed in the sacredness of the land.

   Alternate Question *Select the answer choice from the drop-down list to complete the sentence correctly.*
   When Europeans began claiming land in North America, it was of particular issue to the Native Americans because their religious beliefs taught that land [could not be bought and sold ⇕].

4. **Elaborate** How do experts believe that the pueblos were constructed, and why was this a particularly challenging feat?

   Experts believe that the pueblos were constructed with a high level of social organization and inventiveness. They had to rely on human labor to quarry sandstone from the canyon walls and move it to the site, which was on the side of a tall cliff. That was one reason that this would have been a very challenging feat. Skilled builders had to use mudlike mortar to construct the walls up to five stories high, another challenging feat.

5. **Draw Conclusions** Why did the Eastern Woodland tribes feel it was necessary to form alliances and what was their most famous alliance?

   They felt it was necessary to form alliances because there were often clashes over land. These political alliances helped them ensure the protection of these tribal lands. The best example of a political alliance of these people was the Iroquois League. This was an alliance formed by a group of tribes in the eastern Great Lakes region who spoke similar languages. This alliance's goal was to promote joint defense and cooperation.

6. **Compare and Contrast** What was similar and different about the totems of the various North American Native American clans?

   The totems of these peoples were similar because they were all used as a symbol of the unity of the group or clan. These objects helped to define certain behaviors and social relationships of the group. The totems of the various North American Native American clans were different in how and where they were used. The Northwestern peoples displayed totem symbols on masks, boats, and huge poles in front of their houses. Other groups used totem symbols in rituals or dances associated with marriages, the naming of children, and the planting or harvesting of crops.

ADDITIONAL LESSON CONTENT

Early North American Civilizations Documentary

1. Organize the class into four groups. Assign each group a Native American group that lived in your area.

2. Have each group research and create a documentary about archaeologists studying the group.

3. Have group members work together to write the script. The script should include information on what the work of the archaeologists has revealed about the economics, art and architecture, and family/social structures of those societies.

4. Have students find visuals that support the information being presented.

5. Allow time for the groups to record their documentaries and to show them to the class.

Maya Kings and Cities

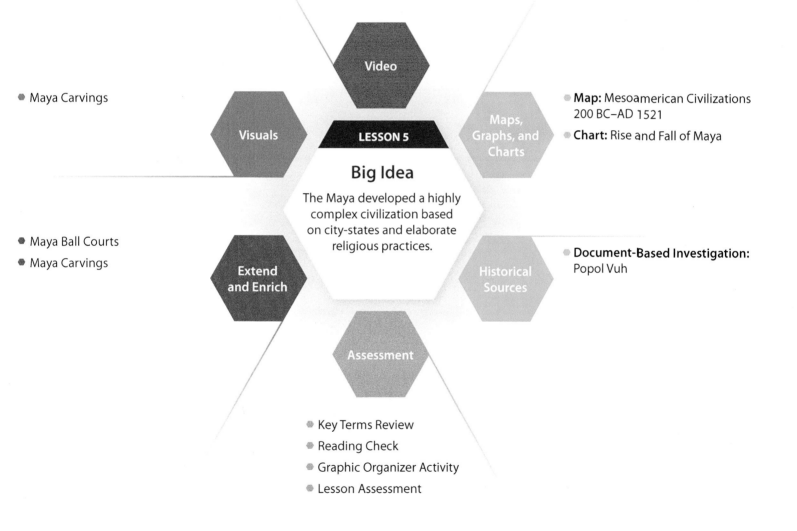

Maya Carvings

Video

Visuals

LESSON 5

Maps, Graphs, and Charts

Map: Mesoamerican Civilizations 200 BC–AD 1521

Chart: Rise and Fall of Maya

Big Idea

The Maya developed a highly complex civilization based on city-states and elaborate religious practices.

Extend and Enrich

Maya Ball Courts
Maya Carvings

Historical Sources

Document-Based Investigation: Popol Vuh

Assessment

Key Terms Review
Reading Check
Graphic Organizer Activity
Lesson Assessment

Online Lesson 5 Enrichment Activities

Maya Ball Courts

Infographic Students read about the Maya ball courts and their political and religious importance. Then students conduct research to find out more about Maya ball courts and draw a diagram or infographic of a Maya ball court with players.

Maya Carvings

Writing Activity Students will research images of Maya carvings and write an analysis of one of the images they find. The activity guides students through prewriting, writing the analysis, and reviewing and proofreading.

Maya Kings and Cities

The Big Idea
The Maya developed a highly complex civilization based on city-states and elaborate religious practices.

Why It Matters Now
Descendants of the Maya still occupy the same territory.

Key Terms and People
Tikal
Pacal
glyph
codex
Popol Vuh

Maya jade death mask, seventh century AD

Setting the Stage
In the early centuries AD, most North American peoples were beginning to develop complex societies. Further south, the peoples of Mexico and Central America were entering into the full flower of civilization. A prime example of this cultural flowering were the Maya, who built an extraordinary civilization in the heart of Mesoamerica.

Maya Create City-States
The homeland of the Maya stretched from southern Mexico into northern Central America. This area includes a highland region and a lowland region. The lowlands lie to the north. They include the dry scrub forest of the Yucatán (yoo•kuh•TAN) Peninsula and the dense, steamy jungles of southeastern Mexico and northern Guatemala. The highlands are further south—a range of cool, cloud-wreathed mountains that stretch from southern Mexico to El Salvador.

While the Olmec were building their civilization along the Gulf Coast in the period from 1200 to 400 BC, the Maya were also evolving. They took on Olmec influences, blending these with local customs. By AD 250, Maya culture had developed into a flourishing civilization. Over time the Maya established cultural patterns and political and economic structures that were similar to those of later civilizations, such as the Aztecs and the Incas.

Urban Centers The period from AD 250 to 900 is known as the Classic Period of Maya civilization. During this time, the Maya built spectacular cities such as **Tikal** (tee•KAHL), a major center in northern Guatemala. Other important sites included Copán, Palenque, Uxmal, and Chichén Itzá (chee•CHEHN-ee•TSAH). Each of these was an independent city-state, ruled by a god-king and serving as a center for religious ceremonies and trade. For example, **Pacal** the Great ruled Palenque in the 600s. During his reign many great buildings were constructed, such as the Temple of

Objectives
You may wish to discuss the following questions with students to help them frame the content as they read.

- What other culture that you have read about consisted of independent city-states? *ancient Greece*

- Why might the Maya have found cacao beans to be a useful currency? *Possible answer: They had an intrinsic value. They were small, like coins, and easily carried.*

More About . . .
Pacal the Great K'inich Janaab Pacal was born in 603. His mother, the queen, stepped down from the throne in favor of Pacal shortly after his 12th birthday. During his reign, Pacal added many buildings to the capital city of Palenque, including the Temple of the Inscriptions, which was used as his tomb. He saw the expansion and growth of Palenque power over the lowland Maya territory, as well as a growth in engineering and arts. Pacal died in 683.

Teach the Big Idea
1. **Whole Class Open/Introduction** Tell students they will learn about Maya calendars. Ask them what they know about their own calendar. *Some students may know that they use the Gregorian calendar, adopted in the American colonies in the 1750s.*

2. **Direct Teach** Read students the Big Idea: *The Maya developed a highly complex civilization based on city-states and elaborate religious practices.* Review the following lesson objectives with students to aid in their understanding of the Big Idea.
   - Describe the key features of Maya kingdoms.
   - Explain Maya beliefs and achievements.
   - Identify reasons for the decline of the Maya.

3. **Whole Group Close/Reflect** Have students create a résumé listing the accomplishments of the Maya civilization.

▷ **ONLINE DOCUMENT-BASED INVESTIGATION**

People and Empires in the Americas
Popul Vuh is the fifth of seven historical sources that students will analyze in the People and Empires in the Americas module. The *Popul Vuh* records the history of the Quiché, a Maya people who lived in Guatemala. Students can use the audio feature to listen to a passage of a Maya creation story.

▷ **ONLINE GRAPHIC ORGANIZER**

Maya Kings and Cities
As students read the lesson, have them use the graphic organizer to take notes. Students can review their graphic organizer notes at the end of the lesson to answer the following question:

Summarize What were the major characteristics of Maya civilization? *urban centers; religiosity; calendars; codices/writing; city-states*

▷ **ONLINE LESSON FLIP CARDS**

Review Key Terms and People
Students can use the flip cards in the Lesson Review at any time to review the lesson's key terms and people: *Tikal, Pacal, glyph, codex,* and *Popul Vuh.*

Mesoamerican Civilizations, 200 BC–AD 1521

Have students explore the map and answer the associated questions.

Region What other civilization areas were eventually incorporated into the Aztec area? *Teotihuacán and Toltec*

In print edition, see map of same title.

1. **Region** Which civilization occupied the Yucatán Peninsula? *Maya*
2. **Region** What other civilization areas were eventually incorporated into the Aztec area? *Teotihuacán and Toltec*

Image with Hotspots: Maya Carvings

Have students explore the image using the interactive hotspots.

Analyze Sources What does this tone panel reveal about the Maya? *that the Maya believed in an afterlife and that they wanted their rulers to be strong and supported*

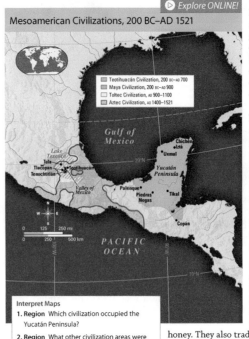

▷ *Explore ONLINE!*

Mesoamerican Civilizations, 200 BC–AD 1521

- ▨ Teotihuacán Civilization, 200 BC–AD 700
- ▨ Maya Civilization, 200 BC–AD 900
- ▨ Toltec Civilization, AD 900–1100
- ▨ Aztec Civilization, AD 1400–1521

Gulf of Mexico

Lake Texcoco
Tula
Tlacopan
Tenochtitlán
Teotihuacán

Valley of Mexico

Palenque
Piedras Negas

Chichén Itzá
Uxmal

Yucatán Peninsula

Tikal

Copán

PACIFIC OCEAN

N
0   125   250 mi
0   250   500 km

Interpret Maps
1. **Region** Which civilization occupied the Yucatán Peninsula?
2. **Region** What other civilization areas were eventually incorporated into the Aztec area?

Inscriptions, where he was laid to rest. Many other Maya cities featured giant pyramids, temples, palaces, and elaborate stone carvings dedicated to the gods and to important rulers. Tens of thousands of people lived in residential areas around the bustling city center.

Archaeologists have identified at least 50 major Maya sites, all with monumental architecture. For example, the Temple IV pyramid at Tikal stretched 212 feet into the jungle sky. In addition to temples and pyramids, each Maya city featured a ball court. In this stone-sided playing field, the Maya played a game that had religious and political significance. The Maya believed the playing of this game would maintain the cycles of the sun and moon and bring life-giving rains.

Agriculture and Trade Support Cities Although the Maya city-states were independent of each other, they were linked through alliances and trade. Cities exchanged their local products such as salt, flint, feathers, shells, and honey. They also traded craft goods like cotton textiles and jade ornaments. While the Maya did not have a uniform currency, cacao (chocolate) beans sometimes served as one.

As in the rest of Mesoamerica, agriculture—particularly the growing of maize, beans, and squash—provided the basis for Maya life. For years, experts assumed that the Maya practiced slash-and-burn agriculture. This method involves farmers clearing the land by burning existing vegetation and planting crops in the ashes. Evidence now shows, however, that the Maya also developed more sophisticated methods, including planting on raised beds above swamps and on hillside terraces.

Kingdoms Built on Dynasties Successful farming methods led to the accumulation of wealth and the development of social classes. The noble class, which included priests and the leading warriors, occupied the top rung of Maya society. Below them came merchants and those with specialized knowledge, such as skilled artisans. Finally, at the bottom, came the peasant majority.

Comparing Civilizations

1. Have students study the information in the text about the Maya city-states.
2. Organize the class into groups of mixed abilities and have groups choose another early civilization they have studied to compare to the Maya.
3. Have groups make a Venn diagram comparing the two civilizations.
4. Invite groups to share their diagrams with the class.

Reading Check
Draw Conclusions
What does the ability
to construct complex
buildings reveal about
a society?

The Maya king sat at the top of this class structure. He was regarded as a holy figure, and his position was hereditary. When he died, he passed the throne on to his eldest son. Other sons of the ruler might expect to join the priesthood.

Religion Shapes Maya Life

Religion influenced most aspects of Maya life. The Maya believed in many gods, and they considered their rulers to be godlike. There were gods of corn, of death, of rain, and of war. Gods could be good or evil, and sometimes both. Gods also were associated with the four directions and with different colors: white for north, black for west, yellow for south, red for east, and green in the center. The Maya believed that each day was a living god whose behavior could be predicted with the help of a system of calendars. The Maya depicted their gods or rulers in art such as through carved statues and bowls, which were made of wood, stone, obsidian, or jade.

Religious Practices The Maya worshiped their gods in various ways. They prayed and made offerings of food, flowers, and incense. They also pierced and cut their bodies and offered their blood, believing that this would nourish the gods. Sometimes the Maya even carried out human sacrifice, usually of captured enemies. At Chichén Itzá, they threw captives into a deep sinkhole lake, called a *cenote* (say•NO•tay), along with gold, jade, and other offerings. The Maya believed that human sacrifice pleased the gods and kept the world in balance. Nevertheless, the Maya's use of sacrifice never reached the extremes of some other Mesoamerican peoples.

Math and Religion Maya religious beliefs also led to the development of the calendar, mathematics, and astronomy. The Maya believed that time was a burden carried on the back of a god. At the end of a day, month, or year, one god would lay the burden down and another would pick it up. A day would be lucky or unlucky, depending on the nature of the god, so it was very important to have an accurate calendar to know which god was in charge of the day.

The Maya developed a 260-day religious calendar, which consisted of thirteen 20-day months. A second 365-day solar calendar consisted of eighteen 20-day months, with a separate period of 5 days at the end. The two calendars were linked together like meshed gears so that any given day could be identified in both cycles. The calendar helped identify the best times to plant crops, attack enemies, and crown new rulers.

The Maya based their calendar on careful observation of the planets, sun, and moon. Highly skilled Maya astronomers and mathematicians calculated the solar year at 365.2420 days. This is only .0002 of a day short of the figure generally accepted today! The Maya astronomers were able to attain such great precision by using a math system that included the concept of zero. The Maya used a shell symbol for zero, dots for the numbers one to four, and a bar for five. The Maya number system was a base-20 system. They used the numerical system primarily for calendar and astronomical work.

Stone panel carved by Maya artists, 8th century BC.

Objectives

You may wish to discuss the following questions with students to help them frame the content as they read.

- How might the belief that each day was a living god affect the daily life of the Maya? *Possible answer: may have chosen to perform specific rituals and tasks on certain days*

- How might the information in the Maya codices be misleading? *Possible answer: Information in the surviving codices may have been minor compared to that in the codices that were destroyed.*

More About . . .

Base Value Explain that the use of numeric symbols implies a *base* value. In a number used in a base 10, or *decimal*, systems (which students use), each place value to the left is equal to 10 times the place value to the right. In the base 20, or *vigesimal* system (used by the Maya), each place value to the left is equal to 20 times the place value to the right. Note that these systems may have originated from the number of digits possessed by humans (10 fingers, or 20 fingers and toes).

Maya Books Most Maya books were burned in the 16th century by Spanish priests, who regarded them as objects of pagan ritual. One priest, Friar Diego de Landa (1524–1579), described how the books appeared to the Spanish priests to contain nothing that did not appear to be a "lie of the devil" and how the priests burned all of the books to the dismay of the Maya. Three remaining codices are kept in museums in Paris, Madrid, and Dresden.

READING CHECK

Draw Conclusions What does the ability to construct complex buildings reveal about a society? *Workers had to be available for more than raising food and had to be highly organized and skilled in the construction of larger buildings.*

Outline Information on Maya Religions

1. Explain that an outline can be used to help recognize main idea and details. Review how to make an outline with students.

2. Have students reread "Religion Shapes Maya Life."

3. Ask students to create an outline for the passage. Encourage them to be consistent in their use of symbols (such as Roman and Arabic numerals) and to pay attention to how these establish a hierarchy of information.

Objectives

You may wish to discuss the following questions with students to help them frame the content as they read.

- What explanations would you consider if you had to investigate the Maya decline? *Possible answers: war, civil war, disease, famine, migrations*

- Would invaders, such as the Toltec, adopt Maya culture? *Possible answer: depends on whether the Toltec could understand the Maya language.*

More About . . .

Maya Decline One theory about the decline of the Maya is that it was caused by a 100-year drought. Researchers have examined sediment layers in the Blue Hole Cave in the Caribbean. By looking at the amount of minerals in the sediments, scientists are able to determine that the area suffered a severe drought from about AD 800 to 900. This natural drought may have been made worse by the Maya practice of slash-and-burn agriculture. This would make the drought worse because cleared lands absorb less radiation from the sun. That means less water is evaporated, causing less clouds and less rainfall. Deforestation also causes more erosion and soil depletion. Since plants need water and soil to thrive, crops would have failed. People would have starved or moved to other areas looking for food.

READING CHECK

Make Inferences How are math, astronomy, and calendars related? *Calendars are based on astronomical observations and are recorded in mathematical terms.*

A detail from the Maya *Codex Troano*

Reading Check
Make Inferences
How are math, astronomy, and calendars related?

Written Language Preserves History The Maya also developed the most advanced writing system in the ancient Americas. Maya writing consisted of about 800 hieroglyphic symbols, or **glyphs** (glihfs). Some of these glyphs stood for whole words, and others represented syllables. The Maya used their writing system to record important historical events, carving their glyphs in stone or recording them in a bark-paper book known as a **codex** (KOH•dehks). Only three of these ancient books have survived.

Other original books telling of Maya history and customs do exist, however. Maya peoples wrote down their history after the arrival of the Spanish. The most famous of these books, the *Popol Vuh* (POH•pohl Voo), recounts the Highland Maya's version of the story of creation. "Before the world was created, Calm and Silence were the great kings that ruled," reads the first sentence in the book. "Nothing existed, there was nothing."

Mysterious Maya Decline

The remarkable history of the Maya ended in mystery. Unlike the Han dynasty and the Roman Empire, evidence does not show that social unrest caused the Mayan Empire to end. Yet, like the Han dynasty and Roman Empire, the Mayan Empire did face invaders. In the late 800s, the Maya suddenly abandoned many of their cities. Invaders from the north, the Toltec, moved into the lands occupied by the Maya. These warlike peoples from central Mexico changed the culture. The high civilization of Maya cities like Tikal and Copán disappeared.

No one knows exactly why this happened, though experts offer several overlapping theories. By the 700s, warfare had broken out among the various Maya city-states. Increased warfare disrupted trade and produced

---

DOCUMENT-BASED INVESTIGATION Historical Source

The *Popul Vuh*

"Then let the emptiness fill! they said. Let the water weave its way downward so the earth can show its face! Let the light break on the ridges, let the sky fill up with the yellow light of dawn! Let our glory be a man walking on a path through the trees! "Earth!" the Creators called. They called only once, and it was there, from a mist, from a cloud of dust, the mountains appeared instantly."

—From the *Popol Vuh*

Analyze Historical Sources
What beliefs did the Maya have about the creation of the earth?

▷ ONLINE DOCUMENT-BASED INVESTIGATION

Popul Vuh

The *Popul Vuh* records the history of the Quiché, a Maya people who lived in Guatemala. Students can play the audio to hear the passage read aloud.

Analyze Sources What beliefs did the Maya have about the creation of earth? *They thought that creators made earth. Then mountains and the sun appeared on their command.*

In print edition, see the Historical Source.

ADVANCED/GIFTED

The Decline of the Maya

1. Have students conduct further research into the decline of the Maya civilization.

2. Have students form a thesis about why the Maya civilization declined and build a case to support it. Tell students they may choose one of the explanations presented in the text, but they need to gather evidence to support their thesis.

3. Have students use software to make multimedia presentations to state their theses and show the evidence used to support them.

4. Allow students to share their presentations with the class. Tell them to be prepared to answer any questions their classmates may have.

Rise and Fall of the Maya		
Traits of Civilization	Strength Leading to Power	Weakness Leading to Decline
Religious beliefs and theocracy	United culture that is loyal to the king	Many physical and human resources funneled into religious activities
Independent city-states with their own power	Wealthy and prosperous urban centers	Frequent warfare occurs between city-states
Intensive agriculture	Production of more food feeds a larger population	Population growth creates need for more land

Interpret Charts
1. **Analyze Effects** Which trait aids in building a sense of loyalty to the ruler?
2. **Draw Conclusions** How can intensive agriculture be both a strength and a weakness?

economic hardship. In addition, population growth and overfarming may have damaged the environment, and this led to food shortages, famine, and disease. By the time the Spanish arrived in the early 1500s, the Maya were divided into small, weak city-states that gave little hint of their former glory.

As the Maya civilization faded, other peoples of Mesoamerica were growing in strength and sophistication. Like the Maya, these peoples would trace some of their ancestry to the Olmec. Eventually, these people would dominate the Valley of Mexico and lands beyond it, as you will learn in Lesson 6.

Reading Check
Analyze Causes
Why did the Maya civilization decline?

Lesson 5 Assessment

1. **Organize Information** Use the web diagram to describe the characteristics of Maya civilization.

How are the characteristics of Maya civilization like those of a typical civilization?

2. **Key Terms and People** For each key term or person in the lesson, write a sentence explaining its significance.
3. **Evaluate** What was the basis of Maya life?
4. **Contrast** What three explanations have been given for the collapse of the Maya civilization, and how were they different from those of the Roman Empire and Han dynasty?
5. **Analyze Effects** Why was trade important to the Maya civilization?
6. **Draw Conclusions** How important do you think the development of advanced mathematics was in the creation of the Maya calendar, and why was it important to Mayan religion?

▶ **ONLINE INTERACTIVE CHART**

Rise and Fall of the Maya

Have students explore the chart and answer the associated questions.

Interpret Charts Which trait aids in building a sense of loyalty to the ruler? *religious beliefs and theocracy*

In print edition, see table of same title.

1. **Analyze Effects** Which trait aids in building a sense of loyalty to the ruler? *religious beliefs and theocracy*
2. **Draw Conclusions** How can intensive agriculture be both a strength and a weakness? *can feed a large population but can result in overused soil*

READING CHECK
Analyze Causes Why did the Maya civilization decline? *warfare among Maya city-states; invasions by neighboring peoples; population growth and overfarming*

Print Assessment

1. **Organize Information** Use the web diagram to describe the characteristics of Maya civilization. How are the characteristics of Maya civilization like those of a typical civilization? *Possible answer: urban centers; religiosity; calendars; codices—Maya science was unusually advanced.*
2. **Key Terms and People** For each key term or person in the lesson, write a sentence explaining its significance. *Explanations of the lesson's key terms can be found on the following pages: Tikal, Pacal, p. 509; glyphs, codex, Popol Vuh, p. 512.*
3. **Evaluate** What was the basis of Maya life? *agriculture, particularly the growing of maize, beans, and squash*
4. **Contrast** What three explanations have been given for the collapse of the Maya civilization, and how were they different from those of the Roman Empire and Han dynasty? *warfare among Maya city-states; warfare with other peoples; food shortages, famine, and disease resulting from population growth and overfarming; Unlike the Roman Empire and Han dynasty, social unrest does not seem to be part of the Maya decline.*
5. **Analyze Effects** Why was trade important to the Maya civilization? *helped unify independent city-states*

People and Empires in the Americas 513

Print Assessment (continued)

6. **Draw Conclusions** How important do you think the development of advanced mathematics was in the creation of the Maya calendar, and why was it important to Mayan religion? *Advanced mathematics was indispensable for recording celestial movements over time, handling large numbers, and calculating solar and lunar years with precision. The Mayan religion was tied into their calendar.*

▷ Online Assessment

1. Why was the game played in the ball court of particular significance to the ancient Maya peoples?
   - ○ They believed it helped bring rain.
   - ○ They believed it gave the king power.
   - ○ They believed it helped keep them safe from enemies.
   - ○ They believed it gave them more natural resources from the earth.

   Alternate Question *Select the answer choice from the drop-down list to complete the sentence correctly.*
   The ancient Maya played a ball game in a stone-sided playing field. They believed that this game helped [*bring rain* ⇕].

2. Why was the development of a calendar significant to worshipers of the Maya religion?
   - ○ It helped them know what god was in charge.
   - ○ It helped them know when to offer sacrifices.
   - ○ It helped them know what weather each day would have.
   - ○ It helped them know when to give their burdens to their gods.

   Alternate Question *Select the answer choice from the drop-down list to complete the sentence correctly.*
   The Maya believed that [*a different god was in charge every day* ⇕], which led to the necessity of developing a reliable calendar system.

3. What are **two** reasons that experts believe the Maya civilization declined into small, weak city-states?
   - ○ warfare
   - ○ drought
   - ○ population growth
   - ○ overthrow of the king
   - ○ arrival of Spanish explorers
   - ○ destruction of holy temples

   Alternate Question *Select the answer choice from the drop-down list to complete the sentence correctly.*
   Experts believe that several factors likely led to the decline of the Maya civilization. [*Warfare* ⇕] disrupted trade and produced an economic hardship. Increased population growth also led to food shortages, famine, and disease.

4. **Elaborate** What did experts originally believe about Mayan agricultural practices, and how have those beliefs changed over time?
   They originally believed that the Maya used slash-and-burn agriculture, which involved burning the existing vegetation and planting crops in the ashes. However, evidence now shows that the Maya also developed more sophisticated methods that included the planting of crops on raised beds above swamps and on hillside terraces.

5. **Draw Conclusions** What evidence shows that the Maya were a highly developed civilization? Use specific examples from the text to support your answer.
   The Maya were highly developed because of their advanced calendar system, their use of mathematics, and their glyph form of writing. The calendar system was developed because of a careful observation of the planets, sun, and moon. They were very close in their calculation of a solar year—only .0002 of a day shorter than the figure that is accepted today. Their mathematic system was one factor that allowed them to be so precise in those astronomical calculations. They included the use of the concept of zero, which was an advanced way of thinking for the time. They also had a highly developed form of writing that used 800 hieroglyphic symbols. They recorded historical events and customs on bark-paper books. One of the most famous is the Popol Vuh, which tells the story of the creation of the world.

6. **Draw Conclusions** How might have the Maya have retained their strong civilizations instead of declining into small, weak city-states?
   They could have avoided warfare, which was one thing that experts believed disrupted their trade and economy. They could have also not overfarmed their land, which could have prevented damage to their environment. They could have also figured out methods of keeping their population growth in check, which (along with improved farming methods) would have helped prevent food shortages, famine, and disease.

ADDITIONAL LESSON CONTENT

COLLABORATIVE LEARNING

Maya City-State Poster

1. Organize the class into four groups. Assign each group a Maya city-state to research, such as Tikal, Palenque, Copán, or Calakmul.

2. Have each group research and create a poster showcasing information about the city-state. Posters should include information about economics, art and architecture, and government.

3. Have each group show their posters to the class.

4. Allow time for the groups to discuss and compare and contrast the information about the different Maya city-states.

History Through Art

Maya Architecture Ask students to carefully examine the Copán stele. Then have them write a brief paragraph that describes the style of the Maya stone carver. Encourage students to contrast the style with other carvings with which they are familiar—the work of Greek artists, for example.

1. **Make Inferences** What does the size and ornamentation of Maya architecture indicate about their society? *Possible answer: Given that many of the structures were heavily decorated and appear to have had religious uses, it seems that the Maya were a deeply religious society and that their architecture was a way of expressing their faith.*

2. **Compare and Contrast** What are some examples of large-scale architecture in the United States? What do they indicate about our culture? *Possible answers: Skyscrapers—They indicate a focus on business. Monuments (such as the Washington Monument and Mount Rushmore)—They indicate a concern for our history and the individuals who shaped that history. Mansions—They indicate an interest in expressing personal wealth. Churches, synagogues, and mosques—Like the Maya structures, large religious buildings today are mean to awe and inspire believers.*

Maya Architecture

Mayan architects created beautiful and monumental structures. The buildings are artistic in structure, as well as in ornamentation. The style and complexity of the ornamentation varies by region, but narrative, ceremonial, and celestial themes are common. Archaeologists and tourists alike are still awed by Maya architecture.

These large structures seem to be designed for ceremonial or religious purposes and dominate the landscapes of the cities. The most recognizable structures are the pyramids, but there is much more to the artful Maya architecture.

▲ **DETAILING**
One characteristic of Maya architecture is the exterior and interior ornamental detailing. This two-headed jaguar throne was found at Uxmal. It represents the jaguar god of the underworld, one of the many Maya gods. An ancient Maya manuscript lists over 160 gods.

▼ **STELE**
Another form of Maya art was the stele (STEE·lee), which is an inscribed or carved marker that is often used to mark special dates or as a building marker. This stele is in the Maya city of Copán and is part of a series of finely carved commemorative steles in the great plaza. The 13th king is represented on most of the steles in ceremonial clothing.

BALL COURT ▲

Ball courts were a feature of ancient Maya cities. The games held deep religious significance, and the same artistic detail is found in the ball courts as in other religious structures. The court shown here is at Chichén Itzá in modern Mexico. It is 545 feet long and 223 feet wide, and it is the largest in the Americas. The ornate hoop is 20 feet off the ground.

The exact rules and method of scoring the game are unknown. However, inscriptions indicate that players could not use their hands or feet to move a solid rubber ball, and that members of the losing team might be sacrificed by beheading.

◄ PYRAMID

Archaeologists have found pyramids at many Maya cities. Pyramids were religious structures and, as in Egypt, could be used as tombs. The pyramid shown here is known as Temple I in the Maya city of Tikal. It is the tomb of Ha Sawa Chaan K'awil, a Tikal ruler. The pyramid is about 160 feet tall. Another pyramid in the city is 212 feet tall. In fact, the Tikal pyramids were the tallest structures in the Americas until 1903, when the Flatiron Building was built in New York City.

Critical Thinking

1. **Make Inferences** What does the size and ornamentation of Maya architecture indicate about their society?

2. **Compare and Contrast** What are some examples of large-scale architecture in the United States? What do they indicate about our culture?

The Aztecs Control Central Mexico

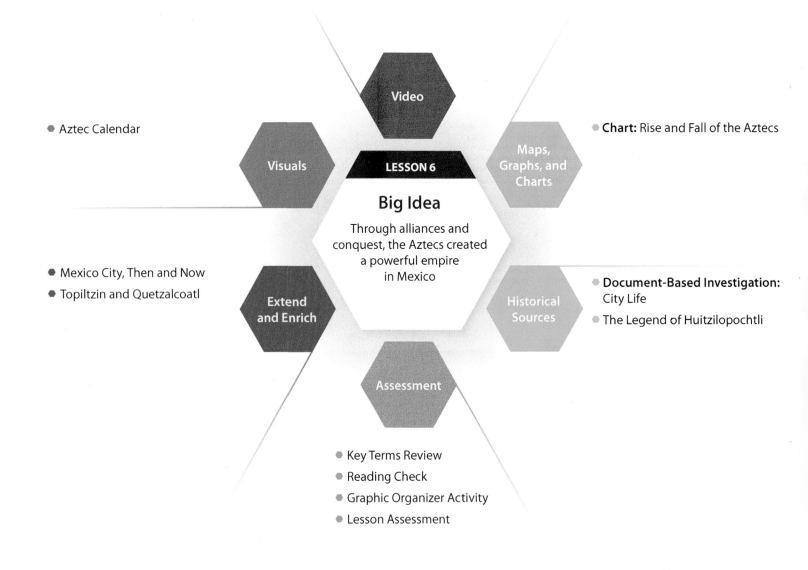

Video

Maps, Graphs, and Charts

● **Chart:** Rise and Fall of the Aztecs

● Aztec Calendar

Visuals

LESSON 6

Big Idea

Through alliances and conquest, the Aztecs created a powerful empire in Mexico

Historical Sources

● **Document-Based Investigation:** City Life

● The Legend of Huitzilopochtli

● Mexico City, Then and Now
● Topiltzin and Quetzalcoatl

Extend and Enrich

Assessment

● Key Terms Review
● Reading Check
● Graphic Organizer Activity
● Lesson Assessment

Mexico City, Then and Now

Digital Table Students will conduct research to add information to a table and then create a digital version of the table that includes audio and images. The activity walks students through preparing, creating, reviewing, and proofreading their tables.

	Tenochtitlán	Mexico City
Area	5.4 square miles	571 square miles
Population	200,000 (Spanish arrival)	20.1 million (2010 Census Bureau)
Population Density	About 27,000 people per square mile	285,500 people per square mile
Capital	Aztec Empire	Mexico
Founded	c. 1325	1521
Government	Empire (emperor)	Federal Republic (president)

Topiltzin and Quetzalcoatl

Legend Students read about the legend of Topiltzin and Quetzalcoatl. They will then make a multimedia presentation showcasing the legend. Their presentations will also address what the legend suggests about the culture it came from.

Teach the Big Idea

1. **Whole Class Open/Introduction** Tell students they will learn about the magnificent Aztec city of Tenochtitlán. Ask students what U.S. cities could be considered among the great metropolises of modern civilization. *Possible answers: Washington, DC, for its monuments and its role as the center of government of a powerful nation; New York, Chicago, Los Angeles for their massive skyscrapers and their role as cultural and financial capitals*

2. **Direct Teach** Read students the Big Idea: *Through alliances and conquest, the Aztecs created a powerful empire in Mexico.* Review the following lesson objectives with students to aid in their understanding of the Big Idea.

   • Describe the Teotihuacán and Toltec cultures of the Valley of Mexico.

   • Describe Aztec society.

   • Describe the city of Tenochtitlán and Aztec urban planning.

   • Explain the importance of religion to the Aztecs.

   • Identify factors that led to the decline of the Aztecs.

3. **Whole Group Close/Reflect** Have students create a poster highlighting aspects of Aztec culture. Students should include text and images with captions on their posters.

▷ **ONLINE DOCUMENT-BASED INVESTIGATION**

People and Empires in the Americas

City Life is the sixth of seven historical sources that students will analyze in People and Empires in the Americas module. In the first excerpt, Hernando Cortés, the Spanish conqueror of Mexico, noted that the market at Tlatelolco was twice the size of the market at Salamanca, the Spanish city where he had attended university. In the second source, Bernal Díaz, one of Cortés's soldiers, describes a bustling urban center in the heart of Mexico. Students can use the audio feature to hear the passages read aloud.

DOCUMENT-BASED INVESTIGATION   HISTORICAL SOURCE

City Life

Hernando Cortés, the Spanish conqueror of Mexico, noted that the market at Tlatelolco was twice the size of the market at Salamanca, the Spanish city where he had attended university. In the second source, Bernal Díaz, one of Cortés's soldiers, describes a bustling urban center in the heart of Mexico.

The Aztecs Control Central Mexico

The Big Idea
Through alliances and conquest, the Aztecs created a powerful empire in Mexico.

Why It Matters Now
This time period saw the origins of one of the 20th century's most populous cities, Mexico City.

Key Terms and People
obsidian
Quetzalcoatl
Triple Alliance
Montezuma I
Montezuma II

This wall hanging is a replica of the Aztec sun stone.

Setting the Stage

While the Maya were developing their civilization to the south, other high cultures were evolving in central Mexico. Some of the most important developments took place in and around the Valley of Mexico. This valley, where modern Mexico City is located, eventually became the site of the greatest empire of Mesoamerica, the Aztec. The Aztecs were preceded by two other important civilizations that traced their ancestry to the Olmec and Zapotec. You learned about the Olmec and Zapotec in Lesson 2.

The Valley of Mexico

The Valley of Mexico, a mountain basin about 7,500 feet above sea level, served as the home base of several powerful cultures. The valley had several large, shallow lakes at its center, accessible resources, and fertile soil. These advantages attracted the people of Teotihuacán (tay•oh•tee•wah•KAHN) and the Toltecs. They settled in the valley and developed advanced civilizations that controlled much of the area.

An Early City-State The first major civilization of central Mexico was Teotihuacán, a city-state whose ruins lie just outside Mexico City. In the first century AD, villagers at this site began to plan and construct a monumental city even larger than Monte Albán, in Oaxaca.

At its peak in the sixth century, Teotihuacán had a population of between 150,000 and 200,000 people, making it one of the largest cities in the world at the time. The heart of the city was a central avenue lined with more than 20 pyramids dedicated to various gods. The biggest of these was the giant Pyramid of the Sun. This imposing building stood more than 200 feet tall and measured close to 3,000 feet around its base. The people of Teotihuacán lived in apartment-block buildings in the area around the central avenue.

COLLABORATIVE LEARNING

Aztec Verse

1. Organize the class into groups of mixed ability.

2. Have students write poems or song lyrics to tell how the Aztecs came to power, what their major achievements were, and what led to their decline.

3. Have volunteers recite their poems or perform their songs for the class.

ADVANCED/GIFTED STUDENTS

Design a Quetzalcoatl Mural

1. Have students research and read a story about Quetzalcoatl. Tell students that they will be designing a mural based on

the selection they read, so they should take notes on significant visual imagery in the passage.

2. Tell students they may illustrate part of the story or the story in its entirety. If wall space is not available for students to create their mural, have them create it on butcher paper. Encourage students to think carefully about the techniques they can use to visually express difficult elements of the story. For example, to show the importance of an event, students might place it in the center of the mural, paint it with bright colors, or increase its relative size.

Teotihuacán became the center of a thriving trade network that extended far into Central America. The city's most valuable trade item was **obsidian** (ahb•SIHD•ee•uhn), a green or black volcanic glass found in the Valley of Mexico and used to make razor-sharp weapons. There is no evidence that Teotihuacán conquered its neighbors or tried to create an empire. However, evidence of art styles and religious beliefs from Teotihuacán have been found throughout Mesoamerica.

After centuries of growth, the city abruptly declined. Historians believe this decline was due either to an invasion by outside forces or conflict among the city's ruling classes. Regardless of the causes, the city was virtually abandoned by 750. The vast ruins astonished later settlers in the area, who named the site Teotihuacán, which means "City of the Gods."

Quetzalcoatl was a god for many ancient Mexican civilizations.

Reading Check
Make Inferences
Why might the followers of the war god rebel against Topiltzin?

Toltecs Take Over After the fall of Teotihuacán, no single culture dominated central Mexico for decades. Then around 900, a new people—the Toltecs—rose to power. For the next three centuries, the Toltecs ruled over the heart of Mexico from their capital at Tula. Like other Mesoamericans, they built pyramids and temples. They also carved tall pillars in the shape of armed warriors.

In fact, the Toltecs were an extremely warlike people whose empire was based on conquest. They worshiped a fierce war god who demanded blood and human sacrifice from his followers. Sometime after 1000, a Toltec ruler named Topiltzin (toh•PEELT•zeen) tried to change the Toltec religion. He called on the Toltec people to end the practice of human sacrifice. He also encouraged them to worship a different god, **Quetzalcoatl** (keht•sahl•koh•AHT•uhl), or the Feathered Serpent. Followers of the war god rebelled, however, forcing Topiltzin and his followers into exile on the Yucatán peninsula. There, they greatly influenced late Mayan culture. After Topiltzin's exile, Toltec power began to decline. By the early 1200s, their reign over the Valley of Mexico had ended.

In time, Topiltzin and Quetzalcoatl became one in the legends of the people of the Valley of Mexico. According to these legends, after his exile from Tula, the god traveled east, crossing the sea on a raft of snakes. He would return one day, bringing a new reign of light and peace. The story of Quetzalcoatl would come back to haunt the greatest empire of Mexico, the Aztecs.

Objectives

You may wish to discuss the following questions with students to help them frame the content as they read.

- Might Teotihuacán have had a defense industry? *Possible answer: It is likely that an industry developed based on the valuable trade item obsidian, used to make weapons.*

- What might inspire a ruler to try to change a state religion? *Possible answer: because of a change in belief or in an attempt to weaken the power of political foes*

More About . . .

Quetzalcoatl The god Quetzalcoatl was a combination of a snake and the brightly colored quetzal bird, which is found throughout the forests of Central and South America. The bird's three-foot-long emerald green tail feathers were highly valued by the Maya and Aztecs. Today, the quetzal appears on the coat of arms of Guatemala. Also, the currency of the country is called the quetzal.

▷ ONLINE GRAPHIC ORGANIZER

The Aztecs Control Central Mexico

As students read the lesson, have them use the graphic organizer to take notes. Students can review their graphic organizer notes at the end of the lesson to answer the following question.

Summarize How did the Aztecs expand their empire so quickly? *through conquest, tribute, and the Triple Alliance*

Rise and Fall of the Aztec Empire
↓
↓

READING CHECK

Make Inferences Why might the followers of the war god rebel against Topiltzin? *They did not wish to worship a different god; perhaps they feared the wrath of the war god if they did not worship him.*

Model Teotihuacán

1. Organize the class into three groups of mixed abilities.

2. Each group will work together to research images of the central avenue of Teotihuacán.

3. Have each group work together to create a three-dimensional model of the central avenue of Teotihuacán. Explain that they can only use readily available materials to build their models.

4. Tell groups to label the city features on their models.

5. Allow groups time to view each others' models. Have them compare the materials they used and the way they constructed their models.

▷ LESSON FLIP CARDS

Review Key Terms and People

Students can use the flip cards in the Lesson Review at any time to review the lesson's key terms and people: *obsidian, Quetzalcoatl, Triple Alliance, Montezuma I,* and *Montezuma II.*

Objectives

You may wish to discuss the following questions with students to help them frame the content as they read.

- Why might stories and myths about origins be important to a nation? *Possible answers: help establish a sense of belonging, a common identity, and a feeling of unity*

- What comparisons and contrasts can you make between the Triple Alliance and the Iroquois League? *Possible answers: Triple Alliance was formed for offense rather than defensive purposes; Iroquois League was a looser confederation, governed a smaller population.*

More About . . .

Aztec Explain that the Aztec name comes from *Aztlán* ("White Land" or "Place of the Herons"), the Aztecs' mythical place of origin in the north. The Aztecs' earlier name for themselves, *Mexica*, gave rise to the country name Mexico.

Aztec Ruins One of the world's largest cities, Mexico City is built on the ruins of Tenochtitlán. Although the lake that surrounded the Aztec capital is gone, many of the ruins of Aztec civilization remain. Most of these ruins lie buried beneath city streets. On February 21, 1978, electric company workers in Mexico City broke through a thick layer of concrete on a city street and uncovered an enormous piece of carved rock. It was a statue of the Aztec moon goddess. The location of the accidental find proved to be the site of the Great Temple of Tenochtitlán, the most sacred Aztec shrine. The Great Temple and a few other Aztec sites in Mexico City have since been excavated and rebuilt.

▶ ONLINE HISTORICAL SOURCE

The Legend of Huitzilopochtli

Invite students to read the excerpt and answer the associated question.

In print edition, see Historical Source titled *An Aztec Legend.*

Analyze Sources Based on what you read from the legend, what geographic feature would be in close proximity to Tenochtitlán? *water source or lake*

HISTORICAL SOURCE

The Legend of Huitzilopochtli
These words capture part of the Aztec legend of Huitzilopochtli, whom they believed was their patron god.

The Pyramid of the Sun dominates Teotihuacán's main highway, the Avenue of the Dead.

The Aztec Empire

The Aztecs arrived in the Valley of Mexico around AD 1200. The valley contained a number of small city-states that had survived the collapse of Toltec rule. The Aztecs, who were then called the Mexica, were a poor, nomadic people from the harsh deserts of northern Mexico. Fierce and ambitious, they soon adapted to local ways, finding work as soldiers-for-hire to local rulers.

According to one of the Aztec legends, the god of the sun and warfare, Huitzilopochtli (wee•tsee•loh•POHCH•tlee), told them to found a city of their own. He said to look for a place where an eagle perched on a cactus, holding a snake in its mouth.

Historical Source

An Aztec Legend

These words capture part of the Aztec legend of Huitzilopochtli.

A statue of an Aztec eagle warrior

"*The place where the eagle screams, where he spreads his wings; the place where he feeds, where the fish jump, where the serpents coil up and hiss! This shall be Mexico Tenochtitlán and many things shall happen!*"

—*Crónica Mexicayotl*

Analyze Historical Sources
Based on what you read from the legend, what geographic feature would be in close proximity to Tenochtitlán?

518 Module 13

STRUGGLING READERS

Illustrate the Aztec Social Order

1. Have students reread "Nobles Rule Aztec Society." Ask them to take notes about Aztec social groups.

2. Encourage students to use a dictionary to understand words such as *artisan* and *elite*. Explain that *class* and *noble* are multiple-meaning words that have different meaning depending on their context.

3. Have students draw a pyramid with the most powerful group on the top and the least powerful group at the bottom.

4. Tell students to write a caption for their pyramids.

5. Allow students to share their completed pyramids with the class.

They found such a place on a small island in Lake Texcoco, at the center of the valley. There, in 1325, they founded their city, which they named Tenochtitlán (teh•noch•tee•TLAHN).

Aztecs Grow Stronger Over the years, the Aztecs gradually increased in strength and number. In 1428, they joined with two other city-states—Texcoco and Tlacopan—to form the **Triple Alliance**. This alliance became the leading power in the Valley of Mexico and soon gained control over neighboring regions. By the early 1500s, they controlled a vast empire that covered some 80,000 square miles stretching from central Mexico to the Atlantic and Pacific coasts and south into Oaxaca. This empire was divided into 38 provinces. Its population may have been between 5 and 15 million people.

The Aztecs based their power on military conquest and the tribute they gained from their conquered subjects. The Aztecs generally exercised loose control over the empire, often letting local rulers govern their own regions. They did demand tribute, however, in the form of gold, maize, cacao beans, cotton, jade, and other products. If local rulers failed to pay tribute or offered any other kind of resistance, the Aztecs responded brutally. They destroyed the rebellious villages and captured or slaughtered the inhabitants.

Nobles Rule Aztec Society At the height of the Aztec Empire, military leaders held great power in Aztec society. Along with government officials and priests, these military leaders made up the noble class. Many nobles owned vast estates, which they ruled over like lords, living a life of great wealth and luxury.

There were two other broad classes in Aztec society, commoners and enslaved persons. Commoners included merchants, artisans, soldiers, and farmers who owned their own land. The merchants formed a special type of elite. They often traveled widely, acting as spies for the emperor and gaining great wealth for themselves. The lowest class, enslaved persons, were captives who did many different jobs.

The emperor sat atop the Aztec social pyramid. Although he sometimes consulted with top generals or officials, his power was absolute. The emperor lived in a magnificent palace, surrounded by servants and his wives. Visitors—even nobles—entered his presence in bare feet and cast their eyes down so as not to look at him.

Reading Check
Compare
How were the Aztecs' methods of controlling the empire like those of other empires you have read about?

Global Patterns

Warriors and Animal Symbols

Some of the highest-ranking Aztec leaders were eagle warriors. In battle, they wore eagle costumes in honor of the sun god, Huitzilopochtli, who often took the form of an eagle.

The use of animal symbols by warriors was a widespread practice in ancient times. The eagle was a favorite among Roman soldiers because they thought it symbolized victory. In many cultures, warriors adopted an animal so that they would inherit the animal's qualities. Celtic fighters, for example, wore boars' heads on their helmets so that they, like the boar, would be strong and fearless. Similarly, many African warriors adopted the lion for its fighting ferocity.

People and Empires in the Americas **519**

COLLABORATIVE LEARNING

Interview the Aztecs

1. Review with students the different Aztec social classes.

2. Organize students into groups of five or six to create a short television talk show about people of the Aztec Empire. One student in each group should be the host and prepare questions to ask people of various social classes about their lives and what they think of the Aztec Empire. The other students should represent the people of the different social classes and should prepare to answer the host's questions about their particular class.

3. Have students rehearse and perform their talk shows for the class

Objectives

You may wish to discuss the following questions with students to help them frame the content as they read.

- Ask students how Tenochtitlán's planners envisioned the city. *Possible answer: as the commercial, religious, and political center of the Aztec empire*

- Ask students what nonfood items vendors might have sold at Tlatelolco. *Possible answers: cookware, religious objects, clothing, animals, weapons, medicine*

More About . . .

Planned and Organic Cities Explain to students that a "planned city" is usually contrasted with an "organic city." A planned city is more or less completely designed and laid out before being built. An organic city grows gradually, developing in response to internal and external pressures—economic and political forces, for example.

▷ **ONLINE DOCUMENT-BASED INVESTIGATION**

City Life

In the first excerpt, Hernando Cortés, the Spanish conqueror of Mexico, noted that the market at Tlatelolco was twice the size of the market at Salamanca, the Spanish city where he had attended university. In the second source, Bernal Díaz, one of Cortés's soldiers, describes a bustling urban center in the heart of Mexico. Students can play the audio to hear the passages read aloud.

Analyze Sources How do the descriptions by Cortés and Díaz of city life in the Aztec Empire differ? Are they both credible sources? Explain. *Cortés's is very straightforward and states the facts. Díaz's is full of wonder and surprise. Yes, even though they have different perspectives they can both be viewed as credible sources.*

READING CHECK

Draw Conclusions How strong do you think the economy of the Aztec Empire was, based on the description of Tenochtitlán? Explain your response. *The Aztec economy was strong because Tenochtitlán was thriving and the market brought many different people and goods to the empire.*

Tenochtitlán: A Planned City

By the early 1500s, Tenochtitlán had become an extraordinary urban center. Much of the building up of the city and some of its growth were achieved under **Montezuma I** (mahn•tih•ZOO•muh). With a population of between 200,000 and 400,000 people, it was larger than London or any other European capital of the time. Tenochtitlán remained on its original island site. To connect the island to the mainland, Aztec engineers built three raised roads, called causeways, over the water and marshland. Other smaller cities ringed the lake, creating a dense concentration of people in the Valley of Mexico.

Streets and broad avenues connected the city center with outlying residential districts. The canals that intersected with these roadways allowed canoes to bring people directly into the city center. Canoes also brought goods from the farthest reaches of the empire to the economic heart of the city, the huge market of Tlatelolco (tlah•tehl•AWL•koh). Visitors to the market also found a great deal of local agricultural produce on display, including avocados, beans, chili peppers, corn, squash, and tomatoes. Most of the fruits and vegetables sold at the market were grown on *chinampas*, farm plots built on the marshy fringes of the lake. These plots, sometimes called floating gardens, were extremely productive, providing the food needed for a huge urban population.

At the center of the city was a massive walled complex filled with palaces, temples, and government buildings. The main structure in the complex was the Great Temple. This giant pyramid with twin temples at the top, one dedicated to the sun god and the other to the rain god, served as the center of Aztec religious life.

Reading Check
Draw Conclusions
How strong do you
think the economy
of the Aztec Empire
was, based on the
descriptions of
Tenochtitlán? Explain
your response.

Religion Rules Aztec Life

Religion played a major role in Aztec society. Tenochtitlán contained hundreds of temples and religious structures dedicated to the approximately 1,000 gods that the Aztecs worshiped. The Aztecs adopted many of these gods, and religious practices related to them, from other Mesoamerican peoples. For example, the Aztecs worshiped the Toltec god Quetzalcoatl in many forms. They saw him as the god of learning and books, the god of the wind, and a symbol of death and rebirth. The Aztecs pictured Quetzalcoatl not only as a feathered serpent, but also as a pale-skinned man with a beard.

Religious Practices Aztec religious practices centered on elaborate public ceremonies designed to communicate with the gods and win their favor. At these ceremonies, priests made offerings to the gods and presented ritual dramas, songs, and dances featuring masked performers. The Aztec ceremonial calendar was full of religious festivals, which varied according to the god being honored.

Sacrifices for the Sun God The most important rituals involved a sun god, Huitzilopochtli. According to Aztec belief, Huitzilopochtli made the sun rise every day. When the sun set, he had to battle the forces of evil to

---

ENGLISH LANGUAGE LEARNERS

Pair Images and Words in a Vocabulary Booklet

1. Have students reread "Tenochtitlán: A Planned City."

2. Ask students to make a list of at least 20 words and phrases from the passage as they read. They will later use the words and phrases to create an image booklet. A list might include the following words and phrases: *Tenochtitlán, London, island, causeway, marshland, valley, canal, canoes, market, avocado, bean, chili pepper, corn, squash, tomato, chinampa, Great Temple, sun god,* and *rain god.*

3. When students are done compiling their lists, have them use the library or the Internet to locate and copy images for words on their list.

4. Have students organize the images in a booklet.

5. Have children write a caption for each image that says something about the image and its relation to Tenochtitlán. For example, a caption for the avocado might read, "People at the Aztec market Tlatelolco sold the avocado, an edible fruit."

The Market at Tlatelolco

Hernando Cortés, the Spanish conqueror of Mexico, noted that the market at Tlatelolco was twice the size of the market at Salamanca, the Spanish city where he had attended university.

> "... [T]here are daily more than sixty thousand souls, buying and selling, and where are found all the kinds of merchandise produced in these countries, including food products, jewels of gold and silver, lead, brass, copper, zinc, stone, bones, shells, and feathers. ... Everything is sold by a kind of measure, and, until now, we have not seen anything sold by weight. There is in this, square a very large building, like a Court of Justice, where there are always ten or twelve persons, sitting as judges, and delivering their decisions upon all cases which arise in the markets."
>
> —Hernando Cortés,
> from *Hernando Cortés his five letters of Relation to the Emperor Charles V, Volume I*

Tenochtitlán—a Bustling City

Bernal Díaz, one of Cortés's soldiers, was amazed to find a bustling urban center in the heart of Mexico.

> "When we saw all those cities and villages built in the water, and other great towns on dry land, and that straight and level causeway leading to Mexico, we were astounded. These great towns and cues [pyramids] and buildings rising from the water, all made of stone, seemed like an enchanted vision. ... Indeed, some of our soldiers asked whether it was not all a dream."
>
> —Bernal Díaz,
> *The Conquest of New Spain*

Analyze Historical Sources
How do the descriptions by Cortés and Díaz of city life in the Aztec Empire differ? Are they both credible sources? Explain.

get to the next day. To make sure that he was strong enough for this ordeal, he needed the nourishment of human blood. Without regular offerings of human blood, Huitzilopochtli would be too weak to fight. The sun would not rise, the world would be plunged into darkness, and all life would perish. For this reason, Aztec priests practiced human sacrifice on a massive scale. Each year, thousands of victims were led to the altar atop the Great Temple, where priests carved out their hearts using obsidian knives.

Sacrificial victims included enslaved persons, criminals, and people offered as tribute by conquered provinces. Prisoners of war, however, were

The Market at Tlatelolco/ Tenochtitlán—A Bustling City

Invite students to read the excerpts and answer the associated question.

Analyze Historical Sources How do the descriptions by Cortés and Diaz of city life in the Aztec Empire differ? Are they both credible sources? Explain. *Cortés's is very straightforward and states the facts. Diaz's is full of wonder and surprise. Yes, even though they have different perspectives they can both be viewed as credible sources.*

Below Level Review with students the reasons why the Aztecs worshipped Quetzalcoatl. Remind them that at ceremonies, dramas, songs, and dances were often performed to communicate with the gods. Have students write a song about Quetzalcoatl.

At Level Have students read the text and describe how the Aztecs saw the god Quetzalcoatl. Have them write a drama depicting a myth involving Quetzalcoatl.

Above Level Ask students to research myths about Quetzalcoatl. They should use the information they find to write a drama that includes songs and a dance about Quetzalcoatl.

Objectives

You may wish to discuss the following questions with students to help them frame the content as they read.

- Why was religion such a central feature of Aztec life? *Possible answer: allowed the Aztecs to feel that they had some understanding of, and control over, their world*

- How might ordinary Aztecs have felt about the blood sacrifices to Huitzilopochtli? *Possible answers: Since they were used to it, it seemed like a normal event. Some must have been horrified but were afraid to protest.*

More About . . .

Aztec Gods and Worlds According to the Aztecs, there had been four worlds that existed before the present one. These worlds, also known as "suns," were each destroyed by a different catastrophe sent by the gods when humankind became too opinionated.

The first world was called Nahui-Ocelotl, or "Four-Jaguar." It came to an end when humankind was destroyed by jaguars, which was a symbol of the creator god Tezcatlipoca.

The second world was called Nahui-Ehécatl, or "Four-Wind." It came to an end when Quetzalcóatl (disguised as the wind god Ehécatl) sent a magical hurricane that turned humankind into monkeys.

The third world was Nahui-Quiahuitl, or "Four-Rain." It was ruled by the god of thunder, Tlaloc, and came to an end in a rain of fire. Only birds survived.

The fourth world was Nahui-Atl, or "Four Water." It ended in a flood.

According to the Aztecs, the age they lived in was is the fifth one and was created by Quetzalcoatl. The Aztecs called this world Nahui-Ollin, or "Four-Earthquake" and predicted that this world would end in a massive earthquake.

▷ ONLINE INTERACTIVE VISUALS

Image Carousel: Aztec Calendar

Have students navigate through the carousel and note similarities and differences among the images or identify a unifying theme.

People and Empires in the Americas   521

Objectives

You may wish to discuss the following questions with students to help them frame the content as they read.

- Why might a rapidly growing population such as Tenochtitlán's be a source of political problems? *Possible answers: If population growth outstrips available resources, there is usually a drop in living standards, causing unrest.*

- What drawbacks might Montezuma II have expected by cutting the number of Aztec officials? *Possible answers: disorder, less information*

More About . . .

Montezuma II and Hernando Cortés When Montezuma II succeeded his uncle to become the ruler of the Aztec Empire in 1502, the empire stretched from what is present-day Mexico to Honduras and Nicaragua. During his reign, civil unrest became more frequent. Spanish conquistador Hernando Cortés arrived during this time. Although Montezuma tried to make a deal with Cortés, it was too late—Cortés had already made alliances with the tribes unhappy with Aztec rule. Cortés believed that he would be safe from the Aztecs if he made Montezuma his prisoner. However, the Aztecs were angry that Montezuma had tried to make a deal with the Spanish and he had lost their respect. How exactly Montezuma died is unclear. According to the Spanish, the Aztecs attacked Montezuma when he tried to speak to them. The Aztecs, however, thought that the Spanish killed their emperor.

READING CHECK
Summarize Why did the Aztecs take so many war captives? *They were needed for sacrifice to the gods.*

This mural, in the National Palace in Mexico City, shows Quetzalcoatl in many forms.

Reading Check
Summarize
Why did the Aztecs take so many war captives?

the preferred victims. As a result, the priests required a steady supply of war captives. This in turn pushed the Aztec military to carry out new conquests. In fact, the Aztecs often went to war not to conquer new lands but simply to capture prisoners for sacrifice. They even adapted their battle tactics to ensure that they took their opponents alive.

Problems in the Aztec Empire

In 1502, a new ruler, **Montezuma II**, was crowned emperor. Under Montezuma II, the Aztec Empire began to weaken. For nearly a century, the Aztecs had been demanding tribute and sacrificial victims from the provinces under their control. Now, with the population of Tenochtitlán growing ever greater, Montezuma II called for even more tribute and sacrifice. A number of provinces rose up against Aztec oppression. This began a period of unrest and rebellion, which the military struggled to put down.

Over time, Montezuma II tried to lessen the pressure on the provinces. For example, he reduced the demand for tribute payment by cutting the number of officials in the Aztec government. But resentment continued to grow. Many Aztecs began to predict that terrible things were about to happen. They saw bad omens in every unusual occurrence—lightning striking

522 Module 13

Montezuma II and Hernando Cortés

1. Share with students information about Montezuma II and Hernando Cortés. Have them find additional information by using library or Internet sources.

2. Organize students into pairs and have them write a dramatic dialogue between Montezuma and Cortés in which the two men discuss their beliefs. Encourage students to think about how the political position of each man might influence what he says.

3. After students complete their dialogues, select pairs to perform their dialogue in front of the class.

4. Have other students in the class provide feedback. Remind students that feedback should be polite and constructive.

Rise and Fall of the Aztecs

Have students explore the chart and answer the associated questions.

Interpret Charts Which trait do you find repeated in the Maya and Aztec empires? *religious beliefs and theocracy*

In print edition, see chart of same title.

1. **Draw Conclusions** How was the tribute system both a strength and a weakness? *It could bring great wealth but also create resentment among the payers.*

2. **Clarifying** How are the army and religious beliefs linked in the Aztec Empire? *The army provides prisoners for the sacrifices to the gods.*

READING CHECK
Make Inferences Why would cutting the number of government officials reduce the need for tribute money? *They would not need to be paid.*

Print Assessment

1. **Organize Information** What steps did the Aztecs take to establish an extensive empire in such a relatively short period of time? *Possible answer: Teotihuacán, Toltec, nomadic Mexica, Triple Alliance, Aztec Empire; Aztecs adapted wisely.*

2. **Key Terms and People** For each key term or person in the lesson, write a sentence explaining its significance. *Explanations of the lesson's key terms can be found on the following pages: obsidian, Quetzalcoatl, p. 517; Triple Alliance, p. 519; Montezuma I, p. 520; Montezuma II, p. 522.*

3. **Evaluate** How did the Aztecs rule their empire, and do you think it was effective? *Possible answer: loosely, allowing local rulers to govern their own regions if they paid tribute; I think it wasn't effective because different leaders might have different ways of leading.*

4. **Find Main Ideas** On what was Teotihuacán's power and wealth based? *trade*

5. **Summarize** How were the Aztecs able to overcome the problems associated with Tenochtitlán's island location? *by building causeways to connect the island and mainland, cutting canals across the island, and converting marshes into floating gardens*

6. **Analyze Effects** How did the Aztecs' growing empire and need for victims for sacrifice lead to problems? *Demands for victims for sacrifice aroused hatred of the Aztecs among conquered peoples. In time, this hatred triggered rebellions.*

Rise and Fall of the Aztecs

Traits of Civilization	Strength Leading to Power	Weakness Leading to Decline
Religious beliefs and theocracy	United culture that is loyal to the emperor	Many physical and human resources funneled into religious activities
Powerful army	More land, power, and prisoners for religious sacrifices	Need for prisoners changes warfare style to less deadly and less aggressive
Empire of tribute states	Provides wealth and power and prisoners for religious sacrifice	Tribute states are rebellious and need to be controlled

Interpret Charts
1. **Draw Conclusions** How was the tribute system both a strength and a weakness?
2. **Clarifying** How are the army and religious beliefs linked in the Aztec Empire?

a temple in Tenochtitlán, or a partial eclipse of the sun, for example. The most worrying event, however, was the arrival of the Spanish. For many Aztecs, these fair-skinned, bearded strangers from across the sea brought to mind the legend of the return of Quetzalcoatl.

Further south in the high mountain valleys of the Andes, another empire was developing, one that would transcend the Aztec Empire in land area, power, and wealth. Like the Aztecs, the people of this Andean empire worshiped the sun and had large armies. However, the society they built was much different from that of the Aztecs, as you will see in Lesson 7.

Reading Check
Make Inferences
Why would cutting the number of government officials reduce the need for tribute money?

Lesson 6 Assessment

1. **Organize Information** What steps did the Aztecs take to establish an extensive empire in such a relatively short period of time?

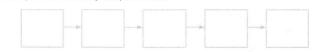

2. **Key Terms and People** For each key term or person in the lesson, write a sentence explaining its significance.
3. **Evaluate** How did the Aztecs rule their empire, and do you think it was effective?
4. **Find Main Ideas** On what was Teotihuacán's power and wealth based?

5. **Summarize** How were the Aztecs able to overcome the problems associated with Tenochtitlán's island location?
6. **Analyze Effects** How did the Aztecs' growing empire and need for victims for sacrifice lead to problems?

▷ Online Assessment

1. Why was Topiltzin forced into exile?
   - ○ He wanted to make razor-sharp weapons.
   - ○ He wanted to trade with the Maya people.
   - ◉ He wanted to change the Toltec people's religion.
   - ○ He wanted to build the largest pyramid in the Americas.

   Alternate Question *Select the answer choice from the drop-down list to complete the sentence correctly.*
   The Toltec people worshiped a god who demanded [*blood and human sacrifice* ⇕]. When a Toltec ruler named Topiltzin wanted to change the worship to a different god, the Toltec people became angry and forced Topiltzin into exile.

2. Why were the merchants considered a special type of elite in the Aztec society?
   - ○ They spoke a variety of languages.
   - ◉ They acted as spies for the emperor.
   - ○ They held many different types of jobs.
   - ○ They traded for weapons of war made from obsidian.

   Alternate Question *Select the answer choice from the drop-down list to complete the sentence correctly.*
   Since merchants traveled widely, they were able to [*spy for the emperor* ⇕], which gave them a special elite status in Aztec society.

3. How were the Aztecs able to provide food for their large urban population?
   - ○ They hunted for wild game.
   - ◉ They grew food on chinampas.
   - ○ They pilfered food from neighboring settlements.
   - ○ They went to war with farming communities nearby.

   Alternate Question *Select the answer choice from the drop-down list to complete the sentence correctly.*
   The Aztecs were able to provide enough food for their large urban population by building [*floating gardens* ⇕] on the marshy fringes of the lake.

4. What was the main purpose of the Aztecs' elaborate public ceremonies?
   - ○ to educate the youth
   - ○ to entertain the peasants
   - ◉ to win the favor of the gods
   - ○ to showcase the king's wealth

   Alternate Question *Select the answer choice from the drop-down list to complete the sentence correctly.*
   Aztec religious practices required elaborate public ceremonies that were designed to [*communicate with the gods* ⇕] and win their favor.

5. What began the period of unrest in the Aztec Empire under the reign of Montezuma II?
   - ○ Montezuma II wanted to build temples for different gods.
   - ◉ Montezuma II called for more tribute and human sacrifice.
   - ○ Montezuma II called for an increase in trade with Mesoamerica.
   - ○ Montezuma II wanted to implement religious practices of other regions.

   Alternate Question *Select the answer choice from the drop-down list to complete the sentence correctly.*
   When Montezuma II demanded that the provinces pay more tribute and supply him with a larger number of sacrificial victims, the [*people rose up in rebellion* ⇕].

6. **Draw Conclusions** What does the extensive trade of obsidian amongst the Teotihuacán people show about the Valley of Mexico in regard to the geography of the area and the culture of the people?

   Obsidian is a green or black volcanic glass that was used to make razor-sharp weapons. The fact that this was one of the most valuable trading items says that this culture was a warlike people or a people who hunted and needed weaponry for those purposes. Since this stone comes from volcanic glass, it says that there were volcanoes or ancient volcanoes in this area.

7. **Evaluate** What evidence supports the idea that the Aztec emperor was extremely powerful and demanded respect from his subjects?

   He lived in a magnificent palace that was filled with servants and wives. He sometimes consulted with his top generals and officials, but his power was absolute. Visitors who came to see him were required to come in bare feet and keep their eyes down so they didn't look directly at him.

8. **Elaborate** What was the economic heart of Tenochtitlán, and what would visitors have found there?

   The economic heart of Tenochtitlán was the market named Tlatelolco. This place was huge and sold a variety of agricultural products that were grown locally on the chinampas on the fringe of the lake. Visitors would have found such things as avocados, beans, chili peppers, corn, squash, and tomatoes at this market, which had all been brought in by canoe on the city's network of canals.

9. **Elaborate** Why was human sacrifice important to the Aztecs?

   They believed that their sun god Huitzilopochtli needed strength obtained by human blood in order to be properly nourished for his nightly battles with the forces of evil. If he was too weak to fight, then the sun would not rise the next day, the world would be plunged into darkness, and all life would perish. In order to prevent this from happening, many people had to be sacrificed daily on the top of the Great Temple.

10. **Evaluate** Why did the Aztecs believe that bad things were about to happen to them? Use examples from the text in your answer.

    They believed that bad things would happen to them because of several reasons. For one, they saw bad omens in nature like lightning striking the temple at Tenochtitlán and a partial eclipse of the sun. Then, the fair-skinned Spanish arrived, which resembled the legend of the return of Quetzalcoatl.

The Inca Create a Mountain Empire

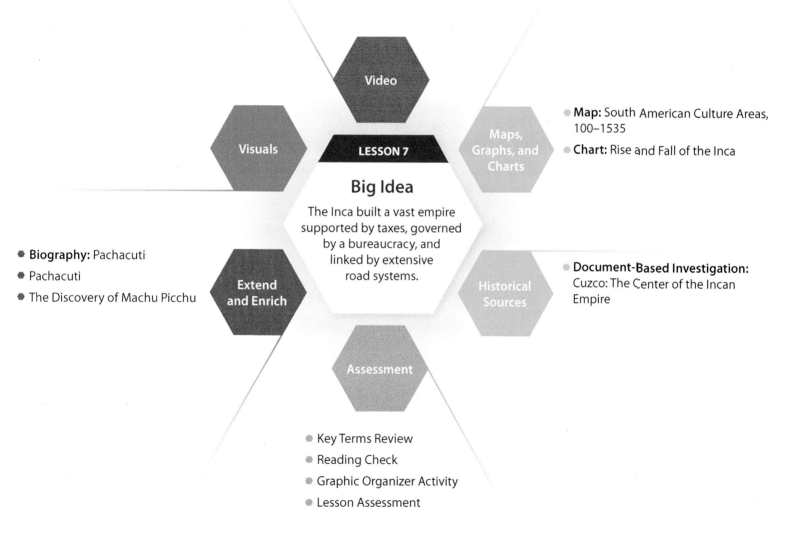

Video

Visuals

LESSON 7

Big Idea

The Inca built a vast empire supported by taxes, governed by a bureaucracy, and linked by extensive road systems.

Maps, Graphs, and Charts

- **Map:** South American Culture Areas, 100–1535
- **Chart:** Rise and Fall of the Inca

Historical Sources

- **Document-Based Investigation:** Cuzco: The Center of the Incan Empire

Extend and Enrich

- **Biography:** Pachacuti
- Pachacuti
- The Discovery of Machu Picchu

Assessment

- Key Terms Review
- Reading Check
- Graphic Organizer Activity
- Lesson Assessment

Pachacuti

Biography Students will read an article about Pachacuti, who became the Incan emperor in 1438. They will then prepare a list of interview questions to ask Pachacuti and role-play an interview with the Incan emperor. Students will record their interview.

The Discovery of Machu Picchu

Article Students will read about the discovery of Machu Picchu by Hiram Bingham, who discovered the ruins in 1911. They will then find a photograph of Machu Picchu and write a paragraph or create an interactive image with hotspots to describe the ruins.

The Inca Create a Mountain Empire

The Big Idea

The Inca built a vast empire supported by taxes, governed by a bureaucracy, and linked by extensive road systems.

Why It Matters Now

The Incan system of government was similar to some socialist governments in the 20th century.

Key Terms and People

Pachacuti
ayllu
mita
quipu

Setting the Stage

While the Aztecs ruled in the Valley of Mexico, another people—the Inca—created an equally powerful state in South America. From Cuzco, their capital in southern Peru, the Inca spread outward in all directions. They brought various Andean peoples under their control and built an empire that stretched from Ecuador in the north to Chile in the south. It was the largest empire ever seen in the Americas.

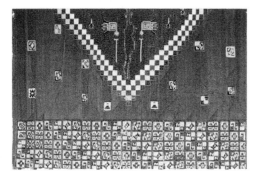

Incan textiles such as this one were a common form of art among early cultures in South America.

The Inca Build an Empire

Like the Aztecs, the Inca built their empire on cultural foundations thousands of years old. Ancient civilizations such as the Chavín, Moche, and Nazca had established a tradition of high culture in Peru. They were followed by the Huari and Tiahuanaco cultures of southern Peru and Bolivia. The Chimú, an impressive civilization of the 1300s based in the northern coastal region once controlled by the Moche, came next. The Inca would create an even more powerful state, however, extending their rule over the entire Andean region.

People and Empires in the Americas **525**

Teach the Big Idea

1. **Whole Class Open/Introduction** Tell students that they will read about a relay mail service developed by the Inca. Ask them if they know of any other relay mail services. *Possible answer: The Pony Express relayed mail between Missouri and California from 1860 to 1861.*

2. **Direct Teach** Read students the Big Idea: *The Inca built a vast empire supported by taxes, governed by a bureaucracy, and linked by extensive road systems.* Review the following lesson objectives with students to aid in their understanding of the Big Idea.

   • Trace the Incan rise to power.

   • Describe how Incan government created unity.

   • Describe Incan religion.

   • Describe discord in the Incan Empire.

3. **Whole Group Close/Reflect** Have students write a short essay comparing and contrasting the Inca civilization with that of the Maya or the Aztecs. Invite students to share their essays with the class.

▷ ONLINE DOCUMENT-BASED INVESTIGATION

People and Empires in the Americas

Cuzco: The Center of the Incan Empire is the seventh of seven historical sources that students will analyze in People and Empires in the Americas module. Cuzco served as the economic center of the Inca. It held an array of temples, plazas, and palaces. Students can click the audio button below the source to listen to a passage describing a conquistador's impression of the city.

Objectives

You may wish to discuss the following questions with students to help them frame the content as they read.

• Was Incan diplomacy effective? *Possible answer: Yes—diplomacy won loyalty of the people and helped ensure longevity of the empire.*

• How important are individual rulers in determining the fate of states? *Possible answer: depends on the strength or weakness of the state's institutions; if these are strong, decisions of an individual have limited impact.*

More About . . .

Inca Expansion According to Inca oral history, the Inca were founded by Manco Capac. With his three brothers and four sisters, Qhapag led their people from the caves at Paqari-tampu on a journey to find land that would support them. No one knows how long this journey took, but eventually they arrived at the land near Cuzco. They attacked the people living there and claimed the land as their own. The second and third emperors did not expand the empire, but the fourth emperor, Mayta Capac, began to conquer other lands. This practice continued slowly until Pachacuti became emperor and expanded the Incan Empire throughout Peru and beyond.

▷ ONLINE GRAPHIC ORGANIZER

The Inca Create a Mountain Empire

As students read the lesson, have them use the graphic organizer to take notes. Students can review their graphic organizer notes at the end of the lesson to answer the following question:

Summarize How did the Inca unify the people they conquered? *small administrative units, roads, mail system, schooling, trade, official language, taxation*

▷ ONLINE LESSON FLIP CARDS

Review Key Terms and People

Students can use the flip cards in the Lesson Review at any time to review the lesson's key terms and people: *Pachacuti, ayllu, mita,* and *quipu.*

BIOGRAPHY

Pachacuti

Have students read the biography of Pachacuti, the Inca leader who ruled from 1438 to 1471, and with the help of his son, Topa Inca, extended the Incan Empire through the use of military force and political alliances.

READING CHECK

Evaluate Do you think that Pachacuti's methods for unifying conquered lands was effective? Explain. *Yes, because people were allowed to keep their own customs and language and that gave them a sense of identity.*

Incan Beginnings The Inca originally lived in a high plateau of the Andes. After wandering the highlands for years, the Inca finally settled on fertile lands in the Valley of Cuzco. By the 1200s, they had established their own small kingdom in the valley.

During this early period, the Inca developed traditions and beliefs that helped launch and unify their empire. One of these traditions was the belief that the Incan ruler was descended from the sun god, Inti, who would bring prosperity and greatness to the Incan state. Only men from one of 11 noble lineages believed to be descendants of the sun god could be selected as Incan leaders.

Pachacuti Builds an Empire At first the Incan kingdom grew slowly. In 1438, however, a powerful and ambitious ruler, **Pachacuti** (pah•chah•KOO•tee), took the throne. Under his leadership, the Inca conquered all of Peru and then moved into neighboring lands. By 1500, the Inca ruled an empire that stretched 2,500 miles along the western coast of South America. The Inca called this empire "Land of the Four Quarters." It included about 80 provinces and was home to as many as 16 million people.

Pachacuti and his successors accomplished this feat of conquest through a combination of diplomacy and military force. The Inca had a powerful military but used force only when necessary. They were also clever diplomats. Before attacking, they typically offered enemy states an honorable surrender. They would allow them to keep their own customs and rulers in exchange for loyalty to the Incan state. Because of this treatment, many states gave up without resisting. Even when force was used, the Inca took a similar approach. Once an area was defeated, they made every effort to gain the loyalty of the newly conquered people.

Reading Check
Evaluate
Do you think
that Pachacuti's
methods for unifying
conquered lands were
effective? Explain.

— BIOGRAPHY —

Pachacuti
(c. 1391–c. 1473)

As the second son of the Incan ruler Viracocha, Pachacuti did not expect to succeed to the throne. However, when Cuzco was attacked in 1438, Viracocha and Pachacuti's older brother fled the city. Pachacuti stayed and drove off the attackers. He then proclaimed himself the new Incan ruler.

Pachacuti, whose name means "World Transformer" or "Earthshaker," ruled for 33 years. During that time, he drew up the plans for the rebuilding of Cuzco and established the Incan system of government.

ADVANCED/GIFTED

Journal Entries of the Conquered

1. Have students review the information in the text about how the Inca conquered and controlled other peoples.

2. Have students write a series of seven journal entries from the point of view of a member of a tribe that has been conquered by the Inca. Suggest that students bring out positive and negative aspects of Inca rule.

3. Have volunteers share their entries with the class.

Incan Government Creates Unity

To control the huge empire, the rulers divided their territory and its people into manageable units governed by a central bureaucracy. The Inca created an efficient economic system to support the empire and an extensive road system to tie it together. They also imposed a single official language, Quechua (KEHCH•wuh), and founded schools to teach Incan ways. Certain social groups were identified by officially dictated patterns on clothing. All of these actions were calculated to unify the variety of people controlled by the Inca.

Incan Cities Show Government Presence To exercise control over their empire, the Inca built many cities in conquered areas. The architecture of government buildings was the same all over the empire, making the presence of the government apparent. As in Rome, all roads led to the capital, Cuzco. The heart of the Incan empire, Cuzco was a splendid city of temples, plazas, and palaces. "Cuzco was grand and stately," wrote Cieza de León. "It had fine streets, . . . and the houses were built of solid stones, beautifully joined." Like the Romans, the Inca were masterful engineers and stonemasons. Though they had no iron tools and did not use the wheel, Incan builders carved and transported huge blocks of stone, fitting them together perfectly without mortar. Many Incan walls still stand in Cuzco today, undisturbed by the region's frequent earthquakes.

Incan Government The Incan state exercised almost total control over economic and social life. It controlled most economic activity, regulating the production and distribution of goods. Unlike the Maya and the Aztecs, the Inca allowed little private commerce or trade. Yet the Inca network of internal trade routes helped unite and strengthen the vast empire.

The Incan social system was based on an age-old form of community cooperation—the ayllu (EYE•loo). The **ayllu**, or extended family group, undertook tasks too big for a single family. These tasks included building irrigation canals or cutting agricultural terraces into steep hillsides. The ayllu also stored food and other supplies to distribute among members during hard times.

The Inca incorporated the ayllu structure into a governing system based on the decimal system. They divided families into groups of 10, 100, 1,000, and 10,000. A chief led each group. He was part of a chain of command. That chain stretched from the community and regional levels all the way to Cuzco, where the Incan ruler and his council of state held court. In general, local administration was left in the hands of local rulers, and villages were allowed to continue their traditional ways. If a community resisted Incan control, however, the Inca might relocate the whole group to a different territory. The resisters would be placed under the control of rulers appointed by the government in Cuzco.

The main demand the Incan state placed on its subjects was for tribute, usually in the form of labor. The labor tribute was known as **mita** (MEE•tuh). It required all able-bodied citizens to work for the state a certain number of days every year. Mita workers might labor on state

Objectives

You may wish to discuss the following questions with students to help them frame the content as they read.

- Incan rulers created schools to teach "Incan ways." Does modern education also serve such a purpose? *Possible answers: No—today's schools focus on practical knowledge. Yes—some might argue that aspects of modern education, such as the Pledge of Allegiance, serve a similar function.*

- Does the U.S. government demand a *mita*, or labor tribute, from its citizens? *Possible answer: No, but some people may argue that taxes serve a similar purpose.*

More About . . .

Incan Relay Messengers The *chasqui* system worked like a modern relay race. A runner would "hand off" a memorized message or package to another runner waiting at a way station. That runner would sprint to the next station along the road. The stations were placed about every mile or so along the main roads, which covered thousands of miles. In this way, a message could travel 150 miles a day. The distance from Cuzco to the coast could be covered in just three days. A century later, the same journey took the Spanish 12 days on horseback! The chasquis who traveled the Incan roads served in 15-day shifts. The job was part of their *mita*.

▷ ONLINE DOCUMENT-BASED INVESTIGATION

Cuzco: The Center of the Incan Empire

Cuzco served as the economic center of the Inca. It held an array of temples, plazas, and palaces. Students can play the audio to listen to a passage describing a conquistador's impression of the city.

Analyze Sources How do you think Cieza de León felt about Inca accomplishments? *He was impressed by their appearance and sophistication.*

DOCUMENT-BASED INVESTIGATION   HISTORICAL SOURCE

Cuzco: The Center of the Incan Empire

Like Tenochtitlán was to the Aztecs, Cuzco served as a center of the Inca. It held an array of temples, plazas, palaces, and was the economic heart of the empire. Spanish conquistadors such as Cieza de León also observed the splendor and offerings of the city.

Incan Record-Keeping

1. Have students review the text "Government Record-Keeping."

2. Organize students into pairs and give each pair lengths of colored strings. (Be sure to indicate in some way the tops of the strings.)

3. Display a color key that identifies which strings are to be used for specific types of accounting. For example: red—student's age; yellow—the time they usually wake up on weekends (rounded to the nearest hour); blue—the average number of hours per week they watch television.

4. Have students use the string to produce their record. Provide students with a way to indicate 10 of something—for example, using special types of knots or coloring the knots with a marker toward the top of the string.

5. When students have finished, have them exchange strings and record their partner's information in a notebook. They can check each other's notes for accuracy.

6. Lead a class discussion after the activity to discuss what problems such a system may have presented to the Inca.

South American Culture Areas, 100–1535

Have students explore the map and answer the associated question.

Place The lands of which earlier South American cultures were included in the Incan Empire? *Moche and Chimú*

In print edition, see map of same title.

1. **Place** The lands of which earlier South American cultures were included in the Incan Empire? *Moche and Chimú*

2. **Human-Environment Interaction** Look at the shape and terrain of the Incan Empire. What problems related to geography might occur in controlling the land? *Distances and terrain make communication and transportation difficult.*

farmlands, produce craft goods for state warehouses, or help with public works projects. Later, the Spanish adopted the mita labor practice but changed it to a system of forced labor.

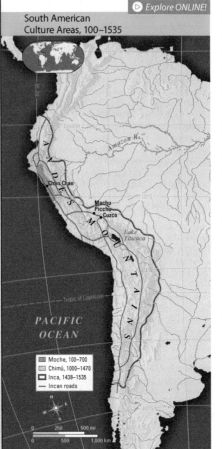

South American Culture Areas, 100–1535

▷ *Explore ONLINE!*

Interpret Maps

1. **Place** The lands of which earlier South American cultures were included in the Incan Empire?

2. **Human–Environment Interaction** Look at the shape and terrain of the Incan Empire. What problems related to geography might occur in controlling the land?

528   Module 13

Historians have compared the Incan system to a type of socialism or a modern welfare state. Citizens were expected to work for the state and were cared for in return. For example, the aged and disabled were often supported by the state. The state also made sure that the people did not go hungry when there were bad harvests. Freeze-dried potatoes, called *chuño*, were stored in huge government warehouses for distribution in times of food shortages.

Public Works Projects The Inca had an ambitious public works program. The most spectacular project was the Incan road system. A marvel of engineering, this road system symbolized the power of the Incan state. The 14,000-mile-long network of roads and bridges spanned the empire, traversing rugged mountains and harsh deserts. The roads ranged from paved stone to simple paths. Along the roads, the Inca built guesthouses to provide shelter for weary travelers. A system of runners, known as *chasquis* (SHAH•skeys), traveled these roads as a kind of postal service, carrying messages from one end of the empire to the other. The road system also allowed the easy movement of troops to bring control to areas of the empire where trouble might be brewing.

Government Record-Keeping Despite the sophistication of many aspects of Incan life, the Inca never developed a writing system. History and literature were memorized as part of an oral tradition. For numerical information, the Inca created an accounting device known as **quipu**, a set of knotted strings that could be used to record data. The knots and their position on the string indicated numbers. They also used a device that functioned almost like a calculator that may have made division and using fractions possible. Additionally, the colors of the strings represented different categories of information important to the government. For example, red strings were used to count warriors; yellow strings

---

STRUGGLING READERS

Examine How the Inca Created Political Unity

1. Have students review the text "Incan Government Creates Unity." Point out how the heading reveals the topic that the passage explores.

2. As they read, have students create a numbered list, with each entry describing a way in which the Incan government promoted unity in the empire.

3. Ask students to write each entry as a complete sentence, and encourage them to use their own words.

COLLABORATIVE LEARNING

Incan Road Plans

1. Before the lesson, obtain topographical maps, preferably of hilly or mountainous regions with rivers or streams.

2. Instruct students how to read topographical maps. Tell them that lines close together indicate a steep area and lines far apart indicate a flatter area.

3. Organize students into mixed-ability pairs. Give each pair a photocopy of a topographical map.

4. Have each pair plan an Incan road that will cross the map, roughly from north to south or from east to west. Students should consider geographic elements to plan logical routes. Have students create a legend and show the location of rope bridges and steps.

Reading Check
Make Inferences
Of all of the methods
used to create unity,
which do you think
would be most
successful? Why?

were used to count gold. However, the meanings of the colors changed depending on the general purpose of the quipu.

Some historians believe that the Inca also developed an elaborate calendar system with two types of calendars, one for night and one for day. They were used primarily for religious purposes. Like the calendars of the Maya and the Aztecs, the two calendars provided information about the gods whom the Inca believed ruled the day and time.

Religion Supports the State

As with the Aztecs, religion was important to the Inca and helped reinforce the power of the state. The Inca worshiped fewer gods than the Aztecs. The Inca focused on key nature spirits such as the moon, the stars, and thunder. In the balance of nature, the Inca saw patterns for the way humans should relate to each other and to the earth. The primary Incan god was a creator god called Viracocha. Next in importance was the sun god, Inti. Because the Incan ruler was considered a descendant of Inti, sun worship amounted to worship of the king.

Machu Picchu lies some 8,000 feet above sea level on a ridge between two mountain peaks.

Objectives

You may wish to discuss the following questions with students to help them frame the content as they read.

- Do you think that the Incan people really believed that the king was a descendant of the sun god? *Yes—They were taught that from an early age. No—some people were probably skeptical.*

- In what ways can architecture be used, as it was in the Incan Empire, to serve the state? *Possible answers: show presence of authority, reinforce the state's values through religious imagery, show wealth and power, promote civic pride.*

More About . . .

The Temple of the Sun Cuzco's Temple of the Sun, or Coricancha, was mostly destroyed by the Spaniards, though a portion remains in a church built on the site. At one point, according to a Spanish conquistador, 700 gold plates were stripped from the walls. When melted down, each plate produced more than four pounds of gold. The total value is more than $11 million in today's currency.

> **READING CHECK**
> **Make Inferences** Of all of the methods used to create unity, which do you think would be most successful? Why? *Probably the strongest answer is language. It allowed easy communication throughout the empire.*

ADVANCED/GIFTED STUDENTS

The Life of Hiram Bingham

1. Have students use the library or Internet to research the life of Hiram Bingham, who discovered the ruins of Machu Picchu.

2. After students have finished their research, have them write a biographical magazine article about Bingham. Provide students with examples of biographical stories in magazines to gather ideas for their feature.

3. Encourage students to write in a lively style and to organize their material so that they will attract and keep readers' attention. Also suggest that they include visuals, such as photographs of Bingham and Machu Picchu, maps, and timelines.

Rise and Fall of the Inca

Have students explore the chart and answer the associated question.

Interpret Charts Which trait do you find repeated in the Maya and Aztec empires? *religious beliefs and theocracy*

In print edition, see chart of same title.

Form and Support Opinions In your opinion, which of the three traits leading to power was the most valuable? Briefly discuss your reasons. *Possible answer: road system unifying the kingdom*

Compare Which trait did you find repeated in the Maya and Aztec empires? *religious beliefs and theocracy*

Traits of Civilization	Strength Leading to Power	Weakness Leading to Decline
Religious beliefs and theocracy	United culture that is loyal to the emperor	Many physical and human resources funneled into religious activities
Major road systems	An interconnected empire that is easier to control	Enemy could also use roads to move troops
Type of welfare state with huge bureaucracy	Able to care for entire population during good and bad times	People struggled to care for themselves with the elimination of the welfare state

READING CHECK
Compare and Contrast How were the Inca and Aztecs alike? *Religion, theocracy, and a united culture that was loyal to the emperor played an important role in their civilizations.*

Rise and Fall of the Inca

Traits of Civilization	Strength Leading to Power	Weakness Leading to Decline
Religious beliefs and theocracy	United culture that is loyal to the emperor	Many physical and human resources funneled into religious activities
Major road systems	An interconnected empire that is easier to control	Enemy could also use roads to move troops
Type of welfare state with huge bureaucracy	Able to care for all people during good and bad times	People struggled to care for themselves with the elimination of the welfare state

Interpret Charts
1. **Form and Support Opinions** In your opinion, which of the three traits leading to power was the most valuable? Briefly discuss your reasons.
2. **Compare** Which trait did you find repeated in the Maya and Aztec empires?

Religious Practices Incan priests led the sun-worship services, assisted by young women known as *mamakuna*, or "virgins of the sun." These women, all unmarried, were drafted by the Inca for a lifetime of religious service. The young women were trained in religious activities, as teachers, spinners, weavers, and beer makers. Young men, known as *yamacuna*, also served as full-time workers for the state and in religious activities. Sacrifice of llamas and exchange of goods were a part of the religious activities. The goods were distributed by the priests to the people as gifts from the gods.

Great Cities The Temple of the Sun in Cuzco was the most sacred of all Incan shrines. It was heavily decorated in gold, a metal the Inca referred to as "sweat of the sun." According to some sources, the temple even had a garden with plants and animals crafted entirely from gold and silver. In fact, gold was a common sight throughout Cuzco. The walls of several buildings had a covering of thin gold sheeting.

Although Cuzco was the religious capital of the Incan Empire, other Incan cities also may have served a ceremonial purpose. For example, Machu Picchu, excavated by Hiram Bingham in 1912, was isolated and mysterious. Like Cuzco, Machu Picchu also had a sun temple, public buildings, and a central plaza. Some sources suggest it was a religious center. Others think it was an estate of Pachacuti. Still others believe it was a retreat for Incan rulers or the nobility.

Reading Check
Compare and Contrast How were the Inca and Aztecs alike?

530 Module 13

Discord in the Empire

The Incan Empire reached the height of its glory in the early 1500s during the reign of Huayna Capac. Trouble was brewing, however. In the 1520s, Huayna Capac undertook a tour of Ecuador, a newly conquered area of the empire. In the city of Quito, he received a gift box. When he opened it, out flew butterflies and moths, considered an evil omen. A few weeks later, while still in Quito, Huayna Capac died of disease—probably smallpox.

After his death, the empire was split between his sons, Atahualpa (ah•tah•WAHL•pah) and Huascar (WAHS•kahr). Atahualpa received Ecuador, about one-fifth of the empire. The rest went to Huascar. At first, this system of dual emperors worked. Soon, however, Atahualpa laid claim to the whole of the empire. A bitter civil war followed. Atahualpa eventually won, but the war tore apart the empire. As you will learn, the Spanish arrived in the last days of this war. Taking advantage of Incan weakness, they would soon divide and conquer the empire.

Reading Check
Evaluate
Do you think that splitting the Incan Empire led to its fall? Explain

---

Lesson 7 Assessment

1. Organize Information Use the web diagram to show how the Inca unified the people they conquered.

Which of the Inca's methods were accepted by the conquered people?

2. Key Terms and People For each key term or person in the lesson, write a sentence explaining its significance.
3. Draw Conclusions How were the Inca able to conquer such a vast empire, and how did they create unity among diverse peoples in their empire?
4. Form Generalizations What role did the mita play in building the Incan Empire?
5. Analyze Motives Why do you think the Inca used the ayllu system as the basis for governing in the empire?
6. Compare and Contrast How were Incan and Aztec religious practices similar? How were they different?

COLLABORATIVE LEARNING

Timeline of the Incan Empire

1. Organize the class into groups of mixed abilities. Give each group butcher paper and markers.
2. Have students review information about the Inca. Encourage them to research more about Incan accomplishments in the library or on the Internet.
3. Have students make a timeline of major events that occurred under the Incan Empire. In addition to dates, have students include summaries of the events, images of the major events, and accomplishments of the Inca.

Objectives

You may wish to discuss the following questions with students to help them frame the content as they read.

- Are modern leaders subject to superstition? *As human beings, some modern leaders probably do have superstitions. As citizens, we hope that their superstitions are not part of their leadership.*

- What are the disadvantages of splitting an empire between two heirs? *The two heirs might fight each other for power and control.*

More About . . .

Incan Succession During the reign of Huayna Capac, Incan custom said that the throne would next pass to the sons of the emperor and his principal wife. If there were more than one such son, they would share power. However, Huayna Capac's principal wife had no children. In this situation, the emperor could ask the gods for guidance by sacrificing a llama and asking which of his sons should inherit the throne. Huayna Capac was aware that he was dying and asked a priest to perform the divination ceremony so he would know which of his sons to appoint. Huayna Capac died before the ceremony could be performed. A priest determined that the emperor's son Ninan Cuyochi should be the next emperor, but the young prince also died of smallpox. This left Ninan Cuyochi's two brothers in charge, which ultimately led to civil war.

READING CHECK

Evaluate Do you think that splitting the Incan Empire led to its fall? Explain. *Yes, because unity kept the empire together before it was split.*

Print Assessment

1. **Organize Information** Use the web diagram to show how the Inca unified the people they conquered. Which of the Inca's methods were accepted by the conquered people? *Possible answer: small administrative units, roads, mail system, schooling, trade, official language*
2. **Key Terms and People** For each key term or person in the lesson, write a sentence explaining its significance. *Explanations of the lesson's key terms can be found on the following pages: Pachacuti, p. 526; ayllu, mita, p. 527; quipu, p. 528.*

(continued)

ADDITIONAL LESSON CONTENT

COLLABORATIVE LEARNING

Aspects of Incan Culture

1. Organize the class into three groups. Assign each group a different aspect of Incan culture: military, religion, and government.

2. Have students create a digital slideshow about their aspect of Incan culture that includes text, images, and audio recordings. Presentations should explain how this aspect of Incan culture led to a strong Incan empire.

3. Have each group present its slideshow to the class.

Social History

Incan Mummies Ask students whether the attitudes and behaviors of the Inca toward the dead have any parallels today in the United States. *Possible answer: Students may mention Memorial Day or Mexican Americans' celebration of the Day of the Dead.* Ask students why might the Inca have buried people in mummy bundles. *Possible answer: Perhaps the Inca viewed the journey to the afterlife as another birth and were preparing the dead for rebirth by arranging their bodies inside womblike sacks.*

1. **Make Inferences** What do Incan mummification practices suggest about Incan culture? *Possible answers: Incan mummification practices suggest that religion was a major part of Incan society. The Incan practice of treating their ancestors as if they were still alive suggests that the dead were very much a part of the daily life of the living.*

2. **Form and Support Opinions** Why do you think mummification is not a common practice in the United States today? *Possible answers: Mummification is not a part of the major belief systems. Prevailing belief systems might view mummification as a violation of those beliefs. Mummification takes time and would probably be expensive. Most of the United States lacks a climate conducive to mummification.*

Incan Mummies

For the Inca, death was an important part of life. The Inca worshiped the spirits and the bodies of their ancestors. They believed in an afterlife, and tombs and the mummies they held were considered holy.

Like the Egyptians, the Inca embalmed their dead to preserve the body. The mummies were bundled with offerings of food, tools, and precious items to help them in the afterlife. These "mummy bundles" were then buried or put in an aboveground tomb to be worshiped. Mummies have been found from many different social classes, and, as you will read, not all of them died natural deaths.

ROYAL TREATMENT ▶
The mummies of Incan rulers were among the holiest objects of Incan religion. The mummies were actually treated as if they were still alive. They had servants, maintained ownership of their property, were consulted as oracles, and were taken to major festivals or to visit other mummies. The mummy shown at right in a 16th-century Spanish codex is being transported in the same manner as the living royalty.

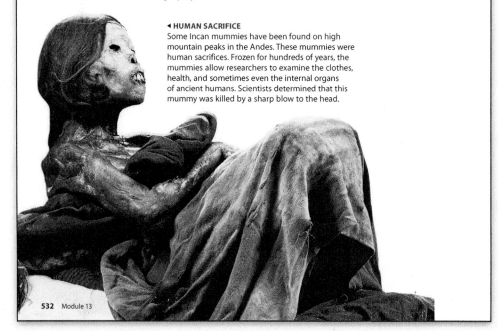

◀ HUMAN SACRIFICE
Some Incan mummies have been found on high mountain peaks in the Andes. These mummies were human sacrifices. Frozen for hundreds of years, the mummies allow researchers to examine the clothes, health, and sometimes even the internal organs of ancient humans. Scientists determined that this mummy was killed by a sharp blow to the head.

532 Module 13

MUMMY BUNDLES ▶

At a site known as Puruchuco, just outside of Lima, Peru, archaeologists discovered a huge Incan cemetery. Some of the mummies unearthed were wrapped in layers of cotton. The outside of the bundle might have a false head made of cloth like the one shown on the right. Inside the bundle were the mummy, religious offerings, and personal items. The illustration shown below re-creates the inside of an actual bundle that archaeologists unwrapped.

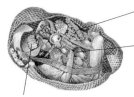

Corn, or maize, was the Inca's most important crop and is often found in Incan burials.

The Inca used gourds as bowls and containers. The gourds found in this bundle held food and cotton.

This man wears a feathered headdress that indicates high social standing.

▲ GIFTS FOR THE DEAD

The Inca sometimes placed mummies in aboveground tombs called *chullpas*. Descendants of the mummy would bring offerings of food and precious goods to honor their ancestor. This mummy is shown as it might have appeared in its tomb.

Critical Thinking
1. **Make Inferences** What do Incan mummification practices suggest about Incan culture?
2. **Form and Support Opinions** Why do you think mummification is not a common practice in the United States today?

AN INCAN GRAVEYARD

The Puruchuco graveyard lies beneath a shantytown in Peru called Tupac Amaru. In 1999, when archaeologists discovered the extent of the site, it was about to be bulldozed. Archaeologists began an emergency recovery effort.

- The remains of over 2,000 men, women, and children were recovered.
- The site may contain as many as 10,000 individuals.
- Some bundles contained up to seven bodies and weighed as much as 400 pounds.
- Between 50,000 and 60,000 artifacts were recovered.
- One of the mummy bundles became known as the "Cotton King." The mummy was wrapped in about 300 pounds of raw cotton.
- The Cotton King's bundle contained 70 artifacts, including food, pottery, animal skins, and sandals. Footwear was not common among the Inca, and sandals were a status symbol.

Print Assessment

Key Terms and People

For each term or name below, brief explain its connection to the early peoples and civilizations of the Americas.

Explanations of the module's key terms can be found on the following pages: Beringia, p. 485; Olmec, p. 490; Zapotec, p. 493; Chavín, p. 499; Moche, p. 501; Mississippian, Iroquois, p. 506; Montezuma I, p. 520; Montezuma II, p. 522, mita, p. 527

Main Ideas

The Earliest Americans

1. Why was corn an important crop to early peoples? *It was nourishing and flourished in the tropical climate.*

2. What were the main differences between hunter-gatherer societies and those based primarily on agriculture? *In a hunting society, people lived in small groups and had to move often to obtain food; in an agricultural society, people grew their own food and thus could live in settled, large communities.*

Early Mesoamerican Civilizations

3. How did the Olmec influence the Zapotec civilization? *Zapotec stone carvings resemble those of the Olmec. Zapotec sites, with their plazas, temples, and pyramids, show Olmec influences*

4. How did the Olmecs' location contribute to the development of their civilization? *abundant resources for making pottery, tools, and monuments; rivers provided transport and fertile land for farming*

Early Civilizations of the Andes

5. In what ways did the Chavín influence other peoples? *Later cultures copied their art styles and religious ideas.*

6. How did the Nazca and Moche develop rich farmland? *They created irrigation systems.*

North American Societies

7. Why were Native American societies in North America so diverse? *They developed in different environments.*

8. What were the three things that most Native Americans in North America had in common? *trade patterns, religious beliefs, social patterns*

Maya Kings and Cities

9. What role did religion play in Maya life? *Religion influenced most aspects of Maya life. The Maya believed in many gods—of corn, of death, of rain, of directions, and of war. To them, each day was a god whose behavior could be predicted with the help of calendars.*

10. What were the three major achievements of the Maya civilization? *solar calendar, advanced system of mathematics that included the concept of zero, writing system*

The Aztecs Control Central Mexico

11. How did the Aztecs build and control their empire? *built through alliances and conquest; controlled by demanding tribute and crushing rebellions*

Module 13 Assessment

Key Terms and People

For each term or name below, briefly explain its connection to the early peoples and civilizations of the Americas.

1. Beringia
2. Olmec
3. Zapotec
4. Chavín
5. Moche

6. Mississippian
7. Iroquois
8. Montezuma I
9. Montezuma II
10. mita

Main Ideas

Use your notes and the information in the module to answer the following questions.

The Earliest Americans

1. Why was corn an important crop to early peoples?
2. What were the main differences between hunter-gatherer societies and those based primarily on agriculture?

Early Mesoamerican Civilizations

3. How did the Olmec influence the Zapotec civilization?
4. How did the Olmecs' location contribute to the development of their civilization?

Early Civilizations of the Andes

5. In what ways did the Chavín influence other peoples?
6. How did the Nazca and Moche develop rich farmland?

North American Societies

7. Why were Native American societies in North America so diverse?
8. What were the three things that most Native Americans in North America had in common?

Maya Kings and Cities

9. What role did religion play in Maya life?
10. What were three major achievements of the Maya civilization?

The Aztecs Control Central Mexico

11. How did the Aztecs build and control their empire?
12. Why did the Aztecs sacrifice human beings to their gods?

The Inca Create a Mountain Empire

13. List three ways in which the Incan government involved itself in people's lives.
14. How did Incan religion reinforce the power of the state?

534   Module 13

▶ ONLINE DOCUMENT-BASED INVESTIGATION

People and Empires in the Americas

Have students complete and review all the DBI activities in **Part 1**.

Use this Informative/Explanatory Essay Rubric to score students' work in **Part 2**.

RUBRIC Students' essays should

- focus on the topic and support it with explanations and facts
- present information logically, clearly, and accurately
- cite at least three sources of relevant, informative text evidence from Part 1 in support of their topic
- be organized into a distinct introduction, a main body consisting of several paragraphs, and a conclusion that sums up the main points

Write an Explanatory Essay

Cultures and civilizations had been thriving for centuries in the Americas before European contact. Were Europeans surprised by what they found and whom they encountered in the Americas? Write an essay in which you synthesize the information you have examined. Be sure to cite specific evidence from at least three sources in your response.

Module 13 Assessment, continued

Critical Thinking

1. **Compare** In a sequence diagram, show how the early Americans' way of life developed through several stages.

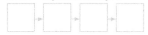

2. **Summarize** What environmental challenges did the first Americans face?

3. **Draw Conclusions** Why do you think the Olmec or Zapotec civilizations might have declined?

4. **Make Inferences** What geographic factors would have made interactions between early Mesoamerican and Andean civilizations difficult?

5. **Formulate Historical Questions** Study the information on the Mound Builders again. What questions might you ask to gain a better understanding of these cultures?

6. **Compare and Contrast** Compare the religious beliefs of the Maya, the Aztecs, and the Inca. How were they similar? How were they different?

7. **Make Inferences** What can you infer about the values of the Inca from the fact that the government provided care for citizens who were aged or unable to care for themselves?

8. **Evaluate** The Maya, Aztecs, and Inca had very similar cultures but also were unique. Do you think that this statement is accurate? Consider their government, economy, art, and religion. Give reasons for your answer.

Engage with History

In this module you examined how killing a mammoth would help you survive and discussed the difficulties of living in a hunter-gatherer society. Now that you have read the module, discuss why the early Americans moved from a hunting to a farming existence. In what ways was food gathering easier in an agricultural society?

Focus on Writing

Write a three-paragraph essay comparing and contrasting American Indian civilizations in North, Central, and South America, such as the Maya, Aztecs, Inca, Pueblo, and Eastern Woodland peoples.

As you plan your essay, consider the following:

- government
- interactions with the environment
- economy
- social life

Multimedia Activity

Write a documentary film script about the Mayan, Aztec, and Incan civilizations, describing cultural patterns, the spread of American cultures, and political and economic structures. Compare and contrast these elements for each group. Provide a definition of *cultural pattern* in your script, and include examples of the following:

- cultural patterns among the Aztec, Maya, Inca, and other peoples of the Americas
- how American cultures spread
- ways in which their political and economic structures were similar and different

---

12. Why did the Aztecs sacrifice human beings to their gods? *The Aztecs believed the sun god Huitzilopochtli made the sun rise every day as long as he was nourished by human blood. Without offerings of blood, the sun would not rise, and all life would perish.*

The Inca Create a Mountain Empire

13. List three ways in which the Incan government involved itself in people's lives. *imposed one official language, founded schools to teach Incan ways, created structured communities, required tribute in the form of the labor, regulated production and distribution of goods, cared for the aged, provided food in times of poor harvest.*

14. How did Incan religion reinforce the power of the state? *The Incan ruler was considered a descendant of the sun god, Inti. Thus, worship of the sun god amounted to worship of the ruler and the state.*

Critical Thinking

1. **Compare** In a sequence diagram, show how the early Americans' way of life developed through several stages. *hunting, gathering, farming, creation of complex societies*

2. **Summarize** What environmental challenges did the first Americans face? *Olmec faced heavy rainfall that often caused severe flooding; Zapotec struggled to maintain an adequate water supply; those in Andes region faced rugged, dry mountain climate.*

3. **Draw Conclusions** Why do you think the Olmec or Zapotec civilizations might have declined? *invaders, civil war, drought*

4. **Make Inferences** What geographic factors would have made interactions between early Mesoamerican and Andean civilizations difficult? *distance, high mountain range*

5. **Formulate Historical Questions** Study the information on the Mound Builders again. What questions might you ask to gain a better understanding of these cultures? *What was the purpose of the mounds? Why were Hopewell mounds bigger than Adena mounds?*

6. **Compare and Contrast** Compare the religious beliefs of the Maya, the Aztecs, and the Inca. How were they similar? How were they different? *Similarities—believed gods ruled over every aspect of life; regarded rulers as divine; used prayer, ritual, and ceremonies. Differences—Maya and Aztecs believed that human sacrifice was necessary, while Inca did not.*

7. **Make Inferences** What can you infer about the values of the Inca from the fact that the government provided care for citizens who were aged or unable to care for themselves? *Inca valued their people at all stages of life and believed it was the state's responsibility to ensure well being.*

Essential Question ESSAY

How did early American civilizations influence future societies and cultures before the arrival of Europeans?

RUBRIC Students' essays should

- respond to the Essential Question with a specific position
- illustrate valid reasoning supporting their position
- cite persuasive evidence supporting their position
- identify key people, events, and/or turning points that demonstrate understanding of the module content
- be organized into a distinct introduction, main body, and conclusion

Write an argument answering this question. Your essay should discuss different early American civilizations and specific examples of how they did or did not influence later civilizations. Be sure to cite evidence to support your point and organize your essay into an introduction, body, and conclusion.

Alternative Activity Instead of writing essays, address the Essential Question through activities such as holding debates, creating multimedia presentations, or writing journal entries.

(continued)

Print Assessment (continued)

8. **Evaluate** The Maya, Aztecs, and Inca had very similar cultures but also were unique. Do you think that this statement is accurate? Consider their government, economy, art, and religion. Give reasons for your answer. *Possible answer: Yes; All three cultures had strong religious beliefs and were theocracies. However, they all had different strengths. The Aztecs had a powerful army and the Inca had good infrastructure.*

Engage with History

In this module you examined how killing a mammoth would help you survive and discussed the difficulties of living in a hunter-gatherer society. Now that you have read the module, discuss why the early Americans moved from a hunting to a farming existence. In what ways was food gathering easier in an agricultural society?

Have students consider that in a hunting society, (1) considerable energy and resources are expended in finding, hunting, killing, and preparing food; and (2) people would rarely know where and how much food was available at any one time. In contrast, agricultural societies could (1) plan their food supplies and control which foods were grown, (2) farm in areas that people could access easily, and (3) expend more energy on preparing food and experimenting with new foods.

Focus on Writing

Write a three-paragraph essay comparing and contrasting American Indian civilizations in North, Central, and South America, such as the Maya, Aztecs, Inca, Pueblo, and Eastern Woodland peoples.

As you plan your essay, consider the following:

- government
- interactions with the environment
- economy
- social life

> **RUBRIC** Essays should
> - discuss the similarities between the American Indian civilizations in North, Central, and South America
> - discuss the differences between the American Indian civilizations in North, Central, and South America

Multimedia Activity

Write a documentary film script about the Mayan, Aztec, and Incan civilizations, describing cultural patterns, the spread of American cultures, and political and economic structures. Compare and contrast these elements for each group. Provide a definition of *cultural pattern* in your script, and include examples of the following:

- cultural patterns among the Aztec, Maya, Inca, and other peoples of the Americas
- how American cultures spread
- ways in which their political and economic structures were similar and different

> **RUBRIC** Scripts should
> - present a concise, well-organized analysis of the spread of culture through trade
> - include clear, imaginative visuals
> - cite sources

▷ Online Assessment

1. Why do some scholars believe that the early Americans could have come from Japan?
   - ○ A footprint found in Monte Verde matched those found in Japan.
   - ○ Pieces of animal hide in Chile matched animals that lived in Japan.
   - ○ A skull found in the Americas looked similar to early Japanese skulls.
   - ○ Spearheads discovered in Mexico resemble those used by Japanese samurai.

2. What caused the end of land travel across Beringia?
   - ○ Glaciers melted.
   - ○ Ships were invented.
   - ○ Tropical forests disappeared.
   - ○ Mammoths were overhunted.

3. *Select the correct button in the table to show whether each statement is true or false about the development of agriculture by the early Americans.*

	True	False
Maize was one of the most important crops in the Americas.	○	○
When agriculture was developed, more people began hunting and gathering than ever before.	○	○
Scholars believe that the Peruvians may have developed their agriculture independently from other areas in the Americas.	○	○
Squashes and apples were other important crops of the people who lived in North and South America.	○	○

4. *Drag each characteristic into the correct position in the table to show whether it describes San Lorenzo or La Venta.*

San Lorenzo	La Venta
earthen mounds, pyramids, and courtyards	100-foot-high mound of earth and clay
colossal sculpted heads	believed to have originated around 900 BC
oldest known Olmec site dating back to 1150 BC	

5. *Select the correct button in the table to show whether each description is associated with San José Mogote or Monte Albán.*

	San José Mogote	Monte Albán
was a main power in Oaxaca in 1000 BC	○	○
was the first real urban center in the Americas	○	○
had a peak population of 25,000	○	○
developed an early form of writing in 500 BC	○	○
constructed stone platforms and monumental sculptures	○	○
built a giant plaza in the center of the city surrounded by pyramids, temples, and palaces	○	○
constructed an observatory for stargazing	○	○

6. Which is a characteristic of the Olmec civilization?
   - ○ They had organized ceremonial centers.
   - ○ They used a cougar motif in their artwork.
   - ○ They used an intricate form of hieroglyphic writing.
   - ○ They had an elaborate way of designing their urban spaces.

7. *Select the correct button in the table to show whether each statement about the Chavín culture is true or false.*

	True	False
The Chavín culture spread quickly across northern and central Peru.	○	○
The Chavín culture flourished in Mesoamerica from 900 BC to 200 BC.	○	○
The Chavín culture built pyramids, plazas, and massive earthen mounds.	○	○
The Chavín culture was considered a "mother culture" for later Andean civilizations.	○	○

8. *Drag each description into the box next to the name of the correct civilization.*

Nazca	○	was known for its beautiful textiles
Moche	○	was a civilization with enormous wealth

9. What are **two** things that experts do not completely understand about the Moche people?
   - ○ why their civilization fell
   - ○ what their religious beliefs included
   - ○ how they took care of people who were ill
   - ○ what kinds of instruments their musicians played
   - ○ why they used semiprecious stones in their jewelry
   - ○ how they benefited by living close to the rivers that flowed from the Andes

10. *Select the correct button in the table to show whether each description belongs to the Pacific Northwest peoples, the Hohokam, or the Anasazi.*

	Pacific Northwest	Hohokam	Anasazi
built large canoes to carry at least 15 people	●	○	○
lived in the area now known as central Arizona	○	●	○
often had conflicts with each other over available farmland	○	●	○
utilized the coastal forests for food and supplies	●	○	○
used pottery instead of baskets	○	●	○
built massive villages on the sides of cliffs	○	○	●
lived in the area stretching from present-day Oregon to Alaska	●	○	○
lived in the present-day Four Corners region	○	○	●
hunted whales for food	●	○	○
used kivas for religious purposes	○	○	●

11. What was the heart of the Cahokia community?
    - ○ cliff-side dwellings
    - ○ palace dwelt in by the king
    - ● tall pyramid topped with a temple
    - ○ large earthen mounds that held tombs

12. What was the basic unit of social organization among North American Native Americans?
    - ○ the clan
    - ○ the tribe
    - ● the family
    - ○ the pueblo

13. *Drag the different parts of Maya society into their correct order from top (highest level of society) to bottom (lowest level of society).*
    - ○ king
    - ○ priests and warriors
    - ○ merchants and artisans
    - ○ peasants

14. *Select the correct button in the table to show whether each statement about the Maya is true or false.*

	True	False
The Maya used a base-20 number system.	●	○
The Maya were known to make sacrifices to their gods.	●	○
The Maya needed a reliable calendar so they could properly worship their gods.	○	○
The Maya had the least advanced writing system of the ancient American civilizations.	○	○

15. What was the significance of the *Popol Vuh*?
    - ● It was a book written by the Maya people.
    - ○ It was an ancient calendar used by the Maya.
    - ○ It was a form of Maya mathematics that included the zero.
    - ○ It was an astronomical observation of the planets, sun, and moon.

16. *Select the correct button in the table to show whether each statement is true or false about the Teotihuacán people.*

	True	False
The Teotihuacán people built a giant Pyramid of the Sun in their city.	●	○
The Teotihuacán people completely abandoned their city by AD 750.	●	○
The Teotihuacán people were at one point ruled by a man named Topiltzin.	○	●
The Teotihuacán people influenced areas of Mesoamerica with their art styles and religious beliefs.	●	○

17. *Drag an answer choice into each box to complete the sentence correctly.*
    The Triple Alliance became the leading power in the [Valley of Mexico ⬍] and soon gained control over neighboring regions. At its height, it had an estimated population of between [5 and 15 million people ⬍].

18. Why might a scholar conclude that waterways were important to the Aztec people?
    - ○ The Aztecs built farm plots along the Pacific Ocean.
    - ○ The Aztecs built their city with massive walls surrounding its perimeter.
    - ● The Aztecs built canals to transport people and goods throughout the city.
    - ○ The Aztecs built a temple in the central plaza that was dedicated to the rain god.

19. To where did all of the roads in the Incan empire lead?
    - ○ the tombs
    - ○ the capital
    - ○ the seaside
    - ○ the farmland

20. *Select the correct button in the table to show whether each statement about the Incan people is true or false.*

	True	False
They sacrificed donkeys and cows to their gods.	○	●
They trained young men to be weavers, teachers, and spinners.	○	●
They covered important religious structures with layers of gold.	●	○
They drafted young unmarried women to a lifetime of religious service.	●	○

21. What ultimately caused the end of the great Incan empire?
    - ○ The Incan military joined forces with the Aztecs.
    - ● The Spanish divided and conquered the empire.
    - ○ The sons of the Incan king refused to take power.
    - ○ The people of Ecuador waged war on the Incan people.

Online Multimedia Connections

In this multimedia connection, students will learn about the ancient Maya civilization by examining the archaeological ruins of central Mexico. They will watch a short video introducing the Maya, examine a map of Palenque, analyze and discuss an image of the temple of Kukulkan, and then watch and discuss a short video clip on King Pakal's tomb.

HISTORY

THE Maya

535 MC1   MULTIMEDIA CONNECTIONS

HISTORY.
Go online to view these and
other **HISTORY**® resources.

The Maya developed one of the most
advanced civilizations in the Americas, but
their story is shrouded in mystery. Around
AD 250, the Maya began to build great cities
in southern Mexico and Central America. They
developed a writing system, practiced astronomy,
and built magnificent palaces and pyramids with
little more than stone tools. Around AD 900,
however, the Maya abandoned their cities, leaving
their monuments to be reclaimed by the jungle
and, for a time, forgotten.

Explore some of the incredible monuments and
cultural achievements of the ancient Maya online.
You can find a wealth of information, video clips,
primary sources, activities, and more through your
online textbook.

"Thus let it be done!
Let the emptiness be filled!
Let the water recede and
make a void, let the earth
appear and become solid; let it
be done . . . "Earth!" they said,
and instantly it was made."

The Popol Vuh
Read the document to learn how the Maya believed
the world was created.

Destroying the Maya's Past
Watch the video to learn how the actions of one
Spanish missionary nearly destroyed the written
record of the Maya world.

Finding the City of Palenque
Watch the video to learn about the great Maya city
of Palenque and the European discovery of the site
in the eighteenth century.

Pakal's Tomb
Watch the video to explore how the discovery of
the tomb of a great king helped archaeologists
piece together the Maya past.

Essential Question Preview

Do art and literature reflect culture, or do they shape it?

Have students consider the Essential Question and capture their initial responses.

Explore the Essential Question

- Explore with students the difference between art and literature reflecting culture versus shaping it.

- Describe to students ways that art and literature reflect culture, using current examples of both to begin a discussion. For example, display images of street art and ask students how it reflects or shapes culture.

Help students plan inquiries and develop their own supporting questions such as

What new ideas and values led to the Renaissance?

How did humanism play a key role in the artistic achievements of the Renaissance?

You may want to assign students to write a short essay in response to the Essential Question when they complete the module. Encourage students to use their notes and responses to inform their essays.

▷ Explore the Online Video

ANALYZE VIDEOS

Da Vinci's World

Invite students to watch the video to learn about the transformation of the world in which Leonardo da Vinci lived: Florence, Italy.

History What is the name of the family that restored Florence? *the Medici family*

PLAY VIDEO 2:18
Da Vinci's World
HISTORY

The Renaissance

Essential Question
Do art and literature reflect culture, or do they shape it?

About the Painting: *The Madonna of Chancellor Rollin,* painted by Jan van Eyck in about 1435, shows the infant Jesus and his mother Mary in a 15th-century European setting. It is painted with oil paints, which were developed during the Renaissance, and uses the technique of perspective.

 Explore ONLINE!

VIDEOS, including...
- Da Vinci's World
- Leonardo Da Vinci's The Last Supper
- Da Vinci: Inventive Genius

✓ Document-Based Investigations
✓ Graphic Organizers
✓ Interactive Games
✓ Image Compare: Perspective
✓ Image with Hotspots: Printing Press

In this module you will learn how European society was revitalized as classical art and ideas were embraced and improved upon.

What You Will Learn ...

Lesson 1 Big Idea

The Renaissance was a rebirth of learning and art.

Why It Matters Now

Renaissance art and ideas still influence thought today.

Lesson 2 Big Idea

The Italian Renaissance was a rediscovery of learning that produced many great works of art and literature.

Why It Matters Now

Renaissance art and literature still influence modern thought and modern art.

Lesson 3 Big Idea

In the 1400s, the ideas of the Italian Renaissance began to spread to northern Europe.

Why It Matters Now

Renaissance ideas such as the importance of the individual are an important part of modern thought.

Lesson 4 Big Idea

The Renaissance was a period of striking achievements in many areas.

Why It Matters Now

The achievements of Renaissance artists, writers, scientists, and thinkers continue to affect people around the world today.

Timeline of Events 1300–1500

▶ Explore ONLINE!

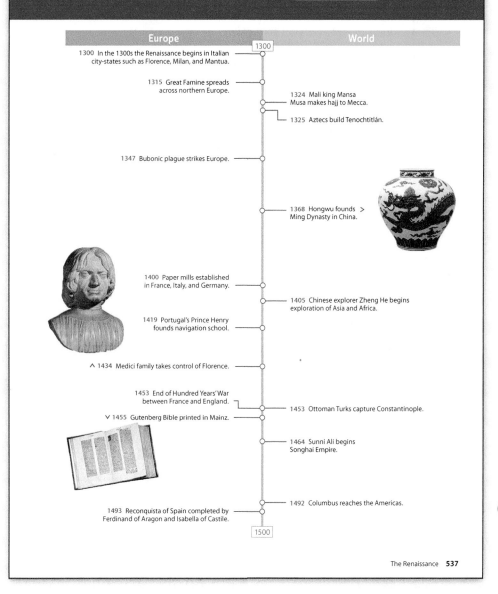

Europe	World
1300 In the 1300s the Renaissance begins in Italian city-states such as Florence, Milan, and Mantua.	
1315 Great Famine spreads across northern Europe.	**1324** Mali king Mansa Musa makes hajj to Mecca.
	1325 Aztecs build Tenochtitlán.
1347 Bubonic plague strikes Europe.	
	1368 Hongwu founds Ming Dynasty in China.
1400 Paper mills established in France, Italy, and Germany.	
	1405 Chinese explorer Zheng He begins exploration of Asia and Africa.
1419 Portugal's Prince Henry founds navigation school.	
∧ **1434** Medici family takes control of Florence.	
1453 End of Hundred Years' War between France and England.	**1453** Ottoman Turks capture Constantinople.
∨ **1455** Gutenberg Bible printed in Mainz.	
	1464 Sunni Ali begins Songhai Empire.
	1492 Columbus reaches the Americas.
1493 Reconquista of Spain completed by Ferdinand of Aragon and Isabella of Castile.	

The Renaissance **537**

Explore the Timeline

Interpret Timelines: The Renaissance 1300–1500

Have students examine the timeline and then answer the following question:

Geography During the 1400s, which areas were scholars forced to leave? *Byzantine Empire, Spain*

Interpret Timeline of Events: The Renaissance 1300–1500

To further explore the timeline, have students discuss the following questions:

1. In what century did the Renaissance begin in Italy? *1300s*
2. Point out that the Gutenberg Bible, the first book printed in the West from movable type, was printed in 1455. Ask what effect this printing technology might have had on the development of new ideas. *The printing press made books more available. As a result, ideas could spread more quickly and easily.*

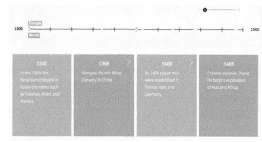

▶ Online **Module Flip Cards**

Use the flip cards as a whole class activity or in student pairs to preview the module's

Key Terms and People. Students can guess the meaning of each word, then review its definition, or do the reverse, using the flip card's toggle button to switch from Term to Definition mode. Students can also use the flip cards at the end of the module as a review tool before taking the Module Assessment.

▶ Online **Sequencing Activity**

Students can use this sequencing activity to review the chronology of events in The Renaissance module. To complete, have students drag each event to the correct year on the timeline.

Year	Event
1300	*Columbus reaches the Americas.*
1400	*Paper mills were established in France, Italy, and Germany.*
1434	*Medici family takes control of Florence.*
1455	*Gutenberg Bible printed in Mainz.*
1492	*The Renaissance begins in Italian city-states such as Florence, Milan, and Mantua.*
1493	*Reconquista of Spain completed by Ferdinand of Aragon and Isabella of Castile.*

The Renaissance 537

Birth of the Renaissance

Video

Islamic Cultural Influences in Spain

Visuals

LESSON 1

Maps, Graphs, and Charts

Map: Europe, 1500

Big Idea

The Renaissance was a rebirth of learning and art.

Biography: Lorenzo de Medici

Trade Fuels City Growth

The Renaissance Man

Extend and Enrich

Historical Sources

Document-Based Investigation: Patrons of the Arts

Renaissance Man

Assessment

Key Terms Review

Reading Check

Graphic Organizer Activity

Lesson Assessment

Trade Fuels City Growth

Plan Students will imagine they are traveling on business and will write a letter describing the journey of a merchant traveling from Venice to Alexandria. This activity walks students through estimating the time the journey will take and describing how people and goods move from one city to the next.

The Renaissance Man

Research Students will read about the Renaissance to learn about characteristics the perfect courtier should possess. They will read about the different attributes and skills Castiglione's book says a courtier should have and analyze how these attributes and skills would be useful for a present-day courtier.

Teach the Big Idea

1. **Whole Class Open/Introduction** Explain that the Renaissance was a time of great creativity. Ask students to describe ways in which they show their own creativity. *Possible answers: through art, music, writing, or type of clothing worn*

2. **Direct Teach** Read students the Big Idea: *The Renaissance was a rebirth of learning and art.* Review the following lesson objectives with students to aid in their understanding of the Big Idea.

   - Identify the specific changes in learning that laid the foundation for the Renaissance.

   - Explain the conditions in Italy that gave rise to the Renaissance.

   - Identify the values and ideas prized during the Renaissance

3. **Whole Group Close/Reflect** Ask students to reference the text and list changes in society that laid the foundation for the Renaissance. Then ask students to use drawing paper and markers to create a visual representation of one or more of the societal changes that contributed to the birth of the Renaissance. Have students present their collage to the class. Let students guess what the change is, and then ask the presenter to explain the change.

▷ **ONLINE DOCUMENT-BASED INVESTIGATION**

The Renaissance

Patrons of the Arts is the first of four document-based investigations that students will analyze in The Renaissance module. Isabella d'Este's excerpt from *Letters* speaks to the relationship between artists and patrons. Students will study the image and evaluate the text.

▷ **ONLINE GRAPHIC ORGANIZER**

Birth of the Renaissance

As students read the lesson, have them use the graphic organizer to take notes. Students can review their graphic organizer notes at the end of the lesson to answer the following question:

Summarize What ideas and events helped lead up to the Renaissance? *increased trade, political independence, rise of merchant class*

Birth of the Renaissance

The Big Idea
The Renaissance was a rebirth of learning and art.

Why It Matters Now
Renaissance art and ideas still influence thought today.

Key Terms and People
Renaissance
humanism
secular
patron

Setting the Stage

During the late Middle Ages, Europe suffered from both war and plague. Those who survived wanted to celebrate life and the human spirit. They began to question institutions of the Middle Ages, which had been unable to prevent war or to relieve suffering brought by the plague. Some people questioned the Church, which taught Christians to endure suffering while they awaited their rewards in heaven. Some writers and artists began to express this new spirit and to experiment with different styles. These men and women would greatly change how Europeans saw themselves and their world.

A Time of Change

From approximately 1300 to 1600, Europe experienced an explosion of creativity in art, architecture, writing, and thought. Historians call this period the **Renaissance** (rehn·ih·SAHNS). The term means "rebirth," and in this context, it refers to a revival of art and learning. People of the Renaissance hoped to bring back the culture of classical Greece and Rome. Yet in striving to revive the past, they created something new. The contributions made during this period led to innovative styles of art and literature. They also led to new values, such as individualism, or a belief in the importance of the individual.

Although the developments of the Renaissance may seem to be a complete departure from the medieval era, they grew out of several important changes in society, politics, economics, and learning. These changes laid the foundation for the Renaissance.

Shifts in Society As a result of waves of famine and disease, Europe's population in 1450 was much smaller than it had been in 1300. With far fewer people to feed, the general standard of living was much higher. People were also

---

COLLABORATIVE LEARNING

New Ideas Represented in Art

1. Have students use the Internet, books, and other resources to examine how the Renaissance marked major changes in science, philosophy, and in society in general, and how the new artistic styles of the time reflect those changes.

2. Then divide students into four groups. Assign each group a Renaissance artist on which to do further research.

3. Have students create electronic presentations, using multimedia software, to explain the cultural developments of the Renaissance and how the work of their assigned artist is reflective of those developments.

4. Tell students to end their presentations with a statement about what they can infer about culture during the Renaissance from the art and the artists of the time.

---

generally better educated. Schools in the growing towns provided at least a basic education, which was extended by recently developed universities. As literacy rates increased, so did the demand for books.

Increased trade led to the development of a new class of people between the nobility at the top and the peasants at the bottom: the middle class. The merchants, bankers, and tradespeople in the middle class had more than enough income to meet their basic needs. They had extra money to buy luxury goods and fine homes, which helped to expand the economy still further.

New Sources of Knowledge After the fall of Rome, knowledge of Greek language and learning all but disappeared in Europe. It was maintained in the Byzantine Empire, which lay at the crossroads of Europe and Asia. In 1453, when the Ottomans captured Constantinople, the capital of the Byzantine Empire, many eminent Byzantine scholars fled to Italy. With their knowledge of the language and learning of classical Greece, they contributed to the new ways of thinking that helped lead to the Renaissance.

Many Greek texts, along with the knowledge to read them, were also preserved in the libraries of the Islamic Empire. The capital of Islamic Spain, Córdoba, was a center of classical learning. Scholars there wrote commentaries in Arabic on the works of Greek writers such as Aristotle and Plato. Jewish scholars in Spain translated these commentaries into Hebrew. Later, these scholars translated into Latin both the original Greek texts and the commentaries. As a result, Western scholars visiting the libraries of Islamic Spain were able to read the works of Greek writers.

Islamic influences in Córdoba include the Moorish-style Alcazar and the cathedral, formerly an Islamic mosque.

The Renaissance **539**

You may wish to discuss the following questions with students to help them frame the content as they read.

- What changes in society and in cities laid the foundation for the Renaissance? *smaller population, changes in politics, economics, and learning*

- In your opinion, which shifts in society had the greatest impact on the Renaissance? *Possible answers: A smaller European population meant fewer people to feed, a higher standard of living for all, a better-educated population, increased trade, and the rise of a middle class.*

More About . . .

The New Middle Class The new middle class celebrated their newfound financial security by investing in comfortable homes, fine art for these residences, and elaborate clothing to signify their wealth in public. All of these investments served to stimulate the economy even further. Many middle-class professions required an investment in education, and people had the time and the means to study the essentials for their jobs as well as for pleasure.

Other Renaissances Since the days of the Italian Renaissance, the word *renaissance* has been used to describe a period of great achievements in art, literature, and culture. During the Harlem Renaissance, which took place in the 1920s in New York City, African American creativity flowered. Writers, painters, and musicians created works of art celebrating African American culture. Some of the best-known artists of the Harlem Renaissance include Langston Hughes, Zora Neale Hurston, Paul Robeson, Duke Ellington, and Bessie Smith.

▷ ONLINE INTERACTIVE VISUALS

Carousel: Islamic Cultural Influences in Spain

Have students navigate through the carousel and note similarities and differences among the images or identify a unifying theme.

ADVANCED/GIFTED

Report on Inventions of the Renaissance

1. Have students research inventions of the Renaissance, such as the printing press, muskets, water closets, or others.

2. Ask students to create a slide show presentation of selected inventions based on their research. Have them include the name of the invention, the inventor, how and when it was invented, and the impact of the invention on society. Encourage students to use images in their presentations along with facts and details.

3. Invite students to share their presentations with the class.

COLLABORATIVE LEARNING

Create a Renaissance Social Media Profile

1. Pair students and tell them to imagine they are living during the early Renaissance. Ask students to create a profile for themselves, similar to a profile on social media.

2. Have students identify their societal status as well as details about their clothes, family, and home. Remind them to use the Internet to conduct further research if necessary.

3. Have each pair use images from their research to accurately illustrate their Renaissance persona.

4. Ask students to share their profiles with the class as a way of describing life in the Renaissance.

Objectives

You may wish to discuss the following questions with students to help them frame the content as they read.

- How did the cities of Italy help create the Renaissance? *City life included wealth, leisure time, exchange of ideas, and so forth.*
- What is your opinion of the Medici family? *Positive—Supported arts and culture. Negative—Publicly executed enemies, ruled as dictators.*

More About . . .

Communication Speed Although Venice established connections with ports around the Mediterranean Sea, the rate of travel and communication remained quite slow by today's standards. It took 9 days for news from Venice to reach Naples, 22 days to reach Sicily, and 37 days for it to reach Constantinople. Even by the year 1500, journeys were typically measured in weeks, not days.

The Bubonic Plague The bubonic plague, also known as the Black Death, originated in China but quickly spread to western Asia and Europe because China was one of the most active trading nations. The plague mainly affected rodents, but fleas then transmitted the disease to humans, causing fever and a painful swelling of the lymph glands. The affected lymph glands are called "buboes," which is how the disease gets its name.

▷ ONLINE LESSON FLIP CARDS

Review Key Terms and People

Students can use the flip cards in the Lesson Review at any time to review the lesson's key terms and people: *Renaissance, humanism, secular,* and *patron.*

READING CHECK

Analyze Effects How did increasing global contact affect Europe? *It exposed Europeans to ideas, inventions, and knowledge from Asia and the Islamic world and reintroduced the knowledge and philosophy of ancient Greece and Rome.*

This painting by Vicente Lopez y Portana shows King Ferdinand II of Aragon and Queen Isabella of Castile receiving Boabdil, the last Muslim ruler of Granada, in 1492.

New Technology Western Europeans also learned the technology of papermaking from Islamic Spain. Paper was first manufactured in China around 105 AD. In 751, technicians in the Abbasid caliphate learned the process. Because paper made it easier to create and store books, its use contributed to the growth of libraries. Papermaking soon spread through the Islamic world. By 1400, paper mills were to be found in France, Italy, and Germany. The availability of paper later helped make possible the development of printing.

A Changing Political Landscape Along with famine and disease, Europe had experienced almost constant warfare. Over the course of the 15th century, peace returned to much of the continent. The Hundred Years' War between France and England ended in 1453. The victory against England confirmed the French king's authority. A period of civil war followed in England, but when Henry VII came to power in 1485, England was again ruled by a strong central power. In Spain, the Reconquista, or Reconquest, was completed in 1493 by Ferdinand of Aragon and Isabella of Castile. This ended Islamic rule and brought to a close 200 years of war on the peninsula.

The Rise of Italian City-States

The final major factor that contributed to the Renaissance was the rise of city-states in Italy. At a time when most of Europe was rural, agricultural, and manorial, Italy was much more urban and commercial. Since cities are often places where people exchange ideas, they were an ideal breeding ground for an intellectual revolution.

Economic Factors Overseas trade, spurred by the Crusades, led to the growth of large city-states in northern Italy. By the year 1000, Italian cities were at the forefront of an impressive economic expansion that would carry on into the Renaissance some 300 years later. Two decades into the 11th century, this financial success would allow Italian cities to begin to

Reading Check
Analyze Effects
How did increasing global contact affect Europe?

540 Module 14

COLLABORATIVE LEARNING

Trader's Log

1. Divide students into small groups and ask them to conduct research to find what products were produced and traded in the 1300s in Florence, Naples, Venice, and Milan.

2. Have each group create a trader's log that describes a journey through each city-state. The log should include a description of the city and its people, the group's mode of transportation, and a list of transactions that occur at each location.

3. Display a class map and have each group reference it as they present their logs to the class.

Venice's waterways, such as the Grand Canal, are still the main thoroughfares of the city.

ignore the German emperor who claimed to control them.

Traditionally, wealth in Europe was based on land ownership. The growth in foreign trade created an economy based on commerce rather than agriculture. Merchants needed financial services, such as the ability to transfer money from one place to another. This led to the rise of banks, which soon became an important part of the city-states' economy. Some crucial aspects of finance, which helped develop the modern economy, were pioneered by the banks of northern Italy.

A wealthy merchant class developed in the Italian city-states. Unlike nobles, merchants did not inherit land and social rank. To succeed in business, they used their wits. As a result, many successful merchants believed they deserved power and wealth because of their individual merit. This belief in individual achievement became important during the Renaissance.

In the 1300s, the bubonic plague struck these cities hard, killing up to 60 percent of the population. This brought economic changes. Because there were fewer laborers, survivors could demand higher wages. With few opportunities to expand business, merchants began to pursue other interests, such as supporting the arts.

Political Factors Political development in Italy was unlike that in other parts of Europe. Whereas countries like England and France steadily moved toward the consolidation of power into the hands of dynastic royal families, Italy remained fragmented. One reason for this was the development of a strong urban nobility that intermarried over time with rising commercial families. These noble families with commercial backing were then able to establish vital, independent bases in a number of Italian cities, mostly in northern and central Italy.

Venice Venice is in the north of Italy, on the Adriatic Coast. The city is built on a lagoon and is made up of over 100 islands where people first moved to find safety from raids after the fall of Rome. It grew into an international powerhouse after shedding the domination of first the Byzantines and then the Franks. The Crusades boosted Venice's standing even further, as Venetian merchants made fortunes supplying and transporting the crusaders. At this time, the city established a Mediterranean empire, controlling Crete and a number of other Greek islands.

Milan As an inland city, Milan lagged behind coastal trading powers such as Venice and Genoa in commercial terms. But it quickly arose as a center

▷ ONLINE INTERACTIVE MAPS

Europe, 1500

Have students explore the map and answer the associated question.

Location Which Italian city shown on the map was located on the coast? *Naples*

ADVANCED/GIFTED

City-State Newspapers

1. Assign each student an Italian city-state.

2. Have students prepare a complete newspaper for their assigned city-states. Newspapers must include articles on politics, current events, and daily life. Have them include one editorial about how society evolved after the Black Death.

3. Students may use the Internet or library for additional research.

4. Refer students to newspaper examples for ideas, and ask them to use features available via word-processing systems to mimic an actual paper.

5. Have students exchange and critique papers and then display them for the class.

Lorenzo de Medici

Have students read the biography of Lorenzo de Medici, a Florentine ruler who supported some of the most talented Renaissance artists. He was known for his patronage and liberal mind.

READING CHECK

Contrast How was Italy unlike other countries in Europe? *Instead of a single nation-state with a strong central government, it included a number of city-states, each with its own ruler.*

---

of manufacturing. Of Milan's four principal industries—cloth, arms, metallurgy, and leather—cloth was the largest. But the trade in arms and metallurgy (tools, utensils, needles) was more profitable. Milanese body armor and weapons were prized throughout Europe and beyond. Trade was boosted in the 13th century by the opening of free passage along roads, canals, and rivers through much of northern Italy.

In Milan, prosperity spurred civic pride and energy and resulted in an upswelling of artistic creativity, public building, and further entrepreneurial endeavor. Unfortunately, this was also a time of frequent warfare—against nearby cities such as Pavia and Como and also the forces of the Holy Roman Empire.

Naples By the late 800s, Naples (in the south of Italy on the west coast) was relatively free from Lombard attacks and able to concentrate on trade, mostly with the Arab world. Increased wealth led to a flowering of architecture, the arts, and scholarship. At the beginning of the 10th century, Naples was a flourishing, independent city-state. This came to an end in the 1130s, when Norman invaders took over southern Italy. Next came the German emperor, Henry VI, to oust the Normans in 1194. Finally, the armies of Charles of Anjou ejected the Germans and established the Kingdom of Naples and Sicily in 1266. The Angevin dynasty ruled from Naples, boosting trade, mostly in arms and luxury goods, and the city's population, which grew to as much as 60,000 by the 1300s. Robert the Wise, king from 1309 to 1343, supported both public building and the arts, but the end of his reign marked the end of Neapolitan prosperity. Earthquakes in 1343 and 1349 and the Black Death in 1348 made sure that Naples limped along toward the Renaissance.

Florence Since the late 1200s, the city-state of Florence had a republican form of government. But during the Renaissance, Florence came under the rule of one powerful banking family, the Medici (MEHD•ih•chee). The Medici bank had branch offices throughout Italy and in the major cities of Europe. Cosimo de Medici was the wealthiest European of his time. In 1434, he won control of Florence's government. He did not seek political

---

BIOGRAPHY

Lorenzo de Medici
(1449–1492)

A rival family grew so jealous of the Medici that they plotted to kill Lorenzo and his brother Giuliano. As the Medici attended Mass, assassins murdered Giuliano at the altar. Drawing his sword, Lorenzo escaped to a small room and held off his attackers until help arrived. Later, he had the killers publicly executed.

More positively, Lorenzo was a generous patron of the arts who collected many rare manuscripts. Eventually the Medici family made their library available to the public.

office for himself but influenced members of the ruling council by giving them loans. For 30 years, he was dictator of Florence.

Cosimo de Medici died in 1464, but his family continued to control Florence. His grandson, Lorenzo de Medici, came to power in 1469. Known as Lorenzo the Magnificent, he ruled as a dictator yet kept up the appearance of having an elected government.

This portrait (c 1490) by Leonardo da Vinci of Cecilia Gallerani is known as "Lady with an Ermine." It was commissioned by Ludovico Sforza, the Duke of Milan and a member of the Order of the Ermine. The duke was a generous patron of the arts and his court became a gathering place for artists, architects, poets, and musicians.

Rome By the mid-700s, Rome was the center of the Papal States—territories controlled by the pope. Rome's wealthy, landholding families controlled the city and the papacy from about 900 until about 1050, when wealthy Romans whose money came from business and banking supported the papacy. In 1143, a revolt resulted in the Roman commune, in which Rome became a self-governing city with a republican constitution.

Reading Check
Contrast How was Italy unlike other countries in Europe?

Classical and Worldly Values

As European scholars studied Greek writers and thinkers, they became more influenced by classical ideas. These ideas helped them develop a new outlook on life and art.

Vocabulary
humanist/ humanities comes from a Latin term that means "studies of human nature"; it refers to the knowledge of culture that every educated person should possess

Classics Lead to Humanism The study of classical texts led to **humanism**, an intellectual movement that focused on human potential and achievements. Instead of trying to make classical texts agree with Christian teaching as medieval scholars had, humanists studied them to understand ancient Greek values. Humanists influenced artists and architects to carry on classical traditions. Also, humanists popularized the study of subjects common to classical education, such as history, literature, and philosophy. These subjects are called the humanities.

Worldly Pleasures In the Middle Ages, some people had demonstrated their piety by wearing rough clothing and eating plain foods. However, humanists suggested that a person might enjoy life without offending God. In Renaissance Italy, the wealthy enjoyed material luxuries, good music, and fine foods.

Most people remained devout Catholics. However, the basic spirit of Renaissance society was **secular**—worldly rather than spiritual, and concerned with the here and now instead of the hereafter. Even church leaders became more worldly. Some lived in beautiful mansions, threw lavish banquets, and wore expensive clothes.

The Renaissance **543**

Focus on Vocabulary

1. Have students create a chart in which they define the key terms in their own words.

2. Ask students to list each term followed by its meaning and an example.

3. For help, have students reference the text.

4. Once the chart is complete, have students exchange work and use the text to check it.

Objectives

You may wish to discuss the following questions with students to help them frame the content as they read.

- How did humanism influence Renaissance ideas? *It focused on people and their achievements, so art and thought became more concerned with the here and now.*

- Why did church leaders and wealthy merchants support the arts? *They showed their importance by having portraits painted and decorating churches and other public places.*

- What were the differences and similarities between upper-class Renaissance men and women? *Both were expected to know the classics, but most women lacked political power.*

More About . . .

Isabella d'Este Isabella d'Este had a privileged upbringing. She could speak Greek and Latin and was an accomplished musician and dancer. An avid collector of art and antiques, she turned her home into an art museum. She had several children but remained involved in politics, governing Mantua while her husband was away and for a short period after he died.

▶ **ONLINE DOCUMENT-BASED INVESTIGATION**

Patrons of the Arts

Isabella d'Este was a devoted patron of many artists, including Leonardo da Vinci. Students can play the audio to hear an excerpt from one of her letters read aloud.

Analyze Sources What role did patrons of the arts play in the development of Renaissance ideas? *They helped support artists financially and, through commissions like Isabella's, helped determine the subjects of many works of art.*

DOCUMENT-BASED INVESTIGATION HISTORICAL SOURCE

Patrons of the Arts

Although Renaissance women were not expected to create art, wealthy women, such as Isabella d'Este, were often patrons of artists. Patrons supported and encouraged artists in various ways, as this letter by Isabella d'Este demonstrates.

The Renaissance Man

Invite students to read or listen to the text, and answer the associated question.

Analyze Sources Do the qualities called for in the ideal Renaissance man seem to emphasize the individual or the group? *The qualities called for seem to emphasize individual achievement rather than group identity. In other words, the qualities require the individual to stand out from the crowd.*

In the print edition, see images titled "The Renaissance Man" and "The Renaissance Woman."

HISTORICAL SOURCE

Renaissance Man

In *The Courtier*, Baldassare Castiglione described the type of accomplished person who later came to be called the Renaissance man.

The Renaissance Man

In *The Courtier*, Baldassare Castiglione described the type of accomplished person who later came to be called the Renaissance man.

"Let the man we are seeking be very bold, stern, and always among the first, where the enemy are to be seen; and in every other place, gentle, modest, reserved, above all things avoiding ostentation [showiness] and that impudent [bold] self-praise by which men ever excite hatred and disgust in all who hear them. . . .

I would have him more than passably accomplished in letters, at least in those studies that are called the humanities, and conversant not only with the Latin language but with Greek, for the sake of the many different things that have been admirably written therein. Let him be well versed in the poets, and not less in the orators and historians, and also proficient in writing verse and prose."

—Baldassare Castiglione, *The Courtier*

The Renaissance Woman

Although Renaissance women were not expected to create art, wealthy women were often patrons of artists, as this letter by Isabella d'Este demonstrates.

"To Master Leonardo da Vinci, the painter: Hearing that you are settled at Florence, we have begun to hope that our cherished desire to obtain a work by your hand might be at length realized. When you were in this city and drew our portrait in carbon, you promised us that you would some day paint it in colors. But because this would be almost impossible, since you are unable to come here, we beg you to keep your promise by converting our portrait into another figure, which would be still more acceptable to us; that is to say, a youthful Christ of about twelve years. . . executed with all that sweetness and charm of atmosphere which is the peculiar excellence of your art."
Mantua, May 14, 1504

—Isabella D'Este, *Letters*

Analyze Historical Sources
Do the qualities called for in the ideal Renaissance man and woman seem to emphasize the individual or the group?

544   Module 14

COLLABORATIVE LEARNING

Justifying the Arts

1. Organize students into pairs.

2. Have students write two letters. The first letter should be to Lorenzo from one of his relatives, criticizing his extravagant spending on the arts. The second should be a reply from Lorenzo, in which he justifies his spending and explains the importance of the arts to the city of Florence.

3. Encourage students to form their own arguments to justify spending on the arts.

4. Have pairs read their letters to the class, with one student taking the position of the relatives and one taking the position of Lorenzo.

Patrons of the Arts Church leaders during the Renaissance beautified Rome and other cities by spending huge amounts of money for art. They became **patrons** of the arts by financially supporting artists. Renaissance merchants and wealthy families also became patrons of the arts. By having their portraits painted or by donating art to the city to place in public squares, the wealthy demonstrated their own importance.

The Renaissance Man During the Renaissance, as the idea of the individual became increasingly important, Renaissance writers introduced the idea of the "ideal" individual. This ideal person was expected to create art and to try to master almost every area of study. A man who excelled in many fields was praised as a "universal man." Later ages called such people "Renaissance men."

Baldassare Castiglione (kahs•teel•YOH•nay) wrote a book called *The Courtier* (1528) that described how to become such a person. A young man should be charming, witty, and well educated in the classics. He should dance, sing, play music, and write poetry. In addition, he should be a skilled rider, wrestler, and swordsman.

The Renaissance Woman According to *The Courtier*, upper-class women should also know the classics and be charming. Yet they were not expected to seek fame. They were expected to inspire art but rarely to create it. Upper-class Renaissance women were better educated than medieval women. However, most Renaissance women had little influence in politics.

A few women, such as Isabella d'Este, did exercise power. Born into the ruling family of the city-state of Ferrara, she married the ruler of another city-state, Mantua. She brought many Renaissance artists to her court and built a famous art collection. She was also skilled in politics. When her husband was taken captive in war, she defended Mantua and won his release.

Reading Check
Compare How were expectations for Renaissance men and Renaissance women similar?

Lesson 1 Assessment

1. **Organize Information** Use a diagram like this one to show the causes of the rise of Italian city-states. Which cause do you think was the most important? Write a sentence explaining why.

2. **Key Terms and People** For each key term or person in the lesson, write a sentence explaining its significance.
3. **Synthesize** What are some of the characteristics of the "Renaissance man" and "Renaissance woman"?
4. **Analyze Causes** What was the attitude of Church leaders and the wealthy toward the arts? Why?
5. **Draw Conclusions** How did study of the classics influence branches of learning such as history, literature, and philosophy?
6. **Compare** What were the differences between medieval and Renaissance attitudes toward worldly pleasures?

Print Assessment

1. **Organize Information** Use a diagram to show the causes of the rise of Italian city-states. Which cause do you think was the most important? Write a sentence explaining why. *Possible answers: Box 1: Increased trade; Box 2: Political independence; Box 3: Rise of merchant class*

2. **Key Terms and People** For each key term or person in the lesson, write a sentence explaining its significance. *Explanations of the lesson's key terms can be found on the following pages: Renaissance, p. 538; humanism, p. 543; secular, p. 543; patron, p. 545*

3. **Synthesize** What are some of the characteristics of the "Renaissance man" and "Renaissance woman"? *Man—Excelled in many fields, charming, witty, educated, politically powerful. Woman— Well-educated in classics, charming, modest, knowledgeable in arts.*

4. **Analyze Causes** What was the attitude of church leaders and the wealthy toward the arts? Why? *They supported the arts because they wanted to beautify their communities and show their own importance.*

5. **Draw Conclusions** How did study of the classics influence branches of learning such as history, literature, and philosophy? *Study of classical texts led to a different outlook on life, one emphasizing human potential and achievements.*

6. **Compare** What were the differences between the Middle Ages and the Renaissance attitudes toward worldly pleasures? *In the Middle Ages, some people believed that denial of worldly pleasures would please God. During the Renaissance, many believed that God intended them to enjoy those things.*

Online Assessment

1. Why was the new technology of papermaking important to the Renaissance?
   - ○ It allowed laws to be written down and distributed to citizens.
   - ○ It caused more efficient record-keeping by bankers and merchants.
   - ● It allowed for the development of printing and easier spread of ideas.
   - ○ It allowed for more criticism to be given to religious and political officials.

   Alternate Question *Select the answer choice from the drop-down list to complete the sentence correctly.* One new technology Europeans learned from Islamic Spain was the making of ⟨ *paper* ⟩. This allowed for the development of printing.

2. How was Italy organized politically before and during the Renaissance?
   - ○ The papacy controlled most of the peninsula, using Rome as a base.
   - ● Wealthy noble families controlled fragments of territory from an urban base.
   - ○ The Medici in Florence forced other ruling families to accept their authority.
   - ○ Foreign kings divided up most of the territory and ruled from their own capitals.

   Alternate Question *Select the answer choice from the drop-down list to complete the sentence correctly.* Renaissance Italy was organized politically into a number of independent states based around a ⟨ *city* ⟩ and ruled by a number of noble families.

3. How was humanism different from intellectual movements during the Middle Ages?
   - ○ It emphasized piety and modesty instead of worldly pursuits.
   - ○ It stressed obedience to local rulers over the national monarch.
   - ● It stressed a secular world view instead of a strict religious view.
   - ○ It emphasized submitting to religious leaders before civic leaders.

   Alternate Question *Select the answer choice from the drop-down list to complete the sentence correctly.* Followers of humanism focused on studying ⟨ *classical texts* ⟩ to understand ancient values.

4. **Sequence** How were western Europeans able to access ancient Greek texts again?

   Possible answer: Ancient Greek texts were preserved throughout the Islamic Empire. Many of these texts were housed in Córdoba, Spain, a center of classical learning in Islamic Spain. Jewish scholars translated these texts, along with commentaries originally written in Arabic, into Latin. Western European scholars could read these translated texts by visiting the libraries there.

5. **Make Generalizations** Why did banking develop in the Italian city-states?

   Possible answer: The economies of the Italian city-states were based on commerce. Merchants needed to be able to transfer money between different places in order to trade different goods. Banks providing this and other financial services filled this need.

6. **Compare and Contrast** How were Castiglione's expectations for young men and young women different?

   Possible answer: In The Courtier, *Baldassare Castiglione explained that young men should be well-educated, witty, and charming. They should be skilled athletes in riding, wrestling, and sword fighting. They should also be capable of dancing, singing, writing poetry, and playing music. Castiglione had much lower expectations for young women. Although he expected young women to be charming and know the classics, he did not think they should seek fame. Similarly, young women should inspire art, but they should not seek to create art themselves.*

The Italian Renaissance

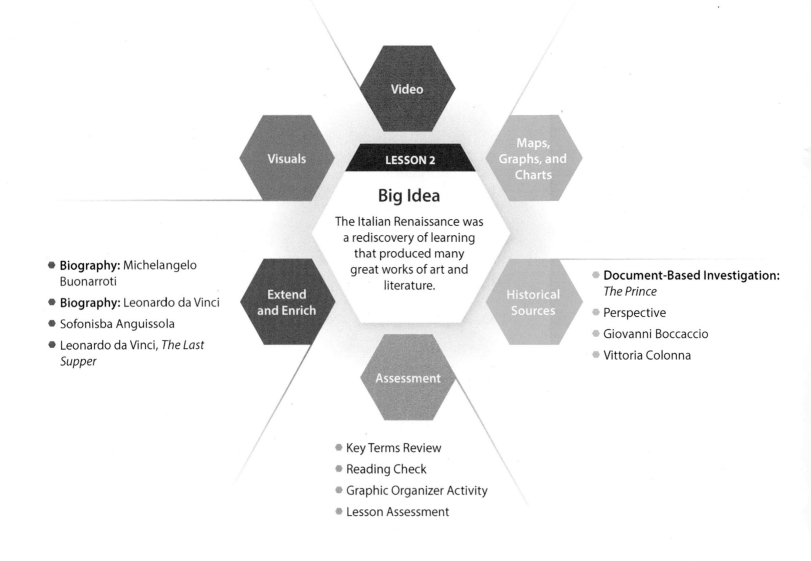

Video

Visuals

LESSON 2

Maps, Graphs, and Charts

Big Idea

The Italian Renaissance was a rediscovery of learning that produced many great works of art and literature.

Extend and Enrich

Historical Sources

Assessment

- **Biography:** Michelangelo Buonarroti
- **Biography:** Leonardo da Vinci
- Sofonisba Anguissola
- Leonardo da Vinci, *The Last Supper*

- **Document-Based Investigation:** *The Prince*
- Perspective
- Giovanni Boccaccio
- Vittoria Colonna

- Key Terms Review
- Reading Check
- Graphic Organizer Activity
- Lesson Assessment

Online Lesson 2 Enrichment Activities

Sofonisba Anguissola

Biography Students will read about Sofonisba Anguissola and her life as a painter. They will create a brochure that describes one of Sofonisba Anguissola's paintings. This activity walks students through evaluating Anguissola's paintings and creating a brochure explaining what is shown in the painting they have chosen and discussing the importance of the work.

Leonardo da Vinci's *The Last Supper*

Video Students will study *The Last Supper* and the way Leonardo used perspective in this painting. Then they will respond to questions about perspective and other devices Leonardo used to create perspective.

Teach the Big Idea

1. **Whole Class Open/Introduction** Explain that many of the artists and writers of the Italian Renaissance are still well known today. Name an artist and a writer from the Italian Renaissance, and ask students if they have previous knowledge of either and to share what they know. *Possible answers: Students may recognize Michelangelo as a painter and sculptor, but they may not know he was also an architect and poet. Students may be familiar with the term* Machiavellian *used to describe a cunning leader as made famous by the actions and writings of Niccolò Machiavelli.*

2. **Direct Teach** Read students the Big Idea: *The Italian Renaissance was a rediscovery of learning that produced many great works of art and literature.*

   Review the following lesson objectives with students to aid in their understanding of the Big Idea.

   - Explain the conditions in Italy that gave rise to the Renaissance.

   - Summarize influential literary works and techniques of key Renaissance writers.

3. **Whole Group Close/Reflect** Have students create a resumé for one of the artists or writers of the Italian Renaissance.

▷ ONLINE DOCUMENT-BASED INVESTIGATION

The Renaissance

An excerpt from Machiavelli's *The Prince* is the second of four document-based investigations that students will analyze in The Renaissance module. Students can use the interactivity of the feature to learn about Machiavelli's philosophy regarding leadership.

DOCUMENT-BASED INVESTIGATION   HISTORICAL SOURCE

The Prince

In *The Prince*, Machiavelli says that a prince can't rely on the loyalty of the people he rules.

▷ ONLINE LESSON FLIP CARDS

Review Key Terms and People

Students can use the flip cards in the Lesson Review at any time to review the lesson's key terms and people: *perspective, Leonardo da Vinci*, and *Michelangelo*.

The Italian Renaissance

The Big Idea
The Italian Renaissance was a rediscovery of learning that produced many great works of art and literature.

Why It Matters Now
Renaissance art and literature still influence modern thought and modern art.

Key Terms and People
perspective
Michelangelo
Leonardo da Vinci

Setting the Stage

The Renaissance began in northern Italy. Italy's city-states were wealthy, with an advanced urban society, and they felt a sense of connection with the classical past of ancient Rome and Greece. During the Renaissance, these city-states were home to some of the world's most extraordinary writers and artists.

Artists of the Italian Renaissance

Supported by patrons like Isabella d'Este, dozens of artists worked in northern Italy. These artists excelled at imitating nature, which became an important aspect of Renaissance painting and sculpture. Medieval artists had used religious subjects to convey a spiritual ideal. Renaissance artists often portrayed religious subjects, but they used a realistic style copied from classical models. Greek and Roman subjects also became popular. Renaissance painters used the technique of **perspective**, a way of showing three dimensions on a flat surface. The introduction of oil-based paints, first developed in Flanders, allowed artists to create more realistic forms and details. Following the new emphasis on individuals, painters began to paint prominent citizens. These realistic portraits revealed what was distinctive about each person.

In Florence, artists such as the sculptor, poet, architect, and painter **Michelangelo** (my·kuhl·AN·juh·loh) Buonarroti used a realistic style when depicting the human body. The sculptor Donatello (dahn·uh·TEHL·oh) revived a classical form in his statue of David, a boy who, according to the Bible, became a great king. Donatello's statue was created in the late 1460s. It was the first European sculpture of a large, free-standing nude since ancient times. David was a favorite subject for sculptors of the period, including Michelangelo.

Leonardo da Vinci, Renaissance Man Leonardo da Vinci (lay·uh·NAHR·doh·duh·VIHN·chee) was a painter, sculptor, inventor, and scientist. A true "Renaissance man," he was

COLLABORATIVE LEARNING

Design Competition

1. Organize students into groups of four to six students. Have each group designate a sculptor, a painter, at least one architect, and a detail person to work out design elements.

2. Tell students that they will compete with other groups to design a city hall of an Italian town during the Renaissance. Have students sketch concepts for each element of the building. Encourage students to create several sketches before they arrive at their final design. Design proposals should include doors, an entry hall, a conference room, and a sample of the exterior façade.

3. Have groups present their design proposals to the class. You may wish to have groups vote on the best design.

4. Ask the class to critique the designs based on characteristics and qualities associated with the Italian Renaissance.

Perspective

Perspective creates the appearance of three dimensions. Classical artists had used perspective, but medieval artists abandoned the technique. In the 1400s, Italian artists rediscovered it.

Perspective is based on an optical illusion. As parallel lines stretch away from a viewer, they seem to draw together, until they meet at a spot on the horizon called the vanishing point. The use of perspective was a feature of most Western painting for the next 450 years.

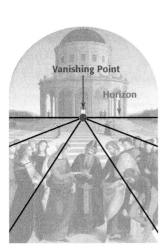

Marriage of the Virgin (1504), Raphael

Analyze Visuals
What is the major difference between the figures in the background of the painting and the figures in the foreground? What is the effect of this difference?

Objectives

You may wish to discuss the following questions with students to help them frame the content as they read.

- In what ways was Renaissance art revolutionary? *use of perspective, revealed the subject's personality*
- How do you think Leonardo's scientific studies helped his art? *They allowed him to make his art even more realistic.*

More About . . .

A Painter of the Spanish Renaissance: El Greco (1541–1614) Domenikos Theotokopoulos, better known as El Greco, meaning "the Greek," was born on the island of Crete. Little is known of his early life as a young artist, but he was inspired by Italian artists Titian and Michelangelo. In 1576 El Greco departed for Spain and soon received a commission to paint *The Assumption of the Virgin* in a church in Toledo. This painting distinguished El Greco's style from that of his Italian teachers. After several church commissions, El Greco painted *The Burial of Count Orgaz,* often considered his masterpiece. El Greco became successful and often entertained friends in his fine home in Toledo. He died in 1614, leaving a rich legacy in his paintings.

Renaissance Rivalry According to several sources, there was a bitter rivalry between Leonardo da Vinci and Michelangelo. When the two artists met in Florence, the young Michelangelo jokingly referred to one of Leonardo's failed projects, a bronze statue of a horse and rider. The comment apparently offended the old master. The two great artists' mutual dislike for one other only increased when they were commissioned to paint battle scenes on opposite walls of the city hall in Florence.

▶ ONLINE HISTORICAL SOURCE

Perspective

Have students explore and compare the images using the interactive slider.

Analyze Sources What is the major difference between the figures in the background of the painting and the figures in the foreground? What is the effect of this difference? *The figures in the background are smaller; the figures in the foreground are larger. This makes the figures in the background seem farther away and the figures in the foreground seem closer to the viewer.*

In print edition, see feature titled Analyze Art Feature.

Michelangelo Buonarroti

Have students read the biography of Michelangelo Buonarroti, an Italian Renaissance sculptor, architect, painter, and poet. He sculpted the *Pietà* and *David*, and he painted the ceiling of the Sistine Chapel.

Leonardo da Vinci

Have students read the biography of Leonardo da Vinci, an Italian painter, sculptor, architect, musician, engineer, and scientist. His interests and talents spanned numerous disciplines, and he painted the *Mona Lisa*.

▶ ONLINE GRAPHIC ORGANIZER

The Italian Renaissance

As students read the lesson, have them use the graphic organizer to take notes. Students can review their graphic organizer notes at the end of the lesson to answer the following question:

Clarify How do the works of Renaissance artists and architects reflect Renaissance ideas? Explain. *Possible answer: The ideas of humanism, realism, and classicism are reflected in Renaissance art. Humanists, who focused on human potential and achievements, were interested in Greek values. Raphael even depicted Greek philosophers in School of Athens. Renaissance artworks glorify the individual and the human body and reflect classical influence. Classical art and architecture influenced Renaissance artists and architects.*

Artist / Architect	Contribution	Writer	Contribution

READING CHECK

Compare How were Leonardo and Michelangelo alike? *Both were "Renaissance men," skilled in painting, sculpture, architecture, and engineering.*

interested in how things worked. He studied how a muscle moves and how veins are arranged in a leaf. His notebooks contain anatomical, mathematical, optical, mechanical, geological, and botanical studies. He sketched designs for machines that resemble modern tanks and helicopters.

Among Leonardo's masterpieces is one of the best-known portraits in the world, the *Mona Lisa*. The woman in the portrait seems so real that many writers have tried to explain the thoughts behind her smile. Leonardo also produced a famous religious painting, *The Last Supper*. It shows the personalities of Jesus' disciples through facial expressions.

Raphael Advances Realism Raphael (RAHF•ee•uhl) Sanzio learned by studying the work of Michelangelo and Leonardo. One of Raphael's favorite subjects was the Madonna and child, whom he portrayed with gentle, calm expressions. He was famous for his use of perspective.

In his greatest achievement, Raphael filled the walls of Pope Julius II's library with paintings. One of these, *School of Athens*, shows the classical influence. Raphael painted famous figures such as Michelangelo, Leonardo, and himself as classical philosophers and their students.

Anguissola and Gentileschi Renaissance society generally restricted women's roles. However, a few Italian women became notable painters. Sofonisba Anguissola (ahng•GWEES•soh•lah) was the first woman artist to gain an international reputation. She is known for her portraits of her sisters and of prominent people such as King Philip II of Spain. Artemisia Gentileschi (jayn•tee•LEHS•kee) was another accomplished artist. She trained with her painter father and helped with his work. In her own paintings, Gentileschi painted pictures of strong, heroic women.

BIOGRAPHY

Leonardo da Vinci
(1452–1519)

Leonardo da Vinci's notebooks—and life—are mysterious. Some 3,500 pages closely covered with writings and drawings survive. His writing is clear and easy to read, but only if you look at it in a mirror. No one knows why he wrote backwards.

Leonardo planned scholarly works and great feats of engineering that were never completed. Only 17 of his paintings survive, and yet the work that Leonardo did produce is so extraordinary that it confirms his genius.

Michelangelo Buonarroti
(1475–1564)

Michelangelo was a true Renaissance man, excelling as a painter, sculptor, architect, and poet.

He is best known for the way he showed the human body. Influenced by classical art, he created forceful, heroic figures. Famous works include his ceiling frescoes in the Sistine Chapel and his sculptures *Pietà* and *David*. His architectural and engineering works include the dome of St. Peter's and the Capitoline Square. This "square" was in fact a trapezoid of sloping ground. Michelangelo created an elegant solution for a difficult site.

548 Module 14

Comparing and Contrasting Art

1. Divide students into groups of two or three.
2. Have groups find images of the *Mona Lisa,* by Leonardo da Vinci, and *Pope Paul III Without Cap*, by Titian, using the Internet.
3. Ask groups to list similarities and differences for these two works of art. Suggest that groups focus on the following: facial expressions, use of color, background, use of light and shadow, amount of detail
4. Ask students, "Based on this analysis and information in the text, what can you conclude about Renaissance art?"

Leonardo's Inventions

1. Show students a variety of Leonardo da Vinci's inventions such as the parachute, diving suit, and armored tank.
2. Have each student research any one of Leonardo's inventions to find illustrations and descriptions of some of his drawings.
3. Ask students to research the impetus for the invention and its evolution.
4. Then ask students to compare Leonardo's invention with its modern version.
5. Have students use technology to share their findings.

Italian Renaissance Architecture Even more than painting and sculpture, Renaissance architecture showed its classical roots. Features included classical Roman forms such as columns and domes. Renaissance architects focused on proportion in their designs. As a result the spaces they designed are clear and easy to comprehend.

One of the pioneers of Italian Renaissance architecture was Filippo Brunelleschi. His designs fused classical elements with the Romanesque style, a mixture of Roman, Byzantine, and local styles. As well as rediscovering the principles of linear perspective, Brunelleschi devised a way to build huge domes, using machines of his own invention.

Reading Check
Compare How were Leonardo and Michelangelo alike?

Venetian architect Andrea Palladio studied surviving Roman buildings as well as the works of Roman architects. He wrote a book with rules and plans for buildings. With its clear, detailed illustrations, his book inspired architects in many countries to design buildings in the same style.

Writers of the Italian Renaissance

The dominant feature of Italian Renaissance writing was humanism. Many Italian writers incorporated classical ideals in their work.

Petrarch and Boccaccio Francesco Petrarch (PEE•trahrk) was one of the earliest and most influential humanists. Some have called him the father of Renaissance humanism. He was also a great poet. Petrarch wrote both in Italian and in Latin. In Italian, he wrote sonnets—14-line poems. They were about a mysterious woman named Laura, who was his ideal woman. (Little is known of Laura except that she died of the plague in 1348.) In classical Latin, he wrote letters to many important friends.

The Italian writer Giovanni Boccaccio (boh•KAH•chee•oh) is best known for the *Decameron*, a series of realistic, sometimes off-color stories. The stories are supposedly told by a group of worldly young people waiting in a rural villa to avoid the plague sweeping through Florence:

> *"In the year of Our Lord 1348 the deadly plague broke out in the great city of Florence, most beautiful of Italian cities. Whether through the operation of the heavenly bodies or because of our own iniquities [sins] which the just wrath of God sought to correct, the plague had arisen in the East some years before, causing the death of countless human beings. It spread without stop from one place to another, until, unfortunately, it swept over the West. Neither knowledge nor human foresight availed against it, though the city was cleansed of much filth by chosen officers in charge and sick persons were forbidden to enter it, while advice was broadcast for the preservation of health."*
>
> —Giovanni Boccaccio, Preface, *Decameron*

The *Decameron* presents both tragic and comic views of life. In its stories, the author uses cutting humor to illustrate the human condition. Boccaccio presents his characters in all their individuality and folly.

Objectives

You may wish to discuss the following questions with students to help them frame the content as they read.

- Why is it important that writers began writing in the vernacular? *more accessible to everyday people, possible to read literature without learning to speak Latin*
- Why do you think Machiavelli's work remains popular? *People are still interested in getting and keeping power.*

More About . . .

Machiavelli "The end justifies the means" is one of the most widely known phrases from *The Prince*. Machiavelli is also probably best remembered for his defense of lies and trickery. "A prince never lacks legitimate reasons to break his promise," he wrote, and "The fact is that a man who wants to act virtuously in every way necessarily comes to grief among so many who are not virtuous." *Machiavellian* describes any crafty or deceitful action used for one's own advantage.

Francesco Petrarch, 1304–1374 Francesco Petrarch's father, a lawyer, forced Francesco to study law in France and then Italy, but his love for literature prevailed. After his father's death, Petrarch stopped studying the law and began pursuing his own interests. In addition to a passion for literature, Petrarch also had a passion for religious faith and virtue. He first saw his mysterious Laura in the Church of St. Clare at Avignon in April 1327 and loved her immediately.

Close Read

The Prince Have students explore the Close Read feature to aid in comprehension and understanding.

▷ ONLINE HISTORICAL SOURCE

Giovanni Boccaccio

Invite students to listen to the recording and answer the associated question.

Analyze Sources What possible causes of the plague does Boccaccio suggest in this excerpt? *It was caused by the stars and planets, or it was a punishment from God for the sins of mankind.*

HISTORICAL SOURCE

Giovanni Boccaccio

The *Decameron* presents both tragic and comic views of life. In its stories, the author uses cutting humor to illustrate the human condition. Boccaccio presents his characters in all their individuality and all their folly.

STRUGGLING READERS

Expressing the Ideas of Machiavelli

1. Pair students and have them read the excerpt in the lesson from *The Prince* by Machiavelli.

2. Have them write down in their own words what they think each sentence means. For example, the first sentence might be rewritten as follows: People wonder whether a leader should try to be loved or feared.

3. Have students discuss what they think of the ideas.

4. Ask students if they can they think of any current rulers who are feared or loved.

▷ ONLINE DOCUMENT BASED INVESTIGATION

The Prince

Machiavelli's excerpt from *The Prince* includes a glimpse into Machiavelli's philosophy regarding leadership. Have students study the image, evaluate the text, and answer the associated questions. Use the interactivity of the feature to help students learn more about Machiavelli.

Analyze Sources Does Machiavelli think that a prince should prefer to be loved or feared? Why? *feared; people are more likely to respond to someone they fear*

DOCUMENT-BASED INVESTIGATION   HISTORICAL SOURCE

The Prince

In *The Prince*, Machiavelli says that a prince can't rely on the loyalty of the people he rules.

▷ ONLINE HISTORICAL SOURCE

Perspectives on War

Invite students to listen to the audio and answer the associated question.

Analyze Sources Why does Colonna say she is afraid and sad while her husband is away? *She is afraid that he will be killed in battle.*

HISTORICAL SOURCE

Perspectives on War

Vittoria Colonna exchanged sonnets with Michelangelo and helped Castiglione publish *The Courtier*. Her own poems express personal emotions. When her husband was away at the Battle of Ravenna in 1512, she wrote to him:

Machiavelli Advises Rulers *The Prince* (1513) by Niccolò Machiavelli (mak•ee•uh•VEHL•ee) also examines the imperfect conduct of human beings. Machiavelli lived in Florence, which was a center of philosophy and the arts. However, it was also the subject of a series of conflicts as different individuals and factions struggled for power. Machiavelli watched as the Medici ruler was driven from Florence by French forces, only to make a triumphant return to power.

The Prince, which was first published after Machiavelli's death, follows a long tradition of books offering advice for princes. However, before Machiavelli, most writers urged princes to model themselves after a good and able ruler. Machiavelli recommended that princes should think for themselves. Rather than identifying what "should" be done, rulers should base their actions on the needs of a given situation. In *The Prince*, Machiavelli was not concerned with what was morally right but with what was politically effective.

In answering the question of how a ruler can gain power and keep it in spite of enemies, he began with the idea that most people are selfish, fickle, and corrupt. To succeed in such a wicked world, Machiavelli said, a prince must be strong as a lion and shrewd as a fox. For the good of the state, he might have to trick his enemies or even his own people.

He pointed out that most people think it is praiseworthy in a prince to keep his word and live with integrity. Nevertheless, Machiavelli argued that in the real world of power and politics a prince must sometimes mislead the people and lie to his opponents. As a historian and political thinker, Machiavelli suggested that in order for a prince to accomplish great things, he must be crafty enough to not only overcome the suspicions but also gain the trust of others:

> "From this arises the question whether it is better to be loved more than feared, or feared more than loved. The reply is, that one ought to be both feared and loved, but as it is difficult for the two to go together, it is much safer to be feared than loved, if one of the two has to be wanting. For it may be said of men in general that they are ungrateful, voluble [changeable], dissemblers [liars], anxious to avoid danger, and covetous of gain; as long as you benefit them, they are entirely yours; they offer you their blood, their goods, their life, and their children, as I have before said, when the necessity is remote; but when it approaches, they revolt. And the prince who has relied solely on their words, without making preparations, is ruined."
>
> —Niccolò Machiavelli, *The Prince*

Niccolò Machiavelli

ADVANCED/GIFTED

Analyzing and Writing Sonnets

1. Introduce the two main forms of sonnets: the Italian or Petrarchan, and the English or Shakespearian sonnet. Explain that each form consists of 14 lines, but that the Petrarchan sonnet is divided into an 8-line octave and 6-line sestet, while the Shakespearean sonnet is divided into three 4-line quatrains followed by a 2-line couplet.

2. Provide students with an example of each sonnet type to analyze the different rhyme schemes (Petrarchan: ABBAABBA CDECDE; Shakespearean ABAB CDCD EFEF GG). Distribute additional sonnets and have students identify their type.

3. Instruct students to compose a sonnet using the Petrarchan or Shakespearean form.

Vittoria Colonna The women writers who gained fame during the Renaissance usually wrote about personal subjects, not politics. Yet some of them had great influence. Vittoria Colonna (1492–1547) was born of a noble family. In 1509, she married the Marquis of Pescara. He spent most of his life away from home on military campaigns.

Vittoria Colonna exchanged sonnets with Michelangelo and helped Castiglione publish *The Courtier.* Her own poems express personal emotions. When her husband was away at the Battle of Ravenna in 1512, she wrote to him:

> *"But now in this perilous assault, in this horrible, pitiless battle that has so hardened my mind and heart, your great valor has shown you an equal to Hector and Achilles. But what good is this to me, sorrowful, abandoned? . . . Your uncertain enterprises do not hurt you; but we who wait, mournfully grieving, are wounded by doubt and fear. You men, driven by rage, considering nothing but your honor, commonly go off, shouting, with great fury, to confront danger. We remain, with fear in our heart and grief on our brow for you; sister longs for brother, wife for husband, mother for son."*
>
> —Vittoria Colonna, *Poems*

Reading Check
Draw Conclusions
Does Machiavelli think that a prince should prefer to be loved or feared? Why?

An ardent humanist and intellectual, Colonna was active in literary, political, and religious life. Her poetry, written in the vernacular, was widely published during her lifetime. Vittoria Colonna was the first secular woman writer to attain high literary status in Italy, and her achievements made her a role model for later women writers.

Lesson 2 Assessment

1. Organize Information Use a Venn diagram like this one to compare medieval and Renaissance art.

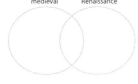

medieval   Renaissance

How were they similar?
How were they different?

2. Key Terms and People For each key term or person in the lesson, write a sentence explaining its significance.

3. Make Inferences How is the humanism of the Renaissance reflected in its art? Explain with examples.

4. Contrast How is Machiavelli's political advice different from the traditional view?

5. Summarize Reread the excerpt from Boccaccio's *Decameron.* What possible causes of the plague does he suggest?

6. Draw Conclusions At a time when few women became artists, what might have helped Artemisia Gentileschi in her chosen career?

Print Assessment

1. **Organize Information** Use a Venn diagram to compare medieval and Renaissance art. How were they similar? How were they different? *Possible answers: Medieval: tried to convey spiritual ideal; Renaissance: imitated nature, followed classical models, realistic, Greek and Roman subjects, portraits of prominent citizens; Both: religious subjects*

2. **Key Terms and People** For each key term or person in the lesson, write a sentence explaining its significance. *Explanations of the significance of the lesson's key terms and names can be found on the following pages: perspective, p. 546; Leonardo da Vinci, p. 546; Michelangelo, p. 546*

3. **Make Inferences** How is the humanism of the Renaissance reflected in its art? Explain with examples. *Renaissance art celebrates the human body and individual achievement.*

4. **Contrast** How is Machiavelli's political advice different from the traditional view? *Machiavelli suggests an individualist, pragmatic approach, focusing on the goal of remaining in power. The traditional view recommended an idealistic approach to ruling.*

5. **Summarize** Reread the excerpt from Boccaccio's *Decameron.* What possible causes of the plague does he suggest? *1. It was caused by the stars and planets. 2. It was a punishment from God for the sins of mankind.*

6. **Draw Conclusions** At a time when few women became artists, what might have helped Artemisia Gentileschi in her chosen career? *Possible answer: Because her father was an artist, he may have recognized her talent and supported her interest in becoming an artist herself.*

History Through Art

Renaissance Ideas Influence Renaissance Art

Ask students how they respond to Leonardo's *Mona Lisa* or Michelangelo's *David*. What do they think the artists were trying to achieve? Ask students if they know anything about any of the artists in this feature. Why do you think the *Mona Lisa* has become such a famous work of art? *Possible answers: realistic yet mysterious style, painted with a high degree of skill, people wonder about her half-smile*

What characteristics of *David* and *School of Athens* indicate that Renaissance artists admired classical works? David *resembles Greek and Roman sculptures;* School of Athens *portrays Greek scholars and shows Greek architecture.*

1. **Draw Conclusions** How do the works of Renaissance artists and architects reflect Renaissance ideas? Explain. *Possible answers: creations reflected a combination of science and art (Leonardo da Vinci), optimism reflected in art and architecture (exploration of light, perspective, color, shape, and dimension), revival of classical arts (Greek and Roman architectural influence, use of human body proportions)*

2. **Synthesize** Look through books on architecture to find examples of American architects who were influenced by the architecture and buildings of the Italian Renaissance. Share your findings with the class. *Answers will vary.*

Renaissance Ideas Influence Renaissance Art

The Renaissance in Italy produced extraordinary achievements in many different forms of art, including painting, architecture, sculpture, and drawing. These art forms were used by talented artists to express important ideas and attitudes of the age.

The value of humanism is shown in Raphael's *School of Athens*, a depiction of the greatest Greek philosophers. The realism of Renaissance art is seen in portraits such as Leonardo's *Mona Lisa*, which is an expression of the subject's unique features and personality. And Michelangelo's *David* shares stylistic qualities with ancient Greek and Roman sculpture.

◄ PORTRAYING INDIVIDUALS
Leonardo Da Vinci The *Mona Lisa* (c. 1504–1506) is thought to be a portrait of Lisa Gherardini, who, at 16, married Francesco del Giocondo, a wealthy merchant of Florence who commissioned the portrait. "Mona Lisa" is a shortened form of Madonna Lisa (Madam, or My Lady, Lisa). Renaissance artists showed individuals as they really looked.

CLASSICAL AND RENAISSANCE SCULPTURE ▶
Michelangelo Influenced by classical statues, Michelangelo sculpted *David* from 1501 to 1504. Michelangelo portrayed the biblical hero in the moments just before battle. David's posture is graceful, yet his figure also displays strength. The statue, which is 18 feet tall, towers over the viewer.

▲ THE IMPORTANCE OF ANCIENT GREECE
Raphael The painting *School of Athens* (1508) was created for the pope's apartments in the Vatican. It shows how highly regarded the scholars of ancient Greece were during the Renaissance. Plato and Aristotle stand under the center arch. To their right, Socrates argues with several young men. Toward the front, Pythagoras draws a lesson on a slate and Ptolemy holds a globe.

RENAISSANCE SCIENCE AND TECHNOLOGY ▶
Leonardo Da Vinci Leonardo filled his notebooks with observations and sketches of new inventions. This drawing from his notebooks shows a design for a spiral screw to achieve vertical flight. Leonardo's drawing anticipated the helicopter.

Critical Thinking
1. **Draw Conclusions** How do the works of Renaissance artists and architects reflect Renaissance ideas? Explain.

2. **Synthesize** Look through books on architecture to find examples of American architects who were influenced by the architects and buildings of the Italian Renaissance. Share your findings with the class.

The Renaissance **553**

▷ Online **Assessment**

1. How did Renaissance architects, such as Brunelleschi, use past styles in their designs?
   - ○ They incorporated Roman forms such as domes and columns.
   - ○ They included rounded doorways used by Arabs in North Africa.
   - ○ They introduced vaulted ceilings pioneered by the ancient Greeks.
   - ○ They installed English styles such as multiple rooms in a smaller space.

   Alternate Question *Select the answer choice from the drop-down list to complete the sentence correctly.* Renaissance architects studied [Roman ⬍] buildings to use similar forms and features in their own buildings.

2. Which of the following was a guiding principle of Machiavelli's *The Prince*?
   - ○ Rulers should take advice from religious leaders in order to avoid making immoral decisions.
   - ○ Rulers should base their actions on similar situations found in the course of historical study.
   - ○ Rulers should allow the needs of a given situation to guide their actions in order to be politically effective.
   - ○ Rulers should be honest with their subjects in order to ensure their trust and consistent obedience.

   Alternate Question *Select the answer choice from the drop-down list to complete the sentence correctly.* In *The Prince*, Niccolò Machiavelli wrote that most people were [selfish ⬍] and corrupt.

3. **Apply Concepts** How was Leonardo da Vinci a "Renaissance man"?

   Possible answer: Leonardo was a master painter and sculptor. In addition to art, he studied diverse fields such as anatomy, mathematics, optics, mechanics, geology, and botany. His notebooks, filled with sketches and notes, were proof of his innovation in and mastery of each field of study.

4. **Apply Concepts** How did Giovanni Boccaccio's *The Decameron* represent a Renaissance outlook and not a medieval one?

   Possible answer: The Decameron reflected a distinctly secular outlook characteristic of the Renaissance. Although some religious topics were present in The Decameron, *it avoided the overall serious, religious tone of the medieval period. Instead, it told realistic stories through different individual characters using humor and tragedy.*

The Northern Renaissance

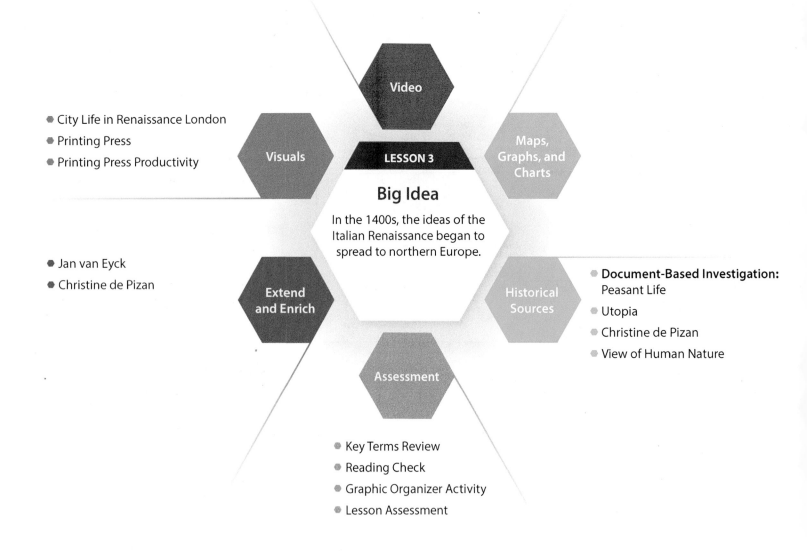

- City Life in Renaissance London
- Printing Press
- Printing Press Productivity

Visuals

Video

LESSON 3

Maps, Graphs, and Charts

Big Idea

In the 1400s, the ideas of the Italian Renaissance began to spread to northern Europe.

- Jan van Eyck
- Christine de Pizan

Extend and Enrich

Historical Sources

- **Document-Based Investigation:** Peasant Life
- Utopia
- Christine de Pizan
- View of Human Nature

Assessment

- Key Terms Review
- Reading Check
- Graphic Organizer Activity
- Lesson Assessment

Jan van Eyck

Biography Students will read about Jan van Eyck's life as a Renaissance artist. They will reference images by Van Eyck to create a collage or poster showing some of the key elements of Van Eyck's style of painting. This activity walks students through evaluating Jan van Eyck's style of painting, creating a collage or poster, and writing a short paragraph to accompany their artwork.

Christine de Pizan

Biography Students will read about Christine de Pizan's life and her work as a poet. Then they will write a letter to Christine's father, explaining the influence her education had on her life and thanking him for giving her the chance to learn.

Teach the Big Idea

1. **Whole Class Open/Introduction** Have students read the Now and Then feature about Shakespeare. Ask students why Shakespeare's plays are still performed today. *They are adaptable to modern themes and settings.*

2. **Direct Teach** Read students the Big Idea: *In the 1400s, the ideas of the Italian Renaissance began to spread to northern Europe.*

   Review the following lesson objectives with students to aid in their understanding of the Big Idea.

   • Explain the origins and characteristics of the northern Renaissance.

   • Trace the impact of the Renaissance on German and Flemish painters.

   • Profile key northern Renaissance writers.

   • Describe the origins of the Elizabethan Age and Elizabethan drama.

   • Explain how printing spread ideas.

3. **Whole Group Close/Reflect** Have students write a journal entry from the point of view of a young German artist traveling through Italy during the Renaissance.

▶ ONLINE GRAPHIC ORGANIZER

The Northern Renaissance

As students read the lesson, have them use the graphic organizer to take notes. Students can review their graphic organizer notes at the end of the lesson to answer the following question:

Draw Conclusions Why was the invention of the printing press so important? *It made more information available not only to scholars but also to ordinary people.*

READING CHECK (Digital)
Synthesize What was the economic base in Flanders? *trade and production*

READING CHECK (Print)
Contrast How did the Northern Renaissance differ from the Italian Renaissance? *stronger interest in realistic art, more of an emphasis on changing society*

The Northern Renaissance

The Big Idea
In the 1400s, the ideas of the Italian Renaissance began to spread to northern Europe.

Why It Matters Now
Renaissance ideas such as the importance of the individual are an important part of modern thought.

Key Terms and People
utopia
William Shakespeare
Johann Gutenberg

Setting The Stage

The work of such artists as Leonardo da Vinci, Michelangelo, and Raphael showed the Renaissance spirit. All three artists demonstrated an interest in classical culture, a curiosity about the world, and a belief in human potential. Humanist writers expanded ideas about individuality. These ideas impressed scholars, students, and merchants who visited Italy. By the late 1400s, Renaissance ideas had spread to northern Europe—especially England, France, Germany, and Flanders (now part of France and the Netherlands).

The Northern Renaissance Begins

By 1450 the population of northern Europe, which had declined due to bubonic plague, was beginning to grow again. When the destructive Hundred Years' War between France and England ended in 1453, many cities grew rapidly. Urban merchants became wealthy enough to sponsor artists. This happened first in Flanders, which was rich from long-distance trade and the cloth industry. Then, as wealth increased in other parts of northern Europe, patronage of artists increased as well.

Unlike Italy, which was divided into city-states, England and France were unified under strong monarchs. These rulers often sponsored the arts by purchasing paintings and by supporting artists and writers. For example, Francis I of France invited Leonardo da Vinci to retire in France, and hired Italian artists and architects to rebuild and decorate his castle at Fontainebleau (fahn•tihn•BLOH). The castle became a showcase for Renaissance art.

As Renaissance ideas spread out of Italy, they mingled with northern traditions. As a result, the northern Renaissance developed its own character. For example, the Renaissance ideal of human dignity inspired some northern humanists to develop plans for social reform based on Judeo-Christian values.

Reading Check
Contrast How did the Northern Renaissance differ from the Italian Renaissance?

Objectives

You may wish to discuss the following question with students to help them frame the content as they read.

• Why and how did an increase in wealth affect the spread of the Renaissance? *Merchants and rulers could sponsor artists and writers.*

More About . . .

Flanders Flanders is believed to mean "Lowland" or "Flooded Land." Louis II, Count of Flanders, died in 1384, leaving Flanders to his daughter Margaret, whose second husband, Philip the Bold, Duke of Burgundy, thereby succeeded to the county of Flanders. This event was the starting point for the eventual political unification of the Low Countries under the dukes of Burgundy.

Artistic Ideas Spread

In 1494, a French king claimed the throne of Naples in southern Italy and launched an invasion through northern Italy. As the war dragged on, many Italian artists and writers left for a safer life in northern Europe. They brought with them the styles and techniques of the Italian Renaissance. In addition, northern European artists who studied in Italy carried Renaissance ideas back to their homelands.

German Painters Perhaps the most famous person to do this was the German artist Albrecht Dürer (DYUR•uhr). He traveled to Italy to study in 1494. After returning to Germany, Dürer produced woodcuts and engravings. Many of his prints portray religious subjects. Others portray classical myths or realistic landscapes. The popularity of Dürer's work helped to spread Renaissance styles.

Dürer's emphasis upon realism influenced the work of another German artist, Hans Holbein (HOHL•byn) the Younger. Holbein specialized in painting portraits that are almost photographic in detail. He emigrated to England where he painted portraits of King Henry VIII and other members of the English royal family.

Flemish Painters The support of wealthy merchant families in Flanders helped to make Flanders the artistic center of northern Europe. The first great Flemish Renaissance painter was Jan van Eyck (yahn•van•YK). Van Eyck used recently developed oil-based paints to develop techniques that painters still use. By applying layer upon layer of paint, van Eyck was able to create a variety of subtle colors in clothing and jewels. Oil painting became popular and spread to Italy.

In addition to new techniques, van Eyck's paintings display unusually realistic details and reveal the personality of their subjects. His work influenced later artists in northern Europe.

DOCUMENT-BASED INVESTIGATION   Historical Source

Peasant Wedding

The Flemish painter Pieter Bruegel's paintings provide information about peasant life in the 1500s. *Peasant Wedding* (1568) portrays a wedding feast.

- **The Bride** The bride sits under the paper crown hanging on the green cloth.
- **The Servers** Men who may be her brothers are passing out plates.
- **The Guests** Several children have come to the party.
- **The Musicians** They are carrying bagpipes. One glances hungrily at the food.

Analyze Historical Sources
In what ways does this painting present a snapshot of peasant life?

Objectives

You may wish to discuss the following questions with students to help them frame the content as they read.

- What factors might have influenced the trend toward a more realistic style of art? *Artists could travel and thereby learn better techniques; oil paints made more realistic, subtle paintings possible.*

- What can be learned about people's daily lives from examining the painting *Peasant Wedding*? *Possible answers: where ordinary people lived, what they ate, how they dressed, how they celebrated*

More About . . .

Jan van Eyck, 1395–1441 Jan van Eyck, the first great Flemish Renaissance painter, included disguised religious symbols in many of his portraits. *The Arnolfini Portrait* is said to be a symbolic recording of the contract of marriage.His masterpiece is the altarpiece in the cathedral at Ghent, *The Adoration of the Mystic Lamb*. Van Eyck was recorded as being the honorary painter of the count of Holland. He worked in the count's palace until the count's death. Van Eyck then served the duke of Burgundy and, on behalf of the duke, undertook a number of secret missions.

▷ ONLINE LESSON FLIP CARDS

Review Key Terms and People

Students can use the flip cards in the Lesson Review at any time to review the lesson's key terms and people: *utopia*, *William Shakespeare*, and *Johann Gutenberg*.

▷ ONLINE DOCUMENT-BASED INVESTIGATION

Peasant Wedding

The painting, *Peasant Wedding*, depicts a scene from a wedding feast in the 1500s. Have students explore the images using the interactive hotspots.

Analyze Sources In what ways does this painting present a snapshot of peasant life? *People are shown in conversation or in mid-movement; the setting and objects are carefully observed and realistic.*

In print edition, see feature titled Peasant Wedding.

COLLABORATIVE LEARNING

The Palace at Fontainebleau: Now and Then

1. Pair students and ask them to research the historical castle at Fontainebleau and the present-day palace.

2. Ask students to create two posters, one with images depicting the historical castle and one with images depicting the palace in the present day.

3. Have students identify how the building has changed over the years and how it has stayed the same.

4. Ask students to present their findings to the class, describing their favorite features from each version of the structure.

ADVANCED/GIFTED

Compare and Contrast

1. Request that students examine the text material on the Italian and the northern Renaissances.

2. Then have them conduct further research on both using the Internet.

3. Ask students to create an outline of similarities and differences.

4. Have students write a compare-and-contrast paper on the Italian Renaissance and the northern Renaissance.

Objectives

You may wish to discuss the following questions with students to help them frame the content as they read.

- What similarities were there in the works of Desiderius Erasmus and Thomas More? *Both wanted to improve society; both believed that greed caused problems.*

- What qualities made Christine de Pizan unusual for her time and place? *few highly educated, outspoken women authors in Europe during the Renaissance*

More About . . .

Utopia, *The Republic* by Plato (427–347 BC) provided Thomas More with many of his ideas for his own "utopia." In Plato's ideal society, the person with the greatest insight and intellect from the ruling class would be chosen as philosopher-king. The theme of More's *Utopia* was social and political equality for all.

Humanists' Views Encourage students to compare the Christian humanists' view of society with that of Niccolò Machiavelli. Ask, "Is it more effective to focus on how society could or should be or to concentrate on how life really is?" *Answers will vary but students should support their opinions with examples from the text or other sources.*

READING CHECK

Summarize What techniques does Bruegel use to give life to his paintings? *rich colors, vivid details, balanced use of space*

 ONLINE HISTORICAL SOURCE

Utopia

Invite students to read or listen to the excerpt and answer the associated question.

Analyze Sources What aspect of the Renaissance economy is More commenting on here? *the increased interest in trade and banking*

 ONLINE HISTORICAL SOURCE

Christine de Pizan

Invite students to read or listen to the excerpt and answer the associated question.

Analyze Sources What kind of reform does de Pizan argue for in this passage? *education for women*

Reading Check
Summarize
What techniques did Bruegel use to give life to his paintings?

Flemish painting reached its peak after 1550 with the work of Pieter Bruegel (BROY•guhl) the Elder. Bruegel was also interested in realistic details and individual people. He was very skillful in portraying large numbers of people. He captured scenes from everyday peasant life such as weddings, dances, and harvests. Bruegel's rich colors, vivid details, and balanced use of space give a sense of life and feeling.

Northern Writers Try to Reform Society

Italian humanists were very interested in reviving classical languages and classical texts. When the Italian humanist ideas reached the north, people used them to examine the traditional teachings of the Church. The northern humanists were critical of the failure of the Christian Church to inspire people to live a Christian life. This criticism produced a new movement known as Christian humanism. The focus of Christian humanism was the reform of society. Of particular importance to humanists was education. The humanists promoted the education of women and founded schools attended by both boys and girls.

Christian Humanists The best known of the Christian humanists were Desiderius Erasmus (dehz•ih•DEER•ee•uhs ih•RAZ•muhs) of Holland and Thomas More of England. The two were close friends.

In 1509, Erasmus wrote his most famous work, *The Praise of Folly.* This book poked fun at greedy merchants, heartsick lovers, quarrelsome scholars, and pompous priests. Erasmus believed in a Christianity of the heart, not one of ceremonies or rules. He thought that in order to improve society, all people should study the Bible.

Thomas More tried to show a better model of society. In 1516, he wrote the book *Utopia.* In Greek, **utopia** means "no place." In English it has come to mean an ideal place as depicted in More's book. The book is about an imaginary land where greed, corruption, and war have been weeded out. In Utopia, because there was little greed, Utopians had little use for money:

"Gold and silver, of which money is made, are so treated . . . that no one values them more highly than their true nature deserves. Who does not see that they are far inferior to iron in usefulness since without iron mortals cannot live any more than without fire and water?"

—Thomas More, *Utopia*

More wrote in Latin. Eventually, his writing was translated into a variety of languages including French, German, English, Spanish, and Italian, making his ideas widely available.

Women's Reforms During this period the vast majority of Europeans were unable to read or write. Those families who could afford formal schooling usually sent only their sons. One woman spoke out against this practice. Christine de Pizan was highly educated for the time and was one

Christian humanist
Thomas More

COLLABORATIVE LEARNING

Renaissance Art: North and South

1. Pair students and have them use the Internet to find Jan Van Eyck's *The Arnolfini Wedding* and Raphael's *The Marriage of the Virgin.*

2. Request that pairs use the Internet to conduct further research on both paintings.

3. Ask pairs to evaluate how differences between the paintings reveal differences between the Northern and Italian Renaissances.

4. Display both paintings and invite pairs to share the differences.

5. Discuss the differences and any similarities as a class.

Christine de Pizan is best known for her works defending women.

Reading Check
Analyze Issues
What kind of reform does de Pizan argue for?

of the first women to earn a living as a writer. Writing in French, she produced many books, including short stories, biographies, novels, and manuals on military techniques. She frequently wrote about the objections men had to educating women. In one book, *The Book of the City of Ladies*, she wrote:

> *"I am amazed by the opinion of some men who claim that they do not want their daughters, wives, or kinswomen to be educated because their mores [morals] would be ruined as a result. . . . Here you can clearly see that not all opinions of men are based on reason and that these men are wrong."*
>
> —Christine de Pizan, *The Book of the City of Ladies*

Christine de Pizan was one of the first European writers to question different treatment of boys and girls. However, her goal of formal education for children of both sexes would not be achieved for several centuries.

The Elizabethan Age

The Renaissance spread to England in the mid-1500s. The period was known as the Elizabethan Age, after Queen Elizabeth I. Elizabeth reigned from 1558 to 1603. She was well educated and spoke French, Italian, Latin, and Greek. She also wrote poetry and music. As queen she did much to support the development of English art and literature.

William Shakespeare The most famous writer of the Elizabethan Age was **William Shakespeare**. Many people regard him as the greatest playwright of all time. Shakespeare was born in 1564 in Stratford-upon-Avon, a small town about 90 miles northwest of London. By 1592 he was living in London and writing poems and plays, and soon he would be performing at the Globe Theater.

Like many Renaissance writers, Shakespeare revered the classics and drew on them for inspiration and plots. His works display a masterful command of the English language and a deep understanding of human beings. He revealed the souls of men and women through scenes of dramatic conflict. Many of these plays examine human flaws. However, Shakespeare also had one of his characters deliver a speech that expresses the Renaissance's high view of human nature:

> *"What a piece of work is a man, how noble in reason, how infinite in faculties, in form and moving, how express and admirable; in action how like an angel, in apprehension [understanding] how like a god: the beauty of the world, the paragon of animals."*
>
> —William Shakespeare, *Hamlet* (Act 2, Scene 2)

Reading Check
Summarize What are two ways in which Shakespeare's work showed Renaissance influences?

Shakespeare's most famous plays include the tragedies *Macbeth, Hamlet, Othello, Romeo and Juliet,* and *King Lear,* and the comedies *A Midsummer Night's Dream* and *The Taming of the Shrew.*

Objectives

You may wish to discuss the following questions with students to help them frame the content as they read.

- How did Elizabeth I contribute to the Renaissance? *She was well-educated and supported writers and artists.*

- How did the Elizabethan Age reflect the values of the Italian Renaissance? *focus on art and literature, positive view of humans and human nature*

More About . . .

The Taming of the Shrew, William Shakespeare *The Taming of the Shrew* is a comedy in five acts describing a topsy-turvy courtship between a shrewish woman, Katharina, and a sharp-witted man named Petruchio, whose motivation is finding a wealthy wife. Petruchio is fiercely determined to tame Katharina and win her hand in marriage. Petruchio is ultimately victorious, wedding Katharina, who even delivers a short sermon on the virtues of wifely obedience.

▷ **ONLINE INTERACTIVE VISUALS**

Carousel: City Life in Renaissance London
Have students navigate through the carousel and note similarities and differences among the images or identify a unifying theme.

READING CHECK (Digital)
Analyze Motives What reasons did humanists give for wanting to reform society? *They wanted people to live a Christian life. To do so they had to give up greed, corruption, and war and provide education for women and children as well as boys and men.*

READING CHECK (Print)
Analyze Issues What kind of reform does de Pizan argue for? *education for women*

READING CHECK
Summarize What are two ways in which Shakespeare's work showed Renaissance influences? *In his work, Shakespeare drew from the classics and displayed a deep understanding of human beings combined with a high idea of human nature.*

TIERED ACTIVITY

Analyze: *The Praise of Folly* by Desiderius Erasmus

Below Level Provide students with a definition of *folly* and a summary of *The Praise of Folly*. Explain that Folly mentions Bacchus and other gods who bring joy and silliness into the lives of mortals. Project a list of the gods (Bacchus, god of wine; Cupid, god of love; Venus, goddess of love, beauty, and fertility; Flora, goddess of flowers and the season of spring). Ask students to choose one god or goddess and create an image of the deity using their imaginations. Have students share images and describe how the deities contribute to joy and silliness.

At Level Provide students with an overview of *The Praise of Folly*. Then ask students to use the Internet to study the text further and answer the following question: How does Erasmus depict Christ? Guide students in creating an outline based on their findings. Have students create an essay based on their outlines.

Above Level Provide students with an overview of *The Praise of Folly*. Then ask students to use the Internet to study the text further. Ask students to analyze the text, focusing on how the three sections of text differ from each other. Have students work in pairs to create a presentation summarizing the three sections and explaining how they differ. Encourage them to use images and citations from the text.

View of Human Nature

Students can activate the audio button beneath the historical source to hear the excerpt read aloud. Invite students to read or listen to the excerpt and answer the associated question.

Analyze Sources How does this speech reflect Renaissance ideas? *It expresses a high view of human nature.*

LEARN MORE ABOUT

Shakespeare's Popularity

Today, almost 400 years after his death, the language of Shakespeare is all around us. Whether we know it or not, we hear and use quotations from Shakespeare every day of our lives. Here are some of the phrases from Shakespeare's plays that have become part of modern English: "at one fell swoop," "foul play," "good riddance," "high time," "lie low," "mum's the word," "neither here nor there," "the game is up," and "vanish into thin air."

READING CHECK
Analyze Effects How did the invention of the printing press affect the dissemination of knowledge and ideas? *It made books readily available and cheap enough for many people to afford.*

Now and Then

Shakespeare's Popularity

Even though he has been dead for about 400 years, Shakespeare remains a favorite with filmmakers. His themes have been adapted for many films, including some in foreign languages. These photos are from movie versions of some of Shakespeare's plays including *Othello* and *Romeo and Juliet* (in period costume); a Japanese film, *Ran*, an adaptation of *King Lear*; and *10 Things I Hate About You*, an adaptation of *The Taming of the Shrew* in a modern setting.

Printing Spreads Renaissance Ideas

The Chinese invented block printing in which a printer carved words or letters on a wooden block, inked the block, and then used it to print on paper. Around 1045, Bi Sheng invented movable type, which uses a separate piece of type for each character in the language. The Chinese writing system contains thousands of different characters, so most Chinese printers found movable type impractical. However, the method would prove practical for Europeans because their languages can be written using a small number of letters.

By the early 1400s in Europe, paper had replaced parchment, a writing material made from animal hides. Parchment was expensive and could not be mass-produced. Paper could be produced quickly and inexpensively. Its availability helped facilitate the printing of whole books.

Gutenberg Improves the Printing Process During the 13th century, block-printed items reached Europe from China. European printers began to use block printing to create whole pages to bind into books. However, this process was too slow to satisfy the Renaissance demand for knowledge, information, and books.

Around 1440 **Johann Gutenberg**, a craftsman from Mainz, Germany, developed a printing press that incorporated a number of technologies in a new way. The process made it possible to produce books quickly and cheaply. Using this improved process, Gutenberg printed a complete Bible, the Gutenberg Bible, in about 1455. It was the first full-sized book printed with movable type.

The printing press enabled a printer to produce hundreds of copies of a single work. For the first time, books were cheap enough that many people could buy them. At first printers produced mainly religious works. Soon they began to provide books on other subjects such as travel guides and medical manuals.

Reading Check
Analyze Effects
How did the invention of the printing press affect the dissemination of knowledge and ideas?

The Printing Press

Many inventions are creative combinations of known technologies. In 1452, Johann Gutenberg combined known technologies from Europe and Asia with his idea for molding movable type to create a printing press that changed the world.

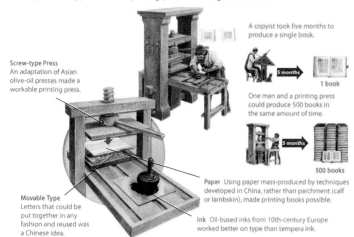

A copyist took five months to produce a single book.

5 months → 1 book

One man and a printing press could produce 500 books in the same amount of time.

5 months → 500 books

Screw-type Press An adaptation of Asian olive-oil presses made a workable printing press.

Movable Type Letters that could be put together in any fashion and reused was a Chinese idea.

Paper Using paper mass-produced by techniques developed in China, rather than parchment (calf or lambskin), made printing books possible.

Ink Oil-based inks from 10th-century Europe worked better on type than tempera ink.

Critical Thinking
1. **Draw Conclusions** About how many books could a printing press produce in a month?
2. **Make Inferences** Which areas of the world contributed ideas that were used in developing Gutenberg's printing press?

Lesson 3 Assessment

1. **Organize Information** Create a timeline showing key events of the Northern Renaissance.

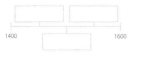

1400   1600

Which of the events listed do you think was most important? Explain.

2. **Key Terms and People** For each key term or person in the lesson, write a sentence explaining its significance.

3. **Form Generalizations** How did Albrecht Dürer's work reflect the influence of the Italian Renaissance?
4. **Analyze Effects** What was one way the Renaissance changed society?
5. **Compare** How were the paintings of the northern painters different from those of Flemish painters? Give examples.
6. **Analyze Motives** What reasons did humanists give for wanting to reform society? Explain.

Effects of the Printing Press

1. Draw a graphic organizer for students showing the effects of the printing press using boxes and arrows and no text.
2. Divide students into small groups and have them draw and complete the graphic organizer.
3. Ask volunteers to complete the class chart.

▷ ONLINE INTERACTIVE VISUALS

Compare Images

Have students explore and compare the images using the interactive slider.

In print edition, see feature titled Global Patterns.

Objectives

You may wish to discuss the following questions with students to help them frame the content as they read.

- Why do you think the Bible was the first book printed with movable type? *Most Europeans were religious.*

- How would you compare and contrast the impact of the printing press with the impact of the Internet? *information easier to access, changes affect society, more ways to access information today, Internet spreads information faster*

More About . . .

Johann Gutenberg Johann Gutenberg was also a blacksmith, which likely helped him develop the metal prisms used to mold the face of the type, which could be cast precisely and in large quantities. Much of Gutenberg's life is a mystery, as there is little recorded information about him. Gutenberg went to great lengths to keep his invention, the printing press, a secret.

▷ ONLINE INTERACTIVE VISUALS

Image with Hotspots: Printing Press

Have students explore the image using the interactive hotspots. You may wish to use the associated question as a discussion prompt.

Analyze Visuals Which areas of the world contributed technologies to Gutenberg's printing press? *Asia (including China) and Europe*

In print edition, see feature titled Global Patterns.

1. **Draw Conclusions** About how many books could a printing press produce in a month? *about 500 books*

2. **Make Inferences** Which areas of the world contributed ideas that were used in developing Gutenberg's printing press? *Asia (including China) and Europe*

Print Assessment

1. **Organize Information** Create a timeline showing key events of the Northern Renaissance. *1450s— Northern Renaissance begins; 1509—Erasmus writes* The Praise of Folly; *1516—More writes* Utopia; *mid-1500s—Elizabethan Age begins; late 1500s— Shakespeare writes plays and poems.*

2. **Key Terms and People** For each key term or person in the lesson, write a sentence explaining its significance. *Explanations of the significance of the lesson's key terms and names can be found on the following pages: utopia, p. 556; William Shakespeare, p. 557; Johann Gutenberg, p. 558*

(continued)

Print Assessment (continued)

3. **Form Generalizations** How did Albrecht Dürer's work reflect the influence of the Italian Renaissance? *He portrayed classical myths, religious subjects, and realistic landscapes.*

4. **Analyze Effects** What was one way the Renaissance changed society? *Possible answer: More people were exposed to ideas because they could read the information in their own language.*

5. **Compare** How were the paintings of the northern painters different from those of Flemish painters? Give examples. *German painters such as Dürer used classic myths and religious subjects. Flemish painters such as Bruegel focused on ordinary subjects and used a great amount of detail.*

6. **Analyze Motives** What reasons did humanists give for wanting to reform society? Explain. *They wanted people to live a Christian life. To do so they had to give up greed, corruption, and war and provide education for women and children.*

▶ Online Assessment

1. How did most monarchs in England and France participate in the northern Renaissance?
   - ○ by creating their own art
   - ○ by establishing law schools
   - ○ by funding humanist universities
   - ⦿ by sponsoring writers and artists

   Alternate Question *Select the answer choice from the drop-down list to complete the sentence correctly.* One way French and English monarchs helped bring the Renaissance to northern Europe was by inviting writers and artists from [*Italy* ⇕] to live in their countries.

2. Which of Jan van Eyck's innovations became very influential to future artists?
   - ○ layering oil-based paints to add subtlety to the colors used
   - ○ studying subjects closely to create incredibly detailed portraits
   - ○ improving woodcutting tools to produce more realistic engravings
   - ○ using multiple subjects to contrast the personalities of different people

   Alternate Question *Select the answer choice from the drop-down list to complete the sentence correctly.* Jan van Eyck influenced artistic style by using [*oil* ⇕] paints to add levels of subtlety to colors.

3. What was the focus of Christian humanism?
   - ○ following tradition
   - ○ increasing trade
   - ○ maintaining peace
   - ⦿ reforming society

   Alternate Question *Select the answer choice from the drop-down list to complete the sentence correctly.* Christian humanists were very concerned with [*education* ⇕].

4. Which characteristic of William Shakespeare's writing followed the style of the Renaissance?
   - ○ working with others to develop stories
   - ○ providing religious lessons in each play
   - ○ writing poems using the local language
   - ○ using the classics for inspiration and plots

Alternate Question *Select the answer choice from the drop-down list to complete the sentence correctly.* William Shakespeare was a Renaissance writer from [*England* ⇕] who drew inspiration and plots from the classics to write plays and poems.

5. Why was Johann Gutenberg's movable type so important to the Renaissance?
   - ○ It made wealthy merchants sponsor copyists by making books luxury items.
   - ⦿ It helped spread ideas by making book printing faster and less expensive.
   - ○ It helped monarchs correspond with other rulers about humanist ideas.
   - ○ It made printing profitable, allowing writers to make more money.

   Alternate Question *Select the answer choice from the drop-down list to complete the sentence correctly.* Johann Gutenberg's development of [*the printing press* ⇕] allowed books to be manufactured more quickly and less expensively.

6. **Cause and Effect** What conditions in northern Europe allowed the middle class to start sponsoring artists?

   Possible answer: Cities in northern Europe started growing during the second part of the 15th century after years of decline due to the bubonic plague and the Hundred Years' War. Urban merchants, such as in Flanders, became wealthy from international trade and the cloth industry. This new wealth allowed them to start sponsoring artists.

7. **Apply Concepts** How did the work of Albrecht Dürer illustrate the style of the northern Renaissance?

   Possible answer: Dürer drew upon religious and classical topics such as myths, much like his contemporaries in Italy and northern Europe. His use of realism helped shape the northern Renaissance's emphasis on it as well.

8. **Summarize** How did Christine de Pizan's position on education disagree with more traditional thinking?

   Possible answer: Like most humanists, Christine de Pizan promoted education. What set her apart from mainstream thinking, though, was her advocating the formal education of both boys and girls. She defended this position by speaking out against the objections of men to the education of women.

9. **Apply Concepts** How was Queen Elizabeth I representative of the Renaissance?

   Possible answer: Queen Elizabeth I was well educated and skilled in many different areas. She wrote poems, composed music, and could speak French, Italian, Latin, and Greek. She helped foster the arts in England during her 45-year reign.

10. **Draw Conclusions** How did the printing press make information more accessible?

    Possible answer: Gutenberg's printing press allowed for books to be printed more quickly and less expensively. This allowed books to be purchased for much less money than before. More people were able to own books and become exposed to more information.

ADDITIONAL LESSON CONTENT

More About . . .

The Palace at Fontainebleau The palace at Fontainebleau is the only royal and imperial residence to have been continuously inhabited for seven centuries. When King Francis I returned from Italy, he ordered extensive work to take place at the castle, which continued throughout the 15th and 16th centuries. The construction of the gallery linking his chamber to the chapel was accompanied by the most renowned décor of the French Renaissance. As a showcase of Renaissance decoration, this gallery was the first of its kind to be built in France, and it is said that the king himself wore the key to it around his neck.

ADVANCED/GIFTED

Becoming a Docent

1. Ask students to define *docent* using background knowledge or the Internet.
2. Explain to students that they will conduct research to become experts in art in preparation for presenting artwork as a docent would in an art museum.
3. Have students choose any work of art from the Northern Renaissance to research. Research should focus on the artist's approach to the subject matter, techniques and visual effects, and when the piece was created.
4. Encourage students to locate unusual or anecdotal information about the artist or the work that a crowd of museum visitors would find interesting.
5. Have students present the artwork as a docent would in an art museum, using technology.

STRUGGLING READERS

Planning a Utopian Community

1. To be sure that students understand the meaning of the word *utopia,* display the word and ask students to brainstorm other ways to describe the same idea. *Possible answers: perfect place, ideal society, city with no problems*
2. Use a word web to help students brainstorm different features of a perfect community.
3. Use the following questions to guide the students in a discussion about utopian communities:
   a. What is special about the society that More imagined? *Possible answers: peaceful, no cheating or stealing, people don't want more than they need*
   b. What ideas of More's should be added to the class's utopian community? *Possible answers: no war, no greed or corruption*
   c. What ideas do you have that could be added? *Possible answers: equality for all races, equality for men and women, free schooling for all*
   d. What makes a utopian community difficult or impossible to create? *Possible answers: People are selfish and imperfect.*

COLLABORATIVE LEARNING

Comparing Book Production Methods

1. Divide students into pairs.
2. Have student pairs copy a paragraph from a book by hand and record how long it takes.
3. Next, ask them to estimate the amount of time it would take to copy the entire page.
4. Tell them to multiply this amount by the total number of book pages. Their answer represents the estimated number of hours required to create a handwritten version of the book.
5. Challenge student pairs to estimate how long it would take to reproduce a set of these books for the entire class.
6. Explain to students that a printing press could do 500 times as much work as a copyist in the same amount of time. Ask students, "What would be the effects of such an invention?"

ENGLISH LANGUAGE LEARNERS

Question Words as Statements

1. Organize students into groups of three or four.
2. Give each group a list of quotations by Shakespeare where *what* and *how* are used as exclamations rather than questions.
3. Explain usage with examples such as that "What a piece of work is a man . . ." could be rewritten as "Man is an extraordinary piece of work!" Point out that the meaning of the sentence remains the same.
4. Ask each group to choose two or three quotations, and direct them to rewrite the excerpt so that *what* or *how* does not begin the phrase.
5. Then have them explain its meaning in their own words.
6. When groups are finished, combine their work into one chart.

COLLABORATIVE LEARNING

Debate: Government Support of the Arts

1. Organize students into groups of three to four students.
2. Ask students to take notes regarding the history of how the government has funded the arts in preparation for a debate.
3. Share information with the students about the Works Progress Administration (WPA), which was formed by President Franklin Roosevelt to help lift the country out of the Great Depression, and the National Endowment for the Arts (NEA), which was created by Congress in 1965 to fund art projects around the United States.
4. Allow the groups time to prepare responses to the following questions: Why would a government provide funding for art? Do students think arts funding is a good use of taxpayer money? Why or why not?
5. Encourage a healthy debate among the groups and remind students to back their viewpoints with claims and examples.

Social History

City Life in Renaissance Europe

Ask students to discuss the similarities and differences between city life in Renaissance London and cities in the United States today. *Possible answers: Crime, sanitation, food, transportation, and entertainment are still important matters. Unlike centuries ago, garbage is picked up, and theatergoers do not throw things at the stage. People in the United States today can beg without being arrested even if they are neither sick nor disabled.*

Also ask students how the problems in London during the Renaissance compare to problems in cities today. *Possible answers: Crime, pollution, joblessness, and crowding still exist in many places today.*

Make Inferences Study the images and captions, as well as the information in the chart. What inferences about the standard of living of London's wealthy citizens can you make from this information? How did it compare to the standard of living of London's common people? *Merchants and other wealthy citizens had a very high standard of living because their yearly income put even luxuries, such as rare spices, easily within their reach. In comparison, it was a struggle for the common people to maintain a decent standard of living because even basic necessities like food took a huge share of their income.*

Compare How does diet in the United States today compare to the diet of Renaissance Europeans? Cite specific examples in your answer. *Comparisons should describe the diet of Renaissance Europeans, describe the diet of modern Americans, and point out what the two diets have in common.*

CITY LIFE IN RENAISSANCE EUROPE
Throughout the 1500s, the vast majority of Europeans—more than 75 percent—lived in rural areas. However, the capital and port cities of most European countries experienced remarkable growth during this time. The population of London, for example, stood at about 200,000 in 1600, making it perhaps the largest city in Europe. In London, and in other large European cities, a distinctively urban way of life developed in the Renaissance era.

▼ **JOBLESSNESS**
Many newcomers to London struggled to find jobs and shelter. Some turned to crime to make a living. Others became beggars. However, it was illegal for able-bodied people to beg. To avoid a whipping or prison time, beggars had to be sick or disabled.

▲ **ENTERTAINMENT**
In Renaissance England, performances at playhouses were often wild affairs. If audiences did not like the play, they booed loudly, pelted the stage with garbage, and sometimes attacked the actors.

▼ **SANITATION**
This small pomander (POH•man•durh), a metal container filled with spices, was crafted in the shape of orange segments. Well-to-do Londoners held pomanders to their noses to shield themselves from the stench of the rotting garbage that littered the streets.

▼ FOOD

A typical meal for wealthy Londoners might include fish, several kinds of meat, bread, and a variety of vegetables, served on silver or pewter tableware. The diet of the poor was simpler. They rarely ate fish, meat, or cheese. Usually, their meals consisted of a pottage—a kind of soup—of vegetables. And the poor ate their meals from a trencher, a hollowed-out slab of stale bread or wood.

Critical Thinking

1. **Make Inferences** Study the images and captions, as well as the information in the tables. What inferences about the standard of living of London's wealthy citizens can you make from this information? How did it compare to the standard of living of London's common people?

2. **Compare** How does diet in the United States today compare to the diet of Renaissance Europeans? Cite specific examples in your answer.

▼ TRANSPORTATION

Many of London's streets were so narrow that walking was the only practical means of transportation. Often, however, the quickest way to get from here to there in the city was to take the river. Boat traffic was especially heavy when the playhouses were open. On those days, as many as 4,000 people crossed the Thames from the city to Southwark, where most of the theaters were located.

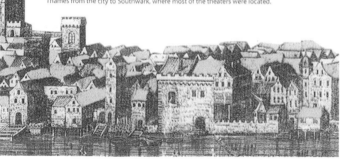

COST OF LIVING IN RENAISSANCE LONDON

These tables show what typical Londoners earned and spent in the late 1500s. The basic denominations in English currency at the time were the pound (£), the shilling, and the penny (12 pence equaled 1 shilling, and 20 shillings equaled 1 pound). The pound of the late 1500s is roughly equivalent to $400 in 2018.

Typical Earnings

Merchant	£100 per year
Skilled Worker	£13 per year (about 5 shillings/week)
Unskilled Worker	£5 per year (about 4 pence/day)
Servant	£1 to £2 per year (plus food and lodging)

Typical Prices

Lodging	4 to 8 pence a week
Beef	3 pence per lb
Chickens	1 penny each
Eggs	2 pence per dozen
Apples	1 penny per dozen
Onions	1/2 penny a sack
Various Spices	10 to 11 shillings per lb

Renaissance Achievements

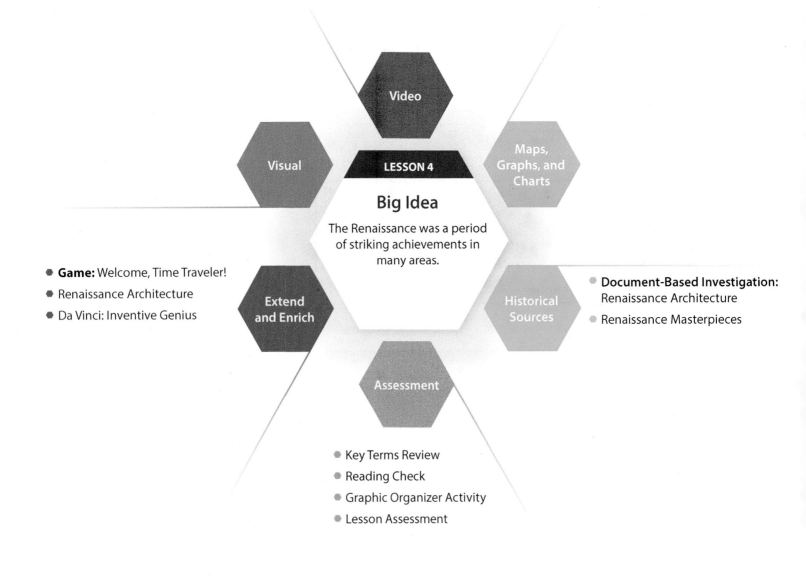

- **Game:** Welcome, Time Traveler!
- Renaissance Architecture
- Da Vinci: Inventive Genius

Video

Visual

LESSON 4

Maps, Graphs, and Charts

Big Idea

The Renaissance was a period of striking achievements in many areas.

Extend and Enrich

Historical Sources

- **Document-Based Investigation:** Renaissance Architecture
- Renaissance Masterpieces

Assessment

- Key Terms Review
- Reading Check
- Graphic Organizer Activity
- Lesson Assessment

Renaissance Architecture

Museum Exhibit Students will create a museum exhibit on the global influence of the Renaissance. They will conduct research to learn about ideas that influenced Renaissance architecture and how, in turn, Renaissance architecture influenced other styles. This activity walks students through planning and creating an exhibit, and reviewing and proofreading the accompanying text.

Da Vinci: Inventive Genius

Video Students will view a video to learn more about Leonardo da Vinci and create a list of questions they would ask him if they had the opportunity to interview him. This activity walks students through watching the video and compiling interview questions.

Teach the Big Idea

1. **Whole Class Open/Introduction** Ask students how the paintings, sculpture, and architecture of the Renaissance are still relevant. *Paintings, sculptures and architecture from the Renaissance are still admired and copied today.*

2. **Direct Teach** Read students the Big Idea: *The Renaissance was a period of striking achievements in many areas.*

   Review the following lesson objectives with students to aid in their understanding of the Big Idea.

   • Describe the artistic breakthroughs and achievements of Renaissance artists.

   • Summarize skepticism and its impact.

3. **Whole Group Close/Reflect** Have students write a letter to a friend explaining how they have adapted skepticism as a new way of thinking and why.

▷ ONLINE DOCUMENT-BASED INVESTIGATION

The Renaissance

Renaissance Architecture is the last of four document-based investigations that students will analyze in The Renaissance module. Students will view a building that shows the influence of Greek and Roman architecture. Students can use the interactivity of the feature to learn more about this influence.

▷ ONLINE GRAPHIC ORGANIZER

Renaissance Achievements

As students read the lesson, have them use the graphic organizer to take notes. Students can review their graphic organizer notes at the end of the lesson to answer the following question:

Analyze Effects What were some long-term effects of the ideas and achievements of the Renaissance? *1. the scientific method; 2. an upheaval within Christianity; 3. the Age of Exploration*

▷ ONLINE LESSON FLIP CARDS

Review Key Terms and People

Students can use the flip cards in the Lesson Review at any time to review the lesson's key terms and people: *vernacular* and *skepticism*.

Renaissance Achievements

The Main Idea
The Renaissance was a period of striking achievements in many areas.

Why It Matters Now
The achievements of Renaissance artists, writers, scientists, and thinkers continue to affect people around the world today.

Key Terms and People
vernacular
skepticism

Setting the Stage

The ideas and innovations introduced during the Renaissance had far-reaching effects. The way people interacted with their world was profoundly altered. Some Renaissance innovations laid the foundation for global changes in the years that followed.

Cultural and Social Achievements

The European Renaissance was a period of great artistic and social change. It marked a break with the medieval ideals that were focused around the Church. The Renaissance belief in the dignity of the individual played a key role in the gradual rise of democratic ideas. Furthermore, the impact of the movable-type printing press was tremendous. Some historians have suggested that its effects were even more dramatic than the arrival of personal computers in the 20th century.

Changes in Art During the Renaissance, artistic styles changed as artists incorporated humanistic ideas in their work. Medieval artists had used religious subjects to convey a spiritual ideal, often arranging saints and Biblical figures in stiff groups. Renaissance painters often portrayed religious subjects, but they used a realistic style copied from classical models. They used light and shadow (called *chiaroscuro*) to give scenes added depth and fullness. As well as creating religious works, painters created secular works. Greek and Roman subjects also became popular.

New techniques and media also changed art. One important change was the introduction of paint that used oils as a binding agent. Earlier types of paint used binders such as eggs, which dry quickly. The longer drying time of oil paint meant artists could continue to add detail to a work for a longer period of time. A key technique was the use of perspective to show three dimensions on a flat surface.

Following the new emphasis on the individual, painters began to paint prominent citizens. These realistic portraits revealed what was distinctive about each person. In addition,

---

COLLABORATIVE LEARNING

Applying the Tradition of Skepticism

1. Organize students into pairs.

2. Explain the five steps in the scientific method: observe and ask questions that lead to a problem, form a hypothesis, test the hypothesis by gathering data, analyze data, reject or accept the hypothesis, form a conclusion.

3. Lead students in a discussion of how the tradition of skepticism relates to the scientific method.

4. Present the hypothesis, "Driving while talking on a cell phone is dangerous."

5. Ask pairs to follow the scientific method to form a conclusion about the hypothesis, conducting further research as needed.

6. Divide pairs into two groups for a debate: one group accepting the hypothesis and one rejecting it.

7. Conclude by leading the class in a discussion about how their conclusions may have been different in the absence of skepticism.

COLLABORATIVE LEARNING

Creating a Website: Renaissance Artists, Architects, and Writers

1. Divide students into pairs.

2. Have pairs choose an artist, architect, or writer from the Renaissance period.

La Primavera, by Italian Renaissance painter Sandro Botticelli

artists used a realistic style when depicting the human body. Sculptors made sculpture more realistic by carving natural postures and expressions that reveal personality.

Changes in Literature Renaissance writers produced works that reflected their time, but they also used techniques that writers rely on today. Some followed the example of the medieval writer Dante. He wrote in the **vernacular**, or his native language, instead of Latin. Dante's native language was Italian. Writing in the vernacular meant that books could be read by anyone, not just people who had been taught Latin.

In addition, Renaissance writers wrote either for self-expression or to portray the individuality of their subjects. In these ways, writers of the Renaissance began trends that modern writers still follow.

Changes in Architecture The study of classical texts showed that the Greeks and Romans used ratios and proportions to give structure to their art. By focusing on ratios, or the relationships between numbers, Renaissance architects created designs that feel balanced and harmonious. Many cities, especially in Italy, are dominated by the impressive domes of Renaissance architecture. The Palladian style, inspired by the work of Andrea Palladio, influenced architecture throughout Europe and in the United States.

As the classical style spread to other countries, it was combined with local traditions. In France, architects combined classical style and French traditions to create a more elaborate French Renaissance style. This style

The Renaissance **563**

Objectives

You may wish to discuss the following questions with students to help them frame the content as they read.

- Why was it important that writers began writing in the vernacular? *more accessible to everyday people, possible to read literature without learning Latin*

- In what ways did Renaissance art connect to the past? *Copied Greek and Roman styles, created religious works* In what ways did it break with the past? *increase in secular art, more realistic style, use of vernacular, emphasis on the individual*

More About . . .

Chiaroscuro The word *chiaroscuro* comes from the Italian *chiaro*, or "light," and *scuro*, or "dark." The technique was first brought to light by Leonardo da Vinci in such paintings as his *Adoration of the Magi*. *Chiaroscuro* became a primary technique for many painters.

▶ ONLINE HISTORICAL SOURCE

Renaissance Masterpieces

Have students explore and compare the images using the interactive slider. You may wish to use the associated question as a discussion prompt.

Analyze Sources What ideas and attributes of the Renaissance period are reflected in these works? *individualism—realistic portraits; renewed interest in ancient Greece and Rome—realistic style copied from classical models, images of Greek philosophers; secularism—portraits of individuals rather than religious subjects; growth of a wealthy merchant class—Mona Lisa commissioned by wealthy merchant; the "Renaissance man"—Leonardo pursued art and scientific inquiry, as seen in Mona Lisa and the sketch of a spiral screw mechanism*

HISTORICAL SOURCE

Renaissance Masterpieces

These two works by Renaissance master artists illustrate the artistic spirit, talent, and techniques that contributed to the lasting legacy of the era.

3. Ask pairs to use the text and additional research to create a website for the person that includes a feature on the person's importance to the Renaissance.

4. Have pairs include a list of achievements and how the person's work reflects the ideas and change brought about by the Renaissance.

5. Ask students to include images of the person and one of his or her works.

6. Have students design the website using a slideshow presentation or posterboard and ask them to present their completed designs to the class.

ADVANCED/GIFTED

The Evolution of Renaissance Maps

1. Ask students to research the evolution of maps beginning with the medieval period through the Renaissance to the present day.

2. Have students create a timeline showing the views, methods, and inventions that shaped the evolution of maps.

3. Encourage students to use technology to organize their timelines.

4. Have students present their timelines.

Renaissance Architecture

This photograph shows Florence's famous cathedral, topped with a dome designed in the Renaissance by Filippo Brunelleschi. Invite students to study the image and answer the associated question.

Analyze Sources

What ideas and attributes of the Renaissance period are reflected in this architectural style? *interest in learning and developing new techniques; reverence for classical styles, like the domes on some Roman temples*

DOCUMENT-BASED INVESTIGATION   HISTORICAL SOURCE

Renaissance Architecture

The dome on Florence's cathedral, built by Filippo Brunelleschi, is a marvel of engineering.

READING CHECK

Analyze Effects How is the influence of Renaissance architecture seen today? *Features like pillars and arches are still used in buildings today.*

The dome on Florence's cathedral, built by Filippo Brunelleschi, is a marvel of engineering.

spread from western Europe through northern and central Europe. In Russia, which was strongly influenced by the Byzantines, the new ruler hired Italian architects and builders to rebuild Moscow. The resulting style was a blend of Italian, Byzantine, and Russian traditions. In Spain, during the centuries of Islamic rule, a style known as Moorish had developed. Elements of Moorish and classical style were combined to create a distinctive Spanish style, with intricately detailed surface ornamentation.

Changes in Society The development of moveable type had a profound effect on society. Within a few years of the introduction of the printing press, the cost of books had fallen dramatically. More people had access to books, which prompted an increase in literacy rates. Also, printing made it easy for people to share new ideas. This facilitated some important changes and reforms in the early modern age as people began to challenge some of the structures of established religion and government.

Printing also made it easier to share new information and discoveries, which often led to further discoveries as other people built on what they read. The ability to print maps and charts made it possible for others to follow in the tracks of explorers.

Reading Check
Analyze Effects
How is the influence of Renaissance architecture seen today?

564 Module 14

The Legacy of the Renaissance

The artists, writers, and thinkers of the Renaissance produced many extraordinary works that still command attention today. However, the Renaissance spirit led to still more advances in the decades that followed.

The Spirit of Inquiry One of the hallmarks of the Renaissance was a questioning attitude. People were no longer willing to blindly follow tradition and accept authority. They wanted to form their own opinions and make up their own minds. As Renaissance humanists rediscovered Greek philosophy, some were drawn by the tradition of **skepticism**. Where medieval thinkers accepted many ideas without questioning them, skepticism questioned everything. The practice of examining everything to check assumptions became part of the scientific method that transformed medicine, physics, and other branches of science. It also led to questions about religion and faith and prompted an upheaval within Christianity.

There was also an increased curiosity about the world. Over the course of the Crusades, thousands of Europeans traveled to the eastern Mediterranean. Crusaders who returned with silk and spices created a market for these items. Merchants addressed this market by extending their trade networks still further. Stories about far-away places made some people wonder what else was out there. As navigational tools improved, this curiosity led to the Age of Exploration.

Because of these fundamental changes, Renaissance ideas continued to have a profound influence on European thought in the decades that followed.

Reading Check
Draw Conclusions
How is the Renaissance emphasis on the individual connected to the renewed interest in skepticism?

Lesson 4 Assessment

1. **Organize Information** Use a cause-and-effect diagram like this one to identify three effects that developed from the Renaissance sense of inquiry.

Which effect do you consider most important? Explain.

2. **Key Terms and People** For each key term or person in the lesson, write a sentence explaining its significance.
3. **Form Generalizations** Explain how the increased availability of books affected the behavior of individuals and groups.
4. **Analyze Effects** What factors combined to make Europeans curious about other places?
5. **Contrast** How did Renaissance artists treat religious subjects differently from medieval painters?

The Effects of Humanism

1. Organize students into diverse learning groups of three or four.
2. Ask students to use their notes and the text to identify the effect humanism had on arts and ideas during the Renaissance.
3. Provide the following list as a guideline: painting, sculpture, architecture, thinkers. *Possible answers: Painting—capture the human spirit; sculpture—more lifelike, showed depth of expression; architecture—reflected humanist love of Greek and Roman culture; thinkers—human mind is almost limitless, focus on individualism*
4. Ask volunteers to share their answers in one category.

Objectives

You may wish to discuss the following questions with students to help them frame the content as they read.

- What advances, aside from those associated with art and literature, came out of the Renaissance? *a questioning attitude, skepticism, increased curiosity*

- How did printing and publishing affect social reforms? *made social reforms more widespread because information, including Christian works, was distributed more widely and freely*

More About . . .

Skepticism Skepticism (from the Greek *skeptesthai*, "to examine") was first held as a prominent view by Democritus, who saw perception as no certain guide to objective reality. The Sophists were the earliest group of skeptics. For René Descartes, skepticism was a methodology that allowed him to arrive at certain truths. He believed that skepticism provided one with a firm ground for knowledge.

GAME

Welcome, Time Traveler!
Have students play the game to test their knowledge of the Renaissance by answering the questions.

READING CHECK

Draw Conclusions How is the Renaissance emphasis on the individual connected to the renewed interest in skepticism? *The focus on the individual made it easier for people to ask questions and make up their own minds.*

Print Assessment

1. **Organize Information** Use a cause-and-effect diagram to identify three effects that developed from the Renaissance sense of inquiry. Which effect do you consider most important? *Possible answers: 1. the scientific method; 2. an upheaval within Christianity; 3. the Age of Exploration*
2. **Key Terms and People** For each key term or person in the lesson, write a sentence explaining its significance. *Explanations of the significance of the lesson's key terms and names can be found on the following pages: vernacular, p. 563; skepticism, p. 565*

(continued)

Print Assessment *(continued)*

3. **Form Generalizations** Explain how the increased availability of books affected the behavior of individuals and groups. *Possible answer: The increased availability of books meant more people learned how to read. With more readers, written communication also increased.*

4. **Analyze Effects** What factors combined to make Europeans curious about other places? *Possible answer: Printing made it easier to share information and discoveries. People had the ability to print maps and charts that others could follow for exploration.*

5. **Contrast** How did Renaissance artists treat religious subjects differently from medieval painters? *Possible answer: Renaissance painters used more natural poses, a realistic style, and light and shadow to give depth to a painting.*

▷ Online **Assessment**

1. How did the style of portraits and sculptures illustrate the ideas of the Renaissance?
   - ○ They incorporated religious themes into vague natural scenes.
   - ○ They created a magical mood by depicting religious figures hovering.
   - ◉ They used realism to reveal the individual personality of their subjects.
   - ○ They emphasized technical aspects to highlight scientific achievement.

   Alternate Question *Select the answer choice from the drop-down list to complete the sentence correctly.* Renaissance artists emphasized [*the individual* ⬍] in depicting the human body in portraits and sculptures.

2. Which of the following ideas was an influence of Greek philosophers on humanism?
   - ○ applying classical thinking to uphold Christian teachings
   - ◉ challenging ideas and assumptions to help form opinions
   - ○ bringing together ideas from Judaism and Christianity to form new ideas
   - ○ applying the needs of a given situation to determine actions without using morals

   Alternate Question *Select the answer choice from the drop-down list to complete the sentence correctly.* A major component of skepticism used by Greek philosophers and humanists was the [*questioning* ⬍] of traditions and sources of authority.

3. **Elaborate** What are two ways that Renaissance writers established trends that are still followed by modern writers?

   Possible answer: Many Renaissance writers wrote in their native languages instead of Latin so that people in their own country could read their writings. They also wrote as a way of expressing themselves. Modern writers continue to follow these trends.

4. **Make Generalizations** How did skepticism during the Renaissance affect science and religion?

   Possible answer: Humanists began to question ideas and to challenge commonly held beliefs about religion and science. This practice of questioning helped lead to establishing a scientific method and transforming different sciences. Its challenging of religious ideas resulted in upheaval in the Catholic Church.

Print Assessment

Key Terms and People

For each term or name below, write a sentence explaining its connection to European history from 1300 to 1500.

1. Renaissance
2. vernacular
3. humanism
4. secular
5. patron
6. perspective
7. William Shakespeare
8. Johann Gutenberg

Explanations of the lesson's key terms can be found on the following pages: Renaissance, p. 538; vernacular, p. 563; humanism, p.543 ; secular, p.543 ; patron, p.545 ; perspective, p. 546; William Shakespeare, p. 557; Johann Gutenberg, p.558

Main Ideas

Use your notes and the information in the module to answer the following questions.

Birth of the Renaissance

1. What economic factor promoted the growth of city-states in northern Italy? *They developed extensive trading networks during the Crusades, which made them financially strong.*
2. What form of government dominated in Western Europe during the Renaissance era? *Strong central monarchies, as in the case of France, England, and Spain*

The Italian Renaissance

3. How did merchants and nobles in northern Italy influence the Renaissance? *They supported artists by becoming patrons of the arts and promoted the development of secular art by commissioning portraits of themselves.*
4. In what ways did literature and the arts change during the Renaissance? *Artists and writers chose secular and classical subjects as well as Christian subjects. Writers started writing for self-expression. Artists painted prominent individuals, glorified the human body, and used new artistic techniques and a more realistic style.*

The Northern Renaissance

5. How did the end of the Hundred Years' War and the French invasion of Italy promote the spread of Renaissance ideas? *The end of the Hundred Years' War led to increased trade in northern Europe. The French invasion of Italy prompted some Italian artists and writers to move to northern Europe, bringing Renaissance ideas and styles with them.*
6. How were the Christian humanist writers of the Northern Renaissance different from the humanist writers of the Italian Renaissance? *Christian humanists adopted humanist ideals but gave them a religious slant and interpreted the ideals based on Christian principles.*

Module 14 Assessment

Key Terms and People

For each term or name below, write a sentence explaining its connection to European history from 1300 to 1500.

1. Renaissance
2. vernacular
3. humanism
4. secular
5. patron
6. perspective
7. William Shakespeare
8. Johann Gutenberg

Main Ideas

Use your notes and the information in the module to answer the following questions.

Birth of the Renaissance

1. What economic factor promoted the growth of city-states in northern Italy?
2. What form of government dominated in western Europe during the Renaissance era?

The Italian Renaissance

3. How did merchants and nobles in northern Italy influence the Renaissance?
4. In what ways did literature and the arts change during the Renaissance?

The Northern Renaissance

5. How did the end of the Hundred Years' War and the French invasion of Italy promote the spread of Renaissance ideas?
6. How were the Christian humanist writers of the Northern Renaissance different from the humanist writers of the Italian Renaissance?

Renaissance Achievements

7. How did the intellectual and philosophical ideas of the Renaissance affect the way people viewed themselves and their place in the world?
8. How was European society as a whole affected by the development of the printing press?

566   Module 14

ONLINE DOCUMENT-BASED INVESTIGATION

The Renaissance

Have students complete and review all the DBI activities in **Part 1**.

Use this Analytical Essay Rubric to score students' work in **Part 2**.

RUBRIC Students' essays should
- present an analysis of the topic that is detailed and relevant.
- develop the analysis logically, clearly, and accurately.
- cite at least three sources of relevant text evidence from Part 1 in support of their analysis.
- be organized into a distinct introduction, a main body consisting of several paragraphs, and a conclusion that sums up the main points.

Write an Analytical Essay Write an essay in which you analyze ways in which the transformations in European life are reflected in Renaissance art and literature. Be sure to cite specific evidence from at least three sources in your response.

Module 14 Assessment, continued

Critical Thinking

1. **Categorize** Create a web diagram to show the major influences on Renaissance thought.

Which one do you think had the greatest influence? Explain.

2. **Analyze Effects** How did the Renaissance expand cultural interaction?

3. **Develop Historical Perspective** What conditions needed to exist before the Renaissance could occur?

4. **Synthesize** How did views of the role of women change in the Renaissance period?

Engage With History

Reread the quotation in Lesson 2 from Machiavelli's *The Prince*. Now that you have read the module, consider the quotation in the context of 15th-century Florence. Machiavelli saw a succession of rulers come and go in Florence. He lost his government position after the Medicis returned to power.

Think about the following questions:

- What opinion does Machiavelli present about people in general?
- Are these statements based on observations of human behavior, or are they assumptions?
- Do you think his advice would be useful to a ruler like Lorenzo de Medici?
- One reason Machiavelli wrote *The Prince* was in the hope of receiving a new post. Does this affect your opinion?

Discuss these questions with a small group.

Focus on Writing

How did the Renaissance revolutionize European art and thought? Support your opinions in a three-paragraph essay.

Multimedia Activity

Use the Internet to find information on the number of books published in print and those published electronically last year. Create a pie graph showing the results of your research.

Renaissance Achievements

7. How did the intellectual and philosophical ideas of the Renaissance affect the way people viewed themselves and their place in the world? *The Renaissance ideas of individualism and skepticism led people to focus more on themselves as individuals and prompted them to question how they fit into the world, both the physical world and the spiritual one.*

8. How was European society as a whole affected by the development of the printing press? *More people learned to read, which meant new ideas could be shared more widely.*

Critical Thinking

1. **Categorize** Create a web diagram to show the major influences on Renaissance thought. Which one do you think had the greatest influence? Explain *Possible Answers: classical Greece; classical Rome; Byzantines*

2. **Analyze Effects** How did the Renaissance expand cultural interaction? *Italian ideas inspired northern artists and writers.*

3. **Develop Historical Perspective** What conditions needed to exist before the Renaissance could occur? *Europe needed to be at peace. Scholars and writers had to be supported. Access to classical works had to be available.*

4. **Synthesize** How did views of the role of women change in the Renaissance period? *Attitudes changed a bit, but not dramatically. Christian humanists viewed women as worthy of education. Some women were writers and painters, while others were patrons of the arts.*

Engage With History

Reread the primary source quotation from Machiavelli's *The Prince*. Now that you have read the module, consider the quotation in the context of 15th-century Florence. Machiavelli saw a succession of rulers come and go in Florence. He lost his government position after the Medicis returned to power.

Think about the following questions:

- What opinion does Machiavelli present about people in general?
- Are these statements based on observations of human behavior, or are they assumptions?
- Do you think his advice would be useful to a ruler like Lorenzo de Medici?
- One reason Machiavelli wrote *The Prince* was in the hope of receiving a new post. Does this affect your opinion?

Discuss these questions with a small group.

Essential Question ESSAY

Do art and literature reflect culture or do they shape it?

RUBRIC Students' essays should
- respond to the Essential Question with a specific position.
- illustrate valid reasoning supporting their position.
- cite persuasive evidence supporting their position.
- identify key people, events, and/or turning points that demonstrate understanding of the module content.
- be organized into a distinct introduction, main body, and conclusion.

Write an argument answering this question. Your essay should include key people, events, and turning points in the Renaissance period. Be sure to cite evidence to support your position and organize your essay into an introduction, body, and conclusion.

Alternative Activity Instead of writing essays, address the Essential Question through activities such as holding debates, creating multimedia presentations, or writing journal entries.

(continued)

Print Assessment *(continued)*

Focus On Writing

How did the Renaissance revolutionize European art and thought? Support your opinions in a three-paragraph essay.

Focus On Writing

RUBRIC Essays should
- discuss how Renaissance scholars looked to classical writers for inspiration.
- note the ways Renaissance artists revolutionized art by using perspective, a more realistic style, and glorifying individuals.

Multimedia Activity

Use the Internet to find information on the number of books published in print and those published electronically last year. Create a pie graph showing the results of your research.

RUBRIC Pie graphs should:
- have a title.
- clearly label data for print and electronic books.
- cite at least two sources.

Online Assessment

1. Which of the following helped cause the Renaissance?
   Select the **four** correct answers.
   - ○ foreign invasions
   - ○ development of papermaking
   - ○ stabilized international politics
   - ○ increased emphasis on religion
   - ○ increased international commerce
   - ○ translations of classic texts into Latin
   - ○ inexpensive mass-produced parchments

2. How did the rise of a middle class in the Italian city-states affect the Renaissance?
   - ○ It provided money to sponsor military campaigns.
   - ○ It created wealth to influence local elections.
   - ○ It provided money to sponsor artists and writers.
   - ○ It created wealth to establish new colonies.

3. Which of the following characterizes humanism?
   - ○ a philosophy based on a strict following of Christian beliefs and teachings
   - ○ an economic system stressing investment in technology and markets
   - ○ a movement focused on human potential and a study of the classics
   - ○ a political system emphasizing democratic ideals and policies

4. Drag the name of the Italian Renaissance artist into the box next to the correct statement.

first woman to achieve an international reputation; known for her portraits	Sofonisba Anguissola
a true "Renaissance man"; known for the *Mona Lisa* and *The Last Supper*	Leonardo da Vinci
known for his use of perspective; often used the Madonna and child as a subject	Raphael Sanzio
known for depicting the human body realistically; sculptures include the *Pietà* and *David*	Michelangelo Buonarroti

5. Drag the name of the Italian Renaissance writer into the box next to the correct description.

early and influential humanist who wrote sonnets in Italian and Latin	Francesco Petrarch
writer whose *The Prince* offered realistic, but not moral, advice to rulers	Niccolò Machiavelli
writer whose *Decameron* described realistic characters through tragic and comedic stories	Giovanni Boccaccio
poet who exchanged sonnets with Michelangelo and helped Castiglione publish *The Courtier*	Vittoria Colonna

6. How was the architecture of Filippo Brunelleschi consistent with the other Renaissance arts?
   - ○ It was strongly influenced by classical architecture.
   - ○ It included portraits of important political leaders.
   - ○ It pioneered the use of new technology and materials.
   - ○ It was financed by wealthy local merchant families.

7. Drag the name of the northern Renaissance artist into the box next to the correct statement.

known for painting incredibly detailed portraits of the English royal family	Hans Holbein the Younger
known for painting scenes of everyday peasant life using rich colors and vivid details	Pieter Bruegel the Elder
known for pioneering oil-based painting, developing new techniques to add subtlety to colors	Jan van Eyck
known for woodcuts and engravings portraying religious subjects, classical myths, and realistic landscapes	Albrecht Dürer

8. Drag the name of the northern Renaissance writer into the box next to the correct statement.

French writer who promoted the formal education of both boys and girls	Christine de Pizan
English playwright who drew upon the classics for stories and inspiration	William Shakespeare
Dutch humanist whose *In Praise of Folly* teased different people in society	Desiderius Erasmus
English humanist whose *Utopia* depicted an imaginary place without war and corruption	Thomas More

9. Why was Johann Gutenberg's printing press significant?
   - ○ It allowed monarchs to communicate laws to their subjects.
   - ○ It made bibles less expensive and led to a revival of religious devotion.
   - ○ It enabled religious writers to reinterpret medieval works.
   - ○ It made books less expensive and encouraged the spread of ideas.

10. Which of the following artistic styles developed during the Renaissance?
    Select the **two** correct answers.
    - ○ using groups of people to show hierarchy in society
    - ○ using water to make shades of color more apparent
    - ○ using marble to show the natural beauty of a subject
    - ○ using perspective to show three dimensions on a flat surface
    - ○ using *chiaroscuro* and other techniques to make work more realistic

11. Why did Dante and other Renaissance writers use the vernacular?
    - ○ It encouraged local leaders to read more books.
    - ○ It made the church view their writing as a threat.
    - ○ It made their writing more accessible to readers.
    - ○ It encouraged readers to learn new languages.

12. How did humanists break with medieval thinkers over the acceptance of tradition and beliefs?
    - ○ Humanists questioned everything in order to form their own opinions.
    - ○ Humanists looked for answers by interpreting religious texts.
    - ○ Humanists relied on political leaders to provide guidance on questions of faith.
    - ○ Humanists incorporated ideas from different countries to find answers.

Essential Question Preview

What new ideas and values led to the Reformation, and what social and political effects did the Reformation cause?

Have students consider the Essential Question and capture their initial responses.

Explore the Essential Question

- Discuss how the ideals of the Renaissance were expressed in the Reformation.

- Describe to students how criticism of the Roman Catholic Church led to a religious movement called the Protestant Reformation.

Help students plan inquiries and develop their own supporting questions, such as:

Why did the new ideas of the Reformation become popular among Europeans?

What were some of the criticisms of the Roman Catholic Church during the 1500s?

You may want to assign students to write a short essay in response to the Essential Question when they complete the module. Encourage students to use their notes and responses to inform their essays.

▷ Explore the Online Video

ANALYZE VIDEOS

Martin Luther Sparks a Revolution

Invite students to watch the video to learn how Martin Luther sparked a religious revolution.

History How did Martin Luther's search to understand his relationship with God contribute to his grievances about certain practices of the Catholic Church? Explain. *Luther's own quest for spiritual purity made him intolerant of the inconsistencies and corruption he saw within the Catholic Church.*

▷ **PLAY VIDEO 2:54**
Martin Luther Sparks a Revolution

Module 15

Reformation and Upheaval

Essential Question
What new ideas and values led to the Reformation, and what social and political effects did the Reformation cause?

About the Photo: In 1517 a Catholic monk named Martin Luther posted his "95-Theses," criticizing the Roman Catholic Church.

In this module you will learn how the Protestant Reformation altered European society, how the Catholic Church responded to the Reformation, and how political and social unrest ensued.

▷ Explore ONLINE!

VIDEOS, including...
- Martin Luther Sparks a Revolution

HISTORY.

- ✓ Document-Based Investigations
- ✓ Graphic Organizers
- ✓ Interactive Games
- ✓ Interactive Map: Religions in Europe, 1560
- ✓ Causes and Effects of the Reformation

What You Will Learn ...

Lesson 1 Big Idea

Martin Luther's protest over abuses in the Catholic Church led to the founding of Protestant churches.

Why It Matters Now

Nearly one-fifth of the Christians in today's world are Protestants.

Lesson 2 Big Idea

Protestant reformers were divided over beliefs, and split into several new Protestant groups.

Why It Matters Now

Many Protestant churches began during this period.

Lesson 3 Big Idea

The Catholic Church made reforms in response to the Protestant Reformation.

Why It Matters Now

Many Catholic schools are the result of reforms in the Church.

Lesson 4 Big Idea

The Protestant and Catholic Reformations caused tremendous political and social unrest throughout Europe.

Why It Matters Now

Nation-states that rose as a result of the Protestant Reformation became many of the leading countries in Europe today.

Timeline of Events, 1400–1600　▶ *Explore ONLINE!*

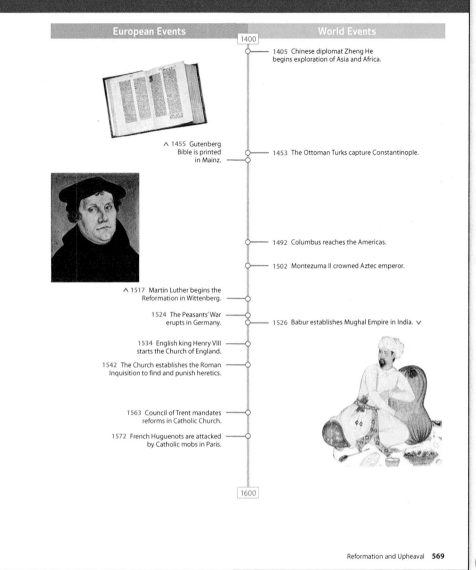

European Events	World Events

1400

1405　Chinese diplomat Zheng He begins exploration of Asia and Africa.

∧ 1455　Gutenberg Bible is printed in Mainz.

1453　The Ottoman Turks capture Constantinople.

1492　Columbus reaches the Americas.

1502　Montezuma II crowned Aztec emperor.

∧ 1517　Martin Luther begins the Reformation in Wittenberg.

1524　The Peasants' War erupts in Germany.

1526　Babur establishes Mughal Empire in India. ∨

1534　English king Henry VIII starts the Church of England.

1542　The Church establishes the Roman Inquisition to find and punish heretics.

1563　Council of Trent mandates reforms in Catholic Church.

1572　French Huguenots are attacked by Catholic mobs in Paris.

1600

Reformation and Upheaval　**569**

Explore the Timeline

Interpret Timelines: Reformation and Upheaval, 1400–1600

Have students examine the timeline and then answer the following question:

History When Henry IV became the ruler of France, which monarch was ruling England? *Elizabeth I*

Interpret Timeline of Events: Timeline of Events, 1400–1600

To further explore the timeline, have students discuss the following questions:

1. How many years passed between the beginning of the Reformation and the reforms in the Catholic Church made at the Council of Trent? *Forty-six years passed.*

2. What can be inferred about the strength of the Reformation from that span of time? *The Catholic Church responded quickly to the Reformation.* If necessary, remind students that he Reformation was strong enough to cause reforms in the huge and wealthy Catholic Church.

▶ Online Module Flip Cards

Use the flip cards as a whole class activity or in student pairs to preview the module's Key Terms and People. Students can guess the meaning of each word, then review its definition, or do the reverse, using the flip card's toggle button to switch from Term to Definition mode. Students can also use the flip cards at the end of the module as a review tool before taking the Module Assessment.

▶ Online Sequencing Activity

Students can use this sequencing activity to review the chronology of events in the Reformation and Upheaval Module. To complete, have students drag each event to the correct year on the timeline.

Year	Event
1455	*Gutenberg Bible printed in Mainz.*
1517	*Martin Luther begins the Reformation in Wittenberg.*
1524	*The Peasants' War erupts in Germany.*
1534	*English King Henry VIII starts the Church of England.*
1558	*Elizabeth I ascends to the throne of England.*
1563	*Council of Trent mandates reforms in Catholic Church.*

Luther Leads the Reformation

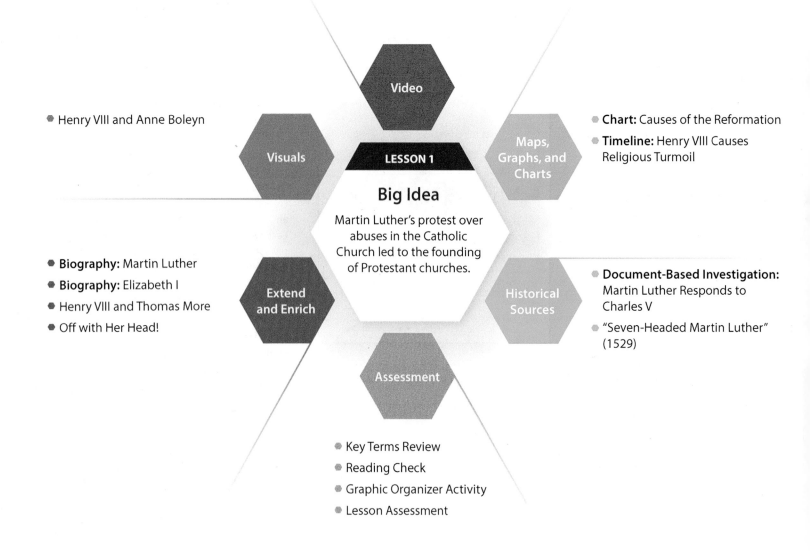

Henry VIII and Anne Boleyn

Video

Visuals

LESSON 1

Maps, Graphs, and Charts

Chart: Causes of the Reformation

Timeline: Henry VIII Causes Religious Turmoil

Big Idea

Martin Luther's protest over abuses in the Catholic Church led to the founding of Protestant churches.

Biography: Martin Luther

Biography: Elizabeth I

Henry VIII and Thomas More

Off with Her Head!

Extend and Enrich

Historical Sources

Document-Based Investigation: Martin Luther Responds to Charles V

"Seven-Headed Martin Luther" (1529)

Assessment

Key Terms Review

Reading Check

Graphic Organizer Activity

Lesson Assessment

Henry VIII and Thomas More

Article Students read about Henry VIII and Thomas More and then create a biographical video about their friendship and conflicts. Their videos should include key aspects about and events in the relationship between these two men.

Off with Her Head!

Multimedia Presentation Students identify and take notes on the six wives of Henry VIII and the controversies surrounding their marriages to the king. Then students create a multimedia presentation that focuses on the wives, the situation each faced during her marriage, and their fates.

Teach the Big Idea

1. **Whole Class Open/Introduction** Ask students how people protest today. *picketing, marching, writing to representatives in government*

2. **Direct Teach** Read students the Big Idea: *Martin Luther's protest over abuses in the Catholic Church led to the founding of Protestant churches.* Review the following lesson objectives with students to aid in their understanding of the Big Idea.

   - Analyze historical forces and religious issues that sparked the Reformation.

   - Trace Martin Luther's role in the movement to reform the Catholic Church.

   - Analyze the impact of Luther's religious revolt.

   - Explain the spread of the Protestant faith to England.

3. **Whole Group Close/Reflect** Ask students to imagine they are Martin Luther before he posted his 95 Theses. Have them write a journal entry in which Luther explains his thoughts and ideas. Invite students to share their work.

▷ ONLINE DOCUMENT-BASED INVESTIGATION

Reformation and Upheaval

Martin Luther Responds to Charles V is the first of four document-based investigations that students will analyze in the Reformation and Upheaval module. In 1521 Charles V told Luther to recant, or take back his statements, but Luther refused. Students can follow the strategies beneath the quote to analyze the primary source.

▷ ONLINE GRAPHIC ORGANIZER

Luther Leads the Reformation

As students read the lesson, have them use the graphic organizer to take notes. Students can review their graphic organizer notes at the end of the lesson to answer the following question:

Analyze Effects What were the effects of Martin Luther's protests? *They led to the Protestant Reformation and the Catholic Reformation.*

▷ ONLINE LESSON FLIP CARDS

Review Key Terms and People

Students can use the flip cards in the Lesson Review at any time to review the lesson's key terms and people: *Martin Luther, indulgence, Reformation, excommunicate, Lutheran, Protestant, Peace of Augsburg, Henry VIII, annul, Elizabeth I, and Anglican.*

Luther Leads the Reformation

The Big Idea
Martin Luther's protest over abuses in the Catholic Church led to the founding of Protestant churches.

Why It Matters Now
Nearly one-fifth of the Christians in today's world are Protestants.

Key Terms and People
Martin Luther
indulgence
Reformation
excommunicate
Lutheran
Protestant
Peace of Augsburg
Henry VIII
annul
Elizabeth I
Anglican

Setting the Stage

By the tenth century, the Roman Catholic Church had come to dominate religious life in northern and western Europe. However, the Church had not won universal approval. Over the centuries, many people criticized its practices. They felt that Church leaders were too interested in worldly pursuits, such as gaining wealth and political power. Even though the Church made some reforms during the Middle Ages, people continued to criticize it. Prompted by the actions of one man, that criticism would lead to rebellion.

Causes of the Reformation

By 1500, additional forces weakened the Church. The Renaissance emphasis on the secular and the individual challenged Church authority. The invention of the printing press helped spread these secular ideas. The printing press was a new device that made printed material more widely available. At the same time, more writers and scholars began to write and translate works into the local vernacular, or common language, instead of using Latin. Together, these changes helped increase literacy, spiritual thinking, individual thought, and perspective among individuals. As individuals found commonalities, new groups of like thinkers formed. In addition, some rulers began to challenge the Church's political power. In Germany, which was divided into many competing states, it was difficult for the pope or the emperor to impose central authority. Finally, northern merchants resented paying church taxes to Rome. Spurred by these social, political, and economic forces, a new movement for religious reform began in Germany. It then swept much of Europe.

Objectives

You may wish to discuss the following questions with students to help them frame the content as they read.

- What were some criticisms of the Catholic Church before the Reformation? *Church leaders too interested in worldly pursuits; abuses of power; placed too much emphasis on Church authority*

- What were some of the forces that challenged the Church's authority by 1500? *printing press, increased literacy, more individual thought*

More About . . .

"The Daughter of Printing" The invention of the printing press greatly affected change during the Renaissance and Reformation. Martin Luther's religious ideas spread quickly by print. Some historians have called the Reformation "the daughter of printing." During Luther's lifetime, about 4,000 editions (books printed from one set of type) of his writings were published. In fact, one-third of the books in Germany were written by him. Luther's *Address to the Christian Nobility of the German Nation*, which appeared in the 1520s, sold 4,000 copies in one week.

Causes of the Reformation

Social	Political	Economic	Religious
The Renaissance values of humanism and secularism led people to question the Church.	Powerful monarchs challenged the Church as the supreme power in Europe.	European princes and kings were jealous of the Church's wealth.	Some Church leaders had become worldly and corrupt.
The printing press was an effective tool that helped to spread ideas critical of the Church.	Many leaders viewed the pope as a foreign ruler and challenged his authority.	Merchants and others resented having to pay taxes to the Church.	Many people found Church practices such as the sale of indulgences unacceptable.

Criticisms of the Catholic Church Critics of the Church claimed that its leaders were corrupt. The popes who ruled during the Renaissance patronized the arts, spent extravagantly on personal pleasure, and fought wars. Pope Alexander VI, for example, admitted that he had fathered several children. Many popes were too busy pursuing worldly affairs to have much time for spiritual duties.

The lower clergy had problems as well. Many priests and monks were so poorly educated that they could scarcely read, let alone teach people. Others broke their priestly vows by marrying, and some drank to excess or gambled.

Early Calls for Reform Influenced by reformers, people had come to expect higher standards of conduct from priests and church leaders. In the late 1300s and early 1400s, John Wycliffe of England and Jan Hus of Bohemia had advocated Church reform. They denied that the pope had the right to worldly power. They also taught that the Bible had more authority than Church leaders did. In the 1500s, Christian humanists like Desiderius Erasmus and Thomas More added their voices to the chorus of criticism. In addition, many Europeans were reading religious works and forming their own opinions about the Church. The atmosphere in Europe was ripe for reform by the early 1500s.

Luther Challenges the Church

Martin Luther's parents wanted him to be a lawyer. Instead, he became a monk and a teacher. From 1512 until his death, he taught scripture at the University of Wittenberg in the German state of Saxony. All he wanted was to be a good Christian, not to lead a religious revolution.

The 95 Theses In 1517, Luther decided to take a public stand against the actions of a friar named Johann Tetzel. Tetzel was raising money to rebuild St. Peter's Cathedral in Rome. He did this by selling indulgences. An **indulgence** was a pardon. It released a sinner from performing the

Reading Check
Summarize
What practices of the Catholic Church in the 1500s might have disturbed ordinary churchgoers?

Reformation and Upheaval 571

ENGLISH LANGUAGE LEARNERS

Political Cartoons

1. Review with students the information in the text about Church abuses, Protestant criticism of the Church, and various Protestant groups.

2. Organize students into small groups.

3. Have students create two political cartoons, one that portrays Protestants as crusaders against the evils of the Church, and the other that shows Protestants as alarmists who overreacted to issues.

4. Have volunteers present their political cartoons to the class.

STRUGGLING READERS

The Importance of Printing

1. Tell students to envision what the world would be like without printing. How would it affect their lives?

2. Have students write a paragraph about what life would be like without books, magazines, or newspapers.

Objectives

You may wish to discuss the following questions with students to help them frame the content as they read.

- Why was Martin Luther unhappy with the sale of indulgences? *Indulgences were pardons for sins. Luther thought that the sale of indulgences would allow people to buy their way into heaven without atoning for their sins.*

- What caused Luther's ideas to spread throughout Germany? *Someone had Luther's words printed; his ideas allowed people to think about and express their own dissatisfaction with the Church.*

More About . . .

Example of Corruption Most Germans who bought indulgences believed that the money would go to the construction of St. Peter's Basilica. The public didn't realize, however, that some of the money was going to Albert of Brandenburg. Albert had purchased the position of archbishop of Mainz but was too young to occupy it according to church law. Pope Leo decided that Albert could take the office provided that he paid the church a large sum of money, which he did by borrowing. Half the money raised through the sale of indulgences in Germany went to Albert to pay off his debt.

▷ ONLINE INTERACTIVE CHARTS

Causes of the Reformation

Have students explore the chart and answer the associated question.

Interpret Charts Which of the following was an event that indirectly caused the Reformation? *invention of the printing press*

Causes of the Reformation

The rapid changes throughout medieval society created an environment ready for reform.

Social

Political

Economic

READING CHECK

Summarize What practices of the Catholic Church in the 1500s might have disturbed ordinary churchgoers? *Popes pursued worldly affairs; some priests drank and gambled.*

Reformation and Upheaval 571

BIOGRAPHY

Martin Luther

Have students read the biography of Martin Luther, the German monk whose protests against the Catholic Church in 1517 led to calls for reform and to the movement known as the Reformation.

READING CHECK

Summarize What were the main points of Luther's teachings? *belief in God's forgiveness; authority of the Bible; equality among all with faith*

Martin Luther
(1483–1546)

In one way, fear led Luther to become a monk. At the age of 21, Luther was caught in a terrible thunderstorm. Convinced he would die, he cried out, "Saint Anne, help me! I will become a monk."

Even after entering the monastery, Luther felt fearful, lost, sinful, and rejected by God. He confessed his sins regularly, fasted, and did penance. However, by studying the Bible, Luther came to the conclusion that faith alone was the key to salvation. Only then did he experience peace.

penalty that a priest imposed for sins. Indulgences were not supposed to affect God's right to judge. Tetzel gave people the impression that by buying indulgences, they could buy their way into heaven.

Luther was troubled by Tetzel's tactics. In response, he wrote 95 theses, or formal statements, attacking the "pardon-merchants." On October 31, 1517, he posted these statements on the door of the castle church in Wittenberg and invited other scholars to debate him. Someone copied Luther's words and took them to a printer. With the support of the printing press, Luther's name and ideas soon were advertised to people and groups all over Germany. His actions began the **Reformation**, a movement for religious reform. It led to the founding of Christian churches that did not accept the pope's authority.

Luther's Teachings Soon Luther went beyond criticizing indulgences. He wanted full reform of the Church. His teachings rested on three main ideas:

- People could receive salvation only by faith in God's gift of forgiveness. The Church taught that faith and "good works" were needed for salvation.
- All Church teachings should be clearly based on the words of the Bible. Both the pope and Church traditions were false authorities.
- All people with faith were equal. Therefore, people did not need priests to interpret the Bible for them.

Reading Check
Summarize What were the main points of Luther's teachings?

The Response to Luther

Luther was astonished at how rapidly his ideas spread and attracted followers. Many people had been unhappy with the Church for political and economic reasons. They saw Luther's protests as a way to challenge Church control.

COLLABORATIVE LEARNING

Press Conference with Martin Luther

1. Organize students into three groups: a small group of speechwriters, a medium-sized group of colleagues, and a large group of the press.

2. Have speechwriters write a speech for Martin Luther to be given a few months after he posted his theses. Have colleagues learn as much as they can about Luther's ideas and prepare to answer questions on his behalf.

3. Guide the press in narrowing down their questions to no more than one question per reporter. Give a copy of the questions to the advisors. Have colleagues discuss how they will answer any tricky questions.

4. Begin the press conference. Choose one of the speechwriters to present the speech. Have members of the press stand up and ask their questions, and have colleagues answer them.

ADVANCED/GIFTED

Research Martin Luther

1. Remind students that Luther's goal was to eliminate corruption in the Church, not to stage a religious revolt.

2. Have students use reference books, the Internet, and other appropriate resources to research Luther as a revolutionary.

3. In a class discussion, have students give examples of Luther's break with tradition, his defiance of authority, and his role in launching a new era.

The Pope's Threat Initially, Church officials in Rome viewed Luther simply as a rebellious monk who needed to be punished by his superiors. However, as Luther's ideas became more popular, the pope realized that this monk was a serious threat. In one angry reply to Church criticism, Luther actually suggested that Christians drive the pope from the Church by force.

In 1520, Pope Leo X issued a decree threatening Luther with excommunication unless he took back his statements. Luther did not take back a word. Instead, his students at Wittenberg gathered around a bonfire and cheered as he threw the pope's decree into the flames. Leo **excommunicated** Luther.

The Emperor's Opposition Holy Roman Emperor Charles V, a devout Catholic, also opposed Luther's teaching. Charles controlled a vast empire, including the German states. He summoned Luther to the town of Worms (vawrmz) in 1521 to stand trial. Charles V told Luther to recant, or take back his statements, but Luther refused:

"I am bound by the Scriptures I have quoted and my conscience is captive to the Word of God. I cannot and I will not retract anything, since it is neither safe nor right to go against conscience. I cannot do otherwise, here I stand, may God help me. Amen."

—Martin Luther, quoted in *The Protestant Reformation* by Lewis W. Spitz

A month after Luther made that speech, Charles issued an imperial order, the Edict of Worms. It declared Luther an outlaw and a heretic because what he believed went against the teachings of the Church. According to this edict, no one in the empire was to give Luther food or shelter. All his books were to be burned. However, Prince Frederick the Wise of Saxony disobeyed the emperor. For almost a year after the trial, he sheltered Luther in one of his castles. While there, Luther translated the New Testament into German.

Luther returned to Wittenberg in 1522. There he discovered that many of his ideas were already being put into practice. Instead of continuing to seek reforms in the Catholic Church, Luther and his followers had become a separate religious group, called **Lutherans**.

Many northern German princes supported Lutheranism. While some princes genuinely shared Luther's beliefs, others liked Luther's ideas for selfish reasons. They saw his teachings as a good excuse to seize Church property and to assert their independence from Charles V.

In 1529, German princes who remained loyal to the pope agreed to join forces against Luther's ideas. Those princes who supported Luther signed a protest against that agreement. These protesting princes came to be known as Protestants. Eventually, the term **Protestant** was applied to Christians who were not Roman Catholic or Eastern Orthodox.

Objectives

You may wish to discuss the following questions with students to help them frame the content as they read.

- Why did Luther's teachings become popular and attract followers? *People saw his protests as a way to challenge Church control, which they were unhappy with.*

- Why do you think Charles V could not force the Protestant princes back into the Catholic Church even after defeating them in war? *Possible answer: Luther's ideas were too strong; the abuses in the Catholic Church caused people to lose faith.*

More About . . .

Connect to Language Arts Point out that the word *excommunication* can be broken into parts. The prefix *ex-* often means "outside" or "away from," and the suffix *-tion* usually means "state of being." The root comes from the Latin *communis*, which means "common, public, or general." Challenge students to think of other words with the same root. *community, Communion, Communist*

Data on Religions Although statistics on religious membership tend to be estimates, it is generally thought that the three largest religions are Christianity, Islam, and Hinduism. The two largest religious denominations, Roman Catholics and Sunni Muslims, account for 33 percent of the world's population.

▷ ONLINE DOCUMENT-BASED INVESTIGATION

Martin Luther Responds to Charles V

In 1521 Charles V told Luther to recant, or take back his statements, but Luther refused. Students can play the audio to hear the excerpt read aloud.

Analyze Sources What evidence did Luther use to support his argument? *the Bible*

DOCUMENT-BASED INVESTIGATION   HISTORICAL SOURCE

Martin Luther Responds to Charles V

Charles V summoned Luther to the town of Worms (vawrmz) in 1521 to stand trial. Charles V told Luther to recant, or take back his statements, but Luther refused:

SYNTHESIZE

Diagram Analysis

1. Point out to students that, like detective work, synthesizing involves putting together clues, facts, and ideas to form an overall picture of a historical event.

2. To answer the question "Why did Luther think it was all right to defy the Pope?" (a synthesis), suggest that students use the following strategy.

3. Have them reread the bulleted list of Luther's teachings and look for information to support the synthesis. Then ask students to create a cluster diagram showing how the synthesis was formed.

COLLABORATIVE LEARNING

Understanding the Response to Luther

1. Divide students into four small groups. Assign each group one of the following roles to research: Martin Luther, Pope Leo X, Holy Roman Emperor Charles V, and Prince Frederick the Wise of Saxony.

2. Have each group reread the sections titled "The Pope's Threat" and "The Emperor's Opposition" and then summarize the viewpoint of their assigned historical figure.

3. Encourage students to take notes in complete sentences. Invite volunteers to present their summaries to the class.

▷ ONLINE HISTORICAL SOURCES

"Seven-Headed Martin Luther" (1529)

Invite students to view the image and answer the associated question.

Analyze Sources Why might this woodcut be an effective propaganda weapon? *Luther is portrayed as an inhuman monster. Several of his heads represent undesirable traits, like fanaticism; heretical thoughts, like declaring oneself pope; and unfavorable references to the Bible, like the thief.*

▷ ONLINE INTERACTIVE CHARTS

Religious Beliefs and Practices in the 16th Century

Have students explore the chart and answer the associated question.

Interpret Charts Which religions believed in salvation by faith alone? *Lutheranism and Anglicanism*

Compare and Contrast Which of the branches on the chart are most different and which are most similar? *Roman Catholicism is most different from Anglicanism. Lutheranism is most similar to Calvinism.*

Analyze Effects Select a Protestant denomination not shown on this page. *Research it and write a paragraph tracing its roots to the Reformation. Students' answers will vary.*

	Roman Catholicism	Lutheranism	Calvinism	Anglicanism
Leadership	Pope is head of the Church	Ministers lead congregations	Council of elders govern each church	English monarch is head of the Church
Salvation	Salvation by faith and good works	Salvation by faith alone	God has predetermined who will be saved	Salvation by faith alone
Bible	Church and Bible tradition are sources of revealed truth	Bible is sole source of revealed truth	Bible is sole source of revealed truth	Bible is sole source of revealed truth
Worship Service	Worship service based on ritual	Worship service focused on preaching and ritual	Worship service focused on preaching	Worship service based on ritual and preaching
Interpretation of Beliefs	Priests interpret Bible and Church teachings for believers	Believers interpret the Bible for themselves	Believers interpret the Bible for themselves	Believers interpret the Bible using tradition and reason

---

Protestantism

Protestantism is a branch of Christianity that developed out of the Reformation. Three distinct branches of Protestantism emerged at first: Lutheranism, based on the teachings of Martin Luther in Germany; Calvinism, based on the teachings of John Calvin in Switzerland; and Anglicanism, established by King Henry VIII in England. Protestantism spread throughout Europe in the 16th century and, later, the world. As differences in beliefs developed, new denominations formed.

THE DIVISION OF CHRISTIANITY

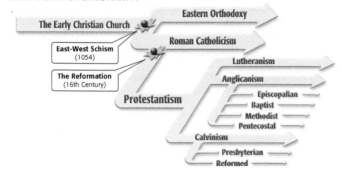

Religious Beliefs and Practices in the 16th Century				
	Roman Catholicism	**Lutheranism**	**Calvinism**	**Anglicanism**
Leadership	Pope is head of the Church	Ministers lead congregations	Council of elders govern each church	English monarch is head of the Church
Salvation	Salvation by faith and good works	Salvation by faith alone	God has predetermined who will be saved	Salvation by faith alone
Bible	Church and Bible tradition are sources of revealed truth	Bible is sole source of revealed truth	Bible is sole source of revealed truth	Bible is sole source of revealed truth
Worship Service	Worship service based on ritual	Worship service focused on preaching and ritual	Worship service focused on preaching	Worship service based on ritual and preaching
Interpretation of Beliefs	Priests interpret Bible and Church teachings for believers	Believers interpret the Bible for themselves	Believers interpret the Bible for themselves	Believers interpret the Bible using tradition and reason

Critical Thinking

1. **Compare and Contrast** Which of the branches on the chart are most different and which are most similar?

2. **Analyze Effects** Select a Protestant denomination not shown on this page. Research it and write a paragraph tracing its roots to the Reformation.

PROTESTANTISM TODAY

Religious Adherents in the United States:

Roman Catholic 22%
Protestant 20%
Non-Christian 18%
Independent Christian 22%
Unaffiliated Christian 15%
Marginal Christian 3%

Sources: *Britannica Book of the Year 2010*

MEMBERSHIP:

- Nearly 400 million Protestants worldwide
- About 65 million Protestants in the United States

BRANCHES:

- More than 465 major Protestant denominations worldwide
- Major denominational families worldwide: Anglican, Assemblies of God, Baptist, Methodist, Lutheran, and Presbyterian
- More than 250 denominations in the United States
- About 40 denominations with more than 400,000 members each in the United States

---

Reading Check
Analyze Causes
Why did Luther's ideas appeal to many northern German princes?

Still determined that his subjects should remain Catholic, Charles V went to war against the Protestant princes. Even though he defeated them in 1547, he failed to force them back into the Catholic Church. In 1555, Charles, weary of fighting, ordered all German princes, both Protestant and Catholic, to assemble in the city of Augsburg. There the princes agreed that each ruler would decide the religion of his state. This famous religious settlement was known as the **Peace of Augsburg**.

England Becomes Protestant

The Catholic Church soon faced another great challenge to its authority, this time in England. Unlike Luther, the man who broke England's ties to the Roman Catholic Church did so for political and personal reasons, not religious ones.

Henry VIII Wants a Son When **Henry VIII** became king of England in 1509, he was a devout Catholic. Indeed, in 1521, Henry wrote a stinging attack on Luther's ideas. In recognition of Henry's support, the pope gave him the title "Defender of the Faith." Political needs, however, soon tested his religious loyalty. He needed a male heir. Henry's father had become king after a long civil war. Henry feared that a similar war would start if he died without a son as his heir. He and his wife, Catherine of Aragon, had one living child—a daughter, Mary—but no woman had ever successfully claimed the English throne.

By 1527, Henry was convinced that the 42-year-old Catherine would have no more children. He wanted to divorce her and take a younger queen. Church law did not allow divorce. However, the pope could **annul**, or set aside, Henry's marriage if proof could be found that it had never been legal in the first place. In 1527, Henry asked the pope to annul his marriage, but the pope turned him down. The pope did not want to offend Catherine's powerful nephew, the Holy Roman Emperor Charles V.

READING CHECK
Analyze Causes Why did Luther's ideas appeal to many northern German princes? *Some supported his ideas but others hoped to secure Church property.*

Objectives

You may wish to discuss the following questions with students to help them frame the content as they read.

- Why did Henry VIII need either a divorce or an annulment? *to marry a woman who could give him a son*
- Elizabeth I came to power at a time of religious turmoil. How did she deal with the question of religion? *She returned England to Protestantism and established a state church.*

More About . . .

Henry VIII Most English people followed Roman Catholicism at the time of Henry's break with Rome. There was a small minority of English dissenters—people who wanted to reform the church. However, Henry was careful to change nothing about the way people worshiped. This explains why there was not greater outcry from his subjects about his actions.

TRACING RELIGIOUS CHANGES IN ENGLAND

Below Level Help students name the religion of each of these English monarchs: Henry VIII, Edward VI, Mary I, and Elizabeth I. Challenge them to identify reasons for each monarch's religious beliefs. Define challenging terms for students.

At Level Have students reread this segment and identify four English monarchs. Ask students to work together and make a chart that shows the rulers, their religions, and the reasons for their religious beliefs.

Above Level Have students independently complete the At Level assignment. Then ask students to write a response to the following question: What was the effect of all these changes? *Possible answer: some people executed; religious confusion; government became unstable*

Carousel: Henry VIII and Anne Boleyn

Have students navigate through the carousel and note similarities and differences among the images or identify a unifying theme.

Henry VIII Causes Religious Turmoil

Have students explore the timeline and answer the associated question.

Analyze Effects How did Henry VIII's personal choices about marriage affect religious history in England? *The Catholic Church was replaced with the Anglican Church to fulfill Henry VIII's personal needs.*

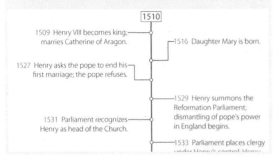

1510

1509 Henry VIII becomes king; marries Catherine of Aragon.

1516 Daughter Mary is born.

1527 Henry asks the pope to end his first marriage; the pope refuses.

1529 Henry summons the Reformation Parliament; dismantling of pope's power in England begins.

1531 Parliament recognizes Henry as head of the Church.

1533 Parliament places clergy under Henry's control; Henry

The Reformation Parliament Henry took steps to solve his marriage problem himself. In 1529, he called Parliament into session and asked it to pass a set of laws that ended the pope's power in England. This Parliament is known as the Reformation Parliament.

In 1533, Henry secretly married Anne Boleyn (BUL·ihn), who was in her twenties. Shortly after, Parliament legalized Henry's divorce from Catherine. In 1534, Henry's break with the pope was completed when Parliament voted to approve the Act of Supremacy. This called on people to take an oath recognizing the divorce and accepting Henry, not the pope, as the official head of England's Church.

The Act of Supremacy met some opposition. Thomas More, even though he had strongly criticized the Church, remained a devout Catholic. His faith, he said, would not allow him to accept the terms of the act and he refused to take the oath. In response, Henry had him arrested and imprisoned in the Tower of London. In 1535, More was found guilty of high treason and executed.

Consequences of Henry's Changes Henry did not immediately get the male heir he sought. After Anne Boleyn gave birth to a daughter, Elizabeth, she fell out of Henry's favor. Eventually, she was charged with treason. Like Thomas More, she was imprisoned in the Tower of London. She was found guilty and beheaded in 1536. Almost at once, Henry took a third wife, Jane Seymour. In 1537, she gave him a son named Edward. Henry's happiness was tempered by his wife's death just two weeks later. Henry married three more times. None of these marriages, however, produced children.

After Henry's death in 1547, each of his three children ruled England in turn. This created religious turmoil. Henry's son, Edward, became king when he was just nine years old. Too young to rule alone, Edward VI was

Henry VIII Causes Religious Turmoil

Henry's many marriages led to conflict with the Catholic Church and the founding of the Church of England.

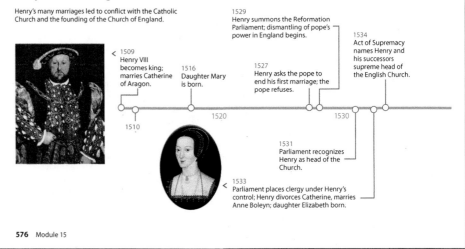

1529 Henry summons the Reformation Parliament; dismantling of pope's power in England begins.

1534 Act of Supremacy names Henry and his successors supreme head of the English Church.

1509 Henry VIII becomes king; marries Catherine of Aragon.

1516 Daughter Mary is born.

1527 Henry asks the pope to end his first marriage; the pope refuses.

1510

1520

1530

1531 Parliament recognizes Henry as head of the Church.

1533 Parliament places clergy under Henry's control; Henry divorces Catherine, marries Anne Boleyn; daughter Elizabeth born.

guided by adult advisers. These men were devout Protestants, and they introduced Protestant reforms to the English Church. Almost constantly in ill health, Edward reigned for just six years. Mary, the daughter of Catherine of Aragon, took the throne in 1553. She was a Catholic who returned the English Church to the rule of the pope. Her efforts met with considerable resistance, and she had many Protestants executed. When Mary died in 1558, Elizabeth, Anne Boleyn's daughter, inherited the throne.

Elizabeth Restores Protestantism Elizabeth I was determined to return her kingdom to Protestantism. In 1559, Parliament followed Elizabeth's wishes and set up the Church of England, or **Anglican** Church, with Elizabeth as its head. This was to be the only legal church in England.

Elizabeth decided to establish a state church that moderate Catholics and moderate Protestants might both accept. To please Protestants, priests in the Church of England were allowed to marry. They could deliver sermons in English, not Latin. To please Catholics, the Church of England kept some of the trappings of the Catholic service such as rich robes. In addition, church services were revised to be somewhat more acceptable to Catholics.

Elizabeth Faces Other Challenges By taking this moderate approach, Elizabeth brought a level of religious peace to England. Religion, however, remained a problem. Some Protestants pushed for Elizabeth to make more far-reaching church reforms. At the same time, some Catholics tried to overthrow Elizabeth and replace her with her cousin, the Catholic Mary, Queen of Scots. Elizabeth also faced threats from Philip II, the Catholic king of Spain.

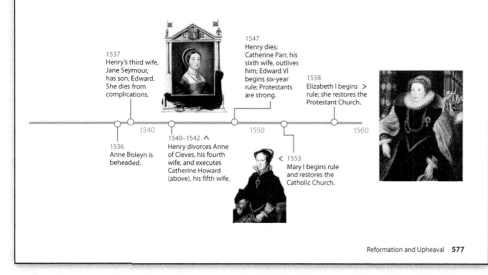

1537
Henry's third wife, Jane Seymour, has son, Edward. She dies from complications.

1547
Henry dies; Catherine Parr, his sixth wife, outlives him; Edward VI begins six-year rule; Protestants are strong.

1558
Elizabeth I begins > rule; she restores the Protestant Church.

1536
Anne Boleyn is beheaded.

1540–1542 ⋀
Henry divorces Anne of Cleves, his fourth wife, and executes Catherine Howard (above), his fifth wife.

< 1553
Mary I begins rule and restores the Catholic Church.

1540   1550   1560

COLLABORATIVE LEARNING

Main Idea Ladder

1. Organize the class into four groups. Assign each group one of the topics in this lesson: Causes of the Reformation, Luther Challenges the Church, The Response to Luther, England Becomes Protestant.

2. Draw four ladders for students to see. Label the tops of the ladders with the names of the topics in this lesson. Have students draw a ladder onto their own paper and label it with their assigned topic.

3. Group members should work together to fill in the rungs of the ladder with the main ideas of their topic.

4. Have each group present and explain its ladder to the class. Allow time for students to view the visuals on their own.

BIOGRAPHY

Elizabeth I

Have students read the biography of Elizabeth I, Queen of England from 1558 to 1603, who was also a skillful politician and diplomat who reasserted Protestant supremacy in England.

READING CHECK

Analyze Effects How did Henry VIII's marriages and divorces cause religious turmoil in England? *As a result, Catholicism was generally abandoned in England, and the Anglican Church was created.*

Reading Check
Analyze Effects
How did Henry VIII's marriages and divorces cause religious turmoil in England?

Elizabeth faced other difficulties. Money was one problem. In the late 1500s, the English began to think about building an American empire as a new source of income. While colonies strengthened England economically, they did not enrich the queen directly. Elizabeth's constant need for money would carry over into the next reign and lead to bitter conflict between the monarch and Parliament. In the meantime, the Reformation gained ground in other European countries.

— BIOGRAPHY —

Elizabeth I
(1533–1603)

Elizabeth I, like her father, had a robust nature and loved physical activity. She had a particular passion for dancing. Her fondness for exercise diminished little with age, and she showed amazing energy and strength well into her sixties.

Elizabeth resembled her father in character and temperament. She was stubborn, strong-willed, and arrogant, and she expected to be obeyed without question. Elizabeth also had a fierce and unpredictable temper. To her subjects, Elizabeth was an object of both fear and love. She was their "most dread sovereign lady."

Lesson 1 Assessment

1. **Organize Information** Make a chart and record the effects of Martin Luther's protests.

cause: Luther protests abuses → effect 1, effect 2, effect 3

   Which effect do you think had the greatest impact? Why?
2. **Key Terms and People** For each key term or person in the lesson, write a sentence explaining its significance.
3. **Summarize** What political, economic, and social factors helped bring about the Reformation?

4. **Find the Main Ideas** From where did the term *Protestantism* originate?
5. **Analyze Effects** What impact did Henry VIII's actions have on England in the second half of the 1500s?
6. **Draw Conclusions** Explain how Elizabeth I was able to bring a level of religious peace to England.
7. **Compare** Do you think Luther or Henry VIII had a better reason to break with the Church? Provide details to support your answer.
8. **Analyze Motives** How did the Catholic Church respond to Luther's teachings? Explain your answer.
9. **Develop Historical Perspective** Imagine Martin Luther and a leader of the Catholic Church are squaring off in a public debate about the Protestant Reformation. Write a brief **dialogue** between the two.

COLLABORATIVE LEARNING

Main Idea Ladder

1. Organize the class into four groups. Assign each group one of the topics in this lesson: Causes of the Reformation, Luther Challenges the Church, The Response to Luther, England Becomes Protestant.

2. Draw four ladders for students to see. Label the tops of the ladders with the names of the topics in this lesson. Have students draw a ladder onto their own paper and label it with their assigned topic.

3. Group members should work together to fill in the rungs of the ladder with the main ideas of their topic.

4. Have each group present and explain its ladder to the class. Allow time for students to view the visuals on their own.

Print Assessment

1. **Organize Information** Make a chart and record the effects of Martin Luther's protests. Which effect do you think had the greatest impact? Why? *Luther excommunicated; Many German princes protested; Lutheran Church founded. The founding of the Lutheran Church had the greatest impact because it has had the most permanent effect.*

2. **Key Terms and People** For each key term or person in the lesson, write a sentence explaining its significance. *Explanation of the lesson's key terms can be found on the following pages: Martin Luther, p. 572; indulgence, p. 572; Reformation, p. 572; excommunicate, p. 573; Lutheran, p. 573; Protestant, p. 573; Peace of Augsburg, p. 575; Henry VIII, p. 575; annul, p. 575; Elizabeth I, p. 577; Anglican, p. 577*

3. **Summarize** What political, economic, and social factors helped bring about the Reformation? *Political: powerful leaders challenged the authority of the Church and pope; Economic: European monarchs were jealous of the Church's wealth, and merchants resented paying taxes; Social: printing press spread new ideas that were critical of the Church*

4. **Find the Main Ideas** From where did the term Protestantism originate? *It was originally used to describe princes who were loyal to Martin Luther and were protesting against the pope and Church.*

5. **Analyze Effects** What impact did Henry VIII's actions have on England in the second half of the 1500s? *led to conflict with the Catholic Church and the founding of the Church of England*

6. **Draw Conclusions** Explain how Elizabeth I was able to bring a level of religious peace to England. *Her church was acceptable to moderate Catholics and moderate Protestants. The church kept some elements of Catholic service.*

7. **Compare** Do you think Luther or Henry VIII had a better reason to break with the Church? Provide details to support your answer. *Luther had legitimate complaints about indulgences and other Church problems; Henry's annulment denied; he needed an heir to prevent another civil war.*

8. **Analyze Motives** How did the Catholic Church respond to Luther's teachings? Explain your answer. *The Church excommunicated him; viewed his teachings as a threat*

9. **Develop Historical Perspective** Imagine Martin Luther and a leader of the Catholic Church are squaring off in a public debate about the Protestant Reformation. Write a brief dialogue between the two. *Dialogues should explain the views of both sides; cite facts and details from the text.*

▷ Online Assessment

1. Why was it difficult for Germany to have any central authority in the 1500s?
   - ○ The country was too geographically vast.
   - ○ The people had many different religions.
   - ○ The people spoke many different languages.
   - ◉ The country was divided into competing states.

   Alternate Question *Select the answer choice from the drop-down list to complete the sentence correctly.* Germany [was divided into competing states ⇕], so it was challenging for rulers such as the pope to exert any kind of central authority in the area.

2. Why did Martin Luther have an issue with Johann Tetzel?
   - ◉ He sold indulgences.
   - ○ He wrote the 95 Theses.
   - ○ He started the Reformation movement.
   - ○ He wanted to rebuild St. Peter's Cathedral in Rome.

   Alternate Question *Select the answer choice from the drop-down list to complete the sentence correctly.* Martin Luther had serious issues with the way that Johann Tetzel tried to raise money to rebuild St. Peter's Cathedral in Rome because he sold [indulgences ⇕].

3. What act ultimately led to Martin Luther's excommunication from the Catholic Church?
   - ○ He wrote the 95 Theses.
   - ○ He encouraged people to study the Bible.
   - ◉ He threw the pope's decree into the flames.
   - ○ He taught that good works were not necessary for salvation.

   Alternate Question *Select the answer choice from the drop-down list to complete the sentence correctly.* Pope Leo [excommunicated ⇕] Martin Luther when Luther threw the pope's decree into the flames of a fire while he was with his students in Wittenberg, Germany.

4. Why did King Henry VIII call the Reformation Parliament in 1529?
   - ◉ He wanted Parliament to end the pope's power in England.
   - ○ He wanted Parliament to finalize his divorce to Catherine of Aragon.
   - ○ He wanted Parliament to make Catholicism the state religion of England.
   - ○ He wanted Parliament to conduct his wedding ceremony to Anne Boleyn.

   Alternate Question *Select the answer choice from the drop-down list to complete the sentence correctly.* In 1529, King Henry VIII called a special session of Parliament, which was later called the Reformation Parliament. In this session, the king asked Parliament to [end the pope's power ⇕].

5. **Make Judgments** Why did people feel that the church leaders were corrupt in the 1500s?

   Possible answer: The popes who ruled during that time period patronized the arts, spent extravagantly on personal pleasure, and fought wars. Pope Alexander VI admitted that he had fathered several children, which was outside the acceptable conduct for popes. Popes were often too busy pursuing worldly affairs to conduct church business. The upper clergy weren't the only ones with problems. The lower clergy were often poorly educated and few could even read, which impacted their ability to teach the people. Other lower priests also broke their vows and married. In addition, they had reputations for drinking to excess and gambling.

6. **Sequence** What series of events was the result of Tetzel's indulgence program?

   Possible answer: Martin Luther was troubled by Tetzel's indulgence program, so he wrote the 95 Theses as a way to prompt a debate by local scholars. However, the 95 Theses was copied by someone and then printed and spread around. Luther's ideas were advertised to the people and groups all over Germany. Luther's actions ended up starting the Reformation. So, in a way, Tetzel's indulgence program was also a cause of the Reformation because it was this program that inspired Luther to write the 95 Theses.

7. **Make Inferences** What impact did Prince Frederick the Wise of Saxony have on the Reformation?

   Possible answer: Prince Frederick the Wise of Saxony had a positive impact on the Reformation. When Martin Luther was declared a heretic by Charles in the Edict of Worms, no one in the empire was supposed to give Luther any food or shelter. All of his books were also to be burnt. However, Prince Frederick disobeyed the emperor. He gave Luther shelter in one of his castles for more than a year. While Luther lived there, he translated the New Testament into German. Had Prince Frederick not done this, there is no guarantee that Luther would have survived, and the Reformation may have been thwarted.

8. **Elaborate** Why did King Henry VIII want his marriage annulled, and why did the pope refuse to do it?

   Possible answer: King Henry VIII wanted to divorce his wife, Catherine of Aragon, because she hadn't produced a male heir, and he didn't think she would be able to because of her age. He could not divorce her according to Catholic Church law, but he thought he could get an annulment. So he asked the pope, but the pope would not annul the marriage because it had been legal from the beginning and was not eligible for annulment. The pope also refused to annul the marriage because he did not want to offend Catherine's nephew who was the Holy Roman Emperor.

The Reformation Continues

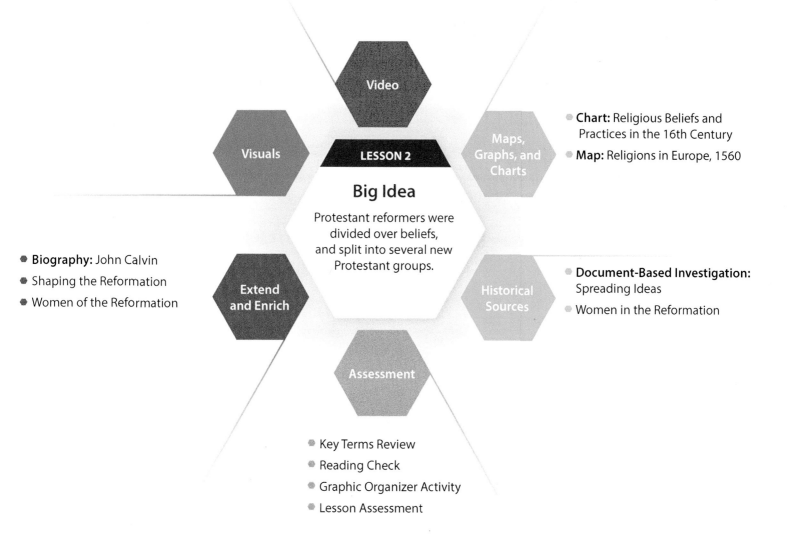

Video

Visuals

LESSON 2

Maps, Graphs, and Charts

- **Chart:** Religious Beliefs and Practices in the 16th Century
- **Map:** Religions in Europe, 1560

Big Idea

Protestant reformers were divided over beliefs, and split into several new Protestant groups.

- **Biography:** John Calvin
- Shaping the Reformation
- Women of the Reformation

Extend and Enrich

Historical Sources

- **Document-Based Investigation:** Spreading Ideas
- Women in the Reformation

Assessment

- Key Terms Review
- Reading Check
- Graphic Organizer Activity
- Lesson Assessment

▷ Online Lesson 2 Enrichment Activities

Shaping the Reformation

Political Cartoon Students draw a political cartoon representing one Protestant reformer's ideas that helped to shape the Reformation. Students are walked through the process of identifying a topic, taking notes, sketching a draft, revising, and making a final draft of the cartoon.

Women of the Reformation

Article Students explore women's roles during the Reformation by preparing interview questions for Katherina Zell. Students imagine they are an editor for a Strasbourg newspaper and write six questions to ask Katherina Zell based on what they know about her life or through additional research.

The Reformation Continues

The Big Idea
Protestant reformers were divided over beliefs, and split into several new Protestant groups.

Why It Matters Now
Many Protestant churches began during this period.

Key Terms and People
Huldrych Zwingli
John Calvin
predestination
Calvinism
theocracy
John Knox
Presbyterian
Anabaptist

Setting the Stage

Under the leadership of Queen Elizabeth I, the Anglican Church, though Protestant, remained similar to the Catholic Church in many of its doctrines and ceremonies. Meanwhile, other forms of Protestantism were developing elsewhere in Europe. Martin Luther had launched the Reformation in northern Germany, but reformers were at work in other countries. In Switzerland, another major branch of Protestantism emerged. Based mainly on the teachings of John Calvin, a French follower of Luther, it promoted unique ideas about the relationship between people and God.

Calvin Continues the Reformation

Religious reform in Switzerland was begun by **Huldrych Zwingli** (HUL·drykh·ZWIHNG·lee), a Catholic priest in Zurich. He was influenced both by the Christian humanism of Erasmus and by the reforms of Luther. In 1520, Zwingli openly attacked abuses in the Catholic Church. He called for a return to the more personal faith of early Christianity. He also wanted believers to have more control over the Church.

Zwingli's reforms were adopted in Zurich and other cities. In 1531, a bitter war between Swiss Protestants and Catholics broke out. During the fighting, Zwingli met his death. Meanwhile, **John Calvin**, then a young law student in France with a growing interest in Church doctrine, began to clarify his religious beliefs.

Objectives

You may wish to discuss the following questions with students to help them frame the content as they read.

- In what ways did Calvin's leadership of the city of Geneva, Switzerland, demonstrate his religious beliefs? *Sinful people need guidance, so everyone obeyed strict rules.*
- Why is John Calvin important today? *His ideas influenced the development of many Protestant churches.*

More About . . .

John Calvin Calvinist ritual, or religious ceremony, differed from that of Catholics and Lutherans. Calvin forbade the clergy to wear rich, colorful religious garments. Many traditional religious objects, such as statues, incense, altars, candles, chants, organ music, and stained-glass windows, were not allowed in Calvinist churches.

Religion in Switzerland Today, the population of Switzerland is approximately half Catholic and half Protestant. The country also has a small Jewish community.

Teach the Big Idea

1. **Whole Class Open/Introduction** Ask students how their lives would be different if they lived in a theocracy like Geneva. *no colorful clothing, no card games, perhaps no computer games, stricter punishments*

2. **Direct Teach** Read students the Big Idea: *Protestant reformers were divided over beliefs, and many Protestant churches began during this period.* Review the following lesson objectives with students to aid in their understanding of the Big Idea.
   - Explore Calvin's Protestant teachings.
   - Describe the beliefs of other reformers and the roles of women in the Reformation.

3. **Whole Group Close/Reflect** Have students write a diary entry of someone their age living during the Reformation. What would his or her life be like? Invite students to share their work.

▷ ONLINE DOCUMENT-BASED INVESTIGATION

Reformation and Upheaval
Spreading Ideas is the second of four document-based investigations that students will analyze in the Reformation and Upheaval module. In *Reformation Europe*, published in 1963, historian G. R. Elton notes the role of geography and trade in the spread of Reformation ideas. Students can click on the audio button beneath the historical source to hear the quote by G. R. Elton read aloud.

▷ ONLINE GRAPHIC ORGANIZER

The Reformation Continues
As students read the lesson, have them use the graphic organizer to take notes. Students can review their graphic organizer notes at the end of the lesson to answer the following question:

Summarize What ideas did other reformers bring to help shape beliefs during the Protestant Reformation? How were they important? *They brought the ideas of predestination and adult baptism, both of which led to the branching out of other Protestant denominations.*

▷ ONLINE LESSON FLIP CARDS

Review Key Terms and People
Students can use the flip cards in the Lesson Review at any time to review the lesson's key terms and people: *Huldrych Zwingli, John Calvin, predestination, Calvinism, theocracy, John Knox, Presbyterian,* and *Anabaptist.*

▷ ONLINE DOCUMENT-BASED INVESTIGATION

Spreading Ideas

In *Reformation Europe*, published in 1963, historian G. R. Elton notes the role of geography and trade in the spread of Reformation ideas. Students can play the audio to hear the quote by G. R. Elton read aloud.

Analyze Sources Why was Germany's location important to the spread of Reformation ideas? *Germany's geographic location at the center of Europe and its position at the center of European trade made the spread of Reformation ideas quick and thorough. Merchants carried ideas and books all over Europe.*

In print edition, see Historical Source titled Location, Location, Location.

DOCUMENT-BASED INVESTIGATION   HISTORICAL SOURCE

Spreading Ideas

In *Reformation Europe*, published in 1963, historian G. R. Elton notes the role of geography and trade in the spread of Reformation ideas.

— BIOGRAPHY —

John Calvin (1509–1564)

A quiet boy, Calvin grew up to study law and philosophy at the University of Paris. In the 1530s, he was influenced by French followers of Luther. When King Francis I ordered Protestants arrested, Calvin fled. Eventually, he moved to Geneva.

Because Calvin and his followers rigidly regulated morality in Geneva, Calvinism is often described as strict and grim. But Calvin taught that people should enjoy God's gifts. He wrote that it should not be "forbidden to laugh, or to enjoy food, or to add new possessions to old."

Calvin Formalizes Protestant Ideas When Martin Luther posted his 95 theses in 1517, John Calvin had been only eight years old. But Calvin grew up to have as much influence in the spread of Protestantism as Luther did. He would give order to the faith Luther had begun.

In 1536, Calvin published *Institutes of the Christian Religion*. This book expressed ideas about God, salvation, and human nature. It was a summary of Protestant theology, or religious beliefs. Calvin wrote that men and women are sinful by nature. Taking Luther's idea that humans cannot earn salvation, Calvin went on to say that God chooses a very few people to save. Calvin called these few the "elect." He believed that God has known since the beginning of time who will be saved. This doctrine is called **predestination**. The religion based on Calvin's teachings is called **Calvinism**.

Calvin Leads the Reformation in Switzerland Calvin believed that the ideal government was a **theocracy**, a government controlled by religious leaders. In 1541, Protestants in Geneva, Switzerland, asked Calvin to lead their city.

When Calvin arrived there in the 1540s, Geneva was a self-governing city of about 20,000 people. He and his followers ran the city according to strict rules. Everyone attended religion class. No one wore bright clothing or played card games. Authorities would imprison, excommunicate, or banish those who broke such rules. Anyone who preached different doctrines might be burned at the stake. Yet, to many Protestants, Calvin's Geneva was a model city of highly moral citizens.

580   Module 15

ENGLISH LANGUAGE LEARNERS

Compare and Contrast

1. Draw a Venn diagram for students to see. Label the diagram Protestant Movements. In the left circle, add the label Zwingli's Movement. In the right circle, add the label Calvinism. In the overlap area, add the label Both.

2. Help students use the text to add information to the left circle. *condemned by Luther; attacked by Church*

3. Help students use the text to add information to the right circle. *predestination; strict laws regulating people's behavior*

4. Encourage students to complete the overlap area on their own. *influenced by Luther; Switzerland; theocracy*

Spreading Ideas

In *Reformation Europe*, published in 1963, historian G. R. Elton noted the role of geography and trade in the spread of Reformation ideas.

"Could the Reformation have spread so far and so fast if it had started anywhere but in Germany? The fact that it had its beginnings in the middle of Europe made possible a very rapid radiation in all directions. . . . Germany's position at the center of European trade also helped greatly. German merchants carried not only goods but Lutheran ideas and books to Venice and France; the north German Hanse [a trade league] transported the Reformation to the Scandinavian countries."

—G. R. Elton, from
Reformation Europe

Analyze Historical Sources
Why was Germany's location important to the spread of Reformation ideas?

Calvinism Spreads One admiring visitor to Geneva was a Scottish preacher named **John Knox**. When he returned to Scotland in 1559, Knox put Calvin's ideas to work. Each community church was governed by a group of laymen called elders or presbyters (PREHZ•buh•tuhrs). Followers of Knox became known as **Presbyterians**. In the 1560s, Protestant nobles led by Knox made Calvinism Scotland's official religion. They also deposed their Catholic ruler, Mary, Queen of Scots, in favor of her infant son, James.

Elsewhere, Swiss, Dutch, and French reformers adopted the Calvinist form of church organization. One reason Calvin is considered so influential is that many Protestant churches today trace their roots to Calvin. Over the years, however, many of them have softened Calvin's strict teachings.

Reading Check
Compare
How did Calvin's ideas about salvation differ from those of Luther?

Other Protestant Reformers

Protestants taught that the Bible is the source of all religious truth and that people should read it to discover those truths. As Christians interpreted the Bible for themselves, new Protestant groups formed over differences in belief.

The Anabaptists One such group baptized only those persons who were old enough to decide to be Christian. They said that persons who had been baptized as children should be rebaptized as adults. These believers were called **Anabaptists**, from a Greek word meaning "baptize again." The Anabaptists also taught that church and state should be separate, and they refused to fight in wars. They shared their possessions.

Viewing Anabaptists as radicals who threatened society, both Catholics and Protestants persecuted them. In 1533, some fled and settled in Münster, Westphalia, in Germany. Among them were Jan Mathijs and

Objectives

You may wish to discuss the following questions with students to help them frame the content as they read.

- What lasting influence did the Anabaptists have? *Anabaptist beliefs influenced the Amish, Mennonites, Quakers, and Baptists of today.*
- How did women influence the Reformation? *protected reformers, managed households, performed good works*

More About . . .

Katherina von Bora In addition to mothering six children with Martin Luther, Katherina von Bora played an active role at the Black Cloister, the monastery at the University of Wittenberg, where they lived. She took care of the animals, her garden, a brewery, and nearby farmland. She also played host to numerous guests and students that stayed in their home. Luther called her "The Morning Star of Wittenberg" because she began her daily chores before the sun came up.

READING CHECK
Compare How did Calvin's ideas about salvation differ from those of Luther? *Calvin believed in predestination, which is the belief that God already selects the people who will be saved. Luther believed that salvation could not be earned but did not believe in this kind of predestination.*

Religions in Europe, 1560

Have students explore the map using the interactive features and answer the associated question.

Region Which European countries became mostly Protestant? *England, Scotland, Denmark, and Sweden*

In print edition, see map of same title.

Location Judging from the way the religions were distributed, where would you expect religious conflicts to take place? Explain. *Possible answer: in the German states and the Swiss Confederation, where there was a mixture of faiths*

Region Which European countries became mostly Protestant and which remained mostly Roman Catholic? *mostly Protestant: England, Scotland, Denmark, and Sweden; mostly Roman Catholic: Ireland, Spain, France, and Italy*

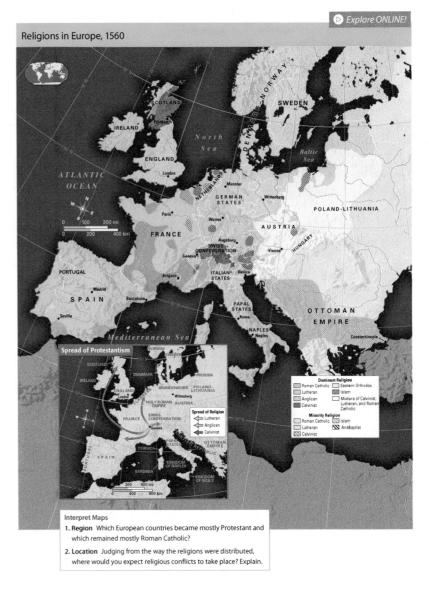

Explore ONLINE!

Religions in Europe, 1560

Interpret Maps

1. **Region** Which European countries became mostly Protestant and which remained mostly Roman Catholic?

2. **Location** Judging from the way the religions were distributed, where would you expect religious conflicts to take place? Explain.

582 Module 15

COLLABORATIVE LEARNING

Data on Religious Groups

1. Divide the class into groups of three to four students. Have them use an online source to count the houses of worship in their community.

2. Then have them create a chart listing up to 10 of the religious groups. For each group, have students note its religious affiliation.

3. Finally, have students note any Protestant churches in the community and explain their direct connection to the Reformation.

John of Leiden, who led the persecution of all non-Anabaptists there. An army comprised of Catholics and Protestants surrounded and later captured the city in 1535. But the Anabaptists survived and became the forerunners of the Mennonites and the Amish. Later, descendants of these people settled in Pennsylvania. Their teaching influenced the later Quakers and Baptists, groups who split from the Anglican Church.

Women's Role in the Reformation Many women played prominent roles in the Reformation, especially during the early years. For example, the sister of King Francis I, Marguerite of Navarre, protected John Calvin from being executed for his beliefs while he lived in France. Other noblewomen also protected reformers. The wives of some reformers, too, had influence. Katherina Zell, married to Matthew Zell of Strasbourg, once scolded a minister for speaking harshly of another reformer. The minister responded by saying that she had "disturbed the peace." Katherina Zell answered the minister's criticism toward the reformer sharply:

"Do you call this disturbing the peace that instead of spending my time in frivolous amusements I have visited the plague-infested and carried out the dead? I have visited those in prison and under sentence of death. Often for three days and three nights I have neither eaten nor slept. I have never mounted the pulpit, but I have done more than any minister in visiting those in misery."

—Katherina Zell, quoted in *Women of the Reformation*

Although Catholic, Marguerite of Navarre supported the call for reform in the Church.

READING CHECK
Make Inferences Why was it easier for women to take part in the earlier stages of the Reformation than in the later stages? *In the earlier stages, most churches did not have formal leaders who could tell women what to do.*

Katherina von Bora played a more typical, behind-the-scenes role as Luther's wife. Katherina had been sent to a convent at about age ten and became a nun. Inspired by Luther's teaching, she fled the convent. After marrying Luther, Katherina had six children. She also managed the family finances, fed all who visited their house, and supported her husband's work. She respected Luther's position but argued with him about woman's equal role in marriage.

As Protestant religions became more firmly established, their organization became more formal. Male religious leaders narrowly limited women's activities to the home and discouraged them from being leaders in the church. In fact, it was Luther who said, "God's highest gift on earth is a pious, cheerful, God-fearing, home-keeping wife."

Reading Check
Make Inferences
Why was it easier for women to take part in the earlier stages of the Reformation than in the later stages?

Now and Then

Martin Luther's criticisms of the Catholic Church grew sharper over time. In recent times, historians have focused more on analyzing the political, social, and economic conditions that contributed to the Reformation. Read the primary source from Martin Luther in Lesson 1 and this secondary source. Discuss them with a partner to evaluate their credibility and perspective based on when they were written.

"Beginning as a protest against arbitrary, self-aggrandizing, hierarchical authority in the person of the pope, the Reformation came to be closely identified in the minds of contemporaries with what we today might call states' rights or local control. To many townspeople and villagers, Luther seemed a godsend for their struggle to remain politically free and independent; they embraced his Reformation as a conserving political force, even though they knew it threatened to undo traditional religious beliefs and practices."

—Steven Ozment in *Protestants: The Birth of a Revolution*

Lesson 2 Assessment

1. Organize Information How did ideas of reformers who came after Luther help shape beliefs during the Protestant Reformation?

Zwingli	
Calvin	
Knox	
Anabaptists	

2. Key Terms and People For each key term or person in the lesson, write a sentence explaining its significance.

3. Draw Conclusions How did the Reformation set the stage for the modern world? Give examples.

4. Find Main Ideas What was Calvin's idea of the "elect" and their place in society?

5. Contrast How were the Anabaptists different from other Protestant groups in their political views?

6. Summarize What role did noblewomen play in the Reformation?

COLLABORATIVE LEARNING

Radio Advertisement

1. Divide students into small groups. Have groups reread the section "Calvin Leads the Reformation in Switzerland."

2. Ask students to imagine that they have been hired by John Calvin to write a radio advertisement encouraging people to visit Geneva. Each group should write a script for a radio commercial lasting 30 to 90 seconds.

3. Groups should consider the following questions:
   - What activities might you find its citizens doing?
   - What activities are not allowed in Geneva? Why?
   - What happens to people who break the rules?

4. Have each group perform its commercial for the class.

Print Assessment

1. **Organize Information** How did ideas of reformers who came after Luther help shape beliefs during the Protestant Reformation? *Zwingli: more personal faith; Calvin: idea of the "elect" and predestination; Knox: adopted Calvin's ideas and set up elders to govern each local church; Anabaptists: adults should be rebaptized*

2. **Key Terms and People** For each key term or person in the lesson, write a sentence explaining its significance. *Explanation of the lesson's key terms can be found on the following pages: Huldrych Zwingli, p. 579; John Calvin, p. 579; predestination, p. 580; Calvinism, p. 580; theocracy, p. 580; John Knox, p. 581; Presbyterian, p. 581; Anabaptist, p. 581*

3. **Draw Conclusions** How did the Reformation set the stage for the modern world? Give examples. *Protestant churches grew, more people left the Catholic Church to join Protestant churches, the church lost some power to the state because of the rise and strength of city states.*

4. **Find Main Ideas** What was Calvin's idea of the "elect" and their place in society? *The "elect" were the few God chose to be saved.*

5. **Contrast** How were the Anabaptists different from other Protestant groups in their political views? *The Anabaptists taught that church and state should be separate, and they refused to fight in wars.*

6. **Summarize** What role did noblewomen play in the Reformation? *Noblewomen, such as Marguerite of Navarre, protected reformers.*

▷ Online **Assessment**

1. What was the main difference between Calvinism and Lutheranism?
   - ○ Calvinism taught that everyone will be saved.
   - ◉ Calvinism taught the doctrine of predestination.
   - ○ Calvinism taught that salvation could not be earned.
   - ○ Calvinism taught that the pope had ultimate authority.

   Alternate Question *Select the answer choice from the drop-down list to complete the sentence correctly.* One of the key precepts of Calvinism was the doctrine of ⌐ *predestination* ⌐ ↕ ⌐, which taught that God has known since the beginning of time who would be saved.

2. Which group was a later offshoot of the Anabaptists?
   - ◉ Amish
   - ○ Calvinists
   - ○ Lutherans
   - ○ Methodists

   Alternate Question *Select the answer choice from the drop-down list to complete the sentence correctly.* Some of the Anabaptists eventually immigrated to the United States and became the forerunners to the Mennonites and ⌐ *Amish* ↕ ⌐.

3. **Make Inferences** Why might a person who didn't believe in Calvinism have felt constrained by living in Geneva in the 1540s?

   Possible answer: The city was run by very strict rules set by Calvin. Everyone had to attend a religion class. No one was allowed to wear bright clothing or play card games. Anyone who broke the rules could be excommunicated from the Church, imprisoned, or banished from the community. Those who preached different doctrines other than Calvinism could be burned at the stake.

4. **Elaborate** What were some of the roles that women played in the Reformation?

   Possible answer: Francis I, Marguerite of Navarre, protected John Calvin from being executed for his beliefs while he lived in France. Other women also protected reformers throughout Europe. Katherina von Bora was Martin Luther's wife. She played a behind-the-scenes role in his life. However, she also believed that women should have more of an equal role in marriage, an opinion for which she argued frequently with her husband.

The Catholic Reformation

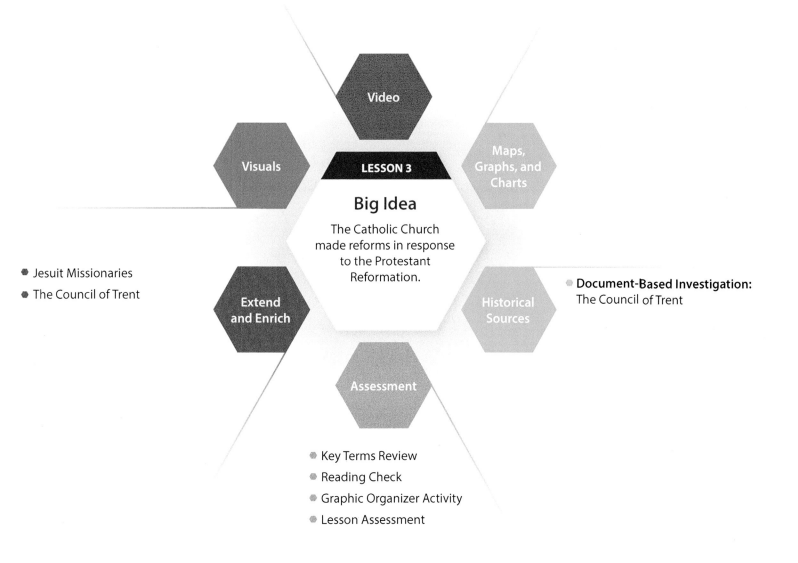

Video

Visuals

LESSON 3

Maps, Graphs, and Charts

Big Idea

The Catholic Church made reforms in response to the Protestant Reformation.

- Jesuit Missionaries
- The Council of Trent

Extend and Enrich

Historical Sources

- **Document-Based Investigation:** The Council of Trent

Assessment

- Key Terms Review
- Reading Check
- Graphic Organizer Activity
- Lesson Assessment

▷ Online Lesson 3 Enrichment Activities

Jesuit Missionaries

Article Students read about the work of Jesuit missionaries and then create a museum exhibit based on what they learn. Students identify a topic for the exhibit and then take notes, referencing credible sources. The activity encourages students to organize the exhibit logically and include visuals to make it more appealing.

The Council of Trent

Report Students read about the Council of Trent and must imagine themselves to be a recorder of the reforms made by religious leaders at the council. Then they write an informational report including key topics and decisions. The report should be factually accurate and include an introduction, a summary of the main reforms, and a conclusion. Students are also reminded to write in everyday language so that everyone can understand it.

Lesson 3

The Catholic Reformation

The Big Idea
The Catholic Church made reforms in response to the Protestant Reformation.

Why It Matters Now
Many Catholic schools are the result of reforms in the Church.

Key Terms and People
Catholic Reformation
Ignatius of Loyola
Jesuits
Council of Trent
heretic
nation-state

Setting the Stage

Protestant reformers were not the only ones who were dissatisfied with the state of the Catholic Church. Even before Martin Luther posted his 95 Theses, some Catholics had been working toward reform of the Church itself.

Early Reformers

While Protestant churches won many followers, millions remained true to Catholicism. Helping Catholics to remain loyal was a movement within the Catholic Church to reform itself. This movement is now known as the **Catholic Reformation**. Historians once referred to it as the Counter-Reformation. Important leaders in this movement included reformers such as Girolamo Savonarola (sahv•oh•nuh•ROH•luh) and **Ignatius of Loyola** (ihg•NAY•shuhs), who founded new religious orders. Two popes, Paul III and Paul IV, took actions to reform and renew the Church from within.

Girolamo Savonarola and Ignatius of Loyola A monk named Girolamo Savonarola was one of the first reformers to try to change the church from within. During the late 1400s, he preached fiery sermons against the abuses of the church. He called for churches to melt down their gold and silver ornaments to buy bread for the hungry and poor members of the church. Savonarola convinced people to gather and burn jewelry and trinkets. This enormous fire was known as "the bonfire of the vanities." Pope Alexander at first allowed Savonarola's work but eventually excommunicated him for spreading ideas that the pope considered dangerous. In 1498, Savonarola was executed in Florence.

Reformation and Upheaval **585**

Objectives

You may wish to discuss the following questions with students to help them frame the content as they read.

- How did Jesuit reforms help the Catholic Church keep its members from becoming Protestant? *Their schools helped educate priests to do better work; students learned more about Catholic theology; missionaries did good works and made converts.*

- Why did the Catholic Church feel the need for reforms, and what did church leaders do? *Protestantism was reducing Catholic membership; Church investigated corruption; supported Jesuits; used Inquisition; called Council of Trent; created Index of Forbidden Books*

More About . . .

Jesuit Missionaries The Jesuits were like a spiritual army, willing to go anywhere in the world in the service of the pope. Jesuit missionaries in Asia adapted their religious teachings to fit the culture of each country. Church officials criticized the missionaries for this approach. Matteo Ricci, for instance, was accused of allowing idolatry when he permitted the Chinese to conduct traditional rituals of reverence for their ancestors.

Teach the Big Idea

1. **Whole Class Open/Introduction** Ask students how the world might be different if the Reformation never took place. *Christianity would have different denominations; fewer religious schools; different nation-states might have more power*

2. **Direct Teach** Read students the Big Idea: *The Catholic Church made reforms in response to the Protestant Reformation.* Review the following lesson objectives with students to aid in their understanding of the Big Idea.
   - Trace reforms in the Catholic Church.
   - Summarize the legacy of the Reformation.

3. **Whole Group Close/Reflect** Have students write a brief opinion paper about the Council of Trent from a neutral observer's point of view. Invite students to share their work.

▷ ONLINE DOCUMENT-BASED INVESTIGATION

Reformation and Upheaval

The Council of Trent is the third of four document-based investigations that students will analyze in the Reformation and Upheaval module. Church leaders consult on reforms at the Council of Trent in this 16th century painting. Students can analyze the image and then answer the associated question.

▷ ONLINE GRAPHIC ORGANIZER

The Catholic Reformation

As students read the lesson, have them use the graphic organizer to take notes. Students can review their graphic organizer notes at the end of the lesson to answer the following question:

Analyze Effects What major reforms were made during the Catholic Reformation, and what were their short and long-term effects? *They ended abuses in the Church, established schools, and asserted that salvation comes through faith and good works.*

▷ ONLINE LESSON FLIP CARDS

Review Key Terms and People

Students can use the flip cards in the Lesson Review at any time to review the lesson's key terms and people: *Catholic Reformation, Ignatius of Loyola, Jesuits, Council of Trent, heretic,* and *nation-state.*

The Council of Trent

Have students analyze the image depicting the Council of Trent and then answer the associated question.

Analyze Sources Based on the image, what are these church leaders doing to help them make informed decisions about reforms in the Church? *They are referring to many sources while they make decisions about reforms to the Church.*

DOCUMENT-BASED INVESTIGATION HISTORICAL SOURCE

The Council of Trent

Church leaders consult on reforms at the Council of Trent in this 16th-century painting.

Church leaders consult on reforms at the Council of Trent in this 16th-century painting.

Ignatius grew up in his father's castle in Loyola, Spain. The great turning point in his life came in 1521 when he was injured in a war. While recovering, he thought about his past sins and about the life of Jesus. His daily devotions, he believed, cleansed his soul. In 1522, Ignatius began writing a book called *Spiritual Exercises* that laid out a day-by-day plan of meditation, prayer, and study.

For the next 18 years, Ignatius gathered followers. In 1540, the pope created a religious order for his followers called the Society of Jesus. Members were called **Jesuits** (JEHZH•oo•ihts). The Jesuits focused on three activities. First, they founded schools throughout Europe. Jesuit teachers were well trained in both classical studies and theology. The Jesuits' second mission was to convert non-Christians to Catholicism. So they sent out missionaries around the world. Their third goal was to stop the spread of Protestantism. The zeal of the Jesuits overcame the drift toward Protestantism in Poland and southern Germany.

586 Module 15

MAIN IDEA AND DETAILS

Learn Details About the Jesuits

Draw the graphic organizer below for students to see.

The Jesuits	
started by	
goals	
achievements	

Have students copy and complete the chart, using information from the text. Invite volunteers to complete the class chart.

Reforming Popes Two popes took the lead in reforming the Catholic Church. Paul III, pope from 1534 to 1549, took four important steps. First, he directed a council of cardinals to investigate indulgence selling and other abuses in the Church. Second, he approved the Jesuit order. Third, he used the Inquisition to seek out heresy in papal territory. The Inquisition was a Roman Catholic tribunal for investigating and prosecuting charges of heresy. This sometimes extended to targeting specific groups such as Jews. Fourth, and most important, he called a council of Church leaders to meet in Trent, in northern Italy.

From 1545 to 1563, at the **Council of Trent**, Catholic bishops and cardinals agreed on several doctrines:

- The Church's interpretation of the Bible was final. Any Christian who substituted his or her own interpretation was a **heretic** (a person accused of having a religious belief that was contrary to the official teachings of the Church).
- Christians needed faith and good works for salvation. They were not saved by faith alone, as Luther argued.
- The Bible and Church tradition were equally powerful authorities for guiding Christian life.
- Indulgences were valid expressions of faith, but the selling of indulgences was banned.

The next pope, Paul IV, vigorously carried out the council's decrees. In 1559, he had officials draw up a list of books considered dangerous to the Catholic faith. This list was known as the Index of Forbidden Books. Catholic bishops throughout Europe were ordered to gather up the offensive books (including Protestant Bibles) and burn them in bonfires. In Venice alone, followers burned 10,000 books in one day.

Reading Check
Summarize
What reforms were passed by the Council of Trent?

READING CHECK
Summarize What reforms were passed by the Council of Trent? *reforms addressed clergy's corruption, regulated priests' training, curbed financial abuses, condemned sale of indulgences*

Global Patterns

Jesuit Missionaries

The work of Jesuit missionaries has had a lasting impact around the globe. By the time Ignatius died in 1556, about a thousand Jesuits had brought his ministry to Europe, Africa, Asia, and the Americas. Two of the most famous Jesuit missionaries of the 1500s were Francis Xavier, who worked in India and Japan, and Matteo Ricci, who worked in China.

One reason the Jesuits had such an impact is that they founded schools throughout the world. For example, the Jesuits today run about 45 high schools and 28 colleges and universities in the United States. Four of these are Georgetown University (shown here), Boston College, Marquette University, and Loyola University of Chicago.

COMPARE AND CONTRAST

Identify Contributions

1. Have students identify a man and a woman mentioned in this lesson. Tell them to take notes about their importance and what each contributed to the Reformation or Counter Reformation.

2. Encourage students to make a Venn diagram to compare and contrast the two individuals they chose.

3. Ask students to write a brief paragraph describing the biggest similarities and differences between these two people.

4. Challenge students to identify what limitations, if any, were placed on what these people could achieve.

Objectives

You may wish to discuss the following questions with students to help them frame the content as they read.

- What roles did women play in the Catholic Reformation? *They worked among the poor, orphaned, and sick; trained women to become teachers; began a network of schools for girls.*

- How did Teresa of Avila demonstrate her religious beliefs? *She ran away to a convent, followed her own strict rules regarding fasting and prayer, and reformed the Carmelite order.*

More About . . .

Teresa of Avila Teresa was only 2 years old when Luther began the Reformation. Her father was very strict and religious, and she grew up convinced that she was a horrible sinner. She eventually learned to enjoy her life at the convent, partly because it was much less strict than her father.

READING CHECK

Compare and Contrast How did the influence of women and men differ during the Catholic Reformation? *Women took on more subordinate roles and focused on helping girls, tending to the sick, and reforming religious orders, while men founded schools, religious orders, and implemented new doctrines in the Church.*

Women Reformers

During the Renaissance, many women in religious orders began to take on more active roles in the Church. Most of them lived together in convents that were secluded, but by the late Middle Ages it was acceptable for nuns to help and work among the poor, orphaned, or sick.

Teresa of Avila Perhaps the most famous female spiritual leader was Teresa of Avila. Born in Spain in 1515, Teresa decided to become a nun around the age of 20. Her father opposed her plan, but Teresa ran away to a convent around 1536. At the convent, after deciding that the practices were too lax, she followed her own strict rules regarding fasting, prayer, and sleep. Eventually the church gave her permission to reform the Carmelite order. Teresa's deep spirituality, reported visions of Jesus, and fervor for the Catholic faith inspired many would-be Protestants to remain in the church.

Other Women Leaders Many other women had a profound and important influence during the Catholic Reformation through their work with the Church. In 1535 Italian nun Angela Merici began the Company of Saint Ursula, an order of women dedicated to teaching girls. Jane of Chantal and Francis of Sales cofounded the Visitation of Holy Mary order, which trained women to be teachers. Mary Ward of England began a network of schools for girls throughout Europe. At first her work was denounced by anti-Jesuits and the church because Ward's ideas about women were considered dangerously new. Later, however, her missionary influence was formally recognized by the Church.

Reading Check
Compare and Contrast How did the influence of women and men differ during the Catholic Reformation?

Teresa of Avila

COLLABORATIVE LEARNING

Women and the Church

1. Tell students that women have always been involved in the Catholic Church, although their roles have changed over the years. Certain types of involvement by women have been and continue to be controversial.

2. Assign each student a famous Catholic woman, such as Mother Teresa or Catherine of Siena.

3. Have students conduct research on their assigned person. Research should focus on the person's actions, her faith, and her relationship to the Catholic leadership.

4. Have students make a short presentation about their assigned person.

MAIN IDEA

Analyze Reforms

1. Ask students to think about which reform had the most impact.

2. Have students make a list of different reforms from this lesson, including Zwingli, Calvin, Anabaptists, and Catholic Reformers.

3. Tell students to organize their thoughts in a graphic organizer and arrange the reforms according to their impact.

4. Invite volunteers to share their thoughts with the class.

The Legacy of the Reformation

The Reformation had an enduring impact. Through its religious, social, and political effects, the Reformation set the stage for the modern world. It also ended the Christian unity of Europe and left it culturally divided.

Religious and Social Effects of the Reformation Despite religious wars and persecutions, Protestant churches flourished and new denominations developed. The Roman Catholic Church itself became more unified as a result of the reforms started at the Council of Trent. Both Catholics and Protestants realized the role that education served as a way to promote their beliefs. This led to the founding of parish schools and new colleges and universities throughout Europe.

Some women reformers had hoped to see the status of women in the Church and society improve as a result of the Reformation. But their status remained the same under both Protestantism and Roman Catholicism. Women were still mainly limited to the concerns of home and family.

Political Effects of the Reformation As the Catholic Church's moral and political authority declined, individual monarchs and states gained power. This led to the development of modern **nation-states**. In the 1600s, rulers of nation-states would seek more power for themselves and their countries through warfare, exploration, and expansion.

Questioning of beliefs and authority during the Reformation also laid the groundwork for the Enlightenment. This intellectual movement would sweep Europe in the late 18th century. It led some to reject all religions and others to call for the overthrow of existing governments.

Reading Check
Analyze Effects
What were the effects of the Reformation, and which one had the most lasting impact?

Lesson 3 Assessment

1. **Organize Information** Make a chart similar to the one below. Show key Catholic reforms that were made during the Catholic Reformation and their effects.

Catholic Reform	Effect

2. **Key Terms and People** For each key term or person in the lesson, write a sentence explaining its significance.
3. **Analyze Effects** How did the Council of Trent help to reform the Catholic Church?

4. **Summarize** What were the goals of the Jesuits?
5. **Compare** How did the steps taken by Paul III and Paul IV to reform the Catholic Church differ from Protestant reforms? Support your answer with details from the text.
6. **Analyze Causes** What caused women's roles to change in the Catholic Church during and after the Counter-Reformation?
7. **Evaluate** Were the effects of the Protestant and Catholic reformations mostly positive or negative with regard to their social, religious, and political impact? Explain your answer.

Objectives

You may wish to discuss the following questions with students to help them frame the content as they read.

- How did education benefit from the Reformation? *schools established, clergy better educated*
- What political changes started by the Reformation are present today? *Nations developed that exist today; wars to expand territory began; church political power declined.*

More About . . .

The Council of Trent The Catholic hierarchy called the Council of Trent to counter the Protestant Reformation and protect the Church. Some significant results of the Council of Trent were:

- disregard for Christian humanism and liberal movements within the church
- better educated Catholic bishops and clergy
- clearly defined Catholic doctrine

READING CHECK

Analyze Effects What were the effects of the Reformation, and which had the most lasting impact? *Religious and social: Catholic Church was more unified; more emphasis on education; rise of new intellectual movement; Political: rulers and leaders gained more power; rise of nation-states in Europe; the emphasis on education because it led to the rise of new school and universities, which advanced learning and an intellectual movement.*

Print Assessment

1. **Organize Information** Make a two-column chart to show the key Catholic reforms that were made during the Catholic Reformation and their effects. *Reforms: Council of Trent, new schools, new religious orders; Effects: redefined Catholic doctrines, established high-quality education; improved unity within the Catholic Church*
2. **Key Terms and People** For each key term or person in the lesson, write a sentence explaining its significance. *Explanation of the lesson's key terms can be found on the following pages: Catholic Reformation, p. 585; Ignatius of Loyola, p. 585; Jesuits, p. 586; Council of Trent, p. 587; heretic, p. 587; nation-state, p. 589*
3. **Analyze Effects** How did the Council of Trent help to reform the Catholic Church? *It helped stop the spread of Protestantism and redefined Catholic doctrine.*

SUMMARIZE

Identify Responses

1. Remind students that many Catholics were leaving the Church and becoming Protestant. The Catholic Church needed to do something to keep its members.
2. Review with students the steps the Church took to respond to the Reformation. Have students make a chart like the one here to identify the responses.

Actions by the Catholic Church	Reasons
Set up a meeting of Cardinals (called a council)	To investigate the selling of indulgences and other abuses
Set up a meeting of church leaders (the Council of Trent, which met for more than 10 years)	To state Catholic beliefs clearly
Approved the order of Jesuits	To support this new religious order which established schools and did missionary work
Started the Inquisition	To punish people who broke the rules of the Church

(continued)

Print Assessment (continued)

4. **Summarize** What were the goals of the Jesuits? *improve Catholic education, convert non-Christians, stop spread of Protestantism*

5. **Compare** How did steps taken by Paul III and Paul IV to reform the Catholic Church differ from Protestant reforms? Support your answer with details from the text. *Protestant reformers attacked abuses and developed new religious beliefs; reformers in Catholic Church stayed within the Church to correct abuses.*

6. **Analyze Causes** What caused women's roles to change in the Catholic Church during and after the Catholic Reformation? *Women were not as secluded and could help girls, the poor, and the needy during the Reformation. They also helped to reform religious orders. The leaders of the Catholic Church probably gave women this freedom so that they would not leave the Catholic Church.*

7. **Evaluate** Were the effects of the Protestant and Catholic Reformations mostly positive or negative with regard to their social, religious, and political impact? Explain your answer. *Mostly positive because education improved, as did intellectual thinking, and this affected religious ideas. However, there were also negative effects because Christianity was divided in Europe. The Church had weakened political power, which led to the rise of nation-states and power-hungry rulers.*

4. **Elaborate** What was the turning point in Ignatius of Loyola's life?

Possible answer: The turning point was when he was injured in war in 1521. While recovering, he had time to think about his past and about the life of Jesus. He believed that his daily devotions cleansed his soul. In 1522 he wrote Spiritual Exercises, *a book that explained his day-to-day plan of meditation, prayer, and study. For the next 18 years, he gathered followers and started a Society of Jesus. The members were called Jesuits.*

5. **Elaborate** Who was Teresa of Avila, and what were her contributions?

Possible answer: Teresa of Avila became a nun at age 20. At the convent, she felt that the rules were too lax, so she started her own rules on fasting, prayer, and sleep. She reformed the Carmelite order. Her deep spiritualism and fervor inspired many people who would have left the Church to become Protestants to stay in the Church.

6. **Cause and Effect** What led to the founding of parish schools and new colleges and universities in Europe?

Possible answer: The Council of Trent provided an opportunity for the Catholic Church to become more unified as a result of the reforms that were started. Both Catholics and Protestants gave more emphasis to the role of education in promoting their beliefs, leading to more parish schools, colleges, and universities.

▷ Online Assessment

1. What was the main tenet of Savonarola's teachings?
   ○ He thought the Church should excommunicate heretics.
   ◉ He thought the Church should spend its wealth on the poor.
   ○ He thought the Church should give more power to the pope.
   ○ He thought the Church should allow everyone to own a Bible.

   Alternate Question *Select the answer choice from the drop-down list to complete the sentence correctly.* Savonarola was one of the first reformers who tried to change the Church from within. He felt that the Church abused its power and should (melt its gold and silver ⇕) to buy bread for the poor.

2. What did Angela Merici, Jane of Chantal, and Francis of Sales have in common?
   ○ They denounced anti-Jesuits.
   ○ They worked as missionaries.
   ◉ They were dedicated to education.
   ○ They reformed the Carmelite order.

   Alternate Question *Select the answer choice from the drop-down list to complete the sentence correctly.* Angela Merici, Jane of Chantal, and Francis of Sales were all dedicated to (educating females ⇕).

3. What was the main result of the Council of Trent?
   ◉ The Catholic Church became more unified.
   ○ The Catholic Church eliminated nation-states.
   ○ The Catholic Church gave women more authority.
   ○ The Catholic Church prohibited education at parish schools.

   Alternate Question *Select the answer choice from the drop-down list to complete the sentence correctly.* The reforms started at the Council of Trent allowed the Catholic Church to become (more unified ⇕).

ADDITIONAL LESSON CONTENT

Council of Trent Poster

1. Review with students the information in this lesson about the Council of Trent.

2. Organize students into small groups.

3. Have students create a poster that summarizes the decisions made at the Council of Trent. Encourage students to conduct additional research and include photos, illustrations, and other visuals to make the poster appealing.

4. Have volunteers present their posters to the class. Display the poster in a classroom exhibit for everyone to see and appreciate.

Social Unrest

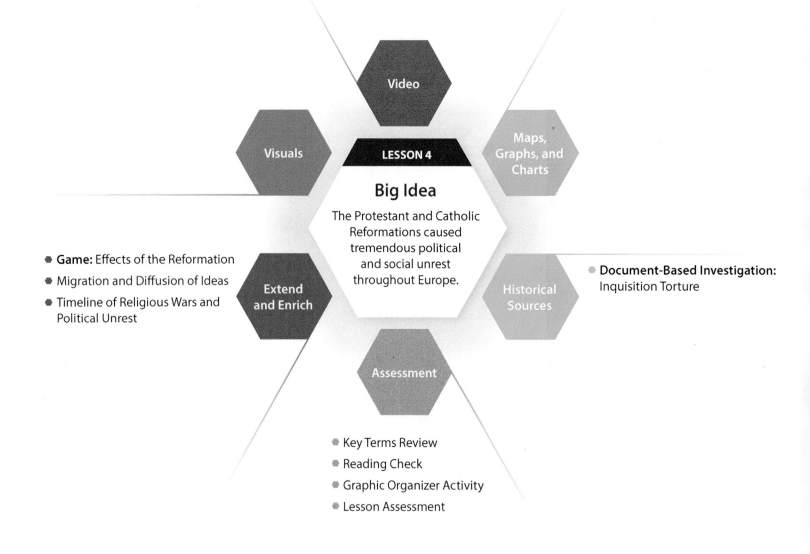

Video

Visuals

LESSON 4

Maps, Graphs, and Charts

Big Idea

The Protestant and Catholic Reformations caused tremendous political and social unrest throughout Europe.

- **Game:** Effects of the Reformation
- Migration and Diffusion of Ideas
- Timeline of Religious Wars and Political Unrest

Extend and Enrich

- **Document-Based Investigation:** Inquisition Torture

Historical Sources

Assessment

- Key Terms Review
- Reading Check
- Graphic Organizer Activity
- Lesson Assessment

▷ Online **Lesson 4 Enrichment Activities**

Migration and Diffusion of Ideas

Article Students read about the effects of Gutenberg's press on print and the Reformation. They then create a chart to illustrate similarities and differences between the printing revolution and the Internet revolution. Students also should write a paragraph describing how the Internet has changed how information is shared.

Timeline of Religious Wars and Political Unrest

Timeline Students create a timeline of the political and social unrest that resulted from the Reformation. They will identify several key events to include on the timeline and take notes on each. The timeline should include factual events with accurate dates, and students should review and proofread their work.

Teach the Big Idea

1. **Whole Class Open/Introduction** How did the Reformation and Catholic Reformation affect politics and government? *softened harsh rule of colonial governments; encouraged independent states; political power separated from churches*

2. **Direct Teach** Read students the Big Idea: *The Protestant and Catholic Reformations caused tremendous political and social unrest throughout Europe.* Review the following lesson objectives with students to aid in their understanding of the Big Idea.

   - Explain the social and political impact of the Reformation.

   - Explain how religious wars and unrest resulted from the Reformation.

3. **Whole Group Close/Reflect** During the Reformation, Europeans began to change how they looked at the world. Write a brief essay about key events and how they changed people's ideas.

▷ ONLINE DOCUMENT-BASED INVESTIGATION

Reformation and Upheaval

Inquisition Torture is the fourth of four document-based investigations that students will analyze in the Reformation and Upheaval module. This image depicts the torture that was used during the Inquisition to make people recant their Protestant beliefs. Students can analyze the image and then answer the associated question.

▷ ONLINE GRAPHIC ORGANIZER

Social Unrest

As students read the lesson, have them use the graphic organizer to take notes. Students can review their graphic organizer notes at the end of the lesson to answer the following question:

Summarize What major events of the Reformation and Catholic Reformation caused social and political unrest in Europe in the 1500s and early 1600s? *Peasants' War, witch hunts, Inquisition, persecution of Jews*

▷ ONLINE LESSON FLIP CARDS

Review Key Terms and People

Students can use the flip cards in the Lesson Review at any time to review the lesson's key terms and people: *Inquisition, heresy,* and *Huguenots.*

Social Unrest

The Big Idea
The Protestant and Catholic reformations caused tremendous political and social unrest throughout Europe.

Why It Matters Now
Nation-states that rose as a result of the Protestant Reformation became many of the leading countries in Europe today.

Key Terms and People
Inquisition
heresy
Huguenots

Setting the Stage

Religious turmoil increased after the Protestant and Catholic Reformations. Catholics persecuted non-Catholics and non-Catholics persecuted both Catholics and non-Catholics of denominations other than their own. Catholics and Protestants persecuted Jews, Muslims, and other non-Christian religious groups. Those who did not convert were forced out of parts of Europe.

Social and Political Impact

The Catholic Reformation affected the whole world. Although the Roman Catholic Church continued to take measures to stop the spread of Protestantism, it was no longer the only religious authority in Europe. Still, its policies influenced governments and societies wherever the Church existed.

The Inquisition To fight Protestantism, the Catholic Church established a Church court called the Roman **Inquisition** in 1542. The main purpose of the Inquisition was to impose religious uniformity, especially on converted Jews and Muslims, and later, on Protestants. The Roman Inquisition used harsh methods, including torture, to force confessions and punish **heresy**, or a denial of Church teachings. The Inquisition tried people who were accused of being Protestants, of practicing witchcraft, or of breaking Church law.

In Spain, Muslims (called Moors) controlled most of the country until 1100. In 1492, the Christian army conquered the last Muslim kingdom in Spain at Granada. Then, Spanish monarchs Ferdinand and Isabella used an Inquisition to increase their power. Jews were forced to convert to Catholic Christianity or leave Spain. In 1500, Muslims faced the same choice. Many Jews resettled in eastern and southern Europe. The majority of the Jews who had earlier converted to Christianity and were members of the educated elite stayed in Spain. In many areas of Europe where Jews were allowed

---

COLLABORATIVE LEARNING

Debate Impact of Religious Conflicts

1. Divide students into three groups, and assign each group one of the religious wars mentioned in this lesson: Italy (Italian Wars), Germany (Peasants' War), France (Huguenot wars).

2. Explain to students that they will take part in a class debate and argue that their assigned conflict had the most significant impact on religion at the time.

3. Encourage students to conduct additional online research, if necessary. Students should work together to identify key events, main ideas, and important people.

4. Act as moderator for a class debate among all three groups. Ensure that all students who wish to contribute have an opportunity to do so.

This scene depicts torture used in the Inquisition.

to stay, they were not as restricted as they had been during the Middle Ages. However, some places forced them to live in a particular part of the city, called a ghetto. The ghettos were walled and their gates closed at a certain time each evening.

In time, accounts of torture and executions by the courts damaged the church's image. The Inquisition's actions during the Catholic Reformation are still seen as an abuse of the Church's power.

Witch Trials Across Europe, many people feared that witches roamed the land, killing children and cattle and working with the devil. Their fears increased in times of poor harvests or other hardships. The fears inspired hysteria in which accused witches were rounded up and tried for their alleged wrongdoing.

The penalty for practicing witchcraft at this time was often death, and many innocent victims were executed for alleged witchcraft. The majority of executions for witchcraft occurred between 1580 and 1660. Thousands of people, most of them women or poor, were killed.

Objectives

You may wish to discuss the following questions with students to help them frame the content as they read.

- What was the purpose of the Inquisition, and why was it an abuse of power? *Its purpose was to impose religious uniformity on everyone. It was an abuse of power because it put people on trial unfairly and used torture and executions.*
- What were the religious and social effects of the Catholic Reformation? *changes in both Catholicism and Protestantism; persecution of non-Catholics, Jews, and Muslims; formation of independent states and nations*

More About . . .

The Inquisition In Catholic countries, the Inquisition stepped up its activities, threatening Protestants and heretics with imprisonment or death. Even the most faithful believers might be reported to the Inquisition by their enemies. Ignatius of Loyola himself was brought before the Inquisition several times. However, he was always found innocent.

▶ ONLINE DOCUMENT-BASED INVESTIGATION

Inquisition Torture

This image depicts the type of torture that was used during the Inquisition to make people recant their Protestant beliefs. Students can analyze the image and then answer the associated question.

Analyze Sources Why do you think that torture was used during the Inquisition? *to force people to tell the truth and confess about their beliefs*

DOCUMENT-BASED INVESTIGATION   HISTORICAL SOURCE

Inquisition Torture

During the Inquisition, torture was not uncommon. This scene depicts the type of torture that was used. Sometimes it could be an effective tool. Many people recanted their Protestant beliefs under torture.

Objectives

You may wish to discuss the following questions with students to help them frame the content as they read.

- What wars occurred because of the Catholic Reformation? *Italian Wars, Peasants' War, fighting in France between Protestants and Catholics*

- How did Martin Luther's reaction to the Peasants' War affect the Catholic Reformation? *It prevented the Reformation from becoming a social revolution as well.*

More About . . .

Winning Followers During the Catholic Reformation Catholic efforts to regain followers often took the form of restoring splendid churches or commissioning new works of art. On the other hand, Protestants produced works of literature and writings on doctrine.

Peasants Remind students that a peasant is a farm laborer. Most peasants farmed land that belonged to the local lord. They had to provide goods and services in exchange for working the land. The lord had a great deal of control over their lives.

READING CHECK

Evaluate How did religious turmoil affect European society during the late 1500s and early 1600s? *caused changes in religion, fear of persecution of different religious groups, the creation of independent states*

GAME

Effects of the Reformation

Have students play the game to test their knowledge of facts about the Reformation.

Myth and Reality

Effects of the Reformation

There are many surprising facts about the effects of the Reformation.

As statements appear, decide whether they are TRUE or FALSE.

Reading Check
Evaluate How did religious turmoil affect European society during the late 1500s and early 1600s?

Political Effects A rising sense of national identity was interwoven with a decline in the power of the Catholic Church. The Protestant Reformation indirectly encouraged the formation of independent states and nations. Both rulers and merchants wanted the Church to be less involved in state and business affairs, which they sought to control on their own. Political power became separated from churches, although nations and churches often aligned themselves with one another to increase their own influence in a region. As a result, modern nation-states began to emerge, with their own independent governments and populations united by a shared culture, language, and national pride. Nation-states, such as Spain and Portugal, would extend their power in the 1600s.

THE REFORMATION	
CAUSES	**EFFECTS**
• Humanist values led people to question Church authority. • Some clergy were corrupt, worldly, or poorly educated. • Martin Luther posted his 95 Theses. • The printing press helped spread Reformation ideas.	• Many Protestant sects developed. • Church leaders reformed the Catholic Church. • Religious intolerance and anti-Semitism increased. • Religious conflicts spread across Europe.

Religious Wars and Unrest

Trade, which had begun to flourish during the Renaissance, better connected regions of Europe through extensive trade routes and trading partners in the East. Italy, England, France, and Germany specialized in making certain products and traded for the products they could not produce. Through trade, ideas spread and daily life improved.

In the years after Luther published the 95 Theses, religious wars erupted within and between countries in Europe. These wars changed historic alliances, pitting against each other countries that had fought together in the Crusades.

Italy In 1494 King Charles VII of France invaded Italy. This began a series of wars in which France and Spain vied for control of the Italian Peninsula. During the Italian Wars, control of Italy bounced between these two powers. England also eventually became involved, as did several popes. The fighting finally culminated in the sack of Rome by the Spaniards and Holy Roman Emperor Charles V, who was a devout Catholic, in 1527. The Italian Wars officially ended in 1559. The most significant impact of the Italian Wars was that they helped expose the rest of Europe to the ideas of the Italian Renaissance. Troops returned home filled with ideas they had encountered in Italy. In addition, artists from Italy fled to the north, bringing new techniques and styles with them.

LINK TO GEOGRAPHY

Conduct Research

1. Have students conduct Internet research using reliable websites to find the percentages of religious followers in the United States in these categories: Protestants, Roman Catholics, Nonreligious or Atheists, Orthodox Christians, Independent Christians, and Other Religions.

2. Then have them research these percentages in your home state.

3. Have students create basic pie graphs of their findings.

4. Have students write a paragraph describing how the percentages of religious followers in the United States compares to percentages in your home state.

Germany With new ideas circulating among a growing population, peasants were becoming more disgruntled by high taxes and a lack of power. At the same time, Reformation preachers supported the idea of freedom. Stirred by these factors, tens of thousands of German peasants stormed castles and monasteries in 1524, a rebellion known as the Peasants' War. The nobles harshly suppressed the uprising. Martin Luther, accused of beginning the unrest, denounced it. The peasants, he wrote, "rob and rage and act like mad dogs." Luther's refusal to side with the peasants prevented the Reformation from spilling over into a social revolution that encouraged social equality.

France In France, Calvin's followers were called **Huguenots**. Hatred between Catholics and Huguenots frequently led to violence. The most violent clash occurred in Paris on August 24, 1572—the Catholic feast of St. Bartholomew's Day. At dawn, Catholic mobs began hunting for Protestants and murdering them. The massacres spread to other cities and lasted six months. Scholars believe that as many as 12,000 Huguenots were killed.

Huguenots fought for years against the Catholics. The fighting ended when their leader, Henry of Navarre, became Catholic. His conversion led to political stability by encouraging Catholics to accept him as king. In 1598 Henry's Edict of Nantes granted religious freedom to Protestants.

Reading Check
Analyze Causes
What factors led to the Peasants' War?

Lesson 4 Assessment

1. Organize Information Create a timeline of the major events that caused social and political unrest in Europe in the 1500s and early 1600s. Write a paragraph indicating how any two of these events are related.

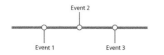

Event 2

Event 1   Event 3

2. Key Terms and People For each key term or person in the lesson, write a sentence explaining its significance.
3. Analyze Causes What led to the persecution of witches across Europe in the 1500s?

4. Find Main Ideas What were the Italian Wars, and how did they end?
5. Analyze Effects How did Luther's reaction to the Peasants' War affect the Catholic Reformation?
6. Summarize Who were the Huguenots, and how did France achieve political stability after years of fighting between the Huguenots and Catholics?
7. Evaluate How did the Protestant and Catholic reformations affect politics and government?
8. Analyze Causes What cause most influenced the spread of ideas and the improvement in daily life?

READING CHECK
Analyze Causes What factors led to the Peasants' War? *peasants pay higher taxes, lack of power, Reformation ideas of freedom*

Print Assessment

1. **Organize Information** Create a timeline of the major events that caused social and political unrest in Europe in the 1500s and early 1600s. Write a paragraph indicating how any two of these events are related. *Possible answer: The invention of the printing press helped spread Reformation ideas. This led to a rising sense of national identity, and many people wanted the Church to be less involved in state affairs. Therefore, the Reformation and the printing press directly led to modern nation-states and independent governments.*

2. **Key Terms and People** For each key term or person in the lesson, write a sentence explaining its significance. *Explanation of the lesson's key terms can be found on the following pages: Inquisition, p. 590; heresy, p. 590; Huguenots, p. 593*

3. **Analyze Causes** What led to the persecution of witches across Europe in the 1500s? *fear of different religious practices*

4. **Find Main Ideas** What were the Italian Wars, and how did they end? *wars between France and Spain (and involved England) over the Italian peninsula; sack of Rome*

5. **Analyze Effects** How did Luther's reaction to the Peasants' War affect the Catholic Reformation? *allowed different religions to coexist*

6. **Summarize** Who were the Huguenots, and how did France achieve political stability after years of fighting between the Huguenots and Catholics? *French Protestants; France's leader, Henry of Navarre, became Catholic. He issued the Edict of Nantes, which granted religious freedom to Protestants.*

7. **Evaluate** How did the Protestant and Catholic Reformations affect politics and government? *encouraged independent nation-states; political power separated from churches*

8. **Analyze Causes** What cause most influenced the spread of ideas and the improvement in daily life? *trade*

▷ Online Assessment

1. What caused many Jews in Spain to resettle in eastern and southern Europe?
   - ◉ They were trying to flee the Inquisition.
   - ○ They were searching for the Promised Land.
   - ○ They were following the teachings of Martin Luther.
   - ○ They were hoping to stop the Reformation movement.

   Alternate Question *Select the answer choice from the drop-down list to complete the sentence correctly.* Jews in Spain were persecuted during the Inquisition, so many of them [resettled in southern and eastern Europe ⬍].

2. Who were the Huguenots?
   - ○ Jews living in France
   - ○ Muslims living in France
   - ○ Catholics living in France
   - ◉ Calvinists living in France

   Alternate Question *Select the answer choice from the drop-down list to complete the sentence correctly.* The Huguenots lived in [France ⬍] and were Protestants who followed the teachings of John Calvin.

3. **Draw Conclusions** Why did fears of witchcraft increase in Europe during times of poor harvests and other hardships?

   Possible answer: People could not explain why natural things occurred because they lacked scientific knowledge. So when bad things happened, they blamed it on the work of the devil and his cohorts. Many people feared that witches roamed the land, killing children and cattle and working with the devil. They believed that when bad things happened, it must be the work of evil forces. These fears inspired hysteria in which accused witches were rounded up and tried, and often executed, for their alleged wrongdoings.

4. **Elaborate** What was the Edict of Nantes, and why was it significant?

   Possible answer: The Edict of Nantes was a royal decree set forth by Henry of Navarre, the king of France, in 1598. Henry had been a Protestant but converted to Catholicism. This conversion led to stability in the country, and the French Catholics finally accepted him as the king. This edict granted religious freedom to Protestants.

Print Assessment

Key Terms and People

For each term or name below, briefly explain its connection to European history from 1400 to 1600.

1. indulgence
2. Reformation
3. Protestant
4. predestination
5. theocracy
6. Catholic Reformation
7. Elizabeth I
8. Henry VIII
9. Council of Trent
10. Inquisition

Explanations of the significance of the lesson's key terms and people can be found on the following pages: indulgence, p. 571; Reformation, p. 572; Protestant, p. 573; predestination, p. 580; theocracy, p. 580; Catholic Reformation, p. 585; Elizabeth I, p. 577; Henry VIII, p. 575; Council of Trent, p. 587; Inquisition, p. 590

Main Ideas

Use your notes and the information in the module to answer the following questions.

Luther Leads the Reformation

1. On what three teachings did Martin Luther rest his Reformation movement? *People could win salvation only through faith, not good works. Church teachings should be based on the Bible only, not on a combination of the Bible and Church tradition. People did not need priests to interpret the Bible for them.*
2. Why did the Holy Roman emperor go to war against Protestant German princes? *He wanted to force the Protestant German princes to rejoin the Catholic Church.*
3. Why did Henry VIII create his own church? *Henry's desire for a male heir pushed him to split with the Church and create the Church of England.*

The Reformation Continues

4. In what ways was John Calvin's church different from the Lutheran Church? *believed in predestination, followed strict rules, promoted theocracy*
5. How did Protestant teaching lead to the forming of new groups? *It encouraged people to discover their own truths in the Bible.*
6. Why did Catholics and Protestants persecute Anabaptists? *Possible answer: They viewed Anabaptists as radicals because the Anabaptists believed in adults being rebaptized after having already been baptized as children. They believed that this went against the doctrine of the Church.*

Module 15 Assessment

Key Terms and People

For each term or name below, briefly explain its connection to European history from 1400 to 1600.

1. indulgence
2. Reformation
3. Protestant
4. predestination
5. theocracy
6. Catholic Reformation
7. Elizabeth I
8. Henry VIII
9. Council of Trent
10. Inquisition

Main Ideas

Use your notes and the information in the module to answer the following questions.

Luther Leads the Reformation

1. On what three teachings did Martin Luther rest his Reformation movement?
2. Why did the Holy Roman Emperor go to war against Protestant German princes?
3. Why did Henry VIII create his own church?

The Reformation Continues

4. In what ways was John Calvin's church different from the Lutheran Church?
5. How did Protestant teaching lead to the forming of new groups?
6. Why did Catholics and Protestants persecute Anabaptists?

The Catholic Reformation

7. What was the goal of the Catholic Reformation?
8. What was the Council of Trent?
9. What are three legacies of the Reformation?

Social Unrest

10. Why did the Catholic Church convict Protestants of heresy?
11. What were the political effects of the Reformation on Europe?
12. After studying the religious wars in Europe during this time, what do you think might happen next on this continent?

594   Module 15

ONLINE DOCUMENT-BASED INVESTIGATION

Reformation and Upheaval

Have students complete and review all the DBI activities in **Part 1**.

Use this Compare/Contrast Essay Rubric to score students' work in **Part 2**.

RUBRIC Students' essays should
- identify similarities and differences appropriate to the topic
- attempt comparisons from parallel categories of items
- cite at least three sources of appropriate text evidence from Part 1 in support of their comparisons
- be organized into a distinct introduction, a main body consisting of several paragraphs, and a conclusion that sums up the main points

Write a Compare and Contrast Essay

The Catholic Church responded in different ways to the Protestant Reformation. Write an essay in which you compare and contrast the responses of the Catholic Church to the challenges made by Protestant ideas and leaders. Be sure to cite specific evidence from at least three sources in your response.

Critical Thinking

1. **Analyze Effects** How did the Reformation lead to great changes in European ideas and institutions?
2. **Draw Conclusions** How did the printing press help spread the Reformation and democracy to individuals and groups?
3. **Analyze Effects** How did the Reformation expand cultural interaction within Europe?
4. **Make Inferences** How were the Jesuits effective in areas where people were not Christians?
5. **Analyze Motives** Why did the Catholic Church create a list of forbidden books?
6. **Develop Historical Perspective** Why did the Catholic Church want to punish Protestants as heretics?
7. **Synthesize** How did views of women and the role of women change as a result of the Reformation?

Engage with History

In the module, you reviewed several primary and secondary sources that criticized the Catholic Church from different points of view. Now, consider the context of each criticism and answer the following questions:

- How does the time period in which the source was written affect its criticism?
- Which criticism was best supported with evidence?
- Which criticism had the greatest impact?

Discuss these questions with a small group.

Focus on Writing

Review the information about Protestantism in the Analyze Key Concepts and other features in this module. Write a three-page essay that analyzes the effects of Protestantism on the Christian Church.

- Examine its impact on the number of denominations.
- Explain the different beliefs and practices it promoted.

Multimedia Activity

Work with a partner to use the Internet to research major religious reforms of the 20th century. You might search for information on changes in the Catholic Church as a result of Vatican II or major shifts in the practices or doctrines of a branch of Hinduism, Islam, Judaism, or Protestantism.

Compare the 20th-century reforms with those of the Protestant Reformation. Present the results of your research in a well-organized paper. Be sure to

- apply a search strategy when using directories and search engines to locate Internet resources
- judge the usefulness and reliability of each website
- correctly cite your Internet sources
- peer-edit for organization and correct use of language

Essential Question ESSAY

What new ideas and values led to the Reformation, and what social and political effects did the Reformation cause?

RUBRIC Students' essays should
- respond to the Essential Question with a specific position
- illustrate valid reasoning supporting their position
- cite persuasive evidence supporting their position
- identify key people, events, and/or turning points that demonstrate understanding of the module content
- be organized into a distinct introduction, main body, and conclusion

Write an argument answering this question. Your essay should include examples of these new ideas and values, as well as their effects. Be sure to cite evidence to support your points and organize your essay into an introduction, body, and conclusion.

Alternative Activity Instead of writing essays, address the Essential Question through activities such as holding debates, creating multimedia presentations, or writing journal entries.

The Catholic Reformation

7. What was the goal of the Catholic Reformation? *The goal was for the Catholic Church to reform itself so that it could retain loyal Catholics.*
8. What was the Council of Trent? *It redefined Catholic doctrines and examined criticism made by Protestants.*
9. What are three legacies of the Reformation? *Possible answers: Religion no longer united Europe; paved the way for the modern nation-states; laid the groundwork for later rejection of Christian beliefs; Catholic Church became more unified; new schools founded*

Social Unrest

10. Why did the Catholic Church convict Protestants of heresy? *because they denied the teachings of the Catholic Church*
11. What were the political effects of the Reformation on Europe? *Division of Christianity led to weakening of the power of the church and growth of power of rulers and rise of nation-states.*
12. After studying the religious wars in Europe during this time, what do you think might happen next on this continent? *Possible answer: more wars between Protestants and Catholics*

Critical Thinking

1. **Analyze Effects** How did the Reformation lead to great changes in European ideas and institutions? *Religious: split the church; divided Protestants into many groups, established Church of England. Political: monarchs and states gained power; modern nation-states developed. Social: peasant revolts, demands to end serfdom*
2. **Draw Conclusions** How did the printing press help spread the Reformation and democracy to individuals and groups? *It helped disseminate information more quickly and cheaply and printed the Bible in the vernacular language, enabling more people to read the Bible. Most books, including the Bible, were written in Latin before the invention of the printing press. Ideas about democracy and government structure circulated among scholars and ordinary people. It also helped to advertise new ideas such as those listed in Luther's 95 Theses.*
3. **Analyze Effects** How did the Reformation expand cultural interaction within Europe? *Ideas were shared among different Protestant leaders that spread throughout Europe. It paved the way for an intellectual movement, the Enlightenment, which would take root there in the 1600s.*

(continued)

Print Assessment *(continued)*

4. **Make Inferences** How were the Jesuits effective in areas where people were not Christians? *The Jesuits established missions where there were nonbelievers and converted them to Catholicism. Through the use of missionaries they were able to spread Catholicism and contain Protestantism.*

5. **Analyze Motives** Why did the Catholic Church create a list of forbidden books? *Possible answer: If Catholics used the books that were banned or forbidden, they could be convicted of heresy; it also prevented Catholics from free or different thinking that opposed the teachings of the Catholic Church.*

6. **Develop Historical Perspective** Why did the Catholic Church want to punish Protestants as heretics? *Protestants went against the teachings of the Catholic Church, so the Church had to punish them to stop the spread of Protestantism and to instill fear in others who may have considered adopting Protestantism.*

7. **Synthesize** How did views of women and the role of women change as a result of the Reformation? *At first, women had a fairly significant role in the Protestant Reformation because there were few formal leaders to place restrictions on them. That changed as Protestant groups became more formalized. Women's roles did not really improve after the Reformation; they remained largely unchanged.*

Engage with History

In the module, you reviewed several primary and secondary sources that criticized the Catholic Church from different points of view. Now, consider the context of each criticism and answer the following questions:

- How does the time period in which the source was written affect its criticism?
- Which criticism was best supported with evidence?
- Which had the most impact?

Discuss these questions with a small group.

Focus on Writing

Review the information about Protestantism in the Analyze Key Concepts and other features in this module. Write a three-page essay that analyzes the effects of Protestantism on the Christian Church.

- Examine its impact on the number of denominations.
- Explain the different beliefs and practices it promoted.
    - **RUBRIC** Essays should:
    - identify effects of Protestantism on the Christian Church.
    - analyze the cited effects on the Church.
    - have a concluding statement
    - use correct grammar and punctuation.

Multimedia Activity

Work with a partner to use the Internet to research major religious reforms of the 20th century. You might search for information on changes in the Catholic Church as a result of Vatican II, or major shifts in the practices or doctrines of a branch of Hinduism, Islam, Judaism, or Protestantism.

Compare the 20th-century reforms with those of the Protestant Reformation. Present the results of your research in a well-organized paper. Be sure to:

- apply a search strategy when using directories and search engines to locate Internet resources.
- judge the usefulness and reliability of each website.
- correctly cite your Internet sources.
- peer-edit for organization and correct use of language.
    - **RUBRIC** Tables should:
    - contain up-to-date information
    - present information in a clear, easy-to-read format
    - list the sources of information used in building the database

Online Assessment

1. What did John Wycliffe and Jan Hus have in common with each other?
   - ○ They both advocated Church reform.
   - ○ They both lived in Germany in the late 1300s.
   - ○ They both believed that the pope had the right to worldly power.
   - ○ They both taught that Church leaders had more authority than the Bible.

2. *Select the correct button in the table to show whether each statement about Martin Luther's ideas about Church reform is true or false.*

	True	False
Luther believed that people could win salvation by faith in God's forgiveness.	○	○
Luther believed that good works were not needed in order to receive salvation.	○	○
Luther believed that people did not need priests to interpret the Bible for them.	○	○
Luther believed that the Bible, the pope, and Church traditions were false authorities.		○

3. *Drag each description into the correct column in the table. Each description will be used only once.*

Elizabeth I	Mary, daughter of Catherine of Aragon
was requested by Protestants to make church reforms	became queen after her half-brother, Edward VI, died
ran into money problems when she was queen	returned the English church to the rule of the pope
established a state church that she led	was succeeded to the throne by her half-sister
decided to build an American empire as a new source of income	

4. *Select the correct button in the table to show whether each statement about John Calvin is true or false.*

	True	False
Calvin believed that the worst form of government was a theocracy.	○	○
Calvin led the city of Geneva, Switzerland, with a very strict and rigid approach.	○	○
Calvin allowed religious freedom in the community he led in Geneva, Switzerland.	○	○
Calvin ended up having as much influence in the spread of Protestantism as Luther did.	○	○

5. What are **two** beliefs of the Anabaptists?
   - ○ It is wrong to baptize young children.
   - ○ Bright clothing is preferred over plain clothing.
   - ○ Bible authority is less valuable than Church traditions.
   - ○ There needs to be a clear separation of church and state.
   - ○ Individual property ownership is preferred over communal property ownership.

6. What did Martin Luther believe about women's role in the Church?
   - ○ They should teach in public meetings.
   - ○ They should stay at home and keep house.
   - ○ They should dedicate their lives to a convent.
   - ○ They should provide opinions on religious doctrine.

7. *Select the correct button in the table to show whether each statement about the Council of Trent is true or false.*

	True	False
It was acceptable to sell indulgences.	○	○
Christians only needed faith for salvation.	○	○
The Church's interpretation of the Bible was final.	○	○
Church tradition had less authority than the Bible.	○	○

8. *Drag each description into the correct column in the table. Each description will be used only once.*

Teresa of Avila	Angela Merici
ran away to a convent against her father's wishes	began the Company of Saint Ursula
reformed the Carmelite order	was dedicated to teaching girls in the Church
had deep spirituality and reported visions of Christ	

9. What was it about the Reformation that led to the Enlightenment?
   - ○ Social classes became less defined during the Reformation.
   - ○ Muslims attracted more followers during the Reformation.
   - ○ People questioned beliefs and authority during the Reformation.
   - ○ The Catholic Church became more powerful during the Reformation.

10. How are the actions during the Inquisition of the 1500s viewed today?
    - ○ as an abuse of power
    - ○ as a necessary way to punish wrongdoers
    - ○ as a key element that helped people reform
    - ○ as an avenue to discover scientific knowledge

11. *Select the correct button in the table to show whether each statement about the Reformation and the Peasants' War is true or false.*

	True	False
Martin Luther was accused by the nobility of starting the peasant rebellion.	○	○
Martin Luther supported the view of the peasants during the Peasants' War.	○	○
The Peasants' War began in Germany, which is where Martin Luther was from.	○	○
The Reformation helped peasants receive social equality because of Martin Luther's efforts.	○	○

12. What was the most significant effect of the Italian Wars, which ended in 1559?
    - ○ They helped Charles V become more popular in the Italian peninsula.
    - ○ They gave rise to more popularity of John Calvin's teachings throughout Italy.
    - ○ They helped expose the rest of Europe to the ideas of the Italian Renaissance.
    - ○ They caused more Europeans to revolt against the abuses perpetrated by the Catholic Church.

Essential Question Preview

Why were peoples of the Age of Exploration willing to risk lives and fortunes to expand the influence of their homelands?

Have students consider the Essential Question and capture their initial responses.

Explore the Essential Question

Why were peoples of the Age of Exploration willing to risk lives and fortunes to expand the influence of their homelands?

- Tell students that by the early 1400s, Europeans had developed the technology to begin exploring other parts of the world.

- Explain that European exploration resulted in the exchange of new items between the Eastern and Western hemispheres.

Help students plan inquiries and develop their own supporting questions such as:

What fueled the Age of Exploration and why did China and Japan withdraw into isolation?

What was the impact of European exploration and colonization of the Americas?

You may want to assign students to write a short essay in response to the Essential Question when they complete the module. Encourage students to use their notes and responses to inform their essays.

▷ Explore the Online Video

ANALYZE VIDEOS

Life in Jamestown
Invite students to watch the video to learn about the English men and women who settled in Jamestown, Virginia.

Analyze Videos For what reasons did the English leave their homeland and settle in North America? *They were seeking religious and political freedom as well as new economic opportunities.*

PLAY VIDEO 2:44
Life in Jamestown

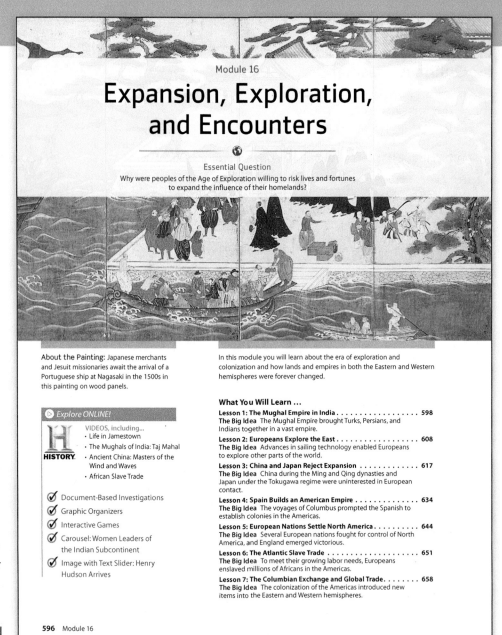

Module 16

Expansion, Exploration, and Encounters

Essential Question
Why were peoples of the Age of Exploration willing to risk lives and fortunes to expand the influence of their homelands?

About the Painting: Japanese merchants and Jesuit missionaries await the arrival of a Portuguese ship at Nagasaki in the 1500s in this painting on wood panels.

In this module you will learn about the era of exploration and colonization and how lands and empires in both the Eastern and Western hemispheres were forever changed.

▷ *Explore ONLINE!*

HISTORY.
VIDEOS, including...
- Life in Jamestown
- The Mughals of India: Taj Mahal
- Ancient China: Masters of the Wind and Waves
- African Slave Trade

☑ Document-Based Investigations
☑ Graphic Organizers
☑ Interactive Games
☑ Carousel: Women Leaders of the Indian Subcontinent
☑ Image with Text Slider: Henry Hudson Arrives

596 Module 16

Lesson 1 Big Idea

The Mughal Empire brought Turks, Persians, and Indians together in a vast empire.

Why It Matters Now
The legacy of great art and deep social division left by the Mughal Empire still influences southern Asia.

Lesson 2 Big Idea

Advances in sailing technology enabled Europeans to explore other parts of the world.

Why It Matters Now
European exploration was an important step toward the global interaction existing in the world today.

Lesson 3 Big Idea

China under the Ming and Qing dynasties and Japan under the Tokugawa regime were uninterested in European contact.

Why It Matters Now
China and Japan's economic independence from the West continues today, though China is pursuing new economic ties with the outside world.

Lesson 4 Big Idea

The voyages of Columbus prompted the Spanish to establish colonies in the Americas.

Why It Matters Now
Throughout the Americas, Spanish culture, language, and descendants are the legacy of this period.

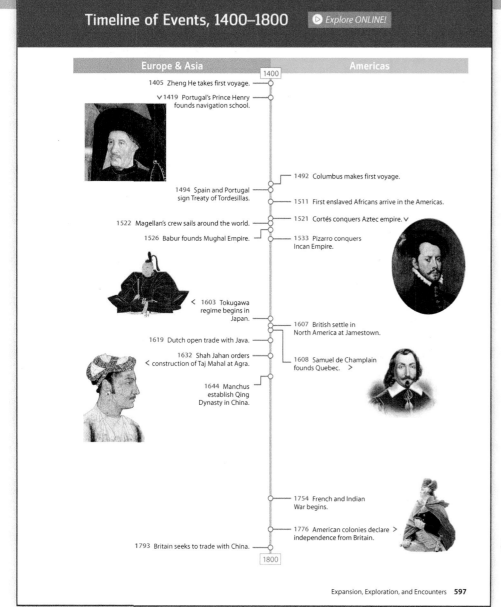

Europe & Asia	Americas

1400

1405 Zheng He takes first voyage.

∨ 1419 Portugal's Prince Henry founds navigation school.

1492 Columbus makes first voyage.

1494 Spain and Portugal sign Treaty of Tordesillas.

1511 First enslaved Africans arrive in the Americas.

1522 Magellan's crew sails around the world.

1521 Cortés conquers Aztec empire. ∨

1526 Babur founds Mughal Empire.

1533 Pizarro conquers Incan Empire.

< 1603 Tokugawa regime begins in Japan.

1607 British settle in North America at Jamestown.

1619 Dutch open trade with Java.

1632 Shah Jahan orders < construction of Taj Mahal at Agra.

1608 Samuel de Champlain founds Quebec. >

1644 Manchus establish Qing Dynasty in China.

1754 French and Indian War begins.

1776 American colonies declare > independence from Britain.

1793 Britain seeks to trade with China.

1800

Expansion, Exploration, and Encounters **597**

Explore the Timeline

Interpret Timelines: Expansion, Exploration, and Encounters, 1400–1800

Have students examine the timeline and then answer the following question:

History Which two major Native American empires did the Spanish conquer in the 16th century? *the Aztec and Incan empires*

Interpret Timeline of Events: Expansion, Exploration, and Encounters, 1400–1800

To further explore the timeline, have students discuss the following questions:

1. When and where did Britain and France establish their first colonies in the Americas? *Britain—1607, Jamestown; France—1608, Quebec* Approximately how long was this after Spain conquered the Aztecs? *86 years*

2. What can you conclude from this timeline about relations among nations of the world? *Possible answer: Many countries, even those in distant parts of the world, were making contact.*

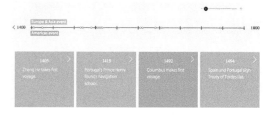

▷ Online Module Flip Cards

Use the flip cards as a whole class activity or in student pairs to preview the module's Key Terms and People. Students can guess the meaning of each word, then review its definition, or do the reverse, using the flip card's toggle button to switch from Term to Definition mode. Students can also use the flip cards at the end of the module as a review tool before taking the Module Assessment.

▷ Online Sequencing Activity

Students can use this sequencing activity to review the chronology of events in the Expansion, Exploration, and Encounters module. To complete, have students drag each event to the correct year on the timeline.

Year	Event
1405	*Zheng He takes first voyage.*
1511	*First enslaved Africans arrive in the Americas.*
1526	*Babur founds Mughal Empire.*
1533	*Pizarro conquers Incan Empire.*
1603	*Tokegawa regime begins in Japan.*
1607	*British settle in North America at Jamestown.*

Lesson 5 Big Idea

Several European nations fought for control of North America, and England emerged victorious.

Why It Matters Now

The English settlers in North America left a legacy of law and government that guides the United States today.

Lesson 6 Big Idea

To meet their growing labor needs, Europeans enslaved millions of Africans in the Americas.

Why It Matters Now

Descendants of enslaved Africans represent a significant part of the Americas' population today.

Lesson 7 Big Idea

The colonization of the Americas introduced new items into the Eastern and Western hemispheress.

Why It Matters Now

This global exchange of goods permanently changed Europe, Asia, Africa, and the Americas.

Expansion, Exploration, and Encounters 597

The Mughal Empire in India

● The Mughals of India: Taj Mahal

Video

● Cultural Blending in Mughal India
● Women Leaders of the Indian Subcontinent

Visuals

LESSON 1

Maps, Graphs, and Charts

● **Map:** Growth of the Mughal Empire, 1526–1707
● **Chart:** Achievements of the Mughal Emperors

Big Idea
The Mughal Empire brought Turks, Persians, and Indians together in a vast empire.

● **Biography:** Babur
● **Biography:** Akbar
● Nur Jahan (1577–1646)
● Europe Discovers the Riches of India

Extend and Enrich

Historical Sources

● **Document-Based Investigation:** Humayun's Tomb

Assessment

● Key Terms Review
● Reading Check
● Graphic Organizer Activity
● Lesson Assessment

Nur Jahan (1577–1646)

Biography Students read about the individualism Nur Jahan showed in a time when women's activities were limited. Then students reflect on a characteristic Nur Jahan had that Jahangir lacked. Students create a Venn diagram that compares and contrasts the emperor Jahangir and his wife Nur Jahan.

Europe Discovers the Riches of India

Article Students read an article about the riches of India. Then they create a journal entry from the point of view of Vasco da Gama describing his experiences in Calicut, consulting maps as necessary.

Teach the Big Idea

1. **Whole Class Open/Introduction** Note that Hindu-Muslim relations are a key issue in this lesson. Discuss the tension between India and Pakistan. (India is mostly Hindu; Pakistan is mostly Muslim. Both want to control Kashmir.) Have students check maps to see how the disputed border of Kashmir is shown.

2. **Direct Teach** Read students the Big Idea: *The Mughal Empire brought Turks, Persians, and Indians together in a vast empire.* Review the following lesson objectives with students to aid in their understanding of the Big Idea.

   • Describe the rise of the Mughal Empire.

   • Analyze the achievements of Akbar.

   • List triumphs and failures of Akbar's successors.

   • Explain why the empire declined.

3. **Whole Group Close/Reflect** Have students write a short biography of one of the emperors of the Mughal Empire. Invite students to share their work.

▷ ONLINE DOCUMENT-BASED INVESTIGATION

Expansion, Exploration, and Encounters
Humayun's Tomb is the first of seven document-based investigations that students will analyze in the Expansion, Exploration, and Encounters module. Mughal emperors brought to India a strong Muslim architectural tradition. Have students view the image.

▷ ONLINE GRAPHIC ORGANIZER

The Mughal Empire in India
As students read the lesson, have them use the graphic organizer to take notes. Students can review their graphic organizer notes at the end of the lesson to answer the following question.

Analyze Effects Which of the emperors on your timeline had a positive effect on the empire? Which had negative effects? *Positive—Babur expanded the empire; Akbar oversaw a flowering of culture. Negative—Jahangir, Nur Jahan, and Shah Jahan sparked religious conflict; Aurangzeb waged costly wars.*

▷ ONLINE LESSON FLIP CARDS

Review Key Terms and People
Students can use the flip cards in the Lesson Review at any time to review the lesson's key terms and people: *Mughal, Babur, Akbar, Sikh, Shah Jahan, Taj Mahal, Aurangzeb,* and *Shivaji.*

The Mughal Empire in India

The Big Idea
The Mughal Empire brought Turks, Persians, and Indians together in a vast empire.

Why It Matters Now
The legacy of great art and deep social division left by the Mughal Empire still influences southern Asia.

Key Terms and People
Mughal
Babur
Akbar
Sikh
Shah Jahan
Taj Mahal
Aurangzeb
Shivaji

Setting the Stage

The Gupta Empire crumbled in the late 400s. First, Huns from Central Asia invaded. Then, beginning in the 700s, warlike Muslim tribes from Central Asia carved northwestern India into many small kingdoms. The people who invaded descended from Muslim Turks and Afghans. Their leader was a descendant of Timur the Lame and of the Mongol conqueror Genghis Khan. They called themselves **Mughals**, which means "Mongols." So, although the Mongols themselves did not directly affect much of India, their descendants had a long-lasting impact on Indian history and culture.

Early History of the Mughals

The eighth century began with a long clash between Hindus and Muslims in this land of many kingdoms, as Muslim groups migrated into various lands, including border areas. For almost 300 years, the Muslims were able to advance only as far as the Indus River valley. Starting around the year 1000, however, well-trained Turkish armies swept into India. Led by Sultan Mahmud (muh•MOOD) of Ghazni, they devastated Indian cities and temples in 17 brutal campaigns. These attacks left the region weakened and vulnerable to other conquerors. Delhi eventually became the capital of a loose empire of Turkish warlords called the Delhi Sultanate. These sultans treated the Hindus as conquered people.

Delhi Sultanate Between the 13th and 16th centuries, 33 different sultans ruled this divided territory from their seat in Delhi. In 1398, Timur the Lame destroyed Delhi. The city was so completely devastated that according to one witness, "for months, not a bird moved in the city." Delhi eventually was rebuilt. But it was not until the 16th century that a leader arose who would unify the empire.

Babur Founds an Empire In 1494, an 11-year-old boy named **Babur**, who counted both Timur the Lame and

Babur's army clashes with the Indian army in the Battle of Panipat.

Objectives

You may wish to discuss the following questions with students to help them frame the content as they read.

• What can you infer about the military balance between Muslims and Hindus between 700 and 1000? *It was roughly even.*

• Do you think the comment on Delhi's ruin is truthful? *may be exaggerated*

• What enabled Babur to found the Mughal Empire? *military power and skill*

More About . . .

Babur From birth, Prince Babur seemed destined to be a conqueror. Babur, whose name means "tiger," was a descendant of both Timur, the great general from Central Asia, and Genghis Khan, perhaps the greatest conqueror in Asian

history. At 11, Babur became king of Fergana, a small territory in Central Asia. By 14, he had led a victorious army to take the city of Samarkand. Babur's ambition was to build a huge empire that rivaled that of his ancestor Timur.

Stampeding Elephants When Babur set out to conquer India, his army was vastly outnumbered by the Indians. In addition, the Indian army included some 1,000 elephants, while Babur's had none. At first glance, the battle appeared to be hopeless. However, Babur's army had a secret weapon—cannons—never before used in India. The first cannon shots astounded the Indians and terrified the elephants, who turned and stampeded through the Indian army. Within a few hours, Babur had won.

Genghis Khan as ancestors, inherited a kingdom in Central Asia. It was only a tiny kingdom, and his elders soon took it away and drove him south. But Babur built up an army. In the years that followed, he swept down into what is now part of Pakistan and northern India and laid the foundation for the vast Mughal Empire.

Babur was a skillful general. In 1526, for example, he led 12,000 troops to victory against an army of 100,000 commanded by a sultan of Delhi. A year later, Babur also defeated a massive Rajput army—soldiers who belonged to regional warrior clans. After Babur's death, his incompetent son, Humayun, lost most of the territory Babur had gained. Babur's 13-year-old grandson followed Humayun.

Akbar's Golden Age

Babur's grandson was called **Akbar**, which means "Great." Akbar certainly lived up to his name, ruling India with wisdom and tolerance from 1556 to 1605.

A Military Conqueror Akbar recognized military power as the root of his strength. In his opinion, a king must always be aggressive so that his neighbors will not try to conquer him. Like the Safavids and the Ottomans, Akbar equipped his armies with heavy artillery. Cannons enabled him to break into walled cities and extend his rule into much of the Deccan plateau. He also appointed some Rajputs as officers. In this way he turned potential enezmies into allies. This combination of military power and political wisdom enabled Akbar to unify a land of at least 100 million people—more than in all of Europe put together.

A Liberal Ruler Akbar was a genius at cultural blending. He continued the Islamic tradition of religious freedom. He permitted people of other religions to practice their faiths. He proved his tolerance by marrying Hindu princesses without forcing them to convert. He allowed his wives to practice their religious rituals in the palace. He proved his tolerance again by abolishing both the tax on Hindu pilgrims and the hated *jizya*, or tax on non-Muslims. He even appointed a Spanish Jesuit to tutor his second son.

Akbar governed through a bureaucracy of officials. Natives and foreigners, Hindus and Muslims, could all rise to high office. This approach contributed to the quality of his government. Akbar's chief finance minister, Todar Mal, a Hindu, created a clever—and effective—taxation policy. He levied a tax similar to the present-day graduated income tax of the United States, calculating it as a percentage of the value of the peasants' crops. Because this tax was fair and affordable, the number of peasants who paid it increased. This payment brought in much needed money for the empire. The Mughals also reformed education for the region's children.

Akbar's land policies had more mixed results. He gave generous land grants to his bureaucrats. After they died, however, he reclaimed the lands and distributed them as he saw fit. On the positive side, this policy prevented the growth of feudal aristocracies. On the other hand, it did not

Objectives

You may wish to discuss the following questions with students to help them frame the content as they read.

- Do you think Akbar's taxes were fair? Why? *Yes—payments increased with wealth. No—some paid more than others.*

- How might Akbar have appealed to bureaucrats to work hard? *Possible answer: permanent land grants*

- How did the stonework created under Akbar reflect his religious tolerance? *Akbar was a Muslim; stonework often portrayed Hindu themes.*

More About . . .

Akbar Sensitive to public opinion, Akbar stood at an open palace window each morning so that his people could see him. He wanted them to feel a connection with their emperor.

BIOGRAPHY

Babur

Have students read the biography of Babur, founder of the Mughal empire of India who invaded Afghanistan and India and established an empire there.

READING CHECK

Analyze Effects What might have happened to the Mughal Empire if Babur had not been such a brilliant general? *The empire might not have come to exist at all; Babur's military successes acquired the land that made up the territory of the empire.*

STRUGGLING READERS

Main Ideas in Pictures

1. Organize students into four groups.

2. Assign each group one of the four topics in the lesson: Early History of the Mughals, Akbar's Golden Age, Akbar's Successors, and The Empire's Decline and Decay.

3. Have each group plan a set of drawings to illustrate the main points of its assigned topic. Each member of the group should have one main point to illustrate.

4. When students have finished their drawings, have them record the main point at the bottom of their papers.

Growth of the Mughal Empire, 1526–1707

Have students explore the map using the interactive features and answer the associated questions.

Movement During whose reign was the most territory added to the Mughal Empire? *Babur's*

In print edition, see map of same title.

Movement During which time period was the most territory added to the Mughal Empire? *before 1605*

Human-Environment Interaction What landform might have prevented the empire from expanding farther east? *the Himalaya Mountains*

BIOGRAPHY

Akbar

Have students read the biography of Akbar, Mughal emperor of India who ruled from 1556 until 1605. Akbar continued the policy of conquest put in place under regent Bairim Khan, enlarging his empire to include nearly all of the Indian peninsula north of the Godavari River.

▷ ONLINE INTERACTIVE VISUALS

Carousel: Cultural Blending in Mughal India

Have students navigate through the carousel and note similarities and differences among the images or identify a unifying theme.

▷ ONLINE DOCUMENT-BASED INVESTIGATION

Humayun's Tomb

Mughal emperors brought to India a strong Muslim architectural tradition. Invite students to view the image and answer the associated question.

Analyze Sources In what way is Humayun's Tomb an example of cultural blending? *The architectural style of the tomb is from Muslim tradition, but it was constructed by Indian workers and artisans, using local (Indian) materials.*

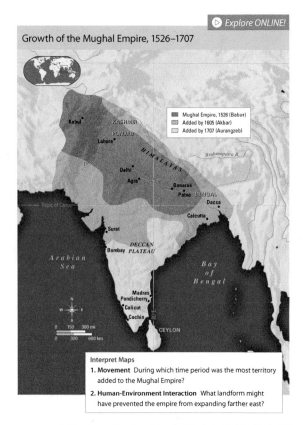

▶ *Explore ONLINE!*

Growth of the Mughal Empire, 1526–1707

Legend:
- Mughal Empire, 1526 (Babur)
- Added by 1605 (Akbar)
- Added by 1707 (Aurangzeb)

Interpret Maps
1. **Movement** During which time period was the most territory added to the Mughal Empire?
2. **Human-Environment Interaction** What landform might have prevented the empire from expanding farther east?

encourage dedication and hard work by the Mughal officials. Their children would not inherit the land or benefit from their parents' work. So the officials apparently saw no point in devoting themselves to their property.

Blended Cultures As Akbar extended the Mughal Empire, he welcomed influences from the many cultures in the empire and from distant lands. This cultural blending affected art, education, politics, and language. Persian was the language of Akbar's court and of high culture. The common people, however, spoke Hindi, a language derived from Sanskrit. Hindi remains one of the most widely spoken languages in India today. Out of the Mughal armies, where soldiers of many backgrounds rubbed shoulders, came yet another new language. This language was Urdu, which means "from the soldier's camp." A blend of Arabic, Persian, and Hindi, Urdu is today the official language of Pakistan.

Vocabulary
Sanskrit ancient Indian language from which multiple modern Indian languages evolved

600 Module 16

ENGLISH LANGUAGE LEARNERS

Understand Idioms

1. Explain that an idiom is a commonly used expression whose intended meaning is different from its literal meaning. For example, if you complain about having a frog in your throat, it means that your voice is hoarse or scratchy. It does not mean you swallowed an animal!

2. Challenge students to find the three idioms in the lesson and determine their meanings.

3. Share students' findings, as well as the following examples from the lesson.
   Akbar's Golden Age > Blended Cultures: Soldiers of many backgrounds "rubbed shoulders," which means they lived and worked together. Paragraph context can help readers understand this idiom—the soldiers spoke a language that was a blend of their different languages.

   Akbar's Successors: Each of the next three emperors after Akbar "left his mark" on the Mughal Empire, which means he made important and lasting changes to it.

   Akbar's Successors > Jahangir and Nur Jahan: Nur Jahan ruled with an "iron hand;" she had power over people.

4. Invite students to share idioms from other languages. For example, in Spanish, *estar a un grito*—literally, "to be on a scream"—means to be in pain.

Akbar
(1542–1605)

Akbar was brilliant and curious, especially about religion. He even invented a religion of his own—the "Divine Faith"—after learning about Hinduism, Jainism, Christianity, and Sufism. The religion attracted few followers, however, and offended Muslims so much that they attempted a brief revolt against Akbar in 1581. When he died, so did the "Divine Faith."

Surprisingly, despite his wisdom and his achievements, Akbar could not read. He hired others to read to him from his library of 24,000 books.

The Arts and Literature The arts flourished at the Mughal court, especially in the form of book illustrations. These small, highly detailed, and colorful paintings were called miniatures. Mughal miniatures combined Persian and Hindu influences. They were brought to a peak of perfection in the Safavid Empire. Babur's son, Humayun, brought two masters of this art to his court to teach others. Some of the most famous Mughal miniatures adorned the *Akbarnamah* ("Book of Akbar"), the story of the great emperor's campaigns and deeds. Akbar was also impressed by European paintings brought to India by Christian missionaries. He encouraged artists to adopt the realistic style of this art into their own works.

Hindu literature also enjoyed a revival in Akbar's time. The poet Tulsi Das, for example, retold the epic love story of Rama and Sita from the ancient Sanskrit poem the *Ramayana* (rah•MAH•yuh•nuh) in Hindi. This retelling, the *Ramcharitmanas*, is now even more popular than the original, having spread to places like the Caribbean, South Africa, and Southeast Asia over the centuries.

Architecture Akbar devoted himself to architecture too. The style developed under his reign is still known as Akbar period architecture. Its massive but graceful structures are decorated with intricate stonework that portrays Hindu themes. The capital city of Fatehpur Sikri is one of the most important examples of this type of architecture. Akbar had this red-sandstone city built to thank a Sufi saint, Sheik Salim Chisti, who had predicted the birth of his first son.

Reading Check
Draw Conclusions
How was Akbar able to build such an immense empire?

Akbar's Successors

With Akbar's death in 1605, the Mughal court changed. The next three emperors each left his mark on the Mughal Empire.

Jahangir and Nur Jahan Akbar's son called himself Jahangir (juh•hahn•GEER), or "Grasper of the World." However, for most of his reign, he left the affairs of state to his wife, who ruled with an iron hand.

Objectives

You may wish to discuss the following questions with students to help them frame the content as they read.

- What evidence shows Nur Jahan's ability to exert power? *Jahangir's family members took orders from her.*

- What caused Shah Jahan to build the Taj Mahal? *the memory of his wife*

- How did Aurangzeb's use of tax money weaken the empire? *He used it for war and repression.*

More About . . .

Nur Jahan According to legend, Nur Jahan was born while her parents were fleeing Persia. They abandoned her under a tree, but a cobra protected her from the hot sun with its hood until her remorseful parents returned. At age 30, Nur Jahan was called to serve at court, where the emperor noticed her. Four years later, he married her.

Mumtaz Mahal According to popular stories, it was love at first sight between Mumtaz Mahal and Prince Khurram, who later became Shah Jahan. On seeing her, the prince reportedly said, "Oh, that I were a glove upon that hand." Mumtaz traveled everywhere with her husband, even on military campaigns. She gave birth on the battlefield to four sons, including the next emperor, Aurangzeb.

Women of Influence Women's patronage of the arts became significant under the rule of shahs Jahangir and Jahan. During the reign of Shah Jahangir, his wife, Queen Nur Jahan, gained more influence in politics and the arts. She made many political decisions, introduced new styles of dress, and commissioned many buildings and gardens. She also arranged her son's marriage. When her son's wife died, his unmarried daughter Jahanara assumed royal duties and commissioned many artistic works.

READING CHECK
Draw Conclusions How was Akbar able to build such an immense empire? *His combination of military might and political wisdom enabled him to get rid of enemies and build allies.*

COLLABORATIVE LEARNING

Policy Debate

1. Review Akbar's instituting of a graduated income tax. Then divide the class into four or six groups.

2. Tell students they will prepare for a classroom debate. Half of the groups should develop arguments in favor of graduated income taxes. The other half should oppose them.

3. Encourage groups to consider issues such as the following:

   • the functions of government

   • the economic impact of a graduated tax

   • the fairness of a graduated tax

   • alternative methods of funding government

   Have groups prepare notes or outlines that address these issues.

4. When groups are ready, select one group from each side and have them debate the issue. Students in the other groups should vote on which side presented its arguments most convincingly.

NOW & THEN

The Sikhs

Sikhs continue to wear turbans today as an expression of their faith and a symbol of their belief in social equality. Like the turban, uncut hair is also a symbol of Sikh identity and faith. To honor the human form as created by God, Sikhs do not cut their hair or beards.

▷ ONLINE INTERACTIVE VISUALS

Carousel: Women Leaders of the Indian Subcontinent

Have students navigate through the carousel and note similarities and differences among the images or identify a unifying theme.

In print edition, see Now and Then of same title.

Women Leaders of the Indian Subcontinent

South Asia has given the world six women prime ministers. Sirimavo Bandaranaike of Ceylon—an island off the southern tip of India that is now called Sri Lanka—was the world's first woman prime minister. She initially took office in 1960. Ask students to speculate on why women have often held political power in this region. *Possible answer: tradition of powerful women dating back to Nur Jahan*

Jahangir's wife was the Persian princess Nur Jahan. She was a brilliant politician who perfectly understood the use of power. As the real ruler of India, she installed her father as prime minister in the Mughal court. She saw Jahangir's son Khusrau as her ticket to future power. But when Khusrau rebelled against his father, Nur Jahan removed him. She then shifted her favor to another son.

This rejection of Khusrau affected more than the political future of the empire. It was also the basis of a long and bitter religious conflict that fostered future disputes over authority and power. Jahangir tried to promote Islam in the Mughal state, but was tolerant of other religions. When Khusrau rebelled, he turned to the **Sikhs**. Sikhism had emerged as a major religion and was gaining followers because of its egalitarian message. It was this message of equality between human beings regardless of their religion, gender, or caste that had drawn Khusrau to the Sikhs. Their prophet, Guru Arjun, sheltered Khusrau and defended him. In response, the Mughal rulers had Guru Arjun arrested and tortured to death. The Sikhs became the target of the Mughals' particular hatred.

Shah Jahan Jahangir's son and successor, **Shah Jahan**, could not tolerate competition and secured his throne by assassinating all his possible rivals.

> Vocabulary
> caste European term used in describing social groups of India

Now and Then

Women Leaders of the Indian Subcontinent

Since World War II, the subcontinent of India has seen the rise of several powerful women. Unlike Nur Jahan, however, they achieved power on their own—not through their husbands.

Indira Gandhi headed the Congress Party and dominated Indian politics for almost 30 years. She was elected prime minister in 1966 and again in 1980. She suspended democracy during an era known as "The Emergency." Gandhi was assassinated in 1984 by her Sikh bodyguards.

Benazir Bhutto took charge of the Pakistan People's Party after her father was assassinated.

She became prime minister in 1988, the first woman to run a modern Muslim state. Reelected in 1993, she was dismissed from office in 1996 and went into exile. She returned from exile in 2007 but was killed by a suicide bomb attack just months later.

Chandrika Bandaranaike Kumaratunga was the fifth president of Sri Lanka. She was first elected in 1994 and served until 2005. She survived an assassination attempt in 1999 and was reelected.

Khaleda Zia became Bangladesh's first woman prime minister in 1991. She was reelected several times, the last time in 2001.

Pratibha Patil, elected in 2007, was India's first female president. She retired from office in 2012.

Indira Gandhi · Chandrika Bandaranaike Kumaratunga · Khaleda Zia · Pratibha Patil

---

ADVANCED/GIFTED

Evaluate Sources

1. Remind students that historians sometimes differ in their opinions because they do not have access to accurate, definitive accounts of an event, the references that are available contradict each other, or accounts of events show bias.

2. Organize students into small groups and have students in each group locate and read three or more primary and secondary articles about the death of Akbar. Have students find what they can about the writer or sponsor of the Internet site and record any indication of possible bias.

3. When students have finished their research, have them review the documents and formulate their own answers to this question: Did Akbar poison his father or not? Have volunteers from each group present their positions and reasoning, supported by research findings, to the class.

He had a great passion for two things: beautiful buildings and his wife Mumtaz Mahal (moom•TAHZ mah•HAHL). Nur Jahan had arranged this marriage between Jahangir's son and her niece for political reasons. Shah Jahan, however, fell genuinely in love with his Persian princess.

In 1631, Mumtaz Mahal died at age 39 while giving birth to her 14th child. To enshrine his wife's memory, he ordered that a tomb be built "as beautiful as she was beautiful." Fine white marble and fabulous jewels were gathered from many parts of Asia. This memorial, the **Taj Mahal**, has been called one of the most beautiful buildings in the world. Its towering marble dome and slender minaret towers look like lace and seem to change color as the sun moves across the sky.

The People Suffer But while Shah Jahan was building gardens, monuments, and forts, his country was suffering. There was famine in the land. Furthermore, farmers needed tools, roads, and ways of irrigating their crops and dealing with India's harsh environment. What they got instead were taxes and more taxes to support the building of monuments, their rulers' extravagant lifestyles, and war.

All was not well in the royal court either. When Shah Jahan became ill in 1657, his four sons scrambled for the throne. The third son, **Aurangzeb** (AWR•uhng•zehb), moved first and most decisively. In a bitter civil war, he executed his older brother, who was his most serious rival. Then he arrested his father and put him in prison, where he died several years later. After Shah Jahan's death, a mirror was found in his room, angled so that he could look out at the reflection of the Taj Mahal.

History in Depth

Building the Taj Mahal

The Taj Mahal in Agra, India, is one of the world's architectural marvels. Some 20,000 workers from all over India and central Asia labored for 22 years to build the famous tomb. It is made of white marble brought from 250 miles away. The minaret towers are about 130 feet high. The spires atop the building guide one's eyes upward.

The design of the building is a blend of Hindu and Muslim styles. The pointed arches are of Muslim design, and the perforated marble windows and doors are typical of a style found in Hindu temples.

The main structure is a dazzling white marble mausoleum that overlooks a garden. The inside of the building is a glittering garden of thousands of carved marble flowers inlaid with tiny precious stones. One tiny flower has 60 different inlays.

Often called the most beautiful building in the world, the Taj Mahal is a monument to love and the Mughal Empire.

▷ **ONLINE ANALYZE VIDEOS**

The Mughals of India: Taj Mahal

Have students watch the video individually or as a class. You may wish to use the associated question as a discussion prompt.

Analyze Videos In what ways is the Taj Mahal a "marvel of engineering?" *It is astonishingly large; it is still standing hundreds of years after it was built; it has never been altered after it was built; 20,000 artisans worked on it; the foundation was built on unstable river soil using underground concrete arches; underground wells were dug to absorb water that otherwise could shift the foundation.*

PLAY VIDEO 4:00
The Mughals of India: Taj Mahal
HISTORY

ENGLISH LANGUAGE LEARNERS

Word and Picture Collage

1. Have students create a collage of images and comments about the Taj Mahal. They can use images from the lesson as well as online sources.

2. Ask students to add their own words and phrases to the collage to answer the question: Why do people find the Taj Mahal so beautiful? For example, students might mention its color, its details, or its symmetry.

3. Encourage students to use a thesaurus to expand their word choice and add to their descriptions.

The Mughal and Ottoman Empires in 1750

By the 18th century, the Mughal and Ottoman empires had waned in power as Europe's economy and influence strengthened.

Compare What impact did commercial activity have on the Ottoman Empire? the Mughal Empire? *The Ottoman Empire economy was hurt by competition from European colonies; the Mughal Empire lost control of Bengal to the English East India Company.*

▷ ONLINE INTERACTIVE CHARTS

Achievements of the Mughal Emperors

Have students explore the chart and answer the associated question.

Interpret Charts Which emperor strengthened the government of the Mughal Empire? *Akbar*

Emperor	Achievements
Babur (1526–1530)	• conquered India • founded the Mughal Empire

READING CHECK

Analyze Effects How did Aurangzeb's personal qualities and political policies affect the Mughal Empire? *He depleted the empire's resources and began the weakening of central power that led to its ruin.*

History in Depth

The Mughal and Ottoman Empires in 1750

By the mid-1700s the Mughal and Ottoman empires were two powerful Muslim states that faced many challenges.

After Suleyman's rule ended in 1566, the Ottoman Empire went through two centuries of economic challenges, social unrest, and, later, limited reform. By the 18th century, Europe loomed powerfully over the Ottoman Empire. Through war, European states won back certain Ottoman territories that had separated from the empire. Other regions became independent when local officials took control. There was a religious angle to the growing European influence as well. Austria and Russia, after defeating the Ottomans in numerous wars, were in a position to provide needed legal support to Christians living under Ottoman rule. Additionally, whereas trade with Europe had once been quite profitable, by the 18th century European colonies were producing sugar, tobacco, cotton, and other goods that Europeans once received through trade with the Ottomans. All of these changes resulted in an Ottoman Empire that saw its power greatly reduced by 1750.

By contrast, the Mughal Empire found itself near collapse by 1750. The splintered, weakened empire that existed at the end of Aurangzeb's reign in 1707 was riddled with political rivalries. Aurangzeb's lack of religious and ethnic tolerance had led to the rise of various factions, including the Marathas and the Sikhs. Both claimed their own state. By the mid-1700s, the Marathas in particular wielded considerable power over much of northern and central India. Another challenge around this time emerged from a collision of politics and trade. The English East India Company had been engaged in commerce with India since 1611. By 1750, the company built an army and assumed control of India's Bengal region, establishing Britain's political seat of imperialist power. By 1803 the Mughal Empire was controlled by the British.

Compare
What impact did commercial activity have on the Ottoman Empire? the Mughal Empire?

Aurangzeb's Reign A master at military strategy and an aggressive empire builder, Aurangzeb ruled from 1658 to 1707. He expanded the Mughal holdings to their greatest size. However, the power of the empire weakened during his reign.

This loss of power was due largely to Aurangzeb's oppression of the people. He rigidly enforced Islamic laws by outlawing drinking, gambling, and other activities viewed as vices. He appointed censors to police his subjects' morals and make sure they prayed at the appointed times. He also tried to erase all the gains Hindus had made under Akbar. For example, he brought back the hated tax on non-Muslims and dismissed Hindus from high positions in his government. He banned the construction of new temples and had Hindu monuments destroyed. Not surprisingly, these actions outraged the Hindus.

The Hindu Rajputs, whom Akbar had converted from potential enemies to allies, rebelled. Aurangzeb defeated them repeatedly, but never completely. In the southwest, a Hindu warrior community called Marathas founded their own state. Their greatest leader was **Shivaji**, an influential warrior king whose government included modern concepts, such as a cabinet of advisers. Aurangzeb captured Shivaji, but he escaped, and the Marathas remained unconquered. Meanwhile, after Aurangzeb executed

604 Module 16

STRUGGLING READERS

Features of Mughal Painting

1. Show students the painting depicting festivities during the coronation of Jahangir, found by entering the phrase in a search engine.

2. Use the following questions to spark a discussion.

   • Based on this painting, what do you think a coronation is? *a ceremony in which a ruler comes to power*

   • What similarities do you see between this miniature and the other examples of art in this chapter? *Possible answer: rich colors, lots of detail, intricate designs*

   • How does this painting show evidence of cultural blending? *People of many different skin colors are pictured, and they are wearing a variety of costumes.*

3. Have students choose one piece of artwork shown in the lesson. Tell students to write a short paragraph describing the artwork and explaining how the artwork shows evidence of cultural blending.

ADVANCED/GIFTED

Shah Political Cartoon

1. Tell students that political cartoonists use their talent to express their opinions and beliefs, both positive and negative, about the actions of national rulers.

Guru Tegh Bahadur for refusing to convert to Islam, the Sikhs continued to develop and transformed themselves into a brotherhood of warriors, emerging as a major power. Sikhism was concentrated in the Punjab, an area in northwest India. A series of military conflicts between the Sikhs and Mughal forces took place there in the early 17th century. Punjab is still the center of Sikhism today.

Aurangzeb levied heavy taxes to pay for these wars against increasing numbers of enemies. He had done away with all taxes not authorized by Islamvic law, so he doubled the taxes on Hindu merchants. This increased tax burden deepened the Hindus' bitterness and led to further rebellion. As a result, Aurangzeb needed to raise more money to increase his army. The more territory he conquered, the more desperate his situation became.

The Empire's Decline and Decay

By the end of Aurangzeb's reign, he had drained the empire of its resources. More than 2 million people died in a famine while Aurangzeb was away waging war. Most of his subjects felt little or no loyalty to him. Meanwhile, the power of local lords grew. After Aurangzeb's death, his sons fought a war of succession. In fact, three emperors reigned in the first 12 years after Aurangzeb died. The Mughal emperor was nothing but a wealthy figurehead. He did not rule a united empire, but a patchwork of independent states.

As the Mughal Empire rose and fell, Western traders slowly built their own power in the region. The Portuguese were the first Europeans to reach India. In fact, they arrived just before Babur did. Next came the Dutch, who in turn gave way to the French and the English. However, the great Mughal emperors did not feel threatened by the European traders. In 1661, Aurangzeb responded to these outsiders by casually handing them the port of Bombay. Aurangzeb had no idea that he had given India's next conquerors their first foothold in a future empire.

Lesson 1 Assessment

1. **Organize Information** Create a timeline similar to the one shown and fill it in with the names and key dates for the following Mughal emperors: Babur (given for you), Humayun, Akbar, Jahangir (and Nur Jahan), Shah Jahan, and Aurangzeb.

1494
Babur

Which of the emperors on your timeline had a positive effect on the empire? Which had negative effects?

2. **Key Terms and People** For each key term or person in the lesson, write a sentence explaining its significance.

3. **Compare** How did Akbar demonstrate tolerance in his empire, and how did his policy compare to earlier interactions between Muslims and Hindus?

4. **Draw Conclusions** What pattern is seen in the ways individuals came to power in the Mughal Empire?

5. **Analyze Causes** Why did the empire weaken under the rule of Aurangzeb?

6. **Summarize** Why were Akbar's tax policies so successful?

7. **Make Inferences** Why was Nur Jahan able to hold so much power in Jahangir's court?

---

2. Have students select one of the shahs discussed in this lesson and create a political cartoon that makes a clear, visual political statement about his actions.

3. When students have had time to complete their work, have volunteers share their political cartoons with the class. Students should explain the reasoning for the viewpoint shown.

Weigh the Value of Patronage

1. Have students name a few of the artistic achievements of the Mughals they read about in this lesson. Make a class list for students to see.

2. Have students select one shah they have studied in this lesson and identify one particular arts project he supported. Have students record these two pieces of information on a piece of paper that has been divided into a three-part chart.

3. On the bottom third of the paper, have students list the costs of the patronage on the left and the benefits on the right.

4. When students have finished, display the charts and guide the class in a discussion of the costs and benefits of art patronage.

Objectives

You may wish to discuss the following questions with students to help them frame the content as they read.

- How large an impact did the famine have on Aurangzeb's empire? *Possible answer: substantial, as the number of deaths equaled the present population of a large city, such as Houston*

- What is a one-sentence summary of the impact of the reign of Aurangzeb? *Possible answer: His aggressive and oppressive policies led to ruin for the Mughal Empire.*

More About . . .

Aurangzeb's Harshness Shah Jahan preferred his mystical, humane son, Dārā Shikōh, over his younger, fiercer son, Aurangzeb. Aurangzeb never forgot this. One legend claims that Aurangzeb jailed his father and had Dārā Shikōh's severed head delivered to Shah Jahan with the message: "Your son sends this [gift] to your majesty to let him see that he does not forget him."

Aurangzeb was strict in less violent ways as well. For example, he forbade parties that involved drinking, singing, and dancing, and he tore down all large-scale pre-Mughal monuments built by Hindus. As a result, the only pre-Mughal architecture remaining in India is in the southern sections that Aurangzeb never conquered.

Indian Painting Artists in regions of India outside of the Mughal Empire developed their own distinctive style of painting. While Mughal artists portrayed contemporary and political themes in their paintings, these other artists used more traditional and spiritual themes. And unlike the naturalism favored by Mughal artists, these artists used a more romantic style.

Technical Terms Encourage students to read more about fabric arts and to keep track of unfamiliar words such as *atelier, dye, motif, palmette, warp,* and *weft.*

Print Assessment

1. **Organize Information** Create a timeline similar to the one shown and fill it in with the names and key dates for the following Mughal emperors: Babur (given for you), Humayun, Akbar, Jahangir (and Nur Jahan), Shah Jahan, and Aurangzeb.

(continued)

Print Assessment *(continued)*

Which of the emperors on your timeline had a positive effect on the empire? Which had negative effects? *Possible answer: 1494, Babur; early 1500s, Humayun; 1556, Akbar; 1605, Jahangir (and Nur Jahan); early 1600s, Shah Jahan; 1658, Aurangzeb. Positive—Babur expanded the empire; Akbar oversaw a flowering of culture. Negative—Jahangir, Nur Jahan, and Shah Jahan sparked religious conflict; Aurangzeb waged costly wars.*

2. **Key Terms and People** For each key term or person in the lesson, write a sentence explaining its significance. *Explanations of the lesson's key terms can be found on the following pages: Mughal, p. 598; Babur, p. 598; Akbar, p. 599; Sikh, p. 602; Shah Jahan, p. 602; Taj Mahal, p. 603; Aurangzeb, p. 603; Shivaji, p. 604.*

3. **Compare** How did Akbar demonstrate tolerance in his empire, and how did his policy compare to earlier interactions between Muslims and Hindus? *He married women from different ethnic groups and abolished the taxes on Hindu pilgrims and non-Muslims. Hundreds of years earlier, especially during the Delhi Sultanate, Muslim sultans treated Hindus as conquered people.*

4. **Draw Conclusions** What pattern is seen in the ways individuals came to power in the Mughal Empire? *new leader killed all opponents*

5. **Analyze Causes** Why did the empire weaken under the rule of Aurangzeb? *He oppressed people, provoked Hindus and Sikhs, and increased taxes to pay for wars.*

6. **Summarize** Why were Akbar's tax policies so successful? *They were fair and affordable, so more people paid.*

7. **Make Inferences** Why was Nur Jahan able to hold so much power in Jahangir's court? *She knew how to use power, and he apparently lacked interest in ruling.*

▷ Online **Assessment**

1. How did the Sultans of Delhi regard the native population of India?

   ○ They considered the Hindus to be a defeated people.

   ○ They thought the Hindu religion was similar to their own.

   ○ They believed the Hindu culture to be superior to their own.

   ○ They respected the Hindus because they were good fighters.

   Alternate Question *Drag the answer choice into the box to complete the sentence correctly.*
   A series of bloody campaigns against Indian armies led by _Mahmud_ led to the creation of the Delhi Sultanate.

2. How did Akbar create an effective government for the Mughal Empire?

   ○ He elevated members of his family to positions of power.

   ○ He appointed officials who demonstrated their personal loyalty to him.

   ○ He allowed Muslim and Hindu women to become high-ranking officials.

   ◉ He promoted Muslims and Hindus based on their ability regardless of their religion.

   Alternate Question *Drag the answer choice into the box to complete the sentence correctly.*
   Akbar's religious tolerance was demonstrated by his appointment of the Hindu _Todar Mal_ to the position of chief financial officer.

3. Why do Sikh men wear turbans?

   ○ to show their belief in social equality

   ○ to demonstrate their love for material possessions

   ○ to show they are a separate denomination of Islam

   ○ to demonstrate devotion to their Punjabi homeland

   Alternate Question *Select the answer choice from the drop-down list to complete the sentence correctly.*
   The wearing of certain garments in the Sikh religion is an outward expression of their belief that all people are (*equal* ⇕).

4. Which statement describes the condition of the Islamic world during the 18th century?

   ○ New Muslim empires grew as the Mughal and Ottoman empires declined.

   ○ Muslims were driven from Turkey and India by rebelling Armenian Christians and Hindus.

   ◉ Europeans colonized territories previously controlled by the Mughal and Ottoman empires.

   ○ Sunni and Shi'a nations agreed to end their bitter feud in order to combat European invaders.

   Alternate Question *Select the answer choice from the drop-down list to complete the sentence correctly.*
   By the beginning of the 19th century, the (*British* ⇕) replaced the Mughals as the ruling power in India.

5. **Draw Conclusions** How did Babur defeat an Indian army that vastly outnumbered his own?

Possible answer: Babur's troops were better equipped than their Indian opponents and were well trained for war. His disciplined troops used cannons in defeating an army that was ten times its size. The cannons frightened the elephants that were being used in battle and thereby routed the Indian army.

6. **Evaluate** How were Akbar's taxation policies viewed by his subjects?

Possible answer: Akbar's chief finance minister created a taxation policy based on one's ability to pay. Peasants, who had their tax burden lessened, were more willing to pay a tax that they considered fair. As well, Akbar abolished the unpopular jizya, a tax on non-Muslims.

7. How was the rule of the Mughal Emperor Aurangzeb different than his predecessor Akbar?

Possible answer: Akbar's reign was characterized by religious tolerance and greater equality for non-Muslims. Aurangzeb reversed many of Akbar's policies. Aurangzeb destroyed Hindu temples and expelled non-Muslims from civil service. He taxed his subjects more and enforced Islamic prohibitions on social vices.

8. **Draw Conclusions** Why did the Mughal Empire decline beginning with the reign of Aurangzeb?

Possible answer: Emperor Aurangzeb was not tolerant of other religions and he lost the support of many of his subjects as a result of his autocratic rule. As many as two million Indians died from famine and disease during his reign and this social upheaval eroded support for his regime. Other groups, such as European traders and the Marathas, became more powerful as the Mughal Empire declined.

ADDITIONAL LESSON CONTENT

COLLABORATIVE LEARNING

Evaluate Aurangzeb

1. Divide students into heterogeneous groups. Explain that Aurangzeb is a controversial figure in Indian history. Historians differ widely on how to evaluate his reign.

2. Have each group find three or more sources describing Aurangzeb. Groups might check general encyclopedias, encyclopedias of history, books on the history of India, biographical dictionaries, and the Internet.

3. Groups should write one-paragraph descriptions of the sources, evaluating how critical or sympathetic each is toward Aurangzeb.

4. Then, as a class, make a list of the sources found by students and rank them from most critical to most sympathetic. Discuss why historians disagree on Aurangzeb. *Possible answer: Aurangzeb was intelligent, serious-minded, and a skilled military strategist. Under his rule, the Mughal Empire reached its largest size. However, his ruthlessness and violence caused great turmoil and contributed to the collapse of the empire.*

History Through Art

Cultural Blending in Mughal India

Have students look at the images in this feature. Ask students which image looks most like their impression of art from India or Southwest Asia. *Possible answer: the building, because of its dome*

1. **Clarify** What does the art suggest about the culture of Mughal India? *The religious tolerance of the early Mughal emperors and the adaptability of the local Hindu population allowed two distinct cultures to produce unusual and innovative pieces of art while forming a united empire.*

2. **Form Opinions** What are some modern examples of cultural blending in art? What elements of each culture are represented in the artwork? Consider other art forms, such as music and literature, as well. *Possible answer: Jazz is a musical form that developed using African American musical styles, American band instruments, and European harmonies and structure. Rap blends poetry and slang with beats, samples, and live music. Modern tragic and comedic theater can be traced to the ancient Greeks, but modern theater has also absorbed modern cultural influences. Japanese animated film has had an influence on animated features in the United States.*

Cultural Blending in Mughal India

Mughal India enjoyed a golden age under Akbar. Part of Akbar's success—indeed, the success of the Mughals—came from his religious tolerance. India's population was largely Hindu, and the incoming Mughal rulers were Muslim. The Mughal emperors encouraged the blending of cultures to create a united India.

This cultural integration can be seen in the art of Mughal India. Muslim artists focused heavily on art with ornate patterns of flowers and leaves, called arabesque or geometric patterns. Hindu artists created naturalistic and often ornate artworks. These two artistic traditions came together and created a style unique to Mughal India. As you can see, the artistic collaboration covered a wide range of art forms.

DECORATIVE ARTS ▶
Decorative work on items from dagger handles to pottery exhibits the same cultural blending as other Mughal art forms. This dagger handle shows some of the floral and geometric elements common in Muslim art, but the realistic depiction of the horse comes out of the Hindu tradition.

▲ ARCHITECTURE
Mughal emperors brought to India a strong Muslim architectural tradition. Indian artisans were extremely talented with local building materials—specifically, marble and sandstone. Together, they created some of the most striking and enduring architecture in the world, like Humayun's Tomb shown here.

▲ PAINTING

Mughal painting was largely a product of the royal court. Persian artists brought to court by Mughal emperors had a strong influence, but Mughal artists quickly developed their own characteristics. The Mughal style kept aspects of the Persian influence—particularly the flat aerial perspective, which demonstrated an artistic ideal. But, as seen in this colorful painting, the Indian artists incorporated more naturalism and detail from the world around them.

▼ FABRICS

Mughal fabrics included geometric patterns found in Persian designs, but Mughal weavers, like other Mughal artisans, also produced original designs. Common themes in Mughal fabrics included landscapes, animal chases, floral latticeworks, and central flowering plants like the one on this tent hanging.

Critical Thinking

1. **Clarify** What does the art suggest about the culture of Mughal India?

2. **Form Opinions** What are some modern examples of cultural blending in art? What elements of each culture are represented in the artwork? Consider other art forms, such as music and literature, as well.

Europeans Explore the East

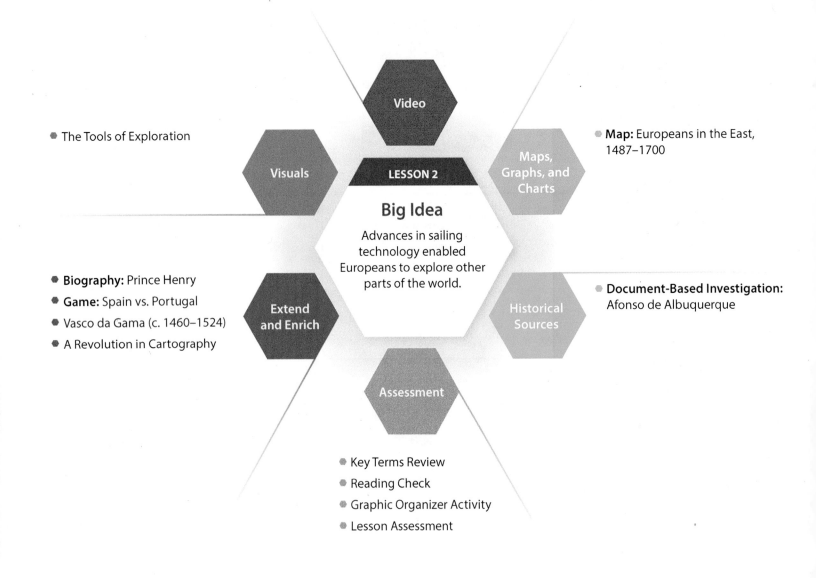

The Tools of Exploration

Map: Europeans in the East, 1487–1700

Visuals

Video

LESSON 2

Maps, Graphs, and Charts

Big Idea

Advances in sailing technology enabled Europeans to explore other parts of the world.

Document-Based Investigation: Afonso de Albuquerque

Biography: Prince Henry

Game: Spain vs. Portugal

Vasco da Gama (c. 1460–1524)

A Revolution in Cartography

Extend and Enrich

Historical Sources

Assessment

- Key Terms Review
- Reading Check
- Graphic Organizer Activity
- Lesson Assessment

Online Lesson 2 Enrichment Activities

Vasco da Gama (c. 1460–1524)

Biography Students read about the ways in which Vasco da Gama displayed courage in his efforts to open a trade route from Portugal to India. They use library and online resources to learn more about Vasco da Gama's first voyage to India. Using their findings, along with information from the text, students write a brief newspaper article about his journey.

A Revolution in Cartography

Article Students read about the advances in mapmaking that were needed to keep up with the flow of information about faraway places. Then they explain why they think the printing press could have such a huge impact on mapmaking and exploration.

Teach the Big Idea

1. **Whole Class Open/Introduction** Explain that a spirit of adventure motivated Europeans to cross oceans and face danger. Ask students what they do to satisfy their sense of adventure. *Possible answer: travel to new places, join in sports, learn new skills*

2. **Direct Teach** Read students the Big Idea: *Advances in sailing technology enabled Europeans to explore other parts of the world.* Review the following lesson objectives with students to aid in their understanding of the Big Idea.

   • Explain what led to European exploration.

   • Describe steps in Portugal's discovery of a sea route to Asia.

   • Explain the rivalry between Spain and Portugal and how the pope resolved it.

   • Identify nations that set up trading empires in eastern Asia.

3. **Whole Group Close/Reflect** Have each student choose one explorer from the time period 1400 to 1800. Then have students write answers to the following questions. What discoveries did the explorer make? What country did he represent? When did he make his explorations? What were the immediate and long-term results of the explorer's discoveries? Have students use the answers to write a paragraph about their chosen explorer.

▷ ONLINE DOCUMENT-BASED INVESTIGATION

Expansion, Exploration, and Encounters

Afonso de Albuquerque is the second of seven document-based investigations that students will analyze in the Expansion, Exploration, and Encounters module. In convincing his crew to attack Malacca, in present-day Indonesia, Portuguese sea captain Afonso de Albuquerque stressed his country's intense desire to crush the Muslim-Italian domination over Asian trade. Have students view the image and read the text.

▷ ONLINE GRAPHIC ORGANIZER

Europeans Explore the East

As students read the lesson, have them use the graphic organizer to take notes. Students can review their graphic organizer notes at the end of the lesson to answer the following question.

Analyze Effects Which of the events that you noted in your web was the most significant? Use evidence from the lesson text to explain. *navigation school because it made explorations possible*

🌏
Europeans Explore the East

The Big Idea
Advances in sailing technology enabled Europeans to explore other parts of the world.

Why It Matters Now
European exploration was an important step toward the global interaction existing in the world today.

Key Terms and People
Prince Henry
Bartolomeu Dias
Vasco da Gama
Treaty of Tordesillas
Dutch East India Company

Setting the Stage

By the early 1400s, Europeans were ready to venture beyond their borders. The Renaissance encouraged, among other things, a new spirit of adventure and curiosity. This spirit of adventure, along with several other important factors, prompted Europeans to explore the world around them. This module describes how these explorations began a long process that would bring together the peoples of many different lands and permanently change the world.

For "God, Glory, and Gold"

Europeans had not been completely isolated from the rest of the world before the 1400s. Beginning around 1100, European crusaders battled Muslims for control of the Holy Lands in Southwest Asia. In 1275, the Italian trader Marco Polo reached the court of Kublai Khan in China. For the most part, however, Europeans had neither the interest nor the ability to explore foreign lands. That changed by the early 1400s. The desire to grow rich and to spread Christianity, coupled with advances in sailing technology, spurred an age of European exploration.

Europeans Seek New Trade Routes The desire for new sources of wealth was the main reason for European exploration. Through overseas exploration, merchants and traders hoped ultimately to benefit from what had become a profitable business in Europe: the trade of spices and other luxury goods from Asia. The people of Europe had been introduced to these items during the Crusades, the wars fought between Christians and Muslims from 1096 to 1270. After the Crusades ended, Europeans continued to demand such spices as nutmeg, ginger, cinnamon, and pepper, all of which added flavor to the bland foods of Europe. Because demand for these goods was greater than the supply, merchants could charge high prices and thus make great profits.

COLLABORATIVE LEARNING

School for Navigators

1. Organize students into small groups. Tell students they work for the admissions department of a navigation school in the late 1400s.

2. Have each group create a set of posters, brochures, advertisements, and other materials to recruit students for the school. Recruitment materials should provide information about the school's programs and explain how they will prepare students for a maritime career.

3. Have volunteers from each group share their recruitment materials with the rest of the class.

4. Ask students to discuss and vote on which school they would choose to attend based on the presentations.

This early globe depicts the Europeans' view of Europe and Africa around 1492.

The Muslims and the Italians controlled trade from East to West. Muslims sold Asian goods to Italian merchants, who controlled trade across the land routes of the Mediterranean region. The Italians resold the items at increased prices to merchants throughout Europe.

Other European traders did not like this arrangement. Paying such high prices to the Italians severely cut into their own profits. By the 1400s, European merchants—as well as the new monarchs of England, Spain, Portugal, and France—sought to bypass the Italian merchants. This meant finding a sea route directly to Asia.

The Spread of Christianity The desire to spread Christianity also motivated Europeans to explore. The Crusades had left Europeans with a taste for spices, but more significantly with feelings of hostility between Christians and Muslims. European countries believed that they had a sacred duty not only to continue fighting Muslims, but also to convert non-Christians throughout the world.

Europeans hoped to obtain popular goods directly from the peoples of Asia. They also hoped to Christianize them. Bernal Díaz del Castillo, an early Spanish explorer, explained his motives: "To serve God and His Majesty, to give light to those who were in darkness and to grow rich as all men desire to do."

Technology Makes Exploration Possible While "God, glory, and gold" were the primary motives for exploration, advances in technology made the voyages of discovery possible. During the 1200s, it would have been nearly impossible for a European sea captain to cross 3,000 miles of ocean and return again. The main problem was that European ships could not sail against the wind. In the 1400s, shipbuilders designed a new vessel, the caravel. The caravel was sturdier than earlier vessels. In addition, triangular sails adopted from the Arabs allowed it to sail effectively against the wind.

Europeans also improved their navigational techniques. To better determine their location at sea, sailors used the astrolabe, which Islamic astronomers and mathematicians had perfected. The astrolabe was a brass circle with carefully adjusted rings marked off in degrees. Using the rings to sight the stars, a sea captain could calculate latitude, or how far north or south of the equator the ship was. Explorers were also able to more accurately track direction by using a magnetic compass, a Chinese invention. Some historians believe the magnetic compass was exchanged between the Chinese and other groups during journeys that ran along various transportation routes.

The Portuguese are credited with perfecting a 16-point wind rose, a tool that showed from which direction the wind was blowing. Captains wrote down the measurements obtained from these tools, as well as observed ocean current patterns, in pilot books, or navigation charts, for use during future voyages.

Reading Check
Summarize How might the phrase "God, glory, and gold" summarize the Europeans' motives for exploration?

Objectives

You may wish to discuss the following questions with students to help them frame the content as they read.

- Why were merchants able to sell spices at a high price? *Many people wanted spices but supplies were limited, which drove up prices.*

- How did the Muslims unintentionally help the Europeans take over trade with eastern Asia? *They didn't keep their sailing technology secret.*

More About . . .

The Astrolabe Sailors of the 1500s had only a few simple tools—such as the astrolabe—to guide them. Using the position of the sun and stars, these explorers sailed the oceans of the world. They could plot and hold a course and measure their progress. Astrolabes helped them estimate where they were with respect to land. These devices, which take their name from the Greek word for "star," were usually made of brass or iron. To use the astrolabe, a sailor would sight a star along the attached bar. By lining up the bar with markings on a disk, he could figure out the latitude of his ship's position. Astrolabes were used until the 18th century, when they were replaced by the more accurate sextant.

The Spice Islands Many voyages of exploration were inspired by the desire to find an easier route to the Spice Islands. The fabled Spice Islands attracted many sailors and explorers from afar. Zheng He was no exception. The Moluccas are located in the eastern part of Indonesia and are now called the Maluku Province. Cloves, nutmeg, and mace are all grown on the small volcanic islands. Archaeologists have discovered evidence that cloves were traded in Persia over 3,000 years ago. In medieval Europe, spices were prized for their medicinal use, as well as to add interesting flavors to edibles. Spices were very expensive because of the great distance they had to be shipped.

READING CHECK
Summarize How might the phrase "God, glory, and gold" summarize the Europeans' motives for exploration? *European explorers wanted to spread Christianity, bring fame to themselves and their country, and become rich.*

▷ **ONLINE INTERACTIVE VISUALS**

Carousel: The Tools of Exploration

Have students navigate through the carousel and note similarities and differences among the images or identify a unifying theme.

Analyze Visuals Why did inventors and sailors develop better tools for navigation? *They wanted to sail into the wind and to cross large bodies of water more efficiently. Often, this meant sailing far out of sight of land, so better navigation tools were needed.*

▷ **ONLINE LESSON FLIP CARDS**

Review Key Terms and People

Students can use the flip cards in the Lesson Review at any time to review the lesson's key terms and people: *Prince Henry, Bartolomeu Dias, Vasco da Gama, Treaty of Tordesillas,* and *Dutch East India Company.*

Objectives

You may wish to discuss the following questions with students to help them frame the content as they read.

- Why did Henry found a navigation school as a means to gain access to the riches of East Asia? *Europeans had to learn how to sail great distances to reach East Asia and its wealth.*

- Why did the Portuguese have to explore the coast of Africa so many times before finally sailing around the tip into the Indian Ocean? *They didn't know where the tip of Africa was or how far they had to travel to reach it.*

More About . . .

The Sextant The sextant incorporated a telescope, mirrors, and an arc of a circle calibrated in degrees. With this device, a mariner could read the angle of elevation above the horizon of the moon, the sun, or another star. With this information, plus the exact time of day and published tables, the ship's latitude could be determined.

Food for the Voyage Sailors were often at sea for six months or more. Meat was salted to preserve it. Biscuits, also called hardtack, were a hard bread baked to remove all moisture. Water went bad in a few weeks, but beer and wine lasted much longer. Sailors received daily rations of each.

Vasco da Gama In July 1497, da Gama sailed from Lisbon with four ships. Ten months later, he arrived in Calicut. Da Gama announced that he came seeking "Christians and spices." He found spices but no Christians. Instead, he found an ancient seagoing commerce run mainly by Muslims.

BIOGRAPHY

Prince Henry

Have students read the biography of Prince Henry of Portugal and patron of exploration. Prince Henry made no voyages himself but spent his life directing voyages of discovery along the African coast.

Prince Henry
(1394–1460)

For his role in promoting Portuguese exploration, historians call Prince Henry "the Navigator." Although he never went on voyages of discovery, Henry was consumed by the quest to find new lands and to spread Christianity. A devout Catholic, he wanted "to make increase in the faith of our lord Jesus Christ and bring to him all the souls that should be saved."

To that end, Henry used his own fortune to organize more than 14 voyages along the western coast of Africa, which was previously unexplored by Europeans. As a result, Henry died in debt. The Portuguese crown spent more than 60 years paying off his debts.

Portugal Leads the Way

The leader in developing and applying these sailing innovations was Portugal. Located on the Atlantic Ocean at the southwest corner of Europe, Portugal was the first European country to establish trading outposts along the west coast of Africa. Eventually, Portuguese explorers pushed farther east into the Indian Ocean.

The Portuguese Explore Africa Portugal took the lead in overseas exploration in part due to strong government investment. The nation's most enthusiastic supporter of exploration was **Prince Henry**, the son of Portugal's king. Henry's dreams of overseas exploration began in 1415 when he helped conquer the Muslim city of Ceuta in North Africa. There, he had his first glimpse of the dazzling wealth that lay beyond Europe. In Ceuta, the Portuguese invaders found exotic stores filled with pepper, cinnamon, cloves, and other spices. In addition, they encountered large supplies of gold, silver, and jewels.

Henry returned to Portugal determined to reach the source of these treasures in the East. The prince also wished to spread the Christian faith. In 1419, Henry founded a navigation school on the southwestern coast of Portugal. Mapmakers, instrument makers, shipbuilders, scientists, and sea captains gathered there to perfect their trade.

Within several years, and with considerable investment from the monarchy, Portuguese ships began sailing down the western coast of Africa. By the time Henry died in 1460, the Portuguese had established a series of trading posts along western Africa's shores. There, they traded with Africans for such profitable items as gold and ivory. Eventually, they traded for African captives to be used as slaves. Having established their presence along the African coast, Portuguese explorers plotted their next move. They would attempt to find a sea route to Asia.

SCIENCE AND TECHNOLOGY

The Tools of Exploration

Point out that early sailors never willingly sailed out of sight of land. However, following the coast added many miles to a long journey. Have students look at the map titled Europeans in the East, 1487–1700 in the last section of this lesson. Ask why da Gama's route was more efficient than Dias's route. Then discuss the inventions in this section. Have students tell how each invention helped sailors follow da Gama's route.

Analyze Motives Why did inventors and sailors develop better tools for navigation? *Possible answer: They wanted to sail into the* *wind and to cross large bodies of water more efficiently. Often, this meant sailing far out of sight of land, so better navigation tools were needed.*

Summarize What types of navigational or other tools do sailors use today? Choose one type of tool and write a brief explanation of what it does.

> **RUBRIC** Students' summaries should:
> - be clear and concise.
> - list the specific functions of the tool.
> - explain the benefits of the tool.

The Tools of Exploration

Out on the open seas, winds easily blew ships off course. With only the sun, moon, and stars to guide them, few sailors willingly ventured beyond the sight of land. In order to travel to distant places, European inventors and sailors experimented with new tools for navigation and new designs for sailing ships, often borrowing from other cultures.

▲ Here, a French mariner uses an early navigation instrument that he has brought ashore to fix his ship's position. It was difficult to make accurate calculations aboard wave-tossed vessels.

1. The average caravel was between 65 and 75 feet long. This versatile ship had triangular sails for maneuverability and square sails for power.

2. The large cargo area could hold the numerous supplies needed for long voyages.

3. Its shallow draft (depth of the ship's keel below the water) allowed it to explore close to the shore.

▲ This 17th-century compass is typical of those taken by navigators on voyages of exploration. The compass was invented by the Chinese.

◄ The sextant replaced the astrolabe in the mid-1700s as the instrument for measuring the height of the stars above the horizon to determine latitude and longitude.

Critical Thinking
1. **Analyze Motives** Why did inventors and sailors develop better tools for navigation?
2. **Summarize** What types of navigational or other tools do sailors use today? Choose one type of tool and write a brief explanation of what it does.

ENGLISH LANGUAGE LEARNERS

Use Nouns as Adjectives

1. Write the following sentence on the chalkboard: "The Portuguese believed that to reach Asia by sea, they would have to sail around the southern tip of Africa." Underline the word *sea*, and tell students that the word is a noun. Then write this sentence on the board: "They would attempt to find a sea route to Asia." Ask, What part of speech is *sea* in this sentence? (adjective)

2. Explain that nouns are sometimes used as adjectives. Often, nouns are used without a change in form, as in this example. At other times, nouns are changed to the possessive form, as in the sentence "Da Gama and his crew were amazed by the spices, . . . that filled Calicut's shops."

3. Next, have students identify nouns used as adjectives in the lesson section Portugal Leads the Way. Create a two-column chart and record students' answers in the first column. Have students provide sentences using the noun as a noun. Write their sentences in the second column.

4. Have students work on their own and create a similar chart for the remainder of the section.

Objectives

You may wish to discuss the following questions with students to help them frame the content as they read.

- How did Columbus expect to get to Asia by sailing west? *He believed the world was round. By sailing west, he would eventually reach Asia.*

- How might Columbus have mistaken the Caribbean for the East Indies? *He didn't know another continent blocked the route to Asia.*

More About . . .

Maritime Trade Even before the Europeans, the Chinese sought to establish maritime trade routes. Between 1405 and 1433 the Chinese Muslim navigator Zheng He led seven naval expeditions in Chinese ships that visited Southeast Asia, India, East Africa, and Arabia to secure trade with these regions. A change in the Chinese government's foreign policies, however, prohibited additional expeditions. China returned to using other nations' commercial fleets to carry its goods.

READING CHECK

Analyze Effects How did Prince Henry's experiences in Africa impact his decision to open a navigation school? *The riches he saw in North Africa motivated him to form a navigation school that would teach and encourage Portuguese explorers to discover the source of the riches and claim those lands for Portugal.*

GAME

Spain vs. Portugal

Have students play the game to test their knowledge of facts about the relationship between Spain and Portugal during the time of Columbus.

True or False

Spain vs. Portugal

History in Depth

A Ship's Rations

The captain of a 17th-century sailing vessel, with a crew of 190 sailors, would normally order the following food items for a three-month trip:

- 8,000 pounds of salt beef; 2,800 pounds of salt pork; 600 pounds of salt cod; a few beef tongues
- 15,000 brown biscuits; 5,000 white biscuits
- 30 bushels of oatmeal, 40 bushels of dried peas, 1 1/2 bushels of mustard seed
- 1 barrel of salt, 1 barrel of flour
- 11 small wooden casks of butter, 1 large cask of vinegar
- 10,500 gallons of beer; 3,500 gallons of water; 2 large casks of cider

Portuguese Sailors Reach Asia The Portuguese believed that to reach Asia by sea, they would have to sail around the southern tip of Africa. In 1488, Portuguese captain **Bartolomeu Dias** ventured far down the coast of Africa until he and his crew reached the tip. As they arrived, a huge storm rose and battered the fleet for days. When the storm ended, Dias realized his ships had been blown around the tip to the other side. Dias explored the southeast coast of Africa and then considered sailing to India. However, his crew was exhausted and food supplies were low. As a result, the captain returned home.

With the tip of Africa finally rounded, the Portuguese continued pushing east. In 1497, Portuguese explorer **Vasco da Gama** began exploring the east African coast. In 1498, he reached the port of Calicut, on the southwestern coast of India. Da Gama and his crew were amazed by the spices, rare silks, and precious gems that filled Calicut's shops. The Portuguese sailors filled their ships with such spices as pepper and cinnamon and returned to Portugal in 1499. Their cargo was worth 60 times the cost of the voyage. Da Gama's remarkable voyage of 27,000 miles had given Portugal a direct sea route to India.

*Reading Check
Analyze Effects
How did Prince Henry's experiences in Africa impact his decision to open a navigation school?*

Spain Also Makes Claims

As the Portuguese were establishing trading posts along the west coast of Africa, Spain watched with increasing envy. The Spanish monarchs also desired a direct sea route to Asia.

In 1492, an Italian sea captain, Christopher Columbus, convinced Spain to finance a bold plan: finding a route to Asia by sailing west across the Atlantic Ocean. In October of that year, Columbus reached an island in the

612 Module 16

ADVANCED/GIFTED

Understand the Treaty of Tordesillas

1. Have students work in a small group to research the Treaty of Tordesillas and the location of its Line of Demarcation.

2. Using a world map or globe, have students locate the Cape Verde Islands off the coast of West Africa and decide where the Line of Demarcation would be drawn. (Explain that a league is approximately 3 statute miles.)

3. Tell the group to discuss the significance of the treaty to Spain and Portugal. Was the Line of Demarcation fairly drawn?

4. Next, have the group explain the Treaty of Tordesillas to the class. The group should explain the agreement and show where the Line of Demarcation would be drawn on a modern map. Have students reach conclusions about the fairness of the division to Portugal and to Spain.

Caribbean. He was mistaken in his thought that he had reached the East Indies. But his voyage would open the way for European colonization of the Americas—a process that would forever change the world. The immediate impact of Columbus's voyage, however, was to increase tensions between Spain and Portugal.

The Portuguese believed that Columbus had indeed reached Asia. Portugal suspected that Columbus had claimed for Spain lands that Portuguese sailors might have reached first. The rivalry between Spain and Portugal grew more tense. In 1493, Pope Alexander VI stepped in to keep peace between the two nations. He suggested an imaginary dividing line, drawn north to south, through the Atlantic Ocean. All lands to the west of the line, known as the Line of Demarcation, would be Spain's. These lands included most of the Americas. All lands to the east of the line would belong to Portugal.

Pope Alexander VI

Reading Check
Analyze Issues How did the Treaty of Tordesillas ease tensions between Spain and Portugal?

Portugal complained that the line gave too much to Spain. So it was moved farther west to include parts of modern-day Brazil for the Portuguese. In 1494, Spain and Portugal signed the **Treaty of Tordesillas**, in which they agreed to honor the line. The era of exploration and colonization was about to begin in earnest.

Trading Empires in the Indian Ocean

With da Gama's voyage, Europeans had finally opened direct sea trade with Asia. They also opened an era of violent conflict in the East. European nations scrambled to establish profitable trading outposts along the shores of South and Southeast Asia. All the while, they battled the region's inhabitants, as well as each other.

Portugal's Trading Empire In the years following da Gama's voyage, the Portuguese monarchy's investment in global exploration began to pay off. Portugal built a bustling trading empire throughout the Indian Ocean. As the Portuguese moved into the region, they took control of the spice trade from Muslim merchants. In 1509, Portugal extended its control over the area when it defeated a Muslim fleet off the coast of India, a victory made possible by the cannons they had added aboard their ships. Five years later, Portugal established control of the Strait of Hormuz, connecting the Persian Gulf and Arabian Sea, and helped stop Muslim traders from reaching India. The Portuguese also oversaw the destruction of mosques and Hindu temples in the lands they took, forcing locals to convert to Christianity.

In 1510, the Portuguese captured Goa, a port city on India's west coast. They made it the capital of their trading empire. They then sailed farther east to Indonesia, also known as the East Indies. In 1511, a Portuguese fleet attacked the city of Malacca on the west coast of the Malay Peninsula. In capturing the town, the Portuguese seized control of the Strait of Malacca. Seizing this waterway gave them control of the Moluccas. These were islands so rich in spices that they became known as the Spice Islands.

Expansion, Exploration, and Encounters   **613**

Objectives

You may wish to discuss the following questions with students to help them frame the content as they read.

- Why were the Portuguese determined to prevent Muslim traders from continuing their spice trade? *The Portuguese would make higher profits if they didn't have any competitors.*

- How was the Dutch East India Company able to drive out the English and Portuguese? *It had ships, money, and armies.*

- Why didn't the Europeans have more influence on the countries of Southeast Asia? *They controlled only port cities, not inland areas.*

More About . . .

Afonso de Albuquerque Afonso de Albuquerque was more than just a sea captain. He gained fame as "the Portuguese Mars" (Mars was the Roman god of war) for his leadership of the armed fleets that took Goa and the Strait of Malacca. Albuquerque also served as the viceroy of India, governing the Portuguese holdings there for six years. He died at sea in 1515 while returning to Portugal after the new king had replaced him and ordered him home.

Pedro Cabral On his visit to Calicut, Pedro Cabral encountered problems with the Arab merchants controlling the port. The Arabs attacked the Portuguese trading booths, killing some of the sailors. Cabral bombarded the city and then sailed south to the rival city of Cochin to trade.

Ferdinand Magellan Ferdinand Magellan was convinced that he could reach the Spice Islands in East Asia by sailing west. The circumnavigation of the globe by his fleet was not only a great achievement of navigation and courage, it was also the first proof that the world was round.

READING CHECK
Analyze Issues How did the Treaty of Tordesillas ease tensions between Spain and Portugal? *It appeased both nations by granting them their own territories to colonize.*

COLLABORATIVE LEARNING

Recruit Explorers

1. Organize students into small groups. Tell students it is the 15th century and their king has asked them to help him recruit explorers.

2. Have each group think of characteristics that would make a good explorer—personality, education, background, etc.—and write a job description for the position. Job descriptions should mention risks involved in the profession, as well as compensation (salary, bonuses, and other benefits such as insurance and pension plans).

3. Next, have each group create a newspaper display advertisement to attract applicants. Student display ads might include artwork, and should list main points from the job description.

4. Have volunteers from each group share their job descriptions and newspaper ads with the rest of the class.

Afonso de Albuquerque

In convincing his crew to attack Malacca, in present-day Indonesia, Portuguese sea captain Afonso de Albuquerque stressed his country's intense desire to crush the Muslim-Italian domination over Asian trade. Have students view the image and read the text.

Analyze Sources What did Albuquerque see as the outcome of a Portuguese victory at Malacca? *the end to Muslim domination of the Indian Ocean trade*

Afonso De Albuquerque

In convincing his crew to attack Malacca, in present-day Indonesia, Portuguese sea captain Afonso de Albuquerque stressed his country's intense desire to crush the Muslim-Italian domination over Asian trade.

In convincing his crew to attack Malacca, Portuguese sea captain Afonso de Albuquerque stressed his country's intense desire to crush the Muslim-Italian domination over Asian trade:

"If we deprive them [Muslims] of this their ancient market there, there does not remain for them a single port in the whole of these parts, where they can carry on their trade in these things. . . . I hold it as very certain that if we take this trade of Malacca away out of their hands, Cairo and Mecca are entirely ruined, and to Venice will no spiceries . . . [be] . . . conveyed except that which her merchants go and buy in Portugal."

—Afonso de Albuquerque, from *The Commentaries of the Great Afonso Dalboquerque*

Portugal did break the old Muslim-Italian domination on trade from the East, much to the delight of European consumers. Portuguese merchants brought back goods from Asia at about one-fifth of what they cost when purchased through the Arabs and Italians. As a result, more Europeans could afford these items.

In time, Portugal's success in Asia attracted the attention of other European nations. As early as 1521, a Spanish expedition led by Ferdinand Magellan arrived in the Philippines. Spain claimed the islands and began settling them in 1565. By the early 1600s, the rest of Europe had begun to descend upon Asia. They wanted to establish their own trade empires in the East.

Other Nations Challenge the Portuguese Beginning around 1600, the English and Dutch began to challenge Portugal's dominance over the Indian Ocean trade. The Dutch Republic, also known as the Netherlands, was a small country situated along the North Sea in northwestern Europe. Since the early 1500s, Spain had ruled the area. In 1581, the people of the region declared their independence from Spain and established the Dutch Republic.

In a short time, the Netherlands became a leading sea power. By 1600, the Dutch owned the largest fleet of ships in the world. Pressure from Dutch and also English fleets eroded Portuguese control of the Asian region. The Dutch and English then battled one another for dominance of the area.

Both countries had formed an East India Company to establish and direct trade throughout Asia. These companies had the power to mint money, make treaties, and even raise their own armies. The **Dutch East India Company** was richer and more powerful than England's company. As a result, the Dutch eventually drove out the English and established their dominance over the region.

COLLABORATIVE LEARNING

Understand the Effect of Competition

1. Remind students that as a result of Portugal's success in establishing a trading empire in Southeast Asia, the cost to consumers of Asian goods fell to about a fifth of their former price.

2. Have students make a chart listing a variety of consumer goods that come from Southeast Asia today. Examples might include automobiles, televisions, cameras, and computer games. Students should show the regular retail price of these items and 20 percent of the retail price. (They might find prices for such goods in newspaper advertisements or department store fliers.)

3. Have students meet in a group to compare their charts and discuss the following questions:

   • How would such a drop in prices affect what you bought?

   • How would it affect U.S. companies?

   • How would it affect the people of Southeast Asia?

   • What would be the effects on the economies of countries in Southeast Asia?

Europeans in the East, 1487–1700

▶ Explore ONLINE!

Interpret Maps

1. **Place** Why would a fort at Hormuz help the Portuguese to stop trade between the Arabian Peninsula and India?
2. **Location** How many miles was the trade route between the Portuguese trading post on the Cape Verde Islands and the Cape of Good Hope?

While the Dutch were similar to Spain and Portugal in their desire to develop profitable trade, they were different in other ways. For one, the Dutch East India Company was founded by the government, not a monarch. Another difference was that the Dutch were not seeking to spread the Christian faith. They were only interested in expanding economically.

Dutch Trade Outposts In 1619, the Dutch established their trading headquarters at Batavia on the island of Java. From there, they expanded west to conquer several nearby islands. In addition, the Dutch seized both the port of Malacca and the valuable Spice Islands from Portugal. Throughout the 1600s, the Netherlands increased its control over the Indian Ocean trade. With so many goods from the East traveling to the Netherlands, the nation's capital, Amsterdam, became a leading commercial center. By 1700, the Dutch ruled much of Indonesia and had trading posts in several Asian countries. They also controlled the Cape of Good Hope on the southern tip of Africa, which was used as a resupply stop.

British and French Traders Also by 1700, Britain and France had gained a foothold in the region. Having failed to win control of the larger area, the

▶ ONLINE INTERACTIVE MAPS

Europeans in the East, 1487–1700
Have students explore the map and answer the associated questions.

Location How far was the trading post on the Cape Verde Islands from the Cape of Good Hope? *about 5,000 miles*

In print edition, see map of same title.

Place Why would a fort at Hormuz help the Portuguese to stop trade between the Arabian Peninsula and India? *Hormuz is on the strait connecting the Persian Gulf and the Arabian Sea. Any ship carrying goods to or from the gulf would have to pass by Hormuz.*

Location How many miles were there between the Portuguese trading post on the Cape Verde Islands and the Cape of Good Hope? *about 5,000 miles*

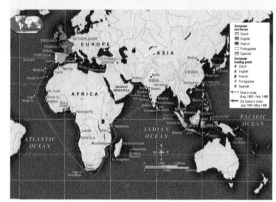

Expansion, Exploration, and Encounters   615

Print Assessment

1. **Organize Information** Create a timeline similar to the one shown and write on it the names and dates of the following key events in the European exploration of the East: Portuguese gain control of Strait of Malacca; Dias sails around tip of Africa; Prince Henry founds navigation school; Da Gama reaches Calicut. Which event is the most significant? *Possible answer: 1419—Prince Henry founds navigation school; 1487—Dias sails around tip of Africa; 1498—Da Gama reaches Calicut; 1511—Portuguese gain control of Strait of Malacca. Most significant—navigation school because it made explorations possible*

2. **Key Terms and People** For each key term or person in the lesson, write a sentence explaining its significance. *Explanations of the lesson's key terms can be found on the following pages: Prince Henry, p. 610; Bartolomeu Dias, p. 612; Vasco da Gama, p. 612; Treaty of Tordesillas, p. 613; Dutch East India Company, p. 614.*

3. **Synthesize** What was Prince Henry's goal and who actually achieved it? *Prince Henry wanted to explore new lands, find treasures, and spread the Christian faith; Bartolomeu Dias, Vasco da Gama.*

4. **Make Inferences** What did the Treaty of Tordesillas reveal about Europeans' attitudes toward non-European lands and peoples? *Europeans believed that non-European lands and peoples were fair game for conquest and exploitation.*

5. **Analyze Motives** What were the motives behind European exploration in the 1400s? Explain. *Possible answer: Europeans wanted to explore new lands to increase their wealth and to spread the Christian faith.*

6. **Recognize Effects** In what ways did Europeans owe some of their sailing technology to other peoples? *Possible answer: Europeans adopted some technology from other peoples: triangular sails of the Arabs, magnetic compass of the Chinese, and astrolabe of the Muslims.*

Now and Then

Trading Partners

Global trade is important to the economies of Asian countries now just as it was when the region first began to export spices, silks, and gems centuries ago. Today, a variety of products, including automobiles, electronic goods, tea, and textiles, are shipped around the world. (Hong Kong harbor is pictured.)

Regional trade organizations help to strengthen economic cooperation among Asian nations and promote international trade. They include the Association of Southeast Asian Nations (ASEAN) and the South Asian Association for Regional Cooperation (SAARC).

English East India Company focused much of its energy on establishing outposts in India. There, the English developed a successful business trading Indian cloth in Europe. In 1664, France also entered the Asia trade with its own East India Company. It struggled at first, as it faced continual attacks by the Dutch. Eventually, the French company established an outpost in India in the 1720s. However, it never showed much of a profit.

As the Europeans battled for a share of the profitable Indian Ocean trade, their influence inland in Southeast Asia remained limited. European traders did take control of many port cities in the region. But their impact rarely spread beyond the ports. From 1500 to about 1800, when Europeans began to conquer much of the region, the peoples of Asia remained largely unaffected by European contact. European traders who sailed farther east to seek riches in China and Japan had even less success in spreading Western culture.

Reading Check
Recognize Effects
How did the arrival of the Europeans affect the peoples of the East in general?

Lesson 2 Assessment

1. Organize Information Create a timeline similar to the one shown and write on it the names and dates of the following key events in the European exploration of the East: Portuguese gain control of Strait of Malacca; Dias sails around tip of Africa; Prince Henry founds navigation school; Da Gama reaches Calicut. Which event is the most significant?

1400 — 1800

2. Key Terms and People For each key term or person in the lesson, write a sentence explaining its significance.

3. Synthesize What was Prince Henry's goal and who actually achieved it?

4. Make Inferences What did the Treaty of Tordesillas reveal about Europeans' attitudes toward non-European lands and peoples?

5. Analyze Motives What were the motives behind European exploration in the 1400s? Explain.

6. Recognize Effects In what ways did Europeans owe some of their sailing technology to other peoples?

NOW & THEN

Trading Partners

Trade with Asia has long been a fast-growing segment of U.S. foreign trade. The United States used to be the world's biggest exporter. However, Asian economies are expanding. Now China is the world's biggest exporter. From 2008 to 2013, China's exports have increased at a rate of 6.8 percent per year, from $1.62 trillion to $2.25 trillion.

▷ Online **Assessment**

1. Which of the following motivated 15th-century European monarchs to find a sea route to East Asia?
   - ○ the desire to learn their native languages
   - ○ the desire to adopt new religions and traditions
   - ○ to create new markets for European wool and textiles
   - ◉ to eliminate the high cost of trading with Italian merchants

   Alternate Question *Drag the answer choice into the box to complete the sentence correctly.*
   Western European nations sought a sea route to East Asia that bypassed the Middle East because Italian and __*Arab*__ merchants increased the price of spices.

2. Why was Portugal the first western European nation to travel to India by sea?
   - ◉ The Portuguese royal family invested large sums of money in naval exploration.
   - ○ Portuguese captains hired Muslim sailors who were familiar with the east coast of Africa.
   - ○ The Portuguese invented the triangular sail, allowing them to sail against ocean currents.
   - ○ Portuguese soldiers discovered maps of Africa after they conquered the Muslim city of Ceuta.

   Alternate Question *Drag the answer choice into the box to complete the sentence correctly.*
   Inspired by the immense wealth of Muslim cities, _*Henry the Navigator*_ nearly bankrupted the Portuguese royal family by investing in sea exploration.

3. Which of the following resulted directly from the voyages of Christopher Columbus?
   - ○ increased piracy in the Caribbean
   - ◉ increased tension between Portugal and Spain
   - ○ opening of new trade routes to China and Indonesia
   - ○ lowering of the price of spices imported from East Asia

   Alternate Question *Drag the answer choice into the box to complete the sentence correctly.*
   The Treaty of Tordesillas allowed _*Spain*_ to colonize lands west of the treaty line.

4. Which of the following reasons primarily motivated the Netherlands to colonize Southeast Asia?
   - ○ The Dutch hoped to convert Asians to their religion.
   - ○ The Dutch wanted to create new markets for their goods.
   - ◉ They expected to make large profits sending spices back to Europe.
   - ○ They wanted to conquer large areas of land in order to spread their culture.

   Alternate Question *Drag the answer choice into the box to complete the sentence correctly.*
   A major difference between the Netherlands, France, Portugal, and Spain in establishing overseas colonies was that the _*Dutch*_ were not very interested in converting others to Christianity.

5. **Analyze Information** Which technological advancements made it possible for European sailors to reach the Far East?

   Possible answer: Europeans built larger oceangoing ships that used a triangular sail allowing them to sail against the wind. As well, Europeans began using the astrolabe, which allowed them to find their location at sea. With the adoption of the magnetic compass, European sailors could figure out in what direction they were sailing.

6. **Draw Conclusions** Why did explorers seek the support of European monarchs to launch their naval voyages?

   Possible answer: Judging by the amount of foodstuffs and equipment that was required by crews for long voyages, the cost of the voyages was usually beyond the capability of an individual. Prince Henry the Navigator spent vast sums of money funding early explorations. As well, Europeans were building larger, more expensive ships with large cargo space, which could survive long and difficult ocean passages.

7. **Draw Conclusions** How did the Roman Catholic Church influence colonization in the New World?

   Possible answer: Competition between Spain and Portugal for land in the New World threatened to bring the two countries to war. Since both of these nations were devoutly Catholic, they respected Pope Alexander VI's moves toward peace. The resulting Treaty of Tordesillas gave half of South America to the Portuguese and the lands west of the treaty line to Spain.

ADDITIONAL LESSON CONTENT

The Technology of Exploration

1. Have students create a four-column chart about technology that aided overseas exploration in the 1400s. The first column should identify the technological advances. The second should describe each advance and the third should explain how it aided exploration. In the fourth column, students number the advances to rank their importance.

2. Review student charts, and then create a master chart. How did students rank the advances? Was there a consensus, or did student opinions vary widely?

3. Discuss the ways in which technological advances combined with the drive to explore.

ENGLISH LANGUAGE LEARNERS

Voyages of Discovery

1. Have students create charts of the explorers mentioned in this lesson. Student charts should include the explorers' names, dates, country for which they explored, and achievements or discoveries.

2. Display a master chart. Have each student relate facts from their chart and add them to the master chart.

3. For emerging English learners, provide the following sentence frames: *In the year _____ , _____ explored for the country of _____ . He discovered _____ .*

China and Japan Reject Expansion

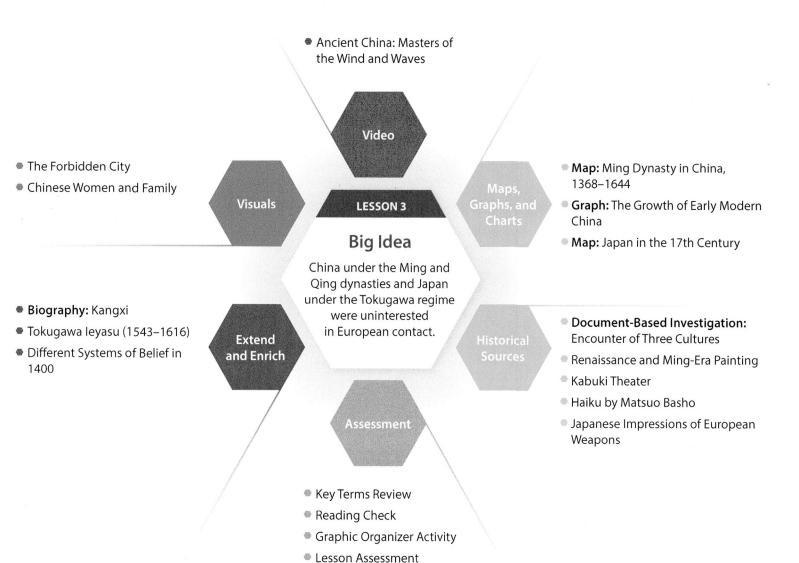

● Ancient China: Masters of the Wind and Waves

Video

● The Forbidden City
● Chinese Women and Family

Visuals

LESSON 3

Big Idea

China under the Ming and Qing dynasties and Japan under the Tokugawa regime were uninterested in European contact.

Maps, Graphs, and Charts

● **Map:** Ming Dynasty in China, 1368–1644
● **Graph:** The Growth of Early Modern China
● **Map:** Japan in the 17th Century

● **Biography:** Kangxi
● Tokugawa Ieyasu (1543–1616)
● Different Systems of Belief in 1400

Extend and Enrich

Historical Sources

● **Document-Based Investigation:** Encounter of Three Cultures
● Renaissance and Ming-Era Painting
● Kabuki Theater
● Haiku by Matsuo Basho
● Japanese Impressions of European Weapons

Assessment

● Key Terms Review
● Reading Check
● Graphic Organizer Activity
● Lesson Assessment

Tokugawa Ieyasu (1543–1616)

Biography Students read about Tokugawa Ieyasu, who was characterized by historians as having "self-control and a truly marvelous patience." Then they explain whether or not Ieyasu always acted honorably, giving examples to support their answer.

Different Systems of Belief in 1400

Map Activity Students create a map that shows the extent of the Eastern Hemisphere's Muslim, Confucian, and Christian realms around the year 1400.

China and Japan Reject Expansion

The Big Idea

China under the Ming and Qing dynasties and Japan under the Tokugawa regime were uninterested in European contact.

Why It Matters Now

China and Japan's economic independence from the West continues today, though China is pursuing new economic ties with the outside world.

Key Terms and People

Ming Dynasty
Hongwu
Yonglo
Zheng He
Manchus
Qing Dynasty
Kangxi
daimyo
Oda Nobunaga
Toyotomi Hideyoshi
Tokugawa Shogunate
haiku
kabuki

Setting the Stage

The European voyages of exploration had led to opportunities for trade. Europeans made healthy profits from trade in the Indian Ocean region. They began looking for additional sources of wealth. Soon, European countries were seeking trade relationships in East Asia, first with China and later with Japan. By the time Portuguese ships dropped anchor off the Chinese coast in 1514, the Chinese had driven out their Mongol rulers and had united under a new dynasty.

China Under the Powerful Ming Dynasty

China had become the dominant power in Asia under the **Ming Dynasty** (1368–1644). In recognition of China's power, vassal states from Korea to Southeast Asia paid their Ming overlords regular tribute, which is a payment by one country to another to acknowledge its submission. China expected Europeans to do the same. Ming rulers were not going to allow outsiders from distant lands to threaten the peace and prosperity the Ming had brought to China when they ended Mongol rule.

The Rise of the Ming A peasant's son, **Hongwu**, commanded the rebel army that drove the Mongols out of China in 1368. That year, he became the first Ming emperor. Hongwu continued to rule from the former Yuan capital of Nanjing in the south. He began reforms designed to restore agricultural lands devastated by war, erase nearly all traces of the Mongol past, and promote China's power and prosperity. Hongwu's agricultural reforms increased rice production and improved irrigation. He also encouraged fish farming and growing commercial crops, such as cotton and sugar cane.

Hongwu used respected traditions and institutions to bring stability to China. For example, he encouraged a return

Objectives

You may wish to discuss the following questions with students to help them frame the content as they read.

- Why might Hongwu have become a tyrant when problems developed? *When people resisted change, he used forceful methods.*

- What probably would have been the effect when Zheng He sailed into a foreign port with his large fleet? *People would have been in awe of China's power.*

More About . . .

Zheng He Zheng He's (1371–1433) parents were Muslims of Mongol and Arab descent. As a young man, he was drafted into the army. When his commander usurped the Chinese throne and became Emperor Yonglo, Zheng was promoted. Later, in 1405, he led the first

of his explorations. Zheng He's ships were among the largest wooden vessels ever built. The rudderpost of a treasure ship was found in 1962. Scientists calculate that the ship might have been 500 feet long.

Matteo Ricci Matteo Ricci (1552–1610) had an immense impact on Chinese thought. He introduced trigonometry and astronomical instruments to China. He also wrote and translated several books into Chinese, including *Euclid's Elements*. Ricci is still well known in China. In 1983, the 400th anniversary of his arrival in China was celebrated by official radio programs and magazine articles.

Teach the Big Idea

1. **Whole Class Open/Introduction** Point out that the Chinese of the 1400s and 1500s resisted interaction with outsiders because they wanted to preserve their culture. Ask students if they have ever shared these feelings and why.

2. **Direct Teach** Read students the Big Idea: *China under the Ming and Qing dynasties and Japan under the Tokugawa regime were uninterested in European contact.* Review the following lesson objectives with students to aid in their understanding of the Big Idea.

   - Identify the successes of the early Ming emperors.

   - Describe China and Korea under the Qing Dynasty.

   - Describe life in Ming and Qing China.

   - Summarize how three powerful daimyo succeeded in unifying feudal Japan.

   - Describe Japanese society and culture during the Tokugawa Shogunate.

   - Explain how Japan's policies toward Europeans changed.

   - Explain the purpose and effect of Japan's closed country policy.

3. **Whole Group Close/Reflect** Have students write a postcard from the point of view of a person living in either China or Japan during the periods studied during this lesson.

▷ ONLINE DOCUMENT-BASED INVESTIGATION

Expansion, Exploration, and Encounters

Encounter of Three Cultures is the third of seven document-based investigations that students will analyze in the Expansion, Exploration, and Encounters module. Japanese merchants and Jesuit missionaries await the arrival of a Portuguese ship at Nagasaki in the 1500s in this painting on wood panels. Have students view the image and read the text.

▷ ONLINE LESSON FLIP CARDS

Review Key Terms and People

Students can use the flip cards in the Lesson Review at any time to review the lesson's key terms and people: *Ming Dynasty, Hongwu, Yonglo, Zheng He, Manchus, Qing Dynasty, Kangxi, daimyo, Oda Nobunaga, Toyotomi Hideyoshi, Tokugawa Shogunate, haiku,* and *kabuki.*

to Confucian moral standards. He improved imperial administration by restoring the merit-based civil service examination system. Later in his rule, however, when problems developed, Hongwu became a ruthless tyrant. Suspecting plots against his rule everywhere, he conducted purges of the government, killing thousands of officials.

Porcelain vase from the Ming Dynasty

Yonglo Hongwu's death in 1398 led to a power struggle. His son **Yonglo** (yung•lu) emerged victorious. Yonglo continued many of his father's policies, although he moved the royal court to Beijing.

Yonglo also had a far-ranging curiosity about the outside world. In 1405, before Europeans began to sail beyond their borders, he launched the first of seven voyages of exploration. He hoped they would impress the world with the power and splendor of Ming China. He also wanted to expand China's tribute system.

The Voyages of Zheng He A Chinese Muslim admiral named **Zheng He** (jung-huh) led all of the seven voyages. His expeditions were remarkable for their size. Everything about them was large—distances traveled, fleet size, and ship measurements. The voyages ranged from Southeast Asia to eastern Africa. From 40 to 300 ships sailed in each expedition. Among them were fighting ships, storage vessels, and huge "treasure" ships measuring more than 400 feet long. The fleet's crews numbered over 27,000 on some voyages. They included sailors, soldiers, carpenters, interpreters, accountants, doctors, and religious leaders. Like a huge floating city, the fleet sailed from port to port along the Indian Ocean.

Everywhere Zheng He went, he distributed gifts such as silver and silk to show Chinese superiority. As a result, more than 16 countries sent tribute to the Ming court. Even so, Chinese scholar-officials complained that the voyages wasted valuable resources that could be used to defend against barbarians' attacks on the northern frontier. After the seventh voyage, in 1433, China withdrew into isolation.

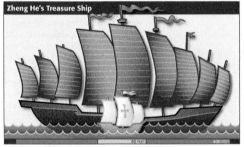

Zheng He's Treasure Ship

Zheng He's treasure ship compared with Christopher Columbus's *Santa Maria*

COLLABORATIVE LEARNING

Strengthen China

1. Explain to students that under the Mongols, China grew weak. Tell students that they will act as advisers to Hongwu.

2. Organize students into small, mixed-ability groups. Have students use information from the lesson to list things that needed to be improved in China during the late 1300s. Have students use their ideas to create a plan to improve the Chinese government and economy. When students have prepared their plans, have them create a petition that they could present to the Chinese emperor.

3. Have volunteers share their petitions with the class. You might wish to provide students with parchment paper and have them write their petitions in black ink.

4. Have the class discuss the strongest elements of the petitions they saw and what specific techniques strengthened each argument.

History in Depth

The Forbidden City

When Yonglo moved the Chinese capital to Beijing, he ordered the building of a great palace complex to symbolize his power and might. Construction took 14 years, from 1406 to 1420. Red walls 35 feet in height surrounded the complex, which had dozens of buildings, including palaces and temples. The complex became known as the Forbidden City because commoners and foreigners were not allowed to enter.

Hall of Supreme Harmony ❶
Taihe Hall, or the Hall of Supreme Harmony, is the largest building in the compound. It measures 201 by 122 feet and stands about 125 feet high. This hall was used for important ceremonies, such as those marking the emperor's birthday or the day the crown prince took the throne.

Hall of Central Harmony ❷
Zhonge Hall, or the Hall of Central Harmony, was a smaller square building between the two main halls. It was a sort of private office where the emperor could stop to rest on his way to ceremonies.

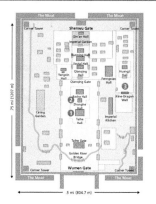

Nine-Dragon Wall ❸
This wall, or screen, of glazed tiles shows nine dragons playing with pearls against a background of sea and sky. From ancient times, the dragon was the symbol of the imperial family. This is the largest of three famous nine-dragon screens in China.

Interpret Visuals
1. **Analyze Motives** Why do you think the emperor wanted to keep common people out of the Forbidden City?
2. **Draw Conclusions** What aspects of the Forbidden City helped to convey the power of the emperor?

Expansion, Exploration, and Encounters **619**

Compare Ships

1. Remind students that many explorers sailed in search of land and wealth. They sailed different ships and traveled to different areas. Have students compare the voyages of Zheng He with those of Christopher Columbus.

2. Organize students into small groups. Have students collect data about the ships of each explorer. Students should document the sources of their data, especially when it conflicts with another source.

3. Next, have students record their information in bar graph form. Display completed work.

4. Discuss the difference in the estimated ship sizes. Finally, have students write a paragraph discussing whether size matters when comparing ships of Columbus and Zheng He.

▷ ONLINE INTERACTIVE VISUALS

Image with Hotspots: The Forbidden City

Have students explore the image using the interactive hotspots. You may wish to use the associated question as a discussion prompt.

Analyze Sources What aspects of the Forbidden City helped to convey the power of the emperor? *The immense size of the complex, the ornate thrones and elaborate art, and the mystery surrounding a forbidden zone all helped convey his power.*

In print edition, see History in Depth of same title.

Point out that the Forbidden City was the seat of government as well as the home of the Chinese emperor. The buildings and walkways of the complex were created to evoke awe at the power of the emperor and the wealth of China. Invite students to compare it with modern seats of government, such as Washington, DC.

Analyze Motives Why do you think the emperor wanted to keep common people out of the Forbidden City? *Possible answer: He thought that commoners were not worthy to be near him. He feared for his safety. He thought he would seem more like a divine being if he was inaccessible.*

Draw Conclusions What aspects of the Forbidden City helped to convey the power of the emperor? *The immense size of the complex, the ornate thrones and elaborate art, and the mystery surrounding a forbidden zone all helped convey his power.*

▷ ONLINE GRAPHIC ORGANIZER

China and Japan Reject Expansion

As students read the lesson, have them use the graphic organizer to take notes. Students can review their graphic organizer notes at the end of the lesson to answer the following question.

Synthesize Which individuals from China and Japan were the most significant? Explain. *China— Hongwu because of long-term reforms; Japan— Ieyasu because he established rule of law.*

	Key Leader (1) and Accomplishments	Key Leader (2) and Accomplishments (if applicable)	Characteristics of Life and Culture
China: Ming Dynasty (1368–1644)			
China: Qing Dynasty (1644–1912)			

Ancient China: Masters of the Wind and Waves

Have students watch the video individually or as a class. You may wish to use the associated question as a discussion prompt.

Analyze Videos In what ways did Zheng He's voyages influence Christopher Columbus? *Columbus's ships employed Chinese innovations, such as rudders and batten sails. Also, China and the Far East were Columbus's destination when he set out on his voyages.*

PLAY VIDEO 4:42
Ancient China: Masters of the Wind and Waves

History in Depth

Different Realms Circa 1400

By the year 1400, the size and power of the world's Muslim, Confucian, and Christian realms varied widely across the Eastern Hemisphere.

Islam Muslim dynasties and empires occupied lands across the Middle East, large portions of Africa, and parts of Europe. The Ottoman Empire controlled land around the Mediterranean Sea, including present-day Turkey and Greece. Around 1400, it was expanding into territories of the Byzantine Empire. The Delhi Sultanate in present-day India had begun breaking up by 1400. The wealthy Songhai Empire of West Africa had a powerful military that controlled the trans-Saharan trade routes in the region. Predominantly Muslim trading cities like Mogadishu and Kilwa dotted Africa's east coast.

Confucianism In 1400, there was a renewed focus on Confucianism in China under the Ming dynasty. Ming China covered the eastern half of modern-day China and was powerful enough to demand tribute from surrounding states, such as Korea. Korea, too, was a Confucian state in 1400.

Christianity The Christian realm in the year 1400 could be divided into two broad parts: Western Christianity, which referred to Catholicism in Europe, and Eastern Christianity, which included Eastern Orthodox and Oriental Orthodox Christian populations. Catholicism was in the midst of a division called the Great Western Schism. Two popes had been elected and their followers were split along national lines. This exacerbated rivalries between various European Christian states. Eastern Orthodoxy was prevalent in Russia, Hungary, Greece, and parts of Turkey, but the Byzantine Empire had already suffered more than 100 years of decline and lost much territory. Oriental Orthodoxy was found in Egypt, Ethiopia, pockets of the Middle East, and a region of India.

Ming Relations with Foreign Countries China's official trade policies in the 1500s reflected its isolation. To keep the influence of outsiders to a minimum, only the government was to conduct foreign trade, and only through three coastal ports: Canton, Macao, and Ningbo. In reality, trade flourished up and down the coast. Profit-minded merchants smuggled cargoes of silk, porcelain, and other valuable goods out of the country into the eager hands of European merchants. Usually, Europeans paid for purchases with silver, much of it from mines in the Americas.

Demand for Chinese goods had affected the economy. Industries such as silk-making and ceramics grew rapidly. Manufacturing and commerce increased. But China did not become highly industrialized for two main reasons. First, the idea of commerce offended Confucian beliefs. Second, Chinese economic policies traditionally favored agriculture. Taxes on agriculture stayed low. Taxes on manufacturing and trade skyrocketed.

Christian missionaries accompanied European traders into China. They brought Christianity and knowledge of European science and technology, such as the clock. The first missionary to have an impact was an Italian Jesuit named Matteo Ricci. He gained special favor at the Ming court through his intelligence and fluency in Chinese.

ADVANCED/GIFTED

Zheng He and Spices

1. Tell students that several common spices come from India. It is likely that Zheng He's travels along the Malabar Coast led to the spread of spices.

2. Have students make a list of at least five of their favorite spices. Then have students conduct outside research to discover the origins of the spices. Students should record the sources of their information.

3. Have students share their lists and the results of their research with the class. As volunteers provide the information, place a label on the map for the origins of each spice discussed.

4. Have students write a paragraph about the spices, explaining why they think explorers were interested in finding them.

Still, many educated Chinese opposed the European and Christian presence.

"But I was careful not to refer to these Westerners as 'Great Officials,' and corrected Governor Liu Yin-shu when he referred to the Jesuits Regis and Fridelli . . . as if they were honored imperial commissioners. For even though some of the Western methods are different from our own, and may even be an improvement, there is little about them that is new. The principles of mathematics all derive from the Book of Changes, and the Western methods are Chinese in origin: this algebra—'A-erh-chu-pa-erh'—springs from an Eastern word. And though it was indeed the Westerners who showed us something our ancient calendar experts did not know—namely how to calculate the angles of the northern pole—this but shows the truth of what Chu Hsi arrived at through his investigation of things: the earth is like the yolk within an egg."

—Kangxi, quoted in *Emperor of China: Self-Portrait of K'ang-Hsi*

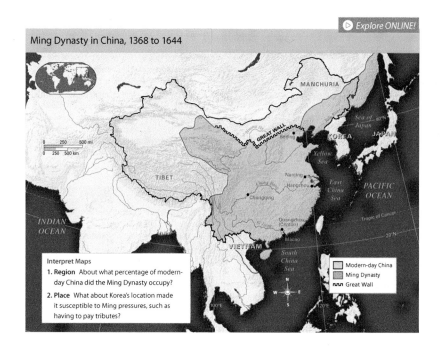

Ming Dynasty in China, 1368 to 1644

Interpret Maps

1. **Region** About what percentage of modern-day China did the Ming Dynasty occupy?

2. **Place** What about Korea's location made it susceptible to Ming pressures, such as having to pay tributes?

Ming Dynasty in China, 1368–1644

Have students explore the map and answer the associated questions.

Interpret Maps About what percentage of modern-day China did the Ming Dynasty occupy? *about half*

In print edition, see map of same title.

Region About what percentage of modern-day China did the Ming Dynasty occupy? *about half*

Place What about Korea's location made it susceptible to Ming pressures, such as having to pay tributes? *It shared its northern border with Ming China.*

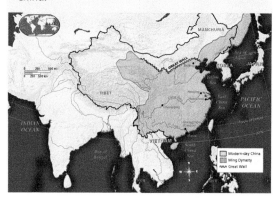

READING CHECK
Make Inferences What do you think the people of other countries thought about China after one of Zheng He's visits? *that China must be very powerful to send so many ships, men, and goods on such a voyage and, therefore, they should pay tribute*

The Great Wall of China was begun during the Qin Dynasty, but it was during the Ming Dynasty that it was rebuilt and extended into the wall that we see today.

Ming China's relationship to its neighbors was reflected in its expansion of the Great Wall. The wall had been repaired during previous dynasties, including the Song, but during the Ming, it saw its greatest extension. Fearing a Mongol invasion, Ming leaders ordered the wall to be maintained and strengthened.

A Stable and Diverse Society After Hongwu expelled the Mongols, he reorganized the government, replaced the Yuan laws with new codes based on Confucian teachings, and established the emperor as the head of the state. Because he was a strong leader, this arrangement created a stable government. It would work less well for later, ineffectual leaders.

The Ming government required candidates for high civil office to pass an official examination based on Confucian traditional texts. This ensured that administrators were highly literate and led to the appointment of many competent officials who were well versed in the Confucian ideals promoted by the Ming.

An institution called the Hanlin Academy, established during the Tang dynasty, issued the official interpretation of primary Confucian books. Hanlin scholars advised the Chinese emperor on history and Confucian thought. Under Hongwu, this Tang-era institution became more political. In his effort to exert direct control over Chinese provinces, Hongwu transformed the Hanlin Academy into an institution of six secretaries that governed various aspects of the empire. These secretaries reported directly to Hongwu.

By 1430, a department called the Censorate was created to enforce anti-corruption laws. Officials of the Censorate traveled to the provinces to complete inspections and could remove corrupt officials from office. Knowing they could be punished by the Censorate encouraged officials to obey the laws and deal honestly with others.

In more diverse provinces, Ming leaders used the military to manage China's ethnic diversity. For example, in hopes of strengthening Ming control of Yunnan province, whose population included both Han Chinese and non-Han Chinese, the military pushed more Han into the area.

During the Ming era, religion flourished, particularly Buddhism, Confucianism, and Taoism. Temples and other new places of worship were built, and monks taught and wrote about religious ideas. Ming politics and society reflected the dynasty's religious diversity. For example, officials had Daoist priests perform rituals at the imperial court and for common

Reading Check
Make Inferences
What do you think
the people of other
countries thought
about China after one
of Zheng He's visits?

people. Daoist priests also composed official hymns at the request of the emperor. The Jesuit missionaries arriving from Europe blended into Chinese society and served as musicians, astronomers, and cartographers at the imperial court. Buddhist monks were officially sanctioned to perform rituals for common people. Many Buddhist and Daoist sects integrated Confucian ideals into their own teachings.

Manchus Found the Qing Dynasty

By 1600, the Ming had ruled for more than 200 years, and the dynasty was weakening. Its problems grew—ineffective rulers, corrupt officials, and a government that was out of money. Higher taxes and bad harvests pushed millions of peasants toward starvation. Civil strife and rebellion followed.

Northeast of the Great Wall lay Manchuria. In 1644, the **Manchus** (MAN•chooz), the people of that region, invaded China and the Ming Dynasty collapsed. The Manchus seized Beijing, and their leader became China's new emperor. As the Mongols had done in the 1300s, the Manchus took a Chinese name for their dynasty, the **Qing** (chihng) **Dynasty**. They would rule for more than 260 years and expand China's borders to include Taiwan, Chinese Central Asia, Mongolia, and Tibet.

China Under the Qing Many Chinese resisted rule by the non-Chinese Manchus. Rebellions flared up periodically for decades. The Manchus, however, slowly earned the people's respect. They upheld China's traditional Confucian beliefs and social structures. They made the country's frontiers safe and restored China's prosperity. Two powerful Manchu rulers contributed greatly to the acceptance of the new dynasty.

The first, **Kangxi** (kahng•shee), became emperor in 1661 and ruled for some 60 years. He reduced government expenses and lowered taxes. A scholar and patron of the arts, Kangxi gained the support of intellectuals by offering them government positions. He also enjoyed the company of the Jesuits at court. They told him about developments in science, medicine, and mathematics in Europe.

—— BIOGRAPHY ——

Kangxi
(1654–1722)

The emperor Kangxi had too much curiosity to remain isolated in the Forbidden City. To calm the Chinese in areas devastated by the Manchu conquest, Kangxi set out on a series of "tours."

"On tours I learned about the common people's grievances by talking with them. . . . I asked peasants about their officials, looked at their houses, and discussed their crops."

In 1696, with Mongols threatening the northern border, Kangxi exhibited leadership unheard of in later Ming times. Instead of waiting in the palace for reports, he personally led 80,000 troops to victory over the Mongols.

STRUGGLING READERS

The Ming and Qing Dynasties

1. Organize students into small groups. Assign groups one of the two dynasties, Ming or Qing.

2. Have groups record the main facts about their dynasty. For each red heading in the lesson, have students write a one-sentence generalization and three supporting details.

3. Have volunteers share their generalizations and supporting details. Tell students to keep these notes and add to them as they study the lesson.

Objectives

You may wish to discuss the following questions with students to help them frame the content as they read.

- Why did the Manchu emperors take a Chinese name for their dynasty and uphold Chinese traditions? *to earn the people's loyalty*

- Why did the British resent China's trade restrictions? *Possible answer: They were eager to make profits from trade with China.*

- Why did the Korean attitude toward China change after the Manchu invasion? *Possible answer: They developed strong feelings of nationalism.*

More About . . .

Kowtow Point out the word *kowtow* in the lesson and explain that the word comes from Mandarin, the principal language spoken in China. It means, literally, "to bump, or knock, one's head."

The Gobi Desert The great Gobi Desert of Central Asia is known as *Yintai shamo* in Mandarin. It is sandy in the western part, but in the east, it is very rocky. Fierce winds from the northwest whip sand into dangerous dry storms. The very edge of the desert supports grasses and a small number of nomadic tribes who raise sheep and goats. It is about 1,000 miles wide.

Tip for English Language Learners Point out the phrase "existed in China's shadow" in the paragraph titled Korea Under the Manchus. Explain that the phrase means "to follow after" or "be under the influence of" something else. Here, the meaning is that Korea existed under the influence of China.

BIOGRAPHY

Kangxi

Have students read the biography of Kangxi, Chinese emperor of the Qing Dynasty from 1661 to 1722. His reign was one of relative internal peace; he constructed many public works and was a patron of the arts.

Objectives

You may wish to discuss the following questions with students to help them frame the content as they read.

- How were women's responsibilities important in Chinese society? *Educating children affected future generations; handling the family finances affected the economy.*

- What was one negative effect of the emphasis on tradition in Chinese art? *Creativity was not encouraged.*

More About . . .

Cao Zhan Cao Zhan (1717–1763) is believed to have written the first 80 chapters of *The Dream of the Red Chamber*. The novel is autobiographical, telling of the fall of a wealthy family and of a scandalous love affair between Baoyu and his cousin Lin Daiyu. Many consider it to be China's greatest novel. Like the family in the novel, Cao's own family experienced a decline in fortunes. His grandfather was one of the wealthiest men in China before the family's financial fall. When Cao died, another writer took over and finished the novel.

READING CHECK

Make Inferences Why do you think the kowtow ritual was so important to the Chinese emperor? *It reaffirmed for him the Chinese belief that their culture was vastly superior to others.*

Under his grandson Qian-long (chyahn•lung), who ruled from 1735 to 1795, China reached its greatest size and prosperity. An industrious emperor like his grandfather, Qian-long often rose at dawn to work on the empire's problems. These included armed nomads on its borders and the expanding presence of European missionaries and merchants in China.

Manchus Continue Chinese Isolation To the Chinese, their country—called the Middle Kingdom—had been the cultural center of the universe for 2,000 years. If foreign states wished to trade with China, they would have to follow Chinese rules. These rules included trading only at special ports and paying tribute.

The Dutch were masters of the Indian Ocean trade by the time of Qian-long. They accepted China's restrictions. Their diplomats paid tribute to the emperor through gifts and by performing the required "kowtow" ritual. This ritual involved kneeling in front of the emperor and touching one's head to the ground nine times. As a result, the Chinese accepted the Dutch as trading partners. The Dutch returned home with traditional porcelains and silk, as well as a new trade item, tea. By 1800, tea would make up 80 percent of shipments to Europe.

Great Britain also wanted to increase trade with China. But the British did not like China's trade restrictions. In 1793, Lord George Macartney delivered a letter from King George III to Qian-long. It asked for a better trade arrangement, including Chinese acceptance of British manufactured goods. Macartney refused to kowtow, and Qian-long denied Britain's request. China, in the emperor's view, was self-sufficient.

In the 1800s, the British, Dutch, and others would attempt to chip away at China's trade restrictions until the empire itself began to crack.

Korea Under the Manchus In 1636, even before they came to power in China, the Manchus invaded Korea and made the country change its allegiance from the Ming to the Manchus. Although Korea remained independent, it existed in China's shadow. Koreans organized their government according to Confucian principles. They also adopted China's technology, its culture, and especially its policy of isolation.

When the Manchus established the Qing dynasty, Korea's political relationship with China did not change. But Korea's attitude did. The Manchu invasion, combined with a Japanese attack in the 1590s, provoked strong feelings of nationalism in the Korean people. This sentiment was most evident in their art. Instead of traditional Chinese subjects, many artists chose to show popular Korean scenes.

Life in Ming and Qing China

In the 1600s and 1700s, there was general peace and prosperity in China. Life improved for most Chinese.

Families and the Role of Women Most Chinese families had farmed the land the same way their ancestors had. However, during the Qing Dynasty, irrigation and fertilizer use increased. Farmers grew rice and new crops,

Reading Check
Make Inferences
Why do you think the kowtow ritual was so important to the Chinese emperor?

ENGLISH LANGUAGE LEARNERS

Compare Ming and Qing Dynasties

1. Point out to students that both the Ming and Qing Dynasties ruled China for hundreds of years. There were many similarities between the two dynasties as well as some important differences.

2. Display a large Venn diagram. Label one circle "Ming Dynasty" and the other "Qing Dynasty."

3. Then ask the following questions:

   • When did the Ming Dynasty rule China? *1368–1644*

   When did the Qing Dynasty rule China? *1644 to about 1911*

   Write the answers in the correct circles on the diagram.

4. Then tell students to copy the diagram and continue finding facts from the text and entering them in the correct portion of the diagram. For help, you may wish to have students use the Guided Reading Workbook.

5. When students have completed their diagram, meet with them as a group to review their diagrams. Encourage students to describe information on their diagrams, prompting them with questions or sentence starters if necessary.

China's Population Boom

China's population grew dramatically from 1650 to 1900. General peace and increased agricultural productivity were the causes.

The Growth of Early Modern China

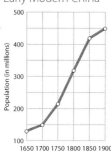

A Chinese family prepares for a wedding in the 1800s.

Interpret Graphs
Compare By what percentage did China's population increase between 1650 and 1900?

such as corn and sweet potatoes, brought by Europeans from the Americas. As food production increased, nutrition improved and families expanded. A population explosion followed.

These expanded Chinese families favored sons over daughters. Only a son was allowed to perform vital religious rituals. A son also would raise his own family under his parents' roof, assuring aging parents of help with the farming. As a result, females were not valued, and many female infants were killed. Although men dominated the household and their wives, women had significant responsibilities. Besides working in the fields, they supervised the children's education and managed the family's finances. While most women were forced to remain secluded in their homes, some found outside jobs such as working as midwives or textile workers.

Cultural Developments The culture of early modern China was based mainly on traditional forms, and these traditions were apparent in all areas of the humanities. The great masterpiece of traditional Chinese fiction was written during this period. *Dream of the Red Chamber* by Cao Zhan examines upper class Manchu society in the 1700s. Most artists of the time painted in traditional styles, which valued technique over creativity. In pottery, technical skill as well as experimentation led to the production of high-quality ceramics, including porcelain. Drama was a popular entertainment, especially in rural China where literacy rates were low. Plays that presented Chinese history and cultural heroes entertained and also helped unify Chinese society by creating a national culture.

Vocabulary
midwife a woman trained to assist women in childbirth

Expansion, Exploration, and Encounters **625**

China Today and Yesterday

1. Guide students in a discussion of the ways that rulers of China struggled to defend its borders.

2. Have students use maps in this module and other sources to draw a large outline map of modern-day China and the surrounding countries.

3. Have students draw the border of early China in a color. Next, have students draw the border of modern China in a second color and modern Mongolia in a third color. Tell them that the land north of the Great Wall was part of Mongolia at the time the wall was built.

4. Have students use a physical map to identify the geography and natural features of the land controlled by the Chinese and Mongols in the 1400s, and the land they control today.

The Growth of Early Modern China

Have students explore the graph and answer the associated question.

Interpret Graphs By what percentage did China's population increase between 1650 and 1900? *about 250 percent*

In print, see graph of same title in Social History feature.

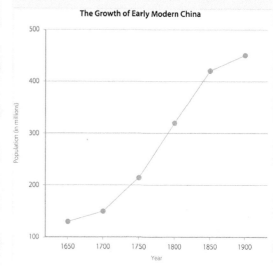

The Growth of Early Modern China

Source: Colin McEvedy and Richard Jones, *Atlas of World Population History*

Renaissance and Ming-Era Painting

Have students explore and compare the images using the interactive slider. You may wish to use the associated question as a discussion prompt.

Analyze Sources Which details in the paintings demonstrate that both artists were looking back to earlier styles and traditions for inspiration? *Ming era: landscapes and calligraphy; Renaissance: arches and columns*

Carousel: Chinese Women and Family

Have students navigate through the carousel and note similarities and differences among the images or identify a unifying theme.

Objectives

You may wish to discuss the following questions with students to help them frame the content as they read.

- Why might people have opposed Nobunaga's effort to unify Japan? *They feared his rule would be ruthless.*

- How did Ieyasu's "alternate attendance policy" help unite Japan? *It helped prevent daimyo from conspiring against him and rebelling.*

More About . . .

Tokugawa Ieyasu One of Ieyasu's goals was to keep his rival daimyo disorganized and weak. He not only forced them to live in Edo, he also kept them busy. In 1604, Ieyasu put the daimyo to work enlarging the castle at Edo. Thousands of ships carried logs and stones to Edo. Thousands of workers turned those materials into the world's largest castle, with tall stone walls, massive gatehouses, and moats. Ieyasu forced the daimyo to help pay for this project.

Shogun The word *shogun*, loosely translated, means "commander in chief." According to tradition, the first shoguns in Japanese history served under Emperor Sujin in the third century AD. In order to put down a rebellion, Emperor Sujin sent four armies into the far corners of Japan. The four generals appointed to lead these armies were given the title *shogun*.

Tip for Struggling Readers Point out the following sentence near the end of the section A New Feudalism Under Strong Japanese Leaders: "the rule of law overcame the rule of the sword." Ask students to paraphrase it. *(A centralized government established order in Japan.)*

READING CHECK
Make Inferences What was the effect of the emphasis on tradition in early modern China? *restored a national Chinese culture and provided stability in time of change and helped unify Chinese society*

Comparing Renaissance and Ming Cultures

The cultural expansion that occurred under the Ming and Qing dynasties can be compared to the European Renaissance in a few general ways. The movements were similar in that they both sought to connect to their own cultural traditions. The subject matter of these traditions, however, was different.

For example, the Ming court asked painters to imitate the styles and subjects of earlier dynasties. In Italy, Renaissance thinkers and artists focused on classical Roman and Greek topics like astronomy and philosophy for inspiration. Interest in Christianity, which was held by Northern European Renaissance figures, was not shared by Chinese thinkers, who looked instead to traditional Confucian teachings and texts.

These 12th-century Chinese women work outside the home, making silk.

One shared value was a focus on individual artistic expression. For example, many Chinese artists developed their own style of calligraphy. In calligraphy, the painting of Chinese characters attains great beauty. The personal style of a calligrapher was not unlike a Renaissance artist's own painterly style.

A deep exploration of human nature was characteristic of both movements, as well, especially in works of literature. *Dream of the Red Chamber* has been praised for its rich characters as much as Shakespeare's plays have. Chinese writers, like their Renaissance counterparts, also excelled at writing in the vernacular.

Architecture was an area where China and Europe diverged. Achievements in European Renaissance architecture centered largely on Christian churches and cathedrals. The main notable work of Chinese architecture is the Forbidden City, built for the glory of the emperor. One more area in which the two cultures differed was patronage. Wealthy patrons supported Renaissance artists, but in China, the court directed all cultural activities.

Vocabulary
calligraphy the art of writing

Reading Check
Make Inferences What was the effect of the emphasis on tradition in early modern China?

A New Feudalism Under Strong Japanese Leaders

In the 1300s, the unity that had been achieved in Japan in the previous century broke down. Shoguns, or military leaders, in the north and south fiercely fought one another for power. Although these rival courts came back together, a series of politically weak shoguns lost control of the country. The whole land was torn by factional strife and economic unrest.

Local Lords Rule In 1467, civil war shattered Japan's old feudal system. The country collapsed into chaos. Centralized rule ended. Power drained away from the shogun to territorial lords in hundreds of separate domains. A violent era of disorder followed. This time in Japanese history, which lasted from 1467 to 1568, is known as the Sengoku, or "Warring States,"

Political Terms

1. Have students find the term *political alliances* in the text. Ask students what *political* means *(having to do with affairs of government)*. Then ask what an *alliance* is *(a union of people with the same purpose)*. Now help students develop a definition for the combined term *(a union of people in government who have the same purpose)*.

2. Have students work in pairs and complete charts with additional political terms. Urge them to use dictionaries as necessary.

Term	Meaning
political alliance	a union of people in government who have the same purpose
unification	a joining of independent states into a state with one government
power base	place where a leader has political allies or other advantages
centralized government	a single government that has all of the power

A samurai warrior

period. Powerful samurai seized control of old feudal estates. They offered peasants and others protection in return for their loyalty. These warrior-chieftains, called **daimyo** (DY·mee·OH), became lords in a new kind of Japanese feudalism. *Daimyo meant* "great name." Under this system, security came from this group of powerful warlords. The emperor at Kyoto became a figurehead who had a leadership title but no actual power.

The new Japanese feudalism resembled European feudalism in many ways. The daimyo built fortified castles and created small armies of samurai on horses. Later they added foot soldiers with muskets (guns) to their ranks. Rival daimyo often fought each other for territory. This led to disorder throughout the land.

New Leaders Restore Order A number of ambitious daimyo hoped to gather enough power to take control of the entire country. One, the brutal and ambitious **Oda Nobunaga** (oh·dah-noh·boo·nah·gah), defeated his rivals and seized the imperial capital Kyoto in 1568.

Following his own motto "Rule the empire by force," Nobunaga sought to eliminate his remaining enemies. These included rival daimyo as well as wealthy Buddhist monasteries aligned with them. In 1575, Nobunaga's 3,000 soldiers armed with muskets crushed an enemy force of samurai cavalry. This was the first time firearms had been used effectively in battle in Japan. However, Nobunaga was not able to unify Japan. He committed *seppuku,* the ritual suicide of a samurai, in 1582, when one of his own generals turned on him.

Nobunaga's best general, **Toyotomi Hideyoshi** (toh·you·toh·mee-hee·deh·yoh·shee), continued his fallen leader's mission. Hideyoshi set out to destroy the daimyo who remained hostile. By combining brute force with shrewd political alliances, he controlled most of the country by 1590. Hideyoshi did not stop with Japan. With the idea of eventually conquering China, he invaded Korea in 1592 and began a long campaign against the Koreans and their Ming Chinese allies. When Hideyoshi died in 1598, his troops withdrew from Korea.

Tokugawa Shogunate Unites Japan One of Hideyoshi's strongest daimyo allies, Tokugawa Ieyasu (toh·koo·gah·wah·ee·yeh·yah·soo), completed the unification of Japan. In 1600, Ieyasu defeated his rivals at the Battle of Sekigahara. His victory earned him the loyalty of daimyo throughout Japan. Three years later, Ieyasu became the sole ruler, or shogun. He then moved Japan's capital to his power base at Edo, a small fishing village that would later become the city of Tokyo.

Japan was unified, but the daimyo still governed at the local level. To keep them from rebelling, Ieyasu required that they spend every other year in the capital. Even when they returned to their lands, they had to leave their families behind as hostages in Edo. Through this "alternate attendance policy" and other restrictions, Ieyasu tamed the daimyo. This was a major step toward restoring centralized government to Japan. As a result, the rule of law overcame the rule of the sword.

Vocabulary

shogunate the administration or rule of a shogun

STRUGGLING READERS

Compare Feudalism in Japan and Europe

1. Remind students that the feudal system in Japan was similar to European feudalism, yet unique. Display a blank Venn diagram with the left circle labeled "Japanese," the right circle labeled "European," and the overlapping portion labeled "Both."

2. Have students use the information in their text and conduct additional research to complete their own version of the diagram.

3. When students have finished, complete the class diagram and have students correct their work. *Possible answer: Japanese—shogun governs, military class governs, only most powerful samurai receive land for services; Both—lords or daimyos, knights or samurai, feudal system based on portioning land to vassals; European—no central governing figure, civil aristocracy or church authorities govern, knights paid with land grants*

Objectives

You may wish to discuss the following questions with students to help them frame the content as they read.

- Why did merchants have such low status in Tokugawa society? *Possible answer: Society valued warriors and farmers more highly. Merchants didn't produce anything.*

- What can you infer about Japanese society from the development of realistic stories and the kabuki theater? *Possible answer: People of the lower classes—the peasants, artisans, and merchants— were beginning to enjoy art.*

More About . . .

Basho As a youth, Matsuo Basho loved haiku. In this type of poetry, simple descriptions of nature evoke a powerful emotional response. At 22, Basho put down his samurai sword and devoted himself to poetry. He refined the traditional haiku, turning what was considered a trifle into a respected literary form. Basho is known for his simple, evocative descriptions and his ability to bring together unrelated images in a style that suggests Zen Buddhism.

READING CHECK

Draw Conclusions How would the "alternate attendance policy" restrict the daimyo? *families held hostage, financial burden of maintaining two residences, time wasted moving back and forth*

▶ **ONLINE INTERACTIVE MAPS**

Japan in the 17th Century

Have students explore the map and answer the associated questions.

Interpret Maps About what percentage of Japan was controlled by Tokugawa in the early 1600s? *about 20 percent*

In print edition, see map of same title.

Place Why might Edo have been a better site for a capital in the 17th century than Kyoto? *It was accessible by water.*

Region About what percentage of Japan was controlled by Tokugawa or related households when Tokugawa Ieyasu took power in the early 1600s? *about 20 percent*

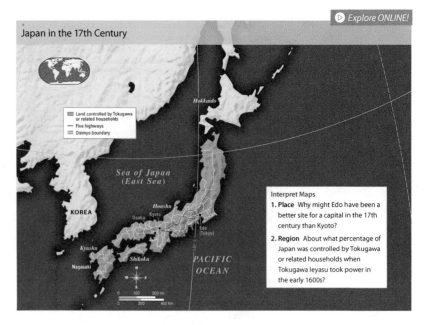

▶ Explore ONLINE!

Japan in the 17th Century

- ▭ Land controlled by Tokugawa or related households
- —— Five highways
- ▭ Daimyo boundary

Interpret Maps

1. **Place** Why might Edo have been a better site for a capital in the 17th century than Kyoto?

2. **Region** About what percentage of Japan was controlled by Tokugawa or related households when Tokugawa Ieyasu took power in the early 1600s?

Reading Check
Draw Conclusions
How would the "alternate attendance policy" restrict the daimyo?

Ieyasu founded the **Tokugawa Shogunate**, which would hold power until 1867. On his deathbed in 1616, Ieyasu advised his son, Hidetada, "Take care of the people. Strive to be virtuous. Never neglect to protect the country." Most Tokugawa shoguns followed that advice. Their rule brought a welcome order to Japan.

Life in Tokugawa Japan

Japan enjoyed more than two and a half centuries of stability, prosperity, and isolation under the Tokugawa shoguns. Farmers produced more food, and the population rose. Still, the vast majority of peasants, weighed down by heavy taxes, led lives filled with misery. The people who prospered in Tokugawa society were the merchant class and the wealthy. However, everyone, rich and poor alike, benefited from a flowering of Japanese culture during this era.

Society in Tokugawa Japan Tokugawa society was very structured. The emperor had the top rank but was just a figurehead. The actual ruler was the shogun, who was the supreme military commander. Below him were the daimyo, the powerful landholding samurai. Samurai warriors came next. The peasants and artisans followed them. Peasants made up about four-fifths of the population. Merchants were at the bottom, but they gradually became more important as the Japanese economy expanded.

LINK TO LANGUAGE ARTS

Write Haiku

1. Have students look closely at the poem in the historical source Haiku by Matsuo Basho. Discuss the poem.

2. Then explain that haiku follow very strict rules:

   - constructed of three lines with five syllables in the first line, seven in the second, and five in the last line

   - refer to or imply a season or month of the year

   - use images from nature

3. Additionally, haiku are written in two parts, which are divided by what is called the "cutting word." In the example in the text, the cutting word (or phrase) is "My dreams." Everything that comes before (the first line) is one thought. Everything that follows the cutting word (the last two lines) is a separate thought. The cutting word may fall in different places in a haiku. The purpose of the cutting word is to enable the reader to respond personally to the poem by filling in the gap created by the cutting word.

4. Help students identify these elements in the example haiku. Then challenge students to write their own haiku.

The Tokugawa era was marked by a return to Confucian values and ideas. This philosophy came to Japan in the medieval age from China. In Japan, as in China, Confucian values influenced ideas about society. According to Confucius, the ideal society depended on agriculture, not commerce. Farmers, not merchants, made ideal citizens. In the real world of Tokugawa Japan, however, peasant farmers bore the main tax burden and faced more difficulties than any other class. Many of them abandoned farm life and headed for the expanding towns and cities. There, they mixed with samurai, artisans, and merchants.

By the mid-1700s, Japan began to shift from a rural to an urban society. Edo had grown from a small village in 1600 to perhaps the largest city in the world. Its population was more than 1 million. As Japan's urban population grew, social structures changed. In these rapidly growing cities, people worked as manufacturers and wholesalers. Eventually, a class of wealthy merchants emerged. In turn, the daimyo and samurai, dependent on taxing a shrinking farmer class, saw their influence wane.

The rise of large commercial centers also increased employment opportunities for women. Women found jobs in entertainment, textile manufacturing, and publishing. Still, the majority of Japanese women led sheltered and restricted lives as peasant wives. They worked in the fields, managed the household, cared for the children, and each woman obeyed her husband without question.

Culture Under the Tokugawa Shogunate Traditional culture continued to thrive. Samurai attended ceremonial *noh* dramas, which were based on tragic themes. They read tales of ancient warriors and their courage in battle. In their homes, they hung paintings that showed scenes from classical literature. But traditional entertainment faced competition in the cities from new styles of literature, drama, and art.

Townspeople read a new type of fiction, realistic stories about self-made merchants or the hardships of life. The people also read **haiku** (HY·koo), 3-line verse poetry with a 5-7-5-syllable pattern. This poetry presents images rather than ideas.

Historical Source

Haiku

This poem was written by Matsuo Basho (1644–1694), Japan's greatest haiku poet.

On a journey, ailing—
My dreams roam about
Over a withered moor.

—Matsuo Basho, from
Matsuo Basho

Tabi ni yande
Yume wa Kareno o
Kakemeguru

—Matsuo Basho,
in Japanese

Analyze Historical Sources
How is Matsuo Basho's haiku a poem about death?

▷ ONLINE HISTORICAL SOURCE

Haiku by Matsuo Basho

Invite students to read the poem and answer the associated question.

Analyze Sources How is Matsuo Basho's haiku a poem about death? *Basho writes about being ill and on a journey perhaps toward death.*

HISTORICAL SOURCE

Haiku

Matsuo Basho was Japan's greatest haiku poet. Before his death in 1694, he wrote the following haiku.

COLLABORATIVE LEARNING

Meeting Between Cultures

1. Have students work in pairs and review aspects of feudalism in Europe so they can compare it to life in Japan during the Tokugawa Shogunate. Tell students to imagine that they are living during the period when the first Europeans visited Japan.

2. Then have partners each take a role, such as that of a European noble and a Japanese samurai. Instruct them to discuss their roles and decide how each of the characters would see his or her place in society.

3. Students should then write a dialogue in which the two characters discuss events from the perspective of their different cultures. Topics might include:

   • the introduction of firearms into Japan

   • the building of castles and the growth of towns

   • the power of the daimyo and shoguns

4. Have students practice and present their dialogue to the class.

Objectives

You may wish to discuss the following questions with students to help them frame the content as they read.

- How did the building of castles attract merchants, artisans, and others? *People came to the castles to help build them; others came to feed and support the workers and their families.*

- How did the Japanese response to missionaries differ from the Chinese response? *Both initially accepted the missionaries, but Japan later banned Christianity altogether.*

More About . . .

Francis Xavier Francis Xavier epitomized the missionary spirit of the Jesuits. Through selfless devotion, he helped establish Christianity in India, Malacca, and the Spice Islands. His strong beliefs and aura of goodness attracted many converts. In 1549, he sought a new challenge among the Japanese, whom he called "the best people yet discovered."

Osaka Osaka, with a population of more than 2.5 million people, is the third largest city in Japan after Tokyo and Yokohama. With its many canals and rivers, it was called the "Venice of the East." Because of the shortage of land, many of Osaka's shopping centers have been built underground. Today, Osaka Castle houses a museum.

▷ ONLINE HISTORICAL SOURCE

Kabuki Theater

Have students explore the image by revealing additional information using the interactive slider. You may wish to use the associated question as a discussion prompt.

Analyze Sources What aspects of kabuki theater do you observe in both the contemporary image and the historical image? *Both actors make use of extravagant costumes, masklike makeup, and exaggerated postures and gestures.*

In print edition, see Now and Then of same title.

Originally women played female roles in kabuki drama. In 1629, however, authorities noticed that men were taking too much interest in the female actors, so they banned women from acting. Male actors immediately took over the female roles. The ban on women was lifted in the 19th century, but the tradition of men playing the female roles was so strong that women still have not taken back their parts.

Now and Then

Kabuki Theater

Kabuki is a traditional form of Japanese theater. It makes use of extravagant costumes, masklike makeup, and exaggerated postures and gestures. The illustrations show a contemporary actor and a 19th-century performer playing warriors.

Although kabuki was created by a woman, all roles, both male and female, are performed by men. Kabuki plays are about grand historical events or the everyday life of people in Tokugawa Japan.

For 400 years, kabuki has provided entertainment for the Japanese people. More recently, kabuki has been performed for audiences around the world, including the United States. Major centers for kabuki theater in Japan are Tokyo, Kyoto, and Osaka.

Reading Check
Summarize How did the Japanese express themselves culturally under the Tokugawa shoguns?

Townspeople also attended **kabuki** theater. Actors in elaborate costumes, using music, dance, and mime, performed skits about modern life. The paintings people enjoyed were often woodblock prints showing city life.

Contact Between Europe and Japan

Europeans began coming to Japan in the 16th century, during the Warring States period. Despite the severe disorder in the country, the Japanese welcomed traders and missionaries, first from Portugal and, later, other European countries. These newcomers introduced fascinating new technologies and ideas. Within a century, however, the aggressive Europeans had worn out their welcome.

Portugal Sends Ships, Merchants, and Technology to Japan The Japanese first encountered Europeans in 1543, when shipwrecked Portuguese sailors washed up on the shores of southern Japan. Portuguese merchants soon followed. They hoped to involve themselves in Japan's trade with China and Southeast Asia. The Portuguese brought clocks, eyeglasses, tobacco, firearms, and other unfamiliar items from Europe. Japanese merchants eager to expand their markets were happy to receive the newcomers and their goods.

Back in Japan, the daimyo, too, welcomed the strangers. The daimyo felt that European goods could provide an advantage over their rivals. For example, they were particularly interested in the Portuguese muskets and cannons. One of these warlords listened intently to a Japanese observer's description of a musket:

READING CHECK

Summarize How did the Japanese express themselves culturally under the Tokugawa shoguns? *kabuki plays, popular stories, haiku poetry, and woodblock prints*

"In their hands they carried something two or three feet long, straight on the outside with a passage inside, and made of a heavy substance. . . . This thing with one blow can smash a mountain of silver and a wall of iron. If one sought to do mischief in another man's domain and he was touched by it, he would lose his life instantly."

—Anonymous Japanese Writer, quoted in *Sources of Japanese Tradition* (1958)

The Japanese purchased weapons from the Portuguese and soon began their own production. Firearms forever changed the time-honored tradition of the Japanese warrior, whose principal weapon had been the sword. Some daimyo recruited and trained corps of peasants to use muskets. Many samurai, who retained the sword as their principal weapon, would lose their lives to musket fire in future combat.

The cannon also had an impact on life in Japan. Daimyo had to build fortified castles, like the Himeji Castle, to withstand the destructive force of cannonballs. The castles attracted merchants, artisans, and others to surrounding lands. Many of these lands were to grow into the towns and cities of modern Japan, including Edo (Tokyo), Osaka, Himeji, and Nagoya.

Christian Missionaries in Japan In 1549, Christian missionaries began arriving in Japan. The Japanese accepted the missionaries in part because they associated them with the muskets and other European goods that they wanted to purchase. However, the religious orders of Jesuits, Franciscans, and Dominicans came to convert the Japanese.

Francis Xavier, a Jesuit, led the first mission to Japan. He wrote that the Japanese were "very sociable. . . and much concerned with their honor, which they prize above everything else." Francis Xavier baptized about a hundred converts before he left Japan. By the year 1600, other European missionaries had converted about 300,000 Japanese to Christianity.

The success of the missionaries upset Tokugawa Ieyasu. He found aspects of the Christian invasion troublesome. Missionaries scorned traditional Japanese beliefs and involved themselves in local politics. At first, Ieyasu did not take any action. He feared driving off the Portuguese, English, Spanish, and Dutch traders who spurred Japan's economy. By 1612, however, the shogun had come to fear religious uprisings more. He banned Christianity and focused on ridding his country of all Christians.

Ieyasu died in 1616, but repression of Christianity continued off and on for the next two decades under his successors. In 1637, the issue came to a head. An uprising in southern Japan of some 30,000 peasants, led by dissatisfied samurai, shook the Tokugawa shogunate. Because so many of the rebels were Christian, the shogun decided that Christianity was at the root of the rebellion. After that, the shoguns ruthlessly persecuted Christians. European missionaries were killed or driven out of Japan. All Japanese were forced to demonstrate faithfulness to some branch of Buddhism. These policies eventually eliminated Christianity in Japan and led to the formation of an exclusion policy.

Reading Check
Compare and Contrast How was the treatment of Europeans different in Japan and China? How was it similar?

▷ ONLINE HISTORICAL SOURCE

Japanese Impressions of European Weapons

Invite students to play the audio to hear the excerpt read aloud and answer the associated question.

Analyze Sources What is the writer referring to—or perhaps predicting—with the phrase "mischief in another man's domain"? *years of armed conflict between Europeans and the Asian nations they sought to colonize and control*

READING CHECK
Compare and Contrast How was the treatment of Europeans different in Japan and China? How was it similar? *The Japanese were more receptive at first to European contact than the Chinese were; however, both countries eventually rebuffed European influences and entered an age of isolation.*

STRUGGLING READERS

The Rise and Fall of Christianity in Japan

1. Remind students that Christianity was introduced into Japan in 1549 by missionaries. Following a series of events, the Tokugawa shoguns banned Christianity and closed the country to Europeans.

2. Draw a large flow chart with nine boxes; each box should have an arrow pointing to the next. Tell students this chart will show sequence of events. Have students copy the chart on their own paper.

3. Write "Missionaries arrive in Japan, 1549" in the first box. Then elicit the following sequence of events that led to the closing of Japan to Europeans.
   • 300,000 Japanese converted by 1600
   • shogun fears religious uprisings
   • shogun bans Christianity
   • 1637, uprising by 30,000 peasants
   • shogun forces all Japanese to accept Buddhism
   • Christianity eliminated in Japan
   • closed country policy adopted

   Write the events on the chart and have students copy them into their own charts.

Objectives

You may wish to discuss the following questions with students to help them frame the content as they read.

- How did the closed country policy strengthen the Tokugawa shoguns? *Possible answer: eliminated European ideas that undermined Tokugawa authority; limiting trade produced monopoly and high profits*

- What might have been the long-term effect of Japan's closed country policy? *Possible answer: missed technological advances; stagnation of ideas*

More About . . .

Japanese Swordmaking When Fujiyasu Masahira makes a sword, he follows the exacting traditional method of master craftsmen from hundreds of years ago. He makes his own charcoal, which he uses to smelt iron oxide sand into steel. When he has made a sufficient amount of steel with the right carbon content, he stacks pieces to form the blade. He wraps the stack in rice paper and dips it in clay before heating it in the forge. Some silicon from the rice straw ash becomes part of the steel. The metal is heated, folded and pounded flat repeatedly. It is then filed into a rough shape and tempered by repeated heating and quenching in water. After careful shaping and polishing, a custom sword guard and scabbard are made. Masahira is one of only 14 Mukansa smiths. Mukansa smiths have won so many first prizes in their craft that they can no longer take part in competition.

▷ ONLINE DOCUMENT-BASED INVESTIGATION

Encounter of Three Cultures

Japanese merchants and Jesuit missionaries await the arrival of a Portuguese ship at Nagasaki in the 1500s in this painting on wood panels. Invite students to study the image and answer the question.

Analyze Sources What did each group depicted in the painting seek to gain from another group? *Japanese merchants wanted to purchase European goods; the Portuguese wanted to sell their goods in a new market; Jesuit missionaries wanted to convert local Japanese people to Christianity.*

DOCUMENT-BASED INVESTIGATION   HISTORICAL SOURCE

Encounter of Three Cultures

Japanese merchants and Jesuit missionaries await the arrival of a Portuguese ship at Nagasaki in the 1500s in this painting on wood panels.

The Closed Country Policy

The persecution of Christians was part of an attempt to control foreign ideas. When Europeans first arrived, no central authority existed to contain them. The strong leaders who later took power did not like the introduction of European ideas and ways, but they valued European trade. As time passed, the Tokugawa shoguns realized that they could safely exclude both the missionaries and the merchants. By 1639, they had sealed Japan's borders and instituted a "closed country policy."

Japan in Isolation Most commercial contacts with Europeans ended. One port, Nagasaki, remained open to foreign traders. But only Dutch and Chinese merchants were allowed into the port. Earlier, the English had left Japan voluntarily, while the Spanish and the Portuguese had been expelled. Since the Tokugawa shoguns controlled Nagasaki, they now had a monopoly on foreign trade, which continued to be profitable.

This painting on wood panels depicts Japanese merchants and Jesuit missionaries awaiting the arrival of a Portuguese ship at Nagasaki in the 1500s.

ADVANCED/GIFTED

Samurai Sayings

1. Before class, print out a variety of quotes or samurai sayings. They are easily found on the Internet. Remind students that samurai considered themselves to be philosophers, and have left behind a number of their ideas.

2. Have students choose one samurai quotation to analyze. Have students copy their chosen quote and explain its meaning. Remind students to consider the time it was written and if it might still be meaningful to people today.

3. Have volunteers share the quotations they selected and their analyses.

STRUGGLING READERS

Changes in Political Stability

1. Tell students that the rise and fall of power were the result of chains of events. Tell students they will create two such chains in class.

2. Write the following title for all to see: "The Collapse of Central Government." Have volunteers share an event or situation that led to the collapse of centralized government in Japan during the feudal period, and add each event to the chain. When finished, arrange the events in order of occurrence and have students copy the information.

3. Next, repeat this process with the following title: "The Establishment of Peaceful Rule."

History in Depth

Zen Buddhism

The form of Buddhism that had the greatest impact on Japanese culture was Zen Buddhism. It especially influenced the samurai.

Zen Buddhists sought spiritual enlightenment through meditation. Strict discipline of mind and body was the Zen path to wisdom. Zen monks would sit in meditation for hours, as shown in the sculpture. If they showed signs of losing concentration, a Zen master might shout at them or hit them with a stick.

For more than 200 years, Japan remained basically closed to Europeans. In addition, the Japanese were forbidden to leave, so they would not bring back foreign ideas. Japan continued to develop, but as a self-sufficient country, free from European attempts to colonize or establish their presence.

Europeans had met with much resistance in their efforts to open the East to trade. But expansion to the West, in the Americas, would prove much more successful for European traders, missionaries, and colonizers.

Reading Check
Form Generalizations Do you think Japan's closed country policy effectively kept Western ideas and customs out of Japan?

Lesson 3 Assessment

1. **Organize Information** Create a two-column graphic organizer similar to the one shown. Fill it in with the names of the Chinese emperors you learned about and a fact or two from the text about each. Which emperor was most influential? Explain by using your facts.

Emperor	Facts
1.	1.
2.	2.
3.	3.

2. **Key Terms and People** For each key term or person in the lesson, write a sentence explaining its significance.

3. **Analyze Effects** What did Christian missionaries bring to China?

4. **Summarize** What was the structure of society in Tokugawa Japan?

5. **Analyze Causes** How did Beijing become the capital of China?

6. **Compare and Contrast** In what ways was the European Renaissance similar to and different from the flowering of Chinese culture during the Ming and Qing dynasties?

7. **Draw Conclusions** Why do you think that the emperor had less power than a shogun?

Print Assessment

1. **Organize Information** Create a two-column graphic organizer similar to the one shown. Fill it in with the names of the Chinese emperors you learned about and a fact or two from the text about each. Which emperor was most influential? Explain by using your facts. *Possible answer: Hongwu—defeated Mongols; ruled 1368–1398; first Ming emperor; encouraged agriculture, Confucian standards, administrative reforms; became brutal. Yonglo—1398, assumed throne; moved capital to Beijing; built Forbidden City; sponsored first Zheng He voyage; increased tributaries. Kangxi—ruled 1661–1722; first Manchu emperor; lowered taxes; defeated Mongols; patronized arts. Qian-long—1736–1795; hard-working; dealt with border unrest and Europeans. Possible explanation: Hongwu because of long-term reforms*

2. **Key Terms and People** For each key term or person in the lesson, write a sentence explaining its significance. *Explanations of the lesson's key terms can be found on the following pages: Ming Dynasty, p. 617; Hongwu, p. 617; Yonglo, p. 618; Zheng He, p. 618; Manchus, p. 623; Qing Dynasty, p. 623; Kangxi, p. 623; daimyo, p. 627; Oda Nobunaga, p. 627; Toyotomi Hideyoshi, p. 627; Tokugawa Shogunate, p. 628; haiku, p. 629; kabuki, p. 630.*

3. **Analyze Effects** What did Christian missionaries bring to China? *Christianity and European inventions*

4. **Summarize** What was the structure of society in Tokugawa Japan? *emperor at the top; next, the shogun; large landowners, the daimyo, followed; next, the samurai warriors; peasants and artisans, followed; merchants at the bottom*

5. **Analyze Causes** How did Beijing become the capital of China? *Yonglo moved the royal court to Beijing.*

6. **Compare and Contrast** In what ways was the European Renaissance similar to and different from the flowering of Chinese culture during the Ming and Qing dynasties? *Possible answer: both tried to connect to earlier traditions; both allowed artists to express themselves; each explored different subjects*

7. **Draw Conclusions** Why do you think that the emperor had less power than a shogun? *Possible answer: The emperor had no army, no control of land; shogun was supreme military commander.*

Expansion, Exploration, and Encounters **633**

---

4. Have students write a paragraph about the causes and effects involved in changes in political stability.

ENGLISH LANGUAGE LEARNERS

Social Structure Chart

1. Organize students into mixed-ability pairs. Tell students that the feudal social structure under the Tokugawa Shogunate was quite rigid.

2. Copy the chart below for students to see, omitting the italicized items. Next to the chart, draw an up-arrow labeled "Most important" and a down-arrow labeled "Least important" to indicate that the higher the role is on the chart, the higher that role was in society.

Have students copy and complete the chart. the higher that role was in society. Have students copy and complete the chart.

Feudal Social Structure	
Title	**Role**
Emperor	*Figurehead ruler*
Shogun	*True ruling power*
Daimyo	*Warlord landowners, owed loyalty to shogun*
Samurai	*Warriors, served the daimyo*
Peasants	*Farmers*
Artisans	*Made goods like armor and swords*
Merchants	*Sold goods, not honored*

▷ Online **Assessment**

1. How did China change following the voyages of Zheng He?
   - ○ China expanded by conquering its neighbors.
   - ○ China opened its borders to foreign settlement.
   - ○ China invited many foreign countries to establish trading outposts.
   - ◉ China closed its borders, fearing barbarian invasions from the north.

   Alternate Question *Select the answer choice from the drop-down list to complete the sentence correctly.*
   Ming emperors rebuilt and expanded sections of the Great Wall because of the continued threats of [*Mongol* ⬍] invasion.

2. Why was the Chinese population slow to accept the Manchu Qing emperors?
   - ◉ The Chinese were resistant to rule by foreigners.
   - ○ The Manchus tried to create a new social structure.
   - ○ The Manchus failed to keep barbarians from invading the south.
   - ○ The Chinese feared that their new rulers would move the capital again.

   Alternate Question *Drag the answer choice into the box to complete the sentence correctly.*
   Rebellions characterized the first years of the Qing Dynasty because the Chinese refused to accept the foreign rule of the _Manchurians_ .

3. Which of the following describes the status of women during the Ming Dynasty?
   - ○ Women were valued as wise political and religious leaders.
   - ○ Women were able to marry for love and divorce their husbands.
   - ○ Women were given greater freedom to travel and own businesses.
   - ◉ Women were expected to care for their children and maintain the household.

   Alternate Question Which jobs were available to women during the Ming Dynasty? Select the three correct answers.

   - ◉ farmers
   - ○ scholars
   - ◉ midwives
   - ○ court advisors
   - ◉ textile workers
   - ○ foreign ambassadors

4. How did Tokugawa Ieyasu pacify Japan after years of internal divisions and warfare?
   - ○ He ruthlessly eliminated all rivals in his government.
   - ○ He defeated his enemies at the decisive Battle of Edo.
   - ◉ He forced the daimyo and their families to live at the capital city.
   - ○ He hired Chinese soldiers to keep the peace throughout the country.

   Alternate Question *Select the answer choice from the drop-down list to complete the sentence correctly.*
   Tokugawa Ieyasu assumed the title of [*shogun* ⬍] after he became the military leader of Japan following the Battle of Sekigahara.

5. Which statement characterizes Tokugawa society?
   - ◉ The shogun controlled the government.
   - ○ Peasants owned more land than the samurai.
   - ○ Merchants were more respected than warriors.
   - ○ The emperor was the most powerful ruler in the country.

   Alternate Question *Drag the individual from Tokugawa society from the highest to lowest rank in the Japanese social pyramid.*

○ emperor	○ shogun
○ daimyo	○ samurai
○ peasant	○ merchant

6. Which development caused the Japanese to become isolationists by the beginning of the 17th century?
   - ○ the importation of the Portuguese cannon
   - ○ the adoption of Chinese cultural influences
   - ○ the continued threats of Mongolian invasion
   - ◉ the growing influence of Christian missionaries

   Alternate Question *Select the answer choice from the drop-down list to complete the sentence correctly.*
   Tokugawa Ieyasu expelled [*Christian* ⬍] missionaries from Japan fearing the growing influence of that religion on his people.

7. Which statement characterizes Japanese commercial policies after 1639?
   - ○ Japan began a period of economic expansion.
   - ○ Japan completely isolated itself from foreign contact.
   - ◉ Japan continued to trade with the Netherlands and China.
   - ○ Japan welcomed Portuguese and Spanish military suppliers.

   Alternate Question *Drag the answer choice into the box to complete the sentence correctly.*
   By the beginning of the 17th century, Japan continued to trade with the _Dutch_ while other European nations were excluded from entering Japanese ports.

8. **Analyze Information** How did the first Ming emperor improve China after he expelled the Mongols?

   Possible answer: Hongwu brought prosperity to a war-ravaged China by restoring the agricultural production of the country. He improved the government by restoring the merit-based promotion system and returning to the moral ideals of Confucius for guidance. Hongwu continued to keep the capital at Nanjing in the south, thus avoiding the upheaval of the resettlement of hundreds of officials.

9. **Compare and Contrast** How did the Dutch and British trading policies with China differ?

   Possible answer: The Dutch traded with the Chinese through ports established and controlled by China. As a result, the Netherlands enjoyed a virtual monopoly of European trade with China and became very wealthy as a result. Great Britain did not like the Chinese trade restrictions and sought to create a market for British goods in China.

10. **Compare and Contrast** How were artistic styles of the Ming and Qing dynasties similar to those of the European Renaissance?

Possible answer: Both Chinese and European artists looked to earlier cultural accomplishments for inspiration and to make a historical connection with their pasts. The artists expressed their individuality either through a personal style of Renaissance painting or through Chinese calligraphy. Both movements stressed the interaction of human nature and art.

11. **Make Judgments** How did the samurai erode the power of the central government during the period of the Warring States?

Possible answer: The samurai were a class of warriors who controlled the peasant population of Japan often through the threat of violence. Samurai served a chieftain, called the daimyo, who controlled rival states throughout Japan. These states continuously fought each other over territory until they were subdued at the Battle of Sekigahara, and the power of the central government under the shogun was restored.

12. **Evaluate** How did Chinese philosophy shape Japanese society during the Tokugawa period?

Possible answer: Confucian philosophy was adopted by the Japanese during the feudal period and it greatly influenced Japanese culture and values. Japanese government was guided by Confucian values. Since the ideal citizen in Confucian philosophy was the hard-working peasant and not the merchant, Japanese society respected peasants more than merchants during the Tokugawa Shogunate.

13. **Cause and Effect** How did contact with Europeans change Japanese warfare?

Possible answer: Prior to contact with the Portuguese, Japanese military technology was primitive. While the samurai were skilled warriors, they relied on bows, arrows, and spears as their weapons of war. When the Portuguese introduced the cannon and muskets to Japan, the medieval style of warfare that had dominated the islands for hundreds of years ended. As well, defensive fortifications were not as effective with the introduction of the cannon.

14. **Evaluate** How did Japanese leaders control the flow of western ideas into their country?

Possible answer: By 1639, the Japanese had closed their ports to all western countries with the exception of the Netherlands. The Netherlands was more interested in trading with Japan and less interested in spreading Christianity. For two hundred years, Japan was isolated and did not allow its citizens to travel abroad. Western influence was closely controlled, and limited to the port of Nagasaki.

Spain Builds an American Empire

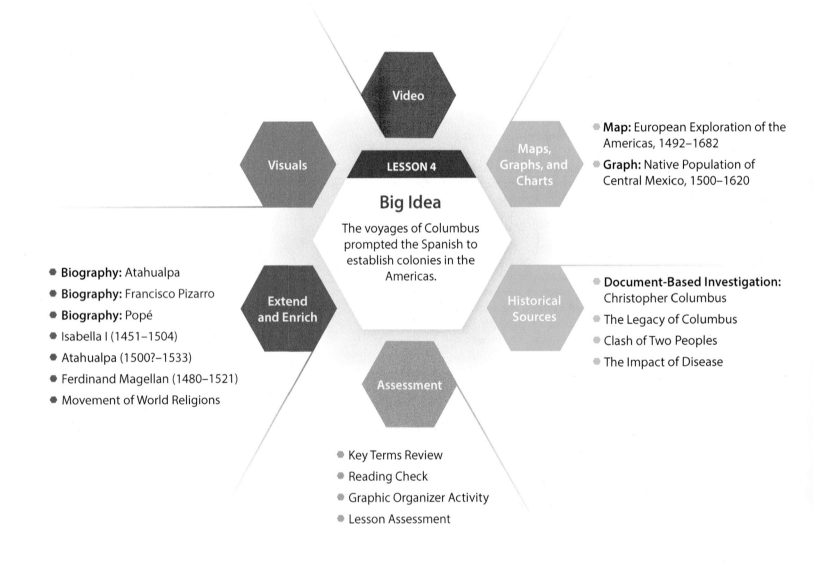

Video

Map: European Exploration of the Americas, 1492–1682

Graph: Native Population of Central Mexico, 1500–1620

Visuals

LESSON 4

Maps, Graphs, and Charts

Big Idea

The voyages of Columbus prompted the Spanish to establish colonies in the Americas.

- **Biography:** Atahualpa
- **Biography:** Francisco Pizarro
- **Biography:** Popé
- Isabella I (1451–1504)
- Atahualpa (1500?–1533)
- Ferdinand Magellan (1480–1521)
- Movement of World Religions

Extend and Enrich

Historical Sources

- **Document-Based Investigation:** Christopher Columbus
- The Legacy of Columbus
- Clash of Two Peoples
- The Impact of Disease

Assessment

- Key Terms Review
- Reading Check
- Graphic Organizer Activity
- Lesson Assessment

▷ Online Lesson 4 Enrichment Activities

Isabella I (1451–1504)

Biography Students read about how Isabella I showed cooperation as she and her husband co-ruled Castile and Aragon. Then students work with a partner to learn more about the reign of Isabella, and create a poster that represents one area in which Isabella had an important effect on life in her kingdom.

Atahualpa (1500?–1533)

Biography Students read about what Atahualpa did to become the sole ruler of the Inca Empire. Then they imagine that they are a reporter at the feast honoring Atahualpa. Students write a paragraph for a newspaper or magazine article about the event.

Ferdinand Magellan (1480–1521)

Biography Students read about Ferdinand Magellan, the Portuguese explorer who led the first circumnavigation of the globe. Then students work in small groups to write a play of Magellan's voyage.

Movement of World Religions

Infographic Students create an infographic that analyzes major territorial transformations and movements of world religions at the end of the 18th century.

Teach the Big Idea

1. **Whole Class Open/Introduction** Ask students how they have experienced Spanish influence in the Americas. *Possible answer: Mexican food, salsa music, language, architecture*

2. **Direct Teach** Read students the Big Idea: *The voyages of Columbus prompted the Spanish to establish colonies in the Americas.* Review the following lesson objectives with students to aid in their understanding of the Big Idea.

   - Describe the voyages of Columbus and his contemporaries.

   - Describe the Spanish conquest of the Aztecs.

   - Explain how the Spanish conquered the Incan Empire in Peru.

   - Identify the effects of Spanish colonization on the Americas.

   - Trace the level of resistance to Spanish rule by indigenous people.

3. **Whole Group Close/Reflect** Have each student choose one of the explorers and write a résumé of his accomplishments. (If necessary, review standard résumé formats with students or provide sample résumés for them to imitate.)

▷ **ONLINE DOCUMENT-BASED INVESTIGATION**

Expansion, Exploration, and Encounters

Christopher Columbus is the fourth of seven document-based investigations that students will analyze in the Expansion, Exploration, and Encounters module. In his journal, Christopher Columbus recounted his first meeting with the native peoples he encountered upon landing in the Caribbean. Students can play the audio to hear the excerpt read aloud.

▷ **ONLINE GRAPHIC ORGANIZER**

Spain Builds an American Empire

As students read the lesson, have them use the graphic organizer to take notes. Students can review their graphic organizer notes at the end of the lesson to answer the following question.

Analyze Effects Which event in the history of Spanish and Portuguese empire-building in the Americas was the most significant? *Columbus's arrival*

Spain Builds an American Empire

The Big Idea
The voyages of Columbus prompted the Spanish to establish colonies in the Americas.

Why It Matters Now
Throughout the Americas, Spanish culture, language, and descendants are the legacy of this period.

Key Terms and People
Christopher Columbus
colony
Hernando Cortés
conquistador
Francisco Pizarro
Atahualpa
mestizo
encomienda

Setting the Stage

Competition for wealth in Asia among European nations was fierce. This competition prompted a Genoese sea captain named **Christopher Columbus** to make a daring voyage from Spain in 1492. Instead of sailing south around Africa and then east, Columbus sailed west across the Atlantic in search of an alternate trade route to Asia and its riches. Columbus never reached Asia. Instead, he stepped onto an island in the Caribbean. That event would bring together the peoples of Europe, Africa, and the Americas.

The Voyages of Columbus

The *Niña*, *Pinta*, and *Santa María* sailed out of a Spanish port around dawn on August 3, 1492. In a matter of months, Columbus's fleet would reach the shores of what Europeans saw as an astonishing new world.

First Encounters In the early hours of October 12, 1492, the long-awaited cry came. A lookout aboard the *Pinta* caught sight of a shoreline in the distance. "*Tierra! Tierra!*" he shouted. "Land! Land!" By dawn, Columbus and his crew were ashore. Thinking he had successfully reached the East Indies, Columbus called the surprised inhabitants who greeted him *los indios*. The term translated into "Indian," a word mistakenly applied to all the native peoples of the Americas. In his journal, Columbus recounted his first meeting with the native peoples:

"I presented them with some red caps, and strings of glass beads to wear upon the neck, and many other trifles of small value, wherewith they were much delighted, and became wonderfully attached to us. Afterwards they came swimming to the boats where we were, bringing parrots, balls of cotton thread,

---

COLLABORATIVE LEARNING

Objective Reporting

1. Divide students into small groups. Tell students each group will create a news segment reporting on one event involving the Spanish conquest of the New World. The report should be directed toward the citizens of Spain and take place shortly after the event occurs.

2. Have group members assign themselves roles as researchers, writers, reporters, and anchors.

3. Give students time to research and prepare their news segments. One or more students in each group should prepare visuals to present as part of the newscast.

4. Have each group present its newscast to the class. Afterward, allow the class to critique the objectivity of the news report. Students should assess whether they think the report took into account the perspectives of both the Spaniards and native populations.

5. Ask students to discuss whether they think it's likely that historians have access to enough source materials to construct an objective report of these events.

javelins, and many other things which they exchanged for articles we gave them . . . In fact they accepted anything and gave what they had with the utmost good will."

—Christopher Columbus, *Journal of Columbus*

Portrait of a Man Called Christopher Columbus (1519) by Sebastiano del Piombo

Columbus had miscalculated where he was. He had not reached the East Indies. Scholars believe he landed instead on an island in the Bahamas in the Caribbean Sea. The natives there were not Indians, but a group who called themselves the Taino. Nonetheless, Columbus claimed the island for Spain. He named it San Salvador, or "Holy Savior."

Columbus, like other explorers, was interested in gold. Finding none on San Salvador, he explored other islands, staking his claim to each one. "It was my wish to bypass no island without taking possession," he wrote.

In early 1493, Columbus returned to Spain. The reports he relayed about his journey delighted the Spanish monarchs. King Ferdinand and Queen Isabella, who had funded his first voyage, agreed to finance three more trips. Their sponsorship was a major motivation for Columbus to continue his explorations.

Columbus embarked on his second voyage to the Americas in September 1493. He journeyed no longer as an explorer, but as an empire builder. He commanded a fleet of some 17 ships that carried over 1,000 soldiers, crewmen, and colonists. The Spanish intended to transform the islands of the Caribbean into **colonies**, or lands that are controlled by another nation. Over the next two centuries, other European explorers began sailing across the Atlantic in search of new lands to claim.

Other Explorers Take to the Seas By the 15th century, the political system in Portugal, headed by King John II, gave strong support to exploration of the Americas. Portugal had already established trading outposts in Africa and Asia, and the Treaty of Tordesillas allowed the king to claim Brazil. In 1500, the Portuguese explorer Pedro Álvares Cabral reached the shores of modern-day Brazil and claimed the land for his country. A year later, Amerigo Vespucci (vehs•POO•chee), an Italian in the service of Portugal, also traveled along the eastern coast of South America. Upon his return to Europe, he claimed that the land was not part of Asia, but a "new" world. In 1507, a German mapmaker named the new continent "America" in honor of Amerigo Vespucci.

In 1519, Portuguese explorer Ferdinand Magellan led the boldest exploration yet. Several years earlier, Spanish explorer Vasco Núñez de Balboa had marched through modern-day Panama and had become the first European to gaze upon the Pacific Ocean. Soon after, Magellan convinced the king of Spain to fund his voyage into the newly discovered ocean.

Objectives

You may wish to discuss the following questions with students to help them frame the content as they read.

- Why were the Spanish interested in establishing colonies in the Americas? *influence, prestige, to gain wealth*
- What actions showed that Columbus had an interest in empire even on his first voyage? *He wanted to take possession of every island he passed and claim it for Spain.*

More About . . .

Magellan Although Balboa was the first European to see the Pacific Ocean, Magellan named it. After sailing through the stormy Atlantic, Magellan rounded the tip of South America and sailed into a quiet sea, which he named *Pacific*, meaning "peaceful."

▶ ONLINE DOCUMENT-BASED INVESTIGATION

Christopher Columbus

Have students study the image and read the excerpt from Christopher Columbus's journal. In his journal, Columbus recounted his first meeting with the native peoples he encountered upon landing in the Caribbean. Students can play the audio to hear the excerpt read aloud.

Analyze Sources How did Columbus characterize his initial contact with the Native Americans he encountered? *Columbus reported that their initial contact was very friendly and positive.*

DOCUMENT-BASED INVESTIGATION   HISTORICAL SOURCE

Christopher Columbus

In his journal, Christopher Columbus recounted his first meeting with the native peoples he encountered upon landing in the Caribbean.

▶ ONLINE LESSON FLIP CARDS

Review Key Terms and People

Students can use the flip cards in the Lesson Review at any time to review the lesson's key terms and people: *Christopher Columbus, colony, Hernando Cortés, conquistador, Francisco Pizarro, Atahualpa, mestizo,* and *encomienda.*

The Legacy of Columbus

Invite students to read the two excerpts and answer the associated question.

Analyze Sources From Samuel Eliot Morison's perspective, was the legacy of Columbus a positive or negative thing? *According to Samuel Eliot Morison, the legacy of Columbus was unreservedly positive.*

European Exploration of the Americas, 1492–1682

Have students explore the map using the interactive features and answer the associated questions.

Interpret Maps Which area of the present-day United States did the English explore? *New England*

In print edition, see map of same title.

Movement How many different voyages did Columbus make to the Americas? *four*

Region Which general region did the Spanish and Portuguese explore? Where did the English, Dutch, and French explore? *The Spanish and Portuguese explored South and Central America; the English, Dutch, French, and Spanish explored North America.*

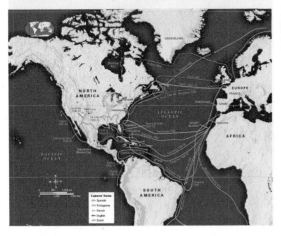

READING CHECK

Make Inferences What was the significance of Magellan's voyage? *It was the first voyage around the globe.*

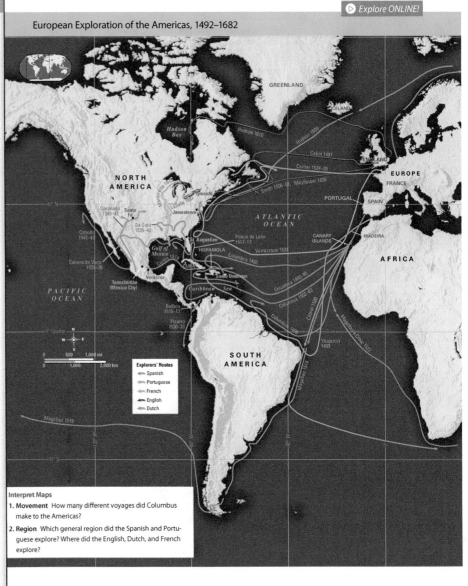

Explore ONLINE!

European Exploration of the Americas, 1492–1682

Interpret Maps
1. **Movement** How many different voyages did Columbus make to the Americas?
2. **Region** Which general region did the Spanish and Portuguese explore? Where did the English, Dutch, and French explore?

636 Module 16

ADVANCED/GIFTED

Eyewitness to History

1. Have students read the excerpt from Columbus's journal in the lesson to get a feel for Columbus's writing. Then have them use the Internet or books to find other primary sources, such as Columbus's letters.

2. Have students create a short news report on the breaking story of Columbus's discoveries. Students may write for any medium they choose—print, radio, or television.

3. Encourage students to think about how to include quotations from their sources and visuals such as illustrations or maps. They could write a straight factual report; an investigative report on some aspect of the story, such as who is profiting from the discovery of gold; or an editorial expressing an opinion about the consequences of this event. Another angle is to write about how news of Columbus's discoveries was spreading across Europe and the impact the story was having.

4. Have students present their reports to the class.

With about 250 men and five ships, Magellan sailed around the southern end of South America and into the waters of the Pacific. The fleet sailed for months without seeing land, except for some small islands. Food supplies soon ran out.

After exploring the island of Guam, Magellan and his crew eventually reached the Philippines. Unfortunately, Magellan became involved in a local war there and was killed. His crew, greatly reduced by disease and starvation, continued sailing west toward home. Out of Magellan's original crew, only 18 men and one ship arrived back in Spain in 1522, nearly three years after they had left. They were the first persons to circumnavigate, or sail around, the world.

Reading Check
Make Inferences
What was the significance of Magellan's voyage?

Spanish Conquests in Mexico

In 1519, as Magellan embarked on his historic voyage, a Spaniard named **Hernando Cortés** landed on the shores of Mexico. After colonizing several Caribbean islands, the Spanish had turned their attention to the American mainland. Cortés marched inland, looking to claim new lands for Spain. Cortés and the many other Spanish explorers who followed him were known as **conquistadors** (conquerors). Lured by rumors of vast lands filled with gold and silver, conquistadors carved out colonies in regions that would become Mexico, South America, and the United States. The Spanish were the first European settlers in the Americas. As a result of their colonization, the Spanish greatly enriched their empire and left a mark on the cultures of North and South America that exists today.

Cortés Conquers the Aztecs Soon after landing in Mexico in 1519, Cortés learned of the vast and wealthy Aztec Empire in the region's interior. After marching for weeks through difficult mountain passes, Cortés and his force of roughly 600 men finally reached the magnificent Aztec capital of Tenochtitlán (teh•NAWCH•tee•TLAHN). The Aztec emperor, Montezuma II, was convinced at first that Cortés was an armor-wearing god. He agreed to give the Spanish explorer a share of the empire's existing gold supply. Though Montezuma hoped that would satisfy Cortés, it did not. Cortés admitted that he and his comrades had a "disease of the heart that only gold can cure." In both the political and economic sense, Cortés wanted more power.

The Aztecs controlled hundreds of smaller surrounding cities. They gained economic power by demanding periodic payments from these conquered communities. The Spaniards disrupted this system of tribute as they invaded areas that had been under Aztec control. Many peoples from these areas were willing to ally themselves with Cortés as he sought to conquer Tenochtitlán.

The Spaniards largely destroyed Aztec culture. For example, the Aztecs maintained a series of painted books called codices. Codices described Aztec history, economy, religious beliefs, and daily life. They were written in a largely pictorial language, and Aztec cultural tradition dictated that a codex was to be read aloud to others. The Spaniards destroyed almost all of the Aztec codices. They also razed temples and other significant places.

Expansion, Exploration, and Encounters **637**

Objectives

You may wish to discuss the following questions with students to help them frame the content as they read.

- What fate was shared by the Aztecs and the natives who fought with the Spanish against them? *Both died from European diseases.*
- Why might Montezuma have thought Cortés was a god? *Possible answer: His white skin made him seem otherworldly. European weapons seemed to work by magic.*

More About . . .

Tenochtitlán In his letters, Hernán Cortés described Tenochtitlán: "This city has many squares where trading is done and markets are held continuously. There is also one square . . . where every kind of merchandise produced in these lands is found. . . . There are shops like apothecaries', where they sell ready-made medicines as well as liquid ointments and plasters. There are shops like barbers' where they have their hair washed and shaved, and shops where they sell food and drink."

Aztec and Inca Unrest in the Aztec and Inca empires contributed to their defeat by the Spanish. Both groups had built their empires in the 1400s, often through the conquest of their neighbors, and both had to put down frequent rebellions in the decades that followed. The Inca were in the midst of a civil war when the Spanish arrived in 1530. Cortés and Pizarro exploited such tensions among native peoples to gain control of both empires.

▷ ONLINE HISTORICAL SOURCES

Clash of Two Peoples

Invite students to view the image and answer the associated question.

Analyze Sources How does the artist depict the clash of Aztec and Spanish cultures? *The two groups are meeting as warriors with weapons drawn.*

▷ ONLINE HISTORICAL SOURCES

The Impact of Disease

Invite students to view the image and answer the associated question.

Analyze Sources Which aspect of the legacy of Columbus does the illustration show? *The illustration shows the effect of smallpox—a disease brought by Europeans to the Americas—upon Native Americans.*

COLLABORATIVE LEARNING

Display Explorers' Sailing Ships

1. Divide students into groups. Have them use the Internet, encyclopedias, or library resources to find out about the design of ships and conditions on board during the time period shown on the map.

2. Next, have students draw pictures or make mockups of the ships.

3. Ask students to think about why there were frequent mutinies on the ships. *(terrible conditions—tight quarters, bad food, lack of fresh water, harsh work, stormy weather—and uncertainty about where they were going)* Help students design a space in the classroom for the mockups or graphics of these ships as well as the accompanying information.

Objectives

You may wish to discuss the following questions with students to help them frame the content as they read.

- What might the Inca have thought of the Spaniards' character? *Possible answer: brutal, untrustworthy*

- What comparisons and contrasts can you make between the Spanish and the Portuguese? *Possible answer: Both established colonies and exploited people to gain wealth—Spanish from gold, Portuguese from sugar.*

More About . . .

The Reconquista Literally meaning "reconquest," the *reconquista* began in the eighth century shortly after the Muslims conquered most of the Iberian Peninsula. The movement peaked in the 11th to 13th centuries. The last state to fall was Granada, defeated under Ferdinand and Isabella in 1492.

Peninsulares *Peninsulares* were Spanish colonists born in Spain, so called because they came from the Iberian Peninsula. In the colonies, they occupied the highest rank on the social scale and discriminated against those of Spanish descent born in the Americas.

▷ ONLINE INTERACTIVE GRAPHS

Native Population of Central Mexico, 1500–1620

Have students explore the graph and answer the associated questions.

Interpret Graphs By what percentage did the population decrease between 1519 and 1605? *96 percent*

In print edition, see graph titled Native Population of Central Mexico, 1500–1620.

Draw Conclusions By what percentage did the native population decrease between 1519 and 1605? *96 percent*

Make Inferences How did the sharp decline in the native population, due greatly to disease, affect the Spaniards' attempts to conquer the region? *The natives offered little resistance.*

READING CHECK
Summarize What factors enabled the Spanish to defeat the Aztecs? *superior weaponry, help from other natives, and the spread of European diseases*

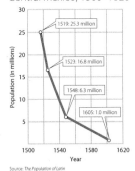

Native Population of Central Mexico, 1500–1620

- 1519: 25.3 million
- 1523: 16.8 million
- 1548: 6.3 million
- 1605: 1.0 million

Population (in millions) / Year

Source: *The Population of Latin America: A History*

Interpret Graphs
1. **Draw Conclusions** By what percentage did the native population decrease between 1519 and 1605?
2. **Make Inferences** How did the sharp decline in the native population, mainly from disease, affect the Spaniards' attempts to conquer the region?

Reading Check
Summarize What factors enabled the Spanish to defeat the Aztecs?

In November 1519, Cortés captured Montezuma II. The following spring, some of Cortés's men killed many Aztec warriors and chiefs while they were celebrating a religious festival. Then, in June 1520, the Aztecs rebelled against the Spanish intruders and drove out Cortés's forces.

The Spaniards, however, struck back. Despite being greatly outnumbered, Cortés and his men conquered the Aztecs in 1521. Several factors played a key role in the stunning victory. First, the Spanish had the advantage of superior weaponry. Aztec arrows were no match for the Spaniards' muskets and cannons.

Second, Cortés was able to enlist the help of various native groups. With the aid of a native woman interpreter named Malinche, Cortés learned that some natives resented the Aztecs. They hated their harsh practices, including human sacrifice. Through Malinche, Cortés convinced these natives to fight on his side.

Finally, and most important, the natives could do little to stop the invisible warrior that marched alongside the Spaniards—disease. Measles, mumps, smallpox, and typhus were just some of the diseases Europeans brought with them to the Americas. Native Americans had never been exposed to these diseases. Thus, they had developed no natural immunity to them. As a result, they died by the hundreds of thousands. By the time Cortés launched his counterattack, the Aztec population had been greatly reduced by smallpox and measles. In time, European disease would truly devastate the natives of central Mexico, killing millions of them.

Spanish Conquests in Peru

In 1532, another Spanish conquistador, **Francisco Pizarro**, marched a small force into South America. He conquered the Incan Empire and destroyed its culture, economy, and society.

Pizarro Subdues the Inca Pizarro and his army of about 200 met the Incan ruler, **Atahualpa** (AH·tuh·WAHL·puh), near the city of Cajamarca. Atahualpa, who commanded a force of about 30,000, brought several thousand mostly unarmed men for the meeting. The Spaniards waited in ambush, crushed the Incan force, and kidnapped Atahualpa.

The Spaniards then moved into the smaller surrounding cities that were under Incan control and plundered them of gold and silver. Not only was this economically devastating for the Incan Empire, but it was also a cultural blow: the gold and silver had adorned Incan temples and buildings that were destroyed during the looting.

STRUGGLING READERS

After 1492

1. Have students create a timeline of events in the Americas in the years immediately following Columbus's arrival.

2. Tell students that their timelines should include the conquest of the Aztec and Inca empires, as well as important explorations that took place during this time.

3. Guide a class discussion about what happened in the Americas between 1492 and 1550. What effects did these events have on Native Americans and Europeans?

While in captivity, Atahualpa offered to fill a room once with gold and twice with silver in exchange for his release. However, after receiving the ransom, the Spanish strangled the Incan king and burned his body, which was culturally forbidden by the Inca.

With these acts, the Spanish debilitated the Incan political organization. It signaled the beginning of the end of Incan culture. The remaining Incan force, demoralized by their leader's death, retreated from Cajamarca. Pizarro then marched on the Incan capital, Cuzco. He captured it without a struggle in 1533. From Cuzco, Pizarro established a new government that offered Incan lands to Spanish conquerors.

As Cortés and Pizarro conquered the civilizations of the Americas, fellow conquistadors defeated other native peoples. Spanish explorers also conquered the Maya in Yucatan and Guatemala. By the middle of the 16th century, Spain had created an American empire. It included New Spain (Mexico and parts of Guatemala), as well as other lands in Central and South America and the Caribbean.

Spain's Pattern of Conquest In building their new American empire, the Spaniards drew from techniques used during the *reconquista* of Spain. When conquering the Muslims, the Spanish lived among them and imposed their Spanish culture upon them. Spanish settlers in the Americas, known as *peninsulares*, were mostly men. As a result,

BIOGRAPHY

Francisco Pizarro
(1475?–1541)

Pizarro was the son of an infantry captain and a young peasant woman. His parents never married. Raised by his mother's poor family, he never learned to read. Ambitious, brave, and ruthless, he intended to make his fortune as an explorer and conqueror.

As Pizarro embarked on a voyage of conquest down the west coast of South America, the governor of Panama ordered him to abandon the expedition to prevent the loss of lives. Pizarro took his sword and drew a line in the dust, inviting those of his followers who desired wealth and fame to cross the line and follow him. Thus began the conquest of Peru.

Pizarro founded the city of Lima, Peru's capital, in 1535. He became governor of Peru and encouraged settlers from Spain.

Atahualpa
(1502?–1533)

Atahualpa was the last ruler of the Incan empire in Peru. After Atahualpa was captured and held for ransom by the Spanish, Incan people throughout the empire brought gold and silver that the Spanish then melted down into bullion and ingots. They accumulated 24 tons of gold and silver, the richest ransom in history.

The Spanish executed Atahualpa despite the ransom paid by his people. As he was about to be burned at the stake, the Spanish offered him a more merciful death by strangulation if he agreed to convert to Christianity, which he did. Thus died the last emperor of the Inca.

BIOGRAPHY

Francisco Pizarro

Have students read the biography of Francisco Pizarro, Spanish conquistador, conqueror of Peru, and founder of Lima, Peru. From 1530 to 1533, he conquered the Inca Empire.

BIOGRAPHY

Atahualpa

Have students read the biography of Atahualpa, the last Incan king.

Express Opinions Visually

1. Have students search for paintings online that depict the meeting of Cortés and Montezuma. Ask students if they think there is any bias in the paintings they found. *(For example, many paintings favored the Spanish because they depicted the Aztecs as submissive.)*

2. Discuss some of the ways the natives might have seen things differently. *(The Aztec and Incan civilizations were advanced, with great cities and much wealth. They saw their offers of friendship met with betrayal. They saw their people dying.)*

3. Then ask students to imagine they are Aztec and Incan artists at the time of the conquest of the Americas. Ask students to draw editorial cartoons that depict the explorers and their actions from the point of view of the people already living in the Americas. The cartoons may be funny or angry, as long as each one expresses an opinion.

4. Display the cartoons in the classroom.

Objectives

You may wish to discuss the following questions with students to help them frame the content as they read.

- How were conquistadors and Spanish missionaries similar? *Both wanted to convert native peoples to Christianity.*

- In what way was Coronado's journey pivotal in Spain's settlement of the southwestern United States? *His failure to find gold caused the Spanish to assign more priests than soldiers there.*

More About . . .

Coronado Coronado came to New Spain in 1535. He was lured to explore the north in 1540 by reports of the fabled wealth of the Seven Golden Cities of Cibola. Instead, he found the Zuni Pueblo. One of the members of Coronado's expedition was the first European to see the Grand Canyon in Arizona.

Spanish Missions Most of the Spanish missions were located in the area between Texas and California. The priests tried to persuade local Indians from miles around to move to these agricultural settlements and adopt Spanish ways, including Christianity. As was true elsewhere, most natives died from European diseases. The more well-known and successful California missions were established in the 18th century. Several became the basis for later cities, including Los Angeles.

READING CHECK

Form Generalizations What was the effect of Portuguese sugar plantations on native peoples in Brazil? *Ever-expanding sugar plantations required workers; the Portuguese captured native peoples in Brazil for that purpose, decimating native cultures in the process.*

---

relationships between Spanish settlers and native women were common. These relationships created a large **mestizo**—or mixed Spanish and Native American—population.

Although the Spanish conquerors lived among the native people, they also oppressed them. In their effort to exploit the land for its precious resources, the Spanish enslaved Native Americans, forcing them to work within a system known as *encomienda*. Under this system, natives farmed, ranched, or mined for Spanish landlords. These landlords had received the rights to the natives' labor from Spanish authorities. The holders of *encomiendas* promised the Spanish rulers that they would act fairly and respect the workers. However, many abused the natives and worked laborers to death, especially inside dangerous mines.

The Portuguese in Brazil One area of South America that remained outside of Spanish control was Brazil. In 1500, the Portuguese king ordered Pedro Álvares Cabral to further explore Africa and Asia, but Cabral landed in Brazil instead. Portugal promptly claimed the land for itself.

Colonization of Brazil took decades to develop because Portugal's political systems there were very poor. Portugal was then at the height of its world power and had bigger concerns than establishing permanent colonies in Brazil.

During the 1530s, however, the Portuguese began settling the country's coastal region. Finding little gold or silver, the colonists grew sugar. Clearing out huge swaths of forest land, the Portuguese built giant sugar plantations. The demand for sugar in Europe was great, and the colony soon enriched Portugal.

By the year 1600, thousands of Portuguese were living in Brazil. Economic and political power was held by a small number of wealthy plantation owners. The plantations required extensive labor, and the Portuguese colonists enslaved both Native Americans and Africans to work them. In time, the Portuguese colonists pushed farther west. They settled even more land for the production of sugar, increasing demand for more native and African slaves.

To find more natives, large groups of Portuguese settlers were organized into *bandeiras*. *Bandeiras* were slave-hunting expeditions that explored western Brazil, searching for natives who could be captured and put to work on sugar plantations. Naturally, the natives resisted, and violent skirmishes often broke out. The *bandeiras* had the dual effect of settling more of Brazil's land for Portugal and destroying the lives and cultures of many native peoples.

Spain's Influence Expands

Spain's American colonies helped make it the richest, most powerful nation in the world during much of the 16th century. Ships filled with treasures from the Americas continually sailed into Spanish harbors. This newfound wealth helped usher in a golden age of art and culture in Spain.

Throughout the 16th century, Spain also increased its military might. To protect its treasure-filled ships, Spain built a powerful navy. The

Reading Check
Form Generalizations
What was the effect of Portuguese sugar plantations on native peoples in Brazil?

ENGLISH LANGUAGE LEARNERS

Understand English Words That Have Spanish Origins

1. Use the Spanish words in this lesson as a springboard to consider the many English words that come from Spanish. Beginning with the words *mestizo* and *encomienda*, students can use a Spanish-English dictionary to find the meaning of each and then write each on a word chart like the one shown below.

2. Then suggest that students consider words that are identified with the American Southwest—*corral, mesa, lariat, mustang, canyon, arroyo, machete,* *tortilla, patio, fiesta, stampede, burro, adobe, padre, plaza,* and others. Have them look up each word in a dictionary to see if the original Spanish word is the same as or different from the form used in English and what the word originally meant. Have them also enter this information on the chart.

English Word/ Definition	Spanish Word	Meaning
Mustang: half-wild horse	mestengo	untamed

Spanish also strengthened their other military forces, creating a skillful and determined army. For a century and a half, Spain's army seldom lost a battle. Meanwhile, Spain enlarged its American empire by settling in parts of what is now the United States.

Conquistadors Push North Dreams of new conquests prompted Spain to back a series of expeditions into the southwestern United States. The Spanish actually had settled in parts of the United States before they even dreamed of building an empire on the American mainland. In 1513, Spanish explorer Juan Ponce de León landed on the coast of modern-day Florida and claimed it for Spain.

This U.S. postage stamp was issued in 1940 to celebrate the 400th anniversary of the Coronado expedition.

By 1540, after building an empire that stretched from Mexico to Peru, the Spanish once again looked to the land that is now the United States. In 1540–1541, Francisco Vásquez de Coronado led an expedition throughout much of present-day Arizona, New Mexico, Texas, Oklahoma, and Kansas. He was searching for another wealthy empire to conquer. Coronado found little gold amidst the dry deserts of the Southwest. As a result, the Spanish monarchy assigned mostly priests to explore and colonize the future United States.

Catholic priests had accompanied conquistadors from the very beginning of American colonization. The conquistadors had come in search of wealth. The priests who accompanied them had religious motives. The priests had come in search of converts, and they found such converts among the native people.

A group's spiritual beliefs are an essential part of its culture. As the priests converted Native Americans to the Catholic religion and Christianity spread, indigenous cultures faced significant consequences. For example, many Native Americans were forced to leave their homes and move somewhere else. Still others were forcefully put to work.

In the winter of 1609–1610, Pedro de Peralta, governor of Spain's northern holdings in New Mexico, led settlers to a tributary on the upper Rio Grande. They built a capital called Santa Fe, or "Holy Faith." In the next two decades, a string of Christian missions arose among the Pueblo, the native inhabitants of the region. Scattered missions, forts, and small ranches dotted the lands of New Mexico. These became the headquarters for advancing the Catholic religion.

Reading Check
Contrast How did Spain's colony in New Mexico differ from its colonies in New Spain?

Opposition to Spanish Rule

Spanish priests worked to spread Christianity in the Americas. They also pushed for better treatment of Native Americans. Priests spoke out against the cruel treatment of natives. In particular, they criticized the harsh pattern of labor that emerged under the *encomienda* system. "There is nothing more detestable or more cruel," Dominican monk Bartolomé de Las Casas wrote, "than the tyranny which the Spaniards use toward the Indians for the getting of pearl [riches]."

Expansion, Exploration, and Encounters **641**

Objectives
You may wish to discuss the following questions with students to help them frame the content as they read.

- How did the end of the *encomienda* system lead to the use of enslaved Africans? *Indians could not be forced to work, so the Spaniards imported Africans.*

- Why was the Pueblo victory over the Spaniards in 1680 significant? *showed that Spain was not invincible and that even after 70 years the Spanish had not subdued the natives*

More About . . .

Pueblo Resistance The Pueblo Indians sought to wipe out all traces of Spanish religion and culture. Popé had his followers burn Christian images, churches, rosaries, and crosses. He did not allow the teaching of the Spanish language, and he destroyed Spanish agriculture.

READING CHECK
Contrast How did Spain's colony in New Mexico differ from its colonies in New Spain? *New Mexico offered little in the way of wealth, so the Spanish were more concerned there with spreading the Catholic religion.*

LINK TO SCIENCE

Gold Deposits and Plate Tectonics

1. Explain to students that if Coronado and his men had had a modern understanding of plate tectonics, they might have found gold in the United States. Geologists have learned that many gold deposits are at the present or former boundaries of the earth's slowly moving plates. The reason for this is not fully known. But a look at a gold distribution map shows that major sources of gold lie along the Sierra Nevada in the western United States and along the Sierra Madre and Andes ranges in Mexico and South America, just where the Aztecs and Inca lived.

2. Have students work in pairs to research the geology of the Sierra Nevada. Ask them to locate gold mines in this region. (It was the center of the 19th-century gold rush.)

3. Then have students research the route of Coronado's expedition. Have them use a physical map of North America to compare Coronado's route and the location of gold.

Popé

Have students read the biography of Popé, the Pueblo who was captured by Spanish colonists but led a successful revolt against them in 1680.

Legacy of Columbus

Invite students to read the excerpts and answer the associated questions.

1. From Samuel Eliot Morison's perspective, is the legacy of Columbus positive or negative? *According to Samuel Eliot Morison, the legacy of Columbus was unreservedly positive.*

2. How does Justin Winsor's opinion show that perspectives about Columbus have evolved over time? What is meant by Columbus's *rectitude*? How does that word support Winsor's perspective? *Justin Winsor, unlike Morison, sees the legacy of Columbus as disastrous. Comparing the two shows that perspectives about Columbus have not always stayed the same. Rectitude refers to one's integrity or virtue. Winsor uses the word to illustrate Columbus's arrogance and overconfidence and support the conclusion that Columbus made disastrous, long-lasting decisions.*

Historical Source

Legacy of Columbus

Historical and contemporary perspectives on Christopher Columbus's voyages have evolved, and the legacy of the voyages is debated. By their nature, interpretations of historical events are limited because they arise from a person's particular frame of reference.

The credibility, or believability, of the participants must be considered as well. For example, you might question the credibility of someone whose writing betrays a clear political bias. Conversely, you may be likely to trust the perspective of someone who lived through a historical event.

Some historians argue that Columbus took heroic first steps in the creation of great and democratic societies, while others claim that Columbus launched an era of widespread cruelty, bloodshed, and epidemic disease.

Samuel Eliot Morison, a supporter of Columbus writing in the 1940s, laments that Columbus died without realizing the true greatness of his deeds.

In 1892, historian Justin Winsor was one of the first American writers to criticize Columbus. William D. Phillips summarized Winsor's critique.

> "One only wishes that the Admiral might have been afforded the sense of fulfillment that would have come from foreseeing all that flowed from his discoveries; that would have turned all the sorrows of his last years to joy. The whole history of the Americas stems from the Four Voyages of Columbus; and as the Greek city-states looked back to the deathless gods as their founders, so today a score of independent nations and dominions unite in homage to Christopher, the stout-hearted son of Genoa, who carried Christian civilization across the Ocean Sea."
>
> —Samuel Eliot Morison, *Admiral of the Ocean: A Life of Christopher Columbus*

> "He [Winsor] portrayed Columbus as a daring mariner with great powers of persuasion and extraordinary dedication to his goals. Winsor also revealed Columbus as an inept administrator, so sure of his own rectitude that he openly disobeyed royal instructions and brought many of his troubles on himself. Among his other failings, Columbus unashamedly waged war against the native inhabitants of the Caribbean and enslaved hundreds of them, hoping to profit from a transatlantic slave trade."
>
> —William D. Phillips, *The Worlds of Christopher Columbus*

Analyze Historical Sources
1. From Samuel Eliot Morison's perspective, is the legacy of Columbus positive or negative?
2. How does Justin Winsor's opinion show that perspectives about Columbus have evolved over time? What is meant by Columbus's *rectitude*? How does that word support Winsor's perspective?

642 Module 16

Aztec and Inca Civilizations

1. Have students research at least one aspect of either the Aztec or Inca civilization at the time the conquistadors first arrived, such as religion, architecture, or agriculture.

2. Tell students that they are members of either Cortés's expedition in Mexico or Pizarro's expedition in Peru, depending on which they researched. Have them write a series of journal entries describing the civilization they discovered from the point of view of a 16th-century European encountering it for the first time.

3. Have volunteers read their entries to the class. Guide a discussion of Aztec and Inca cultures based on students' research. How were these cultures different from the culture of the Europeans who conquered them?

African Slavery and Native Resistance The Spanish government abolished the *encomienda* system in 1542. To meet the colonies' need for labor, Las Casas suggested Africans. "The labor of one [African] . . . [is] more valuable than that of four Indians," he said. The priest later changed his view and denounced African slavery. However, others promoted it.

Opposition to the Spanish method of colonization came not only from Spanish priests, but also from the natives themselves. Resistance to Spain's attempt at domination began shortly after the Spanish arrived in the Caribbean. In November 1493, Columbus encountered resistance in his attempt to conquer the present-day island of St. Croix. Before finally surrendering, the inhabitants defended themselves by firing poison arrows.

As late as the end of the 17th century, natives in New Mexico fought Spanish rule. Although they were not risking their lives in silver mines, the natives still felt the weight of Spanish force. In converting the natives, Spanish priests and soldiers burned their sacred objects and prohibited native rituals. The Spanish also forced natives to work for them and sometimes abused them physically.

In 1680, Popé, a Pueblo ruler, led a well-organized rebellion against the Spanish. The rebellion involved more than 8,000 warriors from villages all over New Mexico. The native fighters drove the Spanish back into New Spain. For the next 12 years, until the Spanish regained control of the area, the southwest region of the future United States once again belonged to its original inhabitants.

By this time, however, the rulers of Spain had far greater concerns. The other nations of Europe had begun to establish their own colonies in the Americas.

Sculpture of Pueblo leader Popé

Reading Check
Analyze Causes
Why did the natives of New Mexico revolt against Spanish settlers?

Lesson 4 Assessment

1. Organize Information Create a graphic organizer similar to the one below and place the following events in chronological order: Pizarro conquers the Inca; Columbus's arrival; conquistadors explore and colonize the southwest United States; Cortés defeats the Aztecs. Which event do you think had the greatest impact?

> Columbus arrives in Americas, 1492

2. Key Terms and People For each key term or person in the lesson, write a sentence explaining its significance.
3. Summarize Why were most of the Spanish explorers drawn to the Americas?
4. Synthesize Which country was the richest and most powerful in the 16th century, and why?
5. Analyze Primary Sources Reread the excerpt from the *Journal of Columbus*. When Columbus described the Taino, what part of his description might have convinced the Spanish that they could take advantage of the natives?
6. Compare and Contrast What might have been some similarities in character between Cortés and Pizarro?

COLLABORATIVE LEARNING

Govern the Spanish Colonies in America

1. Guide students in a discussion of the *encomienda* system. How did the intentions of the *encomienda* system compare with the reality of it?

2. Tell small groups of students they are advisers to the Spanish monarchs charged with developing a new system to replace the *encomienda* system. Have each group write a plan that will treat Native Americans well and still allow development of the colonies.

READING CHECK
Analyze Causes Why did the natives of New Mexico revolt against Spanish settlers? *Spanish attempts to destroy their culture and repressive measures, including beatings*

Print Assessment

1. **Organize Information** Create a graphic organizer similar to the one below and place the following events in chronological order: Pizarro conquers the Inca; Columbus's arrival; conquistadors explore and colonize the southwest United States; Cortés defeats the Aztecs. Which event do you think had the greatest impact? *Possible answer: In order: Columbus's arrival (1492); Cortés defeats the Aztecs (1521); Pizarro conquers the Inca (1533); conquistadors explore and colonize the southwest United States (1540–1541). Greatest impact: Columbus's arrival*

2. **Key Terms and People** For each key term or person in the lesson, write a sentence explaining its significance. *Explanations of the lesson's key terms can be found on the following pages: Christopher Columbus, p. 634; colony, p. 635; Hernando Cortés, p. 637; conquistador, p. 637; Francisco Pizarro, p. 638; Atahualpa, p. 638; mestizo, p. 640; encomienda, p. 640.*

3. **Summarize** Why were most of the Spanish explorers drawn to the Americas? *lured by gold, silver, and land*

4. **Synthesize** Which country was the richest and most powerful in the 16th century, and why? *Spain, because of its colonies and the wealth they provided*

5. **Analyze Primary Sources** Reread the excerpt from the *Journal of Columbus*. When Columbus described the Taino, what part of his description might have convinced the Spanish that they could take advantage of the natives? *Possible answer: the Taino's generosity and peacefulness perhaps seen as gullibility and docility*

6. **Compare and Contrast** What might have been some similarities in character between Cortés and Pizarro? *ambitious, adventurous, ruthless*

▷ Online Assessment

1. Where did Christopher Columbus expect to land?
   - ○ in the islands of East Asia
   - ○ on the southern coast of Africa
   - ○ in the islands of the Mediterranean
   - ○ on the eastern coast of South America

   Alternate Question *Drag the answer choice into the box to complete the sentence correctly.*
   Christopher Columbus named the inhabitants of the New World Indians because he believed he had landed in the East Indies instead of the _Caribbean_ islands.

2. Which statement characterizes the Spanish exploration of Mexico?
   - ○ The lands were largely uninhabited by native populations.
   - ○ The native populations had already converted to their religion.
   - ○ The Spanish had discovered a culture that had little scientific advancement.
   - ○ The Spanish had discovered a civilization that was richer in gold than theirs.

   Alternate Question *Drag the answer choice into the box to complete the sentence correctly.*
   Hernando Cortés made first contact with the Aztec civilization, which controlled the lands and much of the wealth of central Mexico.

3. Which economic activity was profitable for Spain and often the most hazardous for its workers?
   - ○ farming
   - ⊙ mining
   - ○ fishing
   - ○ shipbuilding

   Alternate Question *Drag the answer choice into the box to complete the sentence correctly.*
   The Spanish land grant system, or _encomienda_, relied on the hard work of Native Americans.

4. Which statement characterizes the Spanish colonization of the modern-day United States?
   - ○ The region had large plantations producing cash crops like sugar.
   - ⊙ The region had sparsely populated provinces centered on missions.
   - ○ The Spanish sent few priests to convert the native populations of the region.
   - ○ The Spanish sent many military expeditions to control the wealth of the region.

   Alternate Question *Select the answer choice from the drop-down list to complete the sentence correctly.*
   Since Coronado discovered few material riches in the modern-day southwestern United States, Spanish colonization of the region was organized by [priests ⬍].

5. Which of the following was a result of ending the *encomienda* system?
   - ○ the rebellion of the Pueblo
   - ○ the creation of mestizo culture
   - ⊙ the reliance on African slave labor
   - ○ the return of many native religions

   Alternate Question *Select the answer choice from the drop-down list to complete the sentence correctly.*
   Opposition to Spanish rule in New Mexico erupted into a revolt by the [Pueblo ⬍] that took twelve years to suppress.

6. **Draw Conclusions** Why did Christopher Columbus sail west instead of east?

   Possible answer: Christopher Columbus wanted to find a shorter route to the East Indies than sailing around the southern coast of Africa. Therefore, he sailed west believing that there were no land masses between Europe and East Asia. Columbus landed in the Caribbean islands instead. After he did not find gold, which was his main objective, he sailed back to Spain.

7. **Evaluate** How did European diseases affect the Spanish conquest of Mexico?

   Possible answer: Despite being significantly outnumbered by the Aztecs, Hernando Cortés and his conquistadors were able to wage a successful conquest of the empire. The native populations of the New World had never come into contact with Europeans before and therefore had no immunity to their diseases. Diseases, such as smallpox, ravaged the populations of Mexico. By the end of the Spanish conquest of much of the New World, millions of people had died from disease.

8. **Compare and Contrast** How were the Spanish conquests of the Incan and Aztec empires similar?

   Possible answer: The conquistadors were not satisfied with an enormous amount of gold given to them by Aztec and Incan emperors. Spain demanded complete domination over the conquered people. Spain enslaved both the Aztecs and Incans, and took possession of their lands. As well, Spaniards and native populations intermarried, and created a mestizo culture that contained elements of both the European and New World civilizations.

9. **Evaluate** How did the Spanish conquest of the Americas affect Spain's political position in Europe?

   Possible answer: The immense riches of the Spanish conquests allowed Spain to build a large navy and a powerful army. With its wealth and military might, Spain became the most influential nation in Europe. During the 16th century, Spain dominated European politics and safeguarded Spanish interests.

10. **Make Judgments** How effective were Roman Catholic priests in improving the lives of Native Americans?

    Possible answer: Roman Catholic priests had been vocal concerning the poor treatment of many Native Americans. Church criticism over the encomienda system helped end the harsh treatment of Native American workers. However, abuses still remained, and often the Native Americans rebelled against the loss of their cultural identity as a result of their religious conversion to Catholicism.

European Nations Settle North America

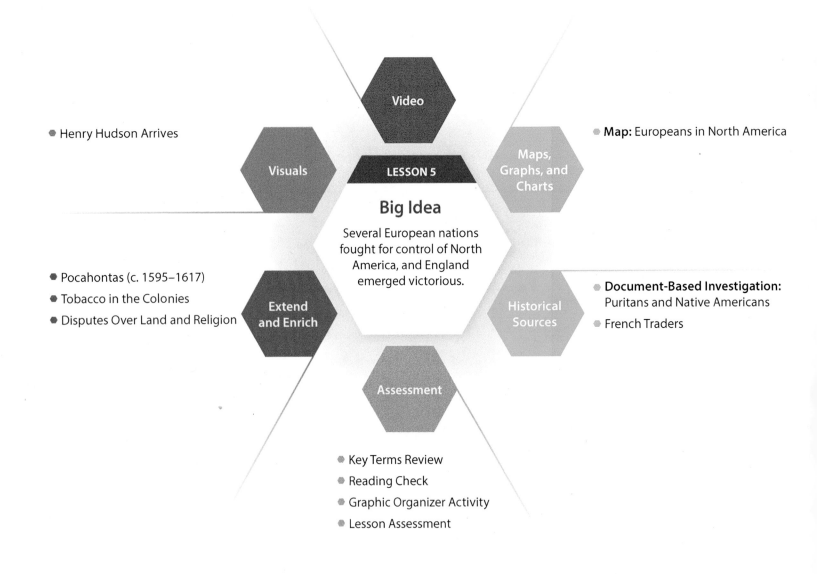

● Henry Hudson Arrives

Video

Visuals

LESSON 5

Big Idea

Several European nations fought for control of North America, and England emerged victorious.

Maps, Graphs, and Charts

● **Map:** Europeans in North America

● Pocahontas (c. 1595–1617)
● Tobacco in the Colonies
● Disputes Over Land and Religion

Extend and Enrich

Historical Sources

● **Document-Based Investigation:** Puritans and Native Americans
● French Traders

Assessment

● Key Terms Review
● Reading Check
● Graphic Organizer Activity
● Lesson Assessment

Online Lesson 5 Enrichment Activities

Pocahontas (c. 1595–1617)

Biography Students read about how Pocahontas's kindness led to peace between the English colonists and Native Americans. Then students write a short paragraph that explains why they think Pocahontas's life story continues to interest people.

Disputes Over Land and Religion

Article Students read about conflicts between Native Americans and English settlers. Then students explain how Native American and European views of land ownership differed and how these differences affected the way both groups viewed land treaties.

Tobacco in the Colonies

Chart Students study a chart and read about the different factors that can affect the price of a product, such as tobacco. Then students explain what happened to tobacco prices between 1618 and 1710 and what they believe caused that trend.

Teach the Big Idea

1. **Whole Class Open/Introduction** Ask students to brainstorm characteristics of modern North America that show that it was once largely controlled by the English. *Possible answer: English language, place names, system of law and government*

2. **Direct Teach** Read students the Big Idea: *Several European nations fought for control of North America, and England emerged victorious.* Review the following lesson objectives with students to aid in their understanding of the Big Idea.

   • Summarize competing claims in North America.

   • Identify English colonial activities in North America.

   • Explain the outcome of struggles among the French, English, and Dutch colonists.

   • Describe the Native American response to land claims made by Europeans.

3. **Whole Group Close/Reflect** Each of the European nations that established colonies in the Americas had its own distinct system of governing its colonies. Have each student decide which nation's colony he or she would have preferred to live in and write a brief essay explaining why.

▷ ONLINE DOCUMENT-BASED INVESTIGATION

Expansion, Exploration, and Encounters

Puritans and Native Americans is the fifth of seven document-based investigations that students will analyze in the Expansion, Exploration, and Encounters module. John Cotton was a Puritan leader who, in 1630, offered some information to fellow Puritans leaving England for Massachusetts. Students can play the audio to hear the passage read aloud.

▷ ONLINE GRAPHIC ORGANIZER

European Nations Settle North America

As students read the lesson, have them use the graphic organizer to take notes. Students can review their graphic organizer notes at the end of the lesson to answer the following question.

Compare and Contrast What did the various European settlements in North America have in common? In what ways were they different? *Similarities—New France and New Netherland had fur-trading posts; New France had missionaries, and Massachusetts Bay had religious refuge. Differences—Plymouth and Massachusetts Bay were founded for religious freedom; the French and the Dutch mostly cooperated with Native Americans, the English did not.*

European Nations Settle North America

The Big Idea
Several European nations fought for control of North America, and England emerged victorious.

Why It Matters Now
The English settlers in North America left a legacy of law and government that guides the United States today.

Key Terms and People
New France
Jamestown
Pilgrims
Puritans
New Netherland
French and Indian War
Metacom

Setting the Stage

Spain's successful colonization efforts in the Americas did not go unnoticed. Other European nations, such as England, France, and the Netherlands, soon became interested in obtaining their own valuable colonies. The Treaty of Tordesillas, signed in 1494, had divided the newly discovered lands between Spain and Portugal. However, other European countries ignored the treaty. They set out to build their own empires in the Americas. This resulted in a struggle for North America.

Competing Claims in North America

Magellan's voyage showed that ships could reach Asia by way of the Pacific Ocean. Spain claimed the route around the southern tip of South America. Other European countries hoped to find an easier and more direct route to the Pacific. If it existed, a northwest trade route through North America to Asia would become highly profitable. Not finding the route, the French, English, and Dutch instead established colonies in North America.

Explorers Establish New France The early French explorers sailed west with dreams of reaching the East Indies. One explorer was Giovanni da Verrazzano (VEHR•uh•ZAHN•noh), an Italian in the service of France. In 1524, he sailed to North America in search of a sea route to the Pacific. While he did not find the route, Verrazzano did discover what is today New York harbor. Ten years later, the Frenchman Jacques Cartier (kahr•TYAY) reached a gulf off the eastern coast of Canada that led to a broad river. Cartier named it the St. Lawrence. Cartier followed the river inward

---

Objectives

You may wish to discuss the following questions with students to help them frame the content as they read.

• How would you compare and contrast New France and New Spain? *both found wealth, converted natives—New Spain: south, gold, cities; New France: north, furs, scattered*

• Why were the Mississippi and St. Lawrence Rivers important to the French? *allowed them to transport furs from the interior and get supplies from Europe*

More About . . .

The Fur Trade From the 1600s to the 1800s, the beaver was hunted until the species was almost extinct. In the late 1600s, one beaver pelt could buy a cooking kettle or a pound of tobacco, and 12 pelts could buy a rifle. Both Canada and the United States have passed laws regulating the hunting season for beavers.

Jacques Marquette explores the Mississippi River in 1673.

until he reached a large island dominated by a mountain. He named the island Mont Real (Mount Royal), which later became known as Montreal. In 1608, another French explorer, Samuel de Champlain, sailed up the St. Lawrence with about 32 colonists. They founded Quebec, which became the base of France's colonial empire in North America, known as **New France**.

Then the French moved further into the North American continent. In 1673, French Jesuit priest Jacques Marquette and trader Louis Joliet explored the Great Lakes and the upper Mississippi River. Nearly 10 years later, Sieur de La Salle explored the lower Mississippi. He claimed the entire river valley for France. He named it Louisiana in honor of the French king, Louis XIV. By the early 1700s, New France covered much of what is now the midwestern United States and eastern Canada.

A Trading Empire France's North American empire was immense. But it was sparsely populated. By 1760, the European population of New France had grown to only about 65,000. A large number of French colonists had no desire to build towns or raise families. These settlers included Catholic priests who sought to convert Native Americans. They also included young, single men engaged in what had become New France's main economic activity, the fur trade. Unlike the English, the French were less interested in occupying territories than they were in making money off the land.

Reading Check
Summarize Why were France's North American holdings so sparsely populated?

The English Arrive in North America

The explorations of the Spanish and French inspired the English. In 1606, a company of London investors received a charter from King James to found a colony in North America. In late 1606, the company's three ships, with more than 100 settlers, pushed out of an English harbor. About four months later, in 1607, they reached the coast of Virginia. The colonists claimed the land as theirs. They named the settlement **Jamestown** in honor of their king.

The Settlement at Jamestown The colony's start was disastrous. The settlers were more interested in finding gold than in planting crops. During the first few years, seven out of every ten people died of hunger, disease, or battles with the Native Americans.

Despite their nightmarish start, the colonists eventually gained a foothold in their new land. Jamestown became England's first permanent settlement in North America. The colony's outlook improved greatly after farmers there discovered tobacco. High demand for tobacco in England turned it into a profitable cash crop.

Objectives

You may wish to discuss the following questions with students to help them frame the content as they read.

- Why was the presence of families such a crucial factor in the success of a settlement? *larger population, more stable lifestyle*
- How would you compare and contrast French and Dutch colonies? *Both—settled along waterways, fur trade; vast French territory, smaller Dutch area*

More About . . .

Jamestown Captain John Smith, one of the original Jamestown colonists, wrote about the lust for gold among the settlers: "No talke, no hope, no worke, but dig gold, wash gold, refine gold, load gold." This was unfortunate, for the colonists found no gold in Virginia.

▷ ONLINE HISTORICAL SOURCES

French Traders

Invite students to view the image and answer the associated question.

Analyze Sources What does the image suggest about the relationship between French explorers and Native Americans? *French explorers often needed Native Americans' help and guidance.*

HISTORICAL SOURCE

French Traders

In this image, Jacques Marquette explores the Mississippi River in 1673. His and others' exploration of the Mississippi helped to establish France's empire in North America. Most people who moved to French colonies in North America were traders, not settlers.

READING CHECK

Summarize Why were France's North American holdings so sparsely populated? *because most of the settlers were priests or fur trappers who had no desire to build towns or start families*

▷ ONLINE LESSON FLIP CARDS

Review Key Terms and People

Students can use the flip cards in the Lesson Review at any time to review the lesson's key terms and people: *New France, Jamestown, Pilgrims, Puritans, New Netherland, French and Indian War,* and *Metacom.*

COLLABORATIVE LEARNING

Colony Life Skits

1. Organize students into small groups. Have each group research life in the early Spanish, Portuguese, French, Dutch, or English colonies in the Americas.

2. Then have students write skits portraying scenes from everyday life in one of the colonies, including typical interactions between native people and the colonists. To ensure variety, you might wish to assign a nation to each group.

3. Have each group present its skit to the class.

4. Guide students in a discussion of life in the various early European colonies in the Americas.

Image with Text Slider: Henry Hudson Arrives

Have students explore the image by revealing additional information using the interactive slider.

Henry Hudson Arrives

Drag the bar for details about Hudson's arrival in North America.

Henry Hudson's ship arrives in the bay of New York on September 12, 1609.

Puritans Create a "New England" In 1620, a group known as **Pilgrims** founded a second English colony, Plymouth, in Massachusetts. Persecuted for their religious beliefs in England, these colonists sought religious freedom. Ten years later, a group known as **Puritans** also sought religious freedom from England's Anglican Church. They established a larger colony at nearby Massachusetts Bay.

The Puritans wanted to build a model community that would set an example for other Christians to follow. Although the colony experienced early difficulties, it gradually began to prosper. This was due in large part to the numerous families in the colony, unlike the mostly single, male population in Jamestown.

The Dutch Found New Netherland The Dutch followed the English and French into North America. In 1609, Henry Hudson, an Englishman in the service of the Netherlands, sailed west. He was searching for a northwest sea route to Asia. Hudson did not find a route. He did, however, explore three waterways that were later named for him—the Hudson River, Hudson Bay, and Hudson Strait.

The Dutch claimed the region along these waterways. They established a fur trade with the Iroquois Indians. They built trading posts along the Hudson River at Fort Orange (now Albany) and on Manhattan Island. Dutch merchants formed the Dutch West India Company. In 1621, the Dutch government granted the company permission to colonize the region

STRUGGLING READERS

Compare and Contrast English Colonies

1. Explain that finding the differences among ideas, institutions, behaviors, and events helps us understand historical events more clearly. Often one concept is easier to grasp if its features can be contrasted with similar features of something else.

2. Have students review the lesson and answer this question: How did the colonies at Jamestown and Massachusetts Bay differ?

3. To help, ask the following questions:
   - Who settled Jamestown, why did they come, and what was their experience? *mostly single males; to make money; hard times*

   - Who founded New England, why did they settle there, and what kind of community did they seek? *Puritans, many families; religious freedom; to build a model community*

4. Have students also use their findings to help them answer the Reading Check question.

History in Depth

Pirates

The battle for colonial supremacy occurred not only on land, but also on the sea. Acting on behalf of their governments, privately owned armed ships, known as privateers, attacked merchant ships of enemy nations and sank or robbed them.

Pirates also roamed the high seas. They attacked ships for their valuables and did not care what nation the vessels represented. One of the best-known pirates was Edward B. Teach, whose prominent beard earned him the nickname Blackbeard. According to one account, Blackbeard attempted to frighten his victims by sticking "lighted matches under his hat, which appeared on both sides of his face and eyes, naturally fierce and wild."

Reading Check
Contrast
How were the Dutch and French colonies different from the English colonies in North America?

and expand the fur trade. The Dutch holdings in North America became known as **New Netherland**.

Although the Dutch company profited from its fur trade, it was slow to attract Dutch colonists. To encourage settlers, the colony opened its doors to a variety of peoples. Gradually more Dutch, as well as Germans, French, Scandinavians, and other Europeans, settled the area.

Colonizing the Caribbean During the 1600s, the nations of Europe also colonized the Caribbean. The French seized control of present-day Haiti, Guadeloupe, and Martinique. The English settled Barbados and Jamaica. In 1634, the Dutch captured what are now the Netherlands Antilles and Aruba from Spain.

On these islands, the Europeans built huge cotton and sugar plantations. These products, although profitable, demanded a large and steady supply of labor. Enslaved Africans eventually would supply this labor.

The Struggle for North America

As they expanded their settlements in North America, the nations of France, England, and the Netherlands battled one another for colonial supremacy.

The English Oust the Dutch To the English, New Netherland separated their northern and southern colonies. In 1664, the English king, Charles II, granted his brother, the Duke of York, permission to drive out the Dutch. When the duke's fleet arrived at New Netherland, the Dutch surrendered without firing a shot. The Duke of York claimed the colony for England and renamed it New York.

Objectives

You may wish to discuss the following question with students to help them frame the content as they read.

- How did the Netherlands and France react differently to English expansion? *Dutch colony was smaller, caught between English colonies and chose to surrender; France fought Britain fiercely, realizing that its vast American empire was at stake.*

More About . . .

The Dutch When the English took over New Netherland, the English language quickly outpaced the Dutch. However, many familiar English words are borrowed from Dutch, including cookie, boss, and crib. Familiar place names originating in Dutch include Rhode Island, Long Island, Brooklyn, the Bronx, Harlem, and Broadway.

> **READING CHECK**
> **Contrast** How were the Dutch and French colonies different from the English colonies in North America? *The English colonies were more populated and begun for religious reasons. Dutch and French colonies were begun mainly for commerce.*

COLLABORATIVE LEARNING

Research the French and Indian War

1. Ask individual students to do research on the Internet or in books to learn more about the French and Indian War.

2. Next, present the following list of topics and have each student choose the one that interests him or her the most:

   - graphic organizer of causes and effects

   - terms of the Treaty of Paris of 1763

   - overview of the phases of the war

   - significance of the fall of Quebec

   - why most Native Americans chose to ally with France

   - what the Iroquois Confederacy was and why it allied with Britain

3. Assign students to groups based on the topic they chose. Make sure every student is in a group or has a partner.

4. Have each group prepare a presentation on the topic. Presentations might be in the form of an oral report, a graphic organizer, a display board, a skit or dialogue, or any other form appropriate to the topic.

5. Have groups present their work to the class.

Europeans in North America

Have students explore the map using the interactive features and answer the associated questions.

Interpret Maps Which nation claimed the largest area of the present-day United States in 1754? *France*

In print edition, see map of same title.

Region Which nation claimed the largest area of the present-day United States in 1754? *France*

Place How did Britain's North American empire change by 1763? *It increased greatly as the British seized most of the French territory and took control of nearly the entire eastern half of the continent.*

READING CHECK

Analyze Issues How did the larger issue of European expansion around the world play out in North America? *The English and French were in conflict all around the world over their expanding empires; in North America, they went to war over territorial disputes.*

Explore ONLINE!

Europeans in North America

Interpret Maps

1. **Region** Which nation claimed the largest area of the present-day United States in 1754?

2. **Place** How did Britain's North American empire change by 1763?

With the Dutch gone, the English colonized the Atlantic coast of North America. By 1750, about 1.2 million English settlers lived in 13 colonies from Maine to Georgia.

England Battles France The English soon became hungry for more land for their colonial population. This economic motive led them to push farther west into the continent. By doing so, they collided with France's North American holdings. As their colonies expanded, France and England began to interfere with each other. It seemed that a major conflict was on the horizon.

In 1754 a dispute over land claims in the Ohio Valley led to a war between the British and French on the North American continent. The conflict became known as the **French and Indian War**. The war became

Reading Check
Analyze Issues
How did the larger
issue of European
expansion around
the world play out in
North America?

part of a larger conflict known as the Seven Years' War. Britain and France, along with their European allies, also battled for supremacy in Europe, the West Indies, and India.

In North America, the British colonists, with the help of the British Army, defeated the French in 1763. The French surrendered their North American holdings. As a result of the war, the British seized control of the eastern half of North America.

Native Americans Respond

As in Mexico and South America, the migration of Europeans to the present-day United States had a great impact on Native American cultures. European colonization brought mostly disaster for the land's original inhabitants.

A Strained Relationship French and Dutch settlers developed a mostly cooperative relationship with the Native Americans. This was mainly due to the mutual benefits of the fur trade. Native Americans did most of the trapping and then traded the furs to the French for such items as guns, hatchets, mirrors, and beads. The Dutch also cooperated with Native Americans in an effort to establish a fur-trading enterprise.

The groups did not live together in complete harmony. Dutch settlers fought with various Native American groups over land claims and trading rights. For the most part, however, the French and Dutch colonists lived together peacefully with their North American hosts.

The same could not be said of the English. Early relations between English settlers and Native Americans were cooperative. However, they quickly worsened over the issues of land and religion. Unlike the French and Dutch, the English sought to populate their colonies in North America. This meant pushing the natives off their land. The English colonists seized more land for their population and their tobacco crops.

Religious differences also heightened tensions. The English settlers considered Native Americans heathens, people without a faith. Over time, many Puritans viewed Native Americans as agents of the devil and as a threat to their godly society. Native Americans developed a similarly harsh view of the European invaders.

Settlers and Native Americans Battle The hostility between the English settlers and Native Americans led to warfare. As early as 1622, the Powhatan tribe attacked colonial villages around Jamestown and killed about 350 settlers. During the next few years, the colonists struck back and massacred hundreds of Powhatan.

Expansion, Exploration, and Encounters **649**

Objectives

You may wish to discuss the following questions with students to help them frame the content as they read.

- Why did many Native Americans ally with the French against the British? *history of better relations between them, wanted to limit settlers on their land*

- What was the overriding attitude of the British toward the Native Americans? *that British civilization was superior, and that they were therefore entitled to take and use native land as they saw fit*

More About . . .

Metacom Like his father, Metacom wanted to maintain peace with the Europeans, but he found it difficult when he saw native land being sold. The uneasy truce of 13 years was shattered when the government of Plymouth executed three natives for killing a man who had informed on the tribe. Metacom led a coalition of tribes for more than a year before he died in battle. To celebrate their victory over Metacom, the Puritans cut off his head and displayed it at Plymouth for many years.

▶ **ONLINE DOCUMENT-BASED INVESTIGATION**

Puritans and Native Americans

John Cotton was a Puritan leader who, in 1630, offered some information to fellow Puritans leaving England for Massachusetts. Students can play the audio to hear the excerpt read aloud.

Analyze Sources How might the last part of Cotton's statement have helped the Puritans justify taking land from the Native Americans? *Puritans could claim natives had wronged them.*

DOCUMENT-BASED INVESTIGATION HISTORICAL SOURCE

Puritans and Native Americans
John Cotton was a Puritan leader who, in 1630, offered some information to fellow Puritans leaving England for Massachusetts. Cotton himself would immigrate to the Massachusetts Bay Colony in 1633.

"Where there is a vacant place, there is liberty for . . . [Christians] to come and inhabit, though they neither buy it nor ask their leaves. . . . Indeed, no nation is to drive out another without special commission from Heaven . . . unless the natives do unjustly wrong them, and will not recompense the wrongs done in a peaceable fort [way]. And then they may right themselves by lawful war and subdue the country unto themselves . . ."

—John Cotton
from "God's Promise to His Plantation"

STRUGGLING READERS

Locate Information on a Map

1. Pair a struggling reader with a more proficient reader. Have them make a list of place names mentioned in this lesson. Then have them use maps to find where they are located.

2. Ask the following questions:
   - How were the Dutch situated relative to the English colonies? *between Virginia and New England*

   - In what modern country is Hudson Bay located? *Canada*

- What country controlled Jamaica in the 17th century? *Britain*

- The Ohio Valley was located along the Ohio River. What French-controlled river did the Ohio flow into? *Mississippi*

3. Ask students to share what they learned from this exercise. Encourage them to consult an atlas when reading information that has geographical references.

Identify Problems Why did the issues of land and religion cause strife between Native Americans and settlers? *Settlers wanted more land for growing population and crops; they also viewed natives as godless devils.*

Print Assessment

1. **Organize Information** Fill in the graphic organizer below with what the given settlements had in common. *Possible answer: New France—St. Lawrence and Mississippi Rivers, fur trade. New Netherland—Hudson River and Hudson Bay, fur trade. Massachusetts Bay—Coastal Massachusetts, religious freedom. Similarities—New France and New Netherland had fur-trading posts; New France had missionaries, and Massachusetts Bay had religious refuge.*

2. **Key Terms and People** For each key term or person in the lesson, write a sentence explaining its significance. *Explanations of the lesson's key terms can be found on the following pages: New France, p. 645; Jamestown, p. 645; Pilgrims, p. 646; Puritans, p. 646; New Netherland, p. 647; French and Indian War, p. 648; Metacom, p. 650.*

3. **Contrast** What was a basic difference between French and English attitudes about the land they acquired in North America? *English wanted to farm; French wanted to take part in fur trade.*

4. **Analyze Effects** What were some effects of European colonization of North America for Native Americans? *Native Americans lost their land and their lives from disease and warfare.*

5. **Draw Conclusions** What need drove the English farther west into the North American continent? *more land for growing population*

6. **Contrast** In what ways did the colonies at Jamestown and Massachusetts Bay differ? *Jamestown—Mostly single males, seeking financial gain. Massachusetts Bay—Numerous families, fleeing religious persecution.*

One of the bloodiest conflicts between colonists and Native Americans was known as King Philip's War. It began in 1675 when the Native American ruler **Metacom** (also known as King Philip) led an attack on colonial villages throughout Massachusetts. In the months that followed, both sides massacred hundreds of victims. After a year of fierce fighting, the colonists were victorious. During the 17th century, many skirmishes erupted throughout North America.

Diseases Strike Native Americans More destructive than the Europeans' weapons were their diseases. Like the Spanish in Central and South America, the Europeans who settled North America brought with them several diseases. The diseases devastated the native population in North America.

In 1616, for example, an epidemic of smallpox ravaged Native Americans living along the New England coast. The population of one tribe, the Massachusett, dropped from 24,000 to 750 by 1631. From South Carolina to Missouri, nearly whole tribes fell to smallpox, measles, and other diseases.

One of the effects of this loss was a severe shortage of labor in the colonies. In order to meet their growing labor needs, European colonists soon turned to another group: Africans, whom they would enslave by the millions.

Reading Check
Identify Problems Why did the issues of land and religion cause strife between Native Americans and settlers?

Lesson 5 Assessment

1. Organize Information Fill in the graphic organizer below with what the given settlements had in common.

Name of Settlement	General Location	Reasons Settled
New France		
New Netherland		
Massachusetts Bay		

2. Key Terms and People For each key term or person in the lesson, write a sentence explaining its significance.

3. Contrast What was a basic difference between French and English attitudes about the land they acquired in North America?

4. Analyze Effects What were some effects of European colonization of North America for Native Americans?

5. Draw Conclusions What need drove the English farther west into the North American continent?

6. Contrast In what ways did the colonies at Jamestown and Massachusetts Bay differ?

Online Assessment

1. Which economic activity was common in New France?
   - ○ gold mining
   - ◉ fur trapping
   - ○ cotton farming
   - ○ cattle ranching

   Alternate Question *Select the answer choice from the drop-down list to complete the sentence correctly.*
   English colonists in North America tended to be farmers, while the French colonists were more interested in [*trade* ⇕].

2. How was the Jamestown settlement different from the Plymouth and Massachusetts Bay colonies?
   - ○ The majority of the Jamestown settlers were married with families, while the Pilgrims and Puritans were young men.
   - ○ The Jamestown settlers were assisted by the Native Americans, while the Pilgrims and Puritans were constantly under attack.
   - ◉ The Jamestown settlers emigrated from England for economic reasons, while the Pilgrims and Puritans were fleeing religious persecution.
   - ○ The majority of the Jamestown settlers were missionaries sent to convert Native Americans, while the Pilgrims and Puritans wanted to be isolated from the outside world.

   Alternate Question *Drag the answer choice into the box to complete the sentence correctly.*
   Englishmen who immigrated to North America for economic reasons first settled in _Jamestown_ .

3. Which of the following was a major cause of the French and Indian War?
   - ○ Britain supported privateers who raided French merchant ships.
   - ◉ France and Britain claimed the same territory in the Ohio Valley.
   - ○ France supported American efforts of independence from Great Britain.
   - ○ Britain and France disagreed over the possession of the Louisiana Territory.

   Alternate Question *Select the answer choice from the drop-down list to complete the sentence correctly.*
   With the help of the American colonists, the [*British* ⇕] were victorious in the French and Indian War and greatly increased the size of their empire in North America.

4. How did Native American relationships with the French and with the English differ?
   - ○ The French forced Native Americans off their land, while the English respected Native American hunting grounds.
   - ○ The French considered the Native Americans to be inferior, while the English intermarried with many of the Native American tribes.
   - ◉ The English viewed the Native Americans as enemies, while the French established good trading partnerships with the Native Americans.
   - ○ The English wanted to convert Native Americans to their religion, while the French sent few missionaries to Native American settlements.

   Alternate Question *Drag the answer choice into the box to complete the sentence correctly.*
   Hostility between Native Americans and the English in Massachusetts erupted into a bloody conflict called (the) _King Philip's_ **war.**

5. **Analyze Information** How did the population density of New France reflect the motivations of the French colonists?

   Possible answer: The colonists who lived in New France were interested in making money from fur trapping, fishing, and trade. Fur trappers usually lived a nomadic lifestyle. Therefore, many French colonists were not interested in creating large settlements. Many of the inhabitants of New France were Christian missionaries who wanted to convert the native population, and therefore did not settle in large towns either.

6. **Draw Conclusions** Why did the first Dutch, English, and French explorers sail into the interior of North America?

   Possible answer: The 17th-century explorers of modern-day Canada were trying to find a northwest passage to East Asia. Henry Hudson did not find a sea route to Asia, but he did explore parts of northern Canada. French and Dutch explorers were equally as unsuccessful at finding a passage, and instead they traded with the Native Americans and established small settlements.

7. **Elaborate** How was the French and Indian War a world war?

   Possible answer: The two main belligerents in the French and Indian War were Great Britain and France. These nations, along with their allies, possessed colonies all over the world. The war determined who would control the eastern half of North America and other valuable colonies in the Caribbean. But the war was part of a larger conflict to decide which European nation would dominate world trade.

8. **Make Judgments** How did religion shape the relationship between the Puritans and the Native Americans?

   Possible answer: Puritans believed Native Americans to be godless savages. This harsh opinion of Native Americans soured the relationship between the two groups and helped justify the English tendency to take Native American lands without compensation or consideration. In turn, Native Americans had little respect for the Puritans, who treated Native Americans as inferior.

ADDITIONAL LESSON CONTENT

French Influence

1. Review the struggles between Britain and France for dominance in North America. Tell students to imagine that France had prevailed in the territory that is now the United States.

2. Have students work in groups to create an alternative history of the United States. Their alternative history should begin at the time of the French and Indian War and continue to the present day. It should imagine what might have happened if France had defeated the British and gained control of North America.

3. Tell groups they should consider not only how language and culture might have been affected but also how the chain of events that make up world history might have unfolded differently.

4. Invite groups to present their work to the class in the format of their choice.

The Atlantic Slave Trade

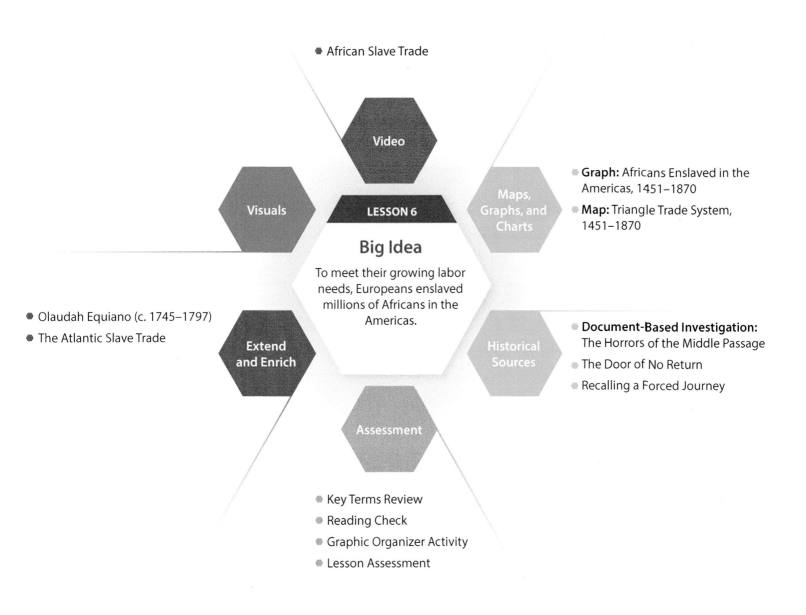

● African Slave Trade

Video

Visuals

LESSON 6

Maps, Graphs, and Charts

● **Graph:** Africans Enslaved in the Americas, 1451–1870
● **Map:** Triangle Trade System, 1451–1870

Big Idea
To meet their growing labor needs, Europeans enslaved millions of Africans in the Americas.

● Olaudah Equiano (c. 1745–1797)
● The Atlantic Slave Trade

Extend and Enrich

Historical Sources

● **Document-Based Investigation:** The Horrors of the Middle Passage
● The Door of No Return
● Recalling a Forced Journey

Assessment

● Key Terms Review
● Reading Check
● Graphic Organizer Activity
● Lesson Assessment

Olaudah Equiano (c. 1745–1797)

Biography Students read about how Olaudah Equiano persevered in becoming a prominent anti-slavery author and speaker. Then students use library and online resources to learn about later slave narratives. With a partner, students discuss how Equiano's autobiography may have influenced these later works. Then students write a brief paragraph that summarizes their conclusions.

The Atlantic Slave Trade

Illustrated Chart Students create a graphic organizer that answers questions about the causes and consequences of the enslavement of Africans. They also write an introduction that summarizes the contents of the graphic organizer.

Lesson 6

The Atlantic Slave Trade

The Big Idea
To meet their growing labor needs, Europeans enslaved millions of Africans in the Americas.

Why It Matters Now
Descendants of enslaved Africans represent a significant part of the Americas' population today.

Key Terms and People
Atlantic slave trade
indentured servitude
triangular trade
Middle Passage

Setting the Stage

Sugar plantations and tobacco farms required a large supply of workers to make them profitable for their owners. European owners had planned to use Native Americans as a source of cheap labor. But millions of Native Americans died from disease, warfare, and brutal treatment. Therefore, the Europeans in Brazil, the Caribbean, and the colonies of North America soon turned to Africa for workers. This demand for cheap labor resulted in the brutalities of the slave trade.

The Causes of African Slavery

Beginning around 1500, European colonists in the Americas who needed cheap labor began using enslaved Africans on plantations and farms.

Slavery in Africa Slavery had existed in Africa for centuries. In most regions, it was a relatively minor institution. The spread of Islam into Africa during the seventh century, however, ushered in an increase in slavery and the slave trade. Muslim rulers in Africa justified enslavement with the Muslim belief that non-Muslim prisoners of war could be bought and sold as slaves. As a result, between 650 and 1600, Muslims transported about 17 million Africans to the Muslim lands of North Africa and Southwest Asia.

In most African and Muslim societies, slaves had some legal rights and an opportunity for social mobility. In the Muslim world, a few slaves even occupied positions of influence and power. Some served as generals in the army. In African societies, slaves could escape their bondage in numerous ways, including marrying into the family they served.

The Demand for Africans The first Europeans to explore Africa were the Portuguese during the 1400s. Initially, Portuguese traders were more interested in trading for gold than for captured Africans. That changed with the

Objectives

You may wish to discuss the following questions with students to help them frame the content as they read.

- How had Africans built up immunity to European diseases? *Possible answer: trading with Europeans for more than 100 years*
- Why were Spain and Portugal the early leaders in the slave trade? *Possible answer: They were the first colonizers and needed labor to work mines and plantations in the Caribbean and in South America.*

More About . . .

Death from Disease Although few European explorers had active diseases, they still carried many germs that were highly contagious to Native Americans. Passing these germs to just a few people could rapidly infect large areas. Large, prosperous towns discovered by Spanish explorers in the early 1540s in what is now the southeastern United States no longer existed in 1560. During this time, Spanish colonists in Florida tried to find these towns to acquire food but diseases brought by the explorers had destroyed them. It is estimated that by the early 1600s, the Mesoamerican Indian population was 90 to 95 percent smaller than it had been a hundred years before.

Teach the Big Idea

1. **Whole Class Open/Introduction** Have students share examples of slaves' stories they've encountered in literature and movies. Ask students to share details they remember about the slaves' experiences.

2. **Direct Teach** Read students the Big Idea: *To meet their growing labor needs, Europeans enslaved millions of Africans in the Americas.* Review the following lesson objectives with students to aid in their understanding of the Big Idea.
   - Identify the causes of African slavery.
   - Trace the spread of slavery throughout the Americas.
   - Explain the triangular trade.
   - Describe the life of enslaved Africans in the colonies.
   - Identify the consequences of the Atlantic slave trade.

3. **Whole Group Close/Reflect** Have students write about the causes and effects of the African slave trade. Then invite students to contribute ideas to a cause-and-effect T-chart on the board.

▷ ONLINE DOCUMENT-BASED INVESTIGATION

Expansion, Exploration, and Encounters

The Horrors of the Middle Passage is the sixth of seven document-based investigations that students will analyze in the Expansion, Exploration, and Encounters module. This diagram of a British slave ship shows how slave traders packed Africans onto slave ships in the hold below decks for the Middle Passage. Invite students to view the image of the diagram.

▷ ONLINE GRAPHIC ORGANIZER

The Atlantic Slave Trade

As students read the lesson, have them use the graphic organizer to take notes. Students can review their graphic organizer notes at the end of the lesson to answer the following question.

Analyze Effects What was the most important consequence of the slave trade in Africa and the Americas? *loss of cultures, because they are difficult or impossible to reconstruct today*

The Door of No Return

Invite students to view the image and answer the associated question.

Analyze Sources In what way is the Door of No Return a powerful symbol of the tragedy of slavery? *It is an actual, physical reminder of what captured Africans endured long ago.*

Africans Enslaved in the Americas, 1451–1870

Have students explore the graph and answer the associated question.

Interpret Graphs Which region of the Americas imported the most Africans? *Caribbean islands*

READING CHECK

Analyze Motives What advantages did Europeans see in enslaving Africans? *Slaves had built up immunity to many diseases; they were experienced in farming; they were in an alien environment that made them less likely to escape.*

---

colonization of the Americas, as native peoples began dying by the millions.

Europeans saw advantages in using Africans in the Americas. First, many Africans had been exposed to European diseases and had built up some immunity. Second, many Africans had experience in farming and could be taught plantation work. Third, Africans were less likely to escape because they did not know their way around the new land. Fourth, their skin color made it easier to catch them if they escaped and tried to live among others.

In time, the buying and selling of Africans for work in the Americas—known as the **Atlantic slave trade**—became a massive enterprise. Between 1500 and 1600, nearly 300,000 Africans were transported to the Americas. During the next century, that number climbed to almost 1.3 million. By the time the Atlantic slave trade ended around 1870, Europeans had imported about 9.5 million Africans to the Americas.

Spain and Portugal Lead the Way The Spanish took an early lead in importing Africans to the Americas. Spain moved on from the Caribbean and began to colonize the American mainland. As a result, the Spanish imported and enslaved thousands more Africans. By 1650, nearly 300,000 Africans were laboring on plantations and in gold and silver mines. By this time, the Portuguese had surpassed the Spanish in the importation of Africans to the Americas. During the 1600s, Brazil dominated the European sugar market. As the sugar industry grew, so too did Portuguese colonists' demand for cheap labor. During the 17th century, more than 40 percent of all Africans brought to the Americas went to Brazil.

Systems of Labor For Spanish colonists, the Atlantic slave trade, like the *encomienda* system, was a way to force others into labor. However, there were key differences. First, in the *encomienda* system, the native laborers were technically not property of the Spanish landlords, but African slaves were. Second, while native peoples were often forced to relocate in order to labor for the Spaniards, African slaves were taken from their homeland and brought to the Americans via horrific transatlantic journeys. Third, the Spanish landlords in the *encomienda* system had to give their word to the Spanish crown that native workers would be treated well (which rarely happened in practice). For African slaves, they made no such promise.

The Atlantic slave trade also differed from other systems of labor during the colonial era. **Indentured servitude** was a system of labor by which a person could work to pay off the cost of coming to the Americas. Indentured servants were usually Europeans who wanted to resettle in the Americas but lacked the means to do so. These Europeans would agree to work for a certain number of years for an employer who paid for their voyage. African slaves, of course, were brought against their will and were usually considered slaves for life. Both groups, however, experienced harsh treatment from their superiors.

Perhaps the starkest difference existed between African slavery and systems of wage labor. Usually, in wage labor, an employer paid workers for

Review Key Terms and People

Students can use the flip cards in the Lesson Review at any time to review the lesson's key terms and people: *Atlantic slave trade, indentured servitude, triangular trade,* and *Middle Passage.*

COLLABORATIVE LEARNING

The Slave Trade

1. Organize students into small groups.

2. Have each group discuss the advantages and disadvantages of the slave trade for one of the following individuals: a plantation owner in the Americas, an enslaved person, the owner of a slave ship, or the ruler of an African kingdom.

3. Have each student write an essay analyzing the different points of view involved in the slave trade.

4. Guide students in a discussion of the slave trade from the points of view that have been presented.

their labor, and the two parties entered into the relationship voluntarily. African slaves, of course, were not paid for their labor and did not volunteer to enter into enslavement. African slaves were kept on the plantations and were given shelter and food.

Slavery Spreads Throughout the Americas

As European nations established colonies, their demand for cheap labor grew. Thus, they began to import large numbers of Africans.

England Dominates the Slave Trade As England's presence in the Americas grew, it came to dominate the Atlantic slave trade. From 1690 until an English law abolished the slave trade in 1807, England was the leading carrier of enslaved Africans. By the time the trade ended, the English had transported nearly 1.7 million Africans to their colonies in the West Indies.

African slaves were also brought to what is now the United States. In all, nearly 400,000 Africans were sold to Britain's North American colonies. Once in North America, however, the slave population steadily grew. By 1830, roughly 2 million slaves toiled in the United States.

African Cooperation and Resistance Many African rulers and merchants played a willing role in the Atlantic slave trade. Most European traders, rather than travel inland, waited in ports along the coasts of Africa. African merchants, with the help of local rulers, captured Africans to be enslaved. Then they delivered the slaves to the Europeans in exchange for gold, guns, and other goods.

As the slave trade grew, some African rulers voiced their opposition to the practice. Nonetheless, the slave trade steadily grew. Lured by its profits, many African rulers continued to participate. African merchants developed new trade routes to avoid rulers who refused to cooperate.

History in Depth

Slavery

Slavery probably began with the development of farming about 10,000 years ago. Farmers used prisoners of war to work for them.

Slavery has existed in societies around the world. People were enslaved in civilizations from Egypt to China to India. The picture shows slaves working in a Roman coal mine.

Race was not always a factor in slavery. Often, slaves were captured prisoners of war or people of a different ethnicity or religion.

However, the slavery that developed in the Americas was based largely on race. Europeans viewed black people as naturally inferior. Because of this, slavery in the Americas was hereditary.

Expansion, Exploration, and Encounters **653**

Objectives

You may wish to discuss the following questions with students to help them frame the content as they read.

- Why does the number of slaves transported by the British to the United States understate the scope of slavery there? *number transported was only about 20 percent of the total*

- How was British involvement in the slave trade similar to that of the Spanish? *Both transported huge numbers of Africans.*

More About . . .

Slavery on Plantations Plantation owners in the British Caribbean colony of Barbados determined that it was more profitable to buy new slaves to replace those who died from disease and overwork than to institute measures to provide for a more humane life for slaves.

▶ ONLINE ANALYZE VIDEOS

African Slave Trade

Have students watch the video individually **HISTORY** or as a class. You may wish to use the associated question as a discussion prompt.

Analyze Videos How did the Atlantic Slave Trade compare to the indigenous systems of African slavery Europeans encountered when they first arrived? *The Atlantic Slave Trade was based on a concept that Africans were to be enslaved not because they were a foreign threat that had to be put down (as was the case with the indigenous systems), but because they were thought to be a lower form of humanity. Further, the Atlantic Slave Trade industrialized the enslavement of Africans; in other words, enslaved Africans were a commodity to be used to increase wealth.*

▶ PLAY VIDEO 3:09
African Slave Trade **HISTORY**

STRUGGLING READERS

Understand the African Slave Trade

1. Pair a struggling reader with a more proficient reader.

2. Explain to students that historians have various ways of expressing time periods. For example, "the 15th century" is another way of saying "the 1400s." Point out that sometimes students need to infer dates by looking at a comparison that an author uses, such as "during the next century" or "with the colonization of the Americas."

3. Have pairs look for chronological references in the lesson. Then have them

make a timeline using the earliest and latest dates mentioned (650 and 1870) as the range. Their timelines might include the following events:

650: *Muslims transport about 17 million Africans to North Africa and Southwest Asia*
1400–1500: *Portuguese explore Africa*
1500–1600: *Spain and Portugal colonize Americas, begin enslaving Africans.*
1600–1700: *Atlantic slave trade grows dramatically under Spain and Portugal.*
1690: *England increases Atlantic slave trade.*
1870: *Atlantic slave trade ends.*

READING CHECK

Analyze Issues Why did many African rulers participate in the Atlantic slave trade? *It was profitable, and they received valuable goods in return.*

Objectives

You may wish to discuss the following questions with students to help them frame the content as they read.

- What pivotal role did the West Indies play in the triangular trade? *principal market for slaves who worked on the plantations, producing sugar and molasses used in making rum that was traded for slaves*

- In what ways did the conditions of the middle passage work against the interests of the European merchants? *contributed to an increased death rate, lowering profits*

More About . . .

The Middle Passage The captain of a slave ship was either a "tight packer" or a "loose packer," referring to the number of slaves he jammed into the ship's hold. Tight packers arranged people in spoon style, lying on top of one another.

▶ **ONLINE INTERACTIVE MAPS**

Triangle Trade System, 1451–1870

Have students explore the map using the interactive features and answer the associated questions.

Interpret Maps Which item was transported from North America to Africa and traded for captured Africans? *rum*

In print edition, see map of same title.

Movement What items were transported to Africa and traded for captured Africans? *tobacco, rum, manufactured goods, guns*

Region According to the graph, which region of the Americas imported the most Africans? Which imported the second most? *Caribbean islands; Brazil*

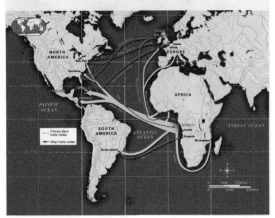

A Forced Journey

After being captured, African men and women were shipped to the Americas as part of a profitable trade network. Along the way, millions of Africans died.

The Triangular Trade Africans transported to the Americas were part of a transatlantic trading network known as the **triangular trade**. Over one trade route, Europeans transported manufactured goods to the west coast of Africa. There, traders exchanged these goods for captured Africans. The Africans were then transported across the Atlantic and sold in the West Indies. Merchants bought sugar, coffee, and tobacco in the West Indies and sailed to Europe with these products.

On another triangular route, merchants carried rum and other goods from the New England colonies to Africa. There they exchanged their merchandise for Africans. The traders transported the Africans to the West Indies and sold them for sugar and molasses. They then sold these goods to rum producers in New England.

▶ *Explore ONLINE!*

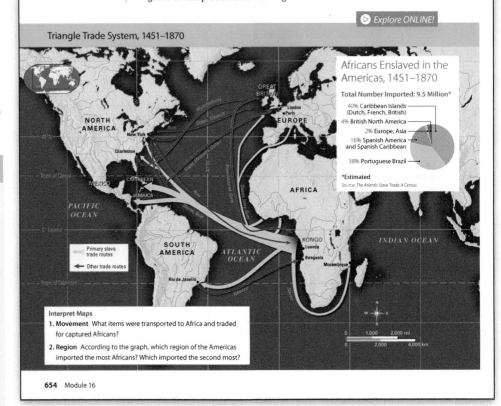

Triangle Trade System, 1451–1870

Africans Enslaved in the Americas, 1451–1870

Total Number Imported: 9.5 Million*

- 40% Caribbean Islands (Dutch, French, British)
- 4% British North America
- 2% Europe, Asia
- 16% Spanish America and Spanish Caribbean
- 38% Portuguese Brazil

*Estimated
Source: The Atlantic Slave Trade: A Census

Interpret Maps
1. **Movement** What items were transported to Africa and traded for captured Africans?
2. **Region** According to the graph, which region of the Americas imported the most Africans? Which imported the second most?

654 Module 16

ADVANCED/GIFTED

Understand Primary Sources

1. Explain to students that Olaudah Equiano told his story in his autobiography, *The Interesting Narrative of the Life of Olaudah Equiano*, which was published in 1789 and soon became a bestseller. It is the first of a genre of world literature written by African slaves, former slaves, and post-slavery African Americans who have described their struggles for freedom. Equiano wrote his story for several reasons. Many white people tried to defend slavery by saying that black people were well suited for heavy work.

They said slaves were well treated and that since they could not read or write, they did not need to be free. Equiano wanted to show these arguments for the lies that they were. He also wanted to provide a model for other black people.

2. Ask students to read Equiano's quotation in the lesson.

3. Then ask them to find additional excerpts from his autobiography using the Internet or library resources.

4. Have students prepare a presentation for the class, with each student reading and explaining a short excerpt.

The Horrors of the Middle Passage

One African, Olaudah Equiano, recalled the inhumane conditions on his trip from West Africa to the West Indies at age 12 in 1762.

"I was soon put down under the decks, and there I received such a salutation in my nostrils as I never experienced in my life; so that, with the loathsomeness of the stench, and crying together, I became so sick and low that I was not able to eat . . . but soon, to my grief, two of the white men offered me eatables; and on my refusing to eat, one of them held me fast by the hands, and laid me across . . . the windlass, while the other flogged me severely."

—Olaudah Equiano, quoted in
*Eyewitness:
The Negro in American History*

This diagram of a British slave ship shows how slave traders packed Africans onto slave ships in the hold below decks for the brutal Middle Passage.

Analyze Historical Sources
1. Why might the white men have forced Equiano to eat?
2. What does the diagram of the slave ship suggest about conditions on board?

Various other transatlantic routes existed. The "triangular" trade encompassed a network of trade routes crisscrossing the northern and southern colonies, the West Indies, England, Europe, and Africa. The network carried a variety of traded goods.

The Middle Passage The voyage that brought captured Africans to the West Indies and later to North and South America was known as the **Middle Passage**. It was considered the middle leg of the transatlantic trade triangle. Sickening cruelty characterized this journey. In African ports, European traders packed Africans into the dark holds of large ships, which were crowded and filthy. On board, Africans endured whippings and beatings from merchants, as well as diseases that swept through the vessel. Slave traders usually did not feed captives well during the journey. Numerous Africans died from disease or physical abuse aboard the slave ships. Many others committed suicide by drowning. Scholars estimate that roughly 20 percent of the Africans aboard each slave ship perished during the brutal trip.

Reading Check
Analyze Causes
Why did so many Africans die during the Middle Passage?

ONLINE DOCUMENT-BASED INVESTIGATION

The Horrors of the Middle Passage

This diagram of a British slave ship shows how slave traders packed Africans onto slave ships in the hold below decks for the Middle Passage. Have students view the diagram and answer the associated question.

Analyze Sources What does the diagram of the slave ship suggest about conditions on board? *Conditions were intolerably crowded and likely to spread disease.*

In print edition, see historical source of same title.

1. Why might the white men have forced Equiano to eat? *He was valuable property that they wished to keep alive.*

2. What does the diagram of the slave ship suggest about conditions on board? *Conditions were intolerably crowded and likely to spread disease.*

DOCUMENT-BASED INVESTIGATION   HISTORICAL SOURCE

The Horrors of the Middle Passage
This diagram of a British slave ship shows how slave traders packed Africans onto slave ships in the hold below decks for the Middle Passage.

ONLINE HISTORICAL SOURCE

Recalling a Forced Journey

Invite students to view the image, read the excerpt, and answer the associated question.

Analyze Sources Why might the white men have forced Equiano to eat? *He was valuable property that they wished to keep alive.*

In print edition, see feature titled The Horrors of the Middle Passage.

READING CHECK
Analyze Causes Why did so many Africans die during the Middle Passage? *They were kept in holds in unsanitary conditions with little food, which helped diseases spread; they were beaten; they committed suicide.*

Objectives

You may wish to discuss the following questions with students to help them frame the content as they read.

- In what ways were enslaved Africans treated as property? *They were bought and sold and owned for life; their children were slaves.*

- How did the preservation of their cultures help people cope with slavery? *Possible answer: It reminded them of their life as humans apart from their current condition.*

More About . . .

Slave Resistance Slave resistance also included ways to supplement a slave's meager food rations. Some took their masters' pigs, buried the hides, and pretended they were eating opossum, which was available to slaves.

READING CHECK

Summarize How did enslaved Africans resist their bondage? *broke tools, uprooted plants, worked slowly, escaped, revolted*

Slavery in the Americas

Africans who survived their ocean voyage faced a difficult life in the Americas. Forced to work in a strange land, enslaved Africans coped in a variety of ways.

A Harsh Life Upon arriving in the Americas, captured Africans usually were auctioned off to the highest bidder. After being sold, slaves worked in mines or fields or as domestic servants. Slaves lived a grueling existence. Many lived on little food in small, dreary huts. They worked long days and suffered beatings. In much of the Americas, slavery was a lifelong condition, as well as a hereditary one.

Resistance and Rebellion To cope with the horrors of slavery, Africans developed a way of life based on their cultural heritage. They kept alive such things as their musical traditions and the stories of their ancestors.

Slaves also found ways to resist. They made themselves less productive by breaking tools, uprooting plants, and working slowly. Thousands also ran away.

Some slaves pushed their resistance to open revolt. As early as 1522, about 20 slaves on Hispaniola attacked and killed several Spanish colonists. Larger revolts occurred throughout Spanish settlements during the 16th century.

Occasional uprisings also occurred in Brazil, the West Indies, and North America. In 1739, a group of slaves in South Carolina led an uprising known as the Stono Rebellion. Uprisings continued into the 1800s.

Consequences of the Slave Trade

The Atlantic slave trade had a profound impact on both Africa and the Americas. In Africa, numerous cultures lost generations of their fittest members—their young and able—to European traders and plantation owners. In addition, countless African families were torn apart. Most were never reunited.

The slave trade devastated African societies in another way: by introducing guns into the continent. One West African empire, the Ashanti, used the guns and weapons acquired from British and Dutch slave traders to expand its lands. Another kingdom, Dahomey, sold slaves to Europeans and gained wealth—and power—enough to acquire new territories. In this way, the slave trade contributed to political changes in Africa.

While they were unwilling participants in the growth of the colonies, African slaves contributed greatly to the economic and cultural development of the Americas. Their greatest contribution was their labor. Without their back-breaking work, colonies such as those on Haiti and Barbados may not have survived. In addition to their muscle, enslaved Africans brought their expertise, especially in agriculture. They also brought their culture. Their art, music, religion, and food continue to influence American societies.

Reading Check
Summarize
How did enslaved
Africans resist their
bondage?

ADVANCED/GIFTED

Slave Songs

1. Have students work individually or with partners to research songs sung by slaves throughout early American history.

2. Encourage students to select one set of song lyrics that they find especially revealing.

3. Have students prepare a written analysis of the lyrics. Tell students they should include specific quotations in their analysis and offer a close reading of what the words might have meant.

4. Discuss which aspects of the songs students found most likely express thoughts and yearnings shared by all slaves.

STRUGGLING READERS

News Flash: Slave Rebellion!

1. Tell students they will write an imaginary news article taking place during the period of colonial slavery across the Americas. Their news account will describe a fictitious slave rebellion.

2. Have students scan the lesson to locate realistic details they can incorporate into their news story. For example, they might choose a location described in the lesson to use as the setting, or incorporate details about the types of work slaves did in their report. Encourage students to include five details from the lesson in their news story.

3. Invite students to share their stories with the class.

The influx of so many Africans to the Americas also has left its mark on the very population itself. From the United States to Brazil, many of the nations of the Western Hemisphere today have substantial populations of African descent. Many Latin American countries have sizable mixed-race populations.

African slaves were not the only cargo transported across the Atlantic during the colonization of the Americas. The settlement of the Americas brought many different items from Europe, Asia, and Africa to North and South America. It also introduced items from the Americas to the rest of the world.

Reading Check
Synthesize How did African slaves contribute to the development of the Americas?

Lesson 6 Assessment

1. **Organize Information** Create an outline and fill it in with key points about the consequences of the slave trade in Africa and the Americas. Then, use your notes to answer the following question: What do you think was the most important consequence of the slave trade in Africa and the Americas?

   Consequences of the slave trade
   I. in Africa
      A.
      B.
   II. in the Americas
      A.
      B.

2. **Key Terms and People** For each key term or person in the lesson, write a sentence explaining its significance.
3. **Cause and Effect** What effect did the spread of Islam have on the slave trade?
4. **Compare and Contrast** How was slavery in the Americas different from slavery in Africa?
5. **Synthesize** What does the percentage of enslaved Africans imported to the Caribbean Islands and Brazil suggest about the racial makeup of these areas?
6. **Make Inferences** Why do you think the slave trade flourished for so long?

Expansion, Exploration, and Encounters **657**

Objectives

You may wish to discuss the following questions with students to help them frame the content as they read.

- In what ways were slaves a source of profit for Europeans? *slave trade—wealth for merchants; slave labor—wealth for owners*
- What made enslaved Africans more attractive than Native Americans to plantation owners? *agricultural expertise versus many Native Americans' hunting-gathering expertise*

More About . . .

The Persistence of Slavery Freed African American slaves from the United States founded the African country of Liberia. There, some of them named settlements after slave states such as Mississippi and Louisiana, cleared land for huge plantations with Southern-style mansions, and modeled their government after that of the United States—complete with slavery. Slavery still exists in Liberia.

NOW & THEN

Uncovering the Legacy of Slavery

The study of remains found in a Manhattan graveyard shows that slaves in New York had been worked to their physical limits and probably lived under terrible conditions.

READING CHECK

Synthesize How did African slaves contribute to the development of the Americas? *through labor, knowledge of agriculture, culture*

Print Assessment

1. **Organize Information** Create an outline and fill it in with key points about the consequences of the slave trade in Africa and the Americas. Then, use your notes to answer the following question: What do you think was the most important consequence of the slave trade in Africa and the Americas? *Possible answer: In order: Columbus's arrival (1492); Cortés defeats the Aztecs (1521); Pizarro conquers the Inca (1533); conquistadors explore and colonize the southwest United States (1540–1541). Most important: Columbus's arrival*

(continued)

Expansion, Exploration, and Encounters **657**

STRUGGLING READERS

The Atlantic Slave Trade

1. Have students make a cause-and-effect chart about slavery in the Americas. Tell students that the reasons the slave trade was started are the causes, while the results, or consequences, of the slave trade are the effects.

2. Review and discuss student charts as a class, having students incorporate additional ideas in their charts.

3. Then, guide students in a discussion of how the development of the American colonies would have been different if slavery had never been introduced in the New World.

Print Assessment (continued)

2. **Key Terms and People** For each key term or person in the lesson, write a sentence explaining its significance. *Explanations of the lesson's key terms can be found on the following pages: Atlantic slave trade, p. 652; indentured servitude, p. 652; triangular trade, p. 654; Middle Passage, p. 655.*

3. **Cause and Effect** What effect did the spread of Islam have on the slave trade? *increase in the slave trade*

4. **Compare and Contrast** How was slavery in the Americas different from slavery in Africa? *Africa—Slaves could escape their bondage. Americas—Most slaves worked for life; slavery was hereditary.*

5. **Synthesize** What does the percentage of enslaved Africans imported to the Caribbean islands and Brazil suggest about the racial makeup of these areas? *great racial diversity*

6. **Make Inferences** Why do you think the slave trade flourished for so long? *Slaves and slavery were sources of wealth.*

▷ Online Assessment

1. Which statement about the treatment of enslaved Africans by Muslims and Europeans is accurate?
   - ○ Enslaved Africans could marry into European families, while Muslims prohibited slave marriages.
   - ◉ Enslaved Africans had the ability to gain their freedom in Muslim society, while Europeans treated them as property.
   - ○ Enslaved Africans could rise to high ranks in European armies, while Muslims assigned them subordinate roles in the military.
   - ○ Enslaved Africans had to work for the remainder of their lives in Muslim nations, while Europeans required them to work for a number of years before gaining their freedom.

   Alternate Question Why did English colonists rely on enslaved Africans as a labor force rather than enslaving Native Americans? Select three correct answers.
   - ○ Africans were readily available.
   - ◉ Africans had experience with farming.
   - ○ Africans had strong kinship ties with their tribes.
   - ◉ Africans had immunities to many European diseases.
   - ○ Africans were distinguishable by the color of their skin.
   - ○ Africans had a familiarity with the surrounding countryside.

2. Which of the following items did European slave traders exchange for enslaved Africans?
   - ○ coal
   - ○ tobacco
   - ◉ guns
   - ○ wool

   Alternate Question *Select the answer choice from the drop-down list to complete the sentence correctly.*
   The international slave trade was very profitable for African ⟨ merchants ⟩, who demanded guns and gold in return for Africans.

3. Which statement describes the Middle Passage?
   - ○ the attempts of French explorers to find a sea route to East Asia
   - ○ the segment of the triangular trade route that transported sugar to New England
   - ◉ the segment of the triangular trade route that brought enslaved Africans to the New World
   - ○ the discovery of the Pacific Ocean by Vasco Núñez de Balboa through the Panamanian isthmus

   Alternate Question *Select the answer choice from the drop-down list to complete the sentence correctly.*
   As part of the triangular trading network, New England imported sugar and molasses from the West Indies and in turn exported ⟨ rum ⟩ to Africa.

4. How did the perception of the institution of slavery change in the American colonies?
   - ◉ Throughout history the color of a slave's skin was often insignificant, while in the colonies race determined slavery.
   - ○ Throughout history people were often enslaved due to their faith, while in the colonies slaves could be freed if they converted to Christianity.
   - ○ Throughout history slaves were forbidden to marry a member of the owner's family, while in the colonies slaves often married white Europeans.
   - ○ Throughout history slaves remained in bondage for life, while in the colonies slaves had many opportunities to improve their status in society.

   Alternate Question *Drag the answer choice into the box to complete the sentence correctly.*
   Slave owners often justified slavery in the American colonies by believing Africans to be __inferior__.

5. In which area did enslaved Africans have the most significant impact in the New World?
   - ○ architecture
   - ○ medicine
   - ○ finance
   - ◉ music

   Alternate Question *Select the answer choice from the drop-down list to complete the sentence correctly.*
   The mixing of African, European, and Native American populations is the most evident in modern-day ⟨ Brazil ⟩.

6. **Compare and Contrast** How were the institutions of slavery and indentured servitude different?

   Possible answer: The most obvious difference between a slave and an indentured servant is that slaves were brought to the New World by force in unimaginable conditions. Both groups were often treated poorly once they arrived in the New World. Indentured servants were required to serve their superior for a number of years to pay for the price of their voyage to the New World, while Africans were forced to live in bondage for the remainder of their lives. Indentured servants were not considered the property of their superior, while slaves could be bought or sold.

7. **Draw Conclusions** How did Great Britain exercise control over the international slave trade during the 18th century?

    Possible answer: After Great Britain defeated France in the French and Indian War, the small island nation expanded its empire throughout the world by creating a large merchant fleet and a powerful navy. It needed a large merchant fleet to be able to transport an estimated 1.7 million slaves to its large plantations in the West Indies. By controlling the seas, Britain controlled the international slave trade.

8. **Elaborate** In which conditions were enslaved Africans transported to the New World?

    Possible answer: Enslaved Africans were transported on large cargo ships in some of the most unimaginably filthy conditions. They were chained to the ship side by side for the few months that it took to sail from the west coast of Africa to the New World. Disease, abuse, malnutrition, exhaustion, fear, and stress killed an estimated 20 percent of the total enslaved Africans who were transported to the New World.

9. **Make Generalizations** How did many Africans demonstrate their opposition to slavery in the New World?

    Possible answer: Africans resisted slavery by violent and nonviolent means. There were periodic slave revolts throughout the Spanish, Portuguese, French, and British colonies that were often suppressed with great difficulty and bloodshed on both sides. Thousands of enslaved Africans ran away from their horrible working conditions in search of freedom. Enslaved Africans more often resisted by breaking farming implements, damaging crops, or working at a slow pace.

10. **Cause and Effect** How did the international slave trade change African society and politics?

    Possible answer: The slave trade devastated the social structure of African tribes and affected the political balance of the continent. Slave traders most often captured young men from African tribes, depriving families of husbands and fathers. Tribes were unable to defend themselves due to the absence of young warriors and they could poorly resist gun-owning Africans. The introduction of large numbers of guns to Africa caused a political shift whereas the more heavily armed tribes, like the Ashanti and Dahomey, gained lands from conquering other tribes and obtained wealth from the slave trade.

ADDITIONAL LESSON CONTENT

COLLABORATIVE LEARNING

Debate: Is It Time to Abolish?

1. Review the causes of the spread of slavery in the Americas and the hardships endured by those enslaved at the time this lesson describes.

2. Organize students into an even number of groups. Tell groups they will prepare for a debate about slavery.

3. Have students imagine that they are colonists at this time who believe that slavery is wrong. Have half the groups take the position that they should work together to end slavery immediately. Have the other half take the position that although they believe slavery is wrong, they don't believe overturning public opinion will succeed at this time and therefore they should wait.

4. Allow groups time to research primary sources in the module and on the Internet to quote during the debate. When the debates are finished, ask students which moments during the debate were most effective in supporting an argument.

The Columbian Exchange and Global Trade

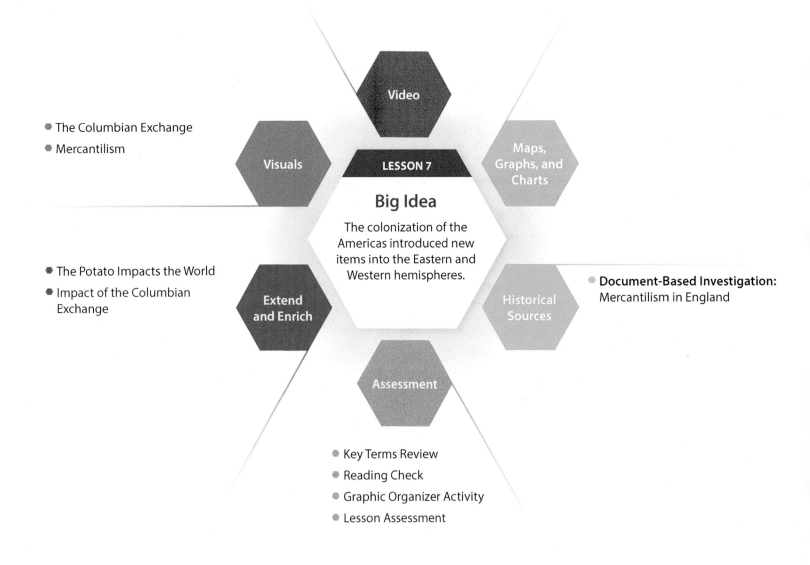

- The Columbian Exchange
- Mercantilism

Visuals

Video

LESSON 7

Big Idea

The colonization of the Americas introduced new items into the Eastern and Western hemispheres.

Maps, Graphs, and Charts

- The Potato Impacts the World
- Impact of the Columbian Exchange

Extend and Enrich

Historical Sources

Assessment

- Document-Based Investigation:
  Mercantilism in England

- Key Terms Review
- Reading Check
- Graphic Organizer Activity
- Lesson Assessment

The Potato Impacts the World

Article Students read about how the potato spread to Europe as part of the Columbian Exchange. Then students create an advertisement that might have appeared in American newspapers in the 1700s describing the merits of potatoes.

Impact of the Columbian Exchange

Chart Activity Students create a chart that explains how certain products in use today resulted from the Columbian Exchange. Students also prepare a brief explanation of the chart to present to a classmate.

Teach the Big Idea

1. **Whole Class Open/Introduction** Ask students to discuss things they own that come from other countries. *Possible answer: consumer electronics, clothes* Then have students brainstorm everyday groceries that might come from other countries. *Possible answer: spices, cheese, produce, soy sauce*

2. **Direct Teach** Read students the Big Idea: *The colonization of the Americas introduced new items into the Eastern and Western hemispheres.* Review the following lesson objectives with students to aid in their understanding of the Big Idea.

   • Explain the Columbian Exchange.

   • Identify factors that led to the development of global trade.

   • Describe the effects of new economic policies on European society.

3. **Whole Group Close/Reflect** Have students answer the following question in a brief essay: Which side gained the most as a result of the Columbian Exchange, or did both sides benefit equally?

▷ ONLINE DOCUMENT-BASED INVESTIGATION

Expansion, Exploration, and Encounters

Mercantilism in England is the last of seven document-based investigations that students will analyze in the Expansion, Exploration, and Encounters module. Thomas Mun, an English author of the time, wrote about the new economic idea of mercantilism. Students can play the audio to hear the passage read aloud.

DOCUMENT-BASED INVESTIGATION   HISTORICAL SOURCE

Mercantilism in England

▷ ONLINE LESSON FLIP CARDS

Review Key Terms and People

Students can use the flip cards in the Lesson Review at any time to review the lesson's key terms and people: *Columbian Exchange, capitalism, joint-stock company, mercantilism,* and *favorable balance of trade.*

The Columbian Exchange and Global Trade

The Big Idea
The colonization of the Americas introduced new items into the Eastern and Western hemispheres.

Why It Matters Now
This global exchange of goods permanently changed Europe, Asia, Africa, and the Americas.

Key Terms and People
Columbian Exchange
capitalism
joint-stock company
mercantilism
favorable balance of trade

Setting the Stage

The colonization of the Americas dramatically changed the world. It prompted both voluntary and forced migration of millions of people. It led to the establishment of new and powerful societies. Other effects of European settlement of the Americas were less noticeable but equally important. Colonization resulted in the exchange of new items that greatly influenced the lives of people throughout the world. The new wealth from the Americas resulted in new business and trade practices in Europe.

The Columbian Exchange

The global transfer of foods, plants, and animals during the colonization of the Americas is known as the **Columbian Exchange**. Ships from the Americas brought back a wide array of items that Europeans, Asians, and Africans had never before seen. They included such plants as tomatoes, squash, pineapples, tobacco, and cacao beans (for chocolate). They also included animals such as the turkey, which became a source of food in the Eastern Hemisphere.

Perhaps the most important items to travel from the Americas to the rest of the world were corn and potatoes. Both were inexpensive to grow and nutritious. Potatoes, especially, supplied many essential vitamins and minerals. Over time, both crops became an important and steady part of diets throughout the world. These foods helped people live longer. Thus they played a significant role in boosting the world's population. The planting of the first white potato in Ireland and the first sweet potato in China probably changed more lives than the deeds of 100 kings.

While these new crops had positive effects, their introduction also created issues in many ecosystems around the world. In the Americas, for example, weeds often accompanied the new plants coming from Europe. These weeds contaminated soil in such a way that other crops had

---

COLLABORATIVE LEARNING

North American Cuisine

1. Have students imagine what it might have been like if, at the time of European colonization of the Americas, the transfer of foods and spices between continents had never taken place.

2. Assign students to groups. Tell each group they will invent three dishes European colonists might have eaten using only ingredients native to North America.

3. Have groups research meals that were popular in each European culture and how European settlers might have re-created or approximated those meals using only American ingredients and spices.

4. Have groups create a poster with their recipes and share them with the class.

Global Patterns

The Columbian Exchange

Few events transformed the world like the Columbian Exchange. This global transfer of plants, animals, disease, and especially food brought together the Eastern and Western hemispheres and touched, in some way, nearly all the peoples of the world.

> "The culinary life we owe Columbus is a progressive dinner in which the whole human race takes part but no one need leave home to sample all the courses."
>
> —Raymond Sokolov,
> *Why We Eat What We Eat: How Columbus Changed the Way the World Eats*

Frightening Foods

Several foods from the Americas that we now take for granted at first amazed and terrified Europeans. Early on, people thought the tomato was harmful to eat. One German official warned that the tomato "should not be taken internally." In 1619, officials in Burgundy, France, banned potatoes, explaining that "too frequent use of them caused the leprosy." In 1774, starving peasants in Prussia refused to eat them.

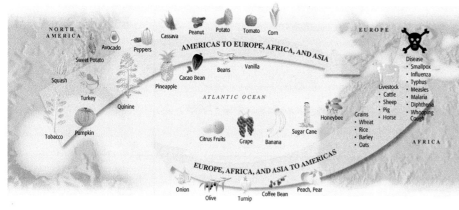

The Geography of Food

Think about your favorite foods. Chances are that at least one originated in a distant land. Throughout history, the introduction of new foods into a region has dramatically changed lives—for better and worse. Dependence on the potato, for example, led to a famine in Ireland. This prompted a massive migration of Irish people to other countries. In the Americas, the introduction of sugar led to riches for some and enslavement for many others.

Critical Thinking

1. **Form Opinions** Have students work in small groups to pose and answer questions about the beneficial and harmful aspects of the Columbian Exchange.

2. **Compare and Contrast** Find out what major items are exchanged or traded between the United States and Asia, Africa, or Europe. How do the items compare with those of the Columbian Exchange? Report your findings to the class.

Expansion, Exploration, and Encounters **659**

Objectives

You may wish to discuss the following questions with students to help them frame the content as they read.

- Why is the Columbian Exchange so called? *because it resulted from Christopher Columbus's initial contact with the Americas*
- How did the introduction of European livestock change the lives of Native Americans? *Possible answer: Horses allowed them to travel farther and faster and were valuable property.*

More About . . .

Colonies Colonies were considered, in part, a dumping ground for Europeans who did not fit in at home. The British poet John Donne told the Virginia Company, a joint-stock company, in 1622, "[Jamestown] shall redeem many a wretch from the jaws of death, from the hands of the executioner. . . . It shall sweep your streets and wash your doors from idle persons and the children of idle persons, and employ them."

Tip for English Language Learners Some students may not know what the items are on the Columbian Exchange chart. Review each term on the chart or have students use an illustrated dictionary to look up each new term.

▷ **ONLINE INTERACTIVE VISUALS**

Image with Hotspots: The Columbian Exchange

Have students explore the image using the interactive hotspots.

Analyze Visuals What was beneficial about the Columbian Exchange? What was harmful? Who benefited most? *Beneficial: both sides received many new foods. Harmful: European diseases killed millions of Native Americans. Benefited most: Europeans.*

GLOBAL PATTERNS

Food Exchange

Tell students that in the United States today, about one-third of the annual harvest is of food crops that had been cultivated by Native Americans prior to the arrival of European settlers. The following six crops each have yearly sales totaling more than $1 billion: corn, cotton, tobacco, potatoes, tomatoes, and peanuts. Have students create a class cookbook of their favorite meals that contain one or more of the four food items in this group.

Form Opinions
Have students work in small groups to pose and answer questions about the beneficial and harmful aspects of the Columbian Exchange. *Possible answer: What was beneficial about the Columbian Exchange? Both sides received many new foods.*

What was harmful? European diseases killed millions of Native Americans. Who benefited the most? Europeans.

Compare and Contrast
Find out what major items are exchanged or traded between the United States and either Asia, Africa, or Europe. How do the items compare with those of the Columbian Exchange? Report your findings to the class. *Suggest that students use various resources to find information about trade between the United States and Asia, Africa, or Europe. For example, students might consult magazines (by means of the Readers' Guide to Periodical Literature), newspapers, current encyclopedias, almanacs (such as Information Please), and the Statistical Abstract of the United States, as well as the Internet.*

The Columbian Exchange and Global Trade

As students read the lesson, have them use the graphic organizer to take notes. Students can review their graphic organizer notes at the end of the lesson to answer the following question.

Analyze Effects Which of the ways that European nations and their colonies affected each other has had the greatest impact on history? *The Columbian Exchange has had the greatest impact because it introduced so many foods that are still grown, eaten, and sold today. Many of the foods also affected millions of lives throughout history; for example, the potato in Ireland, and sugar's contribution to the expansion of slavery.*

The Columbian Exchange		
Causes	→	Effects

Global Trade		
Causes	→	Effects

Mercantilism		
Causes	→	Effects

READING CHECK

Make Inferences Why is the Columbian Exchange considered a significant event? *It greatly improved diets and lifestyles in Europe and Asia and helped prompt an increase in the world's population; it also led to the death of millions of Native Americans from disease.*

---

difficulty growing. Also, agricultural methods created problems for the environment in the Americas. Europeans cut down acres of forests to create farmable land. Of course, plants living in forest environments died.

Traffic across the Atlantic did not flow in just one direction, however. Europeans introduced various live-stock animals into the Americas. These included horses, cattle, sheep, and pigs. Foods from Africa (includ-ing some that originated in Asia) migrated west in European ships. They included bananas, black-eyed peas, and yams. Grains introduced to the Americas included wheat, rice, barley, and oats. Native Americans and Europeans learned from each other how to cultivate crops that were unfamiliar to them. In this way, the Columbian Exchange was an exchange of knowledge as much as an exchange of goods.

Some aspects of the Columbian Exchange had tragic consequences for many Native Americans. Disease was just as much a part of the Columbian Exchange as goods and food. The pathogens Europeans brought with them, which caused diseases like smallpox and measles, led to the deaths of millions of Native Americans. Other diseases Europeans brought with them included influenza, typhus, malaria, and diphtheria.

Global Trade

The establishment of colonial empires in the Americas influenced the nations of Europe in still other ways. New wealth from the Americas was coupled with a dramatic growth in overseas trade. The two factors together

Reading Check
Make Inferences
Why is the Columbian
Exchange considered
a significant event?

Three Worlds Meet, 1492–1700

1500

1492 (Europeans) Columbus embarks on voyage.

1511 (Africans) Africans begin working as slaves in the Americas.

1521 (Americans) The Aztec Empire in Mexico is conquered by Hernando Cortés.

1533 (Americans) The Inca Empire in South America falls to Francisco Pizarro.

1550

1600

1630 (Europeans) Puritans establish the Massachusetts Bay Colony in North America.

1650

1650 (Africans) The number of Africans toiling in Spanish America reaches 300,000.

1675 (Americans) Native Americans battle colonists in King Philip's War.

1700

ENGLISH LANGUAGE LEARNERS

The Columbian Exchange

1. Organize students into small groups. Give each group a list of plants and/or animals from the Food Exchange chart along with a stack of note cards. Each member of the group should have one item and one card.

2. Have groups find pictures of the plants and animals on their lists. Have each student draw and label one of the plants or animals on a card.

3. Create two display areas for all to see and label them "New World" and "Old World."

4. Collect all the cards, shuffle them, and hand them back so that each student gets one card. Have students tack or tape their cards in the appropriate area.

prompted a wave of new business and trade practices in Europe during the 16th and 17th centuries. These practices, many of which served as the root of today's financial dealings, dramatically changed the economic atmosphere of Europe. This economic atmosphere was not dissimilar to the economic issues experienced by Europeans trading with Japan during the 16th century. Just as Portuguese merchants conducted trade with Japan, so too were goods exchanged between colonies in the Americas and European nations.

The Rise of Capitalism One aspect of the European economic revolution was the growth of **capitalism**. Capitalism is an economic system based on private ownership and the investment of resources, such as money, for profit. No longer were governments the sole owners of great wealth. Numerous merchants obtained great wealth from overseas colonization and trade.

Investing in global exploration was important for the development of international trade. A group of investors might fund a transatlantic journey in hopes that a new market might be found with which they could exchange goods and services. The European colonies in the Americas, for example, had become important capital markets in which merchants invested their money. Profits from these investments enabled merchants and traders to reinvest even more money in other enterprises. As a result, businesses across Europe grew and flourished.

The increase in economic activity in Europe led to an overall increase in many nations' money supply. This in turn brought on inflation, or the steady rise in the price of goods. Inflation occurs when people have more money to spend and thus demand more goods and services. Because the supply of goods is less than the demand for them, the goods become both scarce and more valuable. Prices then rise. At this time in Europe, the costs of many goods rose. Spain, for example, endured a crushing bout of inflation during the 1600s, as boatloads of gold and silver from the Americas greatly increased the nation's money supply.

Joint-Stock Companies Another business venture that developed during this period was the **joint-stock company**. A joint-stock company was a partnership of investors who bought shares of stock in the company. In this type of company, a number of people combined their wealth for a common purpose.

In Europe during the 1500s and 1600s, that common purpose was American colonization. It took large amounts of money to establish overseas colonies. Moreover, while profits may have been great, so were risks. Many ships, for instance, never completed the long and dangerous ocean voyage. Because joint-stock companies involved numerous investors, the individual members paid only a fraction of the total colonization cost. If the colony failed, investors lost only their small share. If the colony thrived, the investors shared in the profits. It was a joint-stock company that was responsible for establishing Jamestown, England's first North American colony. As joint-stock companies grew and became more profitable, they adopted characteristics of modern-day corporations.

Reading Check
Make Inferences
Why would a joint-stock company be popular with investors in overseas colonies?

Objectives

You may wish to discuss the following questions with students to help them frame the content as they read.

- How did capitalism change the balance of power in European countries? *Some individuals and some governments had great wealth.*
- How did joint-stock companies reflect the capitalist system? *individuals invested their wealth, shared risk and reward*

More About . . .

Spanish Gold Spain may have been too rich for its own good. Other nations and individuals began to attack Spanish ships and holdings to get some of the gold for themselves and to limit Spain's power. In Spain, the desire for gold meant that fewer people invested in skilled work, farming, and trade.

The New Commercial Economy World exploration led to a new kind of economy in Europe. Goods brought from Africa, Asia, and the New World made many countries in Europe rich. Spices, silks, gold, silver, and precious stones were some of the most sought-after items. The Portuguese, Spanish, and Dutch were the first European powers to build trading empires. Trade and commerce eventually replaced farming as the leading economic activity in Europe. Over time, the new commercial economy generally helped to spread wealth and improve living standards.

READING CHECK
Make Inferences Why would a joint-stock company be popular with investors in overseas colonies? *because they paid only a fraction of the total colonization cost*

The Columbian Exchange and Cuisine

1. Have students obtain or make copies of menus from local Chinese, Italian, or Mexican restaurants.

2. Have each student choose a meal to "order." Then have students find recipes for each item on his or her "order" and make a list of the ingredients. (Tell students they can ignore the amounts needed for each recipe.)

3. Next, have students identify which ingredients came from the New World and which originated in the Old World.

4. Have volunteers share ideas from their lists with the class. For students who need extra help with English, provide sentence frames such as: _____ came from the _____ World, but _____ came from the _____ World.

5. Guide students in a discussion of ways in which these recipes illustrate how cuisines were affected by the Columbian Exchange.

Objectives

You may wish to discuss the following questions with students to help them frame the content as they read.

- Why were strong navies important to European mercantilism? *Possible answer: They protected ships engaged in trade or the transporting of wealth from colonies.*

- Why was self-sufficiency so important to a country practicing mercantilism? *It minimized the amount a country had to import, contributing to a favorable balance of trade.*

More About . . .

The Legacy of Mercantilism The world's nations in 1948 launched a major effort to reduce international tensions in patterns of trade and commerce that emerged during mercantilism. A multinational treaty called the General Agreement on Tariffs and Trade (GATT) created a mechanism to reduce tariffs and other economic barriers between nations. Average tariffs on manufactured goods fell from about 40 percent to less than 5 percent by the 1980s, and regions adopted duty-free trade arrangements like the European Union and the North American Free Trade Agreement (NAFTA). However, some nations have introduced new subsidies or import quotas for certain industries or products in a movement called neomercantilism.

Tip for Struggling Readers *Mercantilism* comes from the word *mercantile*, which refers to anything having to do with merchants.

▷ ONLINE DOCUMENT-BASED INVESTIGATION

Mercantilism in England

Thomas Mun, an English author of the time, wrote about the new economic idea of mercantilism. Students can play the audio to hear the passage read aloud.

Analyze Sources What does Thomas Mun say is the best way for a nation to gain economic power? What approach does he not advocate? *by foreign trade, rather than receiving gifts or taking goods from other nations*

DOCUMENT-BASED INVESTIGATION   HISTORICAL SOURCE

Mercantilism in England

Thomas Mun, an English author of the time, wrote about the new economic idea of mercantilism.

Mercantilism

As you have read, mercantilism was an economic theory practiced in Europe from the 16th to 18th centuries. Economists of the period believed that a country's power came from its wealth. Thus, a country would do everything possible to acquire more gold, preferably at the expense of its rivals. A mercantilist country primarily sought gold in two ways: establishing and exploiting colonies, and establishing a favorable balance of trade with a rival country. In the example, England is the home country, America is England's colony, and France is England's rival.

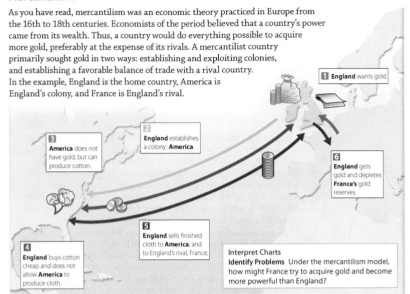

1 **England** wants gold.

2 **England** establishes a colony: **America**.

3 **America** does not have gold, but can produce cotton.

4 **England** buys cotton cheap and does not allow **America** to produce cloth.

5 **England** sells finished cloth to **America**, and to England's rival, France.

6 **England** gets gold and depletes **France's** gold reserves.

Interpret Charts
Identify Problems Under the mercantilism model, how might France try to acquire gold and become more powerful than England?

The Growth of Mercantilism

During this time, the nations of Europe adopted a new economic policy known as **mercantilism**. The theory of mercantilism held that a country's power mainly depended on its wealth. Wealth, after all, allowed nations to build strong navies and purchase vital goods. As a result, the goal of every nation became the attainment of as much wealth as possible.

Balance of Trade According to the theory of mercantilism, a nation could increase its wealth and power in two ways. First, it could obtain as much gold and silver as possible. Second, it could establish a **favorable balance of trade**, in which it sold more goods than it bought. A nation's ultimate goal under mercantilism was to become self-sufficient, not dependent on other countries for goods. An English author of the time wrote about the new economic idea of mercantilism:

"Although a Kingdom may be enriched by gifts received, or by purchases taken from some other Nations . . . these are things uncertain and of small consideration when they happen. The ordinary means

---

COLLABORATIVE LEARNING

Idea Web

1. Have students create an idea web to explore reasons why nations wanted to have colonies. Tell students to label their center bubble "Reasons nations wanted colonies" and to draw additional bubbles around it containing specific reasons.

2. Review student diagrams as a class, filling in a class version of the diagram. Have students correct their own work. *Possible answer: gold and silver; raw materials; new markets*

3. Guide students in a discussion of how raw materials and manufactured goods are related, and why markets are needed for manufactured goods.

ADVANCED/GIFTED

Principles of Mercantilism

1. Tell students that in addition to Thomas Mun, the British mercantilist quoted in the lesson, other leading economic thinkers of the time included the Frenchman Jean-Baptiste Colbert and the Italian Antonio Serra.

2. Ask individual students to research one of these three thinkers on the Internet or in encyclopedias or books. Tell students to learn enough about their chosen person to be able to write a newspaper editorial in that person's voice outlining the reasons mercantilism is good for their country.

therefore to increase our wealth and treasure is by Foreign Trade, wherein we must ever observe this rule: to sell more to strangers yearly than we consume of theirs in value."

—Thomas Mun, quoted in *World Civilizations*

Mercantilism went hand in hand with colonization because colonies played a vital role in this new economic practice. Aside from providing silver and gold, colonies provided raw materials that could not be found in the home country, such as wood or furs. In addition to playing the role of supplier, the colonies also provided a market. The home country could sell its goods to its own colonies.

Economic Revolution Changes European Society The economic changes that swept through much of Europe during the age of American colonization also led to changes in European society. The economic revolution spurred the growth of towns and the rise of a class of merchants who controlled great wealth.

The changes in European society, however, only went so far. While towns and cities grew in size, much of Europe's population continued to live in rural areas. Although merchants and traders enjoyed social mobility, the majority of Europeans remained poor. More than anything else, the economic revolution increased the wealth of European nations. In addition, mercantilism contributed to the creation of a national identity. Also, the new economic practices helped expand the power of European monarchs, who became powerful rulers.

Reading Check
Summarize
What role did colonies play in mercantilism?

Lesson 7 Assessment

1. **Organize Information** Create a three-column chart like the one shown. For each item in the first column, fill in the chart with its place of origin and its effect on the Americas and Europe. Which effect do you think had the greatest impact on history?

Food/ Livestock/ Disease	Place of Origin	Effect
Potato		
Horse		
Smallpox		

2. **Key Terms and People** For each key term or person in the lesson, write a sentence explaining its significance.

3. **Summarize** What were some of the food items that traveled from the Americas to the rest of the world?
4. **Summarize** What food and livestock from the rest of the world traveled to the Americas?
5. **Cause and Effect** What were some of the effects on European society of the economic revolution that took place in the 16th and 17th centuries?
6. **Make Inferences** Why were colonies considered so important to the nations of Europe?
7. **Compare and Contrast** What were some of the positive and negative consequences of the Columbian Exchange?

Expansion, Exploration, and Encounters **663**

▶ **ONLINE INTERACTIVE VISUALS**

Image with Hotspots: Mercantilism

Have students explore the image using the interactive hotspots.

Analyze Visuals Under the mercantilism model, how might France try to acquire gold and become more powerful than England? *It could establish a colony that could provide gold or a raw material; then, France could turn them into a manufactured item and sell to other countries.*

In print edition, see feature titled Analyze Key Concepts.

Under the mercantilist system, the economy was strictly regulated by the government. This regulation extended to a country's colonies. For instance, Britain forbade American colonies to manufacture certain items. Later it required that all American ships pass through British ports on the way to their final destinations. This practice allowed Britain to collect a duty on American shipping.

Identify Problems Under the mercantilism model, how might France try to acquire gold and become more powerful than England? *by establishing a colony that could provide gold or a raw material that France could turn into a manufactured item and sell to other countries*

READING CHECK
Summarize What role did colonies play in mercantilism? *They provided gold and silver, as well as raw materials, and were a market for the home country to sell its goods.*

Print Assessment

1. **Organize Information** Create a three-column chart similar to the one shown. For each item in the first column, fill in the chart with its place of origin and its effect on the Americas and Europe. Which effect do you think had the greatest impact on history? *Possible answer: Potato, Americas, nourished millions; Horse, Europe, transformed transportation; Smallpox, Europe, killed millions. Greatest impact— Potatoes, because people still eat them.*

2. **Key Terms and People** For each key term or person in the lesson, write a sentence explaining its significance. *Explanations of the lesson's key terms can be found on the following pages: Columbian Exchange, p. 658; capitalism, p. 661; joint-stock company, p. 661; mercantilism, p. 662; favorable balance of trade, p. 662.*

(continued)

---

3. Have students write their editorials, making sure they reflect an understanding of the basic principles of mercantilism, incorporate the ideas and style of that historical figure, and are well organized and persuasive.

4. Have students compare the ideas of the three thinkers to see how they all express a similar theory. Ask students if they see any significant differences.

STRUGGLING READERS

The Effects of Mercantilism

1. Have students draw editorial cartoons that illustrate one of the effects of mercantilism, such as the accumulation of gold and silver, creating a favorable balance of trade, establishment of colonial empires, or policies that restricted trade and manufacturing in the home country's colonies.

2. Remind students that since these are editorial cartoons, they should take a clear stand for or against the policy they illustrate.

3. Display student cartoons for the class to see.

4. Guide students in a class discussion of the effects of mercantilism on society and the world.

Expansion, Exploration, and Encounters   663

Print Assessment *(continued)*

3. **Summarize** What were some of the food items that traveled from the Americas to the rest of the world? *Possible answer: potatoes, corn, tomatoes, peppers*

4. **Summarize** What food and livestock from the rest of the world traveled to the Americas? *Possible answer: bananas, coffee, onions, cattle, sheep, pigs, horses*

5. **Cause and Effect** What were some of the effects on European society of the economic revolution that took place in the 16th and 17th centuries? *growth of towns and rise of the merchant class; more social mobility; European nations wealthier*

6. **Make Inferences** Why were colonies considered so important to the nations of Europe? *Possible answer: provided precious metals, raw materials, and markets for European goods, promoting favorable balance of trade for European nations*

7. **Compare and Contrast** What were some of the positive and negative consequences of the Columbian Exchange? *Positive—different foods, both plant and animal, that increased variety of diet and improved nutrition. Negative—warfare, disease.*

▷ Online **Assessment**

1. How did the Columbian Exchange affect the lives of Europeans?
   - ⦿ New sources of food improved their diet and caused a population increase.
   - ○ Weeds from North America destroyed wheat harvests and caused periodic famines.
   - ○ Domesticated animals from South America helped plow fields and increased food production.
   - ○ Diseases from tropical areas led to numerous epidemics and decreased the population by half.

   Alternate Question *Select the answer choice from the drop-down list to complete the sentence correctly.*
   The introduction of corn and (potatoes ⬍) from the New World resulted in greater harvests and fewer instances of famine and disease.

2. How did European colonization help create capitalist economies?
   - ⦿ Colonization increased the world's money supply and products to buy.
   - ○ Colonization decreased competition for natural resources and new markets.
   - ○ Colonization decreased the need for Europeans to emigrate from their homeland.
   - ○ Colonization increased the Catholic Church's control over the newly created wealth.

   Alternate Question *Select the answer choice from the drop-down list to complete the sentence correctly.*
   During the 16th century, Spain imported massive amounts of gold and silver, immediately causing prices to rise and creating economic (inflation ⬍).

3. Which country is following a mercantilist economic policy?
   - ○ Country A manufactures furniture and sells it at a reasonable price to its citizens.
   - ○ Country B's supply of gold is being forcibly removed by its more powerful neighbor.
   - ○ Country C exports cotton to another country but imports more expensive textiles in return.
   - ⦿ Country D's profits from exports of military supplies exceed its costs in importing raw materials.

   Alternate Question *Select the answer choice from the drop-down list to complete the sentence correctly.*
   During the 18th century, countries with mercantilist economies had a(n) (positive ⬍) trade balance.

4. **Elaborate** How did the introduction of the horse affect agricultural production in the New World?

   Possible answer: Native Americans had domesticated only one animal, the llama, for use in farming. However, the llama was not effective as a draft animal to help plow fields. Therefore, with the introduction of the horse, the backbreaking work of tilling the soil was made easier and the fertilizer from horses improved the soil. This allowed plantation agriculture to be introduced to the New World, greatly increasing food production.

5. **Draw Conclusions** How did trade between Europe and the New World change the way business was conducted in Europe?

   Possible answer: Prior to colonization, the national government and the royal families controlled most of the wealth of a country. With the opening of new markets and the overall increase in wealth, businesses were now being owned by private individuals and corporations. Therefore, merchants and business owners were becoming increasingly wealthy. New business practices, such as the formation of joint-stock companies, shared the wealth and the risks involved in capitalist economies.

6. **Cause and Effect** How did the creation of capitalist economies contribute to the growth of European cities?

   Possible answer: Monarchs, bankers, and merchants profited greatly from the new wealth of colonial trade. New businesses were created employing more Europeans managing money. Manufacturing jobs increased, ensuring that countries maintained a favorable balance of trade. Economies slowly shifted from agriculture to manufacturing, and the population shifted from rural areas to towns and cities.

ADDITIONAL LESSON CONTENT

"Interviewing" Words

1. Pair a struggling reader with a more proficient reader and ask them to help each other learn key terms in the lesson

2. Tell students a strategy they can use to remember a term's meaning is to "interview" the term, playing the part of journalists investigating the *who, what, where, when, how,* and *why* of a situation. An example interview question is, "Who are you?" For capitalism, the answer might be, "I am an economic system based on private ownership and the investment of wealth for profit." For joint-stock company, students might ask, "What do you want?" The answer might be, "I want to pool the wealth of a number of different people for a common purpose, such as colonization of the Americas." By asking, "When did you begin?" or "When were you popular?" students can discover a term's historical context.

3. Have students apply this strategy to other key terms in the lesson: *Columbian Exchange, mercantilism,* and *favorable balance of trade.*

Print Assessment

Key Terms and People

For each term or name below, write a sentence explaining how it relates to the era of expansion, exploration, and encounters.

1. Akbar
2. Aurangzeb
3. Bartolomeu Dias
4. Dutch East India Company
5. Ming Dynasty
6. Tokugawa Shogunate
7. conquistador
8. *encomienda*
9. triangular trade
10. Columbian Exchange

Explanations of the module's key terms can be found on the following pages: Akbar, p. 599; Aurangzeb, p. 603; Bartolomeu Dias, p. 612; Dutch East India Company, p. 614; Ming Dynasty, p. 617; Tokugawa Shogunate, p. 628; conquistador, p. 637; encomienda, p. 640; triangular trade, p. 654; Columbian Exchange, p. 658.

Main Ideas

Use your notes and the information in the module to answer the following questions.

The Mughal Empire in India

1. In what ways did Akbar defend religious freedom during his reign? *married two Hindus, a Christian, and a Muslim; abolished taxes on non-Muslims; appointed a Spanish Jesuit to tutor his son; allowed people of all faiths to compete for high office*

2. How did Akbar's successors promote religious conflict in the empire? *Nur Jahan and Jahangir persecuted Sikhs. Aurangzeb reversed Akbar's tolerant policies and levied oppressive taxes on Hindus.*

Europeans Explore the East

3. What factors helped spur European exploration? *desire for new sources of wealth; desire to spread Christianity; technological advancements in sailing and navigation*

4. Why were the Dutch so successful in establishing a trading empire in the Indian Ocean? *The Dutch owned the largest fleet of ships in the world, and the Dutch East India Company was more powerful and better financed than other nation's trading company.*

China and Japan Reject Expansion

5. What are five reasons the Ming Dynasty fell to civil disorder? *ineffective rulers, corrupt officials, bankrupt government, high taxes, bad harvests*

6. Why was the time between 1467 and 1568 called the period of the "Warring States"? *It was an era of disorder when powerful warrior-chieftains, called daimyo, seized control of old feudal estates, set up a new type of feudalism, and often fought each other for territory.*

Spain Builds an American Empire

7. Why did Columbus set sail westward? *to seek an alternate trade route to Asia*

8. What were three goals of the Spanish in the Americas? *to enrich Spain, to colonize the land, to convert Native Americans to Christianity*

Module 16 Assessment

Key Terms and People

For each term or name below, write a sentence explaining how it relates to the era of expansion, exploration, and encounters.

1. Akbar
2. Aurangzeb
3. Bartolomeu Dias
4. Dutch East India Company
5. Ming dynasty
6. Tokugawa Shogunate
7. conquistador
8. *encomienda*
9. triangular trade
10. Columbian Exchange

Main Ideas

Use your notes and the information in the module to answer the following questions.

The Mughal Empire in India

1. In what ways did Akbar defend religious freedom during his reign?
2. How did Akbar's successors promote religious conflict in the empire?

Europeans Explore the East

3. What factors helped spur European exploration?
4. Why were the Dutch so successful in establishing a trading empire in the Indian Ocean?

China and Japan Reject Expansion

5. What are five reasons the Ming Dynasty fell to civil disorder?
6. Why was the time between 1467 and 1568 called the period of the "Warring States"?

Spain Builds an American Empire

7. Why did Columbus set sail westward?
8. What were three goals of the Spanish in the Americas?

European Nations Settle North America

9. What did the Europeans mostly grow in their Caribbean colonies?
10. What was the result of the French and Indian War?

The Atlantic Slave Trade

11. What factors led European colonists to use Africans to resupply their labor force?
12. How did enslaved Africans resist their treatment in the Americas?

The Columbian Exchange and Global Trade

13. Why was the introduction of corn and potatoes to Europe and Asia so significant?
14. What was the economic policy of mercantilism?

664   Module 16

▷ **ONLINE DOCUMENT-BASED INVESTIGATION**

Expansion, Exploration, and Encounters

Have students complete and review all the DBI activities in **Part 1**.

Use this Compare and Contrast Essay Rubric to score students' work in **Part 2**.

> **RUBRIC** Students' essays should
> - identify similarities and differences appropriate to the topic
> - attempt comparisons from parallel categories of items
> - cite at least three sources of appropriate text evidence from Part 1 in support of their comparisons
> - be organized into a distinct introduction, a main body consisting of several paragraphs, and a conclusion that sums up the main points

Write a Compare and Contrast Essay What attitudes did Europeans have toward the other groups they encountered during the age of exploration and colonization? Write a compare and contrast essay in which you consider how Europeans—either individuals or groups—interacted with the people they encountered around the world. Be sure to cite specific evidence from at least three sources in your response.

Module 16 Assessment, continued

Critical Thinking

1. **Compare and Contrast** How were the Spanish and Portuguese colonial empires similar to and different from northern European trading empires? Consider their organization and how they were founded as part of your answer.

2. **Evaluate** Why were the policies of Aurangzeb so destructive to the Mughal Empire?

3. **Make Inferences** Conquest of new territories contributed to the growth of Muslim empires. How might it have also hindered this growth?

4. **Analyze Effects** How might a Chinese emperor's leadership be affected by living in the Forbidden City? Explain and support your opinion.

5. **Develop Historical Perspective** Of the technological advances that helped spur European exploration, which do you think was the most important? Why?

6. **Analyze Causes** What caused Japan to institute a policy of isolation? Defend your viewpoint with evidence from the text.

7. **Draw Conclusions** What factors helped the Europeans conquer the Americas? Which was the most important? Why?

8. **Analyze Effects** Explain the statement, "Columbus's voyage began a process that changed the world forever." Consider all the peoples and places American colonization affected economically.

9. **Compare and Contrast** What might have been some of the differences in the Europeans' and Native Americans' views of colonization?

10. **Compare and Contrast** How was the economic atmosphere of the colonial period similar to that of the Warring States period?

Engage with History

Think about whether or not you would sail into the unknown like the various explorers you read about. Based on what you have read, what are the reasons why you would go? If you would choose not to go, explain your feelings. Discuss your answers with a small group.

Focus on Writing

An English colony would have looked strange and different to a Native American of the time. Conduct historical research on an English colony of the 17th century. Consult at least one primary source and one secondary source. Then write an **essay** describing it, in which you provide details about the following:

- clothes
- food
- shelter
- weapons

Be sure to begin your paragraph with a thesis statement.

Multimedia Activity

Use the Internet, books, and other reference materials to create a multimedia pitch for a television special called "The Voyages of Zheng He." Your pitch should address the historical context of Zheng He's voyages, along with their impact on China and the lands he visited. Be sure to include text, images, audio, and, if possible, video as part of your pitch. During your research, consider the following:

- biographical data on Zheng He
- information about the ships, crews, and cargo
- descriptions of the voyages
- appropriate music and visuals

Essential Question ESSAY

Why were peoples of the Age of Exploration willing to risk lives and fortunes to expand the influence of their homelands?

RUBRIC, Students' essays should
- respond to the Essential Question with a specific position
- illustrate valid reasoning supporting their position
- cite persuasive evidence supporting their position
- identify key people, events, and/or turning points that demonstrate understanding of the module content
- be organized into a distinct introduction, main body, and conclusion

Write an argument answering this question. Your essay should include specific examples of the different places that various nations explored and colonized. Be sure to cite evidence to support your point and organize your essay into an introduction, body, and conclusion.

Alternative Activity Instead of writing essays, address the Essential Question through activities such as holding debates, creating multimedia presentations, or writing journal entries.

European Nations Settle North America

9. What did the Europeans mostly grow in their Caribbean colonies? *sugar and tobacco*

10. What was the result of the French and Indian War? *The English took control of the eastern half of North America.*

The Atlantic Slave Trade

11. What factors led European colonists to use Africans to resupply their labor force? *Native Americans dying; Africans experienced at farming, had built up some immunity to disease, were unfamiliar with the land and could not blend in with the white population, so were less likely to escape*

12. How did enslaved Africans resist their treatment in the Americas? *African slaves resisted by preserving their cultural heritage, sabotaging work efforts, running away, and forming armed rebellions.*

The Columbian Exchange and Global Trade

13. Why was the introduction of corn and potatoes to Europe and Asia so significant? *inexpensive and nutritious and thus improved diets throughout Europe and Asia*

14. What was the economic policy of mercantilism? *Mercantilism held that a country's true power was measured by its wealth, which it acquired by obtaining as much gold and silver as possible and by establishing a favorable balance of trade.*

Critical Thinking

1. **Compare and Contrast** How were the Spanish and Portuguese colonial empires similar to, and different from, northern European trading empires? Consider their organization and how they were founded as part of your answer. *The Spanish empire was driven by a search for wealth and a desire to spread Christianity; the Portuguese empire was mostly driven by a search for wealth, though Prince Henry also wanted to spread Christianity; both were supported by the monarchy and both developed colonies in the Indian Ocean area and Africa as well as the Americas (Caribbean, North America, South America: Spanish; Caribbean, Brazil: Portuguese). The English and the Dutch sought wealth and each established an East India Company that was run like a corporation; both traded in the Indian Ocean area, establishing trading posts and colonies in India, Africa, and East Asia. France traded in the East and established trading posts in India and Africa. All three also sought trade in, and colonized, North America with support from the monarchy, for economic reasons (all) and for religious freedom (English).*

2. **Evaluate** Why were the policies of Aurangzeb so destructive to the Mughal Empire? *He ended policies of tolerance, which led to bitterness and rebellion.*

3. **Make Inferences** Conquest of new territories contributed to the growth of Muslim empires. How might it have also hindered this growth? *Overaggressive empire building may have led to overspending, rebellion, and eventually the decline of the empire.*

(continued)

Expansion, Exploration, and Encounters 665

Print Assessment *(continued)*

4. **Analyze Effects** How might a Chinese emperor's leadership be affected by living in the Forbidden City? Explain and support your opinion. *emperors out of touch; may develop a lack of compassion; heightened contempt for foreigners; pleasure, greed, and court intrigue distract from leadership; corrupt officials may assume power*

5. **Develop Historical Perspective** Of the technological advances that helped spur European exploration, which do you think was the most important? Why? *Answers should show an understanding of the impact of the technological advance selected.*

6. **Analyze Causes** What caused Japan to institute a policy of isolation? Defend your viewpoint with evidence from the text. *The Japanese feared the influence of European ideas and the threat of European colonization of Japan.*

7. **Draw Conclusions** What factors helped the Europeans conquer the Americas? Which was the most important? Why? *Factors—disease, superior weaponry and technology, aid from native allies. Most important—Disease, because it wiped out much of the native population of the Americas.*

8. **Analyze Effects** Explain the statement, "Columbus's voyage began a process that changed the world forever." Consider all the peoples and places American colonization affected economically. *After Columbus, Native American civilizations declined while Europeans prospered. New foods, plants, animals, technologies, and diseases spread to peoples of both hemispheres.*

9. **Compare and Contrast** What might have been some of the differences in the Europeans' and Native Americans' views of colonization? *Europeans: probably positive—they gained land and property and the opportunity to start a new life with more than they had in Europe. Native Americans: probably negative—it deprived them of their property, freedom, and even, in many cases, health and life.*

10. **Compare and Contrast** How was the economic atmosphere of the colonial period similar to that of the Warring States period? *Both periods were marked by economic trade. During the Warring States period in Japan, Japanese merchants traded with Portuguese merchants. During the colonial period, Europeans opened trade with colonial empires in the Americas.*

Engage with History

Think about whether or not you would sail into the unknown as the various explorers you read about did. Based on what you have read, what are the reasons why you would go? If you would choose not to go, explain your feelings. Discuss your answers within a small group. *Some students may say that the rewards were not great enough to go through all the hardship and give up that much time from their lives. Others may say that the opportunity to bring glory and prestige to their country and make some financial gain would be worth the sacrifice.*

Focus on Writing

An English colony would have looked strange and different to a Native American of the time. Conduct historical research on an English colony of the 17th century. Consult at least one primary source and one secondary source. Then write an essay describing it, in which you provide details about the following:

- clothes
- food
- shelter
- weapons

Be sure to begin your paragraph with a thesis statement.

> **RUBRIC** Students' paragraphs should:
> - provide details about clothes, food, shelter, and weapons.
> - use standard grammar and punctuation.

Multimedia Activity

Use the Internet, books, and other reference materials to create a multimedia pitch for a television special "The Voyages of Zheng He." Your pitch should address the historical context of Zheng He's voyages, along with their impact on China and the lands visited. Be sure to include text, images, audio, and, if possible, video as part of your pitch. During your research, consider the following:

- biographical data on Zheng He
- descriptions of the voyages
- information on the ships, crews, and cargo
- appropriate music and visuals

> **RUBRIC** Students' pitches should:
> - portray the voyages accurately and in a dramatic style
> - cover the topic adequately
> - clearly demonstrate an understanding of the material
> - include some historical evaluation of the voyages

▷ Online Assessment

1. Why did the language Urdu develop from Persian, Arabic, and Hindi?
   - ○ The Mughal nobility declared Hindi, Persian, and Arabic to be the state languages.
   - ◉ The Mughal military needed a language understood by soldiers from different nations.
   - ○ Indian merchants dominated Mughal trade and needed to communicate with the nobility.
   - ○ Indian students were expected to learn Persian and Arabic if they wanted to convert to Islam.

2. How did Akbar demonstrate his tolerance for other religions? Select the three correct answers.
   - ◉ by celebrating Christian holidays
   - ◉ by eliminating the tax on non-Muslims
   - ◉ by allowing all faiths to practice their religions
   - ○ by encouraging Muslims to convert to Hinduism
   - ○ by allowing his Indian wives to worship Hinduism
   - ○ by inviting Catholic missionaries to preach in the mosques

3. Which of the following was a characteristic of the Ottoman Empire that led to its downfall?
   - ○ The sultans produced few male heirs to create a clear line of succession.
   - ○ The sultans belonged to a different religion than the majority of their subjects.
   - ○ Their army was composed of foreign soldiers who felt little loyalty to the empire.
   - ◉ There were many nationalities within its borders that wanted to rule themselves.

4. Which statement explains the long-term consequence of the Treaty of Tordesillas?
   - ○ Canada became a French-speaking colony.
   - ◉ Brazil became a Portuguese-speaking colony.
   - ○ The economic power of the Dutch East India Company increased.
   - ○ The influence of the Catholic Church in the New World decreased.

5. How did Western cultures affect Southeast Asia between the 16th and 19th centuries?
   - ○ Many Asians adopted their traditions and began dressing like Europeans.
   - ◉ European colonization was largely limited to port cities and had little impact inland.
   - ○ Many Asians were attracted to the message of Christianity and converted to Catholicism.
   - ○ European architectural styles became popular and were copied throughout the capital cities.

6. *Drag the events into chronological order from top to bottom.*
   ○ Christopher Columbus lands in the New World.
   ○ Spain and Portugal sign the Treaty of Tordesillas.
   ○ Vasco da Gama discovers a sea route to India.
   ○ Portugal captures Goa and establishes the port as its trading capital.
   ○ Spain claims the Philippines as a colony.
   ○ The Netherlands establish a headquarters for the Dutch East India Company in Java.

7. *Drag the answer choices into the boxes to complete the sentence correctly.*
   The Ming dynasty moved its capital from _Nanjing_ in the south to _Beijing_ in the north and constructed an enormous palace complex.

8. Which achievement is associated with the Tokugawa Shogunate?
   ○ the voyages of Zheng He
   ◉ the development of kabuki theater
   ○ the construction of the Forbidden City
   ○ the formation of Confucian philosophy

9. Why did both China and Japan become isolationist?
   ○ They were weakened by continuous warfare between the two countries.
   ○ They were affected by years of famine that reduced the population by half.
   ○ They exhausted their economies by building defenses against Mongol invasions.
   ◉ They feared the loss of their national identities to the influences of European culture.

10. *Drag the explorer into the box next to his discovery.*

Pacific Ocean	Vasco Núñez de Balboa
Caribbean islands	Christopher Columbus
Philippine islands	Ferdinand Magellan
modern-day Brazil	Pedro Álvares Cabral

11. Which of the following were weaknesses of the Aztec Empire that Hernando Cortés used to his advantage in defeating Montezuma II? Select the three correct answers.
    ◉ weaponry
    ○ material wealth
    ○ defensive position
    ◉ hostile neighbors
    ○ number of soldiers
    ◉ lack of immunity to disease

12. How did the Spanish and Portuguese conquests of South America differ?
    ○ The Spanish enslaved the native populations while the Portuguese relied on free labor.
    ◉ The Spanish conquered civilizations rich in gold while the Portuguese discovered few riches.
    ○ The Portuguese established plantations to raise cash crops while the Spanish created small farms.
    ○ The Portuguese exported much of their wealth back to Europe while the Spanish invested in native economies.

13. *Drag the name of the explorer into the box next to the area he explored.*

region of Louisiana	Sieur de La Salle
site of modern-day Quebec	Samuel de Champlain
site of modern-day Montreal	Jacques Cartier
harbor of modern-day New York City	Giovanni da Verrazzano

14. Why did English colonists enslave few Native Americans in the southern colonies and in the Caribbean?
    ○ The English were more interested in trade than creating large plantations.
    ○ English Protestant beliefs prohibited them from owning Native Americans.
    ○ The type of agricultural production in these areas required only a small labor force.
    ◉ Native Americans often died from English contact because they had little immunity to disease.

15. Which statement characterizes the impact of English contact with Native American populations?
    ○ Most Native American tribes converted to Christianity during the colonial period.
    ◉ European diseases killed more Native Americans than warfare with English settlers.
    ○ Most Native American tribes adopted English customs by the end of the colonial period.
    ○ Superior English weaponry convinced Native Americans to leave English settlements alone.

16. Which economic activity relied on the majority of Brazil's enslaved Africans?
    ○ mining   ○ shipbuilding
    ○ fur trapping   ◉ plantation farming

17. *Drag the answer choices into the boxes to complete the sentence correctly.*
    The triangular trading network involving Great Britain, the west coast of Africa, and the West Indies depended on shipments of _sugar_ from the West Indies to Great Britain, _guns_ from Great Britain to Africa, and a supply of _enslaved people_ from Africa to the Caribbean.

18. The causes and effects of African slavery in the New World are numerous. *Drag each development into the table to indicate whether it was a cause or an effect of African slavery.*

Causes of African Slavery	Effects of African Slavery
creation of plantation agriculture	racially mixed populations
need for an inexpensive labor force	creation of negative racial opinions
lack of Native American immunity to European diseases	introduction of different cultural influences
	destruction of African tribal societies

19. The Columbian Exchange introduced many plants and animals to the ecosystems of the Old and New Worlds. *Drag each plant or animal into the table to indicate whether it originated in the Old or New World.*

New World Plant or Animal		Old World Plant or Animal
tobacco	pig	horse
tomato	rice	sheep
turkey		

20. Why did the establishment of some English colonies require the creation of joint-stock companies?
    ○ Colonies were seldom profitable and banks were needed to support them.
    ◉ Colonies were risky and individuals were unwilling to invest all of their money in them.
    ○ Some colonies were attacked by Native Americans and soldiers were needed to defend them.
    ○ Some colonies were founded as royal colonies and the monarchy recruited colonists for them.

21. Which of the following groups experienced a significant increase in economic power with the rise of capitalist economies?
    ○ bishops   ◉ merchants
    ○ farmers   ○ miners

Online Multimedia Connections

In this Multimedia Connection, students will watch and discuss short video clips on de Leon's career. They will identify the nature of the New World in the early 16th century and see how the characteristics of Ponce de Leon enabled him to exploit the native people to become wealthy. They will compare de Leon's motivations for power and riches with the discoveries he made during his journeys.

MULTIMEDIA CONNECTIONS

HISTORY.

Ponce de León

The Spanish conquistador Juan Ponce de León was the first European to set foot on land that later became part of the United States. Ponce de León first sailed to the Americas with Christopher Columbus on his second voyage in 1493. Once in the Caribbean region, he helped conquer what is now Puerto Rico and was named ruler of the island. According to legend, Ponce de León learned about a Fountain of Youth, whose waters could make old people young again. He may have been searching for this fountain when, in 1513, he made landfall on the coast of what today is the southeastern United States. He named the area Florida and claimed it for Spain.

Explore important events in the life of Ponce de León online. You can find a wealth of information, video clips, primary sources, activities, and more through your online textbook.

Caribbean Island Encounters

Watch the video to learn about the first encounters between Spanish explorers and the people of the Caribbean.

Claiming Florida for Spain

Watch the video to learn about Ponce de León's first landing on the coast of what is now Florida.

Ponce de León's 1513 Route

Study the map to learn about the region of the Americas that Ponce de León explored in 1513.